AMERICAN INVASIONS:
CANADA TO AFGHANISTAN:

1775-2010

By

Rocky M. Mirza, Ph.D. (Econ.)

TRAFFORD
PUBLISHING

Order this book online at www.trafford.com
or email orders@trafford.com

Most Trafford titles are also available at major online book retailers.

Printed in the United States of America.

ISBN: 978-1-4269-3848-1 (sc)

Library of Congress Control Number: 2010910229

*Our mission is to efficiently provide the world's finest, most comprehensive book publishing
service, enabling every author to experience success. To find out how to publish your book,
your way, and have it available worldwide, visit us online at www.trafford.com*

Trafford rev. 8/6/2010

North America & international
toll-free: 1 888 232 4444 (USA & Canada)
phone: 250 383 6864 ♦ fax: 812 355 4082

ACKNOWLEDGEMENTS

I wish to thank my friend and colleague Dr. Peter Dunnett for proofreading the manuscript and suggesting minor changes. I wish to thank my brother Shyam Mirza, my son Terry Mirza, and the members of the TGIF singles club for their help in selling the prequel to this book, *Rise and Fall of the American Empire.*

This book is dedicated to the memory of John Lennon: "Give Peace a chance."

CONTENTS

Chapter 4

American Imperialism During and After its Civil War: US Invasions of Nevada, Nebraska, Colorado, Dakota, Montana, Washington, Idaho, Wyoming and Utah: 1864-1896

Chapter 6
The American Empire Completes its Invasions of First Nations Land, Defeats European Imperial Hegemony and Creates the Myth of "Leader of the Free World" While Conquering Central America and the Caribbean

INTRODUCTION

Our primary thesis is that the United States of America was an expansionist empire even before it had secured its own independence from the British Empire which it replaced. Nations become empires by invading and conquering weaker nations. The reasons for an American Empire are the same as Persia, Greece, Rome, Portugal, Spain, France, England, Germany, Russia and all those which came before the American Empire. The American imperial leaders have the same egotistic ambitions as Genghis Khan, Caesar, Alexander the Great, Mark Anthony, Cleopatra, Napoleon, Hitler, Stalin and all of the other imperial conquerors who came before.

The only difference is the fact that it is the most recent empire. As such it is the worst to date. Every empire and imperial conqueror had the ambition to create the biggest, the most ruthless and the most *bad ass* empire the world had ever seen. They all had the single minded obsession of outdoing the biggest and "baddest" which had come before. Their bad and ruthless deeds have all been tempered by their "civilizing" deeds. Many of those so called "civilizing" deeds were aids to their conquests and subjugations of weaker peoples or in response to world-wide criticisms of their excesses which thereby reduced those criticisms and prolonged their survival.

The inspiration for this book came from my research for *Rise and Fall of the American Empire*. As such it is truly a sequel to that effort. During my research for *Rise and Fall* I was struck by how many countries the US had invaded during its relatively short existence as a Nation state. In fact, there has not been a single period of its existence when it did not invade some country or the other. Yet many historians object to calling the US an empire or to accuse it of imperial conquests. If a non-historian like me can so easily recognize the historical facts of these incessant imperial invasions and conquests I can only conclude that the historians who dismiss these facts are part of the cover-up. They are determined to support the American establishment of which they are an integral part. Some historians admit to American imperialism but restrict it to relatively minor "colonial" acquisitions of Spanish territories such as the Philippines.

Our view of American imperialism is quite a departure from any currently accepted thesis. We see American imperialism as the conquest of all territory outside of the original 13 English colonies which declared its independence from England in 1776. Even the land which made up the original 13 colonies could be regarded as conquered territory. However, there can be no question that the lands outside the original 13 colonies were invaded and conquered by the US and turned an independent Republic into an ever expanding empire which continues to invade and conquer to this day. The fact that the US called the initial conquests *territories* rather than *colonies* is purely semantic.

Had England decimated the original inhabitants of India and permitted European immigration to India in sufficient numbers to establish a **White** majority in India which then lobbied the English parliament for a union with England would that make the English conquest of India legitimate? Yet, that is precisely what the US did on the American continent. Had England killed off most of the Chinese population of Hong Kong and peopled it with a majority of **Whites** who voted for Hong Kong to be united with England would that have changed the fact that England took Hong Kong from China by force? What of Napoleon's conquest of Europe and Hitler's conquest of France? Had Napoleon made his conquests states of France or Hitler made France a state of Germany would that have legitimized those conquests? Yet, no historian has ever pointed out that all of the lands outside the original 13 colonies were added to the American Empire by conquests from the original inhabitants, the First Nations.

Having formulated this specific, if somewhat personal, view of American imperialism I was pleasantly surprised to subsequently discover that there was a hint of this "radical" position in the following quote from *The Story of the Usurpation of the Kingdom of Hawaii*, "...the conquest of the mainland United States is never looked upon as a process of colonization, as if the myth of Manifest Destiny was actually a justifiable legal principle. Someday, historians will revisit the process by which new lands were 'acquired' by conquest..." See www.worldfreeinternet.net/archive/arc10.htm.

While the structure of the book progresses in historical sequence from the first invasion of Canada to the current invasion of Afghanistan we intersperse earlier invasions with relevant facts in later invasions. This is a matter of writing style which we hope will appeal to our readers. This style not only caters to those readers who are impatient to get to more current events but also help to support our primary thesis that the current US invasion of Afghanistan is not an aberration of US foreign policy nor the unique disregard for international law by the George W. Bush administration, as many Americans claim, but an inherent characteristic of the US and its founding fathers.

All empires self-destruct for one simple but very important reason. They expand beyond their capacity to fund an ever growing military to control an ever expanding number of colonies. This simple but profound observation explains the fall of every empire, without exception. It is the key reason for the fall of the American Empire which is taking place as you read this book. Despite six centuries of Western propaganda to the contrary, there is not one single historical example where a colonized people have freely chosen the supposed "civilizing" influence of being a colony of a Western empire or the supposed economic gains of being such a colony. Colonies must therefore be held forever by the superior military power of the empire. Of course, military superiority is complemented with propaganda, co-opting some of the colonists, and economic and political blackmail. But colonized people never relinquish their desire to win their independence. They maintain a permanent, if often passive, resistance to being colonized.

You may very well ask why empires do not learn from this constant historical fact and limit their empire to the size they can control with an affordable military. The primary reason for this failure to learn from history is that the process begins with the building of what is currently called a "military-industrial complex." That is clearly the essential foundation for imperial expansion. However, once built, it has a life and momentum of its own. That life and momentum, in the case of the American Empire, is supported by most segments of the American people. Military bases, military communities, military opportunities, military contracts, military personnel and militarized politicians are so integrated and interwoven into American history, culture, thought, geography, employment, education, sports, media and everyday living that it is impossible to restrain its growth much less curtail its appetite for imperial expansion.

In 2010, it is crystal clear to every thinking person that the American Empire cannot afford its wars in Afghanistan and Iraq. But instead of President Obama contracting those wars he is expanding them, while simultaneously creating new wars in Pakistan and Yemen and threatening to start wars with Iran and North Korea. In ignoring reality, President Obama is hastening the inevitable decline of the American Empire. Incompetent leaders are another historical constant which have hastened the inevitable decline of all empires.

An apology to the American people

I have visited the United States on numerous occasions. I have always been struck by the friendly, polite, welcoming and mannerly nature of the American people. It seems almost incomprehensible that such warm, caring people would be capable, as a nation/empire to inflict such evils on the world and on humanity. That is still an unresolved mystery to me. I therefore feel the need to express my sincere view that the truths I have told in this book are not consistent with my personal encounters with individual Americans either in the United States or outside the United States.

CHAPTER 1

Life, Liberty and the Right to Invade and Conquer: The US Invasion of Canada and First Nations Land: 1775-1815

It will come as a huge surprise to the great majority of Americans that military invasion of independent sovereign states by the US was an integral part of the founding of the US as an independent country. US invasions of Afghanistan, Iraq and Vietnam are not exceptions of unprovoked American aggression. They are the norm. Furthermore, they all follow the same pattern.

A naive American electorate is convinced by its leaders that the country to be invaded will be only too happy to be invaded by the US because the people of that country are under some kind of tyrannical rule and will see that the Americans are not invaders but liberators. The Americans will be welcomed with open arms by the citizens of the invaded country because they want the same freedoms and rights which only Americans have. There will be minimal bloodshed because the people will rise up against their tyrannical rulers and support the American liberators to ensure a quick and easy military victory for the US. The US will quickly plant its brand of democracy and republican values which all of the people of the invaded country will support.

In free and fair elections the people of the invaded country will elect leaders who are pro-American in every way. American corporations will be welcomed to develop the economy of the invaded country and establish the sanctity of private property rights, the rule of law and free enterprise. US economic and political "imperialism" will be accepted as a civilizing force which will forge a lasting and peaceful, though subservient, relationship between a grateful people who have been liberated by a country who everyone loves, admires and envies. Americans can take comfort in knowing that their government has brought civilization and American institutions to one more nation on earth. Such unselfish export of US "imperialism" is for the good of all mankind. God bless America.

This false notion of the "good" American liberating independent nation states by military invasion was first tested on Canada. That the idea failed miserably in no way deterred the US from using it over and over again. The most disastrous failures have been Nicaragua, Vietnam, Afghanistan and Iraq. But none of these disastrous failures has deterred American leaders as evidenced by 2008 presidential candidate, Senator John McCain, using the same rhetoric to convince the American voters that Iran should be the next target for America to civilize by military force and liberate the Iranian people from the tyranny of the Shia clerics.

It is astonishing that repeated failures have not changed American aggression, American policy, American rhetoric, American values, American morality, American leadership or the popularity of this failed cause with American voters. Despite vocal criticism of this failed approach by peace demonstrators, draft dodgers, veterans, writers, movie stars, rock stars and other minority views, this entrenched American policy has not wavered throughout the existence of the US as a nation state. The purpose of this book is to document those repeated failures and to show how the US fails to learn from its own history and its own mistakes. Many nations have suffered humiliation, deaths and destruction because of this misguided US policy.

Within the first 40 years of the *Declaration of Independence* from Great Britain the original 13 colonies occupying a **tiny** part of the continent of America would successfully convince the world and historians that it was their "Manifest Destiny" to conquer and rule this entire continent. Never mind that this same land had been previously occupied by the First Nations, Spain, Portugal, France, Great Britain, Holland, Russia and Sweden. The speed and consistency with which the 13 ex-colonies of Britain set about conquering a continent is truly amazing. The success of its propaganda in convincing its inhabitants and many people world-wide that these conquests were not imperialist is mind boggling. The inexcusable justifications for American imperialism across the continent and across the globe provided by historians are truly legendary.

The 13 tiny colonies called their first Congress the **Continental** Congress and their new independent country the United States of **America.** Not yet an independent country, and not militarily powerful enough to seize independence from Great Britain without help from France, these tiny 13 colonies already claimed to be **America.** No one, not even historians, have questioned that assertion or the implicit imperial intent of that assertion.

Historians have rightfully asserted that the European Nations settling colonies in America after Columbus were imperialists. Yet the 13 colonies which stole more of the First Nations lands than any European Nation and exercised political domination of the continent more than any European Nation is seen by historians as non-imperialist, democratic, freedom loving and republican. Within the first 40 years covered in this chapter the 13 tiny colonies not only became the independent United States of **America** but more than doubled its land area by the conquest of Vermont, Kentucky, Tennessee, the Old Northwest Territory and the Louisiana Territory. In addition, it had twice invaded the Canadas and made clear its intention to expand across the continent by military conquests.

A Four Point Plan to Conquer a Continent

The 13 colonies which became the United States had a four part plan to conquer the entire North America continent. First it would trick the English Empire into driving the French Empire out of the Americas. Next it would trick the French Empire into driving the English Empire out of the Americas. With France and Britain out of the way it would conquer as much of the First Nations lands as it could. Finally, it would conquer the lands previously colonized by Spain.

American Invasions began with the Invasion of Canada

Many Canadians, having bought into the missionary zeal of the US as the unquestioned Western source of all that is civilized, will be surprised to learn that the pattern established for American invasions was first tested on Canada when Canada was not so "civilized" by American standards. Indeed, Canada was a mere colony of the "tyrannical" British. The US, in struggling to overthrow the yoke of colonialism itself, will invade Canada to instill those same American republican values which it was bringing to its own thirteen ex-British colonies.

The Canadians would welcome the Americans as liberators, happily join the US in overthrowing their British masters and be forever grateful for the civilizing influence of American culture, language, government, freedom, *African slavery, First Nations subjugation,* capitalism, concentration of wealth through the sanctity of private property, and economic and political power. Canadians would no longer suffer the "humiliation" of having to speak English or French as they would now speak *American* and proudly accept their status as second class Americans bestowed on them by a new generous American republic.

While most people would quickly see the naivety and exaggerated simplicity of the US position when the second Continental Congress of 1775 ordered the invasion of Canada, the great majority of Americans do not. As it was, the Americans were extremely lucky to gain their own independence from England. The idea of successfully capturing Canada at that time was insane. They were unsuccessful, of course, but no lessons were learnt. Having established the precedent of unilaterally invading a sovereign nation without success as part of their birth pangs the Americans became addicted to this notion as an inherent part of their very existence as a nation.

The cure for any perceived threat, real or imagined, to the US would be a military invasion or adventure in some demonized sovereign country. Success would be good but not essential. Failure is temporary since there is always another country to demonize and invade. Failure is also used to lobby for even more resources to be shifted from the relative pittance the United States spend on reducing poverty to feeding its ever expanding military-industrial complex.

Origins of the American Invasion of Canada

The first US invasion of Canada had its origins in the devastating defeat of France by England in the *Seven Years War of 1756-1763*. This French defeat had not come cheaply. The Seven Years War was truly a global war involving the major European nations of the day as well as the European colonies in America, Africa and Asia. England had indebted itself to the tune of 133 million pounds sterling to defeat France and her allies. At the time annual tax revenues in England were miniscule relative to such a large debt, despite the fact that by the end of the Seven Years War English citizens paid the highest taxes in the Western world.

Since the war had been waged mostly to defend the English colonies against French aggression it was natural to impose at least a small part of the tax burden on the colonies. While England's other colonies were willing to help share the cost of the war the 13 American colonies used the imposition of taxes as an excuse for rebellion. While the true motive of the American colonies was to steal First Nations lands made possible by the defeat of France in North America they used the slogan of "no taxation without representation," to justify their theft. This ridiculous slogan has been trumpeted by American historians more often than a talking parrot.

The Seven Years War was started by the 13 colonies when the settlers began to cross the Appalachian Mountains in 1749 to steal the rich agricultural lands in the Ohio valley. Half a million acres of French territory in the Ohio valley was granted to the Ohio Company by King George II and the Virginia Assembly to encourage expanded English settlements in North America. Naturally, France opposed this English incursion into First Nations lands where the French traded with the First Nations. Unlike the English who always settled and established private property rights on stolen First Nations lands, the French were typically interested only in trading rights and not in settling or owning the land. Armed conflict began in 1753 when the young, 22 years old, George Washington arrived at the French Fort LeBoeuf demanding that the French withdrew from the Ohio valley.

Having failed to qualify for a commission in the British army, Washington had to settle for military service with the Virginia militia. It was in this capacity that Washington had been sent by governor Dinwiddie of Virginia. Instead of heeding Washington's demands to withdraw, the French attacked and captured the English fort in the Ohio valley. In response, Washington, with a force of 150 men, ambushed a small French contingent of 33 men, killing 10 men including a French Ambassador, Joseph de Villiers. Washington snuck up on the diplomatic party while they were sleeping and opened fire without warning. The French, who had graciously not killed or captured any of the Americans when they could easily have done so, were outraged. This ambush which took place on May 28, 1754 marked the beginning of the Seven Years War in North America, a full two years before the official Seven Years War of 1756-1763.

At the end of the Seven Years War the 13 colonies lobbied England to keep the French out of North America by returning the rich sugar island of Guadeloupe. At the time the island of Guadeloupe was several times more valuable than all of New France in North America. The representatives of the13 colonies promised to be eternally loyal subjects to the new, young and naïve, English king, George III, if only King George would drive the French out of North America. Despite strong opposition from the more experienced William Pitt, who was largely responsible for England's victory over France, and the powerful West Indian sugar lobby, George III was fooled into believing the lies of the 13 colonies.

The leaders of the 13 colonies wanted France out of North America not to become loyal British subjects but to steal more First Nations lands in the territories previously administered by France through cooperative trade relations with the First Nations. A large part of this territory was in Quebec and the Maritimes. That was the reason for the first invasion of Canada by the US. Such was the greed of the 13 colonies for First Nations lands that it was not sufficient that they would want to steal the lands west of the Appalachian Mountains, which caused the Seven Years War in North America, but also all of the lands governed by New France in Quebec and the Maritimes and by both England and France in Hudson Bay.

It was the French explorers who had explored and conquered the vast Louisiana Territory beginning with the expedition of Louis Joliet and Jacques Marquette in 1673 in search of the famous sea route to the Indies. Rene-Robert de La Salle explored this region from 1679 until his death in 1687. It was France which settled Port Royal or Acadia in the Maritimes and the cities of Quebec City and Montreal in Quebec. It was also the French who competed with the English for the lucrative fur trade in Hudson Bay and James Bay.

The 13 colonies wanted these vast lands settled by the French and English. In pretending loyalty to the English crown to convince George III to remove France from North America by appeasing France with the rich sugar island of Guadeloupe the 13 colonies planned to conquer these lands from England. A rather daunting task at the time since England was the most powerful nation but certainly more feasible than taking on both England and France.

As it turned out the rebellious colonies would only partially succeed in this overly ambitious robbery. They would succeed in the lands which became the United States of America but fail in the lands which became Canada. Even this partial success was due entirely to France aiding the rebellious colonies in a rather sad attempt by France to avenge French honour for England's defeat of France in the Seven Years War. Of course, just as the 13 colonies had lied to England about their long term loyalty to England to secure England's ousting of France from North America so too did the 13 colonies lie to France by signing a long term treaty of alliance with France which was disavowed in the very next war between England and France.

England and France had both forged alliances with the First Nations in their attempts to trade, settle and compete in North America. France claimed the Gulf of St. Lawrence after three voyages by Jacques Cartier who explored 800 miles of the St. Lawrence River from 1534 to 1542. Cartier founded the settlement of *Charlesbourg-Royal* near Quebec City but abandoned it in 1542 because of his failure to recognize the need to negotiate an understanding with the First Nations.

By the late sixteenth century North American beaver pelts were in high demand in Europe. France saw an economic opportunity to exploit its claims to the Gulf of St. Lawrence. French fishermen from Normandy and the French port of Dieppe had been fishing the Grand Banks off Newfoundland since 1504. By setting up "drying stations" along the Newfoundland coast to dry the cod, the French fishermen came into contact with the First Nations with whom they began to trade for furs.

In 1600, a French mariner from the port of Dieppe, Pierre de Chauvin, received monopoly rights to French trade in Canada. Chauvin and another mariner, Francoise Pontgrave, explored the fur trading opportunities in the St. Lawrence and settled on a trading post at *Tadoussac* in Quebec. Chauvin died in 1603 and his monopoly rights to French trade in Canada was turned over to the vice-Admiral of France, Aymar de Chastes. In 1603, Francoise Pontgrave returned to the Tadoussac trading post with Samuel de Champlain who became the founder of New France.

The failure of the Charlesbourg-Royal settlement convinced Champlain that the support of the First Nations was vital for the survival of a French colony or trading post in North America. At the time two major First Nations coalitions competed with each other for the lucrative fur trade. The more powerful of the two groups was the Six Nation *Iroquois League* which was a coalition of Mohawks, Senecas, Cayugas, Oneidas, Onondagas and Tuscaroras. The French formed an alliance with the less powerful Huron Confederacy of Hurons and Algonquins beginning in 1608 when Quebec was first settled by Samuel de Champlain. The French alliance with the Huron Confederacy was cemented in 1609 when Champlain helped the Confederacy defeat the League.

England allied itself with the Iroquois *League* when it challenged France for the fur trade in Hudson Bay beginning in 1670. The First Nations fought alongside their French or English allies in all of the Anglo-French wars in North America. England's First Nations allies were recognized as *British subjects* by the Treaty of Utrecht in 1713. Concerned that the 13 colonies might not adhere to the treaties signed with the First Nations, England called a meeting of representatives from the First Nations and the 13 colonies at the *Albany Congress* of June 1754.

The Albany Plan recommended the formation of a Grand Council of 48 members which would meet annually to ensure peaceful relations between the colonies and the First Nation allies. During the Seven Years War which followed on the heels of the Albany Congress the French were defeated only because of the massive military support to England by its First Nation allies. England's ally, the Iroquois League, was the most formidable First Nation force prior to the American War of Independence.

The First Nations would soon discover that they had made a monumental mistake in supporting the English against the French. As early as 1700 the English population in North America was 250,000 compared to 40,000 French inhabitants. The French warned the Iroquois League that the English would steal their lands for settlement while France only wanted to fish and trade for furs. By the start of the Seven Years War the English settlers were 1.5 million compared to French settlers of 90,000. Of course, in the end, it was the Americans who betrayed the First Nations, the English and the French. They were all lied to and out-smarted by the settlers in 13 tiny colonies along the Atlantic seaboard.

Following Washington's ambush of the French on May 28, 1754, the French attacked Washington's force of 150 men and Washington surrendered. Despite Washington's cowardly ambush of the French Ambassador the French responded generously by sparing Washington's life and allowing him to return to Virginia. This proved to be a mistake. The 13 colonies wanted the French out of North America. The rich farm lands in the Ohio valley would be only the beginning of driving the French out of North America. Furthermore, the colonists were confident that England would continue to pay for the costly wars with the French as England had done in the past.

England could only impose taxes on its citizens in England and on colonists in the Caribbean and India. England dared not impose taxes on the 13 Atlantic colonies since these were the only colonists who would scream "no taxes without representation." This supreme confidence in the 13 colonies that England would never dare impose taxes on them explains the failure of the *Albany Plan*.

One of the recommendations of the Albany Plan was levying taxes to defend the colonies against attacks by France and its First Nations allies. The colonial legislatures voted against the imposition of these taxes.

The French should therefore have anticipated that by allowing Washington to return safely to Virginia that he would only be back with an even larger force to attempt to drive them out of the coveted Ohio Valley. In 1755 Washington attacked the French at Fort Duquesne with a force of 1,500 men under the command of General Braddock but was defeated again. Braddock was killed and Washington retreated with only 500 men.

Another war with France was now inevitable. The more immediate target of the 13 colonies was the Maritimes. The New England colonists, in particular, had never forgiven England for returning the French fortress of Louisbourg on Cape Breton Island in exchange for the English trading post of Madras in India. Now the New Englanders saw an opportunity to get the lands settled by the Acadians in Nova Scotia. They lobbied England to deport the Acadians to French territory in Louisiana and distribute the Acadian lands to them.

England had captured Acadia from France during Queen Anne's war which began in 1702. New Englanders had launched raids into Acadia for many years but it was not until 1710 that Port Royal surrendered to a combined English and colonial force of 3,500 led by Francis Nicholson. Even so, England had to invite its First Nations ally, the Iroquois League, into Nova Scotia to help it keep law and order in the captured French colony. Neither the Acadians nor the Mikmaq First Nation was happy with English rule.

The Treaty of Utrecht of 1713 left Acadia with England. Under English rule trade between Acadia and the New England colonies naturally increased. With increased trade came increased desire for conquest by the New Englanders. Some Acadians wanted to move from Nova Scotia to Louisbourg in Cape Breton to escape English rule but were forbidden to do so by England. The French had built an impressive fortress in Louisbourg and England was fearful of emigrating Acadians adding to the French population in Cape Breton. In Nova Scotia the Acadians remained neutral, not fighting for England or France.

In 1755 a combined English and New England force attacked and captured the French at Fort Beausejour in New Brunswick. Following this victory the Acadians were summoned to a meeting at Grand Pre on September 5, 1755. They were informed that their lands and possessions were being confiscated and over 2,000 Acadians were taken prisoners. Beginning in 1755 between 5,000 and 10,000 Acadians were forcibly put on overcrowded English ships and deported. Their lands were distributed to the New Englanders.

Conquest of the French in the Atlantic Region could not be complete while France held the fortress in Louisbourg. If only England would retake Louisbourg the American colonists would be loyal subjects to the English Crown forever. That was the bait which the New Englanders used to get England to commit to an expensive war with France. After the return of Louisbourg to France in 1748 the English built its own fortress in Halifax. That had not appeased the greedy American colonists. They wanted Louisbourg as well. In June 1758, 12,000 British troops under the command of Jeffery Amherst attacked the 4,000 French troops defending Louisbourg. The French surrendered after a two month siege.

With the French out of the Maritimes the American colonies turned their attention to the mainland colony of Quebec. James Wolfe led a British force of 13,500 against Quebec City on June 12, 1759. While the British fleet pounded Quebec City with their massive guns the American Rangers laid waste to the French settlers along the St. Lawrence, burning homes, looting, scalping and slaughtering livestock. On September 13, 1759, Wolfe scaled the heights of Abraham and attacked the French on the Plains of Abraham. Never expecting the English to climb the steep cliffs the French were taken by surprise and lost the battle after only 15 minutes. Montreal surrendered to a British force of 17,000 led by Amherst on September 8, 1760.

Unfortunately for the future United States of America, Nova Scotia, New Brunswick, Cape Breton and Quebec became part of an independent Canada which the US would have to invade and conquer. But at least the French Empire had been driven out of the Americas and the 13 colonies had achieved the first part of their four part plan. Of course Canada had no more of a legitimate claim to the First Nations land than the American Empire. But that is another book.

The first step of the four part plan also required that England bear the entire cost of ousting the French from North America. When Washington started the Seven Years War by ambushing the French Ambassador on May 28 1754 the American colonists had no intention of paying for a colonial militia to defeat the French. In the past England, and English taxpayers, had paid for the wars started by the colonists.

The colonists were certain that by using frivolous excuses such as "no taxation without representation" or by pretending everlasting loyalty to the English Crown they would once again get England to pay for another costly war with the French. Initially, England was reluctant to start another expensive war with France. English taxpayers were fed up with paying for these expensive wars to protect colonists or expand the empire. We saw that the French easily defeated the force under Washington and Braddock which attacked Fort Duquesne in 1755. This was followed by other French victories over the English in 1756 and 1757.

Fortunately for the American colonists the union of England and Holland under William of Orange had introduced the Dutch financial system to England whereby wars could be funded by borrowing rather than raising taxes to politically unpopular levels. King William's War, the War of the Spanish Succession and the War of the Austrian Succession, had all added to England's National Debt. However, under Sir Robert Walpole's tenure as Chancellor of the Exchequer from 1721 to 1742 England's National Debt had been significantly reduced. This gave William Pitt, the newly elected British Prime Minister, the opportunity to add to the debt to finance another costly war with France.

Pitt was determined to win the war against France by imposing a heavy future burden on English taxpayers. When Pitt took over control of the Seven Years War he secured a commitment from the English Parliament to recruit 55,000 sailors, increase the size of the English navy to significantly exceed that of France and to subsidize England's allies fighting France on the European continent. These commitments were paid for mostly by adding to England's National Debt. Pitt had unwittingly enabled the 13 colonies to succeed in the first step of their four step plan to conquer North America.

William Pitt has been recognized by all historians as the English hero who won the Seven Years War for England. There has been little criticism of the fact that this victory over the French buried England in debt and eventually led to the rise of the American Empire. Likewise there is little criticism today of the fact that the US is waging a war in Afghanistan and Iraq which is largely financed by burying the US in debt. In the case of the Afghan/Iraq war American consumers not only refused to finance it from higher taxes but from savings. Unlike the Seven Years War when Pitt borrowed from Englishmen, Presidents Barack Obama and George W. Bush borrowed from foreign lenders such as China, Japan, OPEC nations and Caribbean bankers. Americans voted for a war which their children and grand-children will pay for.

The second step in the four step plan of the 13 colonies to conquer North America was to get the French to assist the 13 colonies in ousting the English from North America. If the colonies in Canada did not agree with this step of the plan Canada would be invaded and captured. So it was that even before the 13 colonies had successfully defended their unilateral declaration of independence from Britain, George Washington ordered the invasion of Canada. The theme for this invasion, the first of many invasions of foreign countries by the US, would set a lasting precedent for all future invasions.

The theme is that the colonists in the Canadas would welcome the Americans as liberators not invaders. Canadians would thank the Americans for removing the tyrannical English imperialists. In the case of Vietnam the Vietnamese would welcome the American liberators who liberated them from the tyranny of Communist Russia. In the case of Afghanistan the Afghan people would welcome the American liberators who liberated them from the tyranny of the Taliban. In the case of Iraq the Iraqi people would welcome the American liberators who liberated them from the tyranny of Saddam Hussein. This lasting kindergarten mentality that you can fool the people you are invading because you have successfully fooled American voters of your true imperialist intentions is a mystery to me.

The supposedly glorious American Revolution for freedom, equality and substitution of republican values for royal tyranny began with radical leaders like Samuel Adams and James Otis in Boston inciting riots against English custom officers. In 1768, England sent 4,000 troops to Boston but the attacks on the custom officers only escalated. When English troops fired into one of these riots on March 5, 1770, killing five of the rioters, Samuel Adams called this shooting the *Boston Massacre.* England attempted to pacify the colonists by abolishing most of the customs duties and recalling the Boston regiment. A year later England went further in its efforts to discourage future riots by appointing the native born Thomas Hutchinson as the new governor of Massachusetts.

The colonists responded by setting fire to the English schooner *HMS Gaspee* in 1772. England chose not to retaliate against this extreme act of aggression by the colonists. Samuel Adams and his *Sons of Liberty* organization continued to incite riots. The final straw for the overly conciliatory mother country was the dumping of 342 chests of English tea into Boston harbour on December 16, 1773. The tea had been shipped by the very reputable English merchant, Davison, Newman and Company, and was worth over 10,000 pounds sterling. This *cowardly act* by hooligans has been dubbed the "Boston Tea Party," by American historians. Americans have become experts at using language which demonize their victims and glorify their imperialist motives. "Leader of the free world," is the classic example of this gross and shameless misuse of the English language.

The mother country was justifiably appalled by this despicable act of hooliganism by the Boston mobs and their self righteous leaders. England demanded payment for the tea and closed the port in Boston. Sam Adams and his band of brigands dubbed the English response the "Intolerable Acts," and called for a Congress in Philadelphia to rally opposition to the mother country. In May 1774, England sent out General Thomas Gage with 4,000 men to restore law and order in Boston. The colonists went ahead with their Congress calling it the First *Continental* Congress, even though the 13 colonies occupied a very tiny strip of First Nations land along the Atlantic seaboard.

This seemingly infantile use of the word "Continental" should have been a warning to England, France, Spain and the First Nations. It was the first explicit statement of intent by these 13 colonies of their desire to steal a continent through deceit, theft and wars. On September 5, 1774, delegates from all of the colonies except Georgia met at Carpenters Hall in Philadelphia to discuss strategies to oust England from North America and turn over governance of North America to a home grown *aristocracy.*

Fortunately for the rebellious colonists only the First Nations took their threat of conquering a continent seriously. The three European powers, England, France and Spain, were too busy stealing from each other and the First Nations to even consider the absurdity that all of it would end up with 13 tiny colonies who had failed miserably as late as 1754 to support the rather modest Albany Plan of cooperation formulated by their foremost statesman, Benjamin Franklin, and approved by England.

This mistake by the three European powers to take the threat by the rebellious colonists seriously turned out to be the undoing of Europe and the beginning of *American Invasions.*

Not all of the colonial leaders were as radical as Sam Adams. One leader who was more moderate was a younger cousin of Sam Adams, John Adams. John Adams favoured a more conciliatory approach with the mother country. He wrote a Declaration of Rights and Grievances which would be sent to King George III. Events spiraled out of control when the rebels began to acquire military supplies in the town of Concord, 20 miles outside Boston. General Gage was forced to take a stand against this potential threat to law and order. He sent a force of 700 men under Lieutenant Colonel Francis Smith to commandeer the military hardware. With the aid of the newly formed Massachusetts colonial militia called the *Minutemen,* the rebels attacked the English troops and succeeded in preventing them from seizing the military supplies in Concord. Smith's troops were forced to retreat to their ships in Charlestown Harbour after 73 of his men were killed and another 200 were wounded. Armed rebellion against the mother country had broken out and the rebels scored the first military victory. The English were now attacked in New York by another colonial militia and colonial militias across the New England states marched on the English in Boston.

With armed rebellion against the mother country seemingly inevitable the 12 colonies which had met at the First Continental Congress hastily convened a Second, purposely misnamed, *Continental* Congress on May 10, 1775. The primary purpose of the Second Congress was to form a continental army under the leadership of George Washington to defend the rebels. Washington was appointed Commander-in-Chief on June 15, 1775. The man responsible for starting the Seven Years War in North America which removed the French Empire from North America was now leading the charge to remove the English Empire from North America.

It's crucial to any understanding of why there came to be an American Empire to recognize that the rebellion of the 13 English colonies was not simply a rebellion of colonists against English imperialism. It was much more than that. Removing the English Empire from North America meant much more than securing independence for 13 tiny colonies along the Atlantic seaboard. It meant, for starters, taking the colonies ceded to England by France under the Treaty of Paris ending the Seven Years War. This meant declaring war on Canada and that was exactly what the Second Congress did. It declared war on Canada and ordered the invasion of the Canadas, Upper Canada and Lower Canada.

The same George Washington now leading the rebellion had urged **White** settlers to steal First Nations lands in the Ohio Valley by using the military roads built by England during the Seven Years War. He had urged the settlers by saying that "those seeking good lands in the West must find and claim them without delay." Washington, like the other leaders of the rebellion, knew that once the French and English were driven out of North America the third step in the four step plan to conquer a continent would be the removal of the First Nations.

The arguments for invading the Canadas, though proving to be totally fallacious, would become the standard arguments for future invasions, including the current invasion of Iraq and Afghanistan. These arguments were, and are, as follows. The Americans would quickly overwhelm Canada's defense with its far superior military force reminiscent of that argument for the invasion of Iraq. Secondly, most Canadians support the British tyranny because of fear not genuine loyalty much like the people's support of Saddam Hussein in Iraq and the Taliban in Afghanistan. Once the Canadians had observed the quick defeat of their military forces by the Americans they would rush to welcome the Americans as liberators like the Iraqi and Afghan people today.

Thirdly, all freedom loving people, including Canadians, Afghans and Iraqis, envy American freedoms and democratic institutions, *including the freedom to own slaves and subjugate First Nations,* as was the case at the time of the Canadian invasion, or the freedom to tell countries like Britain,

Canada, Mexico, Germany and France, that their voters did not have the democratic right to tell their governments not to support the American invasion of Iraq or that the Palestinian people did not have the democratic right to elect a government like Hamas because the US and Israel objected, as was the case during the Iraqi invasion.

Finally, "love us or we will shoot you." In the case of the Canadian invasion, the slogan was "Liberty or Death." In the case of the Iraqi invasion the slogan changed to, "You are either with us or against us." Make no mistake about it. If you do not at least pretend to love Americans and their narrow definition of democracy, they will kill you. They have both the weapons and the desire to kill you in the mistaken notion of protecting freedom.

Of course, after they have killed you and your wives the next day they will distribute American candy to your orphans making sure the Western media is broadcasting pictures to show the world how peace loving American soldiers are. That Americans would expect Canadians to believe that leaders who owned slaves were freedom loving people is one example of how easy it is to fool Americans. Only Americans can be duped into believing such lies.

Far from succeeding in getting Canadians to support the American invasion of Canada many Americans fled the 13 colonies to seek refuge in Canada. American leaders cannot even fool all Americans much less non-Americans. Is it surprising that more Americans have converted to Islam since *9/11* ratcheted up public rhetoric against Muslims?

The greedy and conceited Americans invaded Canada even before they had declared their independence from England and secured their own borders from an English attack. Fort Ticonderoga was captured on May 10, 1775 the same day the Second Congress was convened. This was the English fort lying between Lake George in New York and Lake Champlain. It was captured by a force called the *Green Mountain Boys* led by Benedict Arnold and Ethan Allen.

Ethan Allen and his two brothers had recruited the Green Mountain Boys since 1770 because of conflicts between White settlers stealing First Nations land in the area which later became the state of Vermont. This area was part of New France ceded to England by the first Treaty of Paris. In 1755 the French had constructed Fort Ticonderoga which they had named Fort Carillon. Five days after Fort Ticonderoga was captured the American colonies declared war on England and proceeded with their invasion of Canada by capturing the English fort at Crown Point on the western shore of Lake Champlain.

Somewhat ironically, the Americans initially succeeded in their invasion of Canada, much as they did later in Iraq. American forces under the leadership of Benedict Arnold and Richard Montgomery occupied parts of the Canadas beginning in September 1775. Montgomery advanced north from Fort Ticonderoga with a force of about 1,700 men on Montreal and captured Fort St. Jean just outside Montreal. The English governor, Sir Guy Carleton, who received his knighthood for successfully defending Canada against the Americans, chose to abandon Montreal to concentrate his defense on Quebec City. By November 12, 1775 the Americans occupied Montreal after Carleton had successfully escaped to Quebec City. The quick victory was as sweet then as the quick defeat of Saddam Hussein was in 2003. As in Iraq initially, the American invasion of Canada went according to the US plan.

Unlike General Wolfe's defeat of the French, the Americans failed to conquer Quebec City. The American plan was for Benedict Arnold to join forces with Montgomery for their assault on Quebec City. However, Arnold's march through the wilderness from the US to Quebec City proved disastrous. Arnold lost 500 of his force of 1,100 men to death and illness from starvation, fatigue, smallpox and other diseases, and from desertion, before reaching Quebec City. With the great majority of French Canadians staying neutral in the coming battle for Quebec City and Canada, the fight was between the English under Carleton and the Americans under Montgomery and Arnold.

The harsh Quebec winter helped the English. The Americans attacked on December 31, 1775 during a blinding snowstorm. Montgomery, like Wolfe before, was killed in the attack. Arnold was injured. Unlike Montcalm in 1759, Carleton successfully defended Quebec City by trapping the Americans between two barricades which he had set up to defend the city. The Americans retreated in disarray losing over 500 men compared with only three men lost by the English. Remnants of the American invasion force camped out on the Plains of Abraham until the spring of 1776. They resorted to looting French Canadians for supplies. As in Iraq, such behviour removed any chance of fooling the people that they were liberators, not invaders. When more British troops arrived in the spring the Americans fled.

The Americans re-grouped for a second attempt at capturing Quebec City by attacking Trois-Rivieres in June 1776. Carleton defeated the Americans again and counter attacked at the Battle of Valcour Island on October 11, 1776. This was a naval battle since there were no roads and access to Valcour Island was via Lake Champlain. The American fleet under Arnold was easily defeated by the far superior English fleet. Arnold was forced to retreat initially to the American held fort at Crown Point and finally, all the way back to Fort Ticonderoga where the planned conquest of the Canadas had begun.

The onset of winter made it impossible for Carleton to re-capture either Crown Point or Fort Ticonderoga. Carleton had driven the Americans out of the Canadas just as they are being driven out of Iraq and Afghanistan by the Iraqi and Afghan people today. Both the English and French in Canada saw clearly that the newly created United States was after their land and the lucrative fur trade while pretending to be liberators of colonial peoples. Both the Shiites and Sunnis in Iraq know very well that the Americans are after their oil and colonization of the Middle East while pretending to be liberators from dictatorship. When will Americans ever learn?

Washington Fails to Expand his Empire into the Canadas but Succeeds in Expanding it into the First Nations Lands

The American plan to conquer North America was succeeding. The 13 colonies had succeeded in the first step of their four step plan by getting England to oust the French with the Seven Years War ending in 1763. The goal of the American War of Independence was expansion into Canada's Maritime Provinces via expansion of the New England states as well as into the mainland via the conquest of Quebec. The conquest of Quebec would enable westward expansion to proceed both from Quebec as well as from the 13 colonies into First Nations land in the Ohio valley and the rich fur bearing regions controlled by the Hudson Bay Company.

To achieve this goal the 13 colonies united under Washington's leadership and sought a military alliance with France to drive the English Empire out of the Canadas and out of First Nations lands west of the Appalachian Mountains where the English had First Nations allies. This second step of the four step plan was only partially successful in that the American alliance with France drove the English Empire from the 13 colonies and the First Nations lands west of the Appalachian Mountains but not from Canada. The Americans would have to postpone the conquest of Canada and move to the third step of their four step plan. This was the invasion of First Nations land. With the English and French out of the First Nations lands surrounding the 13 colonies Washington would move quickly to conquer this territory and expand the US from 13 states to 16 states during his two administrations.

These three new states of Vermont, Kentucky and Tennessee together added 92,500 square miles of First Nations lands to the original 13 colonies. Why is it that historians fail to see such rapid expansionism as anything but imperialistic? Furthermore, this was no minor conquest. The New

England colonies of Massachusetts, New Hampshire, Connecticut and Rhode Island had a total area of only 27,000 square miles. The middle colonies of New York, New Jersey, Pennsylvania and Delaware had a total area of 112,000 square miles. The 13 colonies therefore had a combined area of 342,000 square miles. The conquest of Vermont, Kentucky and Tennessee increased the geographical area of the original United States by a full 27 percent.

More importantly, 92,500 square miles was what the conqueror succeeded in keeping not the total of his attempted conquests. Washington's unsuccessful invasion of the Canadas clearly indicated that he was after much more than the 92,500 square miles he achieved. Washington would push both from the New England states to capture Vermont and westwards to capture Kentucky and Tennessee. Far more important than the conquest of these three states was the founding principle of expansionism and planting the seeds of *Manifest Destiny* to conquer and subjugate a continent. After the American continent was conquered the American Empire would conquer the world and subjugate the entire human race. Such is its insatiable greed and addiction to warmongering.

The idea of world domination by 13 tiny colonies was so far fetched during Washington's presidency that Europe ignored the whims and machinations of the new republic. No one took the threat seriously except for the First Nations. Not even Canada or Spain, the most vulnerable countries, at the time. While the First Nations correctly saw the US as a greater threat to their survival than any of the European Nations which had previously threatened their rights to their lands, culture and way of life, they were militarily too weak to counter that threat. It was especially galling to the once powerful Six-Nations Iroquois League, which had allied itself with the English to protect its lands from the French, only to see England bowing to the new powerful USA even at this early stage of the history of the US as an emerging power.

England developed an incestuous relationship with the independent USA beginning with the second Treaty of Paris which ended the American War of Independence. France was flabbergasted at how forgiving England was to the rebellious colonies, complaining that the English had "bought the peace." Ever since the founding of the US as an independent nation, England turned its back on European unity to pander to the wishes of the Americans and their imperial aspirations. No wonder England's Prime Minister, Tony Blair, was proud to be George W's *poodle* and betray the Iraqi people.

From the very beginning of the Anglo/French conflict in North America the First Nations lost land to both England and France. However, more land was lost to England than France because the English emphasized both trade and settlements while France concentrated relatively more on trade and exploration. The English victory during the Seven Years War replaced France, not with England, but with the USA, as the primary power which would continue the theft of First Nations land. Prior to the Seven Years War the First Nations fought and/or allied with the French and English. After the Seven Years War the First Nations had to choose between the English and the Americans. While it was true that England was much more aggressive than France in conquering and stealing First Nation land the Americans would be even more aggressive and greedy than the English.

Both France and England came to North America for the same four reasons. Firstly, to find a Northwest Passage to the Indies. Secondly, to fish the Grand Banks off Newfoundland. Thirdly, to trade for furs with the First Nations. Fourthly, to settle colonies and expand their empires. When the French arrived early in the seventeenth century to trade for furs in Canada they traded mostly with the Hurons and allied themselves with the Huron Confederacy. Since the British arrived later they allied themselves with the more powerful Iroquois League.

Throughout the many Anglo/French wars in the years of settlement, trade and explorations leading up to the American War of Independence, the Iroquois League remained loyal allies of the British and fought alongside the British against the French. It is therefore fair to say that the 13 colonies were successful in removing the French from North America because of the military power of both England and England's First Nations ally. One of the many problems facing England after the removal of France was the competing interests of England's First Nation ally and those of the 13 colonies. They both wanted the land previously colonized by France. England had anticipated this problem.

In an attempt to pacify both sides England had encouraged the 13 colonies to meet with the Iroquois League at Albany in New York in June 1754. Only 7 of the 13 colonies had sent delegates to the Albany conference. These were New York, Pennsylvania, Maryland and the New England colonies. The First Nations had sent 150 delegates. The delegates recommended the formation of a Grand Council of 48 members which would meet annually to maintain peaceful relations between the colonists and England's First Nation ally. The colonies did not accept this recommendation. They wanted all of the First Nations land and pressured England to abandon the First Nations and assist the colonists in stealing the land.

England was caught between a rock and a hard place. England made a second attempt to keep the peace between the colonists and the First Nations. This was the Royal Proclamation of 1763. This Proclamation prohibited colonial settlements west of the Appalachian Mountains until the land owned by the First Nations in the west was negotiated for settlements by legal treaties between England and the First Nations.

At that time the combined Anglo/French population in North America was under 2 million. The land east of the Appalachian Mountains including Quebec, Nova Scotia and Newfoundland was more than enough for the English and French settlers and traders. The greedy Americans would have none of this peaceful coexistence with the First Nations. In the end England abandoned the First Nations to appease the greedy Americans.

The colonists in the 13 colonies took advantage of the fact that England acquired much more than it could handle with the 1763 Treaty of Paris. The treaty left England with a world-wide empire to administer, including a much expanded presence in India, a largely French population in Canada, demands by its First Nations ally in North America, the desire by the American colonists to expand westwards into new First Nations lands, a huge public debt and high taxes in England and the burning desire of its arch rival, France, to avenge its humiliating defeat in the Seven Years War.

The plan of the American colonists was to harass the mother country wherever it could such as refusing to contribute to the cost of protecting them from First Nations attacks, stirring up rebellion, violating the terms of the Royal Proclamation of 1763 by expanding westwards into the Ohio valley and beyond and threatening the Canadas with invasion or by encouraging Canadians to join with the Americans in rebelling against the English crown.

In the end the Americans succeeded in their greed for more First Nations land only by betraying the mother country through an alliance with England's arch enemy, France. This betrayal of the mother country not only achieved independence for the 13 colonies but led to a second Treaty of Paris in 1783 in which England betrayed its First Nation ally by ceding to the newly independent United States the First Nations lands which were protected by the Royal Proclamation of 1763. All of the lands west of the Appalachian Mountains, which had been specifically declared *Indian Territory* out of bounds to White settlements without prior treaty negotiations, were handed over by England to the United States. It included a part of New France which had not been included in the new English colony of Quebec.

While these lands were not England's to give away the reality was that might was right. Without England's military power to help the First Nations protect their legally owned lands from theft by the Americans, the US succeeded in invading and conquering these lands. The Americans won. France, England, Quebec and the First Nations lost.

This betrayal by England marked the end of the powerful Iroquois League and the gradual theft of all First Nations lands in all of North America. The Iroquois League fought alongside England in the American War of Independence just as it had done in the previous Anglo/French wars including the Seven Years War. The Mohawk chief, Joseph Brant, was a distinguished Captain in the British army during the American War of Independence. Brant was instrumental in getting the Iroquois League to fight alongside the British instead of choosing neutrality.

In August 1779, American troops under General John Sullivan invaded the Iroquois land in New York defeating Brant and forcing the Iroquois to flee to Canada. In August 1781 Brant defeated the Americans in Detroit prior to the British surrender in Yorktown. Most of the *Six Nations* and Joseph Brant re-settled in the Grand River Valley in Ontario on land originally inhabited by Iroquois who had remained neutral during the Anglo/French wars.

The once proud First Nations in both the USA and Canada would be shamelessly killed off or herded into Reservations and left to fight for their treaty rights in long expensive court battles which are continuing to this day. The *Six Nations Reserve* is located south of Brantford in Ontario. First Nations would be stripped of their language and culture, forced to attend residential schools where they would be physically, sexually and mentally abused, forced to live in sub-standard houses with poor sanitation, water and electricity, forced into alcohol and other substance abuse, forced into prostitution, forced into permanent second class citizenships, forced to accept handouts from governments and forced to integrate or die.

What is so incredible to me is that American historians continue to justify the second US invasion of Canada in 1812 by saying that England was responsible for First Nations attacks on US settlers in the Old Northwest. The reality, of course, was quite the opposite. In an attempt to avoid another war with the US, England gave up to the US more and more First Nations lands which it had previously agreed to protect from colonization in exchange for First Nations trading rights and military assistance during the many wars fought with France. The problem was that there was no end to American greed, imperialist ambitions and addictive warmongering. In the period following the *Treaty of Greenville* of 1795 some 48 million acres of First Nations lands were stolen by American settlers who had crossed the Appalachian Mountains by 1809. At the same time the US had acquired the vast Louisiana Territory in 1803. There was absolutely no justification, other than raw imperialism, for invading the Canadas in 1812.

Washington Conquers Vermont, Kentucky and Tennessee, 1791-1796

One of the opening acts of the first US president, George Washington, was the creation of a 1,000 man army to defend the "inalienable rights" of **White** settlers to steal First Nations land west of the Appalachian Mountains. If some people are so naive as to believe the popular rhetoric that Washington invaded the Canadas to free the Canadian people from the yoke of English imperialism there can be no similar naivety regarding the conquest of the First Nations lands. The reason for this difference is unambiguous.

Washington failed to take the Canadas from England and therefore, some will argue that he tried but failed to deliver to the Canadas their independence and freedom. No such argument can be made regarding the US conquest of the First Nations lands in Vermont, Kentucky and Tennessee since these lands were permanently added to what was now an expanding American Empire. There could be no naïve propaganda that First Nations were being granted freedom and equality by a freedom loving United States of America. Nor could there be any claims that colonies were exerting their right to be free of English imperialism as could be claimed in the case of the original 13 colonies.

The evidence is overwhelming that the invasion and conquest of Vermont, Kentucky and Tennessee were acts of aggression and conquest by a new imperial power, the likes of which, the world had never seen. This expansion into Vermont, Kentucky and Tennessee was only a tiny beginning of an insatiable appetite for land, resources, power, control and the unbridled subjugation of human dignity and intelligent discourse by brute force.

The First Nations lands on the border between New York and Quebec was the first to be conquered by the new independent freedom loving American Republic. This area, like Quebec, had been part of New France since 1609. France built Fort St. Anne in 1666, Fort St. Frederic in 1734 and Fort Carillon in 1755. During the Seven Years War the English captured Fort Carillon and re-named it Fort Ticonderoga. Under the terms of the first Treaty of Paris, France ceded this territory to England.

American settlers from the 13 colonies had been moving into this territory as they had been pushing into the Ohio valley confronting both France and the First Nations. The defeat of France made it easier for the Americans as they had one less enemy to deal with. England was caught in the middle trying to keep a delicate peace between its First Nations allies and the greedy American colonists. We saw above that the Americans captured Fort Ticonderoga en-route to invading Quebec. In the summer of 1777 the English under General John Burgoyne re-captured Fort Ticonderoga from the Americans.

However, Burgoyne lost the Battle of Saratoga in New York in October of 1777 and France came to the aid of the colonial rebels. France made the ultimate blunder of supporting colonial rebels only to satisfy its wounded pride as an imperial power. Its humiliating losses to England during the Seven Years War fuelled such a desire for vengeance that it aided rebellious colonists who had no chance of securing their independence from England without the far superior military forces of France. Furthermore, it was these same colonists who had complained bitterly when England had returned the fortress of Louisbourg to France and had since goaded England to start a war that would drive the French out of North America. France should have known that the colonists would not be satisfied with independence but would want all of North America.

France, like England, was too naive to think that 13 tiny colonies could take a continent which England and France had fought over since the sixteenth century. France saw the American War of Independence as a way of increasing French influence, trade and conquests in North America. It foolishly believed that aiding the rebels would mean a new ally in North America against its old enemy, England. The wily colonists out-smarted both England and France by pitting them against each other and then seizing the prize from both of them.

The 92,500 square miles of First Nations land, Vermont, Kentucky and Tennessee, conquered by Washington and incorporated into the new freedom loving American Republic in 1791 was inhabited by several First Nations including the Iroquois, Algonquian, Mohican, Mohawks and Abenaki. When England captured Fort St. Frederick from France in 1759 the Mohawks attacked the fort and burnt it. First Nations feared England more than France because English conquests brought more settlers than French conquests. Immigrants from the neighbouring states of New York, New Hampshire and Massachusetts added to the original French and English settlers and created a new republic called *New Connecticut* on January 18, 1777. Its name was changed to *Vermont* six months later.

In 1791 Vermont became the fourteenth state of the US. Washington had failed to take Quebec but added another New England state to the Union. Vermont's border to the north was Quebec. It would be convenient for future attempts at conquering Canada. The conquest of Vermont was only the first step to taking the continent. In 1791 the US population was just over 4 million. In time many more European settlers would come to America to hasten the theft of First Nations land by the freedom loving Americans.

The Westward Conquests of Kentucky and Tennessee

As early as 1749 settlers from the 13 colonies began to cross the Appalachian Mountains to steal the First Nations lands in the fertile Ohio valley. The lands were the traditional hunting grounds of the *Cherokee* and *Shawnee* First Nations. Most of the settlers were from the neighbouring colonies of North Carolina, Virginia and Pennsylvania.

In an effort to prevent English claims to these lands the governor of New France sent Captain Pierre de Blainville to survey and place French markers over 3,000 miles in the Ohio valley. The French next built a series of forts through the Ohio from Montreal to New Orleans. During the Seven Years War England secured the military help of the First Nations to defeat France by signing the Treaty of Easton in 1758.

This treaty prohibited **White** settlements west of the Alleghany Mountains. At the same time military roads built by the English to prosecute the war against the French were now used by **White** settlers to move into the Ohio valley in contravention of the Treaty of Easton. In response to this invasion of their territory the First Nations attacked England under the leadership of Pontiac and captured 8 of the 11 English forts. England responded with biological warfare using the small pox virus to infect the First Nations. But in October of 1763 England issued a Royal Proclamation prohibiting further English settlements west of the Appalachian Mountains. This kept the peace with the First Nations until the American War of Independence.

The *Cumberland Gap* provided a natural route through the Appalachian Mountains. It was long used by the First Nations. The American, Daniel Boone, began to explore this route in 1769. By 1775, Boone had cut a trail which served as the primary road for American settlers to cross into the First Nations lands. By 1790 some 100,000 Americans had made Kentucky and Tennessee their home.

In 1790 the First Nations defeated an armed invasion by the US under General Josiah Harmar. In 1791, the First Nations defeated another military invasion by the US led by General Arthur St. Clair.

The US, however, had played a clever hand which would ultimately enable it to successfully invade and conquer these First Nations lands. In 1778 the US had signed a long term treaty with France to get France to defeat England so that the US could secure its independence from England. During this *American War of Independence* the *Shawnee* First Nation allied with England to prevent conquest by an independent US. However, once the US had achieved independence it quickly understood that it was not in its self- interest to honour the treaty with France.

If the US were to be successful in conquering the First Nations lands west of the Appalachian Mountains it was essential that the US maintained friendly relations with England, not France. It was England, not France, which now had the military forts in the Ohio Valley. England could use these forts to help the First Nations, its ally up to the second Treaty of Paris, defend against US invasions. The forts were also used by England as trading posts for the lucrative fur trade with the First Nations. It was therefore in the self-interest of the US to renege on its treaty obligations to France so as to successfully negotiate the removal of the English forts in the Ohio Valley.

By 1793 a new war between England and France was imminent. France sent Edmund Charles Genet to the US on April 8, 1793, to confirm that the US would live up to the *long-term* Franco-American treaty signed in1778 and help France defend its Caribbean colonies as well as open US ports to ships captured by France. France quickly learnt that the US had only signed the 1778 treaty to betray England and it was now France's turn to be betrayed by the US. Once a traitor, always a traitor.

On April 22, 1793, President Washington issued a Proclamation of Neutrality in the coming war between England and France. In May 1794, Washington sent his Chief Justice, John Jay, to settle outstanding disputes with England. Jay's important treaty of 1794 secured England's commitment to abandon its forts in the Ohio valley. As the Americans poured into the Ohio valley through the *Cumberland Gap* and the *Wilderness Trail* many bloody wars, including the *Cherokee War,* were fought with the First Nations. However, without British military assistance the First Nations were doomed. *Kentucky* became the 15th state of an expanding US Empire on June 1, 1792.

The colonial settlement of Virginia had pushed the Cherokee Nation south into the area later conquered by Washington's freedom loving republic as the state of *Tennessee.* The Cherokees had settled in the Tennessee Valley alongside the long time inhabitants of this land, the Chickasaw and Choctaw Nations. During the American War of Independence the Cherokee Nation, like the Shawnee Nation, allied with the British to prevent conquest by an independent US. As the First Nations had feared, US independence hastened the conquest of their lands.

In 1787, the North Carolina Road was constructed to make it easier for American settlers to pour into the Tennessee Valley. In 1794 the US defeated the First Nations at the decisive *Battle of Fallen Timbers.* In 1795 the First Nations of the northwest, including the *Shawnee* and *Delaware* Nations were forced to sign the *Treaty of Greenville* with the US. Tennessee was conquered and became the 16th state of the American Empire in 1796. The Cherokee Nation was later forced to migrate westward again because of the American conquest.

The American Empire Invades and Conquers Ohio and Louisiana: 1797-1812

Washington had set the standard for judging the success of American presidents. That standard was territorial conquest and expansion of the American Empire. Future US presidents did not fail Washington until the recent and current presidencies of George W. Bush and Barack Obama whose failed invasions of Iraq and Afghanistan will put an end to American imperialism. The World will finally be able to breathe freedom from US domination. Those who have seen the Hollywood classic, *Ben Hur,* may recall the words of Charlton Heston to Steven Boyd, to the effect that when Rome falls, the world will breathe an air of freedom it has never seen before. How ironic that neither Hollywood nor Heston see the analogy with the American Empire.

The American Invasion and Conquest of Ohio

Territorial expansion continued under the presidency of Thomas Jefferson with the conquest of Ohio which was incorporated into the American Empire on March 1, 1803. This added another 45,000 square miles to the area of the United States and 45,000 square miles less to the lands of the First Nations. The land had been inhabited by several First Nations including the Shawnees, Ottawas, Iroquois, Miamis and Wyandots. It was part of the hunting grounds of the Iroquois confederacy. European colonization had been passed from France to England by the first Treaty of Paris in 1763.

Theft by the US was initially forestalled by Pontiac's rebellion and the resulting Royal Proclamation by the British. England reluctantly ceded some rights to the US by the second Treaty of Paris in 1783. The First Nations, Canada and England continued to oppose the US invasion. The Americans were determined to steal the land. The so called "Continental Congress" passed what it hypocritically called the "freedom ordinance," on July 13, 1787 establishing the right of the US to expand westwards into First Nations lands by adding new states to the Union.

An even more important irony lost on historians was that these planned future states of the Union were conquered by the US **before** there was any significant number of Americans inhabiting these lands. The *Northwest Ordinance,* as the freedom ordinance is more commonly known, ordained that these First Nations lands would become states of the Union once the population of a particular area reached 60,000. "Conquer now and populate later," was the implicit rallying cry of the misnamed *freedom ordinance.*

In 1784, three years before the Continental Congress passed the Northwest Ordinance, Thomas Jefferson suggested names for these new states, one of the names being *Washington.* This ordinance was passed by the government of the same republic which historians claim to be the world's protector of the right to self determination by all people and the country which supposedly protects people around the globe from imperialism. Only American historians can see logic in such hypocrisy.

Only American historians would cling to the false claim that Washington and Jefferson were true republicans fighting for freedom and equality even though both were dedicated slave owners and neither saw the inherent inconsistency of preaching anti-imperialism while conquering First Nations lands. In reality, it was the monarchies of Europe, England and France, chastised by American historians as tyrannical imperialists, which aided the First Nations in resisting the invasions by the American "Republican" Empire.

England eventually abandoned its First Nations allies and the English fur traders in the Old Northwest. American historians take the position that the Old Northwest was American even though it was inhabited by 2,000 English and French traders in addition to the 45,000 First Nations inhabitants. Up until the 1790's English traders alone outnumbered American settlers.

The First Nations, led by Little Turtle of the Miamis Nation and Blue Jacket of the Shawnee Nation had fought many battles against the US military in what has been called the *Northwest Indian War.* Some historians claim that Little Turtle and Blue Jacket inflicted some of the worst defeats of the US military up to that point. But President Washington sealed the fate of the First Nations with Jay's Treaty of 1794. Knowing that England would no longer provide military aid to the First Nations he sent General "Mad Anthony" Wayne to inflict a final blow on the First Nations in the Old Northwest in 1794.

President Washington had laid the groundwork for President Jefferson to create the Ohio state in 1803. Ohio became a part of the US by military conquest. It was split off from the Old Northwest Territory leaving the *Indiana Territory* for future US imperialism and the conquest of states such as Indiana, Wisconsin, Michigan and Illinois. We will address these future conquests later.

The American Invasion and Conquest of Louisiana

The US had refused to honour its obligations to France under the treaty of 1778. As a result, France seized American ships. The US Congress responded by renouncing the 1778 treaty and authorized the US navy to attack French shipping. This undeclared naval war between the US and France ended when Napoleon overthrew the French Directory and signed an agreement with the US in September 1800 to abrogate the 1778 treaty of alliance.

France now had no illusions regarding the imperialist ambitions of the new US Republic. However, as usual, France and England were too busy fighting each other to worry about the conquests of the US which they both regarded as a *puny* nation unworthy of their attention. This would be their undoing. Under the presidency of Thomas Jefferson the Napoleonic War between England and France enabled an even greater land grab of First Nations lands than the Ohio valley. This was the vast Louisiana Territory which doubled the land area of the US with a single acquisition, adding over 800,000 square miles, 5.3 million acres, to the US. Even today, the Louisiana conquest represents almost 25 percent of the area of the US.

The historical justification for this theft of First Nations lands is almost laughable, were it not so criminal. Having stolen the First Nations lands west of the Appalachian Mountains, American historians justify the Louisiana conquest by pointing to the strategic importance of the port of New Orleans and the economics of cheap river transportation of American produce from the newly conquered states of Kentucky, Tennessee and Ohio. This type of American justification of imperialism is almost as bizarre as their justification for stealing First Nations Lands. First they encourage White immigrants to settle on First Nations lands without permission from the First Nations. When the First Nations attack the White settlers that is used as the justification for sending in the US army to butcher the First Nations and steal their land.

Once all of the First Nations land on the US mainland was conquered the American Empire used this same type of double-talk to conquer other lands. For example, the US invades a country in the Middle East to steal their oil. When the people resist the US call them terrorists and use their superior military weapons to steal their country and install puppet pro-American governments justifying the theft in the name of fighting terrorism. The World superficially agrees because everyone, except for a small minority, is afraid of the overwhelming military superiority of the US or is begging for its paltry hand out of foreign aid, a mere 0.2% of its GDP.

French presence in the Louisiana Territory dated back to Louis XIV. The initial exploration of the Mississippi River by Louis Joliet and Jacques Marquette in 1673 led to France claiming the vast Louisiana Territory between the Appalachian Mountains and the Rocky Mountains. In 1682 Rene-Robert La Salle sailed down the Mississippi as far as the Gulf of Mexico. La Salle, Joliet and Marquette, like so many other explorers of the day, were searching for a sea passage to the spices of the Indies. It was La Salle who named the Mississippi valley, Louisiana, in honour of King Louis XIV of France. In 1683 the French built Fort St. Louis on the Illinois River.

France was persuaded to give the Americans a free hand in stealing the First Nations lands in the vast Louisiana Territory by a monetary donation of $15 million to Napoleon's wars in Europe. Despite the hollow claims of the US to be the birthplace of republican values the French revolution was a threat to US slave owners.

Washington, claimed by most Americans to be the father of their country, was a large slave owner, inheriting the Mount Vernon plantation by marriage and for military services to the colony of Virginia. Pennsylvania was not a slave state. Any slave residing in Pennsylvania for over six months had to be freed by law. This posed a huge problem for Washington taking the presidency since the US capital was in Pennsylvania and Washington could not live without his slaves. Washington flouted the law by rotating his slaves at the presidential mansion so that none stayed continuously longer than six months. Washington kept this ploy secret from both his slaves and the American public. He was afraid that at least a few Americans might determine that he was not quite as freedom loving as he preached.

The French revolution emboldened the slaves in France's Caribbean colonies right on America's door step. Slave revolts had a long history in all of the Caribbean colonies where slaves far outnumbered Whites. However, the French revolution led to support for the slaves from many in the mother country. Unlike the American Revolution where freedom was primarily for the few rich aristocrats seeking to grab political power from England, the French Revolution has a more credible history of bringing freedom to the masses.

This scared the living daylights out of the American *slave-owners* because they had lied to the world about their love for freedom and equality. The French revolution exported its call for freedom to the entire Caribbean region but most importantly to the French Caribbean. Since the majority of the population in the Caribbean was **Black,** this call for freedom and equality by the French exposed the hypocrisy of American freedom. American freedom was for **Whites** only.

In 1778, the French Caribbean colonies of St. Domingue, Martinique and Guadeloupe, sent delegates to the Paris meeting of the Estates General agreed to by King Louis XVI. Whites and Blacks were unified in demanding independence from France, unlike the US where the First Nations and Blacks trusted their freedom more with England than with an independent White dominated US. The *Society of the Friends of Blacks* was founded in France to lobby for the abolition of slavery in the French Caribbean colonies. Many non-Whites who had supported the Revolution in Paris journeyed to the French Caribbean colonies to help organize Blacks to revolt against slavery.

On April 4, 1792, the Legislative Assembly in France legalized equality for all free men including Blacks and Coloureds. This was a very significant piece of legislation. The French Caribbean colonies had large numbers of free Blacks and Coloureds, some of whom owned plantations and slaves. In a confrontation with White colonists the free Blacks and Coloureds would join with the Black slaves. In the Caribbean, Blacks far outnumbered Whites, as much as five to one.

America's fear of slave revolts and the abolition of slavery in the 1790's was equivalent to its fear of terrorism today and of Communism in the 1950's. Far from supporting the French revolution as true Republicans, most American leaders hoped that the French revolution would fail. In September 1792, the Jacobin, Leger Sonthonax, arrived in St. Domingue with 7,000 troops to ensure that free Blacks and Coloureds were given greater power in the colonial assemblies. In June 1793, Sonthonax abolished slavery in the French Caribbean colonies in an effort to get support for his cause from all Blacks. On February 4, 1794, the French Revolutionary government abolished slavery in all its colonies. This act by a European colonial power which was militarily much more powerful than the US at the time became America's *worst nightmare.*

American historians ignore America's hypocrisy in their explanations as to why the US did not support the French Revolution. They point to atrocities committed during the French Revolution such as the use of the *guillotine* conveniently ignoring atrocities committed by the US on its Black and First Nations populations. The reality was that Americans were never true Republicans and had much more in common with the English Monarchy than the French Republic.

With the abolition of slavery in the French Caribbean slave revolts increased in the English Caribbean colonies. England and the US had common cause to ally with each other to fight France which dared to give freedom and equality to **non-Whites.** Did the French not know that non-Whites could never be equal to Whites? It was no surprise to anyone except American historians that the US would be reluctant to receive Edmund Charles Genet, the ambassador from the new Republic of France. Alexander Hamilton, the most powerful US politician after President Washington, lobbied hard to deny Genet the right to be received by the US government.

In the end Washington did receive Genet but was not persuaded by Genet to support the new French Republic. France would have to take on England without help from the US. Quite apart from US economic and political interests benefiting from sucking up to England the US saw an economic opportunity to grow and expand its own economy by selling war materials to the combatants. The continuing and incessant wars among the European nations would be the major reason why 13 tiny colonies which became the US would become the most powerful empire the world has ever seen.

England's concern for its sugar barons in its Caribbean colonies led to English troops being sent to the Caribbean to protect the White sugar plantation owners from slave revolts and to even assist White French plantation owners who opposed the manumission policies of the new French Republic. It was a very confusing time in the Caribbean as Blacks were supported by some Whites and France but opposed by some Whites and England in English and French colonies alike.

While the US did not take an active role in the Caribbean during this eventful period it looked on with great concern. It was very much aware that its own constitution and professed claims to freedom, equality and republican values had stirred up its Black population to demand more just treatment. French success in the Caribbean would spill over into the US as Blacks in the US looked to their

West Indian brothers for political support, and also because of the very close economic, political and trade relationships between the US and the Caribbean.

Reneging on its 1778 treaty with France was one way of helping England to win over France and thereby protect US interests. As events developed, US neutrality not only kept slavery and their denial of equality to non-Whites intact it doubled the land area of the US by enabling the US to steal the enormous Louisiana Territory from the First Nations.

Confusion in the Caribbean was compounded when Spain invaded the French colony of St. Domingue in March 1793. A slave by the name of *Toussaint L'Ouverture* recruited a guerilla force of 4,000 Blacks to help the French defeat Spain. England sent troops to support Spain. The Blacks under L'Ouverture defeated both the Spanish and English troops and took control of the most valuable sugar producing colony in the entire world. This successful slave rebellion against two European powers sent shivers across the entire US especially the slave dominated southern states.

Who would have guessed that only a few years later this same successful slave rebellion would play a decisive role in the US acquisition of the Louisiana Territory? Had England and Spain defeated the French and taken control of St. Domingue, as the US hoped, the vast Louisiana Territory would very likely have become an independent French Republic and the US would have been a much smaller and less powerful empire.

L'Ouverture's successful slave rebellion, so feared by the US at the time, turned out to be an enormous gift to US imperialism. In 1798 the English withdrew from St. Domingue after losing 13,000 men. In January 1801, L'Ouverture captured Santo Domingo, the Spanish half of the island of Hispaniola, thereby unifying the French half of St. Domingue with Santo Domingo. Unfortunately for L'Ouverture, England and France singed the *Peace of Amiens* in October 1801. In 1801, St. Domingue was regarded by many as the richest colony in the world because of the high price of sugar and Napoleon, now the supreme leader of France, wanted it back.

Much has been written of Napoleon's disastrous Russian campaign. Less is known of Napoleon's disaster in the Caribbean island that the world now knows as *Haiti* and as one of the poorest and most politically unstable countries in the Western hemisphere. It seems to me that the Haitian disaster was more costly to France than the Russian disaster. It is extremely doubtful that France would have been able to keep Russia as a permanent colony even if Napoleon's invasion had been successful. However, had Napoleon succeeded in Haiti it's almost certain that France would have kept and expanded its Louisiana Territory in America.

Napoleon's European victories had led to the return of the Louisiana Territory to France by Spain. Spain had acquired it from France after the disastrous Seven Years War. Napoleon, like Louis XIV before, had a grandiose vision of a French Empire stretching from the Caribbean to Florida, French Guiana and Louisiana. Napoleon may very well have succeeded in his grand scheme had he not underestimated the hostile tropical climate in St. Domingue, now Haiti, as much as he underestimated the severity of the Russian winter. It must have been especially galling to Napoleon to find out that his plans were thwarted by a slave, Toussaint L'Ouverture.

Despite the efforts of the world famous actor, Anthony Quinn, Hollywood has not yet made the story of L'Ouverture known worldwide. By defeating Napoleon in Haiti, L'Ouverture inadvertently gave the US the opportunity to invade and conquer Louisiana. Napoleon sent a force of 40,000 men to secure his French Empire in the New World. The plan was to quickly secure the Caribbean before moving to the mainland. But the tropical Caribbean climate and tropical disease decimated his troops as it had done to so many French, English and Spanish troops before. Even Napoleon's commander, General Leclerc, succumbed to yellow fever.

Failure in St. Domingue not only ended Napoleon's grand scheme, it forced Napoleon to sell off the Louisiana Territory to the US to finance his defense against the wrath of the seemingly invincible

Royal Navy of Great Britain. A French colony in Louisiana would very likely have been successfully defended against US invasions in the same way as the English colony of Canada was successfully defended against US invasions. Both England and France were militarily more powerful than the US up until the First World War.

President Jefferson's plan to conquer the Louisiana territory was as natural to him as Washington's plan to conquer the Canadas, Kentucky and Tennessee. Both Jefferson and Washington wanted to expand North into Canada and the Maritimes and West and South of the Appalachian Mountains. Washington had succeeded in acquiring Vermont in the North and Kentucky and Tennessee in the West. It was up to Jefferson to continue the precedent set by Washington for US expansion and conquest, the so called "Add a state Plan."

Jefferson's priority was control of the Mississippi River and the port of New Orleans. This was the most natural westward expansion in an age before the railroads when water transportation was the key to territorial expansion. Jefferson had a secret plan to send American explorers into the Louisiana Territory. These secret plans were made public after the "purchase" of Louisiana from Napoleon and became known as the *Lewis and Clark Expedition*. Jefferson's expansionist invasion of First Nations land is unabashedly celebrated by Americans as exemplified by the *Jefferson National Expansion Memorial in St. Louis*. This was designated a National Memorial by the US government on December 21, 1935. The memorial attracts four million visitors annually.

With a budget of $2,500 and the help of 29 men and one woman, Captain Meriwether Lewis and Lieutenant William Clark set off to do the president's bidding in 1804. The primary goal of the expedition was to capture as much of the lucrative fur trade from the French, English and First Nations and lay the foundations for future US invasion and conquest of more First Nations land. The expedition was a resounding success despite the best efforts of Spain to intercept and stop Lewis and Clark.

With the help of the First Nation guide, Sacagawea, and her French Canadian husband, Toussaint Charbonneau, the expedition first followed the Missouri River and then the Columbia River reaching the Oregon territory and finally the Pacific Ocean. Clarke founded the Missouri Fur Company and quickly established trading posts along the Missouri River. Settlers soon followed and by the time of the second US invasion of Canada in 1812, over 75,000 Americans had moved west of St. Louis.

It was somewhat ironic that the official transfer of Louisiana from France to the US would take place at a ceremony in St. Louis, named after the French king, on March 9, 1804. Louisiana was such a huge piece of real estate that the US governed it as two *organized territories*. The precedent for establishing organized territories as a form of government in the US had been established with the Northwest Territory in 1787. In time, several states were carved out of these territories.

The two territories created out of the theft of Louisiana from the First Nations were the *Louisiana Territory* and the *Orleans Territory*. The Orleans Territory was created on October 1, 1804 and became the *eighteenth* US state of Louisiana on March 30, 1812. With the creation of the state of Louisiana the old Louisiana Territory, created on July 4, 1805, was re-named the *Missouri Territory*. While Louisiana was invaded and conquered by President Jefferson, since the state of Louisiana was not officially added to the Union until 1812, President Madison could claim that he had followed faithfully the precedent set by Washington and Jefferson to "add a state" to the Union by military invasions and conquests.

The Second US Invasion of Canada

The second US invasion of Canada, like the first, had its origins in the successful defeat of France by England during the Seven Years War of 1756-1763. There was no question that both England and its 13 colonies found common cause in wanting the French out of America. What changed after the English victory was the opportunity presented to the 13 colonies to seize the continent from England. We explained above how the colonies used France during their War of Independence to implement their plan to seize the continent from England.

The second Treaty of Paris signed on September 3, 1783 enshrined the gains made to that point. We also explained that England was surprisingly generous to the rebellious colonies in that treaty to the detriment of France. This treaty laid the foundation of a long term *special relationship* between England and the United States which continues to this day. While this initially served both England and the US equally well it ended up helping the ascendancy of the US to its current position of supreme world bully at the expense of England taking a leadership position in a united Europe which could have played a more constructive role in the world and acted as a check on the evils of US imperialism.

In 1783, the 13 colonies were a net liability to the English treasury and an unacceptable distraction to its governance of a world-wide empire in India, the Far East, Africa, the Caribbean and North America. It made sense to grant them independence while maintaining good economic and political ties. However, England still wanted to continue the fur trade in North America, continue to defend the English colonies in North America and continue to support its First Nations allies against further thefts of their lands by the US. This was where the interests of the US and England initially collided. Nowhere did these interests collide more than in the defence of Canada against the consistent desire of the US to invade and conquer Canada as part of its goal to steal the entire continent from both the First Nations and Europe.

Canada, like the original 13 American colonies before, was too expensive for England to defend relative to the benefits flowing to England from these colonies. During the second half of the eighteenth century the North American colonies were much less valuable to England than its lucrative sugar producing Caribbean colonies and the riches of its Eastern and African colonies. At the same time these North American colonies were expensive to defend against France, Spain, the First Nations, and now the independent United States. Add to this economic analysis the endemic costs of the military conflicts in Europe and the high taxes paid by the English in England and it is easy to see why an imperialist United States was a serious threat to the survival of the Canadas as British colonies much less as an independent country.

The second opportunity to conquer Canada presented itself to the US when England and France resumed their incessant wars for empire. This time it was the Napoleonic Wars which lasted from 1793 to 1815. This long expensive war between England and France weakened England, reduced the ability of England to defend its North American colonies and simultaneously increased the economy of the US which profited from exports to the European combatants. As the ability of England to defend the Canadas and the Atlantic colonies weakened and the economy and population of the US simultaneously increased it was simply a matter of time before the US invaded.

Canada was ultimately saved from conquest by the American Empire only by Napoleon's disastrous invasion of Russia. The Americans had waited just a little too long to invade. It had made sense for the US to wait since each passing year made the US stronger and England weaker. However, the US, like Napoleon, did not expect the historical turn of events in 1812. The year the US invaded the Canadas was also the year Napoleon was defeated by the Russians.

The defeat of Napoleon by the Russians made it possible for England to send more troops to defend its North American colonies against the invading Americans. As we will briefly explain, even with the defeat of Napoleon by the Russians the defence of the Canadas in 1812 against a very determined imperialist US was a formidable task and victory was never guaranteed. What chance of success would Canada have had if Napoleon had not committed a military blunder by underestimating the power of the Russian winter?

Despite the deafening and irritating rhetoric of Americans, beginning with the founding fathers, of their belief in democracy, self determination, republican values and desire for peace, no one in Canada had any illusions about the imperialist ambitions of the new republic on its southern border. Canadians knew that it was simply a matter of time before the Americans would invade. The British knew this and so did the First Nations.

The British had hoped that the First Nations would have kept the Americans so busy in the west that they would have lacked the resources to wage war on both their western and northern fronts. However, the First Nations resistance was stymied by their defeat in 1794 which forced them to sign the *Treaty of Greenville* in 1795. The military power of the US was growing by leaps and bounds and the expansive English North American colonies with opportunities for fishing, furs, timber and vast settlements were on the US radar even before it had won its independence from England.

The First Nations had feared the English more than the French for good reason. France brought relatively few inhabitants to steal First Nations lands compared with England. But now there was an even greater threat than the English. There was a home made imperial power not one in far off Europe and this home grown imperial power was more ruthless and ambitious than any of the European imperialists, Spain, Portugal, Holland, France and England.

The First Nations therefore knew that England was now the far lesser of the two evils. Despite their feelings of betrayal by England after both the Seven Years War and the American War of Independence they had little choice but to support England and its North American colonies against the new American juggernaut bent on sweeping across the entire continent with no regard for any who came before, First Nations, Spanish, Portuguese, Brazilians, Mexicans, French or English. It was America's god given destiny to conquer and rule the continent. Both god and weapons of mass destruction were on its side.

Talk of invading the Canadas began in typical US fashion. Find a grievance to fool its electorate and the world about its true intentions. This time it would be the British preventing Americans from selling their exports to the combatants in the Napoleonic wars. Americans had a god given right to benefit from all wars around the globe and the English had no right to deny them that benefit. Invade the Canadas to teach England a lesson so that in future wars around the globe America would have the freedom to benefit economically from exports to the combatants.

If the US were to grow relative to other imperial powers it must be allowed to take full economic advantage of all global wars since this was a sure way of gaining an edge. Wars reduce the economy of the combatants while simultaneously increasing the economies of the non-combatants who freely sell much needed war and war related supplies to the combatants. The US must benefit economically from the endemic European wars if it were to achieve its manifest destiny to rule the world.

Canada and the US prior to the US Invasion of 1812

It is useful to summarize the political reality of the two countries prior to the US invasion of 1812. We will begin with Canada, even though Canada did not yet exist as a unified Nation state and the geographical boundaries between states in the American Union and the English colonies which later unified to become Canada were far from well established. In fact, the entire North American continent continued to be in the same state of flux it had been in the three previous centuries when Spain, France, England and the First Nations fought each other for the land.

The only difference now was that there was one more competitor for the same territory. The new competitor was, of course, the United States. It is safe to say that the newly created Nation state of the

USA had an edge over the European imperialists by being on the continent. The US had absolutely no qualms about exploiting that edge to its own advantage using whatever rhetoric and hypocrisy necessary to camouflage its imperialist intentions. Furthermore, by 1812, the European imperialists were beginning to have some feelings of guilt regarding their earlier mistreatment of the First Nations and their introduction of African slavery. Not so for the new imperialist. No such feelings of guilt remotely influenced the behviour of the US as it competed with the European powers for the land.

The Canadian Political Reality before 1812 and the Founding of the new English colony of Upper Canada

England had fought many wars with France prior to the Seven Years War of 1756-63 but the latter war marked the final defeat of France by England. The problem was that neither France nor England wanted the French colony of Quebec. Both preferred the rich sugar island of Guadeloupe. Unfortunately, England had a new inexperienced king, George III, and a new First Lord of the Treasury, Lord Bute. Both came to power in 1760, the year which saw the resignation of the very experienced William Pitt as Chief Minister. George III was only 22 years old.

The 13 American colonies to the south of Quebec were able to convince George III that if he were to give up the sugar prize and take Quebec his loyal subjects in North America would be forever grateful for ridding them of the French menace. Little did King George realize that the 13 colonies had ambitions of their own.

Taking on the governance of the colony of Quebec with its French majority when England had just expanded its world-wide empire across Asia, Africa and the Caribbean and when English taxpayers were revolting against high taxes, was a rather daunting task for the new king. Furthermore, the 13 colonies, far from showing gratitude for expelling the French from North America took advantage of the king's plight to ridicule and question his right to govern them and impose taxes on them to help pay for their own defence against the First Nations whose lands they stole with impunity.

They dubbed him the *Royal Brute* even though it was their continued theft of First Nations lands that led to the chief of the Ottawa Nation, Pontiac, attacking England within a few months of the Treaty of Paris which ended the Seven Years War. England desperately needed a plan which would deal fairly with the English colonists in North America, the French colonists in North America, and England's First Nations allies, if it were to avoid costly wars the English taxpayers rightly rebelled against.

The English plan was the *Royal Proclamation* of October 1763 which provided an abundance of land for expanded English settlements north of the 13 American colonies. West of the Alleghany Mountains the English could trade with the First Nations but not erect permanent settlements. This plan was seen to be fair by everyone except the very colonists who had promised King George III that they would be loyal and obedient British subjects if the King expelled France from North America. They wanted freedom to expand into Quebec, into the Atlantic colonies and into First Nations lands west of the Alleghany Mountains. In essence they wanted England, the First Nations and Spain, out of North America. As early as 1763 they revealed their insatiable greed for the lands of others and their addiction to warmongering.

Pontiac's confederacy of western First Nations was crushed by England towards the end of 1764. The First Nations then recognized that they were militarily incapable of defending their lands against both England and the 13 American colonies. As the 13 colonies became increasingly hostile towards the mother country the First Nations saw their future as better served by allying with England and Quebec against the 13 colonies. That was the lesser of two evils. This choice was reinforced by the pattern of settlement after the Royal Proclamation.

One intention of the Proclamation had been to encourage new **White** settlers into Quebec rather than into the Ohio valley. However, the majority of new settlers disobeyed the Proclamation by moving west into the Ohio valley instead of north into Quebec. These new settlers allied with the 13 colonies against England and the First Nations instead of with England and Quebec.

England's military defeat and ousting of France from North America, far from securing North America for England, led to the division of North America into a new nation far more populous than the French colonies, far more aggressive against both England and the First Nations than France had been, and a string of thinly populated colonies to the north.

It was as if the 13 colonies had become England in North America and England had become France in North America. After the Seven Years War the thinly populated English colonies in the North would have to defend against the far more populous anti-English 13 colonies to the south just as before the Seven Years War, the thinly populated French colonies had to defend against the more populous English colonies.

The other parallel was that just as England fought France for **all** of North America so would the 13 colonies fight England for **all** of North America. While England wanted to trade with the First Nations west of the Alleghany Mountains, just as the French had done before, the 13 colonies wanted settlements, just as England had wanted before. England belatedly recognized this new reality by replacing the Royal Proclamation of 1763 with the *Quebec Act* of 1774.

The Quebec Act was a reluctant recognition by England that it had failed to replace the French majority in Quebec with new **White** settlers loyal to England and simultaneously failed to protect the Ohio valley from theft by the 13 colonies. This theft threatened the lucrative fur trade with the First Nations, England's primary source of revenue from its North American colonies.

It had become increasingly clear to England that no concessions would appease the 13 colonies to the south which were bent on rebellion against the mother country and conquering as much territory in North America as their military power would enable. It would be easier for England to court the allegiance of the French *Canadiens* and expand the territorial boundary of the colony of Quebec than to hold on to the allegiance of the 13 colonies to the south. The Quebec Act, therefore, extended the boundary of Quebec into the Ohio valley and courted the allegiance of the French majority in Quebec to defend England against the increasingly rebellious English colonies to the south.

While the plan accepted the inevitable of the 13 colonies leaving the British Empire it succeeded in preventing the 13 colonies from conquering an expanded Quebec. Many American historians blame the Quebec Act, declared by the rebellious colonies as one of the "Intolerable Acts," as a primary cause of the American Revolution. In fact, the Quebec Act was a farsighted policy by those in England who saw that the 13 colonies were hell bent on rebellion and could only be stopped by military force.

Their alleged grievances against the mother country were fabricated lies to garner world support for their hidden imperialist motives and treachery against the First Nations' inhabitants. Initially, the Quebec Act failed to keep the 13 colonies in the British Empire only because England became embroiled in another costly war with France which the 13 colonies instigated. It was France which enabled a successful American revolt against England.

The Birth of British North America

The loss of the 13 English colonies led to the creation of *British North America* as a way of distinguishing the remaining English colonies in North America from the newly independent nation of the United States of America. As the US imposed its aggressive dominance on the continent it appropriated the name *America* forcing other independent nations, including Canada, to accept lesser status in the continent.

The second Treaty of Paris ending the war with the 13 colonies not only recognized the independence of the 13 colonies but transferred the First Nations lands in the Ohio valley to the United States. This was the first clear and undeniable proof of the imperialist intentions of the 13 colonies. Yet historians continue to treat the American Revolution as purely a revolt by colonies for their own independence. Furthermore, had the 13 colonies succeeded in their invasions of Quebec and Nova Scotia, they would have made every effort to keep those lands as well.

The failure of the 13 colonies to conquer Quebec created a border dispute between Quebec and the United States. Neither Quebec nor the First Nations were happy about the transfer of the Ohio valley to the US. This unity of cause by Quebec and the First Nations was of primary importance in the defence of Quebec against the second US invasion of 1812.

Another important damning piece of evidence against the claims of the new United States that it had created a freedom loving republic was the desire of many **White** settlers to choose English colonial status over US citizenship. This was truly a remarkable slap in the face of this professed freedom loving Republic. If the US was as freedom loving as it professed why would **White** settlers choose English colonial yoke over freedom and equality?

The so called "United Empire Loyalists," who chose "refugee" status in British North America and the British West Indies or returned to England, knew that the United States was founded on hypocrisy, double-talk, lies, militarism, imperialist ambitions and the wholesale disregard for the rights of Blacks, First Nations, non-whites and **poor whites**. Most estimates suggest that one third of the colonists of the 13 colonies opposed the revolt against the mother country. They were called *Loyalists* by the revolutionaries and branded as traitors of the revolution.

The revolutionaries gave themselves the lofty title of *Patriots*. While the majority of Loyalists remained in the independent US about 100,000 Loyalists, roughly 20 percent, fled the US. The *Patriots* were only too happy to confiscate and steal the property of the Loyalists, humiliate and physically attack them. In some cases Loyalists were killed or "tarred and feathered." If you were unfortunate enough to be brought before Judge Lynch, death by hanging was your certain fate. Hence the term, "Lynch mob." While a small minority of Loyalists joined the English army, the great majority were passive throughout the revolution.

During the revolution the British controlled Long Island and New York City. This provided a haven for the Loyalists to escape persecution by the revolutionaries. Life under British *military* rule in New York was preferable to living under the new "freedom loving" republic. US independence led to a massive influx of these Loyalists into the newly created *British North America*. Most of them chose the colony of Nova Scotia which led to the creation of the new colony of New Brunswick in 1784.

The influx of Loyalists into Quebec led to the creation of the new colony of Upper Canada which later became the province of Ontario. It is safe to say that the American Revolution led to the creation of two new independent countries, the USA and Canada, out of the lands belonging to the First Nations.

Colonists, First Nations and slaves, who recognized the lies and propaganda of a wealthy slave owning class led by George Washington, chose the much lesser evil of English colonialism and fled to other English colonies. A few even fled to the Portuguese colony of Brazil. But the great majority chose the colonies in British North America since they were the most accessible and had the most First Nations land for new settlements.

England was more than willing to help the Loyalists move into British North America since England was also not fooled by the lies of the new republic. It knew only too well its imperialist and aristocratic ambitions. Only military force and a growing population would stop the new republic from seizing all of the English colonies in British North America.

The *Constitutional Act* of 1791 recognized the reality of the need for the division of the colony of Quebec into French speaking and English speaking colonies. There had been an influx of English speaking settlers into Quebec after 1763 but it was not sufficient to change Quebec into an English speaking colony as England had hoped. A geographical division was workable because most of the influx of English speaking settlers, including the Loyalists feeing the American Revolution, had settled into the area which became the new English speaking colony of Upper Canada.

The French speaking part of Quebec became Lower Canada. Religion also played an important role in this division of Quebec. Most of the inhabitants of the French speaking Lower Canada were Catholics while most of the settlers of the English speaking Upper Canada were Protestants.

All of the colonies in British North America were united under a single governor general. The Act of 1791 laid the foundation for what later became the independent country of Canada north of a much more powerful and populous USA. The US was determined to use its power to expand west into First Nations lands, south into Spanish colonies and north into English colonies. Nothing but military force could stop the US then as now.

In the period following the creation of an independent USA and the US invasion of Canada in 1812, Americans continued to leave the US for the British North American colonies. The US had signed the second Treaty of Paris in 1783 to secure its independence. However, the US had no intention of abiding by the reciprocal aspect of that treaty which required the US to return lands confiscated from the Loyalists.

The new freedom loving republic would renege on treaties signed with England, with the First Nations and with France. The creation of the new English speaking colony of Upper Canada in 1791 acted as a magnet for American immigrants wanting to escape the lies and hypocrisy of the new republic. This influx of Americans was welcomed by Upper Canada's first lieutenant governor, John Simcoe.

In 1794 England made another attempt to get the US to return the properties of the Loyalists by signing Jay's Treaty with the Americans. The US agreed to return the confiscated properties in exchange for the English forts and trading posts in the Old Northwest. The Americans took the forts but never returned the confiscated properties.

By 1812 the population of the new colony of *Upper Canada* was almost 100,000 due largely to American immigration. Americans of all religious faiths were welcomed and given good First Nations agricultural land for new settlements. Simcoe promoted a *slave free* agricultural economy based on wheat in contrast to the *slave economies* based on cotton and sugar in the freedom loving USA. The 1797 Act prohibited future importation of slaves into Upper Canada. Children of slaves already in the colony were to be freed at age 25. Simcoe also began preparations to defend the colony from the expected US invasion.

England and Canada have not been innocent imperial powers in regard to their treatment of First Nations, African slaves or non-whites. But compared to the USA, the unilateral self-appointed, by military force, "Leader of the Free World," Canada and England have been relatively exemplary.

By 1812 the English colonial population of half a million was ready to face off against the American population exceeding 7 million. It was so reminiscent of the many Anglo/French wars in North America except that the English were now the combatant with the smaller numbers and the Americans would be fighting on home territory. The Americans knew only too well that superior numbers and fighting on home turf had not led to success in their first invasion of the British North American colonies in 1775. They also knew that colonial militias were no match for regular European armies except in guerilla type skirmishes with dense wilderness cover.

Without the French the US would not have defeated England during their War of Independence. Even so, luck was on the American side in that earlier conflict. The French fleet under Comte de Grasse, which had blockaded Charles Cornwallis and prevented his retreat during the middle of a storm, was shortly thereafter decimated by the English Admiral Rodney who had arrived just one week late to relieve Cornwallis in Chesapeake Bay.

The Americans knew that, at the very least, they would have to wait until England was engaged in another major war with France before they could invade any of the English colonies in British North America. In the meantime they would hone their military aggression by attacking softer targets such as the First Nations.

The American Political Reality before its Second Invasion of Canada in 1812

The one constant in US politics has been unbridled expansionism based on military aggression. Strike the weakest military targets first. The weakest military target after American independence in 1783 was the First Nations. Moving quickly against the First Nations, Washington carved out the states of Vermont, Kentucky and Tennessee while Jefferson captured Ohio and the much larger Louisiana Territory. These vast territorial conquests kept the US appetite for war and aggression occupied well into the administration of James Madison beginning in 1809.

It was now Madison's turn to uphold America's warmongering tradition and conquests of new territory. Madison found eager support from a large and growing group of US Congressmen known collectively as the *War Hawks*. US territorial expansion after independence had shifted political dominance from the Atlantic colonies in New England to the western states and territories which had elected the *War Hawks*. The group was led by the Speaker of the House of Representatives, Henry Clay, representing the new state of Kentucky. It has been said that Clay's power was second only to that of the president. Clay appointed War Hawks to all of the important Congressional committees.

Another prominent Congressional War Hawk from Kentucky was Richard Johnson, elected in 1807. Johnson chaired the Committee on Expenditures in the War department. Clay's most powerful ally was Congressman, John Calhoun of South Carolina. Calhoun was elected to the House of Representatives in 1810.

Other notable Congressional War Hawks from South Carolina were Langdon Cheves, elected in 1810 and William Lowndes, elected in 1811. Cheves was appointed as Chair of the Naval Commitee in 1812 and succeeded Henry Clay as Speaker in 1814. Lowndes was Chair of the Ways and Means committee.

Peter Porter was both a Congressional War Hawk and a military commander in the 1812 Canadian invasion. He represented New York and was appointed to the House of Representatives in 1809. George Troup of Georgia was elected to the US Senate in 1805 and chaired the Senate Committee of Military Affairs. As another dedicated War Hawk he lobbied hard for the 1812 invasion of Canada. Troup was ably supported by fellow Senator and War Hawk from Tennessee, Felix Grundy.

The War Hawks had their sights set on the British North American colonies, Spanish Florida and First Nations lands west of the Ohio River. The First Nations had been forced out of Ohio after their defeat by General Anthony Wayne in 1794. In 1811 the War Hawks in the US Congress were after another 3 million acres of First Nations lands to the west. A US force of 1,000 men, led by Governor William Harrison, attacked the First Nations at the Tippecanoe River in 1811 and burnt their village, Prophet's Town, to the ground.

With their backs to the wall the First Nations formed a new confederacy which included Cherokees, Chikasaws, Choctaws and the Red Stick Creeks. The new confederacy was led by the famous Shawnee war chief *Tecumseh* and his less famous brother Tenskwatawa. Since the First Nations knew that American aggression was not constrained to lands in the west but included the British North American colonies to the north, Tecumseh formed an alliance with England to fight the Americans.

Military aggressors like the US invariably overestimate their military prowess and attack one target too many. In the case of the US in 1812 that target too many was Canada. With England weakened by the long war against Napoleonic France, Canada seemed an easy target to a warmonger like the US. The Americans boasted that they could conquer Canada with 1,000 Kentucky riflemen. They planned to defeat both the English and Tecumseh in Canada and steal the lands to the north and to the west. The rich agricultural lands and the valuable fur trade would be theirs.

Next the new American Empire would drive the Spanish out of Florida. Spain was allied with England in the continental struggle against Napoleon. With both England and Spain driven out, all of North America would be theirs. Madison, like Washington and Jefferson before, would be American icons.

In preparation for the second invasion of Canada, American propaganda went into overdrive. They broadcasted that the English were destroying their foreign trade by blockading their ports, impressing their sailors into the Royal Navy and arming the First Nations. These charges against England were grossly exaggerated to fan the flames of war. Their invasion of Canada would be to liberate the people of Canada from English tyranny and bring them American republican democracy based on *slave ownership, decimation of First Nations and aristocratic dominance by large landowners and wealthy merchants.*

As General William Hull proclaimed, "Canadians would be emancipated from English tyranny and oppression and restored to the dignified station of freedom." Since it had been so easy to fool Americans it would not be too difficult to fool Canadians. At least that was what the War Hawks and Madison thought.

In July 1811, President Madison summoned the US Congress for an early session, to be held in November, to discuss preparations for war with England's North American colonies. The War Hawks who had been elected to the twelfth US Congress were ecstatic. However, not all states were equally enthusiastic about another war with the old mother country. Most of the New England states were opposed.

Madison, like most politicians, knew that all wars are extremely popular with the vast majority of the electorate if the war is won. Madison and the War Hawks were convinced that this war would be an easy victory for Madison's administration because Britain had been at war with France since 1792. The coalition of England, Spain, Austria, Prussia and Naples formed in 1792 to fight France had fallen apart by 1797 and a second coalition formed in 1798 also fell apart by 1801. Britain was almost alone in the struggle against Napoleon, who the Americans were proud to finance in exchange for the vast Louisiana Territory.

The European conflict had expanded to the Caribbean and to European colonies across the globe. It was reminiscent of the struggle for European hegemony between France and England during the Seven Years War. With English forces thinly spread across the globe the Americans would march quickly across the border and seize England's North American colonies before England could amass a concerted defence.

As President Jefferson had said, "Conquest of the northern territories was a mere matter of marching." It's a pity Americans never learn. Invasion of Vietnam would be a mere matter of flying

B52 bombers over Vietnam's territory and invasion of Iraq would be a mere matter of toppling the statue of Saddam Hussein in Baghdad.

The divided US Congress debated the planned invasion of Canada for 8 months. The vote in the House of Representatives on June 4, 1812, was 79 in favour of war and 49 against. The US Senate voted 19 in favour and 3 against. Madison declared war on England on June 18, 1812. Congress authorized an increase in the size of the US standing army from 12,000 to 36,000. The standing army would be assisted by the state militias. Financing the war would turn out to be as difficult as financing the later wars in Vietnam, Afghanistan and Iraq. Americans have a huge appetite for war but an equally huge dislike for taxes.

On the other side of the border there were 6,000 regular English troops supported by the colonial militias. However, both the defeated Six-Nations Iroquois League which was forced out of New York to Ontario and the First Nations defeated and forced out of the Old Northwest, now led by Tecumseh, were ready to fight for England against the Americans. The First Nations added about 4,000 men to the 6,000 English Regulars.

The Second Humiliation of the Myth of American Military Invincibility

The myth of American military invincibility like the myth of American democracy and republican values are integral parts of the propaganda used by the military-industrial complex controlling all aspects of American life to get the American people to vote for their unprovoked invasions of any country which the US feels confident enough to conquer. As early as 1814 the US had already suffered two humiliating defeats by populations far smaller and less well armed than the US. In addition, the US military had suffered from many defeats in battles with the First Nations. Yet the American military promoted the myth that it had never been defeated until the Vietnam War.

The American plan for the quick conquest of the British North American colonies in 1812 was to overwhelm Canadian resistance by invading from three sides. Quick victories would deter support for England by the French residents, American settlers in Canada, and the First Nations. The great majority of colonists would see the Americans as liberators and welcome them rather than fight them. Those who resisted would quickly learn to love all things American by looking up at the barrel of a gun pointed at their heads. The three-pronged invasion was to attack Upper Canada from Detroit, a second invasion force across the Niagara border and the third invasion force attacking Montreal from Lake Champlain.

Brigadier-General William Hull, governor of the Michigan territory, led the first attack on Upper Canada from Detroit. Hull arrived at Fort Detroit on July 5, 1812 and attacked on July 12, 1812 with a force of 2,200. His target was the British fort at Amherstburg across the Detroit River. In an effort to prevent an alliance between England and the First Nations, the Canadian "emancipator," Hull, boldly threatened to kill any English prisoner caught fighting alongside an Indian.

Hull crossed the Detroit River and captured Windsor on July 12, 1812, en route to Amherstburg. British forces in Canada were under the command of Sir Isaac Brock who had been stationed in Canada since 1802. Brock had made every effort to improve the defence of the colonies and was familiar with the territory. At the time of Hull's invasion Brock was stationed in York (Toronto). Brock decided to advance to meet the invaders. Hull panicked and retreated to Detroit. Brock reached Amherstburg with a force of 1,500, over half of which were First Nations. Rumour has it that Hull retreated because of his fear of being scalped by a First Nation.

At Amherstburg Brock first met the famous Shawnee war Chief Tecumseh. Together, they decided to carry the fight to the frightened Americans by attacking Hull at his base in Fort Detroit. In doing so, Brock went against the order of the governor of Canada, Sir George Prevost, who strongly warned Brock to stay on the defensive. But Brock crossed the Detroit River with Tecumseh and attacked Fort Detroit on August 14. Brock's cannons were no match for the Fort's fortifications and Brock was unable to shame Hull into facing him in open battle.

Much to Brock's surprise, Hull surrendered the Fort after only 2 days of bombardment and war cries by the First Nations. Hull surrendered a force of over 2,000 begging the English Major General to protect him and his men from England's First Nations allies. Americans had been taught an important lesson. It's much safer to invade far off countries like Vietnam, Grenada or Iraq where the chances of them invading you are relatively remote because of a safe geographical distance. Your marines can then safely return with tall tales of American military invincibility and great fodder for Hollywood movies.

Hull's unexpected surrender provided much needed armaments for Brock's colonial militias. Prior to Hull's surrender the English Captain, Charles Roberts, had captured another American garrison on July 17, 1812, at the key trading post of Michilimackinac which Britain had handed over to the US in 1796 under the terms of Jay's Treaty. This victory effectively kept the Americans out of the lucrative fur trade during their invasion of Canada. Roberts was also able to send men and munitions to Brock.

On July 2, 1812, the supplies of the US schooner, Cuyahoga, had also been captured by Lieutenant Frederick Rolette on the Detroit River. The Americans had also been defeated at Fort Dearborn in Chicago on August 15, 1812 by England's First Nations allies. These four early victories by England destroyed the American plan for a quick and easy conquest of Canada. Their invasion had backfired and put them on the defensive. England had captured Forts Detroit, Dearborn and Michilimackinac from the Americans. Only Fort Niagara along the Canada-US border remained in American hands. Brock transferred most of his troops to the Niagara frontier to meet the second prong of the planned three-pronged US invasion.

The second US invasion force across the Niagara border was led by General Stephen Van Rensselaer. Van Rensselaer commanded a force of 6,500 men, roughly ten times Brock's force. On October 13, 1812, Van Rensselaer crossed the Niagara River with over 3,000 men and attacked Queenston. An English force of only 300 men prevented Van Rensselaer from capturing Queenston. The Americans moved to higher ground and captured Queenston Heights.

With Windsor and Detroit secured after Hull's surrender, Brock led his troops, including 500 Iroquois warriors and a Black militia, to drive the Americans out of Queenston. Brock was killed in the initial attack on Van Rensselaer but the English under Major General Roger Sheaffe, Brock's second in command at Fort George, re-captured the Heights from the Americans taking over 1,000 prisoners and more arms to supply Canadian militias. Van Rensselaer resigned his commission in disgrace. Sheaffe received a knighthood for his efforts.

Success for the US invasion now lay with the third penetration of the Canadian border from Lake Champlain. This third invasion force was led by Major General Henry Dearborn. Dearborn was the senior commander of the planned US invasion of Canada and had the largest of the three invasion forces. Dearborn had served as Jefferson's secretary of war and was the principal architect of the planned removal of the First Nations from the Mississippi Valley. In January 1812, Madison appointed Dearborn to the position of senior Major General in the US army.

Dearborn advanced on Montreal on November 23, 1812 but retreated to Plattsburg when the New York militia refused to follow him into Lower Canada. Like Vietnam, Afghanistan and Iraq, later, the Americans would not score quick easy victories against countries militarily weaker than they were. Yet they would repeat the same mistake throughout their relatively short history as an imperial power.

The US continued to suffer heavy defeats as the invasion continued into 1813. William Harrison, the US general who had attacked the First Nations at Tippecanoe which had led to the alliance between Brock and Tecumseh, formed a second north-western force to re-take territory captured by Brock and invade Upper Canada by capturing Fort Amherstburg. After the English had transferred their primary trading post at Detroit in 1796, under the terms of Jay's treaty, Fort Amherstburg had been built on the other side of the Detroit River. The Fort housed a major shipyard where several large and small vessels were launched after 1796.

Harrison began his march towards Detroit during the winter of 1812 with an invasion force of 6,500. The English under Colonel Henry Procter and First Nations allies crossed the Detroit River on January 17, 1813, and attacked the Americans at Frenchtown on the Raisin River, just south of Detroit. The Americans under Brigadier-General James Winchester were defeated at the Battle of Frenchtown, January 22, 1813. Proctor was promoted to Brigadier General. Both sides suffered major casualties. Proctor and Tecumseh continued to harass the Americans and thereby prevented Harrison from launching a coordinated attack on Amherstburg. Harrison built Fort Meigs and Fort Stephenson to protect the remainder of his invasion force.

On February 21, 1813, the English attacked and defeated the Americans at Ogdensburg. The American garrison at Ogdensburg had been disrupting English supplies on the St. Lawrence River. The defeat of the American garrison ensured English supplies reached Montreal and permitted the resumption of normal trade relations between Americans and Canadians on opposite sides of the river. American farmers disobeyed their warmongering government and supplied food to Canada throughout the invasion.

With so many defeats the Americans formulated a new plan to conquer Canada. If the army fails try the navy. It was a smart if somewhat ironic move by the Americans. With the English blockade of US ports during the Napoleonic wars the Americans had ample supplies of lumber and shipwrights to build ships on the Great Lakes. British command of the seas was England's ace in defending Canada with half a million people against the US with over seven million people. In 1813, the Americans were capable of putting "more boots on the ground," than the British. Yet, England initially won the ground war but lost the initiative because of naval defeats on the Great Lakes.

Commodore Isaac Chauncey was given command of the US navy on the Great Lakes and began building ships at Sackets Harbour on Lake Ontario towards the end of 1812. With seven ships Chauncey attacked the *Royal George* on November 10, 1812 and chased it into Kingston Harbour. Far more daring was Chauncey's attack on York (Toronto) in April 1813 with a fleet of 12 ships. By coordinating his naval attack with the army led by Henry Dearborn they captured York on April 27, 1813.

Dearborn, you will recall, was Madison's senior commander in charge of the invasion of Canada. He had failed to cross the Niagara River and take the English base in Kingston and then proceed to Montreal, as the original invasion plan had called for. York was the capital of Upper Canada but a much softer target than Kingston or Montreal. Dearborn had moved his invasion force from Plattsburg to Sackets Harbour. With close to 2,000 men under Dearborn and heavy naval support from Chauncey, defending York was hopeless.

Sheaffe, as Brock's successor and Lieutenant Governor of Upper Canada, was in charge of the defence but had a combined force of only 400 men including his First Nations allies. After some fierce initial resistance with large casualties on both sides, Sheaffe decided to retreat to Kingston leaving the colonial militia to surrender to the invaders. The Americans had failed to capture the more important military target of Kingston. With so many defeats, capturing York seemed like a major victory to the Americans.

The American marines celebrated by burning the parliament buildings of Upper Canada, desecrating the churches, looting homes and generally behaving like hooligans. They were clearly not accustomed to winning battles and behaved as bullies do when they win a single victory. This kind of cowardly conduct has become the trademark of American soldiers and the American government as evidenced by the *My Lai massacre* of March 16, 1968, prisoner abuses at *Abu Ghraib* and *Guantanamo* and countless atrocities and torture of civilians in Iraq, Afghanistan and in secret American prisons around the world.

The capture of York prompted England to send out Sir James Yeo and five hundred officers to ensure English dominance on the Great Lakes. The problem was that the Americans had the upper hand in that supplies and seamen were abundant and close at hand while England was an ocean away and the English navy was defending the high seas against the French. Yeo was by far a more competent admiral than Chauncey but Chauncey had more ships, more men, more supplies and more powerful guns. Throughout the invasion the two men competed for dominance on the Great Lakes.

The English navy was safe in Kingston harbour where Sheaffe had retreated. Without Kingston, Chauncey could not disrupt British supplies to Lower Canada. On May 27, 1813, the American forces under Dearborn captured Fort George but Brigadier-General Henry Vincent, the English commander on the Niagara frontier, retreated as Sheaffe had done at York. This gave Vincent the opportunity to re-group at Burlington Heights and defeat the pursuing Americans at Stoney Creek on June 5, 1813. Vincent's victory at Stoney Creek enabled British control of most of the Niagara frontier despite the loss of Fort George.

A second attempt by the Americans to expand their control of the Niagara Peninsula turned out to be even more humiliating than their defeat at Stoney Creek. The unfortunate Americans were ambushed at Beaver Dams on June 24, 1813 and pleaded with the English commander, Lieutenant James Fitzgibbon, to save them from the scalping knives of England's First Nations allies, as the frightened Americans under Hull had done before, when Tecumseh had captured Fort Detroit.

In May of 1813, Procter and Tecumseh decided to attack Harrison who had retreated behind the walls of Fort Meigs in Ohio. Procter advanced across Lake Erie and laid siege to Fort Meigs. As with Brock's bombardment of Fort Detroit the year before there was no hope of taking the Fort unless the Americans were shamed into coming out and fighting in the open. Harrison was used to fighting First Nations and was not scared by their war cries into surrendering as Hull had done. Procter had no choice but to pull back to Amherstburg and allow his colonial militias to return to their farms for the spring planting of their crops. Procter made a second attempt to take Fort Meigs in the summer of 1813. Failing to take Fort Meigs, he attacked neighbouring Fort Stevenson without success. The Americans were safely ensconced behind the walls of their forts.

On the Great Lakes, Commodore Oliver Perry used his fleet to prevent supplies reaching the British and their First Nations allies at Fort Amherstburg. With supplies desperately low and Procter frustrated by his failed attacks on Fort Meigs and Fort Stevenson, he pushed Captain Robert Barclay of the British navy to engage Perry. Barclay's defeat at Put-in-Bay on Lake Erie on September 10, 1813 only worsened the Canadian situation in Upper Canada. Barclay was outnumbered with six ships to Perry's nine ships and Perry's ships had the more powerful guns. With the wind shifting suddenly against Barclay, he was forced to surrender his entire fleet to the Americans.

Procter destroyed and abandoned Fort Amherstburg in late September, 1813, disbanded the militia and retreated east with about 800 men to evade Harrison who was now on the attack with 10,000 Kentucky volunteers. Harrison caught the retreating English and their First Nations allies at Moraviantown on the Thames River. Tecumseh was killed at the Battle of Thames River on October 5, 1813. The Kentucky volunteers skinned and mutilated his body. Procter escaped with about 200 survivors to Burlington Heights on the Niagara frontier.

The Americans now controlled both sides of the Lake with Fort Detroit and Fort Amherstburg, which the Americans called Fort Malden. If they could take Kingston their long planned invasion of Montreal and Lower Canada would begin. While Canada was successfully defended by subsequent English victories over the Americans, Tecumseh's death marked the beginning of the end of First Nations resistance to American imperialism. It would be left to Palestinians, Cubans, Vietnamese, Iraqis, Afghans and Iranians to finally defeat US imperialism.

Napoleon's Defeat by Russia Saves Canada from American colonization

Towards the end of 1813 the Americans had recovered from their defeats in 1812 and the first half of 1813 thanks to their naval superiority on the Great Lakes. However, luck was with Canada. Canadian victories in 1812 and early 1813 proved to be the decisive factor in foiling the second US invasion of Canada. The Americans had invaded in 1812 because Britain was at war with France. Their failures in 1812 and early 1813 postponed their opportunity to conquer Canada until Napoleon's defeat by the Russians.

Napoleon's famous *Grande Armee* had captured Moscow on September 14, 1812. But the Russians abandoned the city and the *Grande Armee* died of cold and starvation as it retreated from Moscow. With Napoleon on the defensive in 1813 England could better defend its North American colonies from the American invaders. It would be April 6, 1814 before Napoleon abdicated and England could send 15,000 men to defend British North America. The Americans would have to conquer Canada before the British troop "surge" reached North America.

The Americans made their long planned invasion of Montreal towards the end of 1813. General James Wilkinson sailed from Sackets Harbour on Lake Ontario and joined forces with Major-General Wade Hampton advancing north from Plattsburg on Lake Champlain. Their combined force numbered over 10,000 men. It was Wilkinson's decision to invade Montreal without securing Kingston. The English surprised the Americans again when Lieutenant Colonel Charles de Salaberry with a much smaller force, including First Nations allies, soundly defeated Hampton at the Battle of Chateauguay on October 25, 1813.

Hampton abandoned the plan to join forces with Wilkinson. Wilkinson, commanding a force almost twice the size of Hampton's, fared no better. Lieutenant Colonel Joseph Morrison, again with much smaller numbers than Wilkinson, successfully defended his position when attacked at Crysler's Farm on November 11, 1813. Wilkinson retreated to New York. The Americans had been foiled again. The humiliating defeats of the American forces led the US commander to abandon Fort George on December 10, 1813 and burn Newark and most of Queenston.

Quebec born Lieutenant General Gordon Drummond, second-in-command to Upper Canada's governor, Sir George Prevost, organized raids in the Niagara peninsula in retaliation for what he called *uncivilized* behaviour by the Americans. On December 19, 1813, Drummond captured Fort Niagara and burnt Lewiston. On December 29, 1813, Drummond burnt Buffalo and Black Rock.

The failure of the Americans to take Kingston before invading Montreal allowed the English to launch two new powerful frigates on Lake Ontario. The Americans continued their massive ship building program on the Great Lakes and launched the much more powerful 62-gun *USS Superior*. The British responded by building the even larger 112-gun *St. Lawrence*. Yeo protected the English fleet in Kingston Harbour. The Americans controlled Lake Erie.

American forces numbering 4,500 led by Major-General Jacob Brown and Brigadier-General Winfield Scott crossed the Niagara River at Black Rock on July 3, 1814, and captured Fort Erie. Prior to Major Buck surrendering the Fort and his 200 men, he sent a small force to warn Major-General Phineas Riall, the new commander of British forces in the Niagara Peninsula. Riall and

Drummond engaged the Americans at Lundy's Lane on July 25, 1814 with huge casualties on both sides. Riall was wounded and later captured by the Americans. The Americans withdrew to Fort Erie. Drummond advanced and reached Fort Erie on August 3, 1814. Re-taking Fort Erie was no easy task. Drummond attacked on August 15 without success. Drummond withdrew to Fort George after suffering heavy losses but lack of provisions eventually forced the Americans to surrender the Fort and retreat to Buffalo.

With the arrival of 15,000 British troops following the defeat of Napoleon the English went on the offensive invading the US. On July 11, 1814 the English occupied Eastport in Maine. The border between the English colony of New Brunswick and the district of Maine in Massachusetts had not been firmly established by the second Treaty of Paris of 1783. In September 1814, the English army under Sir John Sherbrooke expanded the territory captured in Maine. On August 19, Major-General Robert Ross landed a force of 4,000 from the British fleet in Chesapeake Bay just outside the American capital.

Admiral George Cockburn had been enforcing a blockade of the Bay since March of 1813. Ross landed on the Patuxent River to begin his march to the American capital. At Bladensburg the 4,000 British Regulars humiliated the 5,000 strong US militia. Sir George Prevost had called for retribution for the burning of York. Ross did not disappoint him. He burnt Washington.

President Madison had to flee the presidential mansion which was subsequently white-washed to cover the scorch marks and re-named the *White House*. Ross and Cockburn advanced to Baltimore but failed to capture the port despite heavy bombardment from the British fleet. Ross was killed. On August 31, 1814, Sir George Prevost led an invasion force of 10,000 into New York reaching Plattsburg. However, Prevost forced a naval encounter between an ill prepared British fleet and a seasoned American fleet in Plattsburg Bay on September 11, 1814. Prevost then used the defeat of the British fleet as his excuse for withdrawing his army intact to defend Canada. Once again the Americans had been rescued by their navy. The British fleet in Chesapeake Bay failed to capture Fort McHenry on September 13, 1814 and sailed to Halifax.

Peace was agreed to on December 24, 1814. The *Treaty of Ghent* returned all captured territories. The return of captured US territory by England was not well received by the Canadians, by England's First Nations allies or by the Loyalists who had still not been compensated for property confiscated by the US during the War of Independence. Fortunately for the warmongering Americans, England was war weary and tired of defending its colonies in North America. There was also the real possibility of renewed conflict with Napoleon in Europe.

The second US invasion of Canada had been as humiliating a failure as their first invasion. In typical US pea-brained logic the US claimed victory by saying it was their second war of independence from British tyranny. This type of pea-brained logic has become a hall mark of US military disasters.

When the US failed to defeat the Communists led by Mao Zedong in China their Chinese collaborator, Chiang Kai-shek, was forced to flee to the island of Formosa, later re-named Taiwan. The pea-brained Americans pretended for years that they had not really lost China to communism because the tiny island of Taiwan was China. Up until President Nixon's visit to China in 1972 the pea-brained Americans and their tightly sanitized "free" media called Taiwan the *Republic of China*. It was the American president who went "cap in hand" to mend fences with Mao Zedong in 1972 to attempt to co-opt China in America's Cold War against the Soviet Union.

CHAPTER 2

American Invasions Before its Civil War: Invasions of Florida, North Africa, Indiana, Mississippi, Illinois, Alabama, Maine, Missouri, Arkansas, Michigan, Texas, Iowa, Wisconsin, California, Minnesota, Oregon and Kansas: 1810-1861

During the century before American independence England and France fought for territory which Spain had not already stolen from the First Nations. These were the lands bordering the Atlantic coast in North America and the Caribbean. Note that while people today think of the Caribbean as a separate region outside America, during the early centuries after 1492 it was considered an integral part of America. This is best exemplified by the fact that those who claim that Columbus discovered America in 1492 meant the Caribbean since that was where Columbus explored in 1492.

After independence, the US invaded the lands to the north, to the west and to the south. Chapter 1 dealt with the earliest invasions to the west and north. This chapter looks at the later invasions further west and to the south. The common theme is that these were First Nations lands. The difference was that the US would now come into conflict more with Spain and less with England.

As in Chapter 1, the US invasion of First Nations lands involved stealing some First Nations lands which had already been stolen by a European imperialist and also stealing First Nations lands which had not been previously stolen by a European imperialist.

The European imperialists had come to America for trade and settlement. They had stolen some land for these settlements, for trading posts and for military forts. However, America was a vast continent. Most of the land, especially in North America, was still in First Nations hands. This changed when the US moved west and south. The US killed off most of the First Nations and imprisoned the few survivors in *Reservations*. The US took all of their land and their hunting grounds.

Unlike the European Nations who had "civilized" their methods of warfare and evolved over the centuries towards fairer trade and interrelationships with the First Nations, Americans were hell bent on extermination of the First Nations by using a method of warfare which the West now calls *genocide*. American wars against the First Nations involved the wholesale and indiscriminate slaughter of civilians, men, women and children. In a recent book, the author, John Grenier, himself a US military officer, describes this wholesale slaughter of innocent First Nations, America's "First Way of War." According to Grenier, the limited wars conducted by the European Nations did not drive the First Nations from all of their lands. By contrast, the US specialized on "extirpative war making."

The American settler became, first and foremost, an Indian fighter. American settlers, individually, in small groups and in large groups, would attack Indian villages, kill their women and children and destroy their crops or means of livelihood. Only when Indians retaliated would the US army intervene on the side of the settlers and engage in wholesale slaughter. This way of war became an ingrained part of the American psyche.

With the First Nations long subjugated, this inherited biological need for war as an integral part of life of the typical American, leads to a constant search for new targets and the use of war as the excuse for killing innocent women and children and proudly referring to it as "collateral damage." When targets on the American continent were eliminated they were found in far off lands like North Africa, China, Japan, Cuba, Latin America, the Philippines, Hawaii, Vietnam, Afghanistan and Iraq.

Background to the Invasion and Conquest of Florida

US conquests began by Washington and Jefferson would be continued by future US presidents. While Washington and Jefferson had made their conquests after election to the presidency, their increased popularity due to those conquests, made it self-evident to every American aspiring to the presidency that wars, conquests and military service were the *primary qualifications* for the job. No American president understood this more than Andrew Jackson. He conquered Florida almost single handedly in his bid for the US presidency.

While previous American presidents may have inherited some of the English traits for hypocrisy with regards to thefts of First Nations land, for double talk and accepted diplomacy when it came to dealing with other "civilized" nations, Jackson was brazenly ruthless and proud to advertise his ruthlessness. He was the first truly *American-made* hero like Davy Crockett and Sam Houston, with whom he rode.

Jackson popularized the American notion that frontier justice had to be quick, bloody and inhumane. Political niceties, international sanction and treaties were for weak minded Europeans who could never understand much less rule Americans. His methods were instantly popular with the new Americans, those who moved west and populated the new American territory conquered after the relative "civilizing" influence of the Spanish, British and French.

Once Spain had conquered the largest islands of the Caribbean, especially Cuba, it was natural that it would attempt to conquer and settle Florida because of its close geographic proximity to Cuba. Cuba was conquered by Spain in 1511. In 1513, Ponce de Leon sailed from the Spanish colony of Puerto Rico and landed in the vicinity of St. Augustine on April 2. He chose the name Florida because *Pascua Florida* is the Spanish term for Easter. He explored most of the east coast of Florida and part of the west coast.

Florida's sub-tropical climate attracted settlers and other explorers. In 1517, Francisco de Cordoba sailed from Cuba to Florida and explored more of its west coast. The Spanish used the name Florida to mean the entire American coastline north of the Gulf of Mexico. Florida became a part of *New Spain*. As with other areas of America the French and English competed with Spain for Florida. French Huguenots founded Fort Caroline in Jacksonville, Florida in 1564. Fort Caroline was at the mouth of the St. John's River which had been discovered by the French explorer, Rene de Laudonniere, two years earlier. In 1565, Spain captured the French fort.

French colonies west of Florida and English colonies north of Florida squeezed the hold of Spain on Florida. As in Canada where the English and French had First Nations allies, Spain and England used the First Nations as allies to compete for the theft of the First Nations lands. The English allied with the Creek and Seminole Nations while Spain allied with the Apalachee and Timucua Nations. Other First Nations inhabitants of Florida included the *Ais, Tocobago and Calusa* Nations.

English settlements began with Jamestown, Virginia in 1607 and pushed steadily southwards along the Atlantic coast to Georgia in 1733. English privateers attacked, looted and burnt the Spanish colony of St. Augustine in Florida frequently. The English colony of South Carolina attacked Florida in 1702. Georgia attacked Florida in 1742.

France began its conquest of the vast Louisiana Territory with the expedition of Louis Joliet and Jacques Marquette in 1673. French explorers charted the tributaries of the Mississippi River and laid claim to the entire Mississippi Delta to the Gulf of Mexico. The French settlements in Biloxi and Mobile were within easy reach of Florida by sea. In 1719, The French Governor of Louisiana captured the Spanish colony of Pensacola, just east of Mobile. The French abandoned Pensacola after the 1722 hurricane.

English victories during the Seven Years War led to the transfer of Canada and part of Louisiana to England by France and part of Florida to England by Spain. Spain had entered the war as an ally of France in 1762. England created two new colonies, East Florida and West Florida. Pensacola became the capital of West Florida which included the cities of Biloxi, Mobile and Baton Rouge. St. Augustine was the capital of East Florida. Spain re-captured West Florida in 1781 and the second Treaty of Paris ending the American War of Independence in 1783 transferred West and East Florida back to Spain. Just as many English loyalists left the US because of the loss of the 13 colonies to the US, many English loyalists left Florida because of its return to Spain. The newly created USA wanted both Canada and Florida and began military invasions against both colonies. Chapter 1 documented the invasions into Canada.

The US Invasion of Florida: 1810-1845

The theft of Florida from the First Nations followed the typical pattern. First, American settlers would gradually encroach on First Nations lands and push them further into the interior. When the First Nations pushed back the US army would step in. As battles ensued the US would send more and more forces. The standard American excuse would be "atrocities committed by the First Nations."

It's ironic that the **White** race can simultaneously consider a non-white race as inferior and primitive and still expect from that primitive inferior race "civilized" behaviour. In fact the primitive "inferior" race is supposed to be honest and **non-violent** at all times even when the civilized "superior" race is dishonest, breaks treaties and uses extreme military force. Just as Americans did not wait for France to be defeated before settling First Nations lands claimed by France, Americans did not wait for Spain to be defeated before settling First Nations lands claimed by Spain.

American settlers began to push into Spanish West Florida and chose the land around Tallahassee, just east of Pensacola, to plant their **slave based** economy. One of the many First Nations near Tallahassee was the *Mikasuki* Nation. Tallahassee was later chosen as the capital city when Florida became a US Territory. Tobacco and cotton plantations using **slave** labour was how American democracy and republican values brought civilized freedom and equality to the "uncivilized" First Nations of Florida.

The plantations prospered because the land was **stolen** rather than purchased and the labour was **slaves** rather than paid labour. The "freedom loving" American Republic was proud to combine colonization with slave labour to prosper. This prosperity based on slave labour meant that it was not long before slaves in the US conquered Territory of Florida were as many as the white settlers. As a **slave state** Florida joined the Confederate states during the Civil War.

Prior to American conquest, Spain had not only rejected a slave-based economy in Florida, Spain welcomed runaway slaves from the bordering English colonies, such as Georgia and South Carolina, and granted them freedom. Many of the free Blacks settled in Fort Mose outside St. Augustine. So much for US lies about freedom and equality.

As American plantations expanded the *Seminole Nation* was among those First Nations pushed off their land. The Seminole Nation had to be forcibly removed. Only **Whites** were entitled to own land. First Nations were forcibly relocated where Whites had not yet settled. It's a policy which the Western world still thinks is fair. Why else would Westerners still apply this same rule to Jews and Palestinians in Israel?

Whites are entitled to the land because they are civilized. Non-whites should go to reservations or refugee camps because they are primitive. Of course, whites also fought among themselves for possession of the land. In the case of Florida, the Americans had to fight Spain as well as the First Nations.

In 1810, President Madison ordered the governor of the Orleans Territory, William Claiborne, to invade West Florida. Americans living in Baton Rouge supported Claiborne. Spain was too weak to defend its numerous American colonies from internal rebellions and military attacks by France, England and the US. In 1810, American settlers declared West Florida an independent Republic. In 1812, the West Florida Republic became part of the newly created *eighteenth* US state of Louisiana.

In 29 years the American Empire had invaded and conquered more territory than it claimed from England by promoting the false notion that its War of Independence was a just war against *imperialism*. It had used false claims about its inherent right to self determination. In reality it had no more legal rights to the First Nations land than the British Empire. That its true motive were *imperial*, not *republican*, is clearly manifested by its invasions and conquests outside the land taken from the British Empire in 1783.

The Presidency of Andrew Jackson

No people love wars as much as Americans. No people love military victories like Americans do. No people celebrate and worship their war heroes as Americans do. Their most celebrated war heroes are usually rewarded with the highest office in the land, the presidency. General Andrew Jackson was to be America's latest war hero and future president for conquering Florida for the US.

Jackson had dedicated his life to destroying the First Nations. Jackson crossed the Cumberland Gap discovered by the American adventurer Daniel Boone to settle in Tennessee in 1787. He profited from land speculation and trading slaves. He used the profits to acquire a cotton plantation called the Hermitage. As a colonel in the Tennessee state militia he honed his military skills by fighting the First Nations. As a prominent land owner he had the required qualification to be elected to the House of Representatives. He became a US Senator in 1797 and a judge of the Tennessee Supreme Court in 1798.

When the US invaded Canada in 1812, Jackson formed an alliance with the Cherokee Nation and the Southern Creek Nation to defeat the Red Stick Creek Nation at the Battle of Horseshoe Bend. The Red Sticks were brutally massacred. Jackson's *search and destroy* military strategy entailed the merciless slaughter of the Red Sticks and destruction of their villages and livelihood. He used this military victory to steal 23 million acres of land from both the Red Sticks and his former allies, the Southern Creeks and Cherokees, earning the nickname, *Sharp Knife Jackson.*

President Madison rewarded Jackson for his conquests of First Nations lands by appointing him a Major-General in the US army and sending him to invade East Florida in 1814. The English colony of East Florida had been returned to Spain in 1783. When the US invaded Canada in 1812, the English used Pensacola in East Florida as a military base. Jackson defeated the English at Pensacola in November 1814.

The Treaty of Ghent signed in 1814 between England and the US guaranteed the return of all First Nations lands stolen from the Creek Nation. As in the case of the Loyalists with the second Treaty of Paris the US did not honour the return of stolen property. In fact, during the following ten years, as Treaty commissioner, Jackson was able to steal 75 percent of Florida from the First Nations. In the process Jackson enriched himself, his family, his friends as well as the freedom loving US Republic.

Any First Nations resistance to his theft was savagely put down with brute military force. He wiped out entire First Nations villages. The Blacks who had escaped slavery from the "freedom loving" US Republic and had been welcomed by Spanish Florida, occupied the Prospect Bluff fort built by England during the 1812-14 War with the US. The Americans called it *Negro Fort* and destroyed it in 1816. US attacks on the Creeks, Seminoles and Blacks continued.

The US attack on the village of Fowltown on November 22, 1817 is regarded as the beginning of the first US war against the *Seminole Nation*. Jackson rebuilt Negro Fort in 1818 and named it Fort Gadsden. Jackson continued his scorched earth policy burning Tallahassee in March 1818. Jackson proceeded to capture the Spanish fort at St. Marks and executed two Englishmen for aiding the First Nations.

In 1818 Jackson defeated both the Seminole and Creek Nations and captured Pensacola from Spain. The US had ignored international law by conquering Spanish territory without a formal declaration of war. When Spain complained the US successfully bullied Spain to transfer all of Florida, including Pensacola, to the US under the terms of the Adams-Onis Treaty of 1819. In 1819, the US population of 9 million was smaller than Spain's but Spain had a world-wide empire to govern and the US had the "home" advantage. Quincy Adams, as Secretary of State, signed the annexation of Florida and the US Senate ratified the annexation.

The US could now concentrate its wrath and military power on the First Nations. The First Nations in Florida had allied with Spain, France and England in the past but now they must stand alone against a militarily superior United States. No European Nation was willing to help them defend against this new "uncivilized" warmongering imperialist.

Jackson was rewarded for his cruel and barbaric treatment of the First Nations by being appointed as the first governor of the US conquered Territory of Florida, by the "freedom loving" US Republic. In the eyes of Americans Jackson was a greater military commander than Napoleon or Wellington. Wars fought by Napoleon and Wellington were too "civilized" for an American war hero like Jackson.

Jackson was elected the seventh president of the US in 1828. His military credentials and brutal killing of First Nations proved to be the highest qualifications for that position. Jackson, more than any other American, made *race* a key motivating factor for US wars. While the widely held Western view of the First Nation as an *inferior race* played an important role in the theft of First Nations lands by Whites, Jackson killed and decimated First Nations more because of his intense hatred of their race than because of their lands which he would steal.

In a rather ironic twist of fate Jackson became president by defeating the incumbent president, John Quincy Adams. Jackson received 178 electoral votes compared with only 83 for Adams. He also received a majority of the popular votes. Adams had saved Jackson's hide only a few years earlier when many Americans, including President James Monroe, wanted Jackson hanged for illegally executing two Englishmen, Alexander Arbuthnot and Robert Ambrister, when Jackson had invaded Pensacola in 1818. Monroe had sent Jackson to kill First Nations not Englishmen, even if the English had shown some sympathy towards the First Nations because of Jackson's barbaric *search and destroy* military campaign. Adams was then Monroe's Secretary of State. Adams spent the rest of his life in the US

Congress dedicated to fighting slavery which Jackson would have happily imposed on First Nations and Blacks alike. No wonder Jackson was revered by so many Americans as "a man of the people."

President Jackson's Indian Removal Act of 1830

In 1823 the US decided to move the entire Seminole Nation into a reservation. The Seminoles resisted but were gradually rounded up and moved by force. Jackson was still unhappy. He wanted the Seminoles removed from Florida. For Jackson, even the dirt poor economic conditions of Indian reservations were too good for First Nations. As president after 1828, Jackson had the absolute power to pursue his intense personal hate of First Nations. He passed the *Indian Removal Act* in 1830. Over 45,000 First Nations were forcibly removed by Jackson and over 130,000 acres of their land stolen during his presidency.

In 1832 the Seminoles in the Florida reservation were told to move west. They protested but in 1835 they were told by Jackson that they would be forcibly removed. Half of the Seminole Nation agreed to move and the other half decided to fight Jackson's Removal Act. This led to the *Second Seminole War* lasting for eight long years. As expected, Jackson's Indian Removal Act was extremely popular with the **White** "freedom loving" Americans. Jackson was returned for a second term in 1832 with an overwhelming majority. Florida became the *twenty-seventh* state of the US on March 3, 1845.

The few remaining Seminoles continued to be in a state of undeclared war with the US.

US Invasion and Conquest of the Mediterranean and North Africa

As we saw in Chapter 1, it was the US navy which had the greatest victories against the English during the War of 1812. Holland, France, England, Russia and Japan, had all recognized the value of a strong navy in the competition for empire. The US was quick to learn that fact. Its desire for a strong navy is yet one more undeniable piece of evidence that the new nation of the United Sates had imperialist ambitions from its very birth.

The US Naval Act which created the US Navy was passed in 1794; only four years after the last of the 13 original colonies formally joined the Union to become the independent USA. The Act authorized the construction of six ships beginning with the USS United States in 1796 and ending with the USS President in 1800. The US also followed standard policy by all other existing empires of using its merchant marine to fully support its war effort during times of war. This policy began with the War of Independence when the merchant marine captured the English schooner, HMS Margaretta, on June 12, 1775.

The US merchant marine has always profited from foreign wars beginning with the Napoleonic wars in 1793. During that conflict between England and France the US boosted its international trade by supplying England, France and their colonies with both peacetime and wartime materials. The US merchant marine increased the number of ships significantly and the numbers of seamen rose proportionately. Attempts by England to reduce American supplies to France and French colonies were one reason for the War of 1812.

One of the six ships built by the US under the Naval Act of 1794, the USS Chesapeake, completed in 1800, was attacked by the English navy in June 1807. President Jefferson responded by placing an embargo on US trade with England and France in December 1807. Jefferson was forced to remove the embargo in March 1809 because of opposition from the US merchant marine.

American Privateers

Much more relevant to exposing the hypocrisy of the American Empire for its invasion of North Africa and the Mediterranean was the **official sanction of piracy** by the US. The Continental Congress and the 13 colonies officially engaged American pirates by issuing special *Letters of Marque.* The legality of using pirates to fight England was formalized by an Act of the Continental Congress as early as March 23, 1776.

American pirates played a significant role during the War of Independence. One estimate suggests that American pirates, including merchant ships provided with *Letters of Marque,* amounted to over 1,600 ships compared with only 60 ships of the Continental Navy. This use of pirates and their ships predated the official US Navy ordered by Congress in 1794. When pirates are commissioned by a government to fight on its behalf they are called *privateers.*

The US Congress has the constitutional power to make use of privateers under Article I, section 8. During the War of Independence, officially sanctioned privateers and merchant seamen far outnumbered members of the Continental Navy. In fact, it has been estimated that there were as many American pirates harassing English shipping as there were soldiers fighting in the Continental Army. By concentrating their attacks on unarmed or lightly armed merchant ships of England the American privateers wrecked havoc on English commerce during the War of Independence.

During the War of Independence, American privateers were almost as successful as Iraqi and Afghan insurgents today. Just as the US is today crying foul because attacks by Iraqi and Afghan insurgents were totally unexpected so did England call the attacks by American privateers on merchant ships **"terrorism."** Whenever a militarily superior nation is surprised by unconventional methods of defence the militarily superior power resorts to propaganda.

American privateers challenged the world's most powerful navy by attacking "**civilians**" during the War of Independence. By using pirates to attack English merchant ships the 13 colonies disrupted English imports of food and war time supplies as well as increasing insurance rates by 500 percent for English ships engaged in international trade. American privateering became so profitable during the War of Independence that American shipbuilders in Baltimore designed a faster ship for pirates, the *schooner.* For a brief period Baltimore became the pirate capital of the world.

American privateers captured over 3,000 English ships during the War. The cost to England has been estimated at over eighteen million dollars. The pirates enriched themselves with the booty while supplying the Continental army with much needed gunpowder and guns. The American pirate, John Manley, supplied 2,000 guns as well as ammunition after capturing a single English ship. Other prominent pirates to fight for American independence included Adam Hyler and Jeremiah O'Brien. Hyler consistently harassed the English fleet anchored in New York harbour. Jeremiah O'Brien captured two ships of the English Navy.

By the time of the American War of Independence in 1776, piracy had a long and well established history. It had been legally and illegally used by England, France and Holland to found the North American colonies, including the 13 English colonies fighting the War of Independence. Dating back to ancient times, piracy got a big boost with the discovery of gold and silver in the New World by Spain. English, French, Dutch and American pirates preyed on the Spanish galleons in the Caribbean and the Atlantic Ocean with the implicit sanction of their governments.

In the ensuing competition for empire, France unleashed its *Corsairs,* Holland unleashed its *Sea Beggars* and England unleashed its *Privateers.* These were the names given to pirates by the respective maritime powers of France, Holland and England, when they were commissioned to work for the Crown to steal the treasures of Spain, to sink the ships of competing empires, to disrupt international trade and to fight for the mother country during the incessant wars. The American Empire was well aware of this fact and signed on fully to this questionable method of expanding its empire.

The American Invasion of Tripoli (Libya): 1801-1805

The Barbary pirates existed long before the US gained its independence from England. Spain's conquest of Granada in 1492 marked the beginning of the rise of Christianity as the dominant religion and the decline of Islam. Many Muslims turned to piracy attacking the Spanish coast in retaliation for the loss of Granada and the exile of the Moors. The Barbary pirates had long attacked the Spanish and Italian coasts as well as North Africa and the Mediterranean. These attacks increased in the sixteenth century.

The home bases of the Barbary pirates were the Muslim states of Algeria, Morocco, Tunisia and Tripoli (Libya), which were semi-independent countries within the Ottoman Empire. While the Christian countries of Spain, France and England concentrated their search for empires during the sixteenth century in the New World the Muslim countries continued to dominate the old trade routes through the Mediterranean and across the Indian Ocean.

Piracy was used by both the Muslim and the Christian countries to expand their empires and spheres of influence. Many of the Barbary pirates were Christians who had converted to Islam. Since piracy was condoned by both Christian and Muslim sovereigns there were only token efforts by countries to stamp it out. Moreover, since piracy took place mostly on the high seas outside territorial waters it was difficult to apply the laws of any country against the pirates without infringing freedom of the high seas.

The US began its current policy of unilaterally invading sovereign states from its birth. Despite long standing conventions by the major empires of the day, including England and France, Thomas Jefferson, then US minister to France, wrote in a letter to John Adams on July 11, 1786, that the US should wage war on the Barbary states instead of paying the tributes which had historically been paid by England, France and other Christian empires. The US was about to defy international law by attacking a sovereign state for the actions of some of its citizens. This was no different from the US invasion of Afghanistan in retaliation for the actions of some of the citizens of Afghanistan.

Had Afghan citizens attacked any country, other than the US, that country would have sought to prosecute those Afghans through internationally accepted legal channels. It would not have invaded Afghanistan. This total disrespect for international law, international rules of conduct, international conventions and the rule of law was the hall-mark of the new American Empire since its birth. The American invasions of Afghanistan, Iraq, Grenada, Vietnam, Laos and Cambodia, were not new to America's unilateral exercise of brute force and military aggression against weaker states. They are examples of the exercise of its birthright beginning with the founding fathers such as Jefferson, Adams and Washington.

Complementing the birthright of the American Empire for unilateral invasion of sovereign states is the American obsession with warmongering. Jefferson hinted at this American trait in his letter of December 26, 1786 to the president of Yale College. In that letter Jefferson noted that taxing Americans to wage a war against the Barbary States would be more popular politically than taxing them to pay tributes. Other Christian empires recognized that tributes were far cheaper than wars. In 2007, Americans were paying $50 billion each month to wage a war in Iraq, rather than spend a much smaller amount on waging peace.

Jefferson became president in 1801 and began a policy of intimidating and provoking the North African Muslim states by flexing its military muscle with a US naval presence in the Mediterranean. This had been the standard American tactic against the First Nations. Provoke them into an attack with taunts, intimidation, theft and humiliation and use that attack to justify all out war. Keep these provocations as secret as possible so that you can claim that the attack was unprovoked. That would make it easier to get the support of Congress and the American people. Thus Jefferson made sure that he did not inform Congress prior to sending the US navy to the Mediterranean.

There is one important proviso. Make sure you pick on a militarily weaker foe. Increase your chance of success by bullying weaker nations to support your cause and invent the notion of "Coalition of the Willing." In 1801, Tripoli was the weakest of the Barbary States. Naturally, the American Empire picked on Tripoli. Sweden, Denmark and Sicily made up the coalition of the willing during that American invasion.

Jefferson sent four ships, the *President, Essex, Philadelphia* and *Enterprise* under the command of Commodore Richard Dale to blockade and bombard Tripoli. Jefferson used as evidence of Tripoli's "unprovoked" attack the seizure of two American ships by Tripoli. These two American ships had *mysteriously* wandered from American bases across an entire ocean, the Atlantic Ocean, and blown *magically* off course into the Mediterranean. How else could they have been seized without provocation by Tripoli since Tripoli had not crossed the Atlantic Ocean to seize them?

Does anyone see the emerging American pattern which played out in the Gulf of Tonkin in 1964? As in the case of the two American ships which had mysteriously entered the Mediterranean in 1801, the two US warships, *Maddox* and *Turner Joy,* had *mysteriously* wandered from their bases in the United States all across the Pacific Ocean to land in Vietnamese waters so that the Vietnamese would cause an unprovoked attack on the US. Or is it simply that the American Empire has the god given right to be in every country's backyard?

Jefferson carefully played his hand pushing Tripoli to declare war on the American Empire in May 1801. In response, Jefferson convinced Congress to pass an Act in February 1802 for a permanent US naval presence in the Mediterranean. In May, 1803, the American Empire sent more ships to strengthen the blockade and enhance the bombardment of Tripoli. In October, 1803, Tripoli captured the *Philadelphia* forcing the US to destroy it rather than have Tripoli add it to its own fleet. In September, 1804, Tripoli destroyed the *Intrepid.*

American reinforcements under Commodore Samuel Barron arrived soon after the loss of the *Intrepid.* With the war going badly for the Americans they hatched a plot to overthrow Tripoli's ruler with his older brother who had been exiled in Egypt. This was the birth of the American policy of *Regime Change.* The original "Dick Cheney" of *Regime Change* was the American consul to Tunis, William Eaton. Eaton raised a mercenary army of Arabs and Greeks and marched 500 miles overland to Tripoli. Unfortunately for Eaton, Jefferson was not as eager as George W. Bush, to support *Regime Change.* Tripoli's ruling pasha, Yusuf Karamanli, decided to negotiate a peace treaty with Jefferson on June 4, 1805, before Eaton could execute his coup.

Jefferson had made up his mind long before he became president that he would convince the American people to wage war on the Barbary States. Western historians, would, of course, claim that this was not a Christian War against Islam, but would make no effort to explain why the US did not criticize Christian States, including itself, for using pirates to expand their empires and spheres of influence.

Moreover, in pointing out the inhumane treatment of captured American sailors by the Barbary pirates as a justification for Jefferson's invasion of North Africa, these American historians conveniently fail to compare such inhumane treatment with the equally inhumane treatment of American privateers captured by England during the War of Independence. The British did not recognize the captured American privateers as prisoners of war just as the US today does not recognize captured al-Qaeda fighters as prisoners of war. They were held in special camps very much like today's Guantanamo,

Abu-Ghraib and other secret US prison camps in Europe. One of the most notorious was the prison ship, *Jersey.*

American Privateers in the War of 1812

Jefferson had made the US position on piracy very clear. The US would be a nation who would go to war to stamp out the evil of piracy. It had made that stance abundantly clear by taking the leadership role in the war on Tripoli waged by the "Coalition of the Willing," when other greater Christian empires such as Britain and France refused to shoulder that responsibility. The World was about to see a new model of civilized behaviour by nation states set by the splendid example of Jefferson's USA.

The motto of this civilized American nation would be to wage war on all sovereign states which harboured pirates much like the "Bush doctrine," of waging war on any sovereign state which harbours terrorists. Of course, the US must exempt itself from the "Jefferson doctrine" if it harboured pirates since no believer in the goodness and honesty of the US would expect the US to wage war on itself just as the US must exempt itself from the "Bush doctrine" since no believer in the goodness and honesty of the US would expect the US to invade itself for harbouring terrorists even if they are as vile as *Timothy McVeigh* or *Luis Posada Carriles.*

This precedent of exempting itself from all international law or rules of "civilized" behavior even when those laws or rules were established and enforced by the US itself, began with Jefferson's attack on piracy, when the US, according to the British media, was only a "puny nation." It should therefore come as no surprise when American historians see no inconsistency when they heap abundant praise on Jefferson for waging war on Tripoli to stamp out piracy and also praise the important role which American pirates played in "saving the new freedom loving republic" during the War of 1812 which they boldly call America's second War of Independence.

Privateers were used by the US during the War of 1812 against England, with Jefferson's approval. President James Madison issued *Letters of Marque* to more than 500 privateers. As in the War of Independence, American privateers concentrated their attacks on unarmed or lightly armed merchant ships of England, sinking over 1,700. Such attacks on "civilians" have never been criticized as cowardly by the US "free" press in the same way that the US media today speak of attacks by insurgents in Iraq or Afghanistan.

The most famous American pirate to serve the new American Empire was Jean Lafitte. Lafitte was engaged by *Sharp knife* Jackson on behalf of the US during the 1812 War with England. Without Lafitte's help and the thousand men he provided Jackson would not have defeated the English in New Orleans in January 1815 to become the hero of New Orleans and thereby qualify for America's top job of *Commander-in-Chief.* Lafitte and his men were pardoned by President Madison for all piracy related charges.

Thomas Boyle was another famous American privateer of the 1812 War. He captured or sank 17 English merchant vessels. Joshua Hailey was another prominent pirate to serve the US during the War of 1812. His ship, the *True Blood Yankee,* was built in France. He sailed from France and preyed on the coastal towns along the English and Irish coasts. He had taken over 25 prizes, large and small, before he was captured by the English. Other famous American pirates included Benjamin Palmer, James Newell and William Dunkin from Massachusetts, all of whom ended up in unmarked graves in Deadman's Island, Nova Scotia, after they were captured by the British.

In the case of Captain John Ordronaux, it was his ship, the *Prince of Neufchatel,* which became famous. The *Prince* was specially designed and built to be a privateer in 1812-1813 and received a *Letter of Marque* in October 1813. It was heavily armed but fast enough to outrun the British navy.

By the time the British navy captured it on December 28, 1814, it had inflicted severe damage on England's international trade.

The American Invasion of Algeria: 1815

You would think that American intellectuals, including American historians, would have been shamed into admitting the double standards employed by the American Empire with regards to piracy as a result of the War of 1812. Unfortunately, these intellectuals understand only too well that they are important ambassadors of American propaganda and are duty bound to promote and embellish the deceit. It should therefore come as no surprise that as soon as the 1812 War ended these same intellectuals would put forth the moral fibre of the new "freedom loving republic" in justifying its invasion of Algeria as taking a stand against piracy.

Commodores Steven Decatur and William Bainbridge were sent with 10 ships to invade Algeria in May 1815. Decatur and Bainbridge had both served in the 1801-05 invasion of Tripoli. The American invasion had very limited success but encouraged invasions by France and England.

The true nature of American hypocrisy became clear when the major empires of England and France, which had profited immensely from embracing piracy, decided that it was time to end this ancient practice. At the end of the Crimean War in 1856, France and England put forward a declaration that nations should not use privateers in future wars. This came to be known as the *Paris Declaration Respecting Maritime Law.* England and France convinced five other nations, Russia, the Ottoman Empire, Austria-Hungary, Prussia and Sardinia, to sign the Paris Declaration. As expected, The American Empire refused to sign.

France and England continue to misunderstand the true extent of American hypocrisy, double-talk and propaganda, to this day. America had no interest in ending piracy. Its interest was in ending piracy by **Muslim** nations in order to gain an edge in its competition for empire. America's subsequent overthrow of England, France and Russia, to become the dominant empire today, was largely due to its advantage in the use of propaganda, hypocrisy and double-talk.

During the American Civil War, Congress once again gave the US president the power to commission privateers and the Confederate states did likewise.

US Invasion and Conquest of Indiana, Mississippi, Illinois, Alabama, Maine, Missouri, Arkansas and Michigan

The new "freedom loving" American Republic born in 1783 out of wars and European competition for lands which legally belonged to militarily weaker Nations, showed an amazing gift for simultaneously invading the English colonies to the north, the Spanish colonies to the south and the First Nations lands to the west and east. Before Florida had become a state in 1845, this new "freedom loving republic" had invaded and conquered sufficient First Nations lands to add **eight** new states to the Union, over and above those added by Washington and Jefferson. Most of these eight states were carved out of the *Old Northwest,* the *Louisiana Territory* and the *Mississippi Territory.*

The US Invasion of Indiana, Illinois and Michigan: 1816-1837

The Northwest Territory had been created by the Northwest Ordinance of 1787. The original Northwest Territory covered 260,000 square miles of First Nations lands. However, on July 4, 1800, a separate Territory called the *Indiana Territory* was carved out of the Northwest Territory to enable the split off of the state of Ohio in 1803. The US invasion of Ohio was explained in Chapter 1. Parts of both the Northwest Territory and the new Indiana Territory were further divided to create the

Michigan Territory in 1805 and the *Illinois Territory* in 1809. Indiana became the *nineteenth* state of the Union in 1816. Illinois became the *twenty-first* state of the Union in 1818 and Michigan became the *twenty-sixth* state of the Union in 1837.

Indiana was home to the Shawnee and Miami First Nations. Americans from Virginia and Kentucky began to steal their land. A few other Americans came from the New England states. The Shawnees and Miamis joined other First Nations to fight the American invaders.

In 1790 President Washington sent General Josiah Harmer with 1,500 men against the Shawnees and Miamis. When Harmer was defeated President Washington sent General Arthur St. Clair the following year. Arthur St. Clair was among the first US settlers at Marietta, Ohio, since 1788. He was appointed as governor of the Northwest Territory. St. Clair was also defeated by the First Nations.

President Washington finally sent General "Mad Anthony" Wayne in 1794 who defeated the First Nations with help from England. When the First Nations lost the Battle of Fallen Timbers in August 1794 they retreated to Fort Miami in Ohio to regroup. Fort Miami was under the control of their English allies. England chose to renege on that alliance and aid the US invasion of the First Nations lands by refusing sanctuary to the First Nations warriors at Fort Miami.

The Treaty of Greenville forced on the First Nations in 1795 because of their defeat by Wayne and betrayal by England led to the American Empire replacing the British Empire in the entire Northwest Territory. The First Nations had defeated invasions by Spain, France and England only to be conquered by the new American Empire.

Slavery in Indiana: The 19th US State

William Harrison was appointed governor of the *Indiana Territory* which had been carved out of the Northwest Territory in 1800. *Indian Territory* had cleverly become *White Territory* by adding a single English letter. Governor Harrison was very determined to permanently "legalize" this theft of First Nations land by having the American Empire recognize *Indiana* as one more state of an ever expanding "freedom loving republic."

But Governor Harrison had a small problem. While most Americans think that owning slaves, especially if the slaves are Black, is not inconsistent with their claim to be civilized and moral beyond reproach a few Americans disagree. The Northwest Ordinance had therefore specified that states carved out of the Northwest Territory could not be *slave-states*.

Harrison decided to resort to typical Western hypocrisy. Slavery in the Indiana Territory was replaced by "voluntary indentured servitude." President Jefferson supported Harrison's decision to allow **White** "freedom loving" American plantation owners in the Indiana Territory to use "slaves." He re-appointed Harrison as governor in 1806.

Unfortunately for the large plantation owners Kentuckians continued to pour into the Indiana Territory to purchase the stolen First Nations lands at $2.00 per acre. These were not plantation owners and had little use for slaves. A move to abolish slavery was led by Jonathan Jennings and the "voluntary servitude" law was repealed.

Indiana became the nineteenth state of the Union on December 11, 1816. Another 37,000 square miles of First Nations land was "legally" added to the American Empire. While the new state abided by the Northwest Ordinance and Jennings was elected as its first governor, Blacks were not welcomed as residents in the latest state to be added to the freedom loving US Republic.

Slavery in Illinois: The 21st US State

The state of Illinois was also carved out of the Northwest territorial lands stolen from the First Nations. It represented a further theft of 58,000 square miles of First Nations lands after the US invaded their hunting grounds. Illinois was home to over 2,000 First Nations including the *Ilini, Fox and Sauk,* Nations.

French explorers, Louis Joliet and Jacques Marquette, had explored the Illinois River since 1673. England succeeded France as the imperial owner by the 1763 Treaty of Paris. The land which became the Illinois Territory in 1809 was first invaded and conquered by Virginia during the American War of Independence. England formally surrendered all claims to lands in the Old Northwest with the Treaty of Ghent in 1814.

Kentuckians moved into Illinois around the same time as other Kentuckians were moving into Indiana. Other Americans came from Virginia and Tennessee. This huge increase of the **White** population within a few years sealed the fate of the First Nations and Illinois became a state on December 3, 1818.

The "freedom loving" Americans settling in Illinois fought the anti-slavery provisions of the Northwest Ordinance as fiercely as their **White** brothers in Indiana. White equality implied the right to own slaves. Denial of this god given right was nothing short of Northern *Yankee* treachery. The problem though was that Blacks were hated as much as the First Nations. Slavery could mean an open invitation to large plantation owners importing thousands of these hated Blacks as slaves.

In the end hatred of Blacks prevented slavery in Illinois but Blacks were no more welcome in Illinois than they were in Indiana. The "freedom loving" US Republic was enforcing its equality rights enshrined in its constitution by insisting on equal *discrimination* against *non-whites* by all states of the Union.

First Nations continued to oppose the theft of their lands. In 1832 the *Fox* and *Sauk* Nations united under the leadership of Black Hawk to wage another full blown war against the invaders. Black Hawk had fought for England during the 1812-14 War. The US invasion of Illinois had forced the Fox and Sauk Nations west across the Mississippi River to Iowa.

The 1832 war was an attempt to reclaim the land stolen by the American Empire. On August 2, 1832 the US army butchered the Sauk Nation at Bad Axe on the Mississippi River. This ended the war and Black Hawk retreated to Iowa where he died in 1837.

Michigan: The 26ᵗʰ US State

Michigan was the home of the *Ottawa, Potawatomi, Huron* and *Chippewa* Nations. The city of Sault Ste Marie, straddling both Michigan and the Canadian province of Ontario, was settled by France in 1641. Michigan was part of New France and lost to England during the Seven Years War. Michigan became part of the new English colony of Upper Canada in 1791.

England surrendered Michigan to the US with Jay's Treaty of 1794. The US government appointed William Hull as governor of the *Michigan Territory* in 1805. England captured the Michigan Territory during the 1812-14 War with the US. It was returned to the US at the peace treaty.

White American settlers poured into the Michigan Territory after the completion of the Erie Canal in 1825. In 1836, the new *Wisconsin Territory* was carved out of the Michigan Territory with the remaining part becoming the state of Michigan. Michigan became the twenty-sixth state of the Union on January 26, 1837. The American Empire stole almost 100,000 square miles of First Nations land to create the state of Michigan.

By 1837, the original Northwest Territory had added **four** states, Ohio, Indiana, Illinois and Michigan, to the Union. Two other states, Wisconsin and Minnesota, would be added later. Each time a new state was added to the Union the First Nations lost more land. Each time they defended the theft of their land they lost lives and livelihood. They were herded into reservations to live as prisoners or moved further west temporarily. Their numbers declined as the **White** population of the

US increased. When the US reached the Pacific there could be no further movement west. Death or reservations were the only choices left. Many chose death.

The US Invasion of Mississippi and Alabama, 1817-1819, and the Creation of an *Internal* Slave-Trade in the "Good Old US of A."

The *Deep South* states of Mississippi and Alabama were carved out of the *Mississippi Territory* which was created by the US in 1798. England had secured imperial conquest rights to the Mississippi after the Seven Years War but was gradually pushed out by the expanding American Empire. Winthrop Sargent was appointed the first governor by President Adams. The land was stolen from the *Biloxi, Natchez, Choctaw, Cherokee, Alabama, Mobile, Creek, Chickasaw* and *Yazoo* Nations.

Jackson's defeat of the Creek and Seminole Nations had made it easier for Americans to occupy this vast expanse of new territory by setting up *slave* plantations to grow cotton and sugar. After the industrial revolution England provided a huge market for American cotton. Cotton price rose steadily until 1819. US cotton production quadrupled between 1810 and 1830. If you were White and not a slave-owner you were seen by your fellow White "freedom loving" Americans as a loser.

White American *slave owners* saw new opportunities for profits with the invasion and conquest of the First Nations' lands in Mississippi and Alabama. This induced many southern plantation owners to move from the old states of Virginia, South Carolina and Georgia, to Mississippi and Alabama, taking their valuable slaves with them. Many other plantation owners profited from the new conquests by simply selling their slaves to the plantation owners in Mississippi and Alabama. During this period the price of slaves rose because of the increased demand from the American *slave-owners* in Mississippi and Alabama.

Being "sold down River" to Mississippi and Alabama became the slaves worst nightmare. This new *internal* slave trade expanded and prospered as the British Navy intercepted ships on the high seas to enforce the law which had made the import of slaves into the "freedom loving" US illegal after 1808. Worldwide opposition to slavery had led to the abolition of the *international* slave trade in 1808. Illegal importation of slaves into the US increased the number of slaves in the US. More than 250,000 slaves were imported illegally into the US.

The invention of Whitney's *cotton gin* in 1794 significantly increased the profits to be made in cotton production in the US. US output of cotton increased from a mere 1,000 tons annually in 1790 to a million tons annually by 1860. *Mobile* became an important port to ship the raw cotton to England. Mobile was first colonized by France in 1702. England had inherited imperial rights to Mobile in 1763 but Spain captured it in 1779 when it became a district in Spanish West Florida. Just as the US had bullied England out of the Mississippi Territory it bullied Mobile from Spain and annexed it to the Mississippi Territory in 1812. The port was also an entry point for new immigrants into Alabama and Mississippi

Sugar plantations were also extremely profitable because the land in Mississippi had the right type of soil and climate for sugar cultivation. With the increased production of cotton and sugar using slave labour the US slave population increased from half a million in 1790 to a staggering 4 million by 1860. This occurred when the majority world opinion was against slavery. How anyone, much less supposedly educated historians, can continue to promote the US as the bastion of freedom and equality when it was the only country fighting to preserve and enhance the vile and evil institution of slavery is simply beyond comprehension.

The US decimates the First Nations to steal their lands. It imports Africans as slaves so that many Americans can own vast acreages of the stolen land and make huge profits by keeping human beings in perpetual servitude. How this is seen by historians as the true mark of a *freedom loving republic* with democratic values boggles the mind? As late as 2005, Blacks made up about 30 percent of the population of these two states despite the fact that many Blacks migrated north after the US civil war to escape the *Jim Crow* laws and the *Ku Klux Klan*.

Mississippi became the *twentieth* state of the Union in 1817 and Alabama became the *twenty-second* state of the Union in 1819. The US invasion and conquest of the states of Mississippi and Alabama transferred close to 100,000 square miles of First Nations' land to the new "freedom loving republic."

The US Invasion of Maine and Missouri, 1820-1821, and the "Missouri Compromise" to Prolong *Slavery* in the American Empire

When the US carved out the state of Louisiana from the Louisiana Territory in 1812, the remaining portion of the Louisiana Territory was renamed the *Missouri Territory*. Intelligent Americans have always opposed the tragic wrongs committed by their country. That is as true today with regards to the US invasion of Iraq and Afghanistan as it was with *slavery* in the USA. It's unfortunate that intelligent Americans have always constituted such a small minority of the population and have never been voted into political office. The majority votes into political office the Barak Obamas, Bill Clintons and George Bushes because they want to keep the American Empire a vile, racist warmongering bully.

The US invasion and conquest of *Missouri* threatened to disintegrate the US over the issue of *slavery*. While the great majority of **White** Americans supported the use of African slaves, slavery had been a source of disunity since the creation of the US. The disunity did not stem from any dislike of slavery by Americans, except for the minority of intelligent Americans mentioned above. It stemmed from constitutional power sharing among states of the Union because some states had slaves and some states did not. Slavery was not profitable in the states which had long grown out of the plantation-based single agricultural crop economy.

The constitutional power sharing had to do with representation of states in the US Congress. Each state, regardless of geographical size or population, had two representatives in the US Senate. Representation in the House was based on population. Slavery had first threatened the union because of representation in the House. The slave states wanted an edge by counting their slaves as part of their population even though slaves were defined as *property* not human beings.

The Union survived this threat by the dastardly act of allowing *slave* states to count a slave as *60 percent human* for representation in the House. This unconscionable act was promoted to the world as a brilliant American "compromise." The new threat to the Union came in 1818 with regards to power sharing in the Senate. In 1818 there were 11 *slave* states and 11 slave-free states. Admission of a new state into the Union would upset the balance of power in the Senate. The American Empire needed another quintessential American "compromise" to prolong the inhumane institution of slavery in their "freedom loving republic." They found it in what many American historians proudly refer to as the "Great Missouri compromise."

To maintain the balance of power in the US Senate new states would be admitted in pairs, one being a *slave* state and the other being a slave-free state. American historians proudly call this solution the great Missouri compromise because **White** American Republicans who dearly love freedom and equality had found a way of preserving the *institution of slavery* in what they touted as the best country in the world. The Union was threatened when Missouri wanted admission to the Union as a *slave* state. At the time Missouri already had 10, 000 slaves.

Missouri dearly wanted admission to the "greatest" country in the world but not if it meant abandoning the God given right of **White** "freedom loving" Americans to own **Black** slaves. According to Senator William Smith of South Carolina, slavery was mandated by God. Senator Smith did not expand on whether God intended the slaves to be Whites or Blacks. Nor could admission to the "greatest" country in the world compensate for the loss of such valuable property.

The slave-free states opposed the admission of Missouri, not because they abhorred slavery, but because it would upset the balance of power in the Senate. They had no qualms with admitting Missouri as a slave state if Maine was admitted as a slave-free state. Maine was therefore admitted as the *twenty-third* state of the Union on March 15, 1820 and Missouri was admitted as the *twenty-fourth* state of the Union on August 10, 1821.

Maine was originally part of the Massachusetts Bay colony settled by England in 1630. There had been some French settlers since 1604. France considered it part of Acadia. It became a part of the state of Massachusetts after the US gained its independence from England. Its final border with the Canadian province of New Brunswick was not settled until 1842 with the *Webster-Ashburn Treaty*. The land was stolen from the *Abenaki, Penobscots* and *Passamaquoddy* Nations.

The Union was saved and so was the *American institution* of slavery. If the Roman Empire could have slaves and be called *civilized,* by God so could the American Empire! President Monroe had been returned for a second term. His second inaugural speech implied that the "Great Missouri compromise" had saved the US from the "defects of the ancient Republics." In his view the preservation of *slavery,* the most vile subjugation of the human condition, made the US a better Republic.

Missouri even banned the entry of free blacks and mulattoes to the new state of the "freedom loving" Union. It had also previously abolished the Catholic Black Code instituted by France to give limited rights to slaves. Any religious leader or abolitionist who spoke against the God given right of Whites to own slaves was physically attacked and killed in some cases. It was the "Manifest Destiny" of Americans to be able to own slaves while preaching freedom and equality to the rest of the world. It was America's "Manifest Destiny" to become "leader of the free world" by subjugating all others, stealing not only their resources and wealth but their dignity and humanity. Missouri added another 70,000 square miles of First Nations land to the US.

The US Invasion of Arkansas: 1836

When Missouri became a state the remainder of the *Missouri Territory* was renamed the *Arkansas Territory* in 1819 with James Miller appointed as the first governor. The area was inhabited by the *Osage, Quapaw* and *Caddo* Nations. Like Missouri, it was admitted to the Union as a *slave* state. It became the *twenty-fifth* state of the Union, and the *thirteenth* slave state on June 15, 1836. Balance of power was maintained in the Senate because Michigan was admitted as a slave-free state the following year.

This completes our documentation of US invasions up to March 3, 1845 when Florida became the *twenty-seventh* state of the Union. The American Empire had more than doubled the number of states in the 62 years between 1783 and 1845. The land area of the new states was much greater than the land area of the original 13 states.

What follows is our documentation of the use of the *Monroe Doctrine* by the US to justify further expansion of its Empire by invading countries in the Americas which had won their independence from Spain or some other European imperialist. This expansion began with the invasion of Texas.

The Monroe Doctrine, Manifest Destiny and the US Invasions of Texas, Iowa, Wisconsin and California:1845-1850

In his annual message to the US Congress, President James Monroe announced on December 2, 1823, that the New World would no longer be open to European colonization. This announcement came to be known as the *Monroe Doctrine.* As usual American historians have hailed this as a blow against imperialism and another example of the desire of the US to protect freedom, equality and self determination.

It was absolutely nothing of the kind. It was a brazen and shameful announcement that the **American Empire** would be the new imperialist in the Caribbean and the Americas. With its home advantage and addiction to warmongering it would be a much more controlling and militarily interventionist imperialist than the Europeans had ever been. Every aspect of life in the ex-European colonies would be controlled by US spies, US troops, US propaganda, US investments, US culture, US threats, US embargoes, US boycotts and US domination.

The American Empire would be the "Roman Empire" of the New World where no one would be allowed to breathe the air of freedom. Big brother would be looking over your shoulder controlling every move, every action and every thought.

While the announcement of the Monroe Doctrine in 1823 was nothing more than an outlandish mouthing off by what England still regarded as a "puny" empire, it set a course for American imperialism which became a reality as the US grew in military and economic stature. It would be the equivalent today of China announcing that Asia was out of bounds to European and American investment and political influence. Both Europe and the US would simply ignore such an announcement by China today. However, China could, in time, develop the muscle to enforce such a doctrine should it want to be as imperialist as the US and Europe.

That was the situation with the US in 1823. Europeans ignored the Monroe Doctrine in 1823 but were unable to after the First World War. By that time the US had the economic and military muscle to enforce it. As early as 1845, Americans began to envisage the reality of the US invading and conquering the entire continent. The editor of the New York Post, John O'Sullivan, called it *Manifest Destiny.*

As in the 2003 invasion of Iraq, O'Sullivan lied about the true meaning of Manifest Destiny. Just as the *neo-cons* in the US promoted a horrendous lie that the US invasion of Iraq was to spread democracy rather than to conquer territory and resources so had O'Sullivan lied in 1845 by promoting the idiotic notion that invasion and conquest of the American continent by the US was to spread liberty instead of **slavery.**

Just as the *neo-cons* in the US tested their doctrine of *pre-emptive war* by unilaterally invading the independent country of Iraq, the US tested the Monroe doctrine and Manifest Destiny by invading the independent country of Mexico and conquering so much land that **five** new states were eventually added to the Union. These were the states of Texas, California, Nevada, Utah, New Mexico and Arizona. Mexico was forced to surrender more than 40 percent of its territory to the "freedom loving" Americans.

Today Mexicans are rightfully reclaiming the land stolen from their fore-fathers. By 2010, Mexicans had become the largest minority in the USA. They cross the border which the American Empire had set in 1848 at the Rio Grande, by invading and "stealing" what had been Mexican land. It's ironic that **White** Americans complain about "illegal" Mexican immigration as if the American Empire had "legally" taken Mexican land when it had invaded in 1845.

The American Empire Invades Texas to Protect and Enhance the Inhumane Institution of African Slavery: 1820-1848

Texas became the *twenty-eighth* state of the US on December 29, 1845, the same year that O'Sullivan coined the term, *Manifest Destiny,* which the US would use to justify its aggression against militarily weaker independent countries in the New World. Florida had been added to the Union earlier that same year by invading and defeating the Spanish Empire in Florida. By adding Texas to the Union the American Empire was invading and conquering ex-colonies of the Spanish Empire which had succeeded in overthrowing the same European imperial yoke the 13 original English colonies had done in 1783.

In 1810, Mexico began its struggle for independence from Spain. In many ways, the colony of Mexico was to Spain what the 13 American colonies had been to England. Mexico was Spain's most populous colony in the New World just as the 13 English colonies which became the US were England's most populous colonies in the New World. The US and the United Mexican States had both wrested independence from a European imperialist. There would have been much to gain from peaceful economic and political cooperation.

This was not to be because the American Empire had an insatiable appetite to colonize, dominate and subjugate militarily, economically, culturally, racially and politically. Moreover, the US had the world's best propaganda machine. It could commit the most heinous crime and still convince many people that the crime had been committed for the good of humanity and to promote a free and just world. In 1823 when the Monroe Doctrine was announced, Mexicans had no hope against the US propaganda machine.

Since then Mexicans have learnt the power and deceit of American propaganda. They are now coming back to take the lands which the US invaded and conquered 150 years before. The US calls 12 million of them *illegal aliens*. Why should that bother the Mexicans? Did the US steal their lands legally?

The Mexican Independence Movement

In 1701, the Bourbon, Philip V, ascended the Spanish throne. Charles II of Spain had named the grandson of Louis IV of France his heir to the Spanish throne. Under the Bourbon kings, Mexico became the most economically developed of all the Spanish colonies. By 1800, output from the silver mines of Mexico was three times the output of silver from Peru.

Mexicans were inspired by both the American War of Independence and the French Revolution. Napoleon's overthrow of the Spanish monarch in 1808 provided an opportunity for Mexico's Revolution. Miguel Hidalgo became Mexico's George Washington. The Revolution began in *Dolores,* Guanajuato state, on September 16, 1810 and advanced to Mexico City on October 30, 1810.

After several setbacks the First Mexican Congress was held in September 1813. Mexico declared itself an independent Republic in October 1814. In August 1821, Mexico signed a treaty with Spain which recognized the independence of Mexico. After a brief stint with Augustin de Iturbide as emperor, Mexico became a Republic in 1824 with Guadalupe Victoria as its first President.

By the time of Mexico's independence in 1821, the US which began as 13 tiny English colonies along a thin strip of land on the Atlantic coast, had invaded and conquered more First Nations land than anyone could have dreamed of. Yet Americans were envious of Mexico and wanted to steal the land which Mexico and Spain had stolen from the *Apache, Cherokee, Comanche, Atakapan, Kiowa* and other First Nations.

Americans invaded the Mexican border state of *Coahuila-Texas,* living as Mexicans much like Mexicans are invading US Border States today and living as Americans. There was one important difference. In the 1820's the Americans brought their **slaves** with them and imported more after settling in Texas.

In 1829, the Independent Republic of Mexico abolished slavery. The American **slave** owners defied Mexican law to continue ownership of slaves and wanted to change Mexican law to allow them to keep their slaves. Americans also proudly claimed racial superiority to Mexicans similar to

White Jews invading Arab lands after the Second World War claiming racial superiority to Arabs. The "freedom loving" Americans were angry that Mexico would deprive them of their freedom to own **slaves** and also bow to their false claim to racial superiority.

The American Invasions into Mexican Territory

In 1836 there were about 50,000 Americans living in Coahuila-Texas, mostly in the North-East part of the state. They revolted against Mexican rule to set up an independent **slave** Republic fashioned after the US **slave** Republic they were so proud of. They called this new Republic *Texas,* with David Burnet as President. The Mexican army led by General Antonio Santa Anna, the new President of Mexico, initially crushed the rebels at the Alamo on March 6, 1836, four days after their formal declaration of Independence.

However, Santa Anna was defeated by Sam Houston on April 21, 1836 at the Battle of San Jacinto. Armed forces from several states of the US had moved into Texas to assist Houston. Houston became President of Texas for defending the American **slave owners.**

American historians proudly defend Sam Houston by claiming that Santa Anna was a dictator. Since most of these historians are **White** and slaves were **Blacks** it is no surprise that these **White** historians would see dictatorship as worse than **slavery.** Moreover, given our criticisms of American democracy and overwhelming misrepresentation of its short comings by American historians, one can question the claims by these historians that Santa Anna was any more dictatorial than the governing oligarchy, and its military-industrial complex, in the US.

On the other hand, African **slavery** was an undisputed fact, not open to any disagreement as to its existence in both the US and the independent Republic of Texas established by American **slave owners.** Santa Anna, on the contrary, was a staunch abolitionist. After his capture of the Alamo he not only spared the lives of women and children but also the life of the slave owned by the "freedom loving" Texan-American commander, Colonel William Travis and the slave owned by the "freedom loving" American legend, Jim Bowie.

The new "freedom loving" Republic of Texas, fashioned after the other "freedom loving" Republic of the USA, formally **legalized slavery** in their constitution. Mexico had chosen to follow world opinion and human decency to abolish slavery. The US, by contrast, fought against world opinion to entrench slavery as a God given right to **White** Americans and invaded Texas both to conquer territory and to expand the institution of slavery.

This view was loudly expressed by ex-president John Quincy Adams who had become an abolitionist. Adams argued against expansion of slavery while the leader of the Whig party, Robert Coombs, reminded Americans that they had already conquered more than enough territory and to check their "lust for dominion." Moreover, when the US Congress voted to annex Texas to the US, the "Ordinance of Annexation," provided for the division of the annexed territory into a maximum of **five** states. This implied that the US invasion and conquest of Texas could add as many as five new **slave** states to the Union. No wonder the northern slave-free states opposed the invasion for fear of losing their balance of power in the US Senate.

American historians have deliberately lied about the facts by promoting the US as the more civilized country when the US invaded Mexico in 1845 to steal Texas. As the largest state, before Alaska, Texas added almost 300,000 square miles of First Nations lands to an already much enlarged USA. American **white supremacy** ideas prevailed. First Nations were subjugated and Blacks enslaved.

Santa Anna was held prisoner by the Americans. As a result he lost the Presidency of Mexico. This was further proof that the invasion of Texas was not due to governance by a dictator as US historians have claimed. Since Americans had captured and imprisoned the "dictator," and the Mexican people had renounced him there was clearly no reason for the Americans to keep Texas if they had only seized control because of the dictatorship of Santa Anna.

The US Congress approved the annexation of Texas to the Union on February 28, 1845. In a desperate attempt to prevent the expansion of **slavery,** Congressman David Wilmot tried to introduce a clause to prohibit **slavery** in the annexed territory. His attempt was, of course, soundly defeated by the "freedom loving" US **slave owners.**

Henry David Thoreau vainly tried another ruse. He refused to pay taxes to support the war against Mexico. He was promptly imprisoned for his efforts. In prison, he wrote the famous essay on *Civil Disobedience.*

President James Polk sent the US army under General Zachary Taylor to organize the defence of the expanded US on its southern border with Mexico. Taylor crossed the Rio Grande and built Fort Brown. As a dedicated warmonger it was not difficult to get the US Congress to approve war with Mexico. The US declared war on Mexico on May 13, 1846. US forces under General Zachary Taylor were instructed to occupy Mexican territory as far south as Monterrey. Taylor captured Monterrey in September of 1846 and continued further south into Mexico to capture Buena Vista on February 22, 1847.

President Polk sent another US army under General Winfield Scott by sea to Vera Cruz. Scott's landing in Vera Cruz was enabled by naval support under Commodore Matthew Perry. Scott marched on Mexico City to become the latest American hero when he captured it on September 14, 1847.

Ulysses Grant, who later became President of the US, participated in the invasion of Mexico. He later expressed his regret for doing so, calling the invasion one of the most unjust wars waged by a militarily stronger nation against a militarily weaker nation. He said that the US Civil War was God's punishment for the US invasion of Mexico.

At the same time that Taylor and Scott invaded Northern Mexico the US attacked Mexico on its Pacific coast with both its Pacific fleet and another army under Stephen Kearney. The goal of this parallel invasion was not Texas but California and New Mexico. Kearney captured Santa Fe in New Mexico before proceeding to California.

The Pacific fleet under Commodore John Sloat captured San Francisco on July 7, 1846. By January of 1847, California had surrendered to the US. The combined US invasions forced Mexico to surrender 500,000 square miles of its territory to the US. This was larger than the area of the initial 13 English colonies which had fought for their independence from England.

American soldiers celebrated by raping Mexican women, scalping civilians, murdering children, burning homes and desecrating churches. Mexico was forced to sign the *Treaty of Guadalupe Hidalgo* on February 2, 1848. The new border with a much reduced Mexico was established at the Rio Grande. The US used the conquered Mexican territory to add the states of Texas in 1845, California in 1850, Nevada in 1864, Utah in 1896, New Mexico and Arizona in 1912, to the Union.

Americans rejoiced and celebrated their dominion over slaves, First Nations and Mexicans. **White** Americans added one more group to the First Nations and the African-Americans who would resist their tyranny. By 2010, the Mexicans had become the most successful group in opposing **White** domination in the US. Mexicans are only now successfully re-conquering their land by legal and "illegal" immigration from Mexico into the captured territory.

Fugitive Slave Acts and the US Invasion of California: 1845-1850

The pace at which the US invaded and added stolen lands to its professed freedom loving Republic was truly staggering. It happened at a time when the three major European imperialists, Spain, France and England, were increasingly pushed out of the New World by US imperialism which was far superior at the use of propaganda. US propaganda succeeded in convincing not only its own citizens, but many fools outside the US, that its invasions and conquests were not imperialist but motivated by a "Manifest Destiny" to protect the weak and exploited from the European imperialists.

The Europeans were caught up both with the American deception and with fighting each other and conquering other empires outside the New World. The ultimate outcome would not have mattered had it not been for the fact that the First Nations lost more land and rights than they would have under the European Empires. As mentioned earlier the European Empires came to the New World both to establish colonies and to trade. As such their settlements were sparsely populated by **Whites** leaving much of the land for the First Nations.

In addition to the disastrous effect of American imperialism on the First Nations the new self-governing independent democracies outside the US, such as Mexico, were crushed by US invasions of the entire continent. Finally, after World War II the US grew to dominate the rest of the world. Its truly sad that even today there are so many fools who still believe that US invasions across the globe are intended for the good of those whose women and children have been slaughtered by Americans and forced to submit to US tyranny.

As the US continues to escalate its enormous production of the most sophisticated WMD's it can still convince many that it needs an even greater arsenal to defend against those who would attack it with sticks and stones and slingshots, never mind IEDs.

The Mexican invasion added 15 percent of the current geographical area of the US. Many Americans saw the 1845-50 invasions into Mexican territory as only the first stage of the eventual conquest of all of Mexico. The *New York Herald* wrote that it was America's destiny to "civilize" Mexico. The implicit assumption was that America was a much greater civilizing force than Spain had been.

As we explained above the American invasion and conquest of Texas in 1845 did not appease America's insatiable appetite for the First Nations' land now ruled by the Mexican Republic. The US invasions into Mexican territory continued until the *state* of California and the *territories* of New Mexico and Utah were added to the American Empire in 1850. Adding the state of California to the American Empire in 1850 raised the never ending power struggle between **slave** states and slave-free states once again. As usual this issue would not be settled by the abolition of slavery but by yet another "Great American Compromise" as American historians proudly call it.

By the time of the US invasions into Mexico, California had about 10,000 Americans living there. Americans revolted against Mexican rule with assistance from the US army led by John Fremont and the US navy under Commodores John Sloat and Robert Stockton. US forces captured San Francisco, Sacramento and Sonoma in Northern California before invading Los Angeles in the south on August 13, 1846. Mexico surrendered California to the invaders on January 13, 1847. Fremont was appointed as military governor.

Gold was discovered at Sutter's Mill east of Sacramento on January 24, 1848 causing a significant influx of Americans into California. First Nations were pushed off their land again by the ever expanding US Empire. California had been home to some 300,000 First Nations prior to the European invasions. White Americans quickly realized that membership in the "freedom loving" United States would guarantee their dominance over First Nations, Mexicans and other non-whites.

The US, always looking for imperial expansion while pretending to uphold the right to self determination, gladly obliged. California became the *thirty-first* state of the Union on September 9, 1850. It added another 160,000 square miles of stolen First Nations/Mexican land to the US.

The Second Fugitive Slave Act of 1850

Article IV of the US Constitution protected the rights of US slave owners. Slaves were the *private property* of White Americans. These White Americans led by their "great father," George Washington, passed the first Fugitive Slave Act on February 12, 1793. Its intension was to deny constitutional rights to slaves who had been emancipated. Under this law **free** Blacks captured as runaway slaves were not allowed to produce proof of freedom in a court of law. It was a federal offense to assist a slave to escape and escaped slaves could be legally apprehended in slave-free states and returned to their slave owners.

Any children born to the mother of a runaway slave could also be arrested and returned to the owner of the mother. Slave catching became a prosperous business since catchers would often forcibly seize **free** Blacks and sell them into **slavery.** It was cheaper than importing them from Africa or the Caribbean.

By 1850, England had abolished slavery in all of its colonies. As we saw above Mexico had also abolished slavery and the *international* slave trade was illegal. The world outside the US was overwhelmingly against this barbaric and inhumane institution. In the US many Americans opposed enforcing the provisions of the 1793 Fugitive Slave Act. In the 1848 presidential elections almost 300,000 Americans voted for the pro-abolitionist Free-Soil party candidate, Martin Van Buren.

Unfortunately, the majority of **White** Americans firmly believed that the freedoms they were guaranteed by the US Constitution included the right to own slaves and were proud of the fact that their democratic republic was a **slave-based** democracy. American **slave owners** saw an opportunity to strengthen the enforcement of the Fugitive Slave Act of 1793 when California wanted to join the Union as a slave-free state. They got the second *Fugitive Slave Act* which guaranteed federal help in returning runaway slaves from **slave** states to slave-free states. Slave-free states no longer provided a haven for runaway slaves and **free** Blacks were captured and enslaved.

This second Fugitive Slave Act of September 18, 1850 served to confirm that freedom continued to be a farce in a **White** dominated United States. The 1850 Act was intended to strengthen the provisions of the 1793 Act by legally forcing the authorities in the slave-free states to search out and apprehend slaves who had escaped from the **slave** states and return them to their owners. Furthermore, a Federal official who did not apprehend a suspected runaway was subject to a fine of $1,000.00. Likewise, anyone aiding a runaway slave could also be fined $1,000.00 and imprisoned for six months.

Since officials who apprehended escaped slaves were paid a fee there was the temptation to arrest **free** Blacks and sell them into slavery. A **free** Black so arrested was not allowed to provide evidence of his/her freedom in a court of law. Many **free** Blacks chose to migrate to Canada and Mexico to escape potential enslavement in the "freedom loving" *civilized* United States.

While the second Fugitive Slave Act was inhumane and barbaric, American historians proudly present it as another Great Compromise, like the other Great Compromises, such as the Missouri Compromise of 1820. By 1850, there had been so many of these Great Compromises to protect the evil institution of slavery that historians ran out of names. This latest one has simply been called the *1850 Compromise.*

By the time of this latest "Compromise" the US was unique in preserving the institution of slavery as a sacred *American* definition of freedom, equality, liberty, democracy and republican values. One more strike for the hypocritical freedom loving USA. The Iraqis and Afghans would be proud to know that democracies planted in their countries by the US would entrench their right to own slaves in their constitutions and arm them to invade their neighbours and steal their lands.

US Invasions of Iowa and Wisconsin, 1821-48, expands the American Empire to 31 states by 1850

The US gained its independence from England in 1783. However, the 13 ex-English colonies joined the Union on different dates beginning with Delaware, Pennsylvania and New Jersey in 1787 and ending with Rhode Island in 1790. It was 1790, therefore, that the US became a fully fledged federal nation made up of 13 states with a total area of 341,668 square miles. Parts of this land area which became the US had been stolen from the First Nations by the British Empire through invasions, wars and conquests.

The US, in turn, seized it from the British Empire by military means. Did the US have a legal claim to this land because it had fought and won a war from an imperial power which had conquered some of the land from the First Nations? It would be difficult to suggest that after years of imperial subjugation by the British the **White** settlers had absolutely no claim to the land and that all of it should have been returned to the First Nations. However, there is no need to answer that question. The **White** Americans who became the citizens of the new nation of the United States had absolutely no intention of sharing **any** of the 341,668 squares miles of land with the First Nations.

The US seized all of it whether it had been previously conquered, stolen or settled. The First Nations were killed off or forcibly evicted out of this area. The few who remained became **second class** citizens, deprived of equal citizenship rights and discriminated against. What would have been a true American revolution ushering in freedom, equality, liberty, justice and republican values, would have been the just treatment of the First Nations as equal partners in a new nation. The reality of the American Revolution was that it was no revolution at all but a regression to a less free and democratic society. First Nations were deprived of their land, non-whites were discriminated against and African **slavery** enhanced. Far from the US being the shining example of a free democratic Republic it was less free or democratic than England, France or other European countries.

The much more important fact resulting from the creation of an independent United States, free of European colonization, was the determined and conscious decision of its citizens to compete aggressively with the European imperialists for its own empire in the New World and later outside the New World. The US became *imperialist* as soon as it became a nation. It had imperial ambitions even before it became a nation as evidenced by its invasion of the English colonies in Canada. However, its attack on the British Empire in Canada failed. It was therefore after it had become a nation that it successfully competed for an empire with the British, French and Spanish empires.

This cannot be disputed. American historians are wrong when they claim that the US never had imperial ambitions. What is surprising is how quickly those imperial ambitions were successful. Assuming we are correct in saying that the US became a fully fledged independent nation in 1790, when Rhode Island was the last of the 13 ex-English colonies to ratify the US Constitution and join the Union, the US began its successful bid for empire status the very next year. In 1791, the US invaded and conquered almost 10,000 square miles of First Nations land in *Vermont* to begin its empire.

Both the French Empire and the British Empire had fought the First Nations and each other for this land. The new American Empire fought both the First Nations and the European Empires for the same land. It is the American Empire which still has it. The American Empire called it a *state* instead of a *colony*. Whether conquered territories are called states or colonies make no difference to those who are invaded and conquered.

In 1775 the US served notice of its imperial ambition by invading Canada. By 1791 the US had succeeded in becoming an empire. Two more states, Kentucky and Tennessee, were quickly added to the American Empire before the end of the century. Within a single decade as an independent nation state the US had acquired an empire consisting of 92,236 square miles of land. At this pace it would quickly overtake the old European empires of Spain, France and England with whom it was competing.

In the first 50 years of the nineteenth century the size of the US Empire exploded with the invasions and conquests of First Nations lands. The 15 states of Ohio, Louisiana, Indiana, Mississippi, Illinois, Alabama, Maine, Missouri, Arkansas, Michigan, Florida, Texas, Iowa, Wisconsin and California were added to the empire in half a century. These 15 states added over a million square miles to the American Empire. With the three states added in the 1790's the US had acquired an empire of 1,149, 381 square miles.

In less than 60 years since its birth as a Nation the US had conquered an empire more than **three times** its own size. This rapid pace of imperial expansion exceeded the pace of any of the European empires which had invaded the New World. The rise of the US Empire would be the fastest the world had ever experienced. Its decline would be just as fast.

US Invasions West of the Mississippi River and the Black Hawk War

As the American Empire pushed westwards from the original New England states and eastward from Texas and California the First Nations were squeezed into a smaller and smaller land area north of Illinois and just east and west of the Mississippi River. It was the home of the *Sauk* and *Fox* Nations. The American Empire would invade these First Nations' land to add the states of Iowa and Wisconsin to its empire before 1850. With California added in 1850 the invasions which made the American Empire an empire of 31 states in 1850 would be complete.

Americans first invaded this area to mine lead. By the 1830's this area produced half the total output of lead in the United States. Other Americans moved from New York and the New England states to settle in the area, using the First Nations' land for dairy farming. The American settlers pushed the First Nations further west and across the Mississippi River. Prior to this invasion First Nations had hoped that the Mississippi River would have provided a natural barrier to further invasions by the American Empire. That was not to be.

The US continued to wage wars on the First Nations to occupy this area. Among those fighting the First Nations here was *Abraham Lincoln*. The First Nations resisted stubbornly under the leadership of Black Hawk. US victory came at the Battle of Bad Axe on August 2, 1832. US forces far outnumbered Black Hawk's 500 braves. Black Hawk made a desperate attempt to out run the US army but his escape across the Mississippi was blocked by more US forces which had arrived by steamboat. Black Hawk and his *Sauk* Nation were trapped. US forces butchered the Sauk Nation including women and children.

After the *Black Hawk War* which killed 100 Americans and 600 First Nations, this area was officially occupied by the US and added to the *Michigan Territory* on June 8, 1834. The Michigan Territory had been created in 1805.

Creation of the Wisconsin Territory, 1836

When Michigan became a state in 1836, the remaining part of the *Michigan Territory* was renamed the *Wisconsin Territory*. The Wisconsin Territory represented a further theft of almost 200,000 square miles of First Nations land under the presidency of Andrew Jackson. Jackson appointed Henry Dodge as governor. The Act creating the Wisconsin Territory was passed by the US Congress on April 20, 1836. The stolen area was large enough to add three more states to the ever expanding Union, Iowa, Wisconsin and Minnesota. First Nations' lands west of the Mississippi River were now being invaded by the US.

The first state carved out of the Wisconsin Territory was Iowa which was west of the Mississippi River. The Mississippi River no longer protected the First Nations from the invaders. Manifest Destiny was about to invade all of the First Nations' lands between California on the west coast and the Mississippi River. Iowa joined the Union as the *twenty-ninth* state on December 28, 1846. It represented almost 60,000 square miles of stolen First Nations' land west of the Mississippi River. The first Americans had migrated west from Indiana, Illinois and Missouri pushing the western frontier of an ever expanding Republic. Wisconsin was the second state to be carved out of the Wisconsin Territory. Its western border is the Mississippi River. Wisconsin became the *thirtieth* state of the Union on May 29, 1848. It represented a theft of over 65,000 square miles of First Nations land. By 1850, the US which continues to claim that its creation was based on a struggle against English colonialism and the replacement of Royal tyranny with Republican freedoms, had expanded from 13 tiny states to 31 states where the new states were much larger in area than the original 13 states.

US Invasions and Conquest of Oregon, Minnesota, Kansas and Arizona

The US invasion of Oregon began as early as 1792, just two years after Rhode Island completed the process of making the US a new independent Nation and only one year after the American Empire began with the successful invasion of Vermont. The 1792 date is based on US claims to Oregon following the discovery of the mouth of the Columbia River that year by Robert Gray. Gray was an American who was the captain of a ship engaged in the fur trade.

The brand new American Empire was already competing with the Russian, Spanish, French and English empires for the lucrative fur trade which the First Nations of the Pacific Northwest controlled. At the time Oregon meant the entire Pacific Northwest. The old empires had no illusions about the imperialist expansionism of the US despite its loud rhetoric to the contrary. However, they were too busy fighting each other to combine forces against the US.

The Lewis and Clark expedition sent by President Jefferson was opposed by Spain. The Spanish governor of Upper Louisiana, Carlos Delassus, refused permission for the expedition to sail up the Missouri River. Delassus was not fooled by the American claim that the expedition was purely scientific. Spain was unable to stop the Americans because of Napoleon's conquest of Spain followed by the successful slave rebellion in the French colony of Haiti. The Lewis and Clark expedition reached the Columbia River in 1805 with the guidance of the French fur trader, Toussaint Charbonneau, and his First Nation wife, Sacajawea. One of the goals of the Lewis and Clark expedition was to set up a fur trade agreement with the First Nations.

General James Wilkinson of the US army became the American governor of Upper Louisiana after the US paid off Napoleon for French imperial rights to Louisiana. Wilkinson sent Captain Zebulon Pike in 1805 to spy on the Spanish colonies along the Mississippi River and on the English fur trading posts. Pike was captured by Spanish cavalry in February 1807 and taken first to Santa Fe and then to the Spanish capital of Albuquerque, Chihuahua. Fearing military reprisals by the US, the Spanish governor, Salcedo, released Pike at the Louisiana border with New Spain. Spain had to content itself with a letter of protest to Washington and breaking off diplomatic relations.

It was just the beginning of the US becoming the world's bully. American fur traders began to cross the Rocky Mountains into Oregon after the Lewis and Clark expedition and Pike's spy mission. The Lewis and Clark expedition promoted the abundance of fur bearing animals in the Pacific Northwest. Beaver pelts were extremely valuable at the time.

In 1811, the Americans built Fort Astoria on the Columbia River as their headquarters for the *Pacific Fur Company*. Their competition against England suffered as a result of the War of 1812.

Fort Astoria was sold to the English who renamed it Fort George. After 1832 the Americans reached Oregon via the famous *Oregon Trail* from Missouri. The Americans were welcomed into Oregon by John McLoughlin, the *Chief Factor* of England's fur trading company, the Hudson Bay Company. Fort Vancouver was the headquarters of the English fur trade throughout the Pacific Northwest.

The number of American fur traders grew steadily until 1840 when the fur bearing animals had been trapped to extinction. As the fur trade declined the number of American settlers in Oregon increased. Missionaries followed the fur traders to assist the American settlers to steal the First Nations land and support the view of the **Whites** that **Red** was an inferior race with their preaching that the religions of the First Nations were inferior. At the same time other Americans entered Oregon by sea to settle or to export the furs from the Pacific coast ports to China.

By 1825, France, Spain and Russia had given up imperial claims to Oregon leaving the US and England to compete with the First Nations for the land. The US naturally wanted all of the land in Oregon as it had wanted all of Canada. Many more American settlers reached Oregon in the 1840's. They went for the free farmland. The American Empire permitted every married American couple to steal as much as 640 acres of good farmland in Oregon from the First Nations.

It was somewhat ironic that many Americans moved to Oregon because disease and epidemics were less common than in the Eastern states but brought with them many infectious diseases, including smallpox, which decimated the First Nations.

American historians not only deny the invasion and theft of First Nations lands in Oregon but foolishly say that many First Nations welcomed the American invaders because they brought increased trade and economic benefits. That would be the equivalent of saying that because many Canadians or Chinese today welcome the economic benefits of trade with the US they would welcome American invasion and conquest of their countries.

We have been consistent in pointing out that First Nations preferred the French to the English because the French Empire in North America was more interested in trade than in settlement. Likewise the First Nations preferred English imperialism to American imperialism because the English Empire in North America was more interested in trade than in settlement compared with the American Empire. At no time would First Nations have welcomed the invasion, conquest and theft of their land by the American Empire.

The majority of First Nations even opposed trade for the same reason as the majority of Canadians today oppose free trade with the US. It's not that Canadians do not want the economic benefits of free trade with the US. They are afraid of US bullying, superior military power, theft of their natural resources and economic domination. It was the same for the First Nations in Oregon. The Spanish, Russian, French and English empires, which had arrived before the American, were not as greedy for every inch of First Nations land as the Americans were.

Adding insult to injury, some American historians stupidly promote American conquest of the First Nations lands as more self righteous than trade. According to these historians the other empires raped the resources of the First Nations by engaging in trade while the great American Empire made the land an integral part of the United States. Using that kind of logic would imply that Canadians who object to free trade with the US would prefer the US to invade and conquer Canada as long as Canada became another state of the US. How ridiculous!

As we have said before, conquest is conquest. Whether you call the conquered a colony or a state matters very little to those conquered? In fact, history has shown that empires have often peacefully returned colonies. The most recent examples are the return of Hong Kong by the British to China and Macau by the Portuguese to China. The US, on the other hand, went to war to prevent the southern states leaving the Union. Likewise, the US calls Mexicans who immigrate into states which were conquered from Mexico, *illegal aliens.* What is the likelihood that they would return any of the stolen states to the First Nations? Would it not have been better if they were treated as colonies and the US had explicitly recognized its imperial conquests? That way the US might be shamed by world opinion to return a few "colonies."

During the 1840's, the US was not militarily capable of defeating England and settled for half of Oregon. In 1846 the US signed the *Oregon Treaty* with England which extended the northern border of the US at the 49th parallel to the Pacific. The US Congress ratified the treaty on June 18, 1846 and created the *Oregon Territory* on August 14, 1848 out of the First Nations land in the Pacific Northwest which England had not taken into the British Empire. The land was large enough to add three new states, *Oregon, Washington and Idaho,* as well as part of *Montana,* to the American Empire.

The state of *Oregon* was added to the American Empire on February 14, 1859. It represented the invasion, conquest and theft of another 100,000 square miles of First Nations' land. The remainder of the Oregon Territory was renamed the *Washington Territory.*

The US Invasion of Minnesota and the Dakota War: 1849-1863

US invasion of First Nations land continued unabated across the continent. Pushing north of Iowa and west of Wisconsin the US invaded Minnesota. The US Congress created the *Minnesota Territory* on March 3, 1849. Alexander Ramsay was the first governor. With the invasion and conquest of Minnesota the American Empire expanded further north into First Nations land. This was possible since Minnesota was west of the Great Lakes which had blocked the northern expansion of the American Empire via states such as Wisconsin or Michigan.

This land was the home of the *Sioux, Dakota, Ojibwe* and *Anishinaabe* Nations. American settlers invaded the land after the US had constructed Fort Snelling in 1820. Prior to the American invasion the English and other Europeans were there to trap animals for furs not to steal First Nations' land for settlements. US military presence expanded with the building of Fort Ridgely, Fort Abercrombie and Fort Ripley. In 1851 the US forced the First Nations to sign treaties giving up their land to the American Empire. The First Nations were forcibly confined to tiny reservations.

Minnesota became the *thirty-second* state of the Union on May 11, 1858. The American Empire had invaded and conquered another 87,000 square miles of First Nations' land. This latest conquest led to another war with the First Nations, the *Dakota War,* in 1862.

The First Nations chief, *Little Crow,* did his best to avert another war with the US which he knew his Nation would lose. He therefore, traveled to Washington after Minnesota was made a state, to negotiate a deal for his people. His pleas were ignored by the US government. Starvation on the reservation forced the First Nations to break into the food warehouse controlled by the Indian agent, Thomas Galbraith, on August 4, 1862. The First Nations were told to eat grass or their own dung. This forced their hand and Chief Little Crow attacked on August 18, 1862.

The war lasted six weeks with the predictable result. The overwhelming military superiority of the US prevailed. America's celebrated President, *Abraham Lincoln,* approved the mass execution of 39 First Nations prisoners after the war ended. Their bodies were skinned before their mass burial. Their skins were boxed and sold as souvenirs. Several other First Nations prisoners were held in US prisons for four years after the Dakota War. Many died in US prisons.

The *Dakota Nation* was expelled from their tiny reservations in Minnesota and a $25 scalp bounty placed on the head of any Dakota Nation person captured in Minnesota. Prior to the mass removal of the Dakota Nation from Minnesota they were held in a US *concentration camp* until 1863. Many died in the concentration camp. Chief Little Crow was captured and killed on July 3, 1863. His body was mutilated and dragged through the main street of the city before being dumped into a pile of garbage.

The US Invasion of Kansas, Popular Sovereignty to protect Slavery and the Gadsden Purchase: 1827-1861

The American Empire expanded westward into Kansas. The US invasion of Kansas provides yet another glaring example of how ridiculous is the claim that America is the birthplace of democratic principles and republican values. In an effort to introduce **slavery** into Kansas after stealing it from the First Nations the Americans invented a new "democratic" term, *popular sovereignty.*

Popular sovereignty meant the "democratic" right of **White** Americans to vote to make **slaves** of Black Americans. How can any sane person think that giving the vote to White **racists** to make slaves of non-whites is democratic or "popular" sovereignty is beyond me? Yet, that is precisely what American historians say. In a true democracy they imply that **White** Americans must be allowed to exercise their democratic right to vote to make Black Americans **slaves** so that Whites can have cheap labour to do all of their dirty work or to enable Whites to become wealthy plantation owners or simply to make Whites feel and act superior.

The shaky balance of power in the US Senate was threatened by invasions and conquests of new states by the American Empire. Each time the US Congress safe-guarded the empire with another ridiculous law to preserve the institution of **slavery,** it proudly called the law another great American compromise. As expected, the invasion of Kansas threatened the empire again. American settlers invaded Kansas after the US army under Colonel Henry Leavenworth built Fort Leavenworth in 1827. The Fort was used as a major base of operations in the wars against the First Nations, including the war against the Cherokee Nation in 1839.

Senator Steven Douglas, Chair of the Senate Committee on Territories, wanted more First Nations' land to build the first railway across the continent. What the American Empire could not steal with its mounted cavalry it would steal with the "iron horse." A transcontinental railway was touted by the American ruling class as one more weapon to enable the invasion and conquest of a continent, since the dawn of the railway age in the 1830's. The US government would use stolen First Nations' land to subsidize the building of the railway by giving large land grants to the railway companies.

President Franklin Pierce, who had fought in the Mexican invasion under Winfield Scott, was as expansionist as any previous US president and supported Douglas's plan. Southwest Kansas had been part of New Spain which the US conquered from Mexico in 1848. Fort Leavenworth was a major US military base throughout the US invasion of Mexico. With the conquest of California and the subsequent California Gold Rush beginning in 1849 pushing the iron horse to the Pacific through California was now inevitable. The railway provided the technological superiority over the wagon trails and canals for America to dominate the continent.

Americans also continued to defend **slavery** against world opinion. American invasion of Kansas provided the opportunity to end the 1820 Missouri Compromise which was intended to prevent the expansion of slavery north of the 37th parallel and keep Blacks out of future states conquered by the American Empire. Many Americans opposed slavery because they wanted nothing to do with Blacks. Those Americans could escape living near Blacks by moving to a newly conquered state free of Blacks. A slave-free state would also mean a **Whites** only state.

The US Congress created the *Kansas Territory* with the Kansas-Nebraska Act of May 30, 1854. The First Territorial Governor, Andrew Reeder, lived and worked from Fort Leavenworth. In an effort to placate the majority of Americans who either supported slavery or discrimination against free Black Americans, the Kansas-Nebraska Act nullified the Missouri Compromise. The Kansas Territory was north of the 37th parallel.

Pro-slavery Americans crossed the border from Missouri to vote in the first elections for members of the Territorial Legislature. The First Legislature therefore supported **slavery** in Kansas. The northern slave-free states were mortified by the possibility of losing the balance of power in the US Senate and not having the opportunity to emigrate to an All-White state. Whether Kansas was admitted to the empire as a slave state or a slave-free state would be decided by allowing White Americans in Kansas to vote on the issue. Trust American propaganda to develop language which would make the most heinous American crime against humanity sound like good old fashioned American democracy. Senator Lewis Cass invented the term, *Popular Sovereignty,* to describe an Act of the US Congress giving **White** Americans the power to enslave Black Americans. No wonder the so called "civilized" world continues to believe the lies about American democracy and republican values.

Americans opposed to having Blacks in new states conquered by the American Empire formed the *Republican Party* on July 6, 1854 in response to the Kansas-Nebraska Act. While the explicit goal of the Republican Party was to end slavery its implicit goals were to maintain the balance of power in the US Senate and create the opportunity for White Americans to live in an All-White society. Having fought so many wars to kill off the *Red* race why should they share the conquered land with the *Black* race?

This new party swept the 1854 mid-term elections. With 108 members elected to the US Congress it was the majority party. White Americans who felt that the new Republican Party was not sufficiently racist formed an even more racist party called the *American Party,* in 1854. In the 1854 elections, 43 members of the American Party were elected to the US Congress.

With so many Americans opposed to having Blacks in Kansas the pro-slavery Southern Senators who had voted for Popular Sovereignty and the Kansas-Nebraska Act, had a real fight on their hands. Anti-slavery and anti-Black Americans, mostly from Northern states, poured into the Kansas Territory to vote against slavery. Pro-slavery Americans poured into the Kansas Territory mostly from neighbouring Missouri and Arkansas to vote for slavery. Both sides were armed for military confrontation. The result came to be known as *Bleeding Kansas.* President James Buchanan and the US Senate supported the creation of a new **slave** state in Kansas. The House of Representatives was opposed and in the end Popular Sovereignty prevailed. Kansas became a slave-free state on January 29, 1861. The American Empire had invaded and conquered another 82,000 square miles of First Nations' land to add the 34th state to the Union.

The invasion and conquest of Kansas was not enough for Senator Douglas and other Americans who wanted First Nations and Mexican land for their transcontinental railway. Another prominent American who had an interest in the railway was James Gadsden. Gadsden, like most Americans, had no love for First Nations. He had fought in the War of 1812 under America's most prominent Indian fighter president, Sharp-knife Jackson. He was one of the commissioners who oversaw the forcible confinement of the Seminole Nation to reservations.

Gadsden became the president of the South Carolina Railroad Company in 1840. In 1853, Gadsden was appointed by President Pierce as US minister to Mexico with the specific task of purchasing land, which Spain had stolen from the First Nations, from the Mexican government and its president, General Santa Anna. Santa Anna had returned as president of Mexico in April 1853, in time to negotiate the land sale with Gadsden.

The *Gadsden Purchase* acquired 30,000 square miles of First Nations land to expand the American Empire. The US built Fort Buchanan in Arizona in 1856 to prevent Mexico or the First Nations re-taking this land. American settlers moved into the area to expand slavery. After the outbreak of the US civil war it became the Confederate Territory of Arizona in 1861.

CHAPTER 3

American Invasions Of China, Japan,
Hawaii And Cuba: 1784-1914

The American Empire recognized from its birth that challenging the European empires of England, France, Spain and Holland, meant expansions and invasions of nations outside the American continent. However, it was not until its invasion of Cuba in 1898 that the world could no longer be fooled into accepting the American Empire's incessant and ridiculous denials of its imperialist ambitions. In this chapter we leave for a while the US imperialist conquests on the American mainland to document some of its earliest imperialist conquests in far off lands. In the next chapter we will return to its mainland conquests during and after its own Civil War.

Just as the US had invaded Canada to expand its mainland empire even before securing its own independence from England it sent ships to China, beginning with the *Empress of China,* in 1784, a full six years before Rhode Island had joined the Union to complete the founding of the USA. At the time only the port of Canton, now the Chinese province of Guangdong on the border with Hong Kong, was open to foreigners. In 1785 the new "freedom loving" republic planted its flag alongside the other European imperialists in Canton. China, like other nations, underestimated the imperial ambitions of the new republic believing that it was only interested in trade.

The American Empire joined forces with the European empires to force a militarily weak China to open more and more of its ports to trade and to open China to colonization by those empires. More importantly, the Americans colluded with England and the other European empires to use the **trafficking in drugs**, specifically, the illegal **opium drug trade,** to force China to trade with the West. As president John Quincy Adams made very clear, the Opium Wars were not so much about controlling the drug trade as it was about using the drug trade to colonize China. This history of using the illicit drug trade to finance US imperialism recurs over and over again without censure from mainstream historians. Today, the US has returned to using the illicit **opium trade** to finance its imperialism in Afghanistan.

American Imperialism in Asia and the Pacific before 1914

The American Empire was not content with invading and conquering the vast lands of the First Nations on the American continent as its invasions of Tripoli and Algeria in North Africa had demonstrated. It surveyed the world looking for easy targets offshore. Such easy targets in the nineteenth century were China and Japan. These two Asian countries had resisted European colonization by closing their ports to foreign trade. However, the European empires had conquered most of Asia and were now ready to use their superior military force to subjugate China and Japan. The American Empire saw this as a golden opportunity to compete with the European empires for this prize. It had scored major gains against the Spanish, French and English empires in North America and felt ready and confident in competing with those empires, as well as with Germany and Russia, in the scramble for China and Japan. It is unbelievable that American historians continue to deny these imperialist ambitions of the United States.

American Imperialism and Military Conquests in China: 1784-1914

In 1784, the first American ship, *Empress of China,* arrived in the Chinese port of Canton. Since the 16th century, China had limited its trade and international exchanges with the West to the single port of Canton. Having subjugated India and other areas of Asia the West was pounding at the gates of China. The American Empire was determined to ensure that it would not be left out of this imperial attack by the West.

It was the search for the spices and silk of China which Marco Polo had documented in his travels and which the Arab caravans brought to Europe that led to the re-discovery of America by Columbus and the other European explorers of the late fifteenth century. Columbus and the other explorers searched for a sea route to the east by sailing west. In the process they stumbled on the Caribbean islands and the American continent.

By the time of American independence from England, Americans were well aware of the value of the spices, teas, silks, porcelains and other exotic goods produced in China and demanded by American consumers. American merchants wanted to control that trade now that England could no longer dictate to America. American leaders wanted to compete with the Europeans to colonize China.

India had become the *jewel in the crown* for the British Empire. Could China become the jewel in the crown for the American Empire? During the sixteenth century Portugal and Spain dominated the Western trade with China. Portuguese ships reached China in 1516 and established the base for trade with the West in Canton. Spain began to trade with China after 1565. Jesuit missionaries arrived in China during the sixteenth century. Christian missionaries had always followed the Western imperialists aiding their colonization of both the indigenous people and their land.

During this earlier period the European powers were not militarily strong enough to challenge the Manchu emperors who ruled China. The Manchus were from Central Asia and had conquered China despite the 1,500 mile Great Wall built to keep them out. They established the *Qing dynasty* beginning in 1616. The Manchus restricted trade with the Europeans to the port city of Canton.

The rise of French and English imperialism coincided with the decline in the Qing dynasty in China. England had defeated the Mughal dynasty in India and colonized India. This had shocked the complacency of the Manchu rulers. England was moving to colonize China by defeating the Qing dynasty using exports of deadly opium from India to China. China would be an even richer prize than India. The Europeans and Americans would initially present a united front to colonize China before fighting each other for dominance. England led the way.

The new American Empire was only too happy to cooperate with the British to colonize China. With the relative decline of the Portuguese, Spanish, Dutch and French empires, England would have had no problem wresting the bulk of the lucrative Western trade with China. However, England was not interested in trade alone. It wanted to colonize China and it wanted a cheap and deadly way to do so. Its plan to use opium from India to make drug addicts of the Chinese people was as simple and as immoral as its use of the **slave trade** before to build its empire.

The American Empire Smuggles Opium into China

Having colonized India, England controlled the production of opium in India, openly selling opium by auction in Calcutta. It would smuggle opium from India into China, make addicts of the Chinese people and sell the opium like any dastardly drug lord. The Spanish had weakened the resistance of the First Nations with small pox and other infectious diseases. The English would weaken the resistance of the Chinese people with opium addiction, increase its wealth by selling drugs to the addicts and use the wealth to defeat the Qing dynasty.

In a rather ironic twist, the Qing dynasty by making opium **illegal** to protect its people from drug addiction, enabled the English drug lords to smuggle the opium into China without having to pay the customs duties which were imposed by China on imports. As in the US today, importing **illegal** drugs into China then was more profitable than importing legal products. The harder the Manchu rulers tried to keep the foreigners out to protect its people the more rebellious its own people became.

The foreigners, including the new American Empire, fully exploited the predicament in which the opium trade had placed the Manchu rulers to further their own imperial ambitions. Ignoring China's centuries of independence, the foreign empires jostled for "spheres of Influence" in their rush to colonize China. The American Empire lobbied hard for what it called an *Open Door Policy* to ensure that the powerful European empires would not exclude the "puny" American Empire from the colonization of China. Where was the "self determination" preached by the hypocritical American leaders?

Opium had long been used in China as a pain killer without problems of drug abuse and addiction. Non-medicinal use began with increased imports by the Portuguese. Most of the imports were from Turkey and India. The Chinese emperor banned imports in 1729 but **illegal** imports by the Portuguese continued. British conquest of India led to increased exports of Indian opium to China by England.

Smuggled imports increased significantly from 200 chests to 1,000 chests between 1729 and the end of the century. Despite the efforts of Chinese officials to crack down on smuggling, illegal imports increased rapidly as other nations, including the US, joined the lucrative drug trade. Drug lords became wealthier than pirates and slave traders.

Americans began trade with China by exporting rum, cheese, ginseng, furs, sea otter pelts, grain and large quantities of Spanish silver to pay for the great variety of Chinese imports favoured by American consumers. Most of the American traders also smuggled **illegal** opium into China from Turkey and India to boost their profits. Prominent Americans who became drug lords in the China trade included FDR's grandfather, Warren Delano, who was a senior partner with *Russel and Company*, a Boston company trading with China.

Warren first sailed to China in 1823 and claimed in his writings that addicting Chinese citizens with opium from Turkey and India was based on "fair and honorable" trade. John Jacob Astor who had founded the *American Fur Company* in 1808 to compete with the British in the Oregon Territory made a fortune exporting furs to the orient. Yet he enhanced his profits by using his exports of furs to smuggle opium into China. Illegal imports of opium into China increased from 1,000 chests to 10,000 chests by 1820 and close to 40,000 chests by 1835. It addicted 12 million men in China including those in the army. The annual value of the opium far exceeded the annual tax revenues of the Chinese government. When China could not pay for the opium with exports of tea, silks and other goods, it was forced to export its silver.

By 1839, the Chinese government had no choice but to come down heavily against the opium trade. It was ruining its people, its tax revenues and its soldiers. When the foreign imperialists resisted,

China closed its doors to foreign trade. The British were confident it could defeat and colonize China with the aid of the Americans and other imperialists.

Britain therefore insisted that British drug lords caught by China smuggling opium into China must be handed over to Britain instead of being punished by China for their crime. At the time opium consumption in England was illegal. This double standard by Britain of protecting its people from the harmful effects of opium while simultaneously profiting from addicting Chinese is typical of the treatment of the East by all Western imperialists, including the US. When China tried to prevent the English merchants from landing in Canton the English Prime Minister, Lord Palmerston, sent the Royal Navy to invade China in June 1840. England started the first *Opium War* with the confidence that it had the full backing of all the foreign empires, including the American Empire, and a technologically superior navy and army.

The American Empire Forces China to sign the Unequal Treaties of Wanghia and Tianjin

By 1842 the foreigners had defeated China and forced China to sign the "Unequal Treaty" of Nanking. This treaty marked the beginning of the forced Western domination of China. The treaty forced China to cede Hong Kong to England and open four ports, *Shanghai, Foochow, Amoy and Ningpo,* in addition to Canton, to foreign trade and imports of opium. China also had to pay a punitive war indemnity of 21 million Mexican dollars to England. Spanish and Mexican currencies were used in China at the time. Furthermore, England would no longer pay China customs duties for its imports into China.

Most humiliating to the Chinese emperor, China had to agree to hand over to England, British **drug lords** caught by Chinese officials smuggling opium into China. Britain could also insist on protecting Chinese drug lords who had worked as partners with the British drug lords. Britain would no longer hide the fact that it was using the illegal drug trade, as it had used the slave trade and piracy, to expand its empire. Drug lords would receive the protection of the Royal Navy which now patrolled Chinese waters and anchored its war ships in Chinese ports.

The Unequal Sino-American Treaty of Wanghia, 1844

Illegal imports of opium into China continued their upward spiral after the Treaty of Nanking. By 1858 imports had reached 70,000 chests. Profits from the illegal drug trade sky rocketed. Hong Kong became the drug capital of the world. China was militarily incapable of defending its own country from the Western drug lords. The colonization of China would take place through the open ports and Hong Kong. The West had colonized India and other parts of Asia. They would now compete for China.

The three leading competitors were England, France and the American Empire. The American Empire benefited from the Treaty of Nanking because it forced China to grant similar concessions to it as those granted to the British Empire. These equivalent concessions were forced on China by the *Sino-American Treaty of Wanghia* of July 3, 1844.

President John Tyler sent Caleb Cushing to "negotiate" the treaty with China fully aware that China could hardly afford a war with the American Empire following on the heels of their defeat by the British. China's most thriving city, Shanghai, was controlled by the Americans, the French and the English. American ships plied the Pacific Ocean expanding its trade and military and economic imperialism in Thailand, India, Java and the Philippines.

The Unequal Sino-American Treaty of Tianjin, 1858

These concessions by China only emboldened the American and European empires to bring about the total capitulation of China. They fought a second *Opium War* with China in 1856. China's defeat in the second Opium War enabled the US to force China to sign an even more "Unequal Treaty," the treaty of *Tianjin*, in June 1858. This treaty forced China to "legalize" the import of opium into China. The "freedom loving" American Republic had made *slavery, piracy* and *opium* legitimate means of imperial conquests. This was quite a coup for a country which is still able to convince the world and American historians that it has never had imperial ambitions.

China was forced to open 23 of its ports to the American Empire and other foreigners. More importantly, China was forced to allow Christian missionaries to penetrate the furthest regions of China spearheading the push of Western colonialism. These Christian missionaries played a crucial role in the colonization process. By converting Chinese citizens to Christianity the American Empire was able to turn many of China's citizens against the Chinese emperors.

The Chinese governments had to fight both the Americans and their own Chinese people who had been brainwashed by the Christian missionaries. The Christian church worked hand in glove with the American Empire to subjugate the Chinese people, weaken their government, steal their wealth and culture and turn them into second class citizens in their own country.

The American Empire Crushes the Boxer Rebellion in China: 55 Days in Peking

As the nineteenth century progressed the power of the Qing dynasty continued its decline as the American Empire and other foreigners demanded more and more concessions and as its own citizens became more confused. While the Chinese who had been brainwashed by the Christian missionaries demanded more concessions for the Americans, patriotic Chinese saw the Qing dynasty as selling out to the "American devils." By the end of the century the patriots felt that the American Empire and other foreign influence on the Qing dynasty had crossed the line.

The American enforced "Open Door" policy of insisting that China be open to all foreigners without limits on their control of the Chinese economy, Chinese culture and Chinese sovereignty, was especially humiliating to Chinese patriots. It is important to note that while most of the existing empires of the day colonized parts of China it was only the American Empire which unilaterally imposed the "Open Door" policy. US Secretary of State, John Hay, solicited support for the US "Open Door" policy from the empires of Britain, France, Germany, Russia and Japan, but was ignored by all of them.

Since the Qing/Manchu dynasty was also a "foreign" dynasty to the extent that the Manchus had invaded and conquered China from Manchuria, it seemed to a growing number of Chinese patriots that the Qing emperors were in cahoots with the "American devils." The patriots decided to take matters into their own hands and start an armed rebellion against their Manchu rulers, against the "American and foreign devils" who had been granted so many privileges and favours in China by the Manchus and against their own Chinese brothers and sisters who had been brainwashed by the American and other Christian missionaries.

The uprising began in Shandong province in March 1898 when the local government, representing the Manchu emperor, turned over a Chinese temple to the Christian missionaries. The American Empire had insisted that missionaries were "above the law," and the Manchu rulers themselves had been subjected to the will of the "American and foreign" devils. In many cases they acted against their own citizens because of fear of reprisals from the American and other powerful foreign empires.

In time the Manchu rulers saw an opportunity to ally themselves with the insurgency to rid China of American imperialism. But they had to proceed with caution. While the insurgency had the numbers, the foreigners had the superior arms and powerful navies. The Manchu support of the insurgency had to be covert rather than overt. If the insurgency was unsuccessful and there was evidence of overt support of the insurgency by the Qing dynasty the penalties imposed on the Manchu emperor by the American Empire would be very severe.

At the time of the insurgency the most influential Manchu leader was the *Empress Dowager, Tzu Hsi.* Tzu Hsi was chosen to be one of the concubines of Emperor *Hsien Feng* when she was 16 years old and took up residence in China's imperial palace, the *Forbidden City.* When Emperor Hsien Feng died in 1861, his five-year old son with Tzu Hsi became emperor of China. The new emperor, *Tung Chih,* ruled with the help of his mother but died in 1875 at a young age without a son to inherit the empire. His mother's power increased after his death. She chose her three-year old nephew, *Kuang Hsu,* to be the new emperor and effectively ruled China.

The *Patriotic Movement* against the American Empire failed because of the superior military power of the American Empire and its allies but also because the Manchus, including Tzu Hsi, did not use the full strength of their imperial forces to support the rebellion. In fact, imperial forces were often used to protect the foreign legations and crush the insurgency because of pressure from the American Empire and fear of reprisals from the foreign coalition. In many cases imperial troops only pretended to attack the "American devils" shooting over their heads or shooting off firecrackers. When the foreign legations in Beijing were under siege from the insurgency and suffered food shortages they were given generous donations of fresh fruit on the orders of the Empress, Tzu Hsi.

The important role of the US Navy in the defeat of the Boxers

We saw in Chapters 1 and 2 that the American Empire recognized from the very beginning that a powerful navy was the key to becoming an imperial power. The US Empire began preparations for military intervention in China as early as 1835 when it began a naval presence in East Asia with its *Asiatic Station* of the US Navy. American warships were stationed in Mirs Bay off the southern coast of China.

The size of the US Navy expanded rapidly after Teddy Roosevelt was appointed as Assistant Secretary of the Navy in 1897. Roosevelt had long been a disciple of Alfred Mahan who had written extensively on the importance of "Sea Power." In 1897, Roosevelt wrote a confidential letter to Mahan stating that the US should build a dozen new battleships and deploy half of them on the Pacific Coast. The US fleet in the Pacific was boosted by the US invasions and conquests of Hawaii in 1893 and the Philippines in 1898.

It was from naval bases in the Philippines that the American Empire was able to play its crucial role in suppressing the armed rebellion of Chinese patriots against foreign domination. These Philippine bases were only 400 miles from China. The American Empire had deployed large numbers of battleships and marines to fight the insurgency in the Philippines following its invasion of the Philippines. These forces were well positioned to move quickly into China. US economic colonization of the Philippines also provided a springboard for US businesses to rape the rich resources of China. What came to be called the *Boxer Rebellion* was the armed revolt of Chinese patriots beginning in 1898. The insurgency was led by members of an ancient Chinese society called the *Righteous Harmonious Fists.* They were called "Boxers" by the Americans because of their use of martial arts. In the late 1890's thousands of China's citizens, if not millions, many of whom were women, joined the insurgency.

US marines from the *USS Newark, USS Oregon* and the *USS Nashville* under the command of Captains John Myers and Bowman McCalla landed at Taku in China in June of 1900 to fight the insurgency. The American Empire euphemistically called this invasion of China the "China Relief Expedition." John Long, the Secretary of the US Navy reported that the *Asiatic Station* had augmented its force and deployed a separate force in Chinese waters in anticipation of US intervention in China. He further reported that this advance preparation by the US Navy meant that the US had adequate naval forces at the nearest seaport town which were sent immediately to protect the US legation in Beijing.

Over 3,000 American marines and soldiers landed in China to fight the Chinese patriots in the city of Tientsin before marching to Beijing. American ground forces led by Major Waller attempted to move men and equipment by train from Taku to Tientsin after landing at Taku on June 18 and 19, 1900. They met fierce resistance from the insurgency but by June 25, 1900 were able to rescue Captain McCalla and his men who had been trapped by the insurgents just outside Tientsin. The *Asiatic Station* commander, Rear-Admiral Louis Kempff, recommended Major Waller for a medal.

The combined US forces and their allies began their assault on the city of Tientsin but failed to capture the city. On June 30, 1900 another US force under Colonel Meade was sent to Taku. He arrived in Tientsin on July 12, 1900 and took over command from Major Waller. With these reinforcements the city was captured two days later. The American troops were part of the frontline of the allied attack on the city. Despite widespread looting of the city the Americans were still able to find over $375,000 of silver bullion not stolen by looters. Major Waller temporarily took over command of US forces in China again after Colonel Meade was incapacitated by rheumatism on July 23, 1900. Colonel Cochrane was sent from Boston on August 1, 1900 to take over the command.

Hollywood's 55 Days at Peking

The primary goal of the US invasion was to capture the Chinese Capital of Beijing, then called Peking. In Beijing all of the foreign legations, including the American legation, were under attack by the insurgents. With the help of their allies the American Empire occupied the Chinese Capital of Beijing on August 14, 1900. The so called "55 day siege," June 20 to August 14, was glamorized by the Hollywood blockbuster *55 Days at Peking* with Charlton Heston leading the US marines to rescue the foreigners. In reality the Americans looted the city, raped Chinese women and plundered the imperial palaces in the Forbidden City.

Despite the generous assistance which the Manchu rulers had given to the Americans and other foreigners against the wishes of the insurgents the Empress Tzu Hsi was forced to flee for her life disguised as a peasant. With its technologically advanced weapons the American Empire forced the Qing emperor to end the insurgency and sign a Peace Protocol on September 7, 1901. The Americans expanded its punitive "Open Door" to apply to all of China not just the ports which had been opened by the "Unequal Treaties." A hefty indemnity of $333 million was imposed on the Chinese government further weakening the power of the Manchus. The American Empire had sown the seeds of the subsequent Chinese revolution led by Dr. Sun Yat-sen which ousted both the Qing dynasty and the American Empire on October 10, 1911.

The American conquest of the Philippines and its forceful intervention in China laid the foundations for its future war with the Japanese Empire for dominance in the Far East and the Pacific. Teddy Roosevelt was explicit in his confidential letter to Mahan in 1897. He told Mahan that the new US battleships should have the capacity for an increased radius of action because "I am fully alive to the danger from Japan." Slavery, the decimation of First Nations, the poisoning of millions of Chinese by feeding them opium and the use of nuclear weapons on civilians, must rank high in any top ten list of human tragedies. Americans are proud to know that they have been willing participants in all four.

Despite these barbaric measures imposed by the West on China purely because of its military superiority, the West, especially the American Empire, continues to promote the propaganda that China has more human rights abuses than the West. Just as England in the nineteenth century used propaganda to justify its military invasion of China so is the American Empire today using propaganda to prevent fair and equal competition by China in global affairs.

America's invasion of Iraq is the worst crime against humanity inflicted by any nation in the history of the world. Yet the US succeeds in promoting the idiotic notion that the world has more to fear from China than the American Empire. The American Empire continues to this day to promote world-wide propaganda intended to prevent China from receiving fair and equal treatment by the world community. In general, the West uses its economic, political, military and media advantage to prevent a level playing field for competition and cooperation between the West and the Third World.

American Imperialism and Military Conquests in Japan: 1797-1914

Japan, like China, had limited foreign trade to a single port, in an effort to deter colonization by Europe and the new American Empire. As events would unfold, the new American Empire would prove to be the most aggressive in terms of Western efforts to colonize Japan and in competing with Japan for dominance in the Pacific. As early as 1791 the American Empire sent two ships to Japan and the American flag was planted by Captain John Kendrick on the Japanese island of *Kii Oshima,* less than two kilometers south of Honshu, Japan.

Aggressive American imperialism would forcibly end two hundred years of self-imposed isolation by Japan. American meddling in the domestic affairs of Japan would lead the Japanese people to rise up against foreign domination. Like Iraq and Afghanistan today the use of superior brute force by the American Empire would bring only temporary conquests for the bully.

In 1797, the American Empire began trading with Japan by obtaining concessions from Holland. Not only had Japan restricted foreign trade to the single port of Nagasaki but dealt officially only with the Dutch. The Dutch had relocated their operations from Hirado to the man-made island of Dejima in Nagasaki after the Japanese had expelled the Portuguese. While other European empires, including the powerful British Empire, reluctantly accepted this arrangement, the new American Empire would challenge it with military force when tact and cunning failed.

American trade with Japan, using the Dutch concessions, increased steadily after 1797. In 1837, the American, Charles King, saw an opportunity to expand his Asian trade in Canton to Japan by dealing directly with the Japanese instead of through the Dutch. He sailed to Japan with three Japanese sailors who had been shipwrecked off the American west coast hoping to convince the Japanese of his Christian virtues by pretending to be the Good Samaritan in returning the Japanese sailors to their homeland. Unlike the First Nations in America, the Japanese were not so easily fooled.

The Japanese fired on his ship and prevented him from landing. The American Empire responded with military force. In 1846, Commander James Biddle was sent with two war ships to force Japan to trade directly with the US. Biddle anchored his ships in Tokyo Bay and threatened the Japanese with his cannons. Next, Captain James Glynn landed at the open port of Nagasaki and signed the first trade agreement with Japan in 1848. On his return to the US Glynn informed the US Congress that the American Empire must flex its naval muscle to coerce Japan to trade with American merchants directly.

The American Empire Wakes a Sleeping Giant with Matthew Perry's Fearsome Black Ships

The expeditions of Biddle and Glynn had paved the way for Commodore Matthew Perry's infamous invasion of Japan in 1853. This was the original "awakening of a sleeping giant." Japan would prove to be a fearsome competitor against the American Empire for dominance in the Pacific until the end of the Second World War.

Perry set sail from the US in 1852 with four technologically advanced war ships with orders from President Millard Fillmore to bomb Tokyo Harbour until Japan signed an "Unequal" trade treaty similar to those forced on China by the Opium wars. The black hulls on these advanced war ships and their much larger than normal size led to subsequent reference to such ships as the fearsome "Black Ships." Perry arrived in Tokyo Harbour on July 8, 1853 and threatened to bomb the city. This show of force convinced Japan to allow Perry to land and present President Fillmore's demands for an "Unequal" trade agreement between the American Empire and Japan. Perry sailed for China and returned to Japan in February 1854 with twice as many war ships. Japan capitulated and agreed to President Fillmore's terms.

The *Convention of Kanagawa,* signed by Perry on March 31, 1854 marked the beginning of American meddling in the domestic affairs of Japan and the forced re-direction of the destiny of the Japanese people by this new "freedom loving" Republic. Japanese military resistance to American imperialism would end only after the American Empire used its nuclear arsenal to kill Japanese civilians including women and children. Since the nuking of Nagasaki and Hiroshima by the evil American Empire Japan has turned to economic means of resisting American imperialism.

The American Empire forced Japan to open the ports of Hakodate and Shimoda to foreign trade, permit the US to have a consulate in Shimoda and, most importantly, forced Japan to allow the US Navy to re-fuel its warships with Japanese coal at coaling stations in Japan. The primary purpose of these coaling stations was to enable the US Navy to dominate the Pacific and thereby expand American trade and colonization of China and the Far East. In the words of US Secretary of State, Daniel Webster, "God had placed coal for steam ships in the depths of the Japanese islands for the benefit of the human family." It was America's "manifest destiny" to steal the Japanese coal.

Townsend Harris was sent to Japan by President Franklin Pierce in July 1854 to man the US consulate in Shimoda. Harris was able to coerce further concessions from Japan. The *Harris Treaty* of July 29, 1858 opened a total of five Japanese ports to foreign trade. Americans were free to reside and do business in Japan but were not subject to Japanese laws. In 1858, the American Empire imposed on Japan the same "unequal" conqueror-conquered relationship it had imposed on China with the Tianjin treaty. In 1860, Japan sent its first official mission to the US hoping to re-negotiate the one-sided terms of the *Kanagawa* and *Harris* treaties.

The Japanese mission quickly learnt that this hypocritical "freedom loving" Republic had no intention of using fair play. The terms remained as unequal as Perry and Harris had acquired by military force and threats of military force. Japan learnt the hard way that it must deter American colonization with military advancement. Americans bow only to military defeats. Peaceful negotiation based on military inferiority does not appeal to American warmongers.

The resistance to the American invasion of Japan would take a form similar to the Boxer uprising in China but would come sooner and be much more successful. The Boxer uprising was directed at both the foreigners and the Qing dynasty which had signed the unequal treaties with the foreigners. Likewise in Japan the resistance to the Americans was directed at both the Americans and the *Tokugawa Shogunate* which had signed the unequal "Perry" and Harris treaties with the American Empire.

In both China and Japan the respective rulers had signed the unequal treaties because of fear of the military superiority of the American Empire and her European allies. Nevertheless the local populations blamed their rulers much as what is taking place in Pakistan, Iraq, Afghanistan, Saudi Arabia and Egypt today. Just as the Empress Dowager, Tzu Hsi, provided guarded support to the Boxers in China so too did the Japanese emperor, *Komei,* support the rebellion against the American invasion.

The Rise of Japanese Opposition to the American Invasion

The Japanese rebellion against the American invasion was led by the *nationalist patriots* who opposed Japan's Shogunate rulers and supported the emperor. The Tokugawa Shogunate rulers had seized power after defeating the pro-imperialist warlords in 1600. Like the Qing dynasty in China, Shogunate rule in Japan was on the decline. Those declines were exacerbated in both countries by the foreign threats as exemplified by the determined efforts of the American Empire to dominate the Pacific with its modern navy.

Japan in the seventeenth century, like England, was a feudal society governed by aristocratic warlords. In Japan the ruling aristocrats had the allegiance of samurai warriors. In general the aristocracy supported the emperor and his imperial court located in Kyoto. Some warlords rose to the rank of *shogun* and carved out their own jurisdictions or *Shogunate.*

While there was a long history of all of the warlords fighting for territory, influence and control, the defeat of the pro-imperial warlords at the Battle of Sekigahara led to the ascendancy of the shogun Tokugawa Ieyasu and the beginning of the *Tokugawa Shogunate* in 1603. This is called the *Edo* period because Ieyasu located his administration in Tokyo which was then called Edo. The emperor and his imperial court in Kyoto retained ceremonial powers but the real seat of government was Tokyo which had grown into one of the world's largest cities during the Edo period.

When Perry invaded Tokyo in 1853 he tried to present President Fillmore's demands directly to Emperor Komei but was prevented from doing so by the ruling Tokugawa Shogunate who controlled both the Japanese military and Japan's foreign policy at the time. Perry's Kanagawa treaty was negotiated with the Tokugawa Shogunate not the Japanese emperor. This would not have mattered had the Tokugawa Shogunate survived as the rulers of Japan. However, the "Perry" and Harris treaties helped to bring down the Tokugawa Shogunate and restore some of the powers of the emperor and the old pro-imperialist nobility.

The Edo period which lasted from 1603 to 1867 was a relatively peaceful period in Japan's long history. The samurai warriors had become mostly bureaucrats and administrators thereby losing some of their military prowess. At the same time the American Empire was modernizing its navy and military. While isolated from the West Japan was well aware of American imperialism in China and had few illusions about American desire and ability to invade and colonize Japan. Perry's "Unequal" treaty of 1854 forced the Tokugawa rulers to recognize the need to protect Japan against American imperialism. Japan needed to modernize its samurai based army and build a strong navy to rival the US navy.

In 1855 Japan established a naval training school in Nagasaki with the help of the Dutch who had been granted special privileges throughout the Edo period. Western steam warships and armaments were also purchased from Holland. The *Kanko Maru* was purchased in 1855 and the *Kanrin Maru* in 1857. This did not deter the American Empire from increasing its colonization of Japan with the Harris Treaty of 1858. In 1859 the naval training school was moved to Tokyo. In 1863 Japan built its first steam warship. In 1865 a French naval engineer was hired to build modern naval arsenals in Japan. By 1867 the Japanese navy had increased its steam warships to eight and invited French advisers to assist with the modernization of the army.

The Satsuma-Choshu Alliance against American Colonization

The inability of the Tokugawa Shogunate to defend Japan against the military invasion of the American Empire emboldened the aristocratic warlords who had lost power to Tokugawa Ieyasu in 1600. They used English military advisers to modernize their navy and army in preparation for battle against their historical rivals. As in Afghanistan and Iraq today, US meddling in the internal affairs of Japan would create a bloody civil war. Harry Parkes, who was the English ambassador at the time, supported the aristocratic warlords, partly because he was opposed to French influence on the Tokugawa Shogunate. Parkes was supported by another British diplomat, Ernest Satow. British arms dealers supplied warships and guns to the rebel forces.

In March 1863 Emperor Komei issued an order to expel foreigners. While the emperor did not have the military resources to enforce such an order it provided a rallying cry for those warlords opposed to the Tokugawa Shogunate. In May 1863 the American embassy in Tokyo was torched and foreign ships in the Shimonoseki Strait were fired on. The leaders of the rebellion were Saigo Takamori and Okubo Toshimichi of *Satsuma* and Inoue Kaoru, Kido Takayoshi, Yamagata Aritomo and Ito Hirobumi of *Choshu*. Satsuma and Choshu formed an alliance to oppose the Tokugawa Shogunate.

The Tokugawa Shogun, Iemochi, who had submitted to the "Perry" and Harris treaties, was forced by the growing power of the pro-imperial forces to issue an order on June 24, 1863 that Japanese ports would be closed to foreigners. This did not sit well with the American Empire. On July 16, 1863 the *USS Wyoming* sailed into Shimonoseki Strait and attacked the rebel fleet. Captain McDougal succeeded in sinking one of the rebel's ships and severely damaging two others. The US was the first of the Western powers to use its navy to enforce the unequal "Perry" and Harris treaties.

In December 1863 Japan sent ambassadors to Europe to get European support for exercising their right to close their ports. But Europe backed America. It's ironic that in 1863 European politicians failed to defy America because they thought that America was an *unimportant* power. In the first decade of the 21st century they fail to defy America because they think America is *too powerful*. Japan, like China, was on its own in taking on the American threat. In September 1864 the US allied with England, France and Holland to attack the rebels in Shimonoseki Strait. The rebels were defeated and the American peace negotiator imposed an indemnity of $3 million on Japan. It was only a temporary victory for the American Empire.

With the defeat of the rebel navy by the allies the Tokugawa Shogunate moved against the rebel forces in Choshu and Satsuma in 1866 but was defeated. This strengthened the power of the emperor and further weakened the Tokugawa Shogunate. That same year Tokugawa Iemochi died and was succeeded by Tokugawa Yoshinobu. With the growing military power of Choshu and Satsuma, Tokugawa Yoshinobu surrendered some of the Shogunate powers to the emperor. It was the beginning of the end of Tokugawa rule and the first American colonization of Japan. The second American colonization of Japan took place after the Second World War.

The Meiji Restoration

In 1867 Emperor Komei died and was succeeded by his son Emperor Meiji. The *Meiji Restoration* beginning on February 3, 1867 refers to the restoration of the historical powers of the Japanese emperor and also the powers of the feudal nobility which had supported the emperors. Those powers had been usurped by the Tokugawa Shogunate after 1600. The Choshu and Satsuma warlords pressed the emperor to abolish the Tokugawa Shogunate.

In November 1867 Tokugawa Yoshinobu officially surrendered all powers to the emperor but resisted handing over effective power. The rebels would have to fight another war against the Tokugawa Shogunate to finally transfer power to the emperor. This was the *Boshin War* of 1868-69. The war began on January 27, 1868 when the forces of the Tokugawa Shogunate attacked the rebels in Kyoto. The rebel forces were backed by imperial forces.

The American Empire and its allies were unsure of which side would win the civil war and decided to stay neutral. America's own civil war of 1861-65 also meant a greater need for the American Empire to focus on its own reconstruction needs before invading more countries. In the end the Tokugawa Shogunate was defeated by the rebel forces. Yoshinobu was removed from power by the emperor.

The Birth of Japanese Imperialism

Under the Meiji Restoration Japan modernized its economy and military to fight American aggression in the Pacific. The Imperial Japanese Navy was created in July 1869 patterned after the Royal Navy of England. By 1920 it was the third largest navy in the world. Conscription was introduced in 1873 for all males over the age of 21. This expanded the base of the military from the smaller samurai warrior class.

The city of Edo was renamed Tokyo in 1868 and the imperial government was moved from Kyoto to Tokyo. A unified central government was developed under the Emperor Meiji. It's unfortunate that Japan did not learn from its own invasion by the American Empire but imitated the imperial aspirations of the American Empire in Asia and the Pacific. It became an empire in its own right colonizing those areas which the Americans, Europeans and Russians never colonized or subsequently lost. This began with its invasions of Taiwan in 1874 and Korea in 1875.

Japan colonized Taiwan and Korea after defeating China in the Sino-Japanese war of 1894-95 and allied itself with the American Empire to help the US put down the Boxer Rebellion in 1900. Japan signed an alliance with England on January 30, 1902. Japan defeated Russia in the Russo-Japanese war of 1904-05 to become the third ranking naval power after England and the American Empire. The Japanese navy acquired its first submarine in 1905. The relative decline of Britain during World War I left the US and Japan as the two dominant Pacific powers. In 1921 Japan built its first aircraft carrier. When World War II began Japan had 10 aircraft carriers compared with the American Empire which had only 7.

American Imperialism and Conquests in Hawaii: 1790-1914

American traders invaded Hawaii in the 1790's following on the heels of the discovery of the islands by the English explorer, Captain James Cook in 1778. Cook, like so many of his contemporaries hoped to find the Northwest Passage to the Indies. Having discovered Tahiti he sailed north from Tahiti on his third voyage to the Pacific and landed in Hawaii which he named the *Sandwich Islands* after Lord Sandwich.

Americans who joined the scramble for trade and conquests in China soon recognized the importance of Hawaii as a stop-over to pick up fresh water and supplies for the long voyage across the Pacific. As the American conquest of China had inspired their conquest of Japan so too would their conquest of China inspire their conquest of Hawaii and other territories in the Pacific such as the Philippines, Guam, Midway Island and Samoa.

The American John Kendrick discovered that Hawaiian sandalwood was in demand in China. As early as 1791, Kendrick began the decimation of Hawaii's sandalwood forest which greedy Americans exploited to extinction by 1825. In 1820, American business interests in Hawaii were formally protected by the US government when the government appointed an Agent specifically assigned to that task. The American military is never far behind American traders and missionaries.

Captain Thomas Jones was sent with the *USS Peacock* to discuss trade with King Kamehameha III. This was followed by regular patrols of Hawaiian waters by warships of the US navy, beginning in the 1820's. In 1841, the editor of a Hawaiian newspaper advocated a US naval base in Hawaii. Hawaii's location in the middle of the Pacific Ocean would provide an important naval base for the American Empire to conquer the Pacific. To rival the British Empire the American Empire needed a strong navy and naval bases in key locations around the globe.

Britain and France Agree *Not* to Colonize Hawaii

The British consolidated their influence in the political affairs of Hawaii by assisting Kamehameha the Great to unite the islands into a single kingdom between 1795 and 1810. British influence could also be seen in the efforts of the Kamehameha dynasty to transform its rule into a constitutional monarchy and Privy Council modeled after the English monarchy.

In 1840, the Kingdom of Hawaii drafted a constitution and established a bicameral parliament under King Kamehameha III. The House of Nobles was modeled on the British House of Lords. The nobles were appointed by the King on the advice of his Cabinet which was the executive branch of the government. The House of Representatives was modeled on the British House of Commons and the legislators were elected by popular vote.

In 1843, England issued a declaration that Hawaii would be an independent state and that Britain would never colonize it. France supported this declaration of independence for the Kingdom of Hawaii but the American Empire did not, even though it was encouraged by England and France to do so. On the contrary, the decision of the two most powerful empires at the time to openly state their intentions never to colonize Hawaii made it so much easier for the American Empire to invade and conquer Hawaii. One more strike for the new "freedom loving" Republic professing not to be an empire.

Christian Missionaries Steal Hawaii for the American Empire

Constitutional changes in 1852 and 1864 reduced the powers of the monarchy and increased the powers of the people's elected representatives. Unfortunately, the people's representatives were mostly Americans as the Americans increasingly got themselves "elected" to the most powerful cabinet positions.

The death of King Kamehameha V without an heir in 1872 ended the relatively stable rule of the Kamehameha dynasty providing the opportunity for the American Empire to complete its invasion and conquest of Hawaii. American missionaries and whalers arrived in Hawaii in the 1820's following the traders. Americans soon dominated Hawaii's whaling industry. Among the Christian missionaries would be the parents of Sanford Dole and Lorrin Thurston, two of the prominent leaders of the American revolt against the Hawaiian people.

Sanford Dole became the President of the Hawaiian Republic after its conquest by the American Empire. The American conquest of Hawaii followed the pattern used on the mainland. The missionaries "civilized" the original inhabitants to make it easier for the American politicians and business men to steal their land, their economy and their culture. While Dole senior controlled the church his son, Sanford, controlled the government and together with his cousin, James Dole, also controlled the economy.

While Sanford made his fortune growing sugar James concentrated on pineapples. As was the case on the American mainland an estimated 80 percent of the Hawaiian people were killed off by the foreigners who had come to "civilize" them, by introducing diseases to which the Hawaiians had no immunity.

The Americans stole their land by preaching the "civilized" virtue of private property over communal property rights. The Puritans fleeing religious persecution who had founded the New England colonies had preached that communal property was sacrilegious. When the Americans first arrived in Hawaii, Hawaiian law prohibited them from purchasing Hawaiian land. By infiltrating the Hawaiian political system Americans not only changed the laws regarding foreign land ownership they soon "legally" owned most of Hawaii. They created a plantation system modeled on the **slave** plantations in the southern American states and imported cheap Asian labour to work their plantations under **slave-like** working conditions. American Christians have always been proud slave owners.

American Sugar Barons in Hawaii

The most profitable colonial product for most of the nineteenth century was sugar cane. The Portuguese had imported the sugar cane from India first to their colonies in the Mediterranean, then to the Madeiras and finally to Brazil. The Dutch took the sugar cane to the Caribbean after competing with the Portuguese in Brazil. The English and French quickly learnt that the extensive coastlines of the tiny Caribbean islands were ideal for growing sugar cane.

The tiny English and French Caribbean colonies became the richest colonies in the world surpassing the value of the North American colonies. The American Empire began growing sugar cane after their conquest of the Mississippi from the First Nations following the Louisiana "sale" by Napoleon and the Lewis and Clark Expedition.

By 1830 the Louisiana sugar plantations produced half the sugar consumed by Americans. Americans settling in Hawaii knew the high value of sugar and had the missionary zeal to profit from this valuable crop. The Christian missionaries would work hand in glove with plantation owners to steal the Hawaiian land, promote the expansion of the American Empire, enslave or kill off the native Hawaiians and import slaves or indentured labour to clear the land, plant the sugar cane and do all of the menial and back breaking work. They would become the *nouveau riche* landed gentry of Hawaii and "lords of the manor," by selling Hawaiian sugar to Americans on the mainland. With their new wealth they would dominate the Hawaiian economic, political and cultural life.

The Missionary Boys Create a Secret Annexation Club

Hawaii's constitution provided for an elected monarchy in the event of the reigning monarch dying without an heir. In 1872, King Kamehameha V died and his only surviving relation, Princess Bernice Bishop, had turned down the King's offer that she succeeds him on the throne. The new monarch, William Lunalilo, was therefore elected by popular vote and by a unanimous vote of the kingdom's legislature.

King Lunalilo died only a year later and was succeeded by King David Kalakaua, the second elected monarch of Hawaii. It was under King David's reign that the American plot to overthrow the legitimate Hawaiian government and set up an American oligarchy patterned after the southern *slave* states on the American mainland, took hold.

The Americans founded a secret society called the *Hawaiian League* to plot the overthrow of the Hawaiian government and annex Hawaii to the American Empire. The leader of this group of prominent American landowners and businessmen was Lorrin Thurston, publisher of the influential *Honolulu Advertiser.*

The League infiltrated the leadership of the *Honolulu Rifles,* Hawaii's volunteer militia. Many of the members of the *League* volunteered for the *Rifles.* The Rifles was nothing more than the military arm of the League which later morphed into the *Annexation Club.* This guaranteed the support of the Hawaiian militia in executing a *coup.* As with any coup, timing is the key to success. A deteriorating economy is usually the best ammunition used by dictators to overthrow popular governments.

In 1874, when David Kalakaua ascended the Hawaiian throne, the Hawaiian economy was depressed. The King was successful in negotiating a trade treaty with the American Empire on January 30, 1875. The treaty enabled the importation of Hawaii's primary crop, sugar, in addition to other products such as rice, duty free into the United States. This preferential treatment of Hawaiian products, especially sugar, gave the Hawaiian economy a much needed boost.

Employment opportunities expanded on the sugar cane plantations and on large scale irrigation projects developed to expand sugar cane production. In search of cheap contract labour, immigration from China, Japan, Korea and the Philippines increased. The local demand for rice by these immigrants gave a boost to the rice industry as well. Exports of sugar and rice paid for imports of American products with the usual dilution of indigenous culture which such imports entail.

Cozying up to the American giant, as many small countries, such as Canada, have learnt, is a double edged sword. American economic imperialism is often a prelude to American political imperialism. King David's good intentions only strengthened the hands of the *Hawaiian League's* traitors by giving them a direct link to Washington. That was possible because many of Hawaii's prominent cabinet ministers were Americans and members of this *secret society,* whose goal was the overthrow of the legitimate government.

Given the inherent expansionist views of the Washington elite which controlled the government of the American Empire they would work hand in glove with the secret *Hawaiian League* to overthrow the Hawaiian government knowing full well that the leaders of the coup would vote for annexation with the American Empire. The empire would expand not only because of the addition of the Kingdom of Hawaii to the empire but also because of the strategic importance of an American naval base in Hawaii to further American conquests in the Pacific and Far East.

The Bayonet Constitution, Legalized Racism, Pearl Harbor and the Overthrow of the Hawaiian Monarchy by the American Empire

The traitors struck in 1887 shortly after the American Empire instructed the US Navy on January 20, 1887 to lease Pearl Harbor for a naval base. The American Empire had previously used Pearl Harbor as a Coal Depot. Lorrin Thurston, the leader of the traitors, was Hawaii's Minister of the Interior. He drafted a new constitution for Hawaii on July 6, 1887, and used the Hawaiian militia, which the traitors controlled, to force King David Kalakaua to sign. Since the King was forced to sign it while looking down the bayonets of the armed militia, it was appropriately called the *Bayonet Constitution.*

The Bayonet Constitution stripped both the Hawaiian people and their elected monarch of all powers and transferred those powers to an oligarchy of wealthy American landowners who had stolen the land of the Hawaiian people, decimated their numbers with their diseases and imported Asians in numbers exceeding the remainder of the indigenous Hawaiian population to work their plantations in a state of semi-slavery. The infamous *Bayonet Constitution* eliminated voting rights for poor Native Hawaiians and all **Asians,** including those Asians previously entitled to vote, while giving the vote to wealthy Americans who were not Hawaiian citizens. Sanford Dole, Thurston's co-conspirator in the coup, became a justice of Hawaii's Supreme Court thereby guaranteeing American **injustice** for Hawaiians. The Americans had taken over the government of Hawaii.

The Missionary Boys import American Racism to Hawaii

Since many of the traitors were children of the missionaries who had come to Hawaii to save souls rather than steal land and become wealthy by exploiting the sacred trust of the Christian Church, they unashamedly called themselves the *Missionary Boys*. The Missionary Boys who already held the most important Cabinet positions in the Hawaiian government would now have the power to elect the Nobles to the House of Nobles, Hawaii's Upper Chamber. Prior to the Bayonet Constitution the Nobles had been appointed by the King.

Neither the King nor the Hawaiians and Asians had the military and economic power to oppose the Missionary Boys. A counter insurgency led by Robert Wilcox and supported by Hawaiians and Asians in 1889 was quickly put down by the superior arms of the Missionary Boys. This relatively small group of Americans had stolen the Kingdom of Hawaii for their personal gain and for the glory of the American Empire.

Imagine that a small group of Americans can change a Kingdom's Constitution in such a way as to deprive its own people of the vote. Under Hawaii's 1864 Constitution, all male Hawaiian citizens, regardless of **colour,** who owned property exceeding $150 in value or had an annual income of $75 or more, had the right to vote. The Bayonet Constitution took away the vote from all **non-Whites,** mostly Asians at the time, except indigenous Hawaiians, and increased the property threshold value for indigenous Hawaiians to $3,000 and the annual income threshold to $600. In addition, **Whites,** who were not Hawaiian citizens, were given the vote and the few indigenous Hawaiians who met the wealth constraint had to take an oath to support the Bayonet Constitution.

This is a classic example of what Americans call democracy. This is their brand name democracy which they claim to have the God given right to enforce by military invasions as "leader of the free world" and for the good of humanity. It is surely a sign of an insane world that so many fools holding high economic, political, media and academic positions in both the American Empire and globally would try so hard to defend the indefensible.

The Bayonet Constitution was another example of a blatantly **racist** oligarchy which Whites established in the United States, Canada, Australia, New Zealand and Israel, after reducing the indigenous populations to minorities in their own countries, and which they continue to promote to this day as the ideal democracy that all free people should aspire to. On the American mainland it was **Africans** who were denied the vote because it was Africans who had been imported to work the plantations and would therefore have had political influence had they been allowed to vote in a true democracy. In Hawaii it was the **Asians** who had been imported to work the plantations and would have had political influence had they been allowed to vote in a true democracy.

Asians were imported into Hawaii since 1852. Most of them stayed in Hawaii after their labour contracts expired and became bona fide long term residents of the Kingdom. Many married Hawaiian women and settled as mixed families, often on land cleared from the Hawaiian interior. Others brought wives and other family members from Asia to settle with them in Hawaii.

The Asians soon outnumbered the Native Hawaiians who had survived the diseases imported by the Americans and Europeans. Denying them the vote was no different from South Africa's *apartheid* policy or Canada's racist immigration policy. The ways in which Whites ensured **White** rule in the United States, Canada, Australia, New Zealand, South Africa, Rhodesia, India, Hawaii and Israel and still perpetuate the myth of democracy, freedom and equality did vary according to the needs of the individual situation but the goal was the same.

The Prize of the US Naval Base of Pearl Harbor

The American Empire formally took possession of the naval base at Pearl Harbor on November 9, 1887. This occupation of Hawaiian territory by the American Empire caused Hawaii to be the central battleground between the American and Japanese empires without a single concern by the international community about the wishes of the Hawaiian people.

American naval bases quickly expanded from Hawaii westward to Midway Island, Wake Island, Guam and the Philippines. The Spanish-American War of 1898 was a prelude to war with the Japanese Empire and another opportunity for **White** Americans to celebrate and glorify their deeply entrenched inherent racism.

By the time the Japanese Empire attacked the American naval base at Pearl Harbor, American propaganda regarding the God given right of the American Empire to wage war on all who dared threaten its hegemony had so saturated the minds of world leaders and citizens globally that there has not been a single mention of the people of Hawaii in that so called "Day of Infamy" of December 7, 1941.

It is as if, it would be a sign of gross ignorance not to publicly claim that Pearl Harbor was ancient and sacred **American** soil which Americans had lived in for millennia long before there were ever a Hawaiian people or Hawaiian Kingdom. Pearl Harbor was as American as apple-pie and Hawaii had never existed. Those who continue to label Muslims who object to American military bases in their countries "terrorists," should remember how a single American military base obliterated the people and Kingdom of Hawaii.

A single American military base in Hawaii removed from the literature and the media the prior existence of an independent state of Hawaii. Everyone, without exception, claims that Japan attacked the United States, not Hawaii, on December 7, 1941. In reality, the American and Japanese empires were fighting for dominance in Asia and the Pacific. Conquest of Hawaii was of immense strategic significance for winning that war. Hawaii was no more American territory than Japanese territory in that war. Both empires wanted to colonize Hawaii because of its strategic importance in the battle for imperial hegemony in Asia and the Pacific.

The failed attempt by Robert Wilcox to restore the powers of King David in 1889 was the last straw for the so called *Merrie Monarch*. With his kingdom stolen by greedy and powerful Americans and his people dispossessed of land and political participation, his health began to fail at the relatively young age of 53 and he died on January 20, 1891, a sad and broken monarch. He was succeeded by his sister, Queen Liliuokalani. In the mean time the Missionary Boys had an economic problem.

In 1890, William McKinley had succeeded in passing one of the highest tariffs in American history. It removed the preferential treatment of imports of Hawaiian sugar and thereby threatened both the wealth of the American oligarchy in Hawaii and their political clout in the Kingdom. At the same time the new monarch had both the desire and energy to fight the Missionary Boys in an effort to restore some of the powers of the monarchy which they had stolen with the Bayonet Constitution.

The dual threat of the McKinley Tariff and Queen Liliuokalani's determination to abrogate the imposed Bayonet Constitution, made the Missionary Boys nervous. They responded by forming the secret *Annexation Club* to lobby Washington to formally annex Hawaii to the American Empire. Lorrin Thurston, who led the Hawaiian League and who now led the Annexation Club, traveled to Washington to talk terms with the "Great White Chief," President Benjamin Harrison. Thurston had given the American Empire a formidable naval base at Pearl Harbor. Now he was delivering the nation from whom he had stolen the land for that base.

The Overthrow of a Queen by the American Empire

Queen Liluokalani forged ahead with her plans for a new Constitution for her people. On January 14, 1893 the Queen asked her Cabinet to support a new Constitution. Since most of the ministers of her Cabinet were members of the "secret" Annexation Club they naturally refused. In typical American hypocrisy, the rebels formed a *Committee of Safety* to overthrow the Queen and invited American troops to support this Committee in ensuring minimal loss of American lives.

Thurston discussed the use of American troops with the American ambassador to Hawaii, John Stevens, prior to his Committee making its move to overthrow the Queen. The American ambassador was only too happy to oblige the Missionary Boys by calling on the troops of the American warship, *USS Boston,* anchored in Honolulu Harbor. On January 17, 1893 the Committee of Safety commandeered 1,500 members of the Honolulu Rifles, the military arm of the "secret" Hawaiian League and stormed the Palace. This action was coordinated with the simultaneous landing of marines from the *USS Boston* fully armed with rifles, cannons, Gatling guns and adequate supplies of ammunition.

It was the unprovoked invasion of Hawaii by the American Empire which forced the Hawaiian monarchy to surrender its Kingdom to the American Empire. As Queen Liliuokalani herself stated, she yielded under protest to the "superior forces of the United States of America," which Ambassador Stevens had landed in Hawaii. That same day the Committee of Safety declared that it was the Provisional Government of Hawaii, having removed the Queen. Sanford Dole was offered the presidency of the Provisional Government by the Committee of Safety.

Imagine a justice of the Supreme Court of Hawaii being one of the main benefactors of a military coup and still embraced by American historians. At the very least I am not aware of him being chastised for such ignoble actions? Are Americans brain-dead or simply gullible? It's simply incredible to me that Americans would think that ordinary people outside their Western sphere of influence would not see such behaviour as raw unbridled imperialism with absolutely no redeeming virtues. No wonder that Americans have become the most hated people on the planet.

Ambassador Stevens immediately gave official recognition to the rebel oligarchy on behalf of the "freedom loving" American Empire. Stevens took the extraordinary step of declaring Hawaii a temporary protectorate, replacing the Hawaiian flag with the American flag. He urged Washington to proceed quickly with the annexation of Hawaii to the American Empire. President Harrison acted on this advice and submitted an annexation treaty to the US Senate. In the meantime, Thurston drafted a Constitution for the temporary protectorate and led a delegation to Washington to lobby for annexation.

As in so many cases of illegal invasions by the American Empire, other Western countries were cowed into supporting American aggression in their rush to defend their up and coming "leader of the free world." Japan initially protested but ultimately fell in line with the Western governments. The West is very dedicated to the notion of unanimity whenever it wants to maintain the pretence that Western opinion is "World opinion," That is why, for example, it pressures both China and Russia today to give at least token support for a Western invasion of Iran. If the West invades Iran it will not be because Russia or China supports such an invasion. Why would Russia and China support another American *uncolony* on their borders? A successful invasion of Iran will make Iran an American *colony*. But since Western historians refuse to call the USA an empire I will refer to American colonies as *uncolonies*.

The Creation of the Illegal Hawaiian Republic

The plans of the rebels were thwarted when President Harrison was defeated by Grover Cleveland in the 1892 presidential elections. Cleveland was no friend of Harrison since Harrison had stolen the presidency from him in 1888 much as George W. Bush stole it from Al Gore in 2000. In the 1888 presidential elections there were gross election irregularities in both New York and Indiana. In addition, Cleveland had a significant majority over Harrison in the popular votes. Cleveland now had an opportunity to get even.

He withdrew the annexation treaty sent by Harrison to the US Senate and appointed James Blount to investigate the legality of the military overthrow of the Hawaiian government. Blount concluded that Ambassador Stevens had acted illegally by using the armed forces of the American Empire to overthrow the Hawaiian Queen. By this time the rebels were in firm control of Hawaii and refused to return the government of Hawaii to the monarch. Despite Blount's conclusion that the overthrow had been an illegal invasion by the American Empire that empire refused to use its military to restore the monarchy.

President Cleveland's half hearted efforts to do the right thing simply emboldened the rebels, confident that the American Empire would only use its military to invade and conquer, never to correct injustices. God forbid that the American Empire would ever use its military power to intervene in a "domestic" issue which is what the Hawaiian situation had now become according to the rebels. In fact, Cleveland had inadvertently done the rebels a huge favour. It forced the rebels to declare Hawaii an independent Republic which gave them the best of both worlds. Had God paid a special visit to President Cleveland as he did to President George W. Bush, perhaps President Cleveland would have intervened on behalf of the Hawaiian people as George W. did on behalf of the Iraqi people.

The Provisional Government led by Thurston and Dole called a Constitutional Convention on May 30, 1894 to draft a Constitution for an independent Republic. A Constitution was drafted by Thurston. The Republic of Hawaii was created on July 4, 1894. Sanford Dole kept the position of president. Those few indigenous Hawaiians who met the high wealth requirement to get the vote had to swear allegiance to the new republic.

There was an unexpected windfall for the rebels stemming from the creation of an independent Republic which had to do with the importation of cheap Asian labour. Annexation to the American Empire was a double-edged sword from the standpoint of the sugar barons who controlled the Hawaiian government. On the one hand it would remove the high duties on sugar exports resulting from the McKinley Tariff since Hawaii would become part of the expanded domestic market of the United States. On the other hand it would prevent the sugar barons from importing cheap Asian labour since the United States had firm laws against **Non-White** immigration.

An independent Republic enabled the Missionary Boys to have their cake and eat it. As an independent Republic Hawaii was free to continue its importation of cheap indentured labour from Asia to work the sugar plantations of the governing oligarchy. At the same time the Missionary Boys gave away large chunks of Hawaiian territory to the American Empire to expand its naval base at Pearl Harbor in exchange for preferential duties on their sugar exports to the US.

With annexation foiled the Hawaiians decided to launch a counter attack against the Missionary Boys. Once again they looked to Robert Wilcox to lead the counter insurgency. But once again Wilcox failed. The military arm of the Annexation Club, the Honolulu Rifles, successfully defended the Missionary Boys against the January 1895 counter insurgency.

The Missionary Boys used this failed counter insurgency to arrest Queen Liluokalani on January 16, 1895 for supporting her people. She was imprisoned in the Iolani Palace. As usual, the American Empire denied any political or military involvement despite the *Blount Report's* conclusion that US ambassador, John Stevens, had authorized the landing of US forces from the *USS Boston* to remove the Hawaiian Queen by force.

President Cleveland washed his hands of the shameful affair despite a personal visit to Washington by the Queen armed with a petition signed by many Hawaiians asking the president to restore their monarch. His successor, William McKinley, sent a new annexation treaty, signed on June 16, 1897 to the US Senate. In a confidential letter to Mahan in 1897, Teddy Roosevelt wrote that, "If I had my way we would annex those islands tomorrow." A petition against annexation was signed by 29,000 Hawaiians and taken to the US Congress by Queen Liluokalani.

The Creation of the Illegal American Territory of Hawaii

The US Congress voted against annexation. However, Hawaii became an American Territory on August 12, 1898 after the US Congress passed a joint resolution, the *Newlands Resolution.* Many have questioned the legality of such a joint resolution. What mattered was that the American Empire had the military power to steal Hawaii from the Hawaiians in the same way as it had stolen the other states of the empire from the First Nations. The American Empire had a secure naval base at Pearl Harbor to wage war against the Spanish Empire and later against the Japanese Empire.

Sanford Dole was appointed territorial governor of the empire's latest conquest. The sugar from his large plantation would now enter the US market duty free. He and Thurston had finally come through for the Missionary Boys and the "Big Five" sugar plantation owners.

Dole's Cousin, James Dole, came to Hawaii in 1899 and invested heavily in Hawaii's pineapple crop. His plantation on the island of Lanai became the world's largest pineapple plantation. With his other pineapple plantations on the island of Oahu he became the "Pineapple King" of Hawaii. His Hawaiian Pineapple Company owned over half of all the Hawaiian land devoted to growing pineapple.

In 1993, the US Congress passed a Resolution which officially apologized for the overthrow of the Hawaiian monarchy by the American Empire but, of course, did not return the stolen islands to the Hawaiian people. This *Apology Resolution* was due largely to the efforts of Hawaii's representatives in the US Senate, Daniel Akaka and Daniel Inouye. Daniel Akaka continues to lead the struggle for recognition of the historical rights of indigenous Hawaiians and the right of the Hawaiian people to self determination.

Hawaiians have never given up on their legal rights to the islands but their demands for justice have become increasingly vocal as people across the globe recognize what a bully the American Empire truly is. In Palestine, Lebanon, Iraq, Afghanistan, Iran, Pakistan, Vietnam, Cuba, Venezuela, Russia, China, and in so many other countries, people today are less afraid to fight American aggression and injustice. So too today, in Hawaii.

The Importance of Cuba in the Rise and Fall of the American Empire

As we saw in Chapter 1, territorial expansion based on military invasions of independent countries or military conquests of colonies of the European empires was an integral part of the future American Empire even before the 13 English colonies gained their independence from England. When the second invasion of Canada in 1812 failed the American Empire learnt from these two military disasters that they must choose **weak** military targets in future.

In the period after 1812, the Spanish colonies were much easier targets than the English colonies because Spain had become a much weaker power than England. While the primary goal of the war of 1812-14 was the conquest of the English colony of Canada the American Empire was happy to take the lesser prize of the Spanish colony of Florida.

Given the long historical link between Spain's colonial conquests of Cuba with that of Florida it does not take too much imagination to see that America's conquest of Florida was but a prelude to its conquest of Cuba and Spain's other remaining Caribbean colony, Puerto Rico. In fact the American Empire invaded and conquered Spain's colonies almost in the same sequence as Spain had initially colonized these territories, except in the reverse order.

The US invasion and conquest of Cuba is of great significance in two somewhat ironic ways. Its initial significance is that it marks the beginning of historians, often reluctantly, to formally recognize that this relatively new country, born out of a proclaimed desire not only to oppose imperialism by European nations, but also never to become an empire, had in fact become an empire. While we have argued that the US became an empire well before its acquisition of Cuba as an American *uncolony* most historians do not share our view.

A much more important reason for analyzing the significant role which Cuba has played in American imperialism is that the current decline of the American Empire has its roots in the long and successful struggle by Cubans against American imperialism. It is truly amazing that 13 tiny English colonies quickly invaded and conquered so much territory to become the very powerful American Empire. But equally, if not more amazing, is the fact that this mighty empire will be defeated not by a more powerful empire, but by smaller states such as Nicaragua, Cuba, Vietnam, Somalia, Afghanistan, Iraq, Iran, North Korea, Pakistan, Yemen and Venezuela.

Cuba must be given full credit for starting that process. How ironic that historians reluctantly date the beginning of American imperialism with its formal "colonization" of Cuba in 1898 when in fact it marks the beginning of the decline of the American Empire.

The Historical Link between Spain's Caribbean Colonies and Spanish Florida

Spain's first colonial acquisition, following the first voyage of Christopher Columbus, was the island of Hispaniola or Santo Domingo which has since been divided into the two sovereign present day countries of Haiti and the Dominican Republic. Spain next colonized Puerto Rico after it was invaded by Ponce de Leon in 1509. Jamaica was colonized after Diego Columbus began a settlement in 1510.

Cuba was conquered in 1511 by Panfilo de Narvaez and Diego Valesquez after fierce resistance from the First Nations. By 1511, Spain had conquered the four largest islands in the Caribbean. Spain's primary objective was not settlements but the search for gold and other precious metals. The discovery of gold in Cuba led to a gold rush in 1512. By 1515 there were six towns in Cuba and Cuba quickly replaced Santo Domingo as Spain's "jewel" in the Caribbean.

Since gold was found in relatively small quantities in the Caribbean, the islands were subsequently used by Spain as a base for conquests, search for precious metals and eventual settlements, on the mainland. Cuba's close geographical proximity to Florida made it the ideal base for exploring the mainland.

Ponce de Leon, the conquistador responsible for subduing Puerto Rico for Spain, was given royal orders to invade Florida in 1513. He explored the entire east coast of Florida while searching for the mythical fountain of youth, *Bimini*. In 1517, another conquistador, Francisco de Cordoba, completed the exploration of the west coast of Florida. While the ultimate goal of all these conquests was the discovery of precious metals, Florida's relatively milder climate compared to the Caribbean islands, soon attracted many more Spaniards to Florida than to the islands.

The Historical Link between the English Caribbean Colonies and the 13 American Colonies

The English came to the Caribbean to plunder the Spanish galleons sheltering in the Spanish Caribbean ports laden with gold and silver from Mexico and Peru, to sell African slaves and to grow sugar. As the English Caribbean increasingly specialized in the world's most profitable product, cane sugar, the 13 English colonies on the mainland became essential suppliers of food and other produce to the islanders.

Without the American colonies the extreme sugar specialization of the islands would have been impossible. Likewise, without the Caribbean market the mainland colonies would not have grown and prospered. To fully appreciate this partnership it must be recognized that in the eighteenth century a tiny sugar producing island was more valuable than the total agricultural output of the mainland colonies. It is in this context that the intense specialization of the islands on sugar made economic sense.

The smaller the island the relatively more profitable is sugar since a small island has a larger percentage of coastline to hinterland and sugar is grown on the coast. For example, the tiny island of Barbados, only 166 square miles, was England's largest sugar producer for many years, overtaking the total output of sugar by the Portuguese and Dutch in Brazil. This was even more remarkable in view of the fact that sugar was first introduced into the New World by the Portuguese in Brazil and Brazil had dominated the world's sugar output until the late seventeenth century.

This close economic dependency between the 13 English colonies on the Mainland and the English Caribbean meant that the future American Empire coveted the relatively rich Caribbean islands even before the birth of the United States. Much as the American Empire coveted the entire Caribbean as it coveted the entire mainland it was militarily much weaker than England throughout the nineteenth century. It therefore settled for the Spanish colonies only.

By the time of the birth of the American Empire the English had already captured Jamaica from Spain. That still left the three largest Caribbean islands, Santo Domingo, Puerto Rico and Cuba for American invasions. Cuba was by far the largest prize. Sugar came late to Cuba but when it did Cuba became the world's largest sugar producer. By the 1880's Cuba's sugar output was three times the total output of all the other Caribbean sugar islands combined.

Think what the American military would do today to steal the oil of the Middle East and you will get an idea of how far the American military went to steal Cuba's sugar. In the end the American Empire was defeated militarily in Cuba, as it had been in English Canada, and would be defeated again and again, in Nicaragua, in Vietnam, in Somalia, in Lebanon, in Iraq, in Afghanistan, in Pakistan, in Iran and in Yemen. Americans will never learn because they are addicted to wars and military invasions.

The American Empire got its first taste of conquests in Cuba during the Seven Years War. England had fought many wars with France over colonies in the New World. In all of these wars the colonists were recruited by the mother countries to fight. The colonists in the 13 Mainland colonies were no exception. When England declared war on Spain in January 1761 at the height of the Seven Years War with France, Cuba was one of the prizes of war. With the help of the colonists, including recruits from the 13 Mainland colonies, the English navy under Admiral George Pocock and the English army under the Earl of Albemarle, invaded Cuba.

By August 1762 the English had captured Havana and seized the largest Caribbean island for the benefit of both the mother country and the Mainland colonies. Trade and economic opportunities would expand for both. The American Empire got its first, albeit short-lived, taste of the riches of Cuba.

More importantly, the brief English occupation of Cuba opened up Cuba to international trade and the slave-based sugar economy of the English Caribbean. Up until the English conquest Cuba was relatively closed to foreign trade and sugar specialization by Spain. Spain had used its Caribbean colonies primarily as naval bases for its fleets transporting gold and silver from Mexico and Peru. The Spanish fleets would seek the safety of the Caribbean ports during the hurricane season.

The brief English occupation brought Cuba into the orbit of the English Caribbean model of economic development whereby the islands would specialize in sugar and the 13 American colonies would specialize in supplies for the sugar barons and their army of slaves. Thousands of slaves were imported to Cuba during the brief English occupation.

Captured colonies are often returned or traded at the peace treaties. The Treaty of Paris ending the Seven Years War in 1763 was no exception. England exchanged Cuba for Florida mostly to appease the Mainland colonists much as England exchanged the captured French islands of Martinique and Guadeloupe for Canada because of the strong lobby from the 13 Mainland colonies. The sugar islands were several times more valuable than all of Florida and Canada.

However, it was the Mainland colonists who had started the Seven Years War when a young and inexperienced George Washington ambushed a small diplomatic French mission and killed 10 members including a French ambassador on May 28, 1754. Likewise, it was the Mainland colonists who sent Benjamin Franklin to London as early as 1757 to lobby England to expand its mainland colonies at the peace treaty.

The American Empire had a secret plan to conquer the American continent but needed England's help to oust the French and Spanish. It succeeded by convincing a young and inexperienced King George III that they would be loyal colonists to the Crown for all eternity. The English acquisition of Florida also enabled the growth of "illegal" trade between the 13 colonies and Cuba because of the close geographical proximity of Florida to Cuba. The Seven Years War was an all round win-win situation for the future American Empire.

Post US-Independence Plans to Invade and Conquer Cuba

As we saw in Chapter 1, all of the US presidents beginning with President Washington considered themselves duty bound to invade and conquer new territory for the sole purpose of expanding the geographical, economic, military and political power of the new empire. By the time of American independence in 1783, American *economic* imperialism had already invaded Cuba. With the loss of the English Caribbean markets following its independence from England, American trade with *Spanish* Cuba and American investment in *Spanish* Cuba, increased significantly.

As we saw with the example of Hawaii, American economic imperialism often precedes military conquest. The protection of American economic interests is an extremely popular election campaign slogan with American voters to justify unilateral military invasions of sovereign states by the American Empire.

The third US president, Thomas Jefferson, was obsessed with adding Cuba to the American Empire. In a letter to President Monroe dated October 24, 1823 Jefferson wrote that Cuba would be the "most interesting" addition to the US of all the remaining Spanish possessions which the American Empire was intending to conquer. He went on to clarify that the addition of Cuba to Florida would give the US control of the Gulf of Mexico and the countries bordering the Gulf as well as the waters flowing into the Gulf.

The sixth US president, John Quincy Adams, was also keen on invading and conquering Cuba. While Secretary of State for President Monroe, Adams sent a letter to Hugh Nelson, American ambassador to Spain, expressing his confidence that the American Empire would annex Cuba within the next 50 years. Adams wrote that Cuba was a "natural appendage" to the American Empire. Its conquest would simultaneously enhance the economic and political power of the American Empire while reducing those of the European empires.

As Secretary of State for President Monroe, Adams was largely responsible for formulating the *Monroe Doctrine* announced by the president in 1823. The *Monroe Doctrine* became the key justification for American invasions of sovereign countries in the New World. In Cuba, as well as other Spanish colonies, these American invasions were preceded by the Americans stirring up revolutionary fervour, discontent, independence movements, rebellions and other mischief in the Spanish colonies.

American meddling in Cuban affairs reached new heights in the 1840's. An important example is the determined efforts of Narciso Lopez who lost his influential position of assistant to the Spanish governor general of Cuba in 1843. Lopez switched sides and joined the American movement to foment revolution in Cuba against Spain.

When Spain tried to arrest Lopez in Cuba he fled to the US in 1848 where he continued to work for American annexation of Cuba. In the US he joined forces with John O'Sullivan, a strong supporter of US expansionism who had the ear of America's eleventh president, James Polk.

Polk, like his predecessors, worked incessantly to expand the empire. He instructed his ambassador to Spain, Romulus Saunders, to determine the monetary payment Spain would insist on if the US assisted the Cuban revolutionaries. The firm reply from Spain was that Cuba was not for sale.

O'Sullivan had worked on behalf of Polk during the 1844 election campaign and used his position as co-editor of the *New York Morning News* to drum up support for Polk. O'Sullivan subsequently became famous for coining the term *Manifest Destiny* in an essay he wrote in July 1845 entitled *Annexation.* The essay talked about the divine right of the American Empire to subjugate the entire continent. Americans have consistently used God and Christianity to justify their selfish desires to conquer and dominate others. *Christianites,* such as President George W. Bush hold very extreme religious views which are supported by a large segment of the American population and the American media to this day.

Lopez found huge support for his cause in the Southern **slave** states of the American Empire. These states saw Cuba not only as fulfilling the manifest destiny of the American Empire and the will of God but as a golden opportunity to expand and entrench the evil institution of slavery.

One of the unique characteristics of the sugar islands of the Caribbean was that slaves outnumbered the relatively small white populations. Unlike the Mainland colonies where many poor whites settled alongside the wealthy plantation owners, relatively few whites immigrated to the Caribbean colonies because of the inhospitable climate. The few whites were the wealthy plantation owners.

The invasion and conquest of Cuba would bring to the south many slaves as well as enhanced economic and political clout in the Union. John Quitman, Governor of Mississippi, for example, was a formidable supporter of Lopez. So was the editor of the *New Orleans Delta,* John Henderson.

With the help of these southerners Lopez recruited an army of volunteers, including Cuban exiles, to invade Cuba in May 1850. When the invasion failed, Lopez found new recruits and invaded again in August 1851. This time Lopez was caught and executed by Spain.

The American Empire denounced Spain's execution of Lopez. However, Europe, as a whole, was wary of American meddling in Cuba. In 1852 England and France asked the US to sign a joint declaration with them to guarantee Spain's right to Cuba. The American Empire, of course, refused. US inspired break-downs of law and order were often used as the pretexts for subsequent US invasions. Restoring law and order or protecting American property and citizens was, and still is, useful propaganda for the American imperialists.

The Ostend Manifesto and the US *Slave* Republic

In 1854, US plans to invade Cuba were leaked by the media. The plan had been hatched by President Franklin Pierce, his Secretary of State, William Marcy, and three of his ambassadors. The US ambassador to England, James Buchanan, ambassador to Spain, Pierre Soule, and ambassador to France, John Mason, were directed by President Pierce to develop a plan to **steal** Cuba from Spain, and from the Cuban people, for the glory of the American Empire and the economic power of sugar. This secretive plan was called the *Ostend Manifesto* because the American ministers first met in Ostend, Belgium on October 8th to October 11th, 1854, to hatch the plot before completing their secret scheme at Aix-la-Chapelle in Prussia.

Naturally, the scheme involved a monetary payment to justify the pretence that it was a "purchase" rather than a theft backed by military threats or high sounding propaganda about the rights of Cubans to self determination. Spain had made it very clear to President James Polk only a few years earlier that Cuba was not for sale at any price. All of the American players, Marcy, Buchanan, Soule and Mason, were well known for expressing their strong support for American annexation of Cuba by any means.

Stealing and **colonizing** Cuba was America's "manifest destiny." Pierre Soule was one of the leaders of a group of influential southern politicians called the *Young Americans*. Like President John Quincy Adams before him, he thought of Cuba as a "natural appendage" to the American Empire.

The institution of **slavery** was as much an ingrained part of the "freedom loving" American Republic as apple pie, militarism and popular deceit. The three American ministers who met in Ostend to discuss the military conquest of Cuba were all die hard supporters of the Republic's **inherent right to slavery** as a fundamental principle of the American definition of freedom. Furthermore, the *Young Americans* justified their planned invasion of Cuba by frightening the freedom loving Americans with the "scary" notion that Cuba might one day become an independent Republic ruled by **Non-Whites.**

Imagine American paranoia today over the tiniest probability of Cuba becoming an **Islamic** republic and you will get a good idea of American paranoia in the 1850's of the tiniest probability of Cuba being governed by **Blacks.** This, more than any other example, symbolizes the American definition of freedom, equality and democracy before its birth as an independent nation and to this day.

The American Empire backed away from a Cuban invasion in 1854 only because the other European empires, including England and France, supported Spain over the manifest destiny of the **slave republic** of the US. Furthermore, the Cuban annexationists had whipped up American warmongering on the basis of the seizure of the American merchant vessel, the *Black Warrior,* by Spain. Spain had seized the vessel in Havana, Cuba, on February 28, 1854, for violating Cuban customs regulations. Once Spain released the vessel the warmongers lost their primary propaganda tool.

Post US Civil War Plans to Invade and Conquer Cuba

The American Civil War of 1861-65 and the domestic turmoil leading up to that conflict made it impossible for presidents Buchanan and Lincoln to go to war with Spain to steal Cuba. However, American control of the Cuban economy continued unabated. By 1860, Cuba had imitated the English and French Caribbean colonies by specializing in sugar. It had become dependent on the United States not only for supplies but for its market for sugar.

While the primary market for the sugar from the English and French colonies was the mother countries the primary market for Cuban sugar was the US. By 1860, the US bought over 80 percent of

Cuban sugar. While still a "political" colony of Spain, Cuba had become an "economic" colony of the US. American investments modernized the Cuban sugar industry to the point that a single modern American sugar factory in Cuba produced more sugar than the entire sugar output of England's largest sugar island, Jamaica.

Just as Spain did not want to grant *political* independence to Cuba so too the US did not want to grant *economic* independence to Cuba. The Cuban people would have to fight two empires for their independence.

Unlike the US which succeeded in wresting its political independence from England with a single War of Independence, albeit with massive military assistance from France, the Cubans had to fight three Wars of Independence against Spain. The first of these was a long *Ten Years War,* 1868-78. The disastrous economic consequences of such a lengthy war increased Cuba's economic dependence on the US. Political independence from Spain was being traded for economic dependence on the American Empire. American investors snapped up sugar estates at very low post-war prices. The revolutionaries failed to strike a decisive blow against Spain and signed a peace treaty on February 10, 1878 known as the *Pact of Zanjon.*

A second War for Cuban Independence broke out in August 1879 but was concluded in 1880 without achieving political independence from Spain. Cuba's third War of Independence was successful because of military assistance from the United States. Just as the US had won independence from England because of French interest in North America so had Cuba won independence from Spain because of US interest in Cuba.

The US was fortunate that continued military conflicts between England and France prevented either European empire from further political or economic interference with American independence. Cuba was not so fortunate. Political independence from Spain was replaced by both political and economic subjugation by the American Empire. After the American conquest of Cuba from Spain American investments quadrupled Cuba's sugar output in the first two decades of the twentieth century.

Fear of another *Black* Caribbean Republic hastens the American Conquest of Cuba

Cuba's third War of Independence began on February 24, 1895. By this time the economic and military power of the American Empire had increased significantly while that of the Spanish Empire had continued to decline. In addition, American paranoia over Cuba becoming an independent **Black** republic got a boost from England's most famous **racist** statesman and future American citizen, Winston Churchill. In an article in the *Saturday Review,* in 1896, Churchill warned the world about the "dangers" of Cuban rebels imitating the Haitian rebels by forming an independent **Black** government in Cuba.

The American investments in expanding the island's output of sugar meant that many more Black slaves had been imported to cultivate the sugar cane. The French Caribbean colony of St. Domingue had become the richest sugar producer in the world before Cuba by importing Black slaves. In 1798 the Blacks overthrew their colonial master and defeated the armed intervention of England to establish an independent republic which we know today as Haiti. That was what Churchill was warning the Americans about.

The Cuban rebels invited the American Empire to aid their struggle for independence just as the 13 English colonies had invited the French Empire to aid their struggle for independence. The American Empire initially supplied the military hardware just as France had done for the 13 English colonies. Next the US media created the necessary propaganda about Spanish atrocities to win public support in the American Empire for war with Spain. President William McKinley demanded that Spain reform its rule of Cuba.

The most **evil** empire, America, was demanding reforms by another, but lesser, evil empire. Where is the incentive for one evil empire to consider the admonitions of another empire which is even more evil? Of course, the American Empire has no shame. It dropped nuclear bombs on Japan and provided nuclear bombs for Israel to nuke any Arab country attempting to liberate Palestine. Yet in 2009 it sends President Obama to China to preach human rights to a legitimate and popular Chinese government of the *People's* Republic of China while in the US it continues to subjugate its First Nations and practice institutionalized and democratic racism against its non-White citizens.

Why should we expect China or Russia today to listen to admonitions about human rights abuses from the West when the American Empire continues its ruthless slaughter of women and children in Iraq, in Palestine, in Afghanistan, in Lebanon, and now in Pakistan and Yemen? As for the use of torture on prisoners there is overwhelming evidence that the American Empire, as well as its allies, Canada and England, have both condoned and encouraged the use of torture on the prisoners captured as a result of its so called "War on Terrorism."

In the late 1890's Americans were asked to give their lives to fight the "evil" empire of Spain just as they are asked today to give their lives to fight the "axis of evil," Iraq, Iran and North Korea. President Obama added Pakistan to President Bush's "axis of evil." In the 1890's the American propaganda was that Cubans would greet the Americans as liberators of Cuba from Spanish imperialism. Today the American propaganda is that Iraqis, Afghans, Iranians, Pakistanis and Yemenis will greet the Americans as liberators from their "non-democratic" governments. The reality is that no humane and civilized people want an American **"slave-based"** warmongering "democracy."

The American media never tire of this false rhetoric. Should an American reporter happen to stray from the canned message he or she is simply fired by the networks. That is the essence of the American definition of freedom of the press. Just ask any CNN reporter today how long he or she would keep his or her job if he or she were to refer to the Peoples Republic of China simply as China instead of *Communist* China even though Chinese reporters never refer to the US as *Capitalist* America.

Even comedians like Bill Maher and country singers like the Dixie Chicks are ostracized for exercising their freedom of speech if it is critical of American invasions of Muslim countries such as Iraq. The United States has a long history of restricting freedom of speech and freedom of expression by artists.

The American Invasion of Cuba and the birth of Yellow Journalism

At the time of the third Cuban War of Independence there was no CNN vying with BBC World News for popular ratings and the almighty dollar. But there was the equivalent of today's profit motivated media competition in the form of two powerful newspapermen, William Hearst and Joseph Pulitzer. In the 1890's newspapers were the equivalent of TV news today.

William Hearst inherited the *San Francisco Examiner* from his father in 1887. In 1895 he purchased the *New York Journal*. In New York he engaged in head to head competition with the *World*. The *World* was owned by Joseph Pulitzer and was the largest circulation newspaper in New York. Wars are the surest way of boosting media attention. Hearst and Pulitzer knew that an American invasion of Cuba and a full blown war with Spain would send newspaper sales through the roof.

William Hearst sent one of his reporters, Frederick Remington to Cuba to "manufacture a war." Once the war began Hearst went personally to Cuba to report on the fighting. The competition between Hearst and Pulitzer for war coverage in Cuba quickly expanded to all of the major US newspapers of the day. Two other leading New York newspapers, the *Herald* and the *Sun,* joined the fray. Chicago newspapers such as the *Times-Herald* and the *Tribune,* joined with the *Boston Herald,* to add to the competition on the east coast.

Hearst took the competition to the west coast with his *San Francisco Examiner.* Since journalists in the US are permitted very little freedom by their corporate advertisers or by their editors to describe the true facts much less express a contrary opinion, all of the American newspapers carried the same propaganda. Spain was a "barbaric" empire and the US was in Cuba to save the Cuban people. They could have reported that same true and tried American propaganda from safe havens in the US. But by pretending it came from journalists on the battlefield in Cuba it got the undeserved legitimacy it needed.

American imperialism in Cuba as in other parts of the globe could never have succeeded without the willing connivance of the American "free" press. It is the American "free" press which stirs the American people to support every new war with false propaganda of atrocities committed by the nation to be invaded combined with the "goodness" of American intervention.

Sure enough many Americans are recruited to war by an innate desire to simply "kick ass," by using superior weapons. But many more are recruited by the true and tried propaganda that Americans are the good guys and only Americans truly know what is best for the entire human race.

The intense media competition for newspaper sales by Hearst and Pulitzer which provided the media support for the America invasion of Cuba was so far out and biased that the American media itself coined a new term, *yellow journalism,* to refer to this kind of biased propaganda unsupported by the facts. "Yellow journalism" by all of the Western media played a significant role in garnering popular support for the **criminal** US invasion of Iraq in 2003 by President Bush.

Teddy Roosevelt and the Washington Syndrome

Another ingredient essential to American warmongering is one or more committed generals shooting for the White House. These are the George Washingtons, the Andrew Jacksons, the Zachary Taylors, the Ulysses Grants, the Ike Eisenhowers and countless others in American history.

In my book on the *Rise and Fall of the American Empire,* I called this essential ingredient of American "democracy" the *Washington Syndrome.* Today it is possible to get to the White House by simply being a vocal war hawk without having served on the battlefield, a Dick Cheney or a Donald Rumsfeld, but being on the battlefield will still improve your chances. In the 1890's the general shooting for the White House was undoubtedly Teddy Roosevelt. While Hearst and Pulitzer produced the hype, Roosevelt provided the military leadership and bravado.

In 1897 Roosevelt became Assistant Secretary of the Navy and ran roughshod over then Secretary of the Navy, John Long. Roosevelt had the ear of President William McKinley because of his close friendship with Senator Henry Cabot Lodge. Lodge was a wealthy Republican from Boston with a Harvard Ph.D. Both Roosevelt and Lodge were highly influenced in their commitment to a powerful US navy by Alfred Mahan. Mahan had consistently urged the US to build a stronger navy to promote its imperialist *birthright* and to wrest naval dominance in the Caribbean from the British. They firmly believed Mahan's views on the importance of sea power as expressed in Mahan's book, *The Influence of Sea Power upon History.* According to Mahan, "colonies attached to the mother-country," was the surest way of supporting sea power.

In a confidential letter to Mahan in 1897, Roosevelt wrote that if he had his way he would "turn Spain out of the West Indies tomorrow." In a letter to Lodge, Roosevelt wrote that "this country needs a war." He was aware that wars make it much easier to get the US Congress to vote the funds to expand the US navy. Setting his sights on Cuba he organized a volunteer invasion force called the *Rough Riders* with the help of Colonel Leonard Wood who was placed in command. Volunteers from both the eastern and western states began training in San Antonio, Texas. Roosevelt secured a military commission as lieutenant colonel and his invasion force was approved by the US Congress on April 22, 1898. Roosevelt took command of the *Rough Riders* after he was promoted to Colonel.

It would not surprise any objective reader of US history to learn that Roosevelt returned to the US as a war hero which got him the governorship of New York in 1898 followed by the vice-president's job in 1901. President McKinley was assassinated by Leon Czolgosz on September 6, 1901 and Roosevelt took over as Commander-in-Chief. Roosevelt was extremely proud of his military commission and his military service in Cuba. He liked to be called the Colonel. What should shock any objective reader is why such a bold outspoken **warmonger** would later receive the Nobel Peace prize?

The Roosevelt Corollary and the Desecration of the Nobel Peace Prize

In 1898 Teddy Roosevelt had to convince President McKinley to start a war with Spain and invade Cuba. In 1903 he was the president and chose to invade Columbia to steal Panama. Cuba provided a rich sugar colony as well as a naval base at Guantanamo. Panama provided a canal to move the US navy quickly from the Atlantic to the Pacific Ocean. In a confidential letter to Mahan in 1897 Roosevelt had explained his desire to steal the Caribbean islands from Spain, annex Hawaii, build the "Nicaraguan" canal and expand the navy to confront Japan.

With the invasions of Cuba and Columbia Roosevelt decided unilaterally that the American Empire had an important international task. That task would be to overthrow legitimately elected governments in Latin America with American military force if those governments were to oppose the self-determined right of American corporations to "colonize" and exploit the economies of those countries. This newly assigned task of the American Empire has been called the *Roosevelt Corollary* to the Monroe Doctrine. The American Empire used the Roosevelt Corollary to overthrow many democratically elected governments in Latin America, the most publicized being the overthrow of the Allende government in Chile and replacing it with the brutal dictatorship of Pinochet.

The primary reason Roosevelt stole Panama to construct a canal was to compete with Japan for a Pacific Empire. US naval bases from Hawaii to the Philippines, combined with the Panama Canal, were all aggressive military threats to the Japanese Empire in the Pacific by the American Empire. How ironic that one of the major architects of this military threat, Teddy Roosevelt, was awarded the Nobel Peace Prize in 1906 because he helped to negotiate a peace treaty between Japan and Russia.

A year later Roosevelt's *Great White Fleet,* as his expanded US navy was called, toured the Pacific to intimidate the Japanese Empire. It is not atypical for a warmonger to intervene in the wars of other nations to pretend to be a peacemaker. Moreover, Roosevelt freely expressed his deeply ingrained **racist** views. He called the First Nations "squalid savages." He called wars against First Nations the "most righteous of wars." Christian wars against the "black, red and yellow races" are essential to promote Americans as the mighty race. "Moslem victories over Christians are a curse."

Roosevelt had an opportunity to combine his desire for warmongering with his inherent racism not only by invading Cuba to prevent the emergence of an independent **Black** republic but also when he waged war on the indigenous *Filipinos.* His three-year war against the *Filipinos,* following the US defeat of Spain in 1898, was far more brutal than the treatment of Cuban rebels by Spain. Bold outspoken warmongering and racism are such ingrained American characteristics accepted by an uncritical world community that they qualify Americans for Nobel peace prizes. No wonder that Teddy Roosevelt is the only person to date to simultaneously receive his country's highest military medal and the Nobel Peace Prize. Only Americans like Roosevelt and Obama can be so "Godlike" that they can be simultaneously war-loving and peace-loving. God bless America.

True to form the five-member Norwegian Nobel Committee continued its long tradition of condoning American warmongering by awarding the 2009 Nobel Peace Prize to the latest American warmonger, President Barack Obama. President Obama's invasion of Pakistan combined with his expansion of President George W. Bush's invasion of Afghanistan clearly inspired the pro-Western Nobel Committee. This "Af-Pak" invasion by the American Empire is correctly referred to as "Obama's War."

By awarding the Nobel Peace Prize to a warmonger like President Obama, instead of a peace activist like Cindy Sheehan, the Norwegian Committee sent a clear, unmistakable endorsement of American warmongering today as it had done during the Vietnam War when it awarded the Nobel Peace Prize to another American warmonger, US Secretary of State, Henry Kissinger, instead of a peace activist like John Lennon.

Canada's dangerous flirtation with the Washington Syndrome

Canada, like most non-US style "democracies" has deliberately steered clear of the *Washington Syndrome* until the US invasion of Afghanistan. With Canada's unusually vigorous political and military support of the *Afghan Mission,* despite its unpopularity both with its NATO allies and the Canadian public, especially in the province of Quebec, Canada has moved dangerously towards the US style "democracy." The Liberal Prime Minister, Jean Chrétien, **secretly** negotiated with the Bush administration a strong presence for Canada's military in Afghanistan when he increased Canada's troop commitment from 500 men and women to 2,500 men and women without even consulting his military commanders much less the Canadian public.

Chretien publicly pretended not to support the US invasion of Iraq. The reality was that the American Empire did not want Canadian forces in Iraq but wanted the Canadian forces to play a leading **combat** role in Afghanistan. President George W. Bush made this very clear to Prime Minister Chretien. In this way the US could more easily concentrate its full attention on Iraq. Canadian soldiers could die in Afghanistan so that the Americans could steal the oil in Iraq. By publicly pretending to oppose the US invasion of Iraq Chretien was able to win Canadian support for the American led Canadian invasion of Afghanistan

The Liberal government promoted the US style and partly US trained general, Rick Hillier, to Chief of Defence Staff **and** public relations officer to sell the War in Afghanistan to Canadians. Under the subsequent Conservative government of Stephen Harper, Hillier was given free rein to be the mouthpiece of the Canadian government and the Canadian people, a dangerous precedent for the Canadian "democracy." Harper and Hillier share similar views as American war hawks such as Bush, Cheney and Rumsfeld. Hillier would be the first Canadian general to emulate the George Washingtons, Andrew Jacksons and Teddy Roosevelts, who see a publicly orchestrated military career as the road to political ascendancy.

In 1995, General Hillier proudly referred to Afghans opposed to the Canadian invasion of their country as "detestable murderers and scumbags." He has consistently defended such foul language by saying that Afghans were out to kill Canadian soldiers. By implication, Canadian soldiers were not in Afghanistan to kill Afghans but simply to swat flies. The reality, of course, is that Canadian soldiers kill far more Afghans, including women and children, than Canadian soldiers are killed by Afghans. Canadian soldiers have the massive and modern firepower to kill and maim, almost at will. Canadians have flown thousands of miles to invade and destroy the homes and livelihood of the Afghan people. Canadians like General Hillier are the aggressors.

Afghans are defending their lives and homes against the superior weapons of an invading Canadian army intent on colonizing, occupying and raping their country. Canadians would do well to remember that the "freedom loving" Republic to the South invaded Canada twice and that Teddy Roosevelt bragged to his mentor Alfred Mahan that he did not fear England because "Canada is a hostage for England's good behavior."

Remember the Maine, to Hell with Spain

The media and the war hawks prepare the American public well in advance of the planned invasion of a sovereign state. The launching of the invasion must wait for an "international incident." The most publicized example of such "international incidents," is of course the September 11, 2001 attack on America's World Trade Center. In the case of the invasion of Vietnam it was the "Gulf of Tonkin," incident. The invasion of Japan was preceded by the Japanese bombing of Pearl Harbor. The "international incident" used by American warmongers to invade Cuba was an unexplained explosion of the American battleship, the *USS Maine,* on February 15, 1898 while anchored in Havana, Cuba.

These "international incidents" used by the American Empire are all the subject of "conspiracy" theories for good reason. Objective minds know that they have all been used as the pretext for unjust wars launched by the American Empire to steal territory, resources such as oil, economic power or to establish military bases for future conquests.

The official explanation for the *USS Maine* to leave its US port in Key West to invade Cuban territorial waters was "protection of American economic interests." Americans had invested over $50 million in the lucrative Cuban sugar industry alone. The true reason, of course, was to intimidate and provoke Spain and to enforce American military presence in a foreign country. The explosion of the *USS Maine* provided the ingredients for William Hurst to "manufacture" his war and for Teddy Roosevelt to shoot for the White House. As Assistant Secretary of the Navy, Roosevelt used his influence to stir up the war hawks of the day, the Dick Cheneys and Donald Rumsfelds of the 1890's.

The battle cry became, *Remember the Maine, to Hell with Spain."* The *USS Maine* was a 6700 ton battleship launched by the US Navy in 1889. It was used to patrol both US waters along the American east coast and foreign waters in the Caribbean. No one dare question the legitimacy of American naval presence in **foreign** waters. The *USS Maine* exploded because the gun powder for its guns stored in the front of the ship had exploded. Four separate official investigations by the US government were unable to explain the reason for the gunpowder igniting.

The American Empire secures another Naval Base at Guantanamo Bay

In the 1896 presidential elections William McKinley had campaigned on the popular slogan, "Free the Cuban people." As president he had an opportunity to fulfill that election promise. He hesitated to start a war to "free the Cuban people," when Spain promised to grant Cuba its independence. Teddy Roosevelt, speaking for the war hawks, said the president had no backbone for war. With the goading from the war hawks and the "Yellow Press" President McKinley asked the US Congress on April 11, 1898 to declare war on Spain.

The US Congress passed the war resolution on April 19, 1898 and The US navy secured Guantanamo Bay on June 6, 1898. With naval support US troops landed in Cuba on June 22, 1898. After an initial defeat at the Battle of Las Guasimas on June 24, 1898 Roosevelt's invasion force defeated the Spanish forces at the Battle of San Juan Hill on July 1, 1898 and at the Battle of Santiago on July 17, 1898. The US navy annihilated the Spanish Caribbean fleet in Cuba's Santiago Harbor and Spain surrendered on July 17, 1898. Spain was forced to hand over Cuba to the American Empire at the Treaty of Paris on December 10, 1898.

During the US Senate debate on the Treaty of Paris, Roosevelt's friend and fellow warmonger, Henry Cabot Lodge, argued that rejection of the Treaty would mean that Americans were "incapable of taking rank as one of the greatest world powers." By voting in favour of the Treaty the US confirmed that it had ambitions to be a great power like England and France.

The *Platt Amendment* to the Army Appropriations Bill passed on March 2, 1901, provided for the American Empire to establish a permanent naval base at Guantanamo Bay. Senator Orville Platt's Amendment also neutralized the *Teller Amendment*. Senator Henry Teller's Amendment to the April 19, 1898 war resolution of the US Congress was intended to prevent the American Empire from colonizing Cuba. That intention was reversed by the Platt Amendment. The American Empire could not stand the thought of a rich sugar island being owned by **Non-Whites.**

Teddy Roosevelt's "Splendid Little War," as US Secretary of State, John Hay, called it, had lasted little more than 3 months. It was sufficient to qualify Roosevelt for both the highest office in the American Empire and a Nobel Peace Prize. But it did cost over 5, 000 American lives in addition to Spanish and Cuban lives. The American taxpayer footed a bill for a quarter of a billion dollars.

The American Empire had stolen the largest and richest island in the Caribbean even though it had arrived in the Caribbean after the Spanish, Dutch, French and English empires. The first European Empire in the Caribbean, Spain, had succumbed to the American Empire. Within the next half century the American Empire would surpass the Dutch, French and English empires in economic, political and military power. Cuba was only the beginning of US acquisitions of *uncolonies* which would not become states of the Union.

Guantanamo was only one of over 700 military bases which the American Empire would set up by force in "sovereign" states across the globe. In many cases it is cheaper to enforce economic imperialism with a military base than taking over the local administration of the *uncolony*. By allowing an indigenous "puppet" government to administer the *uncolony* it is also easier for American politicians to fool the American electorate and keep up the pretence that the US is not a colonial monster.

CHAPTER 4

American Imperialism During and After its Civil War: US Invasions of Nevada, Nebraska, Colorado, Dakota, Montana, Washington, Idaho, Wyoming and Utah: 1864-1896

In this chapter we return to the Mainland invasions of First Nations land which we began in Chapters 1 and 2. These invasions were interrupted when those who lived in the conquered territory and had voluntarily joined a union to dominate and exploit others, found themselves dominated and exploited. They expressed their desire to leave that union but were prevented from doing so by military force. They found out what it was like to fight for their freedom in the same way that the First Nations had fought them before when they were the invaders. The First Nations had lost to their superior numbers and advanced military machine. In the so called *Civil War* these *Southerners* lost to the superior numbers and advanced military machine of their northern conquerors.

Part I: Civil War Conquests: Slavery vs. Empire

The United States of America was in every respect a false union. It was born out of lies, conquests of the lands of peaceful inhabitants, treachery, **slavery,** hypocrisy, militarism and warmongering as well as inequalities of wealth, political power and economic opportunities. It is no surprise to me that such a union would be short lived. Those who live by such false and immoral principles must sooner or later use those same false principles against themselves.

In less than a century after the declaration of independence by the 13 English colonies which first joined a voluntary union to create a *false* republic, some members of that voluntary union wanted their freedom from what they saw as tyranny. The last English colony which voluntarily joined the union was Rhode Island in 1790. It was only a decade later that these same colonies, which had now become states in a union, began to question the wisdom of this union.

The primary reason for questioning the wisdom of the voluntary union was the false premise on which it was born. The colonies had proclaimed widely and loudly that they had rebelled against England to remove themselves from English tyranny and to form a republic of free men with equal opportunities. In reality it was an American aristocracy seizing power by military force from an English aristocracy. The lies quickly led to a competition for power by the American aristocracy.

Two primary alliances quickly emerged. One alliance was among the aristocracy whose power depended on owning large numbers of African **slaves.** The other alliance was among the aristocracy who had a strong desire to rule an ever expanding **empire** achieved by military conquests and held together by force. The **slave-owner** aristocracy was the southern states where economic and political power required large cotton and sugar plantations. The **pro-empire** aristocracy was the northern states where economic and political power required ever expanding markets for industrialization and trade. At the time, colonies were thought to be the best way of securing guaranteed markets and sources of raw materials for industrialization.

While the union of the 13 English colonies, completed in 1790 when Rhode Island joined, was based on numerous lies and falsehoods the key lie that would divide the union was **slavery.** The United States of America was created as a **slave-based** Republic. All of the founding fathers owned slaves or believed firmly that owning slaves was a fundamental right in a "freedom loving" republic. That this was an inherent inconsistency did not seem to have registered with men who have been promoted by historians not simply as educated or intelligent but as brilliant, outstanding, gifted and endowed with enormous foresight.

Another factor often overlooked was the unquestioned **racism** of this "freedom loving" republic. Here I am not referring to slavery though racism and slavery has an important commonality because slaves were non-Whites; Blacks or First Nations. What I am referring to is that in both the **slave** aristocracy and the **pro-empire** aristocracy there was a common hatred of non-Whites. This hatred of non-Whites filtered down to the White masses and was therefore not exclusive to the White ruling class. The inherent **racism** of the new republic added to the North/South conflict for the following reason.

The South favoured importation of Blacks because Blacks were their primary source of slaves. The North opposed importation of Blacks not so much because they opposed slavery but because of their deeply ingrained **racist** personality. The Southern states never quite understood that the strong opposition to slavery by the ever expanding number of **pro-empire** states was not so much due to the White inhabitants, rulers and ruled alike, dislike of slavery as to their much stronger dislike of all **non-White** races.

It's one of the enduring ironies of the White/Black debate in the US that Blacks were not simply in greater numbers in the South than in the North but that Blacks co-mingled up close and personal with Whites in the South but were often highly segregated from Whites in the North.

No one can suggest that there is anything worse than slavery but the complexity of **racism** in the United States is far from explained by slavery alone. In the South, Blacks lived in the same homes as their White masters and often nursed and cared for the children of their White masters. They lived on the same estates in close geographic proximity, rode the same buses, albeit in the back, and often attended the same churches, albeit in separate pews. In the **slave-free** North whole communities were **segregated.** It's ironic that the movies portray Whites from the Northern states marching and protesting post-slavery segregation in the Southern states when segregation began in the northern **slave-free** states.

Slavery was sure to die because of changing world opinion and economics. **Racism** and racial discrimination did not end with the abolition of slavery because White racism against non-Whites was an issue in its own right, in addition to slavery, in the birth and life of the American Republic. It's important that we recognize this if we are to understand why the North needed to colonize the South by force to keep the Southern states permanently in the Union. The North opposed slavery in the South because they were die hard **racists.** Yet they opposed a separate Union of Southern states because they were first and foremost die hard **imperialists.** If imperial expansion meant having non-Whites in the empire so be it.

The American *Slave* Economy

The American aristocracy which seized power from the English aristocracy on July 4, 1776 with the unilateral declaration of independence, UDI, by 12 of the 13 colonies was different in several important respects. The key difference was **not** tyrannical monarchy versus democratic republicanism as Americans would have us believe but **freedom** versus **slavery.**

What the American founding fathers called the tyranny of King George III, the English monarch of the mother country at the time, was a monarch who ruled England with an aristocracy which had accepted the **abolition** of slavery within his kingdom since June 22, 1772 a full four years before American UDI. In chapters 1 and 2 we have already documented how the so called "English tyranny of King George III," fought "freedom loving" American republicanism for better and fairer treatment of First Nations. In this section of this chapter we focus on **slavery** as the most important of the many inherent lies in the founding and expansion of the American Empire.

In the years immediately following UDI in 1776 the 6 **slave-based** colonies of Virginia, Maryland, Georgia, Delaware and North and South Carolina volunteered to join the Union between 1787 and 1789 because they saw themselves as equal partners. These were the *Southern* colonies whose economies had prospered because of cheap **slave** labour.

The **slave** aristocracy which governed these colonies, contrary to the high sounding accolades of wisdom heaped on them by all and sundry, did not even have the foresight to see that the economic advantage of slavery was fast deteriorating. Future wealth and economic development was based on free trade, cheap labour from White and Chinese immigrants and colonial conquests for cheap raw materials and markets. The more these **slave** states expanded slave-based crops such as cotton and sugar to gain an economic advantage over the **pro-empire** *Northern* states the further they widened the economic gap. They were making short-term gains for long-term pain.

The Changing World View of *Slavery*

By 1790 when the American union of the original 13 colonies was completed the European empires had already succumbed to the **anti-slavery** movement. The **anti-slave** crusade, which had long existed in Europe and North America, got an important boost in the 1770's when Methodist and Baptist preachers moved from England to North America and the Caribbean to spread the word.

The Society for the Abolition of the slave trade was founded in England in1787 by Granville Sharp and Thomas Clarkson. The Society was supported by some of the most powerful politicians and businessmen of the day in England. Leading the charge in the English parliament was William Wilberforce. In 1788 the English parliament had already passed an act to ameliorate the horrible conditions on the slave ships during the *Middle Passage* from the European slave depots on the West African coast to the colonies in the New World. This was in response to increasing public disgust over slavery and the slave trade.

The new "freedom loving" Republic of the US acted as if it were totally ignorant of this new world view. It continues to behave today with the same degree of ignorance of changing world opinion, oblivious of world condemnation of its atrocities in Iraq, Afghanistan, Palestine, Lebanon, Yemen and Pakistan. It refuses to learn that military superiority is no guarantee of world domination.

After a failed attempt in 1788 the English **anti-slavery** movement succeeded in convincing the British government to abolish the slave trade in 1807. More importantly, the abolitionists succeeded in getting the Royal Navy, the most powerful navy in the world at that time, to enforce the law and capture and punish illegal slave traders. Fearful of confronting the British navy on the high seas the American Empire fell in line and abolished the slave trade in the following year.

What was hidden by the self righteous American Empire was its **internal** slave trade which expanded as its international slave trade contracted. The growth of the internal slave trade combined with illegal imports led to an increase, not a decrease, in the number of slaves traded by the **evil** empire after 1808. The slave population of the American empire increased from 1 million to 4 million between 1800 and 1850.

Whitney's Cotton Gin and the Second Middle Passage

The internal American slave trade and **illegal** imports of slaves expanded after 1808 due to the conquests of more First Nations land. The **genocide** committed against the First Nations as their land was stolen was combined with the **evil** of enslaving Africans to work the plantations of the American aristocracy.

The first lease on life presented to the southern **slave** aristocracy was the invention of *Whitney's* cotton gin in 1793. By increasing the productivity of **slave** labour in the production of cotton **fifty-fold,** it presented an economic opportunity to cotton producers which the **slave** aristocracy could not resist. Prior to Whitney's invention American cotton output was under 5,000 bales per year. Cotton exports were negligible compared with tobacco. By 1820, the value of cotton exports was four times the value of tobacco exports.

By 1860 output of cotton exceeded 5 million bales per year. Most of it was exported to England where cotton fabrics had replaced woolen fabrics as England's primary textile manufacture. Export revenues reached $200 million making it America's number one export in terms of value. In fact the export value of cotton alone exceeded the value of all other American exports combined.

The second lease on life presented to the **slave** aristocracy was the introduction of sugar to the "colonized" First Nations lands in the Mississippi delta. Sugar was an even more lucrative **slave-based** plantation crop than cotton. The Southern colonies had long profited from exports of tobacco from lands stolen from the First Nations. By 1860, the American Empire had driven off the First Nations from much more land to add cotton and sugar to a growing list of agricultural exports using an ever expanding **slave** work-force.

Despite the greater economic maturity of the North with its specialization on manufactured goods using wage labour the value of agricultural output exceeded the value of manufactures until 1890. This was the essence of the "freedom loving" republic founded in 1776. Agricultural staples using **slave** labour still dominated the American economy. While the Washingtons, Jeffersons, Jacksons, Adams's and Roosevelts, who founded that original **evil** empire have long passed on there has been no shortage of George W. Bushes, Dick Cheneys, Donald Rumsfelds, Condoleezza Rices or Barack Obamas to take their place and enslave the entire world with lies, deception and brute force.

The American *Second Middle Passage*

Everyone who has read of the inhumanity of slavery has heard of the dreaded *Middle Passage* between the European slave stations on the west coast of Africa and the European slave plantations in the New World. Relatively few have heard of what historian Ira Berlin called the *Second Middle Passage,* a unique and quintessential **American** nightmare for African slaves. It ranks right up there with American genocidal atrocities against First Nations and American nuking of Japanese civilians in Nagasaki and Hiroshima.

In the first half century after UDI the **legal** internal slave trade from the old English colonies in the South to the conquered First Nations lands incorporated as new states in the Union more than compensated the American **slave** aristocracy for the loss of legal imports from Africa and the Caribbean. While over half a million African slaves arrived in the US through the *Middle Passage* twice as many experienced America's unique *Second Middle Passage*. American slaves in the Southern colonies feared nothing more than being "sold down the river" and experiencing the inhumane journey of the *Second Middle Passage* to unfamiliar lands, new owners, new tasks and separation from family and friends.

Slaves were bred on *slave farms* by "breeding wenches" and sent through the *Second Middle Passage* to the sugar and cotton plantations in Alabama, Louisiana and Mississippi. This cotton and sugar plantation boom increased the average price of slaves more than four-fold. The price of slaves fit enough to work in the fields increased from under $300 in 1790 to over $2,000 by 1860. Despite the higher price, as mentioned before, the number of slaves in the "freedom loving" republic increased from well under one million in 1790 to over four million by 1860.

Colonization of the Southern States by the American Empire

There was an inherent inconsistency in expanding the empire through the extermination of the First Nations and replacing their lands with **slave** plantations to grow cotton and sugar. This inhumane approach to enriching the aristocrats of the empire widened the gap between the alliance which favoured a **slave** republic and the **pro-empire** alliance which favoured free trade, commerce and **colonies** that would rival the European empires.

Long term economic progress lay with the Northern pro-imperialists using cheap immigrant labour. By 1819 it may have appeared as if the two alliances were evenly matched. The number of **slave** states had increased from 6 to 11 while the **pro-empire** states had expanded from 7 to 11. In reality the 11 states in the pro-empire alliance had more economic and political power and had already begun to "colonize" the **slave-based** states of the union. Virginia, for example, declined significantly from its first place eminence in the Union in terms of population, geographical area and political influence as the oldest and most powerful of the 13 English colonies. Virginians emigrated in large numbers after confederation because of the relative economic decline of their state.

As the more powerful *Northern* alliance increased its political and economic subjugation of the weaker *Southern* alliance these "colonies" of the Northern alliance rebelled against the "Mother" country just as the 13 English colonies had rebelled against England. Unlike the 13 English colonies the rebellion was unsuccessful. The American Empire used military force to subdue the southern "colonial" states in the same way as it had used military force to steal the First Nations land and conquer *uncolonies* outside the American Mainland.

Had the Southern "colonial"states been allowed to leave the Union as freely as they had entered they would have been forced to recognize in time the economic, political and moral folly of a **slave** economy in the modern world. However, the United Sates would have been a smaller and less powerful empire. That was the reason for its use of military force to prevent secession. It was an empire bent on expansion at any cost and by force of arms. It was not the benevolent peace loving freedom fighter it so loudly claimed to be.

The Battle in the US Senate

The battle for independence by the southern states originally began in the US House of Representatives. In the House of Representatives, the Lower House, states elected members in proportion to their population. Since slaves were private property rather than people in the new "freedom loving" Republic this would have disadvantaged the **slave** states where Blacks represented as much as one-third of the total population. In 1790 when the Union of the 13 original colonies was completed, the US had a total population of 4 million. The Black population was almost 20% of the total population. The overwhelming majority of this Black population was slaves and therefore lived in the **slave** states.

During the Philadelphia Constitutional Convention of 1787 the **slave** states succeeded in securing their independence within the Union by having slaves count as 60% human for votes to the US House of Representatives. This amendment to the Articles of Confederation was a victory for the **slave** states. It increased the seats held by the **slave** states in the Lower House from 33 to 47 by 1793. This was the first of many inhumane constitutional amendments which enshrined slavery in the US constitution by those founding fathers who supported slavery as an American birthright. They were called "compromises." This one was called the "three-fifths compromise" and is found in Article 1, section 2 of the US Constitution.

The independence protection secured by counting slaves as 60% human for votes to the Lower House proved to be transitory for two reasons. The founding fathers in the **slave** states had not anticipated the imperial ambition of the slave-free states. This imperial ambition led to the carving out of additional states from conquests of First Nations land outside the original 13 colonies. This threatened the **slave** states in two ways. Firstly, in the Lower House their numbers of elected Congressmen fell as their populations declined. Their relative population declines were largely due to out migration to the newly conquered states of the Union. Representation for Virginia, for example, fell from 23 Congressmen in 1790 to 11 by 1850. The future battle for independence by the **slave** states therefore came primarily in the US Senate or Upper House.

In the Senate each state elected two Senators to the Upper House regardless of population. Balance in the Senate could be maintained even if the population of the Southern states declined relative to the **pro-empire** states. This required increasing the **slave** states in the Union in proportion to the **pro-empire** states. But with the institution of slavery dying from economic disadvantage and world-wide moral outrage it was simply a matter of time before the **pro-empire** states would exceed the number of **slave** states and dominate the US Senate. Moreover, the Northwest Ordinance of 1787 prohibited slavery in the First Nations lands invaded and conquered by the new American Empire. The **pro-empire** states would eventually combine their economic advantage with political advantage in both Houses. The South would be "colonized" economically and politically.

The "Missouri Compromise" postpones the *Colonization* of the Southern *Slave* States by the American Empire

The Southern **slave** states began their battle in the US Senate as early as 1817. At that time the "three-fifths compromise" still gave them an edge in the Lower House. As late as 1833 the "three-fifths compromise" gave the **slave** states an additional 25 seats in the Lower House.

The Senate battle began in 1817 when Missouri voted for membership in the Union. When Indiana joined the Union on December 11, 1816 there were 19 states in the Union. The number of **slave** states had increased from 6 to 9 and the number of **pro-empire** states had increased from 7 to 10. The **pro-empire** states had maintained their one state lead in the Senate thereby partially offsetting the advantage given to the **slave** states in the Lower House by the "three-fifths compromise."

By the time the Bill to admit Missouri came before the Lower House in December 1818, Mississippi had joined the Union as a **slave** state on December 10, 1817 and Illinois had joined the Union as a **pro-empire** state on December 3, 1818. Fearful of losing its one state advantage in the Senate, New York Congressman, James Tallmadge, introduced an amendment on behalf of the pro-empire slave-free states which would result in Missouri being admitted to the Union only as a slave-free state. While the Bill with the Tallmadge amendment passed the Lower House it was rejected in the Senate.

Missouri was temporarily kept out of the Union. On December 14, 1819, Alabama was admitted to the Union as a **slave** state. The **pro-empire** states had now lost their one state advantage in the

Senate. However, that same December of 1819 Congressman John Holmes introduced a Bill in the Lower House to admit Maine as a slave-free state. The **slave** states countered that same day by introducing another Bill to admit Missouri as a **slave** state. Once again the Lower House passed the Missouri Bill with an amendment which would admit Missouri only as a slave-free state. Once again the Bill was defeated in the Senate.

Maine was admitted to the Union on March 15, 1820 returning the one state advantage to the **pro-empire** states in the US Senate. The advantage was short lived. On August 10, 1821, Missouri was admitted to the Union as a **slave** state. There were 24 states in the Union. Half were **slave** states and half were slave-free **imperialist** states. What came to be called the "Missouri Compromise" was another commitment to slavery as an American birthright. It simply postponed the inevitable. The **slave** states were declining in economic and political power as their industrialization lagged the **pro-empire** states and their population declined. Their threat to secede from the Union could not be bought permanently on the backs of African slaves by maintaining the **evil** institution of slavery against world-wide condemnation.

The Road to Civil War: The American Empire Invades the Confederate States

Empires usually collapse from their own weight as greed pushes them to invade and conquer more than they can hold effectively with their stretched military. In the years following the "Missouri compromise" the imperial greed of the US led to conquests of more First Nations land and conflicts with England, Spain and Mexico over other First Nations lands which they had conquered and which the American Empire coveted. We have documented those conquests and conflicts in Chapter 2.

This mad push for an ever expanding empire on the American continent exacerbated the decline in the political and economic influence of the **slave** states as equal partners in this imperial republic. To preserve their independence and prevent their colonization by the more powerful slave-free imperialists they wanted a separate Union of their own. In an effort to keep the larger empire intact the northern imperialists offered the South yet another "compromise" which would once again prove to be a short-term band aid.

The 1850 Compromise and the Second Fugitive Slave Act

The Southern **slave** states had long implored the Northern **pro-empire** states to help them find, arrest and forcibly return runaway slaves. If some free Blacks were mistakenly returned and enslaved in the process that would be a welcome bonus. As the world-wide abolitionist movement infiltrated the "freedom loving" American Republic it lobbied hard and forcefully to deny such assistance to the **slave** states. In the end the greed for empire was stronger than the abolitionist movement and the "compromise of 1850" led to the US Congress passing the most inhumane Fugitive Slave Act.

This act forced the federal government to legally apprehend and assist in the return of runaway slaves to the **slave** states. In 1850 the "freedom loving" US Republic had over 3 million slaves out of a total population of 23 million. Slavery had been abolished in all English colonies since 1834. France had abolished slavery in its colonies during the French revolution but it was restored by Napoleon and finally abolished in 1848. Most of the Spanish colonies in South and Central America had gained their independence from Spain and abolished slavery before 1850.

The Second Fugitive Slave Act was quite a coup for the **slave** states. The economic boom in the Northern states had attracted growing numbers of free Black labour. Runaway slaves found haven in the free Black communities of the North and intermingled with free Blacks. An estimated 20,000 runaways had found haven in the Northern states. The Second Fugitive Slave Act turned the life of all

Blacks into a nightmare. Whereas free Blacks offered help and sustenance to their enslaved brothers and sisters before the Second Fugitive Slave Act now their own hard won freedom was threatened by unscrupulous money hungry slave catchers apprehending free Blacks and sending them to the **slave** states as runaways. Many free Blacks joined the *Underground Railway* taking runaways to Canada or migrated legally to Canada because they feared the slave catchers.

Popular Sovereignty and the End of Peaceful "compromises."

Up until the Second Fugitive Slave Act of 1850 the inherent inconsistency of creating a new imperial super power to rival the European empires and keeping **slave** states as equal partners in this Union was resolved by peaceful means which were called "compromises." That changed with the *Kansas-Nebraska Act* of 1854. Imperial greed for ever expanding conquests of First Nations land led to the Kansas-Nebraska Act to enable the empire to build a railway across the conquered lands. This railway would secure the original Union of 13 colonies along the thin strip of land on the Atlantic seaboard with its massive conquests across the width of the American continent to California and the Oregon Territory. It would secure this vast territory and lay the foundation for even more imperial conquests. A great notion for the imperial slave-free states. The death knell for the decaying **slave** states.

The Kansas-Nebraska *Bill* was the brainchild of Democratic Senator and railway insider, Stephen Douglas. Douglas would be the equivalent of our present day Dick Cheney with connections to big oil through Halliburton combined with political clout in the Oval office. Likewise, Steven Douglas was an influential Senator from Illinois with railway connections through his directorship with the Illinois Central Railroad. Like Cheney's influence with George W. Bush, Douglas had the ear and support of Democratic President Franklin Pierce who had secured the land for Douglas's railroad with the $10 million Gadsden Purchase of Mexican land in 1853.

Pierce had big dreams of empire as evidenced by his conquest of Japan by Commodore Matthew Perry in 1853. Douglas could combine the imperial dreams of President Pierce with his desire for private profit through railroad expansion. It was the unbeatable *Bush-Cheney* combination of the 1850's. Like the *Bush-Cheney* combination it proved to be a very deadly combination for American service men. It led to a war with the southern states almost as disastrous as the *Bush-Cheney* war in Iraq.

With his political clout, Douglas succeeded in getting the American Empire to conquer First Nations land which would add two new states to the Union and provide the land through which his "iron horse" would pass on its way to the Pacific Ocean. The Kansas-Nebraska Act which legalized this theft of First Nations land had to repeal the 1820 "Missouri Compromise" by allowing two new states admitted into the Union to vote on whether they wanted to be **slave** states or slave-free states. The Act effectively removed the power of the US federal government to determine the number of **slave** states in the Union.

The right of the people of the state to vote for or against slavery was called "Popular Sovereignty." The immediate effect of the Act was a huge influx of pro-slavery settlers into Kansas in anticipation of the crucial vote on slavery. Most of the new settlers came from the neighbouring **slave** state of Missouri which had fought a long battle against the American Empire between 1817 and 1821 to earn the right of admission to the Union as a **slave** state. The inhabitants of Missouri were fighting this same battle again to ensure that their neighbour, Kansas, secured that same American birthright.

In 1854 the Kansas-Nebraska Act was seen by leaders of the American Empire as another brilliant "compromise" which reconciled the desire for imperial expansion by the slave-free states with the desire for equal treatment by the **slave** states. Popular sovereignty would provide a way for new **slave** states to enter the Union to preserve the crucial balance in the US Senate. The **slave** states would continue to be empowered as equal partners in the ever expanding Union rather than "colonized" states of the Empire.

Unfortunately, the "Pierce-Douglas" plan for a quick easy transition to the Union for the new state of Kansas suffered a fate comparable to the *Bush-Cheney* plan for Iraq. Just as the *Bush-Cheney* plan for Iraq stumbled from the unexpected eruption of violence so did the *Pierce-Douglas* plan stumble from the unexpected eruption of violence. The *Bush-Cheney* plan brought Al-Qaeda to Iraq to fight the invaders. The *Pierce-Douglas* plan brought abolitionists to Kansas to fight the slavers. Al-Qaeda came heavily armed with suicide bombers and IEDs. The abolitionists came heavily armed with "Beecher's Bibles."

Henry Beecher was the Christian leader preaching armed resistance against those who would dare to take their **evil** institution of slavery to Kansas. The violence which erupted in Kansas came to be known as "Bleeding Kansas." The armed resistance of abolitionists led by John Brown, the Kansas equivalent of Zarqawi in Iraq, turned the *Pierce-Douglas* plan on its head. Far from providing a lasting solution to the power struggle between slavers and imperialists in the American Union it led to a bloody invasion of Southern states by the American Empire. This **imperial** invasion of Southern States which had voluntarily seceded from the Union has been dubbed by historians the "American Civil War."

Bleeding Kansas and the End of the Popular Sovereignty Compromise

The conquests of the American Empire in Mexico, California and Oregon had expanded the opportunities for slave-free states over **slave** states. But the Second Fugitive Slave Act of 1850 had quelled the resulting dissent by the **slave** states. Now the greedy empire had stolen more First Nations lands in Kansas which would once again favour the slave-free states since this land, like most of the Mexican, California and Oregon conquests, was north of the "slave line" agreed to by the "Missouri Compromise" of 1820.

Douglas's "Popular Sovereignty" was the equivalent of the Second Fugitive Slave Act as yet another bribe to keep the **slave** states in a doomed Union. The problem with this bribe, unlike the Second Fugitive Slave Act, was that it required the **slave** states to populate Kansas for it to be an effective bribe. Only by populating Kansas could the **slave** states use "Popular Sovereignty" to make Kansas a **slave** state and thereby keep their political influence in the US Senate.

But how can an empire populate so much land which was stolen because of greed and an obsession with warmongering rather than any economic or population necessity? The empire already had great difficulty populating the land in Mexico, California and Oregon which had led to the "1850 Compromise." The dire lack of people to use so much stolen land was especially acute since the empire only wanted **White** inhabitants. This prevented the empire from peopling the empty land from Asia or Africa.

As soon as the Kansas-Nebraska Act was passed Senator David Atchison of Missouri led the call for "volunteers" to temporarily populate Kansas to win the popular sovereignty vote for the **slave** states. These "Border Ruffians," as they were called, came armed as if they expected violent confrontation. Once they voted they would return to their home state. It was the only way that the **slave** states could use the "Popular Sovereignty Compromise."

What was totally unanticipated by Douglas and others who had dreamed up the "Popular Sovereignty Compromise" was the intervention of the abolitionist movement based in New England. The abolitionists saw "Popular Sovereignty" as an opportunity to prevent new states like Kansas ever becoming **slave** states. They sent their own army of volunteers to fight the "Border Ruffians." The armed confrontation between slavers and abolitionists in Kansas lasted through the second half of the

1850s. The road to ending slavery in the American Empire would prove to be as bloody and violent as UDI, the conquest of First Nations land and American invasions today by President Obama in Yemen, Pakistan, Afghanistan and Iraq.

Armed confrontation between slavers and abolitionists first erupted in Kansas in November 1855 with the *Wakarusa War.* In December of 1855 armed slavers crossed the border into Kansas from Missouri and laid siege to the Kansas town of Lawrence. Abolitionists from New England armed with Sharps rifles and led by John Brown and James Lane defended Lawrence. In retaliation for the attack on Lawrence by the slavers Brown attacked a slave settlement in Pottawatomie Creek in May 1856. This was followed by the Battles of Black Jack in June 1856 and Osawatomie in August 1856.

Despite support for the slavers by President Buchanan the abolitionists won in the end and Kansas was admitted to the Union as a slave-free state on January 29, 1861. The insatiable greed for empire by the slave-free states had finally forced the **slave** states to abandon a Union which no longer guaranteed them equality of political opportunity. Unfortunately this imperial monster which they had helped to create could not relinquish its imperial conquests. They would not be allowed to leave a Union which they had voluntarily joined. Intermittent battles and guerilla warfare continued until this mini "Civil War" in Kansas merged into the much wider "Civil War" between the **empire** and the Southern **slave** states.

Abraham Lincoln and the Birth of the Republican Party

The American Empire had experienced the birth and death of many political parties by 1854. The Kansas-Nebraska Act led to the birth of yet another political party. This was the *Republican Party* which elected George W. Bush and Dick Cheney in 2000 and thereby hastened the demise of the empire. In 1854 the new party chose its name to represent the republican values of freedom and equality which would oppose slavery. It was therefore immediately seen by the **slave** states as against their economic and political interests which depended on the continuation of slavery.

The new party cemented the North-South divide which had long plagued the Union. It entered the 1856 presidential race with John Freemont as their candidate who would represent the economic and political interests of the free trade Northern states. The southern states were represented by a much fragmented Democratic Party led by James Buchanan. Buchanan won the presidency with 174 electoral votes to 114 for Freemont. Freemont did not score a single electoral vote in the South confirming the view of the South that the *Republican Party* was not a National Party but a sectional party representing the desire of the slave-free North for **imperial** expansion and domination. A Republican victory would mean the "colonization" of the South. Buchanan's victory in 1856 only postponed the inevitable secession of the Southern States.

Abraham Lincoln joined the Republican Party and ran against Stephen Douglas in 1858 for the Illinois seat in the US Senate. Lincoln's parents had moved from Indiana to Illinois in 1830. In a highly publicized series of debates with the incumbent, Douglas, Lincoln argued against Douglas's "Popular Sovereignty Compromise." Lincoln may have won the debates but he lost the Senate seat to Douglas. However, the debates raised the profile of Lincoln propelling his political career to the national stage. Having been thrashed by the South in the 1856 presidential race the *Republican Party* was looking for a candidate that would least offend the South. That candidate was Abe Lincoln.

Lincoln's great grandfather was from the founding English colony of Virginia, the Union state which championed the right of the **slave** states for equal treatment in the Union. In his home state of Illinois, Lincoln was a captain of the state militia which had fought the Chief of the Sauk Nation, Black Hawk, during the Black Hawk War. Warmongering, especially against First Nations, was a sure-fire qualification for *Commander-in-Chief* and president.

Most importantly, Lincoln was **against** the abolition of slavery. He disagreed with the anti-slavery views of his father and married Mary Todd, the daughter of a prominent slave holding family from the southern **slave** state of Kentucky. The Republican Party had chosen the republican name for publicity not principle. It was consistent with the hypocrisy which is the most enduring characteristic of the American Empire. Lincoln's anti-abolition stance would be his major qualification for his selection by the Republican Party as their presidential candidate in the 1860 elections.

With his widely publicized anti-abolition stance on the slave issue he would be the least objectionable Republican candidate to the **slave** states. He would save the Union by protecting slavery for the **slave** states. During his debates with Douglas for the Illinois Senate race Lincoln had made it very clear that he did not support political equality for **Blacks.** This is not the impression you get from standard American history which falsely credits Lincoln with the abolition of slavery in the foremost **slave** Republic of the 1860's.

Lincoln's Election and the Secession of Southern States

Despite Lincoln's strong **pro-slavery** views his victory in the 1860 presidential elections led to the secession of the Southern states from the Union. The South was firmly anti-Republican no matter who ran the Republican Party. Furthermore, their loss of Kansas to the abolitionist movement killed the "Popular Sovereignty Compromise" of 1854. South Carolina seceded on December 20, 1860, shortly after Lincoln won the elections on November 6, 1860. On December 26, 1860 South Carolina demanded the removal of federal forces from Fort Sumter. By February 4, 1861 six Southern states had seceded from the Union and met in Alabama to form a new country called the *Confederate States of America*. Jefferson Davis was the Confederacy's George Washington.

It was not difficult for these states to know that the "republican" values of the American Empire and their government under the Republican Party led by Lincoln were pure unadulterated lies. How could they not know that when they had been a party to those lies since the birth of the fraudulent Union? Their hasty decision to leave the Union was proof of their distrust of the integrity of a Union they had concocted to steal First Nations land and conquer all and sundry with the most savage use of brutal force. They rightly feared that the military juggernaut they had so joyously helped to create in order to steal from others and colonize their lands would now be mercilessly unleashed on them.

Their **evil** American Empire gave no quarter to the highly moral and civilized people they conquered. Why would it give any quarter to the inhabitants of immoral **slave** states? The Southern states knew with certainty that if their military defense failed them they were doomed to total subjugation. President Lincoln was quick to declare the secession of the Southern States an illegal act of rebellion. An empire born out of warmongering would fight another bloody war against "rebels." That empire had fought the English because the English were "imperialists." It had fought the First Nations because they were "savages." It would later fight Russia because Russians were "communists" and Iraq because Iraqis were "terrorists." The theme is a familiar one. Demonize those you invade and conquer in order to justify your own **evil** nature. Lincoln's abuse of executive powers to justify his war against the rebels was as extreme as the abuse of executive powers by George W. Bush to fight "terrorism" in the twenty-first century. An **evil** empire will always invent an enemy to justify restrictions on freedoms.

As we have explained before, the American Empire has always underestimated the enemy and paid dearly for selling invasions cheaply to a naive American populace. Wars are popular with the majority of Americans only if Americans are winning. By selling every new war as a cheap quick victory American presidents have easily obtained the support of the American people. However, as soon as the people conclude that the war is going badly their support evaporates. Fortunately for American presidents they can change the rationale for the war and thereby manufacture new support.

Since the American Empire is devoid of any fundamental human principle it is easy to invent new principles as events unfold. Just as George W. Bush could easily sell a new justification for his invasion of Iraq to a gullible American electorate so did Lincoln sell new justifications for invading the Confederate States. Lincoln's initial justification for his war was that the secession was an illegal rebellion. When the war went badly he used the **abolition of slavery** as his justification. When the war continued to go badly he used the fail-safe American justification, "the preservation of democracy and the American way of life."

There were many Americans who warned Lincoln against war just as many Americans warned George W. Bush against the invasion of Iraq. Unfortunately, American *Commanders-in-Chiefs* seem to believe so firmly that it is their duty to expand the territory of the American Empire that the thought of it contracting because of a few "rebels" is simply unacceptable. What's a little war to teach these "rebels" a lesson? At least that's what Lincoln thought.

Like George W. Bush's "slam-dunk" invasion of Iraq, Lincoln soon found out "rebels" fight back as hard as "terrorists," "communists" or "savages." Lincoln's first act of aggression against the Confederacy was sending reinforcements to Fort Sumter instead of withdrawing federal troops. The Confederacy attacked and captured Fort Sumter on April 12, 1861 forcing the federal troops to withdraw. Lincoln's response was typical. Demand tax dollars to expand the armed forces of the empire.

The Confederacy expanded to 11 states, moved its capital from Montgomery, Alabama to Richmond, Virginia and recruited General Robert E. Lee to its cause. Lincoln would have no quick or easy victory. Lincoln's attack on Richmond in July 1861, led by General Irvin McDowell, suffered a humiliating defeat by the Confederacy's generals, Pierre Beauregard and Joseph Johnston. This defeat at the first battle of Bull Run promoted a relatively unknown Confederate general, Stonewall Jackson, to legendary status. American invasions have a habit of producing heroes. Who would have heard of Abu Musab al-Zarqawi if George W. had not invaded Iraq?

The American Empire produced its own hero in the form of General Ulysses Grant. Grant's first victory for the empire at Pittsburg Landing in early 1862 resulted in more casualties than the American War of Independence, the 1812 invasion of Canada and the 1846 invasion of Mexico. It was a proud beginning for American warmongers and its Commander-in-Chief, Lincoln.

Nevertheless, the Robert E. Lee/Stonewall Jackson combination proved to be more than a match for the much larger number of troops Lincoln could buy with the larger economy of the American Empire. His generals, Irvin McDowell, George McClellan, Henry Halleck and John Pope, were all devastated by the Lee/Jackson combination. The Second Battle of Bull Run in August 1862 was as disastrous for Lincoln as the First had been.

Lincoln's desperate search for his American Napoleon stumbled on General Ambrose Burnside who led a much larger army against Lee in December 1862 only to be humiliated by Confederate forces at Fredericksburg. The quick easy victory with which every American president has conned gullible Americans into supporting every new invasion eluded Lincoln as much as it eluded George W. Bush. It was time for Lincoln to shift gears and promote a new "principle" to justify the war. Illegal rebellion, Lincoln's original "principle" had run its course and not produced victory for the warmongers.

Lincoln *used* the Abolition Movement to Conquer the Confederate States of America

When the only intrinsic principle of an empire is *hypocrisy* it is very easy to shift from one principle to another if that promotes your immediate self interest. The invasion of the Confederate states was going as badly for Lincoln as the invasion of Iraq went for George W. Bush. When no weapons of mass destruction were found in Iraq George W. switched gears to "Regime Change." George W. was showing his leadership of the "free world" by removing an evil dictator, Saddam Hussein, for the benefit of the Iraqi people. Likewise, Lincoln recognized his need to shift gears by pretending that he had invaded the Confederate states to promote the abolition of slavery.

Just as it was difficult for those who opposed the empire's invasion of Iraq to argue against the toppling of an "evil" dictator, so too it was difficult for abolitionists who had opposed Lincoln's invasion of the Confederate states to oppose Lincoln's new principle. Both Lincoln and Bush needed to hide their natural American instincts for warmongering and imperial expansion.

There were three important reasons why Lincoln's new found principle would help his cause. These three factors would hopefully turn the war against the "rebels" who were now promoted to **evil** slave holders. Firstly, by promoting the invasion of the Confederate states as a war against slavery instead of a war of conquest, Lincoln would forestall a British removal of the empire's blockade of Confederate ports.

While the land battles were disastrous for the empire the privateers authorized by President Davis since April 1861 were no match for the US navy. The US navy blockaded the Confederate ports across 3,500 miles of coastline from the Carolinas to Texas. President Davis was confident that the British would use the Royal Navy, the most powerful navy at the time, to remove the blockade. British factories needed the Confederate exports of cotton for its booming textile industry.

Lincoln thwarted the hopes of President Davis by playing to the strong abolitionist movement in England. That movement had secured the abolition of the slave trade worldwide since 1807 and had secured the abolition of slaves throughout the British Empire since 1834. It now stopped Britain from removing the blockade since Lincoln was promoting his warmongering as a means of ending slavery in the American Empire. It was a clever, if hypocritical, move by Lincoln and it succeeded. The abolition movement in both England and the United States threw its weight behind Lincoln's invasion.

Secondly, Lincoln needed Blacks in the empire's armed forces. The Confederate army had proved to be too formidable for a "Whites only" US navy and army. When Blacks volunteered for the US army in early 1861 Lincoln turned them away. The shortage of White volunteers forced the US navy to recruit Blacks. The US army later recruited Blacks for non-combat work.

In early 1862, one of Lincoln's generals, David Hunter, recruited an all-Black militia only to be ostracized by Lincoln. However, shortage of White recruits forced Lincoln's generals to find ways around his stubborn all-White policy. General Benjamin Butler, for example, recruited Blacks by using the "freedom loving" Republic's designation of Black slaves as private property. Butler said he was confiscating private property which he could use as he saw fit. Growing shortage of White recruits forced the US Congress to pass an Act in July 1862 to permit the empire to recruit Blacks in both the army and the navy. By the end of the war the US had recruited over 200,000 Blacks. The 20,000 Blacks recruited to the US navy represented 25 percent of sailors in the US navy.

Thirdly, abolition robbed the Confederate states of Black labour which severely hampered their ability to defeat the invaders. The total population of the Confederate states was half that of the empire even when all Blacks were counted. Lincoln's promise of freedom and employment in the empire's armed forces encouraged slaves to escape and free Blacks in the Confederacy to migrate into the armed forces of the empire. It also encouraged slave rebellions and other forms of disobedience and sabotage. Of the 200,000 Blacks who signed up for the armed forces of the empire half were escaped slaves or free Blacks from the Confederacy. An estimated 20 percent of slaves escaped from the Confederacy. This was not simply a gain of 100,000 men for the empire but also a loss of 100,000 workers for the war effort of the Confederacy. It therefore doubled the contribution to Lincoln's successful invasion.

Lincoln *used* the American Empire's most hypocritical line: Protecting Democracy and Freedom

Neither the promised abolition of slavery nor the institution of the draft in March 1863 provided the victory Lincoln had promised the American people. Support for the invasion generated by using the abolitionist cause had run its course without providing victory. Lincoln needed to shift gears again. What new moral principle could he abuse to justify new support for his warmongering? He turned to the old standby of protecting liberty, freedom, equality and democracy itself.

Just as George W's invented "terrorists" threatened the American way of life and the protector of the "free world," the **slave** Confederacy threatened the "freedoms" which the "freedom loving" Republic stood for. The empire must crush the Confederacy without mercy to protect its right to freedom and equality. Lincoln delivered his new found principle for the invasion with the "infamous" Gettysburg Address of November 19, 1863.

The general who would execute Lincoln's new found principle and crush the Confederacy without mercy was General William Tecumseh Sherman. Lincoln's initial principle for the invasion, "crushing rebels," may have failed because he had not found his American "Napoleon" in General George McClellan. In Sherman he found his American "Attila the Hun," which certainly contributed to the hypocrisy of his latest principle, "preserving democracy," producing victory at last.

Sherman captured Atlanta, Georgia on September 2, 1864 and burnt it to the ground. He decimated the Confederate army led by General John Hood and captured Savannah, Georgia before the end of the year. As he marched from Atlanta to Savannah, burning, looting, pillaging and raping, Confederate soldiers deserted in droves. By March 1865 Sherman had reached North Carolina and bloodied another Confederate army led by General Joseph Johnston into submission by April 1865.

After delivering victory to Lincoln, Tecumseh Sherman would later take on the task of providing the "final solution" for the empire's "Indian problem." He was the senior general assigned to destroying the Plains Indians beginning in 1875. This must have given him great satisfaction for providing the opportunity to get back at his parents for naming him after the First Nation Shawnee Chief, Tecumseh, who had defeated the empire when it had invaded Canada in 1812.

While Sherman was breaking the will of the Confederate resistance with his *scorched earth* rampage Lincoln's latest general-in-chief, Ulysses Grant, proved to be a formidable match for Robert E. Lee. By the time Grant was promoted to general-in-chief in March 1864 Lee was desperately short of men and equipment. Grant had more than twice the manpower and equipment of Lee when he crossed into Virginia to attack Lee in May 1864. He could afford the massive losses Lee inflicted on his forces. Lee was forced to surrender on April 9, 1865.

The hollow platitude of "defending freedom and democracy" together with the brutal methods of Sherman combined with the leadership of Grant had produced victory at last for Lincoln's invasion. Lincoln would pay the ultimate price for that invasion. Less than a week after Lee's surrender, Lincoln caught an assassin's bullet on April 14, 1865. Lincoln did not live to learn that violence only begets more violence. A conquered people will find a way to resist even when they face overwhelmingly superior military forces. Americans have never learned that lesson despite their failures in Canada,

Nicaragua, Vietnam, Lebanon, Iraq and Afghanistan. Propaganda may fool a majority of Americans but will not fool the majority of insurgents who resist invaders.

Part II: US Invasions of Nevada, Nebraska, Colorado, Dakota, Montana, Washington, Idaho, Wyoming and Utah

By the time the Southern states seceded from the Union in 1861 the 13 tiny English colonies which became the independent country of the United States in 1776 had invaded and conquered First Nations lands to the west and south. Those invasions had added 21 new states to the Union. The bloody war from 1861 to 1865 to hold the Southern states hostage to the Union should have sent a strong message to the empire that it would be wise to expand no more.

But warmongering was in its nature and in its very soul. It knew not how to be a peaceful nation content with itself. It envied the land of its neighbours and it yearned for more bloody conflicts. Having re-conquered the Confederate states by 1865 the empire was now free to invade and expand further. Before the end of the century it would have invaded and conquered another 925, 000 square miles of First Nations land thereby adding **ten** new states to the empire.

US Invasion and Conquest of Nevada

First Nations land in Nevada would be the empire's first conquest even before victory against the Confederate states was final. First Nations who owned this land included the *Washoe* Nation, the *Paiute* Nation and the *Shoshone* Nation. Americans, including the Mormon followers of Brigham Young, began to move into their land in the 1840's. A few explorers, trappers and traders had arrived since the 1820's. Wagon trains passed through Nevada on their way to California.

Western claims to the land were transferred from Spain to Mexico and then to the American Empire in 1848, after the empire invaded and defeated Mexico. The American Empire created the Utah Territory on September 9, 1850 to administer the land stolen from the First Nations and Mexico. Nevada was part of the Utah Territory. Brigham Young and his Mormon followers had earlier settled in Salt Lake City. Brigham Young was appointed as the first governor of the Utah Territory.

American settlements expanded and reduced the hunting grounds of the First Nations. Conflicts between the tiny numbers of American settlers and the First Nations provided the publicized excuse for the empire to send its army to conquer the state. Armed resistance by the First Nations against the empire began with the *Paiute War* of 1860 at Pyramid Lake, Nevada.

With the empire's invasion of their hunting grounds, fishing in Pyramid Lake by the Paiute was the only way of preventing death from starvation. The Paiute Nation defeated the first attack at Pyramid Lake in May 1860. As usual a victory by the First Nations only meant later facing a much larger imperial force in June, and accepting defeat or wholesale slaughter. The empire built a fort on Lake Pyramid to prevent the Paiute from fishing and thereby causing them to die off from starvation.

The discovery of silver beginning with the *Comstock Lode* in 1859 brought large numbers of American miners and shop keepers into Virginia City, Gold Hill, Austin, Eureka and Pioche. Nevada is still the empire's second largest producer of silver today. The California gold rush of 1849 had brought many miners to the west coast who had passed through Nevada and were now willing to return to Nevada to mine for silver and gold.

This large influx of non-Mormon settlers led to the empire carving out the separate Nevada Territory in the eastern portion of the Utah Territory on March 2, 1861. The increased influx of Americans also led to more wars with the First Nations such as the *Battle of Bear River* in 1863 and the *Bannock War* of 1878. The superior military force of the empire often led to the massacre of

First Nations by US soldiers such as the Bear River massacre of the Shoshone women and children. American invasions also killed off the First Nations with smallpox and other diseases.

Nevada Statehood Helps the Re-Election of Lincoln for a Second Term

The "Civil War" against the Confederate states had clearly not reduced the appetite of the empire for more First Nations land. The creation of the Nevada Territory was the first step towards the addition of one more state to the empire. Lincoln saw this as an opportunity for the new Republican Party and his re-election in 1864.

Lincoln's invasion of the Confederate states had not been popular for him or his Republican Party. Americans love wars when they are winning. By the time of the 1864 presidential campaign Lincoln's war against the Confederacy had yet to be won. The Democratic Party was against the war. When the Southern states were part of the empire they naturally went along with hypocritical claims to protecting freedom, democracy and republican values. Now that they were the butt of that hypocrisy it was impossible to fool them. Lincoln knew this. His Gettysburg Address was directed at his supporters and the permanently brain dead. Lincoln needed new lies to secure re-election.

Lincoln dropped his Vice-president, Hannibal Hamlin, to form a coalition with Democrats by selecting a Democrat from the Confederate state of Tennessee, Andrew Johnson, to be his running mate. He also disavowed his "Republican" roots by calling his party the "National Union Party." The Republican Party was too widely seen to be overtly warmongering to be able to fool a sufficient number of voters. The icing on the cake for his makeover would be securing one more state which publicly supported his cause. Statehood for Nevada would add a further guarantee to his re-election.

Statehood would provide imperial protection to the American miners, shop keepers and settlers against the First Nations whose land they had stolen. In return, Lincoln and his *National Union Party* would gain the support of one more state in the Union against the Southern states. The US Congress hurriedly created the state of Nevada on October 31, 1864 despite the fact that Nevada's population at the time was less than the minimum required to qualify for statehood. A week later on November 8, 1864 Lincoln was re-elected.

With the re-conquest of the Confederate states and the creation of West Virginia as a separate state in 1863, Nevada became the thirty-sixth state of the Union. This added another 111,000 square miles of First Nations land to the empire. This area includes Pah-Ute County which was named after the Paiute Nation of Nevada. Pah-Ute County was added to the state of Nevada on May 5, 1866 after gold was discovered. Nevada's largest city, Las Vegas, is located in what was Pah-Ute County and is now called Clark County.

US Conquests of the Great Plains states of Nebraska, Colorado, North Dakota and South Dakota: 1864-1889

The Great Plains had long been inhabited by over 300,000 First Nations including the Sioux, Cheyenne, Comanche, Arapaho, Crow, Cree, Kiowa, Lakota and Blackfoot Nations. It was explored by the Spanish conquistadors such as Cabeza de Vaca, Marcos de Niza, Francisco de Coronado and Hernando de Soto searching for *Cibola,* the legendary "Seven Cities of Gold," long before the American Empire invaded and conquered it from the First Nations.

It was these Spanish explorers who had brought the horses which enabled the Plains Indians to be some of the best mounted warriors of the day. The large buffalo herds roamed the Plains providing abundant food for all of the First Nations. The American Empire would deliberately slaughter the buffalo herds to starve the First Nations into surrendering their land to an **evil** empire. Americans like Buffalo Bill Cody slaughtered thousands of buffalos to subdue the First Nations.

American conquest of these states is yet another glaring example of the deep seated ingrained **racism** of the American Empire. There was more than enough land to share between Americans and First Nations. The Great Plains constituted an area of 1.4 million square miles. But First Nations were **Red** and the American Empire wanted **Whites** only. The empire butchered or starved the First Nations only because they were not White. The evidence of this is overwhelming since the American Empire had to bribe Whites from Europe with free acreage to populate the land conquered from the **Red** people. It is shameful that so many in the world still boldly defend America as the land of freedom and equality. There is no greater crime against humanity than this denial of reality.

The empire began to establish trading posts on the Great Plains after the Lewis and Clark expedition of 1804. The European empires had long traded for furs with the First Nations inhabiting the Plains. After slaughtering the buffalos the vast grazing land was used as open range for cattle. Next came the railroads and small settlements around the railway stations. President Lincoln passed the Pacific Railway Act in 1862 which gave 10 square miles of First Nations land on each side of the rail tracks to the railway companies.

But it was the Homestead Act of 1862 which led to the massive influx of **White** settlers to replace the **Red** inhabitants. The Homestead Act provided 160 acres of First Nations land free to every White settler. Lincoln used his "Civil War" to get the Homestead Act through the US Congress. The Southern states had opposed free land to small farmers since that would have undermined their "democracy" which was based on large plantation owners using **slave** labour.

When the Confederate states withdrew their representatives from the US Congress Lincoln passed his Homestead Act to replace **Red** First Nations with **White** Europeans. White settlers came from as far as the Ukraine, Scandinavia and Russia in addition to the more traditional European countries such as England, Ireland, France and Germany. After the re-conquest of the Confederate states the empire turned its generals and expanded army to the task of killing or removing all of the First Nations from the Great Plains. This was called the "final Solution" to the "Indian problem." The conquered states of Nebraska, Colorado, North Dakota and South Dakota, added over 330,000 square miles of First Nations land to the empire.

US Invasion and Conquest of Nebraska

Nebraska was the **first** of these four Great Plains states to be conquered following the empire's victory over the Confederate states. It is located in the Northern Great Plains region. The Nebraska Territory was created by the Kansas-Nebraska Act of 1854 which had led to the secession of the Confederate states. The re-conquest of the Confederate states would have been difficult, if not impossible, without the abolition of slavery.

Despite the empire's intense hatred of **Blacks** Lincoln needed Blacks in his armed forces to win the invasion he had foolishly started. With empires the ends always justify the means. America's "Civil War" freed the slaves so that the Confederate states would be deprived of their labour and lose the war. Blacks would take a giant step up the freedom ladder from slavery to **third class** citizens. This was the one good outcome of that brutal **imperial** act.

The need to preserve slavery to keep the empire intact ended with the defeat of the Confederacy. The empire could now expand more quickly as there would no longer be confrontation and hypocritical "compromises" with the **slave** states to preserve balance in the US Senate. More importantly, the unified empire could now devote all of its massive armed forces to slaughtering First Nations.

The empire had already built a series of forts in preparation for its invasion of Nebraska such as Fort Lisa, Fort Crook, Fort Atkinson and Fort Robinson, beginning as early as 1806. Omaha, Nebraska became one of the major cities in the Great Plains and headquarters of the Union Pacific

Railroad. The Union Pacific Railroad was incorporated in the same year that President Lincoln passed his Homestead Act. First Nations land in Nebraska was given away to both the Union Pacific Railroad and the **White** homesteaders.

While the empire slaughtered the First Nations and their buffalo herds the "iron horse" made it much easier to bring large numbers of **Whites** to populate the stolen land. Within seven years the Union Pacific Railroad, together with the Central Pacific Railroad, would cross the entire width of the American continent. That was truly the "final solution" to the "Indian problem." White immigrants could cross the Atlantic by steam ship and quickly reach the furthest western state of the union to inhabit all of the land once inhabited by the First Nations. The White immigrants of Nebraska honoured President Lincoln for his gifts by naming their capital city *Lincoln*. Nebraska was admitted to the empire as the 37th state on March 1, 1867.

US Invasion and Conquest of Colorado

Colorado became the 38th state of the empire on August 1, 1876. This was the contribution of President Ulysses Grant to the expansion of the empire. White settlers had poured into Colorado in large numbers as a result of the Pike Peak gold rush of 1859. This led to the creation of the Colorado Territory on February 28, 1861. First Nations from whom the land was stolen included the Cheyenne, Comanche, Kiowa, Shoshoni, Arapaho, Pawnee and Ute Nations. These First Nations were brutally massacred or forcibly removed from the land after their defeat by the empire in 1865.

Europeans and Americans had begun to establish trading posts and settlements along the Arkansas and South Platte Rivers in the 1830's. American homesteaders arrived after the Kansas-Nebraska Act of 1854. In 1858, William Larimer filed a gold claim on the South Platte which he called Denver City. The empire hastened to establish territorial rights in 1861 to exploit the gold, silver, coal and other mineral wealth of the Rocky Mountains.

The Cheyenne and Arapaho Nations were forced by the empire in 1861 to give up land for **White** miners and homesteaders. Most of the Pike Peak miners settled in Denver which is today Colorado's largest city. The 1860 discovery of gold in Central City caused another influx of miners. Two railroads, the Denver Pacific and the Kansas Pacific brought the "iron horse" to Denver in 1870, sealing the fate of the First Nations. Colorado's silver boom began with the discovery of silver in 1879 at Leadville forcing the Ute and Shoshone Nations off their land.

Open warfare with the First Nations broke out in 1863. The First Nations were being forced to give up more and more of their hunting grounds. The White settlers and Colorado Volunteers of the empire's army had superior arms and defeated the Cheyenne, Kiowa, Comanche and Arapaho by 1865. US Army commander, John Chivington, attacked a First Nations campsite at Sand Creek on November 29, 1864 while all of the First Nations warriors were out hunting. The Colorado militia led by Chivington slaughtered and scalped all of the women, children and elders.

The *Sand Creek massacre* was "investigated" by the empire but it did not stop the removal of the First Nations from their traditional hunting grounds in Colorado. The defeated First Nations were forced to move from Colorado to Oklahoma.

The Ute and Shoshone Nations inhabited the areas in and west of the Rocky Mountains. The gold rush had led to the removal of the First Nations east of the Rocky Mountains. However, there were many small battles between the Whites and the First Nations west of the Rocky Mountains as well. When silver was discovered at Leadville in 1879 it started a silver boom which lasted longer than the earlier gold boom.

This new influx of silver miners led to the *Ute War* and the forced removal of the remaining First Nations from Colorado to Utah. The confrontation began in 1878 when the Indian Agent, Nathan

Meeker, tried to force the Ute Nation off the White River Reservation. Victory by the empire forced the Ute Nation to surrender their land and move to a reservation in Utah.

US Invasion and Conquest of North and South Dakota

The Dakota First Nation, also called the Sioux Nation, had both their land and their name stolen by the ever expanding American Empire. The empire's theft of the Dakotas dates back to the creation of the Louisiana Territory in 1805. Both Meriwether Lewis and William Clark were rewarded with governorships of the Territory for doing President Jefferson's bidding in "exploring" the land for the empire.

The Dakota Nation was one of several First Nations inhabiting the vast Territory. They had tried to stop Lewis and Clark from exploring their land in 1804 but when they were unable to do so peacefully they decided not to resort to violence. Lewis and Clark had clearly signaled their own intention to use violence. The Dakota Nation was forced to surrender most of their land to the empire as Americans moved into the Minnesota Territory.

In 1838 the empire had carved out the separate Iowa Territory from the vast Louisiana Territory. Then in 1849 the empire had carved out the separate Minnesota Territory from the Iowa Territory. Finally, in 1861, the empire had created the Dakota Territory out of what was left of the Minnesota Territory after Minnesota had become a state. As with the invasion of Nebraska the empire built a series of forts including Fort Snelling, Fort Howard, Fort Crawford and Fort Armstrong, to assist Americans willing to steal the land of the Dakota Nation and other First Nations.

In 1851 the empire forced the Dakota Nation to sign two treaties surrendering most of their land in the Minnesota Territory and confining over 7,000 to two reservations. Promised cash payments exceeding $3 million were never made. As usual such surrenders reinforce the empire's use of force to steal more and more land until open warfare annihilates future opposition. This initial surrender of land enabled the empire to create the state of Minnesota in 1858.

The Dakota Nation had lived peacefully with European traders and settlers including the French and English. They were forced into open warfare by the wanton greed of the American Empire beginning with the Dakota War of 1862 referred to in Chapter 2. The Dakota's chief, Little Crow, initially defeated the empire's forces led by Henry Sibley at the Battle of Birch Coulee. Three weeks later Little Crow was defeated by Sibley at the Battle of Wood Lake.

President Lincoln abolished the two treaties signed in 1851 and proceeded to remove the Dakota Nation from the two reservations which had been created by the treaties. They were placed in **concentration camps** before the survivors were moved out of the state of Minnesota to the newly created Dakota Territory. Whites had settled Sioux City and Yankton in South Dakota between 1856 and 1858. The Yankton Treaty of 1858 had forced the Dakota Nation to surrender much of their remaining land in what became the Dakota Territory. This further theft of Dakota land by White settlers helped the Whites in what was still the unorganized portion of the Minnesota Territory gain territorial status in 1861. One of those prominent White settlers to successfully lobby the empire for territorial status was the brother-in-law of Abraham Lincoln. Yankton became the capital of the new Dakota Territory.

The Dakota War of 1862 was only the beginning of two decades of intermittent warfare between the empire and the Dakota Nation. The 1862 war in Minnesota spilled over into the Dakotas and continued until 1865. This was followed by the Red Cloud War of 1866-1868. The Fort Laramie Treaty of 1868 ending the Red Cloud War guaranteed exclusive rights to the First Nations in the Great Sioux Reservation, including the Black Hills which were sacred ground for the First Nations.

Despite these wars White settlers continued to migrate into the Dakotas especially after the Northern Pacific Railroad brought the "iron horse." The Dakota Southern Railroad reached the territorial capital of Yankton in 1873. The empire invited Europeans to populate the land stolen from the Dakota Nation. The land was well suited to the cultivation of wheat.

A gold rush began in 1874 after George Armstrong Custer ignored the Fort Laramie Treaty and invaded the sacred land of the Dakota Nation to steal the gold in the Black Hills. This led to the Black Hills War of 1876-1877. While Lt. Colonel Custer was invading sacred land searching for gold General Philip Sheridan was killing off the buffalo herds.

General George Crook's imperial forces were defeated at the Battle of Rosebud and Custer was defeated a week later at the Battle of the Little Big Horn, June 25, 1876. In the end imperial forces prevailed over the First Nations and the gold rush enabled the empire to steal another 7 million acres of First Nations land in the Black Hills with the peace treaty of 1877. The decade following 1877 was called the *Great Dakota Boom* because there was a massive influx of Whites into the Dakotas.

The US Congress passed an Act on March 2, 1889 which confiscated another 9 million acres of land in the Black Hills forcing the Dakota Nation into six tiny reservations. The influx of Whites together with the confinement of the First Nations led to the creation of the states of North Dakota and South Dakota on November 2, 1889. The empire had expanded to 40 states.

US Invasion and Conquest of Montana

The American Empire continued its theft of First Nations land westward from the Dakotas into Montana. The empire created the Montana Territory in 1864 and built more forts such as Fort Shaw and Fort C. F. Smith to subjugate the First Nations and steal their land. Like the Black Hills gold was found in Montana.

The Battle of Rosebud, June 17, 1876, took place in Montana Territory. Having invaded the Black Hills of Dakota General George Armstrong Custer moved against the Sioux Nation, led by Sitting Bull. The Crow, Blackfoot, Cheyenne, Arapaho and other First Nations had been pushed westward into Montana by an ever expanding empire bent on wiping out every trace of the **Red** race of people. The Crow Nation had migrated north of the Big Horn Mountains more than a century before hoping to escape the wrath of this military juggernaut.

Chief Crazy Horse had led the Lakota and Cheyenne Nations against General George Crook at the Battle of Rosebud. The Cheyenne Nation had joined forces with the Lakota after they had been massacred at Sand Creek in Montana in 1864. Together they had avenged the Sand Creek massacre by inflicting the empire's worst army defeat in the Great Plains on December 21, 1866. Their defeat of George Crook on June 17, 1876 prevented Crook from joining forces with Custer on June 25. At the same time Crazy Horse was able to join forces with Sitting Bull to defeat Custer and his infamous 7th Cavalry in Eastern Montana.

Custer's defeat and humiliation at the Battle of the Little Big Horn on June 25, 1876, did not in any way discourage this ruthless warmongering empire. It was "Custer's Last Stand" and a sweet victory for the First Nations. But it only postponed the inevitable for a fleeting moment in time.

The retaliation of the empire was merciless. Within a year of Custer's defeat the Lakota was forced to surrender the Black Hills, Crazy Horse forced to surrender to the US army, Sitting Bull was forced to flee to Canada and the Cheyenne Nation was forcibly moved south to the Oklahoma Territory. On November 8, 1889, Montana became the 41st state of the Union representing a further theft of 147,000 square miles of First Nations land.

US Invasion and Conquest of the Pacific Northwest States of Washington and Idaho

Despite the aggressive nature revealed by George Washington and the other founding fathers of the American Empire by invading Canada even before independence had been won from England, none of the founding fathers would have imagined that within a century of declaring independence from England their aggressive empire would have been invading and conquering First Nations land in the Pacific Northwest.

It was therefore appropriate to name one of these conquered states after the man who had set the precedent for ruthless and aggressive military expansionism at any cost to human suffering, **George Washington.** So it was that Washington's empire created Washington Territory on February 8, 1853 despite fierce opposition from the First Nations who had been pushed further and further westward and northward by the American juggernaut.

Many a First Nation has been brought to "justice" by the empire for stealing a white settler's cow to feed his starving family. The empire steals an entire continent and the world glorifies its theft in the name of spreading freedom, democracy and civilized behaviour. This double standard simply boggles the mind. The empire would now have to cross the Pacific Ocean to expand westward and it had already begun to do just that. It was on its way to invading and conquering the planet with the blessings of an ignorant or submissive human race. That so many today still holds this **evil** empire in such high regard is a testimony to the naivety of the human race.

US Invasion and Conquest of Washington

American explorers and fur traders arrived by sea in Washington after the Spanish Nootka Convention of 1790. Americans joined the trade in sea otter pelts in 1792. The Lewis and Clark expedition had reached Washington on October 10, 1805. In 1819 the US ousted Spain as an imperial competitor by signing the Adam-Onis Treaty with Spain.

England relinquished its imperial claims to this First Nations land on June 15, 1846 when it signed the Treaty of Oregon with the US. This gave the US a free hand in stealing the land from the many First Nations who had lived here comfortably for centuries fishing and hunting. The Columbia River, in particular, provided a rich harvest of salmon. The abundance of cedar trees provided lumber for homes and canoes and bark for clothing.

Some Americans using the Oregon Trail to California settled north in the Tumwater area of Washington beginning in 1846. White settlers lobbied for territorial status and Isaac Stevens was appointed as governor. Olympia became the territorial capital. As usual this was a prelude to statehood which was achieved on November 11, 1889. The empire had stolen another 71,000 square miles of First Nations land.

US Invasion and Conquest of Idaho

First Nations inhabiting Idaho included the Nez Perce, Shoshone and Coeur d'Alene. Like Washington State, fur traders and missionaries were the first Americans to explore Idaho. The Lewis and Clark expedition reached Idaho about two months before reaching Washington State. Like Washington State, a few Americans using the Oregon Trail to California, settled in Idaho.

England relinquished imperial competition for Idaho with the American Empire, when it signed the Treaty of Oregon in 1846. A sizeable American settlement began in 1856 in Cache Valley. Then gold was discovered nearby in 1862. The influx of miners led to the inevitable war with the First Nations whose land the Americans were stealing. The Battle of Bear River between the empire's army and the Shoshone Nation took place on January 29, 1863. The superior force and equipment of the Union army led by Colonel Patrick Connor quickly defeated the Shoshone Nation.

The Union army did not disappoint the empire when it celebrated its victory by killing the children and raping the women. Connor and his men returned to Fort Douglas in Utah as heroes. Connor was promoted to Major General and sent to fight the Cheyenne and Sioux Nations. President Lincoln celebrated the defeat of the Shoshone Nation by creating the Territory of Idaho on March 4, 1863.

Mormons created several settlements in Idaho beginning with Franklin in 1860. The Territory of Idaho attracted many other "undesirable" second-class and third-class Americans in addition to the Mormons. These included Southern Confederates who had lost the "Civil War," Blacks, Chinese and Irish. The "iron horse" arrived in 1869.

Having conquered Washington State in 1889 the empire moved quickly to steal Idaho from the First Nations. Less than a year after the theft of Washington State President Benjamin Harrison admitted Idaho as the 43rd state of the Union on July 3, 1890. Another 84,000 square miles of First Nations land had been stolen for no reason other than wanton greed, military might and the "inalienable right" of **White** Americans to engage in **ethnic cleansing** and the total subjugation of the **Red** race.

US Invasion and Conquest of Wyoming and Utah

The First Nations land in North America has been fought over by Spain, France, England, Holland, Sweden, Mexico, the United States and Canada. None of these empires had legal title to the lands they were fighting for. Likewise, purchase of illegal goods does not transfer legal ownership to the buyer.

Yet historians have knowingly distorted the legality of American imperialism by using terms like the "Louisiana Purchase" or "cessation by Mexico" or "Treaty of Oregon with England." These distortions have been deliberately used by historians to validate their own selfish goal of sanctifying the theft of First Nations land by the American Empire.

US Invasion and Conquest of Wyoming

Wyoming provides an excellent example of the deliberate misinformation by historians. The First Nations land stolen by the American Empire to create the state of Wyoming had parts which intersected with what historians have misleadingly called the "Louisiana Purchase," (828,000 square miles) what historians have misleadingly called the "Mexican cession," (525,000 square miles) and with what two empires, England and the US, illegally settled with the "Treaty of Oregon," (340,000 square miles).

Stolen goods are always purchased well below legal market values especially when the buyer is fully aware that the goods are stolen. The 98,000 square miles of First Nations land stolen by the American Empire to create the state of Wyoming on July 10, 1890, had been fought over by Spain, France, England, Mexico and Texas.

The First Nations which owned the land in Wyoming included the Shoshone, Crow, Lakota and Arapaho Nations. Despite having no gold or silver the empire still envied their land and created the Wyoming Territory on July 25, 1868 using the name of one of the more famous First Nations, Cheyenne, for the name of its capital city.

The land which became the city of Cheyenne had been stolen from the First Nations a year earlier to build the Union Pacific Railroad. The "iron horse" brought the American settlers to Cheyenne. The Cheyenne Nation had consistently fought the construction of the "iron horse." The empire saw no irony in stealing their name after stealing their land. Cheyenne was a typical railroad town shipping cattle to Eastern consumers and populated by soldiers, gamblers, cowboys, ranchers, prostitutes, saloon owners and storekeepers.

US Invasion and Conquest of Utah

Utah attracted Mormons attempting to escape mainstream American religious and social values. While many American settlers used the Oregon Trail to settle in California and the Pacific Northwest the Mormons chose Utah to escape from their fellow Americans. Nevertheless, they contributed to the theft of First Nations land by assisting the empire in adding yet another state to the Union. Furthermore, while the Mormons settled in a relatively smaller area around Salt Lake City the empire stole the entire state consisting of 85,000 square miles of First Nations land.

The initial group of Mormons led by Brigham Young arrived in Salt Lake on July 24, 1847. Some 80,000 Mormons arrived within 20 years of the initial settlement. They came from other American states as well as from Europe. The empire increased its control of the region by defeating Mexico in the Mexican-American War of 1846-48 and creating the Utah Territory on September 9, 1850.

Salt Lake City became the capital in 1856. The empire further attempted to undermine Mormon and First Nations influence by sending its army to fight both the Mormons and the Paiute Nation in 1857. Brigham Young was forced out as governor of the territory and replaced by the empire's governor, Alfred Cumming. The empire constructed Fort Floyd to station troops in Utah. In 1862 the empire constructed Fort Douglas and invited miners to prospect for minerals in Utah. This led to an increase in the non-Mormon American population and growing opposition by First Nations.

The theft of First Nations land in Utah was so great by 1865 that First Nations were dying of starvation. Others were dying from lack of immunity to "White" diseases such as smallpox and tuberculosis. They united under the leadership of the Ute Chief, Antonga Black Hawk, to fight the empire and the settlers. The First Nations waged war for seven long years against an empire determined to exterminate them. They lost to a militarily superior force and Utah became the 45th state of the empire on January 4, 1896.

Utah was the last state conquered by the empire before the end of the century. In a little more than a century of becoming an independent country based on 13 relatively tiny English colonies along the Atlantic coast the American Empire dominated an entire continent which several powerful European empires had fought for and ultimately lost. It was an incredible military, political and propaganda achievement. But it was only the beginning. The American Empire's conquest of First Nations land would continue in the 20th century. The empire would also expand west across the Pacific Ocean and east across the Atlantic Ocean.

CHAPTER 5

The American Empire Challenges Europe, Britain, Russia and Japan for Imperial Dominance: Invasions in the Pacific, Atlantic, Alaska and Panama

Empires rise and expand not only because they are ruthless and unapologetic in their invasions and conquests but also because they have competent leadership. This was certainly true of the American Empire. Its early invasions and conquests of the tiny islands of Midway and Wake in the expansive Pacific Ocean were good examples of that far sighted leadership.

Empires decline and fall not because they lose their ruthless pursuit of new territories and shameless aggression but because of incompetent leadership. The decline of the American Empire is no exception. George W. Bush's invasions of Afghanistan and Iraq, and his planned invasions of Iran and North Korea, had all of the hallmarks of American aggression and unbridled imperialism. But they severely lacked the competent leadership of the earlier invasions and conquests. Barack Obama's invasion of Pakistan is equally ruthless but also lacks any leadership strategy for success.

After 12 years of pummeling the Iraqi infrastructure with non-stop aerial bombing by itself and Britain following the Gulf War of 1991, George W. Bush was certain that his 2003 invasion of Iraq would be a quick "slam dunk" conquest en-route to the empire's conquest of Iran and North Korea. The unexpected tactics of the resistance not only stopped the most powerful empire dead in its tracks, it has effectively begun the demise of that once formidable **evil** empire.

With an economically more powerful China and an energy rich revitalized Russia under President Putin, the once invincible American Empire appears confused, weak, leaderless, intensely hated and searching for a way to avoid total humiliation and disgrace. Its once mighty greenback is shunned by all as military humiliation in Iraq and Afghanistan is combined with economic woes of sub-prime meltdown and financial bankruptcy. President Barack Obama is so lost that he heaps blame on Pakistan for the empire's failures in Afghanistan, including the empire's failure to capture Osama bin Laden.

As we saw in Chapter 3, the American Empire had made inroads into the Caribbean by invading and conquering the largest island, Cuba, made inroads into the Pacific by invading and conquering Hawaii and tested its naval strength by attempting invasions of China and Japan. None of these invasions were seen as major threats to Britain, France or Germany but were of serious concern to Japan and, to a lesser degree, Russia. In this chapter we will pick up where we left off at the end of Chapter 3 by beginning with American invasions in the Pacific up to the end of the nineteenth century.

Part I: US Invasions and Conquests in the Pacific

While the American Empire was consolidating its domination of the American continent it simultaneously looked for conquests offshore to boost its claims to imperial status at least equivalent to those of England, France, Germany, Russia and Japan. England had called it a "puny" power and the American imperialists were eager to shed that image by invading and flexing their military muscle wherever they could.

By the end of the 19th century the American Empire had stolen enough First Nations land and invaded both its northern and southern neighbours to squelch any possible challenge to its hegemony on the American continent. In addition, the American Empire had pushed westward across the Pacific to conquer Hawaii and the Philippines and to **force** both China and Japan to accept unfair trade treaties.

The successful Spanish-American War had not only transferred the Spanish colonies of Cuba and the Philippines to the American Empire but also the Spanish colonies of Puerto Rico on the Atlantic side and Guam on the Pacific side to this quickly expanding American Empire. It was ready to take on the Europeans, British, Russians and Japanese for world domination. Its *Great White Fleet* was ready to challenge the navies of Japan, Germany, Russia and Britain.

American strategy was to encourage British isolation from Europe and sever the British alliance with Japan. American alliance with Britain would keep Europe disunited while making it easier for the American Empire to challenge Japan and Russia in the Pacific. It was not yet strong enough to challenge a united Europe. Continued European disunity was essential for its progress towards world domination. It had already taken on the Spanish Empire successfully in the Caribbean.

While Europe continued its incessant warfare among member states and Britain carved out its own empire outside Europe the new player was testing the "imperial" waters. This new imperialist had worked alongside the European empires to force China to trade with the West as an economic colony and had single handedly forced Japan to trade and compete with the West.

By 1900 the American Empire had honed its strategy for stealing the lands of First Nations and indigenous peoples on the mainland and in Hawaii by combining military aggression with token financial compensation to European empires such as France, England and Spain. It was about to expand this strategy to Cuba and Puerto Rico in the Caribbean and to the Philippines, Guam, Midway Island, Wake Island and Samoa, in the Pacific. We have already explained its theft of First Nations lands on the American continent and the Caribbean, in Florida, Mexico and Cuba, by defeating the Spanish Empire. We now turn to its theft of the Philippines from Spain and the Filipino people and the expansion of its Pacific empire from Hawaii.

Island Hopping Across the Pacific Ocean to an Asian Empire

It did not take much imagination to see that the American Empire was forming a "sea-bridge" across the expansive Pacific Ocean, from its west coast, to position its navy strategically to take on the Japanese in the Pacific and Asia. Just as Hawaii provided a strategic naval base for the empire some 2,000 miles from its western coast, Midway Island provided the second strategic military base, some 1,300 miles from Hawaii, to fortify America's Pacific Empire and to enable the American Empire to compete with England, Europe, Japan and Russia.

Wake Island is about 1200 miles west from Midway Island. Guam is a further 1500 miles west from Wake Island. The biggest prize was, of course, the Philippines which was a mere 1600 miles west from Guam. American Samoa is about 2600 miles south-west of Hawaii and about 750 miles from Fiji. It was only indirectly part of the "sea-bridge" linking the American west coast to the Philippines via Hawaii, Midway, Wake and Guam. With its excellent harbour, American Samoa provided an important coaling station in Pago Pago Bay for the empire's Pacific fleet.

US Invasion and Conquest of the Midway Atoll or Midway Island

The American conquest of the strategic island of Midway as part of its Pacific expansion from Hawaii originated with the use of *guano* as an agricultural fertilizer. Islands rich in guano deposits were occupied by private citizens of the American Empire after the US Congress passed the Guano Islands Act on August 18, 1856. Under this Act, Midway Island became the personal possession of the American, Captain Middlebrooks, in 1856.

Midway Island was colonized by the American Empire in 1867 when it became an unincorporated territory of the US. Unlike the annexation of Hawaii, which later became a state of the Union, the Guano Islands Act did not anticipate that conquests under this Act would ever become states of the Union. Western historians could therefore not apply the hollow argument that this American conquest was not an imperial conquest because the captured territory never became a state of the Union. Midway Island is therefore one of the many *uncolonies* of the American Empire.

US Invasion and Conquest of Wake Atoll or Wake Island

Wake Island was named after the British sea captain, William Wake, who landed on one of the islets in 1796. Commodore Charles Wilkes surveyed Wake Island for the American Empire in 1841. Wilkes led the US Congress sanctioned Navy's *Exploring Expedition* of the Pacific in1838-42. After landing in Fiji in 1840, where the American Empire burnt Fijian villages and killed almost 100 Fijians, the expedition reached Wake Island in 1841 en-route to the Philippines.

Wake Island was not formally annexed by the American Empire until January 17, 1899. The empire's construction of a military base and military occupation of the island in 1941 was not enough to defend the island against the anticipated Japanese invasion. The American Empire re-colonized the island in 1945, using it as a test site for its anti-missile program, despite claims to the island by indigenous inhabitants of the Marshall Islands.

US invasion and conquest of Guam

The surprising ease with which the American Empire stole Guam from Spain is the best indicator of how the Spanish Empire had declined by 1898. Spain had established "imperial" rights to Guam since 1565. Spain had encroached on Portugal's "half of the world," after Ferdinand Magellan had sailed west from the Spanish Empire in the New World. The papal bull of 1493 had given the East to Portugal.

But Spain was determined to pursue Columbus's dream of finding the riches of the East by sailing west. It was not difficult for Magellan to convince King Charles I of Spain to finance his voyage to find the rich spice islands of the Moluccas. After all, Portugal had set the precedent by encroaching on Spain's "half of the world," when it had landed 13 ships in Brazil in 1500.

Magellan set sail from Spain in September 1519, crossed the Atlantic to Brazil, navigated the difficult Strait of Magellan, sailed west across the Pacific and landed on Guam in 1521. Guam is the southernmost of the Mariana Islands and the largest island in Micronesia. Without supplies from Guam's indigenous inhabitants, Magellan may never have been able to reach the Philippines.

Spain colonized the Philippines, Guam, the Caroline Islands and the Mariana Islands. Guam was strategically located between Wake Island and the Philippines. It was no surprise that the American Empire would capture both Guam and the Philippines from Spain in a single war. The American

Empire ordered Captain Henry Glass to capture Guam. Spain surrendered the island in June 1898 without a fight.

The indigenous *Chamorros* were no more able to fight the Americans than they were able to fight the Spaniards. Their numbers had dwindled significantly during the Spanish occupation. They were destined to be colonized by another Western imperialist. In return for "accepting" their status as a colonized people they have been given a single token, non-voting, representative to the American Empire's House of Representatives. US military bases occupy almost 30 percent of this American *uncolony*.

US Invasion and Conquest of Samoa

The American navy invaded and colonized Samoa in March 1899, less than a year after the conquest of Guam. It reflected the ferocious appetite of the American Empire to steal territory wherever it had the military muscle to succeed. As in Hawaii, the American Empire overthrew the Samoan monarchy to steal the islands. The Samoan *Mau* insurgents were unsuccessful in their efforts to drive out the invaders.

Fortunately for the Samoan people, Germany had captured the western half of the Samoan islands. This had prevented complete US domination. The western half regained its independence in 1962 and was admitted to the UN as Samoa. The American Empire continues to refer to independent Samoa as Western Samoa. This is a mini version of the American Empire's insistence on referring to the tiny island of Taiwan as the Republic of China and to the Peoples Republic of China as Communist China.

During the Second World War the American Empire used Samoan men as *child* soldiers. Like Guam, American Samoa has one token, non-voting, representative in the American Empire's House of Representatives. American business and American consumers benefit from the huge American controlled tuna fishery and commercial port facilities in American Samoa. The tuna fishery is American Samoa's primary industry. American multinationals, such as Del Monte Foods which owns the popular StarKist Tuna brand name, pay less than US minimum wages. These multinationals are exempted from the US minimum wage legislation since American Samoa is an *uncolony* of the American Empire.

US Invasion and Conquest of the Philippines

Roosevelt's "splendid little war" against the Spanish Empire in the Caribbean acquired for the US not only the beginnings of its Caribbean empire but rather unexpectedly a significant boost to its claims to a Pacific empire. The American incentive for starting the Spanish-American War was the rich sugar island of Cuba. However, once war was declared its naval presence in the Pacific provided the opportunity to take the Philippines as well. Given its inherent expansionist nature it would certainly not resist such an opportunity. Adding the Philippines to its empire would be as natural as adding Hawaii or Cuba. Unlike Hawaii, which was destined to be a state of the Union, the Philippines, like Cuba, became an American *uncolony*.

The whole purpose of developing a strong navy was to expand the American Empire offshore. The *uncolonies* added to the American Empire would be determined solely by military superiority. Any country or empire militarily weaker than the American Empire was "fair" game. All territorial expansions provide opportunities for new military bases, sources of raw materials and markets for American produce.

Commodore George Dewey commanded the US Pacific fleet during the Spanish-American War. He attacked and defeated the Spanish fleet at the Battle of Manila Bay. With the help of Filipino forces led by Emilio Aguinaldo the American Empire defeated the Spanish army as well. But, like Cuba, the American Empire would find out that it was easier to defeat the Spanish imperial forces than the subsequent Filipino resistance against American colonization.

The Philippines, like Cuba, wanted independence from colonial status, much like the original 13 English colonies which rebelled against English imperialism. The Filipinos, like the Cubans, were unable to defeat Spanish imperialism without American military assistance, much like the original 13 colonies were unable to defeat English imperialism without the military assistance of France. Unlike France, however, the American Empire used the Filipino people, as it had used the Cubans, to replace Spanish imperialism with American imperialism. Initially, neither Cuba nor the Philippines was militarily strong enough to defeat American imperialism. In time, they both were, and the American Empire was largely, though not totally, defeated by both the Cubans and the Filipinos.

Most historians agree that the Filipino rebellion against imperial rule began in 1892 when Andres Bonifacio and a group of freemasons founded the *Katipunan* revolutionary movement in Manila to overthrow Spanish rule by military force. The revolution was not militarily equipped to defeat Spain. Bonifacio was blamed for the failure and executed by the rebels in May, 1897. Thereafter, the revolution was led by General Emilio Aguinaldo. However, Aguinaldo was no more successful against Spain since failure was due to the superior military forces of the Spanish Empire. In August, 1897, Aguinaldo decided to negotiate an end to the revolution, with Spain. Aguinaldo accepted a monetary payment for voluntary exile in Hong Kong.

Aguinaldo saw an opportunity to continue the revolution with American backing as a result of the Spanish-American War of 1898. The War began on April 23, 1898 and the Spanish fleet in Manila was defeated by the American Empire on May 1, 1898. The Americans facilitated the return of Aguinaldo to the Philippines on May 19, 1898 to continue his leadership of the Filipino revolution against imperial rule. As usual, the American Empire lied about its desire to conquer and colonize the Philippines, as it had done in Cuba.

As in Cuba, the American Empire was forging a coalition with the Filipino rebels to reduce American casualties so as to sell the war to a gullible American electorate. Under the leadership of General Aguinaldo, the Filipinos declared independence from Spain on June 12, 1898. The new Filipino Army under General Aguinaldo quickly defeated the Spanish forces outside Manila.

When the American Empire captured Manila on August 13, 1898 it threatened to open fire on the Filipino Army if Aguinaldo attempted to enter Manila. The American Empire insisted that Spain surrendered the Philippines to the Americans not to the rebels. It would not be difficult to persuade Spain to do that. Empires prefer to exchange colonies during the peace negotiations rather than surrender to rebels.

The one exception was the rebellion of the 13 English colonies, where England chose to negotiate with the rebels over the French Empire. In addition, the American Empire was willing to make a modest financial payment to Spain in exchange for the Philippines as it had done with Napoleon for the Louisiana Territory. In Louisiana, the First Nations fought the American Empire and lost. In the Philippines the Filipinos would fight the American Empire and lose as well.

The Filipino Resistance to the American Invasion

The American Empire invaded the Philippines to colonize it in the same way as it invaded Iraq and Afghanistan to colonize them. As a relative latecomer to imperialist conquests, it would naturally face stiffer resistance from the conquered people than the older European empires. Just as the Cubans and Filipinos had had enough of imperialism under Spain by the time the American Empire arrived, so too had the Vietnamese tired of imperialism under France by the time the American Empire invaded.

In like fashion the American Empire is finding out that the Afghans had had enough of imperialism under the Soviet Union, by the time the American Empire invaded with help from Canada and Britain and that the Iraqis had had enough of imperialism under Britain, by the time the American Empire invaded.

The Philippines declared war on the American Empire on June 2, 1899. The American Empire had not yet invented the term, "terrorist" so the Filipinos were called "bandits" by the invader. It's an upside down world which calls those who defend their country against American invasion, communists, bandits or terrorists. Western civilization continues to degrade itself by latching on to the last remnants of American leadership and American hypocrisy.

The defeat of the First Nations on the American mainland by 1899 enabled the American Empire to send the generals who had defeated the First Nations to fight the Filipinos. An empire must find new wars to keep its generals in steady employment. Idle generals are often tempted to take over the civilian government.

As in Iraq and Afghanistan today, the Filipinos quickly recognized that they would lose a head to head war with a militarily superior American army. Their strategy, like the Iraqi and Afghan insurgents today, was to harass the Americans with hit and run attacks. They had time on their side since it was their country. The Filipinos were there to stay. The Americans needed a quick victory to be able to move to their next imperial conquest.

The imperial government in Washington cannot afford a long drawn out war in a single conquest when there are many more colonies to capture from the other empires. In the competition for imperial dominance you need quick victories. The long Filipino resistance frustrated the American Empire in the first years of the twentieth century almost as much as the long Iraqi/Afghan resistance is frustrating the American Empire today.

The more than100,000 strong Filipino Resistance initially engaged the American imperial troops, despite their inferior weapons and lack of munitions. Both sides suffered huge casualties. Once it was clear that the American Empire had dug its heels in for a protracted war the Filipinos resorted to guerilla warfare to offset their weapons disadvantage. As in Iraq and Afghanistan today, the lack of a quick imperial victory raised doubts about the wisdom of the invasion, in Washington. President William McKinley, who had authorized the imperial expansion, was now under attack in the American Congress.

McKinley had honed his military qualification for America's top job of Commander-in-Chief during the Civil War. He formed a lasting military and political relationship with another war hawk, turned Commander-in-Chief, Rutherford Hayes. In his military career, Hayes, as McKinley's superior officer, helped McKinley become a captain in the imperial army. In his political career, Hayes helped McKinley's election to the empire's lower house.

In Congress, McKinley lobbied hard for the American Empire's annexation of Hawaii. In the 1896 presidential election, McKinley ran on an expansionist imperial ticket against the anti-imperialist, William Jennings Bryan. Winning that election gave him the "mandate" to annex Hawaii and secure the military base in Pearl Harbor. This was an important step in his invasion of the Philippines and imperial conquests in the Pacific. His stated goal for invading the Philippines was to secure a military base to move against China and control Asia.

McKinley's re-election in 1900 gave him the mandate to continue to pursue that goal despite the fierce resistance of the Filipino army. As the American electorate chose the warmongering George W. Bush over John Kerry in 2004, so too did the American electorate choose the warmongering McKinley over William Jennings Bryan in 1900.

The Filipino resistance changed its engagement tactics against McKinley's imperial forces after suffering several defeats by the American Empire during head-to-head combats in 1899. Since the

American electorate had signaled by re-electing McKinley that the American Empire was in the Philippines for the long haul, the Filipino resistance restructured for protracted guerilla warfare against the invaders. The response of the American Empire was brutal. Entire Filipino villages were burnt to the ground.

Tecumseh Sherman had perfected the American Empire's scorched earth war methods during the American Civil War. Think of the American destruction of Fallujah in Iraq in November, 2004 and you get a good picture of American atrocities in the Philippines against the Filipino insurgency. The video, "Fallujah-The day after," documents the horrific devastation of Fallujah, mass graves and all, by the American imperialists. Like the Philippines, the American electorate signaled to the Iraqis and Afghans that the American Empire was there for the long haul when it re-elected George W. Bush in 2004.

The American Empire called the ethnic cleansing of Fallujah, "Operation Phantom Fury." This American barbarism of destroying civilian villages to "save the conquered inhabitants," was practiced in the Philippines and later in Vietnam, Afghanistan and Iraq. To this day the American Empire does not consider **non-whites** as human beings. Their wholesale slaughter is viewed by the American Empire and the Western media as the killing of those who are somehow less than human because their skin colour is not white. The killing of mothers and their children is even "celebrated" by the West as somehow promoting women's rights. That is how twisted the mind-set of the West continues to be.

It was the American Empire which invented *concentration camps* during its occupation of the Philippines. As many as one million Filipinos were killed by American atrocities. American torture and killing of Filipino prisoners was as common in the Philippines as it was in Abu Ghraib and My Lai. American soldiers openly bragged about their use of torture against Filipino civilians. As in Iraq and Afghanistan, American atrocities were justified as "collateral damage" in fighting for what the West proudly calls "freedom and democracy." Foreign journalists who wrote about American atrocities or Filipino kindness to American captives were expelled from the Philippines by the American Empire.

The capture of the leader of the Filipino resistance, General Aguinaldo, combined with the demoralizing effects of American brutality, brought several victories to the American Empire. Filipino resistance continued under General Mariano Trias followed by General Miguel Malvar. By 1902, the American Empire had a firm grip on its colonial conquest. The strength of the insurgency waned and died slowly by 1913.

Annexation of the Philippines to the American Empire was rejected by **White** Americans fearful of an increase in the potential political power of a larger percentage of non-whites who may one day get to vote in democratic elections. American **racism** saved the Filipino people from permanent colonization by the American Empire. According to the American military governor, General Arthur MacArthur, shooting Filipino prisoners was not the correct explanation for the post-war body count of 15 Filipino soldiers killed for every wounded Filipino soldier. It's just that shooting Filipino prisoners killed them because of their "inferior race" compared with the White prisoners. **White** prisoners would have survived a Filipino firing squad because of their superior race.

The temporary American colonization of the Philippines lasted until 1946. Americans confiscated Filipino land previously captured by the Catholic Church and excluded Filipinos from political office by making English the official language. During the Second World War, Japan defeated the American Empire in the Philippines, beginning with the Japanese conquest of Manila on January 2, 1942. General Douglas MacArthur, the son of Arthur MacArthur, was forced by the Japanese invasion to flee the Philippines.

As in China, the American Empire fought both the Japanese and the Filipino communists. The Treaty of Manila granted independence to the Philippines on July 4, 1946. The Second World War had made it difficult for the European and Japanese empires to deny independence to many of their colonies. Likewise the Second World War made it much more difficult for the American Empire to deny independence to some of its *uncolonies.*

Part II: US Invasions and Conquests in the Atlantic, Alaska and Panama

In the period up to and including the First World War the American Empire expanded across two oceans. American victory in the Spanish-American War of 1898 effectively replaced Spain with the US as the empire which would compete with Britain, France, Germany, Russia and Japan, for imperial dominance in the twentieth century. Britain and France would both be severely weakened by the First World War. After 1918, the US would continue to compete with Germany, Japan and Russia.

The Second World War destroyed Germany and Japan. After 1945, the US would have to compete only with Russia. With the collapse of the Soviet Union the American Empire became the world's only super-power. Despite widespread peace demonstrations and Hollywood movies which always push the envelope, the American Empire has never retreated from a war it was winning. The unfortunate reality is that insurgents must sacrifice their lives in massive numbers to defeat American imperialism.

As the American Empire amasses more WMD's while using the propaganda of the entire Western media as well as punitive economic and military sanctions to prevent others, such as Iran and North Korea today, from acquiring WMD's, it becomes more and more difficult to restrain the military aggression of this **evil** super power.

In Part II of this chapter we document the continued expansion of the American Empire from its east coast to the Caribbean, its northern expansion into Alaska and its southern expansion into Panama both before and after the First World War. The Spanish-American War led to American colonization of both Cuba and Puerto Rico in the Caribbean. The First World War led to the American colonization of the Virgin Islands in the Caribbean. We covered the invasion and conquest of Cuba in Chapter 3. Here we focus on the other Caribbean conquests.

We deal with the American invasions of Panama at some length because of its importance in the long history of the American Empire's continued subjugation of Latin America which began immediately after the end of three centuries of Western European subjugation of Latin America. In 2010, Latin America is only now beginning to have some success in rebelling against American imposed dictators, American genocide committed against the indigenous peoples of Latin America, economic imperialism of American multinationals in Latin America, incessant military crimes committed by the US in Latin America and the covert operations by the CIA to defeat any democratic movement by Latin Americans.

US Invasions and Conquests in the Atlantic

While the primary goal of the US war against Spain in 1898 was the conquest of Cuba, it is the inherent nature of imperialism to conquer all that is militarily possible. It was therefore no surprise that the American Empire invaded the Caribbean island of Puerto Rico in July 1898. Prior to landing troops on July 25, 1898, the US navy blockaded San Juan harbour and bombed Puerto Rico's capital city, San Juan, from its ships in the harbour. Spain surrendered Puerto Rico, along with Cuba, the Philippines and Guam, to the American Empire.

While the American Empire envied the entire Caribbean since the infamous Monroe Doctrine of 1823 it bided its time while increasing its military arsenal. At the same time the incessant squabbling among the Europeans reduced their military capabilities. The Europeans returned to open warfare again in 1914. This provided the ideal opportunity for the American Empire to seize strategic chunks of the Caribbean. The Danes were an easy military target and the Danish Caribbean colonies were strategically located to safeguard any naval attack on the Panama Canal.

Denmark was a relatively small player in the European colonization of the New World. During the glory days of the state chartered monopolies such as the Hudson Bay Company, the Dutch and English East India monopolies, there were also West India state monopolies such as the Dutch, French and Danish West India Companies. The Danish West India Company was patterned after the very successful Dutch East India and West India Companies.

The West India state monopolies exploited both the Caribbean and West Africa because of the need for African slaves to enrich the European plantation owners in the Caribbean. It was therefore no coincidence that the Danish West India Company was granted a state monopoly by Denmark to trade in both the Danish Caribbean islands and the Danish conquests in Ghana.

Denmark colonized the tiny Caribbean islands of St. Thomas, St. John, St. Croix and Water Island between 1670 and 1769. While all of the European empires coming after the Spanish engaged in "illegal" trade with the Spanish colonies, especially the very profitable slave trade, it was the Danes who fully exploited "illegal" inter-imperial trade.

This was the age of mercantilism when empires restricted trade to their own colonies and with the mother country. However, it was militarily impossible to enforce mercantilism. The tiny Danish Caribbean colonies were mostly slave depots and safe havens for Danish ships engaged in the lucrative business of transporting African slaves to the Caribbean colonies for sale to the other European empires. Like the other European empires, the Danes colonized the West African coast mostly to secure their slave warehouses where the slaves were forcibly kept before transportation to their Caribbean slave depots.

US Invasion and Conquest of Puerto Rico

Puerto Rico, like most of the Caribbean, was inhabited primarily by the Arawak Nation. During the Spanish colonization from 1508 to 1898, Puerto Rico's Arawak population declined significantly while the numbers of Africans and Europeans increased. Spain had successfully fought off attacks by both the dominant Arawak Nation as well as the next largest First Nation in the Caribbean, the Carib Nation.

Spain had also successfully defended its conquest from the other European empires, England, France and Holland. Like Cuba and other colonies in the New World, Puerto Ricans attempted to rebel against colonialism prior to the US invasion. Spain granted a high degree of autonomy to both Cuba and Puerto Rico on November 25, 1897. Puerto Ricans elected their first semi-independent government under this "Autonomous Charter," on February 9, 1898.

American rhetoric to the contrary, US intervention and conquest of Puerto Rico replaced Puerto Rico's emancipation from Spanish colonialism with entrenched American colonialism. Puerto Rico came under US military rule following the American conquest. US military rule coincided with disastrous hurricanes in August 1899. The destruction of Puerto Rico's economy made it much more difficult for Puerto Ricans to resist American economic imperialism.

US military rule enabled the unbridled access of American multinationals to Puerto Rico's agricultural resources of tobacco, sugar and coffee. The US unabashedly stamped its economic imperialism by making the American greenback the official currency of Puerto Rico and English the official language of the Puerto Rican judiciary. The civilian government established in Puerto Rico in1900 embraced free trade with its new imperial master.

Puerto Ricans were granted US citizenship in 1917 when Puerto Rico became a US territory. This allowed the US to extend the military draft to Puerto Ricans. Over 20,000 Puerto Ricans were drafted to fight for the expansion of the American Empire during World War I. The post-war economic boom helped the Puerto Rican economy. However, this increasing economic integration with the US led to economic disaster during the Great Depression of the 1930's.

Nationalists seeking independence from the American Empire were killed or imprisoned by the pro-American governments installed by the US. Economic stagnation without political independence led may Puerto Ricans to migrate to the US. The Puerto Rico independence movement took its battle to US soil with an attempted assassination of President Harry Truman on November 1, 1950. This forced the American Empire to permit a free vote by Puerto Ricans on a constitution granting the status of *Free Associate State* to Puerto Rico on July 25, 1952. In a free vote on July 23, 1967 Puerto Ricans rejected the option of become a state of the **evil** empire. The Puerto Rican economy has benefited from industrialization and expansion of its tourist sector.

US Invasion and conquest of the Virgin Islands

As in most of the Caribbean the two major First Nations in the Virgin Islands were the Arawak Nation and the Carib Nation. Today the majority of the population is of African descent. Whites are now a larger percentage of the population than First Nations.

The First World War provided the opportunity for the American Empire to steal the Danish Caribbean colonies. If Spain had not been militarily capable of preventing the American Empire from stealing its Caribbean colonies, Denmark was even less militarily capable. Of course, the American Empire would never publicly profess the notion that might was right but that was always the reality of American conquests. Only those who have militarily defeated the American Empire such as Canada, China, Cuba, North Korea, Vietnam, Afghanistan and Iraq, have been saved from American colonization.

The American Empire sweetened the pot by offering the Danes US$25 million in 1917 for a peaceful surrender. Previous offers of purchase by the American Empire had always been rejected by Denmark. The Danes accepted the 1917 offer only because it was clear that the Americans would launch a successful invasion since no European empire, fully occupied by World War I, was free to come to the aid of Denmark.

The American Empire took possession of three of the four islands on March 31, 1917, re-naming the Danish West Indies the *US Virgin Islands.* The fourth island, Water Island, was added in 1944 for an additional payment of US$10,000. The US Virgin Islands is a territory of the American Empire to this day. It has a single token non-voting representative in the American Empire's House of Representatives. Like Puerto Rico, the inhabitants have rejected becoming a state of the **evil** empire.

US Invasion and Conquest of Alaska

The name William H. Seward is as synonymous with America's successful invasion and conquest of Alaska as is the name George W. Bush synonymous with America's failed invasion and conquest of Iraq. What is less well known is that Seward was an important player in America's invasion and conquest of Hawaii, Midway Island, Panama and the Danish colonies in the Caribbean. It was Seward who explicitly lobbied for the invasion and conquest of Midway because of its strategic importance in enabling American ascendancy in the Pacific.

In 1867, Seward lobbied hard for the American Empire to add two of the Danish Caribbean colonies, St. Thomas and St. John, to secure port facilities for the ever expanding US navy. While unsuccessful in convincing Americans to conquer the Danish Caribbean in 1867, it was, nevertheless, quite a career coup for Seward to have added both Midway and Alaska to the American Empire that same year. The ambitious Secretary of State for Abraham Lincoln was expanding the empire both westward and northward.

In 1867, only a few Americans could relate to Seward's long-term goal of World domination by the American Empire. By 1867, America had invaded and conquered more land than it could ever populate. The conquest of Alaska was called "Seward's Folly," by Americans who did not yet dream of America dominating the world. Acquiring so much more land, over half a million square miles, made no sense to those who could not share Seward's vision of conquering the entire continent.

Smart Canadians knew what Seward's agenda was. The Canadians and British had stolen land from the First Nations which the Americans envied. Alaska was a stepping stone to relieving the Canadians of that land as the Americans had done in Mexico. Canada's so called sovereignty relies heavily on us doing the bidding of the **evil** empire to the south. Currently we fight for the American Empire in Afghanistan. Canadian soldiers kill Afghans for no reason other than fear of American aggression against their own country. Likewise, Canadian governments of all stripes endanger the lives of all Canadians by waging an illegal and immoral war against the Afghan people only to keep the Americans from confiscating our fresh water and oil.

Pre-American Alaska

Alaska was home to the Inuit and First Nations such as the Haida, Aleut and Athabascan Nations. They hunted the caribou, bear, rabbits, sea lions, whales and sea otters and fished for salmon.

The Russians invaded and conquered Alaska to exploit the profitable fur trade in sea otter pelts after Vitus Bering and Alexei Chirikov reached Alaska with two ships of the Russian Navy in 1741. The Russians, like the French in North America, were in Alaska for trade rather than colonization. They established trading posts. Like the French in North America, the Russians enslaved and destroyed the livelihood of the Natives. As in North America, many died from diseases for which they had no natural immunity.

In 1799, the *Russian-American Company* received a charter from Tsar Paul I to monopolize and expand Russian trade with Alaska and the Aleutian Islands. Such monopolies were commonly used by empires at that time to trade with far off lands which had not yet been fully colonized by the empire. Forts were constructed to protect the trading posts from both the indigenous inhabitants and competition from the Americans and British.

In 1812, the company constructed one fort, *Fort Ross,* as far south as Sonoma County in California, to protect its trading monopoly along the west coast of North America. The Russian settlement around Fort Ross represented the southernmost reach of the Russian Empire in the Pacific Northwest. While Fort Ross was one of several Russian fur trading posts in the Pacific Northwest, the surrounding settlement was expanded to grow food and other supplies for the Russian trading posts in Alaska. The later decline of the fur trade led the Russians to abandon the settlement in 1841.

The American Invasion and Conquest

Americans competed with the Russians in the valuable trade in sea-otter pelts. The first Americans to explore California came to challenge the Russians for the lucrative market for sea-otter pelts in China. A single pelt could fetch a price of $300 in China. Together with the Russians, the Americans fished the sea-otter to extinction.

By 1867, the commercial value of Alaska to the Russians had fallen significantly. At the same time, the First Nation and Inuit population had been decimated by disease and loss of livelihood.

The Russian invasion of Alaska had made it easy for the American conquest in 1867. The Russians were happy to relinquish imperial competition with the US for the $7.2 million they received from the Americans.

The American Empire added over 663,000 square miles of Inuit and First Nations land on October 18, 1867. The American Empire clearly had no limit to its greed for First Nations land and its desire to ethnically cleanse the conquered land for **White** domination. Despite the relatively small influx of Whites, the decimation of the indigenous population has led to Whites outnumbering First Nations and Inuit, 5:1. In 1959, Alaska became the largest state of the Union, over twice the size of Texas. This large conquest of land makes Alaska one of the least densely populated states of the Union.

Most Americans may not have understood Seward's hunger for First Nations and Inuit land in 1867. But all Americans understand the value of gold. American miners poured into Alaska in the 1890's after the discovery of gold. Gold was first discovered in Nome in 1898. A year after this discovery the population of Nome exceeded 10,000. A decade later the population of Nome doubled to 20,000. In 1902, gold was discovered in Fairbanks. Fairbanks soon overtook Nome as Alaska's largest city. By 1912, the **White** population of Alaska was deemed sufficient by the American Empire to grant it territorial status.

The Second World War boosted Alaska's fortunes in the American Empire. The Japanese Empire retaliated against American encroachment in the Pacific by attacking Hawaii and capturing three of the Aleutian Islands nearest to Japan. The American Empire responded with military bases in Alaska and the construction of the Alaska Highway. Construction of the Alaska Highway began in March 1942. Canada had little choice but to accept the American highway through Canadian territory.

Most Canadians also believe the rather idiotic notion that the US is the self-appointed leader of the free world. The self-styled "freedom loving empire" had no qualms about using its military bases in Alaska to supply the US designated "evil empire" of the Soviet Union with war materials during the Second World War. The Soviet Union and Josef Stalin were conveniently **not** evil or communist when they were helping the American Empire defeat Germany and Japan.

Alaska struck gold again in 1968. This time it was "black gold." Oil was discovered in Prudhoe Bay in 1968. Pipeline construction began in March 1974. Native land claims which had been languishing since the American invasion of 1867 suddenly became urgent. Agreement was reached with the original inhabitants in December 1971 to enable the construction of the pipeline. The original inhabitants of Alaska were given legal title to about 10 percent of Alaska in addition to a monetary compensation of $96.5 million.

The First US Invasion and Conquest of Panama

We have seen that the American Empire expanded off the American Mainland both eastwards and westwards across two oceans. This prompted the American Empire to find a way of connecting its Pacific and Atlantic empires by sea. Water transportation remains one of the cheapest modes of transporting military and economic supplies. Prior to the coming of the railroads the American Empire had used canals to expand and hold its conquests of First Nations lands across the Mainland. The European empires had built the Suez Canal to consolidate and hold their empires. The American Empire would build its own canal to consolidate and hold its Pacific and Atlantic empires.

The conquest of Panama would also consolidate the American Empire's southern expansion across the American continent. Panama, like Cuba, would become another everlasting love-hate relationship with the American Empire. Its invasion and conquest will be a "work in progress." In a rather twisted irony, the US invasions of both Cuba and Panama provided the opportunity for Cubans and Panamanians to struggle for their independence from imperial domination before and after the US invasions. Both Cuba and Panama were caught up in the forefront of the Latin American struggle for independence, first from Spain, then from the US.

Spain had investigated the feasibility of a canal across the narrow Isthmus of Panama as early as 1529. Such a canal would have been invaluable for the transportation of gold and silver from the Spanish mines in Peru to Spain. Panama was an integral part of the Viceroyalty of New Granada established by Spain in 1717. New Granada revolted under the leadership of Simon Bolivar and created the Republic of Columbia in 1819-21. Spain had not succeeded in constructing a canal before this revolution. As with other Spanish colonies which had revolted successfully from Spain, the Republic of Columbia was in a **semi-colonial** status with a United States bent on enforcing the *Monroe Doctrine* of 1823.

In 1831, Venezuela and Ecuador became independent states reducing the size of Colombia. Panama also wanted independence from Colombia but the US intervened to prevent Panamanian independence. By 1900, the US had intervened a record **13 times** to prevent Panama from gaining its independence from Colombia. It would be the US decision to build the Panama Canal which would finally give Panama independence from Colombia but also colonial dependence on the American Empire.

By the time the US expanded its dominion over Columbia the railroad age had been born. Since railroads replaced canals as a cheaper and more reliable means of transportation, the US abandoned Spain's desire for a canal in favour of a railway. The American Empire built the Panama Railway in 1848-55. While railroads were superior to canals for connecting two land masses, such as two American states, it was not as efficient for connecting two oceans. The reason was simple. Cargoes would have to be unloaded and loaded again to the two different ocean carrying ships. This increases the transportation cost immensely. Once this was recognized, interest in a canal returned.

One of the reasons Spain had failed to build the canal was the technical problems. The completion of the Suez Canal in 1869 gave a huge boost to the technical feasibility of a Panama Canal. It was not surprising that France would promote the idea and ask Ferdinand de Lesseps to supervise the project. De Lesseps had successfully completed the Suez Canal with French and Egyptian finance.

Unfortunately, de Lesseps was not the right man for the Panama Canal project. The Panama terrain was totally different from the Suez terrain. De Lesseps began construction in 1880 using Caribbean labour. Technical problems and huge labour force deaths from malaria and yellow fever bankrupted the French project. The American Empire took over the French project in 1902. This required the Americans to negotiate a concession with Colombia as France had done in 1878.

Since the American Empire had been a strong ally of Colombia and had intervened militarily to prevent Panama from seceding from Colombia it may have appeared to President Teddy Roosevelt that a concession from Colombia was a done deal. To Teddy's surprise the Colombian Senate did not ratify the treaty he signed with the Colombian government in 1903.

Roosevelt quickly changed American policy from preventing Panamanian independence to military intervention to guarantee Panama's independence. All Roosevelt needed was a single battleship, the *USS Nashville,* to signal to the Colombian government that the American Empire would not hesitate to use force to obtain the land to build the Panama Canal. In the process, Panama became an "independent" state, with the Americans controlling the *Canal Zone,* five miles of land on both sides of the canal. American firepower stood ready to ensure a pro-American Panamanian state. Panama had become an American *uncolony,* much like the Philippines and Cuba before Fidel Castro.

The American Empire formally recognized the "Republic of Panama" on November 13, 1903. The US signed the *Hay-Bunau Varilla Treaty* on November 18, 1903. Colombia made a last ditch effort to appease the American Empire by offering to grant the land concession to build the canal and moving Colombia's capital from Bogota to Panama City. The American Empire had the firepower to humiliate Colombia and it did just that by shunning all overtures. Moreover, Colombia's attempt to express independence had offended the innate American need for super-power allegiance and also provided the excuse to acquire one more *uncolony* for the empire.

We have seen time and again that the American Empire has no hesitation in dumping its allies if it fits with its latest short-term economic, military and political interests. Colombia learnt that harsh lesson when it tried to negotiate with the American Empire as if it were an independent country. At that time it was, in general, only countries in the New World which had no political independence from the American Empire. After the Second World War, no country in the entire world had complete political or economic independence from the American Empire.

The people of this planet would be fooled time and again by the media rhetoric that each new American invasion was a unique isolated event brought about by some tiny despicable foe that was a military threat to the most powerful empire in history. In every case the American Empire would have planted a somewhat nasty dictator in the puny country which had suddenly become this global threat. Removal of this nasty dictator was a duty of the American Empire since no other nation had the moral fortitude to do it. The media would conveniently ignore the fact that it was the American Empire which had installed the nasty dictator, until many years after the American invasion and conquest.

Historians would then conveniently re-write the truth that it was the American Empire which had manufactured the justification for the American invasion. By that time the American Empire would have moved on to another "unique, isolated, invasion," using exactly the same justification it had used before. It would be another ten years later that the historians would tell the truth about the latest invasion. Even Hollywood, often the institution doing its best to shed some light on the crimes against humanity by the "ugly American," waited seven years to release *Green Zone*, a movie based on the fact that the American Empire had fool proof intelligence that Saddam Hussein had fully dismantled its WMD program since 1991. Matt Damon played the lead role of the naïve American sent on a wild goose chase by his **evil** superiors to search for the non-existent WMD's in Iraq. This cycle of initial lies and later truths would repeat itself endlessly. It is all part of a Western conspiracy to maintain the hegemony of the West since the fifteenth century. Whether you tune in to CNN, BBC or CBC they tell the same professionally packaged lies over and over again.

Today, the focus of the world is on the American invasion of Iraq. The Western media is slowly beginning to reduce the lies it told about that invasion. But the Iraqi invasion has many similarities with the earlier invasion of Panama. In both cases, as in so many others, the American Empire invaded to remove a dictator it had previously installed. The Panamanian dictator was removed by President George Herbert Bush and the Iraqi dictator was removed by President George W. Bush. How much more evidence of continuity in American foreign policy does anyone need? Yet, every invasion is touted by the Western media as an isolated *exception* to America's dedication to peace, non-intervention and republican values of freedom and equality. How many times can the Western media peddle such outrageous propaganda?

The Rise and Fall of General Manuel Antonio Noriega: The Second US Invasion and Conquest of Panama

Teddy Roosevelt had inspired the Spanish-American War which had acquired the American *uncolonies* of Cuba and Puerto Rico in the Atlantic and the Philippines and Guam in the Pacific. As president he had stolen Panama from the First Nations and Colombia. Colombia received a belated monetary bribe of $25 million in 1921 to recognize American sovereignty over Panama.

The First Nations were treated as irrelevant. With Panama as the latest American *uncolony* Teddy had constructed the Panama Canal and operated it as American property even though the $250,000 annual payment to Panama was supposed to be rent. In the US, tenants who pay rent do not have private property rights. The landlord does. Unfortunately, if your tenant happens to be the American Empire you will not have the military muscle to evict him.

Initially, the Panamanian people welcomed the US invasion since it gave them independence from Colombia as well as economic advantages. The American Empire paid the $10 million it had offered to Colombia to Panama as well as annual rent of $250,000. The construction of the canal brought employment and economic opportunities, especially to Panama City.

Panama City had been founded by the Spanish since 1519. It boomed during the years when it became the "transit city" for Peruvian gold and silver in transit to Spain. It got another boost in the 1850's when the US built the railway to enable Americans easier access to the California goldfields. But colonies have a habit of growing up and rebelling against imperialism. Why would Panama be any different?

It should not surprise anyone that the first signs of colonial rebellion against the American Empire came during the poor economic conditions resulting from the Great Depression of the 1930's. The depressed economic conditions made it easier for the leaders of the January 2, 1931 coup against President Florencio Arosemena to gain popular support. The leaders of the coup were the pro-nationalist Arias brothers, Arnulfo and Harmodio.

Harmodio had written a book which had denounced the Monroe doctrine. He won a landslide victory in the 1932 elections, much to the dismay of the American Empire. With major economic problems at home, President Franklin Roosevelt decided against military intervention to remove Harmodio. Roosevelt's *Good Neighbor Policy* of 1936 only emboldened Panamanian dissidents. The centre of Anti-American discussions and rallies was the new University of Panama established by President Harmodio. In 1940, Arnulfo Arias took over the presidency. Arnulfo was even more openly anti-American than his brother.

The Second World War provided an excuse for the American Empire to oust Arnulfo Arias from the presidency. While outside Panama during a visit to Cuba in 1941 the Americans organized a coup which **temporarily** removed Arnulfo from the presidency. Economic prosperity returned to Panama with the construction of American military bases during the Second World War. These bases were constructed on Panamanian land outside the Canal Zone. This increased occupation of Panamanian land only increased Panamanian hostility to American imperialism.

An attempt to permit the American Empire to keep the military bases permanently with the *Filos-Hines Treaty* of 1947 was soundly rejected by the Panamanian people. President Harry Truman was forced to retreat behind the Canal Zone. It was a temporary victory for Panama's independence. The 1955 *Eisenhower-Remon Treaty* recognized the Canal Zone as Panamanian property and allowed the Panamanian flag to fly alongside the American flag within the Canal Zone. President Eisenhower's seemingly inconsequential concession to Panamanian sovereignty to permit the Panamanian flag in the Canal Zone turned out to be very significant when Panamanian students rallied around their flag in 1964.

Martyrs Day and Panama's Revolt against American Imperialism

Students often provide leadership in demonstrations against imperialism. Panama was no exception. We have already mentioned the leadership against American imperialism in Panama by the students of Panama University. High School students were also in the forefront of demonstrations against US imperialism. In 1947, students of Panama's highest ranked High School, *Instituto Nacional,* had led protests against the Filos-Hines Treaty. In those demonstrations the Panamanian flag had been used as a symbol of Panama's independence from the American Empire.

In January 1964, American students attempted to raise the American flag at Balboa High School. This prompted students from Instituto Nacional to march to Balboa High School carrying the Panamanian flag as a symbol of Panama's sovereignty over the Canal Zone. The Instituto Nacional's students were prevented from raising Panama's flag at Balboa High School by American students and American police. The Americans outraged the protestors by causing the Panamanian flag to be torn. This desecration of Panama's symbol of independence brought out crowds of Panamanians to support the Instituto Nacional's students.

The anger of the Panamanian people was initially vented on the "Berlin Wall" built by the American Empire to keep Panamanians out of the Canal Zone. However, the resistance soon spread outside Panama City across the nation. The American response to this demand by the Panamanian people for independence from American imperialism was typical. The American Empire said that it was a *Communist* plot. In the 1960's, *Communism* was the empire's buzz word just like *terrorism* today. These words become so powerful that no defense is permitted. To be accused of Communism in the 1960's or of terrorism today is carte-blanche justification for the American Empire to put you away in the worst hell holes of *Abu-Ghraib* and *Guantanamo* without question from any civil rights group in the universe.

In 1964, the American Empire was still competing for hegemony with the Soviet Union. It therefore came in for much more international criticism for its colonial practices in Panama than its invasion of Iraq. By the time the American Empire invaded Iraq it was the only super-power. International criticism would have been futile. Ironically, it was Venezuela which led the protests from Latin America in 1964 and is doing so again in 2010 under President Hugo Chavez.

Panama broke off diplomatic relation with the US. It marked the beginning of negotiations between Panama and the American Empire for Panamanian property rights over the Canal Zone and the Panama Canal. Panama negotiated the *Torrijos-Carter Treaty* in September 1977 which set a timetable for the return of the Canal Zone and the Panama Canal to Panama and the removal of all US military bases from Panama by 1999.

Most Americans objected to the treaty as a sell out by President Carter to Panamanian extremists who had planned to blow up the canal if the American Empire had not returned it to Panama. Americans have never given up the hope of returning Panama to the empire through military intervention. On the other side, General Omar Torrijos, who had negotiated the treaty with President Carter, was hailed a leader of the Third World who had successfully taken on the world's most powerful and **evil** empire.

The Bush-Reagan-Noriega Drug Years

General Manuel Noriega rose to power in Panama after a plane crash took the life of General Torrijos in 1981. Noriega had served the American Empire as a paid CIA operative since the 1960's. Like Saddam Hussein, this Panamanian dictator would rise to power with the military and political support of the American Empire only to be brought down by that same empire when he had outlived his usefulness.

As Director of the CIA, George Herbert Bush played an important role in the rise of both Saddam Hussein and Manuel Noriega. As president, George Herbert Bush played an equally significant role in the fall of both Saddam Hussein and Manuel Noriega. Herbert Bush was Director of the CIA from 1976 to 1977, Vice-President from 1981 to 1989 and President from 1989 to 1993.

Manuel Noriega rose to prominence during the rule of General Torrijos. He assisted Torrijos in deposing Arnulfo Arias in 1968 and effectively succeeded Torrijos in 1981. They were both strong military leaders who dominated Panama's political leadership from 1968 until the Second US invasion of Panama in 1989. The American Empire did not mind the fact that Noriega was a double agent. The empire was aware of this fact and used it to its advantage. In 1971, for example, President Nixon asked Noriega to visit Cuba to seek the release of two Americans detained by Fidel Castro. The fact that Noriega was also a drug dealer, money launderer and gun runner made him a valuable CIA agent because of his many important connections with the under-world.

Noriega became an even greater asset to the American Empire when President Ronald Reagan escalated the Cold War against Communism. Reagan needed an intermediary to supply arms to the *Contras* who were waging a guerilla war in Nicaragua. Noriega was his man, given Noriega's connections with gun-runners and arms dealers.

The pro-Communist *Sandinista National Liberation Front* came to power in Nicaragua in 1979 with some assistance from Cuba. When Reagan became president in 1981 his priority was to wipe the communists off the globe. Nicaragua was a good place to start his global war on *communism,* laying the foundations for Bush's later global war on *terrorism.* Even today it's unclear whether Americans are more afraid of terrorism or communism. Given their total ignorance of what either concept means it is safe to say that Americans are simply afraid of any form of fear-mongering which their misguided leaders place into their gullible heads with cheap propaganda.

Regan began his war on Nicaragua by suspending economic aid in January 1981. Next, the president supplied arms and money to the *Contras* based in Honduras and Costa Rica. The economic squeeze from the American Empire combined with the military raids into Nicaragua by the US supported Contras devastated the Nicaraguan economy. Nicaragua had not yet recovered from the devastating earthquake which had hit Managua in 1972. The Sandinistas had taken over a bankrupt economy in 1979. Now that same economy was being pummeled by the American Empire much like Iraq and Afghanistan today. The only example of the American Empire ever using economic aid rather than military destruction to "win hearts and minds" was the *Marshall Plan* aid to the **White** population of Western Europe.

In April 1985 the American Empire began a total embargo on trade with Nicaragua. In 1986, President Reagan persuaded a suspicious US Congress to vote $100 million for military supplies to Reagan's *Contras.* What the US Congress did not know was that the president was illegally funneling additional funds to the *Contras* from sales of drugs and weapons. This public revelation, as well as the later public revelation of George Herbert Bush's connivance with Manuel Noriega, far from ending the political career of Reagan or Bush, ended the political career of Manuel Noriega. Many Americans are so gullible that the most heinous crimes by their leaders can be turned to political advantage with cheap propaganda.

President Reagan, Iran, Lebanon and American Hostages

The Iran hostage crisis ended the presidency of Jimmy Carter while boosting the political fortunes of President Reagan. However, all American leaders focus on short term solutions to political fiascos. It should not therefore surprise anyone that President Reagan was also haunted by a hostage crisis, the one in Lebanon.

In 1980, the American Empire's military *Operation Eagle Claw,* failed to rescue the 52 American hostages held by Iranians in retaliation for the American invasion of Iran in 1953. The 1953 American invasion had replaced the democratically elected Prime Minister of Iran, Mohammed Mossadegh, with the pro-American Shah, Mohammad Reza Pahlavi. The primary motivation for the American invasion was the theft of Iran's huge oil reserves.

It was not until 1978 that the Iranian people were able to overthrow the American installed puppet. Iranian students saw an opportunity to humiliate the American Empire for its 1953 invasion by holding the 52 American diplomats hostage in the US embassy in Tehran. The failure of President Jimmy Carter to rescue the hostages in April 1980 with *Operation Eagle Claw* lost him the 1980 presidential elections to Ronald Reagan. With the failure of the military mission the American Empire was forced to negotiate the release of the hostages.

The Republican Party consorted secretly with the Iranian government to delay the release of the American hostages until President Reagan had won the elections. A premature release of the hostages would have favoured Jimmy Carter. The Iranian government agreed to release the hostages on the day of President Reagan's inauguration in exchange for the unfreezing of Iranian assets in the US and the supply of weapons to Iran by the US.

Apart from ensuring Reagan's victory in the 1980 elections the **secret** negotiations with Iran meant that Reagan was able to use this "victory" to launch his vigorous *War on Communism*. He would be the tough talking US President who would convince the world that it was the Soviet Union, not the American Empire, which was the *evil empire*. The so called Cold War would become "hot" wars in countries like Guatemala, Lebanon, Afghanistan, Libya and Grenada.

In 1981, President Reagan saw an opportunity to prosecute his *War on Communism* by sanctioning the Israeli invasion of Lebanon. But Israel's invasion turned out to be a military and political disaster for "the Gipper," as Reagan liked to be called. Israel's invasion of Lebanon began with the usual aerial bombardment typical of American and Israeli superior firepower. It was followed by Israeli ground forces. But Israel did not get the quick victory it expected. In fact, heavy casualties were inflicted on Israel by both Palestinian and Hezbollah forces.

The Lebanese Defense Forces were also able to attack the American Empire directly by bombing its Embassy in Beirut, Lebanon on April 18, 1983, killing most of the embassy staff, including 8 CIA operatives. There could be no doubt that Israel's invasions of Palestinian and Arab lands were correctly identified as American invasions. The US Embassy was moved to East Beirut only to be attacked again on September 20, 1984. The US Embassy in Kuwait was also bombed on December 12, 1983.

More devastating to President Reagan was the bombing of American soldiers in Lebanon on October 23, 1983, killing 241 in a single attack. Reagan was forced to withdraw American ground forces from Lebanon in February 1984. But worse was yet to come. The Lebanese resistance to American/Israeli aggression had learnt the power of taking hostages from the Iranian students and the willingness of American political parties to make secret deals for political control of the American government.

The Lebanese Resistance began capturing American hostages in Lebanon in 1982. As more and more hostages were captured the Reagan team made another secret deal with the Iranians. Publicly, Iran was America's enemy number one. Privately, the Reagan team was negotiating all kinds of illegal deals with the Iranians. This latest one blew up in their faces and became Reagan's "Watergate."

President Reagan's Iran-Contra Fiasco

President Reagan had lied to the American people with the time-honoured Western propaganda that America does not negotiate with its enemies. He had falsely claimed that he had secured the release of the American hostages held by Iran by being tough on Iran, tough on Iran's allies and calling the Soviet Empire an evil empire in every public speech he made. The reality was that President Carter, who Reagan had characterized as *soft* on America's enemies, was the president who had successfully **negotiated** the release of the hostages by Iran.

With the hostage taking in Lebanon, Reagan's propaganda effectiveness was being undermined. His tough talk had no effect on the Lebanese Resistance. He once again resorted to a secret deal with Iran to hang on to the White House. He would once again sell arms illegally to Iran in exchange for hostages. This time it was American hostages in Lebanon, not Iran. Reagan's very public tough denunciation of Iran had the expected result that Iran would support the Lebanese Resistance to American/Israeli imperialism. Hence the recognition by President Reagan that Iran would have the political clout to secure the release of hostages held by the Lebanese Resistance.

Reagan saw an opportunity to double the political mileage from the secret arms sales to Iran by using the funds, illegally, to add to the $100 million he had convinced the US Congress to vote for his *War on Communism* in Nicaragua. Reagan would boost his image as the tough talking *Commander-in-Chief* whose methods forced America's enemies to shudder and release hostages. At the same time the funds from the secret arms sales would pay for the arms which General Noriega was helping to secure for his Contra guerrillas in Honduras and Costa Rica. There is no question that these secret illegal dealings with Iran, Noriega and the Contras boosted the political careers of both President Reagan and his Vice-President, George Herbert Bush.

It is useful for us to pause and reflect on why the American media is so gung ho on supporting the lies and cheap propaganda of American politicians. The inconsequential political consequence to Reagan or Bush of the media publicizing the truth of the trade of arms for hostages with Iran and the illegal dealings with Noriega and the Contras reduce the incentive for journalists to expose the lies and deceit of Western politicians.

On the other hand, supporting cheap and disgustingly untrue Western propaganda often lead to substantial monetary gains in terms of promotion and job offers for Western journalists. Why offend the establishment when there is no compensation for digging for the truth? Why not support the establishment, even when you know it is lying, if there are such obvious financial rewards? In fact you can easily double the financial rewards by publishing the truth much later in a guaranteed best seller as George W's press secretary, Scott McClellan, did in May 2008.

The secret Iran-Contra negotiations were picked up by the Western media after the story broke in a Lebanese magazine, *Ash-Shiraa,* on November 3, 1986. When it became crystal clear that this scandal was so large that it not only discredited the Gipper's tough talking credibility of "not negotiating with terrorists," but threatened possible impeachment of the Gipper, Reagan disassociated himself and his top administrators by publicly announcing that the despicable plan had been concocted and executed by two lower level administrators, Oliver North and John Poindexter.

This was sufficient to appease the American public. Reagan may have lost some international credibility but no legal action was taken against him or other members of his administration. Many of Reagan's top administrators continued to hold high political office in later administrations. These include George Herbert Bush, Dick Cheney, John Bolton, David Addington, Robert Gates, John Negroponte and Edwin Meese.

In fact, Robert Michael Gates has so impressed Americans that he not only served both Republican presidents Herbert Bush and George W. Bush but continues as US Secretary of Defense in Democratic President Barack Obama's administration. Gates continuation as US Secretary of Defense is only one of many examples of how Barack Obama lied when he campaigned for change. His administration is filled with the same people who served Presidents Bill Clinton and George W. Bush, many of whom were responsible for both the disastrous foreign policy in Iraq and Afghanistan as well as the disastrous domestic financial crisis.

An important lesson is that the American public sees their president first as *Commander-in-Chief.* His job is to wage war and do whatever it takes to expand the empire's military power and aggression against all nations, large and small. Honest members of Congress or of the media are obstacles which a tough *Commander-in-Chief* must maneuver around. If he has to bend the rules to do so that is accepted by the American public as a necessary part of his job. America's image in the world as the dominant "kick-ass" super-power requires a tough talking *Commander-in-Chief* who can always count on the support of the American people.

George Herbert Bush vs. Manuel Noriega

George Herbert Bush had emerged unscathed by the Iran-Contra debacle. He had coveted the White House since the presidential elections of 1979 but had lost out to Reagan. The Gipper had served his two terms and George Herbert got his second chance in the 1988 presidential elections. It was during these elections that the *Noriega Connection* haunted him. As early as June 1987, the US Senate had called for Noriega's removal in response to public demonstrations in Panama. By the 1988 presidential elections public opinion in the US was moving quickly against American support for Manuel Noriega.

Bush needed to distance himself from Noriega to win the US elections. He had no qualms denouncing Noriega publicly as an evil dictator, drug lord and communist spy. The problem was that his credibility suffered somewhat when a picture of him with Noriega surfaced in the media. Bush had claimed publicly that he had never met Noriega. Some investigative journalism produced a picture Bush had taken with Noriega during his second visit to Panama. As CIA Director at the time, Bush first met with Noriega in Panama on December 8, 1976. He was cozying up to Noriega because Noriega was a valuable CIA asset. Bush had met with Noriega again in Panama as late as 1983. Then Vice-President, he was the envoy of President Reagan in seeking Noriega's help in Reagan's *War on Communism.* Noriega was Reagan's conduit for arms to Reagan's Contra guerrillas invading Nicaragua.

George Herbert Bush continued to support his boss, President Reagan, during the 1984 Panamanian elections. Nicolas Barletta, a puppet of both President Reagan and Manual Noriega, was fraudulently elected as Panama's new president who would willingly support Reagan's *War on Communism.* Barletta was hand-picked by Reagan's Secretary of State, George Schultz. Schultz had been Barletta's professor at the University of Chicago's Graduate School of Business.

The Reagan Administration's support for Noriega began to sour when Noriega tried to play hardball with the American Empire. Dictators like Noriega, Saddam Hussein or Ferdinand Marcos underestimate how ruthless and **evil** American leaders are. Like the good guys, they too believe the propaganda and lies spewed out by American leaders about freedom, democracy, good governance, upholding the law, due process and other hollow platitudes.

Their downfall is often due to their mistake in believing that they could even come close to matching, much less surpassing, the evil, ruthlessness and lack of conscience, of American leaders. They fail to recognize that American leaders have played the same ruthless game since the time when America had not yet gained independence from England. American leaders honed their ruthless skills over more than two centuries, killing First Nations, enslaving Blacks, discriminating against non-Whites, waging wars on their neighbours and on Spain, England and France. All through these centuries that unchanging ruthless leadership was combined with the same high sounding propaganda about freedom, equality and desire for peace. Most importantly, American leaders never fail to use overwhelming brute force to punish any and all who question their foul motives.

The Iran-Contra Affair had revealed that Lt. Colonel Oliver North had convinced the Reagan Administration that Noriega would be willing to provide military assistance to the Contras in addition to his earlier assistance in funneling the funds from the illegal arms and drug sales by the American Empire. In reality, Noriega proved to be unwilling to "take care of the Sandinistas," as North had boasted in an e-mail to his boss, John Poindexter, in August 1986.

Noriega had straddled a fine line between his personal ideals for the Communist cause and his unsavoury dealings with the American Empire. In the past the American Empire had found Noriega's friendship with Fidel Castro useful. That was no longer a consideration. CIA Director, William Casey, personally explained to Noriega on November 1, 1985, that Panama must stop its international trade with Cuba. The American Empire's focus had shifted to the more immediate task of overthrowing the Sandinistas in Nicaragua. If Noriega would not fully commit to that cause the American Empire would replace him. Noriega, like Saddam Hussein later, underestimated the force of American media propaganda and the gullibility of the American people.

American leaders know that they can count on the fact that the people of any country despise American imposed dictators. Whenever the American Empire wants to remove an American imposed dictator it simply has to turn the pent up hatred of the people on that dictator. The fact that the dictator had been imposed on the people by the American Empire is history. It does not blunt the desire or willingness of the people to use the military, economic or propaganda support of the American Empire to remove the despised dictator. That was what George Herbert Bush counted on when he decided to depose Manuel Noriega. Noriega had become a liability to Bush's campaign for the White House in 1988. He had also resisted full commitment to Reagan's *War on Communism*. It was time to replace him with a more malleable asset whose image was also not as tarnished.

In 1986, American journalists, including Pulitzer Prize journalist, Seymour Hersh, began to report Noriega's connections with the CIA and Cuba. In 1987, the Reagan Administration decided to fund the creation of a people's protest organization in Panama called the *Civic Crusade* to organize public demonstrations against Noriega.

The US embassy sent members of the *Civic Crusade* to the Philippines to be coached in demonstration tactics by those who had worked with the US to overthrow Ferdinand Marcos. Marcos, like Noriega, was an American backed dictator who had outlived his usefulness to the empire. President of the Philippines and dedicated American ally since 1965, Marcos lasted less than two years after Reagan began to turn on him in 1984.

The *Civic Crusade* accused Noriega of the murder of Hugo Spadafora, who had been an outspoken critic of Noriega. Spadafora had accused Noriega of drug trafficking and was found in a body bag in September 1985. The *Civic Crusade* also accused Noriega of rigging the 1984 presidential elections to get Barletta elected.

The Reagan Administration indicted Noriega of drug trafficking in February 1988 and imposed a trade embargo and financial squeeze in March 1988. In April 1988 the American marines arrived in Panama, as they usually do when the American Empire wants to "negotiate peacefully." The Reagan Administration then began to execute several coups to oust Noriega, the de facto leader of Panama since 1983. When all of these attempted coups failed Panama braced itself for a full scale US invasion. But the US invasion would have to wait for President Bush to assume office. George Herbert Bush used the invasion of Panama to prove to the American people that when it comes to war and naked aggression he was no "wimp."

George Herbert Bush Invades Panama: Operation "Unjust" Cause

Bush began his administration by executing another series of failed coups to depose Noriega and tightening the economic and financial sanctions against Panama. He had vilified Noriega during the presidential race and the American people had cheered. Wars are essential to feed America's insatiable military industrial complex and no American *Commander-in-Chief* could survive much less get re-elected without taking care of the Pentagon and the military brass.

It would be unthinkable for the world's only super-power not to wage wars. To maintain your super-power status you must beat other nations into submission. This keeps your generals happy and provides young American punks the opportunity to kick ass in foreign nations populated by **non-Whites** who are viewed as inferior human beings, even less than human. The higher the human body counts the greater the glory. The wars keep the American economy ticking over nicely with munitions factories and related industries. Conquered territories provide oil and raw materials to keep American consumers happily over consuming cheap food to way past gluttony, and over consuming every conceivable useless gadget to excessive pollution and planetary degradation levels.

In November 1989, Bush announced publicly that Panama was added to Cuba and Guatemala, as immediate targets of American fear mongering, just like Iran today. The American media upped its propaganda campaign against Noriega to prepare the Panamanian people for the invasion. It's ironic that decades of anti-American resentment by the Panamanian people against American colonialism in Panama could turn temporarily to acquiescing to American intervention to oust General Noriega.

This temporary acquiescing to the American invasion should never be interpreted as a preference for American brutality over the brutality of a home grown dictator. It's simply a recognition by conquered peoples that fighting a brutal behemoth like the American Empire is often a hopeless cause. Better to surrender and accept their token economic aid and removal of sanctions since their economic sanctions had created the poverty and starvation in the first place. That the Cubans, Vietnamese, Afghans and Iraqis fought successfully against such incredible odds is truly a huge testimony to their determination, sacrifice, courage and bravery.

Bush launched his military invasion on December 20, 1989, inflicting the usual Western media "collateral damage," by killing and maiming thousands of innocent Panamanians. Dick Cheney was Bush's defense secretary. For Cheney, Panama's invasion was just a trial run for his main prize, Iraq. In both invasions, Bush and Cheney declared that their purpose was to spread democracy. "Listen up people! Accept American democracy or 2000 pound bombs will rain down from our new Lockheed F-117A military jets. The heavens are on our side."

It took five days for Bush to conquer Panama, a small developing nation with hopes for economic and political independence. His approval rating in the US skyrocketed. The World's most powerful empire mercilessly squashed the hopes and dreams of the Panamanian people as well as the people of Latin America and the Caribbean. Americans were proud of their newly elected ass kicking *Commander-in-Chief.*

Ever since the Monroe Doctrine of 1823, the people of this region have lived under the yoke of American imperialism. The Organization of American States made a grandiose gesture by passing a resolution condemning the US invasion. America's puppet international body, the UN, refused to pass a resolution asking for the withdrawal of American forces from Panama. The American Empire had the right to self defense for its invasion force. American logic boggles the mind.

The General Assembly of the UN passed a token resolution condemning the invasion. Lawyers argued the international illegality of the invasion as if the American Empire cared a hoot about international law. The American Empire moved on boldly to its next "illegal" invasion and conquest. But its military failures in Iraq and Afghanistan, combined with its financial crisis and relative economic decline, made it much more difficult for President Obama to sustain the American Empire's economic and political colonization of Latin America after 2010.

Chapter 6

The American Empire Completes its Invasions of First Nations Land, Defeats European Imperial Hegemony and Creates the Myth of "Leader of the Free World" While Conquering Central America and the Caribbean

By the end of the nineteenth century the 13 tiny states of the Union had expanded to 45 states by invading and conquering First Nations land. Prior to the start of World War I another three states were added to the union. These were Oklahoma, New Mexico and Arizona. The First World War simultaneously weakened the European empires of Britain, France and Germany while providing a market for war supplies by the American Empire.

While the Europeans had fought incessantly among themselves since the re-discovery of America by Columbus, the First World War had an important difference. It was much less a war over colonies than the previous wars. However, it was still a war for imperial hegemony. The irony was that while Britain, France and Germany were battling for imperial hegemony they destroyed themselves and enabled the American Empire to seize hegemony from all European empires for the first time since Columbus. The European empires never recovered sufficiently from their self made disaster of World War I though Germany came close to doing so under Adolf Hitler.

Part I: American Invasion and Conquest of Oklahoma, New Mexico and Arizona

The American invasions and conquests of the three states of Oklahoma, New Mexico and Arizona, completed the ethnic cleansing of the First Nations began by Columbus in 1492. The 13 tiny English colonies which had deceived the once mighty French Empire to fight Britain to secure their independence had invaded and conquered more land from the First Nations than either France or Britain had envisaged or aspired to. In the process of doing so it had driven both France and Britain, as well as Spain, from mainland America between Canada and Mexico.

While this in itself was a very surprising achievement it would be only the beginning of America's lust and greed for every small nook and cranny of the planet we call Earth. No nation, small or large, would be safe from American aggression. America's ethnic cleansing of the First Nations had only whetted its appetite for ethnically cleansing all other nations inhabiting the planet.

Fighting the European empires of Spain, France and Britain was no picnic for the First Nations. However, with the European empires the First Nations always had home advantage. No matter how powerful a navy the European empires built it would be difficult and uneconomical to penetrate inland across such a vast continental land area to completely conquer the First Nations. Furthermore, it was not clear that any of the European empires desired total conquest. They were always torn between trading with the First Nations and stealing their land.

With the American Empire, the First Nations lost the home advantage. Furthermore, there was no question that the American Empire desired total conquest and theft of all of their land. When the American Empire combined naval power with air power there was no corner of the globe safe from the **evil** empire's reach.

When the Spanish explorers, such as Cabeza de Vaca, Marcos de Niza and Francisco de Coronado, reached the American Southwest in search of the mythical *seven cities of gold* they discovered a First Nation civilization responsible for building the *pueblos*. Coronado began a war with the Pueblo Nations, including the Zuni and Hopi Nations, in 1540. Imported Spanish diseases and superior Spanish weaponry led to Spain's conquest of New Mexico by 1598. The Pueblo Nations revolted successfully against the Spanish occupation in 1680 but were re-conquered by Spain in 1694. Many of the Pueblo Nations were recruited by Spain to fight the other First Nations inhabiting the Southwest, including the Apaches. Apache is the Zuni word for *enemy*.

Conquest of the Apache Nation

The Apache Nation inhabited all of the three states, Arizona, New Mexico and Oklahoma, invaded and conquered by the American Empire between 1907 and 1912. The Apache Nation inhabited other areas of the southwestern US and many other First Nations inhabited these three states alongside the Apache Nation. However, it is appropriate to begin this final conquest of First Nations land by the American Empire with the Apache Nation.

The Apache Nation was the last of the First Nations to be confined to reservations by the American Empire. Hollywood movies have portrayed the Apache as the most formidable warrior to fight the white menace and have made heroes of Geronimo, Cochise, Taza, Naiche, Victorio, Chato and other Apache warriors. Chato betrayed his people by helping the American Empire to defeat Geronimo and the Apache Nation. His reward by the **evil** empire was 27 years of imprisonment. First Nations, like many whites, have never learnt the depth of American deception.

The Apache Nation, like the other First Nations, had fought the Spanish and Mexican occupations, prior to the American occupation. Americans first arrived in the Southwest following the Lewis and Clark expedition of 1804 and Zebulon Pike's exploration of 1807. Most of the early Americans were fur trappers. The American Empire invaded and conquered the *New Mexico Territory* in 1846 during the Mexican-American War. The Pueblo Nations revolted against the American occupation in 1847 but were defeated.

During the Mexican-American War the Apache Nation was led by Mangas Coloradas. In the decades leading up to the Mexican-American War the Apache Nation had waged war on Mexico. Mangas saw an opportunity to join forces with the American Empire to defeat Mexico. American soldiers were escorted safely through Apache controlled territory on their way to wage war on Mexico. Mangas signed a peace treaty with the US in 1846 after the American conquest of New Mexico.

The peace lasted only so long as the American Empire did not envy the Apache land. Once American miners learnt that gold could be found on Apache land in the Santa Rita Mountains an excuse was found for the American Empire to break yet another peace treaty with First Nations. In 1851, Mangas himself was captured and severely beaten by American miners. That act guaranteed reprisals by the Apache Nation. The miners were well aware that First Nations attacks on Whites would bring American troops to their defence.

After the defeat of Mexico the Apache Nation began its long war against the American occupation. The American Empire built Fort Buchanan in 1856 and Fort Beckinridge in 1860 to fight the Apache, Navajos and other First Nations. The First Nations were far from united. Even the Apache Nation was made up of ten or more different tribes. Some of the more familiar tribes were the Chiricahua, the Kiowa and the Mescalero.

One of the ways in which Mangas had tried to unite the Apache Nation was to marry his three beautiful daughters to chiefs of the other tribes. His most famous son-in-law was Cochise, chief of the Chiricahua Apaches. Cochise had waged war on Mexico as fierce as Mangas had done. The Apache Nation gained the advantage again during the American Civil War when American troops were forced to leave the forts. This left the American miners more vulnerable.

In 1861, The US army captured and hung Cochise's brother and five of his warriors. In 1862, the Apache Nation defended its territory against a US attack led by General James Carleton during the Battle at Apache Pass. The American Empire built Fort Bowie to continue the war against the Apache Nation. In 1863 Mangas surrendered under a flag of truce to the US army but was nevertheless tortured and **beheaded** by the **evil** empire, anticipating equally horrific reprisals by today's enemies of the American Empire such as the recent beheadings by Iraqi insurgents. But the American Empire boiled the head of Mangas to ensure that its barbaric deeds could never be matched by its enemies.

Cochise, with his sons Taza and Naiche, continued the Apache War against the American Empire until 1873 when Cochise signed another peace treaty which the **evil** empire broke after his death in 1874. The 1873 peace treaty guaranteed the land at Apache Pass to the Chiricahua Apache. But in 1876, they were forcibly removed from the land at Apache Pass to the barren San Carlos Reservation.

With the death of Cochise oldest son, Taza, in 1876, the leadership of the Apache War against the empire passed to Cochise younger son, Naiche, and Geronimo, whose wife was Chiricahua. His wife's brother, Juh, was a Chiricahua chief. By the time Geronimo took up the war against the American Empire the Apache Nation was on the defensive. Geronimo became the most famous of the Apache leaders because he fought against such overwhelming odds and also because he was the last of the great Apache warriors to be captured by the American Empire.

Since Geronimo and Naiche had waged war on both the American Empire and Mexico, the American Empire combined military forces with Mexico to hunt down and wipe out the Apache Nation. Despite the overwhelming American and Mexican forces combining their efforts to capture Geronimo they could not have succeeded without the help of Apache scouts such as Chato, who had fallen victim to the American Empire's lies and deceit. When Naiche surrendered in 1883, Geronimo continued the war for another three years.

The End of *Indian Territory*

The decision to prohibit **White** settlements on First Nations land within part of North America began with the Royal Proclamation of 1763 by the British Empire. When Britain arrived in North America the French were already there and had formed a strong alliance with the Huron Confederacy. England could not have succeeded against France without a similar alliance with an equally strong First Nations Confederacy. England therefore formed an alliance with the six nations Iroquois League.

The Iroquois League was the most formidable First Nations Confederacy in North America and contributed significantly to the defeat of France during the Seven Years War. Britain's obligation for this military support was the exclusion of British colonial settlements west of the Appalachian Mountains. This was a win-win agreement for both Britain and the Iroquois League.

As mentioned before, the European empires were heavily dependent on naval power to secure and defend colonies. In the New World the British Navy could defend the colonies along the Atlantic coast and in the Caribbean. Britain did not have the desire or military ability to conquer and defend colonies deep into the heartland of the American mainland. In that area the First Nations had a decisive military advantage.

On the other hand the Iroquois League, like other First Nations which had survived the onslaught of the European empires, reluctantly recognized the sad reality that they could not defend the coastal areas from the European invaders. The Appalachian Mountains formed a natural geographical division between the English colonies and *Indian Territory.*

We have further explained that the First Nations military "home advantage" disappeared once the three home grown empires, Canada in the North, USA in the Centre and Mexico in the South, replaced the European empires of Britain, France and Spain. Our central thesis has consistently been that the USA was never founded because of some innate desire for freedom, equality and the right of self determination. It was founded because of the innate ambitions of a home grown aristocracy for conquests of First Nations land.

Americans violated the Royal Proclamation of 1763 by settling in *Indian Territory* west of the Appalachian Mountains before their War of Independence. After the War of Independence new states were added to the American Empire by pushing the First Nations further and further into the interior of the American Mainland.

American settlements in California and Oregon began to push the First Nations from the Pacific Ocean until *Indian Territory* was reduced to Oklahoma. President Jackson's *Indian Removal Act* of 1830 formalized the unofficial policy of the American Empire to steal every inch of First Nations land as soon as it was militarily feasible. The first step was to forcibly move the First Nations to Oklahoma.

Wars, diseases and starvation reduced the First Nations population and weakened their ability to resist forceful removal. The First Nations who survived to make Oklahoma their home were desperately trying to make the best of an atrocious situation by coming together and saving a tiny part of the American Mainland to call home. With the American Empire still fighting those First Nations who resisted removal to Oklahoma and with its own Civil War ongoing the American Empire pretended to support this home for First Nations in Oklahoma. But once the Civil War was over there was no military necessity for maintaining this pretence.

After the Civil War the American Empire reduced the land in Oklahoma set aside for the First Nations by 3 million acres. This would enable White settlers to move into what had been designated as *Indian Territory.* In 1890, half of what had been *Indian Territory* became the Oklahoma Territory. The First Nations recognized that this was one more step in achieving the ultimate goal of the American Empire. That goal, of course, was the empire's theft of every inch of First Nations land.

The First Nations made a desperate attempt to secure the last remnants of *Indian Territory* by asking for statehood within the Union. This movement was led by the so called *Five Civilized Tribes.* This Five-Nation Confederacy of Cherokees, Creeks, Seminoles, Choctaws and Chickasaws was reminiscent of the initial Five-Nation Iroquois League whose members had been granted the status of British subjects in 1713 by the Treaty of Utrecht. At the Albany Congress of 1754, the English colonies had met with the Iroquois League to form a joint Union. Benjamin Franklin was so impressed with the governing structure of the Iroquois League that he recommended to the colonial delegates to the Albany Congress that it could serve as a model for a constitution for the proposed Union.

The *Five Civilized Tribes* had adopted Western life styles to placate White Americans in the hope of being accepted into the Union as "Equals." In 1902 they reached agreement among themselves to call their proposed state *Sequoyah.* In 1903 they held their first constitutional convention. In 1905 they drafted a constitution. Despite the best efforts of the *Five Civilized Tribes* to present to President Teddy Roosevelt and the American Empire's Congress as non-threatening and as "White" a state as humanly possible, the First Nations were turned down flat.

Americans could never accept or even tolerate a First Nation state within their **lily white** Union. To prevent any future president or Congress from ever contemplating such a "Non-American" act the American Empire made all of Oklahoma the 46th state of the Union in 1907. Another 70,000 square miles of First Nations land had been stolen by the **evil** empire.

New Mexico and Arizona Completes the American Empire's Mainland Conquests

The New Mexico Territory was created in 1850 out of the First Nations land captured by the empire from Mexico. The New Mexico Territory of 1850 had been greatly expanded by the Gadsden Purchase of 1853. Santa Fe, founded by the Spanish since 1609, was the largest White settlement. The American railroad reached Santa Fe in 1880, replacing the old Santa Fe Trail and ushering in the cattle boom. In time Albuquerque far outgrew Santa Fe to become the largest city.

The territory was plagued by conflicts between the First Nations, the Mexicans and the Americans. There were also conflicts between American ranchers and American homesteaders. The surrender of Geronimo in 1886 ended the long war with the Apache Nation. In January 1912, New Mexico became the 47th state of the Union adding another 123,000 square miles of First Nations land to the American Empire.

Conflicts between Americans and Mexicans have heated up again in the 21st century as Mexicans migrate from Mexico into New Mexico to re-claim the land that many of them felt was stolen from them by the American Empire. New Mexico has the largest percentage of *Hispanics* of any American state. Hispanics account for about 42% of the population and is growing with immigration from Mexico. Americans often misleadingly refer to the Mexican immigrants as *illegal Aliens* as if they were coming from Mars. The reality is that the Mexicans occupied New Mexico before the Americans. It is the American occupation which is illegal.

First Nations still account for about 12% of the population of New Mexico. They must be looking at the current rhetoric between the Mexicans and Americans with cool resignation, wondering why no American or Western media or historian is willing to point out that both the Americans and the Mexicans stole New Mexico from the First Nations. The First Nations had fought and lost against Spain, Mexico and the American Empire.

Arizona: The Empire's Final Mainland Conquest

We ended Chapter 2 by recognizing the creation of the Confederate Territory of Arizona in 1861. In 1863 the Arizona Territory was carved out of the Western half of the New Mexico Territory where the First Nations had maintained greater control. But gold was discovered in Prescott in 1863 and Prescott became the first Capital of the new territory of Arizona. Gold, like oil today, is always guaranteed to get the American Empire to invade and conquer land legally owned by others.

American miners and other settlers arrived by steam boats down the Colorado River, beginning in the 1850's. Gold was first discovered in Arizona in1857. The largest American settlement was Yuma at the border between the American Empire and Mexico. The *Desert Land Act* of 1877 boosted

American immigration into Arizona. This Act sold up to 640 acres of "desert" land at the price of $1.25 per acre. Brigham Young expanded his *Mormon Commonwealth* into Arizona settling towns like Mesa and Snowflake in 1878.

The American railroad reached Arizona in 1881. The railroad enabled a huge expansion in the gold, silver and copper mining industry. The mining companies set the precedent for hiring Mexican labour which is currently causing White Americans so much pain in controlling the influx of Mexican immigrants into the southern states which had been part of the Mexican Empire. The so called *porous* American border with Mexico dates back to the 1850's when the American Empire invaded and conquered Texas, California, New Mexico and Arizona from the Mexican Empire.

With Hispanics accounting for over 30 percent of the current population and growing much faster than Whites, Arizona is well on its way to becoming the first state of the Union with a Hispanic majority.

The Apache Nation was not, by any means, the only First Nation to defend their homes in Arizona against the American Empire. Wars were fought against the Navajo, Mohave, Yuman and Pai Nations. In 1871, the American Empire coordinated its military offensive against the First Nations in Arizona under the command of General George Crook. Crook hired Apache scouts to locate the First Nations' hide-outs. The First Nations were hunted down and killed by Crook. Their food supplies and weapons were destroyed. Those who survived the wars, diseases and starvation were forced to march to the barren San Carlos reservation. Many perished on the march.

Living conditions at the San Carlos reservation were inhumane. The First Nations, forced to live together in a single reservation, fought among themselves for the meager handouts of rations provided by the American Empire. It was a deliberate effort to humiliate and destroy the will of the First Nations. But even this barren piece of land was envied by **White** settlers after they found out that it could be mined for copper.

Mexico had often joined forces with the American Empire to hunt down and kill the First Nations in the Southwest. In 1882, Crook received permission from the Mexican government to pursue the First Nations across the border into Mexico. Crook moved his operations into Northern Mexico. Once again Apache scouts were used by Crook to locate the First Nations' hide-outs in Mexico. Despite the superior weapons of the US military and the invaluable help of the Apache scouts, Crook was unable to give the American Empire the total victory it demanded. Crook was frustrated and forced to resign and hand over command to General Nelson Miles.

The First Nations today account for about 6 percent of Arizona's population and 10 percent of the total First Nations population of the American Empire. Ignoring Alaska, Arizona became the last Mainland state of the Union in February 1912, the same year that New Mexico became the 47th state. This increased the land area of the American Empire by another 114,000 square miles. As in New Mexico the First Nations today are looking on at the renewed battle between the American Empire and Mexicans for control of Arizona.

With the invasion and conquest of Arizona the American Empire had expanded fully across the width of the American continent and wiped out resistance from the First Nations, the Spanish, the French, the British, the Mexicans and its own "Confederate" states. The American Empire had begun looking outside the American Mainland long before its conquest of Arizona in 1912. We have documented many of these invasions in our earlier chapters. The First World War provided the opportunity for the American Empire to expand even faster as the War reduced competition from the European empires. We now turn our attention to American invasions and conquests leading up to the First World War and into the 1930's.

Part II: World War I Opportunities for American Hegemony

The First World War was the ultimate disaster for European hegemony and the golden gift for American domination. Visionary American leaders had dreamt of world domination while America was still under imperial control by the mother country, England. They had cleverly used colonial control to their own advantage. By pitting the French against the English they had weakened French imperialism in the New World.

By pretending to be good colonial servants they had secured British help in stealing the First Nations land and weakened the resistance of the First Nations. With French help they had weakened English imperialism in the New World. With superior military forces they had conquered the Spanish colonies world-wide and reduced the threat from Mexico.

In the Pacific, American leaders had competed with Japan. By 1914, America was the dominant nation in the New World and had made some inroads into the Pacific. But it did not have the world-wide empire of England or France. The First World War handed over that world-wide empire to America on a silver platter. England and France had wrested European hegemony from Portugal and Spain. By 1914, England and France were under threat from a new European power, Germany. European conflicts between Spain, Holland, France and England had given the American Empire the New World. That continued European conflict, this time between England, France and Germany, would hand over the Old World to America.

Teddy Roosevelt had secured for the American Empire the Spanish Caribbean and Pacific colonies by starting the Spanish American War. In 1904 he had sent US marines to Tangiers in Morocco to help him win the 1904 presidential election. The *Roosevelt Corollary,* enunciated in Teddy's annual address to the US Congress in December 1904, had given the American Empire an excuse to colonize the entire New World. Roosevelt had also built the Panama Canal to connect America's Atlantic and Pacific Empire. He had built the *Great White Fleet* and sent it into the Pacific to threaten and terrorize the Japanese Empire and China. "Carry a big stick," was Teddy's motto.

For these and other actions of a dedicated **warmonger** he had secured for himself the Nobel Peace Prize in 1906. He was the first but by no means the last American **warmonger** who would receive the hypocritical Nobel "Peace" Prize. America's latest recipient, President Barack Obama, outdid Teddy Roosevelt by getting the 2009 Nobel Peace Prize while waging wars in Afghanistan, Iraq, Pakistan and Yemen. In his acceptance speech in Oslo, President Obama proudly proclaimed that his wars in Afghanistan, Pakistan, Yemen and Iraq were "just" wars. He did not even deny that he was a **warmonger.**

The fact that President Obama was so proud to acknowledge that **warmongers** like him are deserving of the Nobel Peace Prize shows the depth to which the members of the Nobel Committee have lost touch with reality. There are absolutely no "just" wars, none whatsoever. We can go back a hundred centuries and I challenge anyone to give a single example of a war which can be justified as unavoidable. Every war has its root cause in imperial and territorial expansion. Killing innocent men, women and children in Iraq, Afghanistan and Pakistan by the American Empire with its highly advanced military arsenal of planes, bombs, manpower and guns, is barbaric, inhumane and insane. President Obama's modest statement in his acceptance speech that the unrecognized masses who fight for peace are "far more deserving," is itself a commentary on how *brain dead* the members of the Nobel Committee are.

Al Gore may not have been as dedicated a warmonger as Teddy Roosevelt or Henry Kissinger or Barak Obama. However, he received the Nobel Peace Prize during the criminal US invasion of Iraq even though he never publicly criticized that invasion. Many peace activists who sacrificed their careers in America, Britain and elsewhere, to criticize the illegal US invasion of Iraq were deemed less deserving than a non-peace activist like Al Gore. Peace activists like Cindy Sheehan still get less respect in the Western media than **warmongers** like George W. Bush, Britain's Tony Blair and Barack Obama.

Most importantly, Teddy Roosevelt had determined that *non-White* races were inferior and that it was the destiny of **White Empires,** like the American Empire, to conquer, colonize and rape all of the lands populated by non-Whites. As skin colour had been a key motive for decimating the First Nations, enslaving Blacks and demonizing Asians on the Mainland, it was now a key motivation in determining which new colony the American Empire would subjugate. America's key ally in expanding its race-based empire would be the British Empire. The British Empire willingly handed over the "policing" of the New World to the Americans. Tony Bair's coalition with George W. Bush was no accident. Neither is President Obama's "White" image for himself and his family, while occupying the White House.

Since the industrial revolution, relative economic power was measured by the output of three products, iron, coal and steel. In 1914, the American Empire had already surpassed the individual outputs of the three major European combatants, Germany, Britain and France. As these three European empires turned their factories to producing war materials the American Empire met their expanded needs with American exports. Never had markets for American products been so abundant or lucrative.

The First World War was the single most undeserving opportunity for profits provided to American entrepreneurs by the idiocy of war. Taking full advantage of the markets provided by World War I and the devastation of the European economies, America's industrial output had grown to 40 percent of the World's output by 1920. It had become the largest economy in the world. It was this massive economic base that enabled it to support the costly military base with which to dominate and subjugate the world.

American Imperialism in Central America and the Caribbean

We have documented American expansion north into Canada and Alaska and south into Mexico. President Teddy Roosevelt had invented the *Roosevelt Corollary* to justify American military intervention in Latin America and the Caribbean. President Howard Taft complemented Roosevelt's "Corollary," with *dollar diplomacy*.

President Woodrow Wilson invaded Honduras, Nicaragua, Haiti, the Dominican Republic and Costa Rica while presiding over a 400 percent increase in US trade with Latin America. Wilson's willingness to follow in the footsteps of all American presidents in waging wars and invading independent countries secured him the Nobel Peace Prize in 1919. He would join the ranks of the Barack Obamas, Teddy Roosevelts and Henry Kissingers who could so easily convince the members of the Nobel Committee that American leaders must be encouraged to wage endless wars to secure peace.

Military intervention in Central America and the Caribbean would be complemented and supported by economic and financial control of Latin American and Caribbean economies. Americans invested in sugar, coffee, bananas, tobacco, railways, ports, postal services, radio, telecommunications, banking, and in every conceivable business venture in Latin America and the Caribbean.

American corporations and the American military dictated how these ex-Spanish, and ex-English, colonies would be governed. Latin American and Caribbean culture, identities and nationalism were brutally stamped out by Corporate America, American imperialism, White supremacist views, anti-Communist propaganda, Christian dogma and Western biases.

Latin America and the Caribbean provided markets for American products while supplying to American consumers agricultural products, such as sugar, coffee and bananas, produced by American Corporations with cheap local labour. The **slave** plantation owners of the Southern US states and the business aristocracy of the northern US states had effectively expanded their conquests of First Nations lands outside the borders of the United States of America.

Cotton plantations in the American south and sugar plantations in Mississippi had enriched the landed gentry of the emerging American Empire. It seemed a simple matter for this privileged class to transform Central America into coffee and banana plantations as it had transformed Cuba into sugar plantations. The low wages paid to the agricultural workers by American Corporations would be even cheaper than using **slaves.** To this day rich North American consumers pay 50 cents or less for a pound of bananas produced by cheap labour employed by American Corporations in the Caribbean and Latin America.

During the nineteenth century, the British Empire dominated the Caribbean and Latin America as much as it dominated the rest of the world. However, it had acquiesced to the Monroe Doctrine of 1823 because its economic and political interests coincided with those of the emerging American Empire. As a result of this partnership in global exploitation and shared principles for Anglo hegemony, the American Empire was allowed by the British to expand its relative share of trade, foreign investment, foreign financial controls, infrastructure investments and political control in Latin America and the Caribbean.

By the outbreak of World War I, America had become the dominant empire in the Caribbean and Latin America, the so called, *Colossus of the North.* The First World War forced the British to sell off most of their remaining assets in the Caribbean and Latin America to the American Empire. By the end of the First World War, the American Empire had a virtual monopoly on the colonial exploitation of the Latin American and Caribbean economies. Their investments soon exceeded that of the British. The American Empire controlled banking, transportation, communications, ports, public utilities, tariffs, education, health services and public works.

US Invasions of the Central American Republics of Honduras, Nicaragua, Guatemala, El Salvador and Costa Rica

American invasions and interventions in the Central American states of Honduras, Nicaragua and Guatemala in the first decades of the twentieth century are somewhat reminiscent of US invasions and interventions in the Middle East states of Lebanon, Iran and Iraq in the second half of the twentieth century. As in Lebanon, Iran and Iraq, the American Empire exercised economic and political dominance in Honduras, Nicaragua, El Salvador and Guatemala. As in Lebanon, Iran and Iraq, the American Empire often encouraged and exploited the neighbourly squabbling of Honduras, Nicaragua, El Salvador and Guatemala to advance its own desire to dominate and control these countries. For example, when Nicaragua invaded Honduras in 1907, American marines quickly used this as an excuse to invade Honduras.

As we will see, these Central American invasions by the American Empire are not only linked with each other, but also with invasions by the American Empire throughout Latin America and the Caribbean. In the case of the *Iran-Contra Affair,* invasions in Panama were linked with invasions in Honduras, Nicaragua, Costa Rica, Iran and Lebanon. Honduras and Costa Rica were the military bases for the American funded Contras to launch their attacks in Nicaragua.

The Lebanon "Hostage Crisis" was the inspiration to sell arms to Iran. The money from the arms sales to Iran went to the Contras. The supply of arms and funds from drug trafficking to the Contras were facilitated by General Manuel Noriega of Panama. These links were never planned by the American Empire. They were simply opportunities presented to an **evil** empire whose only single-minded goal was world domination by military force.

Honduras, Nicaragua, Guatemala, Costa Rica and El Salvador won their independence from the Spanish Empire in 1821. This was the signal for the American Empire to infiltrate their post-colonial governments and undermine their struggle for economic and political independence. In Hawaii, pineapple production was the key to American domination. In the Central American states it was bananas.

Just as the Dole Pineapple Corporation dominated the Hawaiian economy, two American banana producers, *United Fruit Company* and *Standard Fruit Company,* dominated these Central American economies. Honduras, Nicaragua, Guatemala and El Salvador quickly became four of many American dominated "Banana Republics," dancing to the tune of the "Yankee Dollar." The United Fruit Company produced pineapples as well as bananas and typically had the advantage over the Standard Fruit Company.

The United Fruit Company also owned or controlled the railways, shipping, postal, telegraph and radio transportation and communications sectors of the Central American states. It owned large chunks of real estate in Honduras, Nicaragua, Guatemala, Costa Rica, El Salvador, Panama, Venezuela and Columbia. The combined GDP of the seven Central American *uncolonies* of the American Empire never exceeded one percent of the GDP of the USA. One reason is the ridiculously low price they receive for bananas in their primary market, the USA.

After the Second World War, the American Empire found another cause to justify its invasions in Central America. The Soviet Union had emerged from the Second World War as the only country capable of challenging the American Empire for hegemony. The American Empire immediately began a very successful propaganda campaign to persuade the Western World that *communism* was evil. Since communism replaced private property with communal property, America's attack on communism simultaneously protected the private property rights of the American Corporations in Central America. However, it was easier to fool the world by pretending to invade a country to stamp out the evil *communism* than to protect rich American Corporations.

Two important ironies of using the scapegoat of the supposed *evil* of communism as America's war cry were firstly, that the very exploitation of the First Nations and mixed races of Central America by American Corporations provided the greatest incentive for these poor people, whose land had been stolen by the American Empire, to seek out the communist ideal of shared communal property rights. The ideas of Marx, Lenin and Mao Ze Dong, became the intellectual inspiration of Central American leaders opposed to the evils of American imperialism.

Secondly, the loss of Cuba to communism under Fidel Castro, while a serious blow to America's ego, became the American Empire's most convincing rallying cry to dupe its own citizens. "Not another Cuba," was the most convincing propaganda used by the American Empire to get Americans to support the most vicious military invasions of every democracy in the New World.

US Invasions of Honduras

When I first wrote this section of the book, the "2009 Honduran constitutional crisis," of June 28, 2009, had not yet occurred. I will comment on this crisis at the end of this section. However, it is a timely reminder of America's historical domination of Latin America and of the continuing struggle of the people of Latin America to break free from American imperialism. The encouraging sign is that most of Latin America's leaders today are less fearful of distancing themselves from the American Empire. As of 2010, the only Latin American leader still openly pro-American Empire is the president of Columbia. Quite a reversal from the 1980's when only the Cuban leader openly opposed the American Empire.

In Honduras, Americans controlled the mining industry in the 1880's, producing gold, silver and copper. Americans began to grow bananas in Jamaica and Costa Rica in the 1870's. The United Fruit Company inherited the banana trade from the Boston Fruit Company in 1899. Together with the Standard Fruit Company, it expanded the production of bananas in Honduras along the north coast.

In 1903, US marines landed at Puerto Cortes in Honduras to protect US economic interests and support any dictator who suppressed the Honduran people for the benefit of the American Empire and a tiny percentage of wealthy Hondurans. US marines landed at Puerto Cortes again in 1907. The American Empire sent its military again into Honduras in 1911, 1912, 1919, 1924 and 1925. A total of **seven** invasions between 1903 and 1925.

Honduras, the second largest country in Central America, became the world's largest exporter of bananas. By 1930, bananas accounted for 80% of the value of Honduran exports. At that time, the United Fruit Company was the largest employer in all of Central America.

The military forces of the American Empire stood ready to prevent national governments from reducing American economic dominance or for indigenous employees to strike for decent wages. More often than not, it was the American installed dictators who carried out the American Empire's dirty work. For example, pro-American dictator, General Tiburcio Carias, banned the Communist Party of Honduras in 1935 and viciously crushed strikes by farm workers against the American banana corporations.

Another ploy of the American Empire was to ensure that the pro-American dictators in the region supported each other. Thus the pro-American dictators in the four Central American states invaded by the American Empire between 1903 and 1933, Honduras, Nicaragua, Guatemala and El Salvador, fully supported each other in protecting American economic interests in the region, thereby guaranteeing their own military survival. With the support of American Corporations, the American military and fellow pro-American dictators in Nicaragua, Guatemala and El Salvador, pro-American dictator, General Carias, presided over Honduras for a second term from 1933 until 1949.

General Carias benefitted from America's *lend-lease* military aid during World War II while the American Empire secured a Central American ally against Germany. US military aid to Honduras increased after World War II. In 1954, Honduras signed a *military assistance agreement* with the American Empire. The Honduran army was trained by the Americans at the US *Army School of the Americas.* US financial assistance to the Honduran military increased throughout the 1950's and 1960's. This continued military aid to Honduran dictators proved invaluable to President Reagan's new War on Communism in the 1980's.

Pro-American military dictators continued to govern Honduras after 1949. During the Reagan presidency, Honduras became the prime military base for Reagan's new War on Communism in Central America and against the Sandinista government in Nicaragua. While every American president was anti-Soviet Union, with President Reagan, the Soviet Union was an obsession. His intense hatred of the Soviet Union spewed out of every speech he gave. For Reagan, it was the USSR, not America, which was the *evil* empire.

The first civilian Honduran president elected in 1981, Roberto Suazo Cordoba, was as pro-American as his military predecessors. President Cordoba received military advisers, weapons and financial aid from the Reagan Administration. The US and Honduran forces conducted joint training exercises. The American Empire recruited General Alvarez Martinez to create the *Battalion 316 Death Squad.* Alvarez had honed his skills in the use of torture in Argentina.

Key members of *Battalion 316 Death Squad* were brought into the US for specialized training in the use of torture methods which the CIA had perfected in Vietnam. President Reagan invited General Alvarez to the White House and awarded him the Legion of Merit for his outstanding leadership in using death squads and torture to prosecute the American Empire's dirty war in Honduras and Nicaragua.

A US military training facility was established in Honduras. American military aid increased from $6 million in 1969 to $282 million in 1985. American economic and political imperialism expanded under future civilian presidents. In 1987, the American Empire simulated an invasion of Nicaragua from Honduras and Costa Rica. More American troops were sent in 1988 to support Reagan's 15,000 Nicaraguan *Contras* in Honduras.

President Reagan's point man on the ground to assist General Alvarez in the use of *human rights abuses and torture* of Hondurans to support his new War on Communism was none other than **John Negroponte.** Negroponte replaced Jack Binns as US Ambassador, because Binns had expressed some concerns regarding the extreme torture methods used by Alvarez.

Negroponte would later use his Central American experience to torture and abuse Iraqis to "win hearts and minds" for the American invasion of Iraq. Far from questioning the methods of General Alvarez he honed his own skills in the use of torture from the General. *Abu-Ghraib and Guantanamo* are simply more well publicized examples of a long history of the use of torture by the American Empire.

American use of torture did not begin with President George W. Bush. It's just that America today has less power to suppress *freedom of the press* outside the Western World. Negroponte's covert Honduran operations were ably supported in Washington by then Director of the CIA, William Casey. Together, they falsified reports to the American people and the American Congress. Not that it takes much to "fool" those who govern an **evil** empire. But it is wise to distort the facts just in case.

Honduras continued to be used as a military base for the American Empire after the fall of the Soviet Union. The *War on Communism* has been replaced by the *War on Terrorism.* In 2003, President Ricardo Maduro was forced to send Honduran troops to support the US invasion of Iraq. With an unemployment rate close to 30 percent and the US its primary market for its bananas, coffee and citrus fruits, no Honduran president dared offend the American Empire.

Despite opposition from Honduran farmers, Honduras ratified membership in the US-Central American Free Trade Agreement in 2006. Apart from popular opposition to American imperialism in Honduras, small businesses, farmers and workers feared competition from heavily subsidized US agricultural imports into Honduras.

Honduras remains a poor country after more than a century of American colonization. The majority of its population lives in poverty. In 2010 at least one-third of the population lives on less than $US 2.00 per day. Even in the Mexican style *maquiladoras* wages are less than a dollar per hour. Its external debt exceeds its annual GDP. As a "Heavily Indebted Poor Country," it qualified for debt relief in 2005.

Under public pressure, the two US Corporations, United Fruit and Standard Fruit, returned some of their vast uncultivated land holdings to landless Honduran peasants in the 1960's and 1970's. However, these new small land owners had to market their crops through the American Corporations at prices intended to keep them in poverty. They also cleared and cultivated land in the hills which caused disastrous mudslides which killed many Hondurans when Hurricane Mitch devastated the economy in 1998.

Economic damage was estimated at US$3.0 billion. Ninety percent of the banana crop was lost. Thousands became homeless after Hurricane Mitch damaged or destroyed close to 100,000 houses.

Half a century of modest economic growth was wiped out. There is not a single shred of evidence to show that American imperialism benefitted the people of Honduras.

The 2009 Military Coup in Honduras

Military regimes ended in Honduras with the "democratic" election of President Cordoba in 1981. But neither the military nor the American Empire left Honduras in 1981. As we saw above as late as 2003 the "democratically" elected President Maduro was forced by the American Empire to send the Honduran military to aid the American Empire's illegal and immoral invasion of Iraq.

With the American Empire occupied in Iraq, Afghanistan, Iran, North Korea, Palestine, Lebanon, Pakistan, Somalia and Yemen, true, non-western, people's democracy has breathed new life in Latin America. Under the leadership of Venezuela, Cuba, Brazil, Argentina, Bolivia and Nicaragua, Latin America is desperately trying to drive the American Empire out of Latin America and the Caribbean. Evo Morales, the President of Bolivia, said in a speech in Cuba on December 14, 2009, that in a short time "there will be no pro-US president or government in Latin America," and that the American Empire will be defeated in Latin America as it had been in Vietnam.

On June 28, 2009, President Jose Manuel Zelaya Rosales was deposed in a military coup led by General Romeo Velasquez. President Barack Obama publicly denounced the coup but it is simply not credible that the Honduran military would have returned Honduras to military rule in today's increasingly democratic Latin America without connivance and support from the American Empire. Manuel Zelaya was the seventh "democratically" elected president of Honduras since military rule ended in 1981. Zelaya was elected in 2005 and inaugurated in January 2006. His term would have ended in January 2010.

As we have explained, while the presidents, beginning with Cordoba in 1981, were elected by the people of Honduras, they were under the thumb of the American Empire which had significant control of the economy and military. But with the growing anti-Americanism of Latin American leaders (the people were always anti-American), such as Hugo Chavez, Evo Morales, Daniel Ortega, Rafael Correa, Lula da Silva and Cristina Kirchner, President Zelaya found the courage to reduce American imperialism in Honduras. It was President Zelaya's efforts to make Honduras less of a puppet democracy of the American Empire and implement policies which had popular support from the majority of the Honduran electorate that led to the military coup which the American Empire must have implicitly approved.

FTAA, ALBA, UNASUL and American Military bases in Columbia

The key to understanding the military coup in Honduras lies in recognizing the efforts to exclude the American Empire from new free trade areas being created to integrate the economies of Latin America combined with the publicly expressed concerns by Latin American leaders, including heavyweights such as Brazil's Lula da Silva and Argentina's Cristina Kirchner, of the American Empire expanding military bases in Latin America under the guise of fighting terrorism and drug trafficking.

During the Reagan administrations the American Empire had tightened its control over the Latin American economies under the guise of fighting communism. Following the success of the North American Free Trade Agreement, NAFTA, the American Empire promoted a Free Trade Area between the US and Latin America, the so called Free Trade of the Americas, FTAA. At the time the idea was floated in 1994 most Latin American leaders felt impelled to support it. The American Empire still ruled the global economy and could crush any country which did not publicly support its imperialist ambition. No Latin American leader was willing to suffer the fate of Cuba. Not so in 2010.

In 2010, the American economy is but a shadow of its size and influence in 1994. Disastrous wars combined with economic mismanagement have sucked the dynamism out of its entrepreneurial prowess at a time when the global shift has enriched the Third World, especially Asia and Latin America. True people's democracy in the Third World requires good governance which harnesses the entrepreneurship of free enterprise, international trade and foreign investment, while obstinately and forcefully rejecting Western imperialism. In the previous five centuries that was impossible. In 2010, it is not. China has shown the way.

Latin American leaders are aware of the importance of trade and investment. But to get trade and investment without American imperialism they need a free trade area which excludes the US. That is why they oppose the FTAA and that is one reason for the US backed coup in Honduras. If the Obama administration can install a puppet government in Honduras it could use Honduras and Columbia to undermine other democratic regimes in the region. That also explains why Latin American leaders object strongly to the US military bases in Columbia. It is therefore the combined opposition to the FTAA and military bases in Columbia by Latin American leaders that explains the private US support for the military coup in Honduras.

Empires like the American Empire never quit their expansionist militarism because their economies are collapsing. They continue to the bitter end. A simpleton can easily recognize today that the American Empire is over extending itself across the globe with disastrous consequences for its own people, never mind the people outside the US. But it has no system or leadership which has the intelligence and power to change course. Each disaster only encourages its leaders to steer a course that will lead to greater disaster. Its long time allies, Britain and Canada, do not have the foresight to disengage from the sinking ship. Currently they are jostling to see which of the three "asses of evil" can proudly lose more soldiers, per capita, in Afghanistan.

An important alternative to the FTAA which would exclude the US was proposed by none other than American nemesis, President Hugo Chavez. **ALBA** began modestly as an agreement between the leaders of Venezuela and Cuba in 2004. It now boasts nine members, Venezuela, Cuba, Bolivia, Nicaragua, Ecuador, Dominica, Saint Vincent and the Grenadines, Antigua and Barbuda and *Honduras*. Yes, Honduras joined this anti-American group in October 2008. Like the millions who supported the candidacy of Barack Obama because they hoped for a better world, President Manuel Zelaya naively believed that President Barak Obama would not be just another gun-toting American gringo who viewed Latin America as an appendage to the "colossus of the North," to be exploited at will for the benefit of the empire.

UNASUL is a much older alternative to the FTAA which would exclude the US. Modeled along the lines of the European Union it is much more ambitious that the FTAA or NAFTA. UNASUL began as two smaller free trade areas, *Mercosur* and the *Andean Community*. In addition to Venezuela, Bolivia and Ecuador, which are members of ALBA, UNASUL includes the larger Latin American countries such as Brazil, Argentina, Chile and Peru as well as smaller ones such as Colombia, Guyana, Uruguay, Paraguay and Suriname.

US Invasions of Nicaragua

America's dictator in Nicaragua was General Jose Santos Zelaya Lopez. Jose Zelaya took over the presidency of Nicaragua in 1893 and looked after American economic interests. He protected American investments in coffee, sugar, rubber and banana plantations as well as in Nicaraguan mining and lumber. However, like Saddam Hussein in Iraq and Manuel Noriega in Panama, the American Empire "regime changed" him in 1909, when he tried to play hard ball.

Jose Zelaya had the audacity to propose that American Corporations pay taxes in Nicaragua. US warships arrived in Nicaragua in November, 1909 to "protect American property." Only the American Empire has the god given right to claim private property rights in any country in the world and to use military force, not laws or judicial arguments, to brutally enforce those *illegal* private property rights.

Prior to the construction of the Panama Canal, the American Empire was investigating the feasibility of constructing a canal through Nicaragua. American marines surveyed the route in 1887 and the Maritime Canal Company was founded in 1889 to construct the canal. As late as 1901, the American Empire pursued the canal route through Nicaragua.

In 1878, a French company had obtained a concession from Columbia to build a canal across Panama. However, the French effort was on the verge of bankruptcy and sold its Panama route to the American Empire in 1902. This effectively killed the route through Nicaragua. When the American Empire learnt that their Nicaraguan puppet, General Zelaya, was talking to Germany and Japan about a canal through Nicaragua they deposed Zelaya and sent in troops in 1910 to protect their new puppet, Adolfo Diaz.

US Military Occupation and the Somoza Dictatorships

Nicaragua, the largest country in Central America, became a military *uncolony* of the American Empire from 1909 to 1933. The American Empire had sent its troops into Nicaragua in 1894, 1896, 1898, 1899 and 1907. The **seventh** invasion of 1912 was to be much longer than the American Empire envisaged. The American Empire's troops were bogged down in Nicaragua because of a very determined Nicaraguan insurgency against the **evil** empire. The empire's troop surge in 1927 was no match for the insurgency. During this extended military occupation the American Empire trained a local pro-American National Guard to protect American investments. That ploy to save humiliation by pretending to hand over the invasion to local forces failed in Nicaragua, as it failed later in Vietnam, Afghanistan and Iraq.

The American Empire found a new dictator in Commander Anastasio Somoza Garcia. American marines had been badly bloodied by a six-year war against the insurgents, led by the formidable General Augusto Sandino. They needed to return to the US to lick their wounds and re-group for an easier invasion in another country. A year after the American forces withdrew in 1933, Somoza assassinated General Sandino and, two years later, took over the presidency of Nicaragua from Juan Sacasta. With Somoza safely installed by the American Empire, first as Director of the pro-American National Guard and later as President of Nicaragua in 1936, American troops could safely be withdrawn from Nicaragua for conquests elsewhere.

Like Carias in Honduras, Somoza saw the American Empire through its final battle for hegemony during the Second World War. The American Empire armed Somoza to fight the Germans as well as protect himself from any uprising by his own people. German owned property in Nicaragua became the property of the Somoza family. President Franklin Roosevelt was proud to refer to Somoza as "**our** son of a bitch."

Somoza governed Nicaragua with an iron fist until his assassination in 1956. As the Somoza family enriched itself at the expense of both Nicaragua's middle class and the large lower class popular opposition to American imperialism increased. The expansion of a US style "plantation economy," together with cattle ranching created a growing class of landless peasants. Cattle ranching supplied beef to American consumers. As the people of Nicaragua became increasingly pro-Communist, American determination to prevent "another Cuba," in Nicaragua only increased.

President Reagan's New War on Communism

The Somoza family dictatorship continued to rule Nicaragua until it was overthrown by the Sandinistas in 1979. The Sandinistas had been waging a war against the Somoza dictators since 1961. Garcia's oldest son, Luis Somoza, took over the presidency until his death in 1967. Garcia's second son, Anastasio Somoza Debayle, became the president in May 1967 and was assassinated in July 1979.

When the Sandinista forces overthrew the Somoza dictatorship in 1979, President Jimmy Carter refused to expand American military aid to rescue Somoza. By this time the American media had become increasingly anti-Somoza, exposing American support for a very repressive dictatorship. On the other hand it was clear that the Sandinistas had the overwhelming support of the Nicaraguan people.

The election of Ronald Reagan in 1980 turned American public opinion around once again. The American media propaganda was ramped up to convince Americans that any government deemed anti-American must also be anti-democratic. It's not difficult to fool westerners since they have little idea as to what democracy really means. In their view democracy meant that the souls of the Nicaraguan people needed to be saved by the god-fearing American *Christianites* while their land was stolen by American plantation owners willing to use dirt-cheap labour to produce bananas and coffee at ridiculously low prices for American consumers.

President Reagan emphasized America's determination to fight the "evil" of communism and protect American property and business interests. President Reagan cut off all American aid to Nicaragua and then armed the Contras to overthrow the popular Sandinista government. The American Empire mined the harbours in Nicaragua and expanded its military aid and training of the Contras in Honduras and Costa Rica.

At the same time, pro-American Nicaraguan politicians, such as Arturo Cruz and Enrique Bolanos, were funded by the CIA to contest the same democratic elections which the American Empire had deemed non-democratic. It was a clever two-pronged approach to overthrow the popular Sandinistas. Try to win at the polls if you can but reserve the option to overthrow the elected government if you lost. If you lose at the polls declare the process non-democratic. If you win at the polls declare the process democratic. Who would dare argue with Western logic?

President Reagan popularized the notion that the Contras were America's new "founding fathers." They were indeed the equivalent of the founding fathers of the American Empire but not the way in which Reagan believed. They were more like the Virginia dynasty of plantation owners, such as Washington, Jefferson, Madison, Monroe and Tyler, who saw no contradiction in owning slaves and supporting the god given right to own slaves, while boasting about Christian values, freedom and equality. It was this "proudly" southern, American-style plantation economy which President Reagan was using America's military muscle to defend in Nicaragua. Devastated by America's own Civil War, these southern "founding fathers" needed new lands to exploit and new non-whites to enslave.

Many Contra members had been National Guards under the Somoza dictatorship. Like the Mujahideen fighters Reagan armed in Afghanistan, the Contras were Reagan's *freedom fighters* in Nicaragua. They were well trained by the CIA in the art of torture and disrespect for human suffering or human life. Reagan was fighting the Soviets in Latin America, in Angola, in the Caribbean, and in Afghanistan, using America's wealth and superior air power. Reagan's "freedom fighters" terrorized the civilian population of Nicaragua, raping, beating, murdering, kidnapping and torturing at will. They targeted schools, medical clinics, infrastructure, farms and businesses. Over 13,000 civilians lost their lives to the Contras during the 11 year American instigated civil war in Nicaragua.

President Reagan imposed a total embargo on trade with Nicaragua in 1985 after the Sandinistas, under Daniel Ortega, won the 1984 elections, deemed free and fair by international observers. This total economic embargo was intended to bring an already devastated war-torn Nicaraguan economy, to its knees. The Nicaraguans would be forced to beg for redemption from the "Leader of the Free World" and his Christianite fundamentalists. The fact that the American Empire had toppled another **democratic** government in no way led the West to cease referring to America as "Leader of the Free World." Only the brain-dead continues to believe that Western freedoms mean anything other than American dictatorship.

In 1986 President Reagan persuaded the US Congress to vote another US $100 million dollars for military supplies to the Contras. American tax payers have always been more willing to pay for wars and military conquests than for health care and social welfare. President Reagan also opened up the American market to importing illegal drugs from his Contra drug lords fighting the Sandinistas. Americans have been indoctrinated to fear communism more than the plague. Better to increase the number of Americans suffering from drug addiction than to increase the number of Americans who do not fear communism. Since the fall of the Soviet Union American leaders have been sufficiently wise to replace communism with terrorism.

Those who naively believed that American imperialism would wane with the fall of the Soviet Union are sadly mistaken. The American Empire will be stopped by military defeats and the economic rise of Asia not by the fall of communism. Communism was a convenient scapegoat for military domination. Scapegoats are easy to find when you have gullible voters. That is why it was so easy to replace fear of communism with fear of terrorism.

American funding of the Contras began to decline after it was discovered that the Reagan Administration had been selling arms to Iran and using those funds for additional military supplies for the Contras. Public scandals such as the *Iran-Contra* scandal usually force the leaders of the American Empire to look for new "secret" wars to fight. After all, the *military industrial complex* must be supported at all cost. American presidents can never lose sight of the fact that they are first, *Commander-in-Chief,* and only secondly, President. Furthermore, the term, *Commander-in-Chief,* is an American euphemism for *Warmonger.*

The media constantly reminds Americans that the American Empire must use superior military force to be the *Leader of the Free World.* As we will see later, the invasion of the tiny island of Grenada became President Reagan's diversion for the *Iran-Contra* scandal and for continued warmongering by the military industrial complex.

President Reagan had successfully out-spent the USSR into economic oblivion. This was the tried and true policy of past and succeeding presidents. It served President George Herbert Bush when Herbert invaded Panama shortly after the departure of Reagan. Unfortunately it failed Herbert's son, George W. Bush, miserably.

With massive defeats, first in Vietnam, and now in Afghanistan, Iraq and Lebanon, military victories are becoming more expensive and more difficult to achieve. As American *Commander-in-Chiefs* divert more and more of the empire's economic resources to fighting the superior enemy on the ever expanding global battlefields, its once mighty economic stature is daily eroded. Like the British Empire after World War II the American Empire in 2010 is a debt ridden behemoth struggling desperately to forestall its inevitable decline. It is clueless and leaderless. Those Americans who have the intelligence to lead are shut out by the voices of the ignorant, the incompetent, the fear mongers, the fearful, the insane, the compulsive liars, the fanatic *Christianites,* the racists and the talk-show lunatics.

In 1986 the World Court ruled that the US was responsible for the pain inflicted on the Nicaraguan people by sabotaging its economy through actions which disrupted its shipping, international trade, oil supplies, economic aid and funding the Contra rebellion. The US was ordered by the Court to pay reparations to Nicaragua. In 1988, Senator John Kerry's *Committee on Foreign Relations,* made public the use of profits from drug trafficking by the Reagan Administration to fund the Contras.

Kerry's report further eroded public support for America's invasion of Nicaragua and signaled the need for Reagan's successor to find a new "secret" war to feed America's addiction to warmongering. The future colonization of Nicaragua would revert to American Corporations as it had been prior to 1909. Mexican style *maquiladoras* sprung up in Nicaragua in the 1990's. Nicaragua signed on to the US-Central American Free Trade Agreement in 2006. This would ensure that the USA would remain Nicaragua's largest export market. This continued economic dependency would be the American Empire's security against anti-Americanism in Nicaragua.

Somewhat ironically, Daniel Ortega, who led the first Sandinista government in 1979, was re-elected president in November 2006. Ortega had previously won the 1984 presidential elections but lost in 1990, 1996 and 2001 because the US heavily financed opposition candidates and threatened the Nicaraguan people with economic sanctions if they elected Ortega. After winning the presidency again in 2006 he was congratulated by America's old enemy, Fidel Castro, as well as America's new enemies, Hugo Chavez of Venezuela and Mahmoud Ahmadinejad of Iran.

Ortega compared the Nicaraguan struggle against American imperialism to that of Iran's, during a visit of the Iranian president to Nicaragua. In 2008, the leaders of Nicaragua, Venezuela, Columbia and Ecuador met in the Dominican Republic to show their solidarity against American imperialism in Latin America. Like Honduras, Nicaragua remains a poor country after more than a century of American colonization. Its economy had also been devastated by hurricane Mitch in 1998. However, American imperialism is the primary cause of poverty and destitution in Nicaragua.

US Invasions of Guatemala

By the time of Teddy Roosevelt's presidency, Guatemala was led by a ruthless dictator, Manuel Cabrera. Cabrera was pro-American and invited the *United Fruit Company* into Guatemala in 1901. Big business practically enslaved the people of Guatemala. They worked for minimum wages on the coffee and banana plantations. Attempts on Cabrera's life were unsuccessful.

When Cabrera was overthrown in 1920 the American Empire invaded Guatemala. Another pro-American dictator, Jorge Ubico, took over the presidency of Guatemala. Under Ubico's presidency, the American Empire consolidated its economic colonization of Guatemala. Ubico expanded the domination of Guatemala's economy by the *United Fruit Company.* The American multinational giant diversified its investments in Guatemala by investing in ports, railways, telegraph and electricity. By 1940, 90 percent of Guatemala's exports went to the United States.

During the Second World War the American Empire removed German control over Guatemala's coffee industry. Coffee had become the life blood of Guatemala's economy since the 1870's. By World War I, Germans had controlled 50 percent of Guatemala's coffee production. The removal of the German competition gave absolute economic control to the American Empire. The further impoverishing of the Guatemalan people during the Great Depression of the 1930's and the disruption of European trade during the Second World War led to the popular overthrow of the American puppet, Ubico, in June 1944.

The American Empire continued to undermine democratic governments elected by the Guatemalan people after 1944. No less than 25 coups were instigated by the American Empire against the democratic government of Juan Arevalo. US Secretary of State, John Foster Dulles, and CIA Director, Allen Dulles, led the attack by the American Empire on democracy in Guatemala. Both brothers were shareholders in the United Fruit Company.

President Dwight Eisenhower fully supported the under-cover work of the CIA in Guatemala. "Operation Success," as it was branded, included US trained assassins who would target government officials and prominent supporters of the Guatemalan government. Eisenhower launched a full scale military invasion in 1954, including aerial bombing of Guatemala City. President Jacobo Arbenz, who had succeeded President Arevalo, was "regime changed" by Eisenhower with another pro-American dictator, Colonel Carlos Armas.

Arbenz was branded a communist by the American Empire when he nationalized some of Guatemala's land previously stolen by the United Fruit Company. It mattered little to the American Empire that the United Fruit Company had stolen so much of Guatemalan land, 550,000 acres, that it could only profitably cultivate 15 percent of its holdings. The American Company claimed 40 percent of the **best** land in Guatemala and Arbenz had only nationalized land not cultivated by the Company. As Supreme Allied Commander during World War II, General Eisenhower heaped praise on Josef Stalin and the Communists in fighting the evil of Nazism. As President of an equally **evil** empire Eisenhower had no qualms about turning on his communist allies.

Arbenz had also committed the "democratic" sin of allowing a pro-labour party, *The Guatemalan Labor Party*, to contest free and open elections to win four of the 58 seats in Guatemala's legislature. President Eisenhower made an example of President Arbenz. He sent a clear message to Latin Americans that the American Empire would not tolerate democratic governments, only vicious pro-American dictators. There was no greater threat to the human race than the tiny possibility of another pro-USSR "Cuba" in Guatemala. Such remote possibilities must be viciously crushed by the *Leader of the free world*. Why else would American presidents such as Eisenhower fund America's military industrial complex instead of waging war on poverty and human misery?

America's "War on Communism," and search for world domination created chaos and instability in Guatemala. The American Empire poured its wealth and military prowess into a growing insurgency creating the same economic and political disaster we see in Afghanistan, Pakistan and Iraq today. The American Empire created a civil war in Guatemala lasting from 1960 to 1996. The infamous "death squads," which haunt civilians in all of Central America, were first introduced to Guatemala by the American Empire in 1966. They tortured and executed 200,000 civilians on behalf of the American Empire. Most of them were poor First Nations whose land had been stolen. President Reagan supported the dictatorship of General Rios Montt and his one-million strong conscript Guatemalan army. The worst human rights abuses occurred during Montt's dictatorship. Some four hundred Mayan villages were wiped off the map during the US backed genocidal war.

Peace accords signed in 1996 ended the long bloody conflict. In 1999, President Bill Clinton admitted to America's role in creating the chaos, kidnapping, human rights abuses and repression in Guatemala. President Clinton's apology to the Guatemalan people was motivated by the public testimony of Alvaro Ramos. Ramos managed to escape his captives and testified to the Inter-American Commission on Human Rights. Many Guatemalan army officers were paid by the CIA.

The American Empire is still Guatemala's largest trading partner. President Portillo, elected in 1999, continued the economic ties with the American Empire. Oscar Berger, the new president since 2004, was also pro-American. Under his presidency Guatemala joined the US-Central American Free Trade Agreement in 2005. The World Bank estimated that over half of Guatemalans still lived in dire poverty. Its rate of economic growth is still a disappointing 2.5 percent.

The evidence is overwhelming that American imperialism brought nothing but chaos and poverty to the people of Guatemala. Guatemala's economy was also affected by hurricane Mitch in 1998 and again by hurricane Stan in 2005. Like other Latin American countries, Guatemala, now led by President Alvaro Colom since 2007, is looking to Asia for a way out of American domination.

US Invasions of El Salvador

El Salvador, like Guatemala, became a predominantly, one crop coffee economy by the 1850's. It was a plantation economy like the Southern United States. The "landed gentry" was made up of 14 families. Dirt cheap non-White workers substituted for the slave labour of the American plantations. A landless, dirt poor, peasant class, was economically exploited for the benefit of the American Empire. The American Empire created the ideal breeding ground for a socialist revolution so that it would have an excuse to invade to save it from communism.

Armed with weapons from the American Empire, General Maximiliano Martinez overthrew the pro-labour government of Arturo Araujo in December 1931. An insurgency led by Farabundo Marti in January 1932 was easily crushed and Marti was executed. Martinez went on a rampage killing 30,000 civilians. Warships from the American Empire arrived in El Salvador to deter any who would dare threaten American imperialism. If you are labeled a communist by the American Empire, the Western World turns a blind eye to American atrocities against you. Such is the power of American propaganda. As many as four percent of El Salvador's population was brutally slaughtered to win America's War on Communism.

President Reagan invaded El Salvador again in 1981 to fight communism. American air strikes, ground forces and CIA operatives were combined with "death squads" to kill, maim and terrorize "communist sympathizers." The assassination of Archbishop Oscar Romero is only the most publicized of many such assassinations of those opposed to American imperialism in El Salvador. Mass executions and rape became commonplace occurrences. This American invasion, like the current invasion of Afghanistan and Iraq, led to a bloody civil war which took another 75,000 lives, mostly civilians, in El Salvador. Reagan poured millions of dollars of military aid into El Salvador to arm his "freedom fighters." Salvadorans lost their lives to Reagan's new War on Communism. As many as one million Salvadorans were forced to flee their homes.

While El Salvador is no longer a one-crop coffee economy, the United States remains its largest trading partner. With 70 percent of its exports going to the US, American domination of El Salvador will increase with the *US-Central American Free Trade Agreement*. The US dollar is its official currency. As in Vietnam today, the American Empire complements its military aggression with its Americanization of Salvadoran consumption behavior. McDonalds is but one example of the proliferation of American brands, American culture, music, movies and American products from toothpaste to software. Low income Salvadorans are induced by American advertising to purchase higher priced American imports over lower priced domestic goods. The poorer you are the more you view local produce as inferior to American goods.

The most vicious example of American imperialism in El Salvador is the forced contribution of Salvadoran troops to America's immoral and illegal invasion of Iraq. Imagine colonizing a people and forcing them to help you colonize other peoples for the expansion of your empire! Salvadorans, like Mexicans, are migrating into the United States to get better wages. The theft of their land by pro-American corporations forced Salvadorans to work for low wages on the coffee plantations. By migrating to the US they can work for higher wages and better support their families in El Salvador by sending a substantial portion of their income to El Salvador.

The fact that the lowest wage in the US exceeds what they can earn as colonized people in their own land is a good measure of the degree of exploitation by the American Empire. Once again, the evidence is indisputable. American imperialism impoverished El Salvador. Even with the remittances from families working in the US, at least half of Salvadorans live in poverty. It's a sad irony that this poverty is increasingly due to Salvadorans using the remittances to purchase high priced American imports rather than cheaper Salvadoran products. They support an empire which exploits them and dream of migrating to America as their only hope of escaping poverty.

US Invasions of Costa Rica

As in the other Central American economies, Costa Rica specialized on bananas and coffee destined for markets in the USA. The American owned *United Fruit Company* is as dominant in Costa Rica as in the other Central American republics. The American, Minor Keith, expanded banana plantations after securing ownership to Costa Rican real estate in exchange for building railways in the 1880's.

The American War on Communism heated up in Costa Rica in 1948. The anti-American government led by Calderon Guardia was overthrown with military and financial assistance from the American Empire in April 1948. Costa Rica's Communist Party was outlawed, Calderon was forced into exile in Mexico and 2,000 Costa Ricans lost their lives. Costa Rica, like Honduras, was used as a military base for President Reagan's new War on Communism in Central America.

Costa Rica is a member of the US-Central American Free Trade Agreement. A total of seven countries have signed up for CAFTA-DR. These are the United States, Guatemala, El Salvador, Nicaragua, Honduras, Costa Rica and the Dominican Republic. Eco-tourism now competes with banana and coffee exports for economic development in Costa Rica. Americans see Costa Rica as a safe haven for real estate investment. They are currently buying up large chunks of Costa Rican real estate.

US imperialism in Belize

The American Empire was somewhat more hesitant in invading Belize because of their common Anglo-imperial bond with Great Britain. While the American Empire treated the ex-Spanish colonies as its "manifest destiny" to invade and conquer it recognized that it could not enforce the "Monroe Doctrine" without British support. Implicit in this Anglo-American alliance was the acceptance by the American Empire that English colonies in the New World were not fair game for American imperial expansion.

Belize, then British Honduras, was formally recognized as a British colony in 1862. Since independence from Britain in 1981, American influence has naturally increased. Sugar and bananas remain its most important exports and the USA its most important market. Like Costa Rica it is now focusing economic development on a growing tourism sector.

Caribbean Invasions of Haiti and the Dominican Republic

The largest islands of the Caribbean, Cuba, Hispaniola, Puerto Rico and Jamaica, had been colonized by Spain after the voyages of Columbus. At the time of the Spanish American War, Jamaica was a colony of England and Hispaniola had been divided into Haiti and the Dominican Republic. As we have explained before, English colonies were not up for grabs by the American Empire before the decline of the British Empire. Having captured Cuba and Puerto Rico from Spain, the next Caribbean targets were Haiti and the Dominican Republic.

The Spanish Caribbean Empire had been under constant threat from pirates and from the other European empires of Holland, France and England. The Spanish colony of Hispaniola was gradually encroached on by the French Empire forcing the division of the island into the French colony of St. Domingue and the Spanish colony of Santo Domingo. The capture of Cuba and Puerto Rico had emboldened the American Empire. American invasions would now have the sanctity of the *Roosevelt Corollary* of 1904. Two years later the world community had seen it fit to award the Nobel Peace prize to Teddy Roosevelt despite his history of warmongering on behalf of American expansionism. Roosevelt's wars and invasions in the Caribbean and the Pacific had been sanctified as peaceful by Western hypocrites.

The Birth of the Independent Republic of Haiti

Haiti presented a unique threat to the emerging American Empire after it became an independent **Black** republic. While still fighting for its own independence from European colonialism the emerging American Empire invaded the English colony of Canada. This was the first sign that the creation of an independent union of 13 English colonies would also create one of the world's most ambitious empires. That empire would not only expand north into Canada and west into the First Nations land but also south-east into the very lucrative Caribbean.

At the start of the American War of Independence in 1775, the European colonies in the Caribbean were far more valuable than the English colony of Canada. The American invasion of Canada as early as 1775, was therefore the "easy" target before getting to the real prize of the rich sugar islands in the Caribbean, including what is now Haiti.

Of course, Canada proved to be no soft target because Canadians and First Nations chose English imperialism over American imperialism. This ingrained American arrogance is one of the many ways of supporting its military industrial complex. Failure never deters future military disasters. The invasion of Iraq in 2003 was the "easy" target on the road to Iran and North Korea. By 2003 Iraq had been softened by 12 years of "coalition" bombing by the American and British empires. Just as "failure" in Canada in 1775 only galvanized the empire to further militarization so does its "failure" in Iraq today increase its expenditures on the military.

The rhetoric quickly changes from, "Iraq is an easy "victory," to "we cannot afford to lose in Iraq." With more than two centuries of conditioned warmongering under their belt American voters support wars for easy victories as much as they support wars *we cannot afford to lose.* The military industrial complex wins either way.

In 1775, Haiti was still the French colony of St. Domingue. In 1697 Spain ceded the western portion of the colony of Hispaniola to France under the *Treaty of Ryswick*. It became the French colony of St. Domingue. Since Spain had colonized the largest Caribbean islands, England, Holland and France had to make do with the smaller islands. But colonies were exchanged at peace treaties. That is how England acquired the large Caribbean island of Jamaica and France acquired a third of the larger Caribbean island of Hispaniola.

The Dutch were the first to recognize the economic value of the smaller islands. With a high proportion of coastline to total geographical area they were ideal for sugar cane cultivation which Holland and Portugal had introduced to Brazil. St. Domingue was only one third of Hispaniola. But a third of Hispaniola was larger than the islands which had not been colonized by Spain.

By 1775, the French colony of St. Domingue had become the richest colony in the world because of the high price of sugar. This economic value alone would have made it a target for the emerging American Empire. However, the American Empire needed the superior French navy on its side to defeat England during its War of Independence, 1775-1783. St. Domingue was therefore not as easy a military target as Canada at that time. It had to wait for an opportunity when France was not its ally and also sufficiently weakened militarily not to protect its colony from an American invasion. As events unfolded the American Empire would have an urgent political motive for invading Haiti over and above the hugely titillating economic motive.

The emerging American Empire had signed a long-term alliance with the French Empire during its War of Independence against the English Empire. However, the American Empire's self interest was best served by reneging on this long-term alliance only 10 years later when England and France were at war again for the fifth time during the 18th century, 1793-1815. The long-term alliance with France had served the emerging American Empire well in its War of Independence. Without the French alliance it had absolutely no chance of wresting independence from England.

At the time, neither France nor England had the tiniest inkling that this ex-English colony would have imperial ambitions greater than they dreamed of. America's betrayal of France and the French revolution was an unexpected blow to France. However, it was a strategic move by the emerging American Empire intended to improve its imperial standing while France and England were reducing theirs. Since all of these wars included wars in their Caribbean colonies, the emerging American Empire was well placed to enhance its expansion into the Caribbean while France and England degraded their colonial wealth.

Since the arrival of Spain in the New World the European empires of Spain, Portugal, Holland, France and England, had waged incessant wars over their colonial possessions. These wars led to colonial exchanges among the European empires. Both the American War of Independence, 1775-1783, and the Napoleonic War, 1793-1815, had an important difference. At the end of the 1775-1783 war, colonies were exchanged. But the 13 English colonies which became the independent United States of America were not. This was a unique occurrence. Likewise, colonies were exchanged during the 1793-1815 war. But the French colony of St. Domingue was not. It became the independent country of Haiti.

Those who are forever doomed to be fooled by American propaganda would have naively believed that the newly independent republic of the United States of America would have welcomed and embraced the second independent republic in the New World, Haiti. Far from it. The emerging American Empire immediately saw an independent Haiti as a "soft" military target for its own territorial expansion. Canada, Haiti, Mexico and Spanish colonies in Florida and the Caribbean were quickly seen as "soft" targets for American imperial expansion. At the time, Haiti was by far the richest prize.

By the start of the Napoleonic War in 1793, St. Domingue produced more sugar than all of the English Caribbean colonies combined, including the large island of Jamaica which England had conquered from Spain in 1655. During the *Treaty of Paris* ending the Seven Years War in 1763, England would have gladly traded a much smaller French Caribbean island, Guadeloupe, for all of Canada.

A rather disturbing fact for the new American **slave** empire was that the second independent republic in the New World, Haiti, had abolished slavery. While the American Empire was succeeding in fooling the brain dead that a **slave** republic could be *Leader of the free world,* there was another republic on its doorstep, which the world did not recognize as freedom loving as the US **slave** republic but which had in fact abolished the **evil** institution of slavery.

The institution of slavery in the New World was an integral part of White colonization and **White** racism. African slaves were imported into the New World by White slave traders and bought by White plantation owners. There was an important difference between the English and French colonies in the Caribbean compared with their colonies in North America. In the Caribbean colonies the African slaves far outnumbered the White settlers and plantation owners. In the North American colonies Whites outnumbered Blacks.

The newly independent USA was therefore a **White** republic which owned **Black** slaves and practiced an extreme form of White racism against every non-White race. The newly independent Haiti was a republic where the majority was Black and which did not practice slavery. Having experienced slavery by the White imperialists it now had the political and military power to enslave the Whites but chose the moral high ground and abolished slavery.

Not so with the hypocritical "freedom loving" American republic. It hung on to slavery after every European empire had abolished slavery. Had it not been for its Civil War which President Lincoln wanted to win at all cost, slavery would still have been institutionalized. Lincoln needed the support of all Blacks, including the Black slaves in the Southern states, to win the Civil War. His abolition of slavery was the price Lincoln was willing to pay to win the Civil War. But ending slavery did not end America's extreme forms of racial discrimination against its non-White population. **White** racism is an integral part of the American Empire to this day.

Haiti, like the USA, secured its independence from the European empires while these empires were busily engaged fighting each other. At the outbreak of the French revolution in 1793, St. Domingue was populated by Whites, Mixed Race children of Whites and Blacks, Free Blacks and Black slaves. Both the British and Spanish empires attempted to conquer St. Domingue after war broke out in 1793. By 1798 however, the European empires were defeated and St. Domingue became the independent republic of Haiti.

Napoleon attempted to re-conquer the colony in 1802 but his forces were defeated by the Haitians. In the new Haitian republic all citizens were considered Black, regardless of the colour of their skin. Whites were not allowed to own property but had a far superior status than Blacks in the American Empire. Many American Blacks immigrated into Haiti in the 1820's to escape White American racism. Haiti received diplomatic recognition by France and became increasingly attractive to investments from Germany.

The American Empire was very concerned about the influence of Haiti in fomenting slave rebellions in the "land of the free." It was not until it was forced to abolish slavery to win the Civil War that it gave Haiti diplomatic recognition in 1862. With its European connections Haiti managed to forestall American invasion until the beginning of the 20th century.

US Invasions of Haiti

Haiti had been on the American Empire's radar ever since it became an independent republic. A rich sugar republic on America's doorstep without protection by a strong European Empire was more than enough temptation for an expansionist warmonger like the US. But Haiti was also a **Black** republic which had freed its Black slaves. This sent the wrong signals to the American aristocracy who believed firmly in the institution of slavery but professed to the world that they believed in freedom, democracy and republican values more than European empires which had also abolished slavery. Haiti was simply a thorn in the side of America's strong belief in hypocrisy and propaganda. American colonization of Haiti began with Haiti's tiny off-shore island of Navassa.

US Invasion of Navassa Island: 1857

The two square mile island of *Navassa,* 35 miles from Haiti, is extremely rich in *guano* deposits. In the previous chapter we explained the American incursion into the Pacific by way of Midway Island. Under the Guano Islands Act which had enabled Captain Middlebrooks to claim Midway Island for the American Empire, Navassa Island was claimed by Captain Peter Duncan in 1857, despite protests by the independent republic of Haiti.

Haiti rightly claimed that Navassa was an integral part of Haiti since it had been an integral part of the French colony of St. Domingue. Navassa is recognized as an integral part of Haiti in its constitution and in many books on Haitian history. Haitian fishermen had been fishing the coast around the island before the American invasion. When Haitian emperor Faustin I sent his gun boats to threaten the Americans the American Empire responded with its much more powerful war ships.

The American Empire employed Blacks under a state of semi-slavery to mine the rich guano deposits. In 1889 the Blacks rebelled against their White semi-slave masters. The American Empire sent a warship to rescue the Whites and capture the Blacks for trial in the US. The trial publicized the torture, beatings, enslavement and deaths of the Blacks on the island.

The American Empire appointed Governor James Woodward to administer the island. In 1917 the American Empire built a lighthouse on the island to protect American ships passing between Haiti and Cuba en-route to the Panama Canal. The American Empire continues to oppose Haiti's legal claim to the island. A recent estimate suggests that the guano deposits are worth over two billion dollars today. Guano continues to be a very valuable organic fertilizer.

US Invasion of 1915

While Haiti had been a prime target for an American invasion since the Napoleonic War the American Empire had kept itself extremely busy elsewhere carving up the Spanish colonies, Mexico, First Nations lands, Alaska, the Pacific and Central America. The rise of the German Empire in the second half of the 19th century and the threat of World War I provided the opportunity for an American invasion of Haiti safe from European opposition.

President Woodrow Wilson sent an invasion force to Haiti on July 28, 1915. As in all other invasions, the American Empire invaded to protect American lives and American property. American economic imperialism in Haiti was the excuse for military invasion and conquest. American Banks, in particular, had invested in the Haitian banking sector and wanted political control of Haiti to exercise economic and financial control.

When Haitians rebelled against pro-American dictator, Guillaume Sam, the American Empire invaded and established a military government. Haiti became another American *uncolony*. The evidence is overwhelming that the American occupation was not only exploitative but very brutal. The Americans created a local police force, the *Gendarmerie d'Haiti,* to do its dirty deeds of torture and intimidation. The American occupation naturally opened up the Haitian economy to even more American investment. Americans could now purchase land. Purchase of Haitian land by Whites had been prohibited by the independent Haitian republic to prevent any return to American-style **slave** plantations. With American land ownership, Haitian peasants were returned to a semi-slavery condition and forced to build roads for the American *uncolony*.

An insurgency which began in 1919 was initially led by Charlemagne Peralte. When the Americans killed Peralte, the insurgency continued under a new leader, Benoit Batraville. The Americans were forced to bring more troops to support their local militia. After killing Batraville and 15,000 Haitians, the Americans prevailed. Haitians were forced to live under the same type of extreme "Jim Crow" racism practiced in the US after Lincoln was forced to abolish slavery to win the Civil War.

Many Haitians found partial escape from American imperialism by working as farm labour in Cuba and the Dominican Republic. In the 1990's Haitians became the new "boat people." Like Vietnam before, the American Empire had failed miserably in its efforts to conquer Haiti. Instead it had created another group of refugees willing to risk their lives to sail away from the devastation of their homeland by an **evil** and callous empire. The American Empire has still not completely ended its occupation of Haiti. Haiti, like the Central American republics invaded and conquered by an **evil** American Empire, has nothing but extreme poverty to show for its American occupation.

US Invasions of the Dominican Republic

After the Haitian revolution created the independent Haitian republic, Spain had a very difficult time keeping Santo Domingo as a colony. Spanish colonies in the Caribbean and on the Mainland were fighting for independence from Spain. Santo Domingo was about twice the size of Haiti but was much poorer because of economic neglect by Spain. The Black general, Toussaint L'Ouverture, who had defeated the British and thereby gained independence for Haiti, abolished slavery in the Dominican Republic in 1801.

In doing so he was enforcing the will of the French Republic following the French revolution in France. The French National Convention had abolished slavery in all French colonies in 1794. The act took effect immediately in Haiti and led to supplying arms to the freed slaves who helped to defeat the British invasion of 1798. By 1801, L'Ouverture had conquered the Dominican Republic, thereby enabling him to enforce the abolition act of the Revolutionary government.

Napoleon wanted the wealth of the richest ex-French colony of Haiti to pay for his wars in Europe. He sent a massive invasion force in 1802, under the leadership of his brother-in-law, Charles Leclerc, to re-capture the rich sugar island and to return slavery to the French Caribbean colonies. Leclerc resorted to treachery by capturing L'Ouverture during a peace negotiation but Leclerc and over half of his men died of tropical diseases such as yellow fever.

L'Ouverture's second in command, Jean-Jacques Dessalines, easily defeated Leclerc's successor, Vicomte de Rochambeau in November 1803. Haiti's independence was confirmed in 1804 with Dessalines as emperor. Napoleon was forced to sell Louisiana to the American Empire to replenish his war chest. He received far less than what the exports of sugar from Haiti would have brought him. The defeat of Napoleon's Caribbean force by Haiti was largely responsible for his later defeat by Wellington and the eventual demise of the French Empire in the New World.

An even more important fact ignored by historians was that Napoleon's defeat made the abolition of slavery in the Dominican Republic by L'Ouverture, a permanent reality which the **slave** republic of USA had to contend with. Napoleon's defeat by Haiti had gained the massive Louisiana Territory for the American Empire but it had also left one more threat to the **evil** institution of slavery which was so sacred to the American Empire. The American Empire's expansion into the vast Louisiana Territory enhanced the profitability of slavery in the American Empire by creating new sugar and cotton plantations requiring large numbers of African slaves.

As slavery declined in the Caribbean because of the French and Haitian revolutions it simultaneously increased in the American Empire. Western historians unabashedly claim this increased entrenchment of slavery in the American Empire as a major qualification for America to be "Leader of the Free World." This rather pathetic view of freedom by Western historians is consistent with the notion that the West was chosen by God to dominate over all others and therefore America's determination to maintain slavery when Europe was less willing to, implies that leadership of the "free" must pass from Europe to America.

It was under the dictatorship of Lilis Heureaux, beginning in 1882, that the American Empire increased its economic colonization of the Dominican Republic. The American Empire formally took control of the Dominican Republic's economy in 1905 after pro-American dictators had bankrupted the country. A 50 year treaty was signed in 1906. This enabled increased American investment and control of the Dominican Republic's sugar industry.

Dominican resistance to American economic colonization led to the US military invasion of May 15, 1916, less than a year after the US invasion of Haiti. President Wilson's public lies about the "right to self-determination," applied, at best, to the White race only. As in Haiti, an American military government was imposed on the people of the Dominican Republic. The Dominican insurgency continued a guerilla war against the US occupation. The Americans created and trained a highly centralized indigenous police force to use brutal tactics to crush the insurgents.

Many small peasant farmers in the Dominican Republic lost their land to the American plantation owners. By the end of the US occupation in 1924, American plantations owned over 80 percent of the sugar producing land in the Dominican Republic. The American Empire formed an alliance with the Dominican Republic's dictator, Rafael Trujillo, in 1940. Trujillo became America's anti-communist warrior in the Caribbean. When Trujillo became a liability to the American Empire the CIA was ordered by President Eisenhower to assassinate him in 1961.

The original Spanish colony of Hispaniola had become two American *uncolonies.* The three largest islands of the Caribbean, Cuba, Hispaniola and Puerto Rico, colonized by Spain for over three centuries had become part of an ever expanding American Empire before the end of World War I. It was one more indication that World War I would mark the relative decline of the European empires and the ascendancy of the American Empire. The American Empire would expand by conquering the colonies of the European empires as each of those empires was weakened by wars among themselves. Spain was the first target as it was weaker than France, England or Germany.

The second US invasion of the Dominican Republic took place on April 28, 1965. *Operation Power Pack,* as the empire's invasion was aptly named, lasted about 18 months. The key motivation for this second US invasion was the prevention of democratically elected governments which would nationalize American corporations. "Another Cuba," could not be allowed in the Caribbean.

The Dominican Republic had elected Juan Bosch after the assassination of Trujillo. Bosch was not sufficiently anti-communist for President Lyndon Johnston. A successful invasion of the Dominican Republic would also take some heat away from Johnston's military failures in Vietnam. Americans love a warmongering Commander-in-Chief, but only if he is winning. Johnston imposed a naval blockade of the island and landed an invasion force of 42,000. The US puppet, Joaquin Balaguer, was installed as president in June 1966.

The American Empire could safely draw down its forces for other conquests. Rather than nationalizing American corporations Balaguer welcomed increased American investment in the Dominican Republic. In 1978, President Jimmy Carter refused to invade again to protect Balaguer against the democratically elected Antonio Guzman.

American colonization has left a legacy of poverty in the Dominican Republic. As in other parts of Latin America, Dominicans must emigrate to the US mainland to find low paying jobs to support their family in the Dominican Republic. New York is only a short distance from the Caribbean. They join the immigrants from Mexico, Central America, Puerto Rico and other American *uncolonies* to create a new political force in the American Empire.

By over extending itself with its insatiable greed for more and more territory the American Empire is sowing the seeds of its own destruction from within and without. White Americans speak of illegal immigration as if they entered the New World legally. Whites stole the land from the First Nations and the Non-Whites are returning the favour. By 2004, the Dominican Republic could sense the relative decline in the power of the American Empire. It safely thumbed its nose at American imperialism by pulling out the 300 soldiers it was coerced into sending to Iraq just a year earlier.

CHAPTER 7

Taking on the Big Guns: US Invasions of Russia, China and Japan: 1917-1945

The European empires did not know it at the time but the First World War marked their demise and the simultaneous rise of the American Empire as the dominant international player. Prior to World War I, the American Empire was expanding relatively close to home in Central America, the Atlantic and the Pacific. It finished off the ailing Spanish Empire while challenging Japan. But it did not go head to head with Britain, France, Germany or Russia. All that changed with the First World War. The Europeans had engaged in one war too many and it wiped them out. The First World War simultaneously gave a huge boost to the emerging American Empire by providing it with massive economic opportunities to supply the warring Europeans with armaments, raw materials, food and loans.

The US had invaded China and Japan before. But it had done so in co-operation with the dominant European empires of Britain and France in pursuit of its so called *Open Door Policy*. Expansion of international trade with China and Japan had been its over-riding objective. In the post-1917 period the American Empire invaded Russia, China and Japan as part of its global onslaught on communism and its quest for hegemony. Hegemony was the over-riding objective but "War on Communism," was its public propaganda.

We begin with Russia since it was the birthplace of the communist revolution which swept the globe after the Russian revolution of 1917. China and Japan will be dealt with both as a single entity and individually. Our treatment of China and Japan as a single entity will be yet another major departure in our interpretation of history and American invasions.

The fact that Russia was an ally of the American Empire in 1917 did not in any way discourage the Americans from invading. The American Empire signed many alliances with the First Nations. That did not deter its many invasions and conquests of First Nations land. The American Empire had signed an Alliance with France to help them win their independence from Britain. That did not deter its invasions and conquests of French colonies. The American Empire promoted dictators like Saddam Hussein, Manuel Noriega and Rafael Trujillo. That did not deter the CIA from arranging their assassination or demise when the short-term interest of the American Empire changed.

The American Empire had longed for hegemony ever since it had been 13 tiny colonies of the British Empire. The incessant European wars played into its hands. All it needed now was a cause which it could use to justify its military madness. That cause was the communist revolution in Russia in 1917. It was the perfect gift. Communism was "evil." No one has to be convinced that evil must be destroyed. More importantly, no one has to be convinced that those who destroy evil must be "good." Add to this good vs. evil nonsense the fact that most of the American allies fighting this "evil" were in the West and were **White** whereas most of the Russian allies were in the East and were **Non**-Whites, and you have one of the most formidable combination of media propaganda, covert racism, moral hyperbole and military-industrial complex, the world has ever had to contend with. This formidable coalition of the willing has so infected mankind since 1917 that the West has failed to produce a single statesman with sufficient clout to stand up to American genocide, wars, invasions and general destruction of freedoms, humanity and the human spirit.

It's important to emphasize that in **every** case, no exceptions, the American Empire is the aggressor and the invader. That needs emphasis because few are bold enough or wise enough to cast the American Empire in the role of aggressor. The world makes ridiculous excuses for American aggression and American invasions. No country has yet invaded the USA. That is certainly true of the three countries, Russia, China and Japan, which we are highlighting in this chapter. The Japanese attack on Pearl Harbour was not an invasion of the US. Pearl Harbour is Hawaiian territory. The USA has no more legal rights to Hawaiian territory than the Japanese.

How the West made Communism a banned substance?

Only a demented civilization like the Western civilization could have turned a worthwhile human goal such as communism into something so evil that no Western nation dare permit a Communist Party in their so called democratic system. Diehard Western communists meekly call themselves *socialists* to minimize the "fire and brimstone" that would be rained on them by their so called democratic governments and by most segments of their brain-washed "free" electorate. Emerging Nations like China and Russia have to do as much as possible to deny their belief in the ideals of communism to gain admission to Western clubs such as the WTO and Western controlled international financial markets. CNN reporters are forced to say Communist China whenever they mean the *Peoples Republic of China* to keep their jobs in the "land of the free" and "the home of the brave."

The American propaganda has so intimidated Western intellectuals that they pretend to forget that the ideals of socialism and communism were born, not in Russia or China, but in Western Europe, and France, in particular. They were a continuation of the ideals of the French revolution to search for a more egalitarian and just society than *Monarchy, Aristocracy and Capitalism.* The French revolution had overthrown the monarchy and the aristocracy. But the revolution would not be complete if a tiny percentage of the people owned most of the wealth and consumed most of the goods and services. Capitalism had produced this tiny upper class because of the sanctity of *private property.* By the nineteenth century Western intellectuals were rightly convinced that *communal property* was a far better ideal for the human race to strive for.

The sanctity of communal property scared the living daylights out of the American Empire and its aristocratic landed gentry and capitalist class. Unlike the French, Russian and Chinese revolutions, the American Revolution had simply replaced the imperial aristocracy of England with a home grown American aristocracy. Despite the Western rhetoric to the contrary, **capitalism** is inherently **un-democratic.** How can the concentration of wealth among a few create a democracy? The reality is that the West has become so caught up with demonizing communism that it has totally lost sight of what democracy is? In the West, democracy has come to mean having more than one political party. In the United States, as in most Western countries, the system has forced the people to choose between two parties with minimal difference in policies. Yet Americans are now fed the latest Western propaganda that China and Russia cannot be democratic because those countries only have one political party.

Economists from Adam Smith to Milton Friedman have contributed to the false notion that democracy is impossible without capitalism. This line of reasoning suggests that true democratic freedom requires free enterprise and free markets, two of the characteristics of capitalism. Western ideologues who falsely use economics to justify their rant against communism conveniently omit universally accepted economic theories which conclude that capitalism, free enterprise and free markets lead to huge inequalities of income and wealth. Unless the state intervenes to redistribute income and wealth capitalism is inconsistent with democracy.

Sure enough there have been numerous dissenting voices in the West, but they have all been marginalized and silenced by the overwhelming desire of the West to dominate. Their bravery and wisdom in challenging the American madness has been largely ignored. The propaganda has been so pervasive that they are often portrayed as whacoes. On the other side of the coin, for every activist, intellectual, Hollywood celebrity and Human Rights organization which criticize the American Empire for its abuses there is an equal number who deliberately take the spotlight off the United Sates, Canada and other Western countries by scapegoating countries supportive of communism.

Over the years these scapegoats have shifted back and forth between Russia, China, Myanmar, Iraq, Iran, Cuba, North Korea, Japan, Venezuela and several countries in Africa. Canada today, for example, treats its First Nations far worse than China treats its minorities. Yet Canada is touted as having a far better human rights record than China. The world falsely believes this to be true because China dared to embrace the civilized goal of "communal" property.

White Americans had stolen First Nations land by military force but also by denying their "communal rights" to the land. Private property was the very essence of an empire founded on stolen land. Unlike the French Revolution, the American Revolution was a false revolution. Having "legalized" the stolen First Nations land by promoting the superiority of private property over communal property it pretended to be a revolution against monarchy, aristocracy and a privileged wealthy class. In reality it was a revolution against a foreign English aristocracy in favour of a domestic American aristocracy.

A small upper class, mostly in Virginia and Massachusetts, gave themselves private property rights to most of the stolen First Nations land. This home grown landed gentry fooled the American masses about their true intentions in order to get their support to overthrow British colonialism and start their own empire. This empire, founded on a tiny strip of land in the New World, would become the most militaristic, warmongering, expansionist, greedy, cowardly, unprincipled and inhumane empire the world had ever experienced. It made the atrocities committed by the earlier European empires pale by comparison.

The birth of communism in the nineteenth century in Europe and its successful revolution in Russia in 1917 posed a dilemma for the false American Revolution. It could not deny the egalitarian principles of socialism and communism without condemning the public principles of its own revolution. It therefore chose to continue to lie about the true nature of its own revolution and publicise a second false notion that communism was evil and ungodly. Every Western leader has bought into this falsehood. They have bought into this falsehood to such a degree that every American military invasion of peaceful countries has been supported by these brain dead Western leaders as a fight against the "evil" of communism.

The Americans have convinced every Western person that communism is inconsistent with democracy. No Western person even questions or looks for contrary evidence when the Americans equate communism with dictatorship. Western "democracies" are far from democratic. Yet their people blindly assume that countries which are not unquestionably allied to this false Western democracy are non-democratic. The reality is that it is the people of these non-Western countries, such as the people of China today, who are the ones searching for a truly democratic society.

There are, of course, Westerners who criticize the United States and even their own copycat American democracy. They typically fall into two categories. There are those who console themselves with the idiotic notion that their democracy may not be perfect but it's still the best. There are others who pretend that they have not copied America. Canadians are a good example of the second group. They are very critical of many things American. But their actions, views, politics, media and institutions are as American as apple pie.

Whether you get your news and views from CBC, BBC or CNN matters very little. The newscasters may be different but the message is identical. They even use the same exact words, fearing that any slight change of language may confuse the precision of the intended propaganda. The propaganda is clear. The West is superior in every respect compared to others. The West is democratic and free. Others are not. Better to have a broken, lying, deceitful, warmongering, inhumane Western democracy than what the "others" have. The key to our continued hegemony is to stay on this message regardless of the consequences. We must support the American Empire at all cost. Only America can guarantee our continued sense of **White** superiority.

Not that the American Empire gave the West much of a choice. Western countries either ally themselves with the US and support the empire's propaganda or risk being invaded and have regime change imposed on them. By controlling all Western institutions such as the capital and financial markets, the World Bank, the WTO, the G-8, the IMF the UN, economic blackmail by the American Empire is usually sufficient to get compliance. But military invasion with the world's most sophisticated arsenal of weapons is always signalled as an option which the American Empire will not hesitate to use to "protect its way of life."

The Communist Revolution in Russia and the Zimmerman Telegram: 1917

The American Empire had been careful not to join the European empires in their incessant wars against each other. In doing so it saw its own power grow relative to the European empires. Instead of suffering economic devastation by participating in the conflict it made significant economic gains by supplying the warring empires. But in 1917 it was drawn into the European war begun in 1914, which we now call the First World War. It was this war which ended the rule of the Czars in Russia and created the opportunity for the American Empire to invent the "evil" of communism to justify its own military conquest of the world.

In return for American assistance to rebuild their war destroyed economies and for international trade and economic cooperation with the Americans, European leaders had to crush all intellectual dissent. No European intellectual would be allowed to promote the virtues of socialism and communism over capitalism as they had done in the nineteenth century. Socialists and communists throughout Western Europe would be hunted down and harassed. Any European government which was not publicly pro-American and pro-Capitalist was deemed a communist sympathiser by the American Empire. Born in Western Europe after the French Revolution, socialism and communism were stamped out by Western European leaders because of their fear of the Americans. Communism could only flourish where the long arm of the ugly American was out of reach. This was Russia and China. To this day the American juggernaut has failed to impose its will on these two giants who continue to fight for everyone's freedom by standing up to the American bully.

The Americans had stayed out of the European conflict as long as it was economically and strategically beneficial for them to do so. While supplying the belligerents in Europe it strutted and flexed its military muscle in the Caribbean and in Latin America. Mexico had been an easy target for American expansion. As we saw in Chapter 2, the American Empire had already invaded and conquered half of Mexico. The First World War provided an opportunity to conquer the rest of Mexico while the Europeans were busy beating up on each other. Mexico was in turmoil since the beginning of its own revolution in 1910.

Taking advantage of a weakened Mexico and the war in Europe the American Empire invaded Mexico again in 1916. Its forces were led by General John Joseph, *Blackjack,* Pershing. However, this invasion of Mexico backfired when Germany saw an opportunity to form an alliance with Mexico. The now infamous *Zimmerman Telegram* of January 19, 1917, was intercepted by British intelligence and passed on to the Americans. Germany was offering the Mexicans an alliance to regain territory conquered by the American Empire since the 1840's. Fearing an alliance between Mexico and Germany which may even have swayed Japan to switch sides, General Pershing was ordered by President Wilson to high tail it out of Mexican territory to fight the Germans in Europe.

The term *socialism* first appeared in the English language in 1832 while the term *communism* first appeared in the 1840's when the *Communist League* was founded. While having the common goal of distributing income and wealth more equally than *capitalism,* the American Empire focused its wrath on communism because communists believed in the abolition of private property. While both socialists and communists blamed private property for the unequal distribution of income and wealth under capitalism, communists were seen as more extreme in their condemnation of the "evil" of private property.

Two prominent German members of the *Communist League* were Karl Marx and Friedrich Engels. They co-wrote the *Communist Manifesto* in January 1848. Born in Western Europe, socialism and communism reached Russia much later in 1898 with the founding of the *Social Democratic Labour Party.* The Party organized a demonstration by 200,000 workers against Czar Nicholas II in 1905 in St. Petersburg. Russian peasants also rose up against the Czar. The workers founded local councils called *soviets.* These *soviets,* especially the *soviets* in St. Petersburg and Moscow, would later play the leading role in the Russian revolution. "Power to the soviets," became the rallying cry of the revolution. Such demonstrations had taken place in Western Europe much earlier in 1848.

It was Russia's humiliation in World War I which gave the workers and the peasants the courage to establish the first communist state in the world. World War I brought military defeats and widespread starvation. Russia lost 9 million men in combat alone. Starvation killed many more Russians. The country was ripe for revolution. Vladimir Lenin and his wife, Krupskaya, were dedicated Russian Communists. Lenin campaigned for the overthrow of the Czar while exiled in Switzerland. In 1903, Lenin had founded the *Bolshevik Party* which would lead the revolution against the Czar. While the war had been a disaster for Russia, by 1917 the Germans were ready for a peace treaty with Russia to fight the Americans who had now entered the war as a result of the Zimmerman telegram. Whupping the Americans was now more strategically important to Germany than conquering Russia. Lenin was able to convince the Germans that if the Bolsheviks overthrew the Czar he would sign a peace treaty with Germany and cede valuable Russian territory to Germany.

Germany arranged for Lenin and key members of the Bolshevik Party to be smuggled into Russia on April 3, 1917. Czar Nicholas II had already abdicated on March 2, 1917 following massive demonstrations by Russian workers and disloyalty by the Czar's forces. The communist revolution established a provisional government led by Alexander Kerensky since Lenin was still in exile. Lenin took control of the revolution as soon as he arrived in St. Petersburg, with the slogan, *Peace, Bread and Land.* Peace for Russia's war weary and demoralized army, bread for the starving poor and land for Russia's peasants. Russian peasants flocked to Lenin's *Bolshevik Party.* With the help of Leon Trotsky and the Russian army, Lenin was able to overthrow the Kerensky government and lead the first truly Communist government on October 26, 1917. Lenin's Bolshevik Party was later renamed the *Communist Party.*

America's worst nightmare had come to pass in Russia. The American Empire would no longer fight only for the land of others. It would now have to fight for its false revolution founded on the sanctity of *private property* and aristocratic values based on wealth and privilege. Canada and Mexico would be saved from future invasions by the American Empire. They would become America's allies in its global war on communism.

The evidence is overwhelming that without the priority of waging war on communists everywhere, the American Empire would have invaded and conquered the ex-English and ex-French colonies in the New World as it had already invaded and conquered the ex-Spanish colonies in the New World. When Canadians sound off on Russia and China, as they obsessively do with pride and glee, they would be wise to remember that it was the communist revolutions in Russia and China which saved them from certain American invasion and conquest.

Having said that, those Canadians who long for true independence rightly despise their satellite status to the American Empire. At every turn Canadians must kowtow to the explicit and implicit threats of the American Empire to retain the little sovereignty which the American Empire permit them to have in exchange for Canada's implicit and explicit support of the American wars on communism and terrorism. For example, some naïve Canadians wondered why Canadians paid more attention to the US presidential race in 2008 than their own federal election. The truth is, why bother about who wins in Ottawa when Canadian policies will be dictated by Washington?

US Invasion of Russia: 1918-20

The American Empire was so obsessed with the threat of communism to their false sense of identity that they could not wait for the end of World War I to invade Russia. The American Empire had entered the First World War on the side of the allies after the *Zimmerman telegram.* Russia, still ruled by the Czars, was fighting the Germans on the Eastern front and receiving war supplies from the allies. On entering the war, the American Empire also began to send war supplies to its Russian ally. Despite its professed republican and democratic values the American Empire had absolutely no hesitation allying itself with the Czarist monarchy of Russia to safeguard its conquered Mexican territory in California, Arizona and New Mexico.

In terms of the reality of the American political system, the Russian-American alliance of 1917 was a perfect fit. Czarist Russia had abolished serfdom in 1861 but many Russians still lived semi-servile lives as landless labourers. Likewise, the American Empire had abolished slavery in 1865 but many Americans continued to live in a state of semi-slavery. The popular overthrow of the Czar in March 1917 caught the Americans by surprise. While the American Empire preaches a love for democracy and freedom it secretly abhors free democratic societies and is threatened by true democracy.

The American Empire had entered into an alliance with Russia because Czar Nicholas II oversaw a Russian government with the same ideals as the American Empire. Of course the American Empire publicly professed otherwise but what mattered was the reality of how the two countries were governed not the rhetoric and hypocrisy. In 1917, Russia and America were aristocracies with small governing elites. They ruled over a small middle class who supported the governing elite and a large under class with very limited freedom and economic opportunities. The American ruling elite was no different from the Russian ruling elite. They shared the same lifestyles, goals and aspirations. The American elite were simply better at their propaganda skills. They were better able to fool Americans and the world as to their true intensions. Germany had threatened the territory controlled by the Russian elite and in 1917 Germany threatened the territory controlled by the American elite. It was only natural that they would form an alliance to defeat Germany.

Shortly after this natural Russian-American alliance, the Russian people dealt a deadly blow to American hypocrisy. The Russian underclass revolted against the Russian ruling elite. Like the French and Haitian revolutions before, the Russian revolution challenged the survival of the American aristocracy. Far from allying itself with the new Russian reality the American Empire was now forced to invade the new Russia and overthrow its very popular **democratic** government. And that is precisely what it did in September 1918, only a year after it had allied itself with the former Czarist regime. As with so many failed invasions beginning with its first invasion of Canada, the American Empire over-estimated the power of its propaganda in swaying the "hearts and minds" of the Russian people in aiding the American invasion. As the Russian people saw through the false promise of American freedom, Russian support for the invading forces collapsed and forced the American Empire to retreat in the face of military defeat.

When Czar Nicholas I abdicated on March 2, 1917 the initial strategy of the American Empire was to support the establishment of a pro-American populist government. While the American Empire would prefer an elitist regime which shared similar values as those of the American aristocracy it would support a more democratic regime if such a regime was pro-American. The reality, however, is that popularly elected democratic governments can hardly support American imperialism and still remain popular. Before long, therefore, the American Empire was at war with the new government chosen by the Russian people. As we would expect, the elitists overthrown by the Russian people aided the Americans. The American invasion led to a bloody civil war in Russia, not unlike the civil wars in Iraq, Afghanistan and elsewhere, which erupted after American invasions.

Bolshevism to Communism

Public American policies for invading countries are naturally unclear, contradictory and malleable since these public policies are always intended to deceive the American people and the international community. The Russian invasion was no exception. Public reasons given by President Wilson for the 1918 American invasion of Russia included the usual American hyperbole of saving the Russian people from tyranny in addition to preventing war supplies from falling into German hands, maintaining the Trans-Siberian railway, enabling the safe evacuation of Czech soldiers from Russian soil, keeping the Japanese Empire in check and fighting *Bolshevism*. The "evil" *Communists* had not yet threatened American hegemony. But the *Bolsheviks* were.

It matters very little whether American hegemony is threatened by *Communists, Socialists, Terrorists, Bolsheviks,* or *Peaceniks*. What matters is for us to understand that whatever threatens American hegemony will become the new unquestioned evil word. The American Empire can then use that single word to justify its launch of a thousand missiles against defenceless women and children without any world leader questioning its motives. While American leaders are themselves often confused about the specific reasons behind a given invasion, these specific reasons are unimportant in assessing the truth behind any given American invasion.

It is sufficient for us to focus only on the single over riding reason for any and all American invasions. That singular reason is world domination through the use of its military superiority. The American Empire only retreats from this singular goal when it loses the military advantage, as it so often does. But it is only temporarily deterred. Its defeat spurs it on to even greater military spending. Its withdrawal from a losing war enables it to rebuild its military superiority to invade another day. Its military-industrial complex never loses.

Lenin's *Bolshevik Party* came to power in Russia prior to the end of the First World War. Russia had been an American ally against Germany. As the defeat of Germany became imminent, the American Empire was quick to recognize that the threat to its hegemony would come from Russia, not Germany. It had to invent a propaganda war against Russia to win public support in America for yet another war, even before the First World War had ended. That propaganda war was to convince the American people that they had much to fear from the "evil" *Bolsheviks*.

In fact, *Bolshevism* was so evil that it had satanic powers to miraculously fly all the way from Russia to reach into the very homes of the American people. Distance would not save the American people from such powerful evil. The Russians would not need ships or planes or missiles to reach American soil since the "evil" of *Bolshevism* was such a powerful force. That is the reason why Americans must invade Russia and kill *Bolshevism* before it infects the entire galaxy.

American invaders have always allied with local opportunists. The Russian invasion was no different. Given America's long history of **White** subjugation of the **Red** First Nations, it was natural for the American invaders to ally themselves with the **White** Russians against the **Red** *Bolsheviks*. Race and colour is never outside American politics, culture, history, discussion, opportunity and daily life. The American media quickly associated the Bolsheviks with Jews and Blacks.

President Wilson was careful to restrain his own inherent racism by having his outspoken Secretary of State, Robert Lansing, make the more strident racist comments. As in Iraq later, the American instigated civil war in Russia was much more costly in terms of Russian lives than in American lives. The Russian Civil War, begun by the Americans in 1918, lasted until 1923 and took an estimated 15 million Russian lives. Later American instigated civil wars in Latin America, China, Korea, Palestine, Lebanon, Vietnam, Afghanistan, Iraq, Iran and Pakistan were equally costly in terms of human lives. Yet the world community openly sanctions American invasions and atrocities in the name of democracy, freedom and other *Western* fantasies.

The American Expeditionary Force

As part of its propaganda to "win hearts and minds," the American Empire uses invasion language which is intentionally deceptive. That is why its initial invasion force into Russia was called an "Expeditionary Force." When this "Expeditionary Force," was soundly beaten by the Russians, the American Empire could more easily deny military defeat by pretending to withdraw an "expeditionary" force rather than its marines. Frequent military defeats of its marines would sap morale in future invasions.

This so called "expeditionary" force was made up of 5,500 marines under the command of Lieutenant Colonel George Stewart. It arrived at the Russian port of *Archangel*, on August 2, 1918, over three months before the Allies ended the First World War on November 11, 1918. The German threat to American hegemony had stalled the American Empire's second invasion of Mexico. With the end of World War I in sight the American Empire had to find a new military target for its military industrial complex.

The First World War had severely weakened Russia. Russia had suffered more than any of the other Allies. It had suffered the most humiliating military defeats by Germany, lost over 2 million men and brought famine to the Russian people. It had been forced to surrender vast amounts of territories and resources to Germany. The treaty of *Brest-Litovsk,* signed on March 3, 1918 from a position of weakness, effectively transferred 70 percent of its industries and a third of its people and farm land to Germany and its allies. This smaller weakened Russia looked like an easy target for an American Empire hungry for world domination. There was no time to lose. It had to strike before France, England, Germany and Japan could re-vitalize their economies and challenge it for shared imperial hegemony.

Colonel George Stewart joined forces with the Canadians, British, French and the *White* Russian opportunists to defeat the Russians in the North. As usual, the Americans over-estimated local support for their cause and over-estimated their military prowess. Within two months of their optimistic invasion they were forced on the defensive by the superior Russian forces. But it was really the cold Arctic winter in Northern Russia which devastated the American marines and sent them packing by June 27, 1919.

They would have left earlier if American ships had had the technology to penetrate the frozen ice blocking entry into the Russian port of Archangel. They retreated in humiliation as they had done before from Canada and as they would do later from Vietnam, Afghanistan and Iraq.

With such a humiliating military defeat, President Woodrow Wilson would have to ramp up the verbal propaganda war against *Bolshevism*. During his eight year term from 1913-1921, President Wilson had previously invaded Mexico, China, Cuba, Panama, Turkey, Haiti, Honduras, Guatemala, Yugoslavia, the Dominican Republic and Nicaragua. The West sanctified his warmongering by presenting him with the Nobel Peace Prize in 1919 while he was at war in Russia. Wilson was given the maligned "Peace Prize" for fighting communism just as Barack Obama was given the "Peace Prize" for fighting terrorism. In reality they were both fighting for American domination of the world.

Wilson's plan had been to overthrow the Bolsheviks and establish a pro-American military dictatorship in Russia as he had done elsewhere. The American electorate love wars and invasions, but only when they are winning. President Warren Harding distanced himself from the Russian invasion by blaming President Wilson for the military misadventure. The disgraced American marines consoled themselves by pretending that they had been on a "Polar Bear" hunt. The *Expeditionary Force* became the *Polar Bear Expedition*.

The Trans-Siberian Railway

One obvious way of holding a nation at ransom after you invade it is to control its transportation life line. In the case of Russia that life line was the *Trans-Siberian Railway*. Imports into Russia through the ports of Archangel and Vladivostok were only accessible to the Russian people via the Trans-Siberian Railway. President Wilson sent a second invasion force into Russia to capture the Trans-Siberian Railway. This was an 8,000 strong force under the command of Major General William Graves. Graves was assisted by John Stevens, a railway engineer.

This second invasion force arrived in the Russian port of *Vladivostok* between August 15 and September 1, 1918, less than a month after the first invasion force. As with the *Polar Bear Expedition,* there was a small contingent of Canadians eager to join the American "Siberian" force in helping to stamp out the "evil" of *Bolshevism* and show solidarity with their American cousins. While this second, somewhat larger American force, fared a little better than the "Polar Bears," in the end, it was also defeated by the Russians and forced to retreat.

Both President Wilson and his Secretary of State wanted to send a much larger force to Russia. But the American people were war weary from the First World War and Russia seemed much further away in 1918 than in 2010. It was the same in Vietnam, Afghanistan and Iraq. Warmongers such as Wilson and Bush are fortunately constrained by the limits of the numbers of Americans willing to put their lives on the line even when they support American invasions. As in Iraq in 2008, the "Siberian" marines complained about their extended tour of duty. They had served under combat conditions longer than any American unit in World War I. Conditions in Siberia were as miserable as those in Iraq. Extreme cold in Siberia and extreme heat in Iraq. There were shortages of ammunition, fuel, food and other supplies. Wars are costly on American taxpayers. Losing Congressional support for an unwinnable invasion, Wilson pulled the Siberian contingent out in April 1920.

The American invasion did succeed in promoting the fortunes of a military dictator in Russia. American presidents are often proud of the fact that the military dictators they install in the remotest corners of the globe are "their SOB's." But in the case of Russia, Josef Stalin was not an American SOB, despite all their efforts to woo him to their side, even to the point of convincing the American media to refer to him as "Uncle Joe." Sadly, the world only thinks badly of dictators like Stalin, Noriega and Saddam Hussein after they refuse to be puppets of the **evil** American Empire. "Uncle Joe" was courted by the American Empire during World War II when Germany once again threatened American hegemony. When Britain, France, Germany and Japan capitulated to American dominance it was Russia and "Uncle Joe" who stood alone against American tyranny.

The Second US Invasions of China and Japan

The American Empire had signalled its true intentions towards Russia when it invaded in 1918. However, both Germany and Japan had recovered sufficiently from the economic devastation of World War I to successfully challenge the American Empire for hegemony. America's invasion and conquest of Russia was put on hold because of the threat from Germany and Japan. As the American Empire had allied with France to defeat Great Britain during its War of Independence so it would ally with Russia to defeat Germany and Japan during the Second World War before attempting its defeat of Russia after WWII. In the meantime, it would make a second attempt to invade and conquer China and Japan simultaneously. We covered the first invasion in Chapter 3.

America's first invasion of China and Japan in the nineteenth century was based on imperial expansion through forced international trade with China and Japan. By the time of its failed invasion of Russia in 1920, China and Japan were much more open to an alliance with the West. Like Russia, they had joined the allies against Germany, during the First World War. A weakened Britain and France were amenable to such an alliance between Asia and the West. The American Empire, however, saw its conquest of China as an opportunity to seize hegemony in Asia and the Pacific from Japan.

The American Empire correctly understood that the threat to its goal of hegemony would not come from Britain or France but from Japan and Russia. By conquering China it would strengthen its hand in defeating the looming challenge from Japan and Russia. This is the context in which we suggest that the second American invasions of China and Japan were a single unified strategy to colonize both China and Japan. The Western view that the American Empire went to war with Japan to safeguard Chinese independence is pure unadulterated propaganda.

America's Capitalism vs. China's Communism:
Rhetoric trumps Substance

It is extremely important for us to be very clear that the American Empire's invasion of Russia and China had absolutely nothing to do with fighting communism or fear of communism. It had to do with America's dedicated pursuit of world domination. American leaders, beginning with Washington, Adams, Jefferson, Madison and Monroe, and continuing through to Reagan, Bush I, Clinton, Bush II and Obama, were united in their position that American hegemony must be based on lies, deceit, propaganda and military conquests. In the early years the lies and propaganda were based on demonizing the "Red Savage," and Blacks. Today it's "Islamists." In the twentieth century it was "Communists."

There is absolutely nothing evil about communists or communism. Communism is far more democratic than capitalism. Western intellectuals are unanimous in their view that communism and socialism are far superior goals for civilized societies than capitalism. In 2009, the United States has a far larger communist sector than China. The most recent transfer of America's financial sector from the private capitalist sector to the public communist sector by Bush II in 2008 has led some Western intellectuals to refer to President Bush facetiously as "Comrade Bush."

However, facts and truths are no match for Western propaganda, media compliance, military dominance, world institutional dominance of the WTO, G8, World Bank, IMF and the UN, control of shipping lanes and air space, superior technology and wealth. Most important is America's overwhelming possession of WMD's. American intelligence did not fail to determine that Saddam Hussein had no WMD's. Twelve years of incessant bombing by the US and Britain had wiped out Iraq's WMD's, capability to make WMD's, economic infrastructure, health care and scientific manpower. The American Empire invaded precisely because its intelligence had identified Iraq's **lack** of WMD's as well as limited conventional weapons. This is precisely why President Bush and his *Neo-cons* chose Iraq over North Korea or Iran to test drive the *Wolfowitz/Bush* doctrine of regime change by pre-emptive strikes.

The American Empire's threat from its enormous nuclear arsenal is complemented by its enormous propaganda campaign to prevent states, other than its Western allies, from acquiring nuclear deterrents against American invasions. The latest casualties of this propaganda campaign may be North Korea and Iran. Years of American economic blackmail has so weakened the North Korean economy that North Korea agreed to abandon its nuclear deterrent in October 2008. It has subsequently asked to re-negotiate terms.

Iran is still resisting the American blackmail. If it succeeds without military confrontation, that will be due largely to the economic and financial decline of the American Empire. If Iran fails and military confrontation happens, Iran will have to resort to the same "primitive" weapons as Palestine, Vietnam, Afghanistan and Iraq, to defeat the **evil** American Empire. Such a military confrontation will bring massive pain and suffering to the Iranian people. But it would be another mistake by the American Empire to doubt the resolve of the Iranian people as they doubted that of the Palestinians, Vietnamese, Afghans and Iraqis. When American bombs are raining down from the skies on your women and children, on your hospitals, schools and homes, because of the superior technology of American planes piloted by Americans safely ensconced out of range, people are no longer fooled into believing that suicide bombers are cowards, no matter how loud the Western media shouts its propaganda.

China's Embrace of Communism and Democracy

With the overthrow of the Qing Dynasty on February 12, 1912, the Chinese people ended 2,000 years of imperial rule by creating the *Republic of China, ROC*. Like the Russians, they chose a Communist form of government for their new Republic, precisely because they wanted a more **democratic** form of government than American Capitalism. They also accepted Vladimir Lenin's interpretation of the **inherent imperialism** in Capitalism. Lenin had added this key feature to Marxism. According to Lenin, Capitalism would require colonies for supplying raw materials and providing markets. Capitalist countries would also use **warmongering** to compete for colonies. The Chinese people had no interest in such imperial pursuits.

Americans, Russians and Chinese have one goal in common. They all want goods and services. This universal goal is what links the political system with the economic system. Communism and Capitalism are political systems. Both of these political systems can be democratic or dictatorial. The Western association of Communism with dictatorship and Capitalism with democracy is purely Western propaganda. This Western propaganda is partly fuelled by the two different *economic* systems inherent in the two different *political* systems. It is therefore incumbent upon us to clarify the inherent difference in the *economic* systems in order to debunk the Western propaganda that Communism means dictatorship while Capitalism means democracy.

Capitalism uses the market to direct the resources of the economy towards producing those goods and services which consumers prefer. The richest consumers get most of the goods and services produced by Capitalism. Monetary reward is the key incentive used to ensure that the economy's resources are used efficiently. Communism uses a Central Planning Bureaucracy to direct the economy towards producing those goods and services which consumers prefer. Communal and social incentives as well as monetary incentives are used to achieve economic efficiency. The Centrally Planned System is extremely complex to manage. However, it is no more prone to abuse or dictatorship than the Capitalist system.

The West has used the Central Planning inherent in a Communist *economic* system to support its propaganda that Communism implies dictatorship. This is combined with the simplistic Western view that democracy requires more than one political party, as long as there are, of course, no **Communist** parties. The Communism practised in both Russia and China, on the other hand, insists on the Communist party being the only political party. The West's insistence on more than one political party is no guarantee of democracy. Likewise Russia and China's insistence on a single political party does not necessarily prevent the existence of democracy.

Democracy is much more complex than Western dogma. In fact, the Western view of democracy is one which is inherently undemocratic. Quite apart from its insistence on the inequalities inherent in the sanctity of *private property* its deep seated **racism** which dates back to the Crusades deny equality of opportunities and respect for its **non-white** citizens. In America today, as in Canada and other Western "democracies," Whites openly defend their **racist** democracies by arguing loudly and proudly how racism today is not as bad as in the past. They would proudly counter charges of racism with: "Surely, you cannot deny that racism today is much less than it was before." Quite apart from the impossibility of finding an objective measure of the degree of racism, why would a non-white citizen care about this ridiculous argument as to whether there was more or less racism? They care only about the fact that it exists. If your non-white citizens and your low-income citizens are second class citizens you do not have a democratic system. You can white-wash it all you want with meaningless platitudes.

By the time of the Chinese revolution in 1912 the *Communist Manifesto* of Marx and Engels had circulated worldwide for over half a century. Communism offered new hope to countries like China which had experienced so much exploitation by the capitalists of the American Empire. It was the attempt by China to sever the colonial stranglehold of the American Empire that would lead to the second invasion of China by the American Empire. Communism was both the means by which China would seek its independence from American imperialism and the excuse used by the American Empire for invading China and participating in its civil war. China's civil war lasted much longer than the Russian civil war and American intervention lasted well beyond the end of China's civil war.

As with the Russian revolution, two factions competed to replace the deposed emperor. As in Russia, the American Empire naturally supported the faction which was **less** democratic and therefore better able to ally itself with American capitalism and continued exploitation of the masses. Democratic movements, whether communist or not, require popular support. Pro-American governments can never get popular support since the American Empire is the symbol of imperialist exploitation of the masses. The American Empire has succeeded in fooling its own electorate with its massive propaganda campaign. But it has never succeeded in fooling the electorate in countries where the majority of the population is non-white.

Whites may not always be fooled by the rhetoric of the American Empire. Nevertheless, they have a vested interest in supporting the American Empire since that empire ultimately maintains the military, economic, political and financial domination of Whites over non-whites. Non-whites have no equal vested interest but may be forced to support American propaganda because of military, financial and economic threats from the American Empire. It's simply amazing how many non-whites profess their great love for America and American institutions when American marines point a gun and say, "love me or I will shoot you."

The Birth of Communism in China

Communism in China is associated with the name of Mao Zedong as much as Lenin is associated with communism in Russia, Ho Chi Minh in Vietnam and Fidel Castro in Cuba. While Marx and Engels developed the theories in Western Europe, it was leaders like Lenin, Mao Zedong, Ho Chi Minh and Castro who put the Marxian theories into practice in countries which were outside the birthplace of the communist theories. It was 1918, one year after the Russian revolution and six years after the Chinese revolution, when Mao Ze Dong founded a society in Beijing, to study Marxism.

During the Chinese revolt against the Qing emperor, Mao joined the revolution by enlisting in his local Hunan regiment in 1911. China, like the US, initially stayed out of World War I. The revolutionary government was weak and divided. Japan, one of the allies in World War I, took advantage of China's internal turmoil to invade and conquer China. The American Empire was naturally opposed to the Japanese invasion since Japanese occupation of China would make it more difficult for the American Empire to colonize China. When the American Empire entered World War I on the side of the allies it persuaded China to do the same as a way of countering the Japanese threat to its independence. China therefore entered World War I on the side of the allies on August 13, 1917; four months after the American Empire had joined the allies.

As usual, the American Empire did not support China during the peace negotiations following the defeat of Germany. The American Empire was as keen as Japan on carving up China to promote its own imperial hegemony. If anything, President Woodrow Wilson drove China closer to Japan than the American Empire when he vetoed according equal **racial** status to Japanese and Whites in his League of Nations proposal. This sent a clear message to China and Japan that the American Empire had no interest in treating the "Yellow" race any better than it had treated the "Red" and "Black" races. President Wilson's proposal of "self determination" for all was as hollow as American propaganda about freedom and equality.

China's entry into World War I had not helped its fight against colonialism. It would have to fight both the American and Japanese empires for its independence. Article 156 of the *Treaty of Versailles,* giving Shandong to Japan, was strongly protested by China. On May 4, 1919, students in Beijing started the *May Fourth Movement,* to protest strongly against China signing the *Treaty of Versailles.* China rejected the allied *Treaty of Versailles* and later signed its own peace treaty with Germany. The *Treaty of Versailles* and the *May Fourth Movement* gave a huge boost to the birth of Communism in China. Neither the American Empire nor its allies could be trusted to secure China's independence from imperialism, either from Japan or the West. On the contrary, we will show that Japan's invasion of China was in the interest of the American Empire. Firstly, it prevented Asia from uniting against American imperialism. Secondly, a China weakened by years of wars against Japan would be an easy target for American imperialism.

At the first Congress of the *Communist Party of China, CPC,* held in Shanghai in July 1921, Mao Zedong was one of 53 delegates who attended. Mao was one of two delegates from Hunan. A rival political party, the *Kuomintang,* or *KMT,* had been founded since August 1912, following the abdication of the Qing emperor in February 1912. In 1921, the *KMT* had a membership of 150,000 compared to the *CPC's* membership of only 300. It was led by the popular nationalist, Dr. Sun Yat-sen and supported by the Russian Communist Party.

When Sun died in 1925, the leadership of the KMT passed to General Chiang Kai-shek. Unlike Sun, who had worked closely with the Communist Party of Russia, Chiang Kai-shek was a **capitalist.** He was dedicated to using military force to wipe out communism in China. Communists were purged from the KMT and ties with the Russian Communist Party severed. Chiang would provide the propaganda which the American Empire would use to invade and colonize China. The American Empire would use Chiang Kai-shek to lie to the American people and the world that its military forces in China were there to support Chiang as the chosen leader of the Chinese people.

The Second US Invasion of China

The American Empire chose to fuel a civil war in China, as it had done in Russia, by providing military and financial support to General Chiang Kai-shek. The American Empire never fully removed its military threat to China after it forced China to sign the "Unequal" Sino-American Treaty of Wanghia on July 3, 1844. At the time of the Chinese revolution in 1911-12, the American Empire had gunboats patrolling the Yangtze River and the South China Sea. Both marines and army personnel were stationed on Chinese soil, such as the 15th Infantry in Tientsin. Its military base in the Philippines was never far away. However, it is appropriate that we separate the 19th century American invasions of China from those of the 20th century.

America's 19th century invasions, which we documented in Chapter 3, were in cooperation with the more powerful British and French empires. In the 19th century, the American Empire invaded China to ensure its presence in the Pacific alongside Britain, France, Japan, Russia and Germany. The propaganda used was "Open Door" international trade. In the 20th century, the American Empire invaded China to dominate it as its exclusive colony, much as it had done with the Philippines, and would later do with Japan, South Korea and Taiwan. The propaganda used was "fighting the evil of communism."

We have documented many examples of the American Empire using a local strong man to aid their invasions and conquests. In China, their strong man was Generalissimo Chiang Kai-shek. Chiang had risen to the top of the KMT after rescuing Sun Yat-sen and Sun's second wife, Soong **Ching-ling,** in 1923. The governor of Guangdong, Chen Jiongming, attempted to assassinate Sun on June 16, 1923, and may have succeeded had it not been for Chiang's intervention. Chiang strengthened his position in both the KMT and the United States by marrying Soong **May-ling,** the sister of Sun's second wife, in 1927. Sun had obtained US citizenship after living and studying in Hawaii.

There is much evidence that Chiang had bought into the American propaganda about "freedom and equality." Likewise, Soong May-ling was educated and respected in the US. Madame Chiang Kai-shek had the unquestioned support of a growing "China lobby" group in the United States. More than ever, Chiang became their man in China who could easily be swayed by American lies and American hyperbole. He commanded the best trained military force after the fall of the Qing dynasty and had a Christian wife who had been brainwashed in the United States. While Madame Sun Yat-sen remained true to China's struggle against American imperialism after Sun's death, her sister, Madame Chiang Kai-shek was a diehard American capitalist and emigrated to the US after Chiang's death.

It was for these reasons that the KMT fell into the hands of a pro-American capitalist general. Long standing leaders of the KMT, such as Wang Jingwei and Zhou Enlai, were forced to join the relatively new CPC to fight the Americans and Japanese for China's independence. While Chiang's leadership of the KMT improved America's chance of succeeding in its second invasion of China, Chiang's leadership simultaneously improved the membership and leadership of the CPC as well as the CPC's support from the Russian Communist Party. In 1927, the left wing leaders and members of the KMT who opposed Chiang's pro-American capitalism, officially broke with the KMT and joined the CPC. They established a rival government in Wuhan.

The KMT's base was in Southern China where Sun had established a military government in Guangzhou since 1921. Sun had also created a military academy in Guangdong with Chiang as its Commandant. The goal of the academy was to train an army to defeat the warlords who controlled most of China from Beijing since the 1912 revolution. On July 27, 1926, with the aid of the American Empire, Chiang launched a military campaign to subdue Northern China. Chiang also moved the KMT base from Guangzhou to Nanjing. Since the American Empire was firmly behind Chiang, the KMT's government in Nanjing received worldwide recognition as the legitimate government in China. In 1927, it looked as if the communists and the Chinese people had lost while the American Empire and General Chiang had won.

Mao Zedong defeats the American Empire

The American Empire, time and time again, underestimates the power of the people. American leaders are so used to a docile, ignorant and politically naïve electorate at home that they foolishly attribute the same qualities to the people of the Third World. In the USA, leaders take pride in dumbing down the American electorate to the level of the Oprah Winfrey talk shows and "Joe the Plumber," Samuel Wurzelbacher. They proudly claim that democracy must cater to the lowest common denominator. That's well and good for the American electorate if they "freely" choose to live in ignorance. But American presidents should learn from constant failures that it most certainly does not work with the people they wish to colonize.

The American Empire has also, time and again, overestimated its military prowess. This combination of underestimating the intelligence of the people of the Third World and overestimating the fighting skills of the American forces explain why most American invasions have failed. True enough, many American invasions have succeeded. American invasions succeeded in Hawaii, Puerto Rico, the Philippines, Japan and South Korea, for example. But they failed in Canada, Cuba, Russia, China, North Korea and Vietnam, among others. It's not a coincidence that American failures have typically been in countries where the people have used the strength and spirit of a combined *communal* resistance to American imperialism.

At a time when the communist movement in China was disintegrating before the forces of American imperialism and the capitalist General Chiang Kai-shek, the relatively unknown delegate to the first CPC Congress, from Hunan province, Mao Zedong, staged a peasant revolt in Hunan. Mao's goal was to create an "army of the people" to resist the army of Chiang and his imperial overlord. It was the peasant revolt in Russia which had enabled the Russian Communist Party to defeat the American Empire. Likewise, Mao was determined to use the Chinese peasants to drive the American Empire out of China. In Russia, Lenin had concluded that the 1848 revolutions in Western Europe had failed because the communist leaders had not harnessed the power of the peasants. Mao was about to build on Lenin's example by promoting the power of rural over city, farm labour over industrial proletariat, communal ownership over private property.

Mao was determined to build his resistance to the foreign domination of China from rural China. That was where the great majority of the Chinese people lived and earned their livelihood. China's industrial proletariat was far too small to mount a successful revolution against Chiang and the American or Japanese empire. Like Lenin had done in Russia, Mao would combine his resistance to imperialism with the simultaneous emancipation of the Chinese peasants from feudalism and semi-serfdom. Mao, like Lenin before, would give the Chinese peasants a powerful self-serving reason to fight the capitalist imperialists. Mao would turn this invincible force first against the Japanese and afterwards against the American Empire.

The American Empire's strategy in China was the same as they had used in Cuba, Puerto Rico and the Philippines. Sell the very successful American propaganda that the American Empire sent its forces into China to protect American lives and assist the Chinese people fight the "evil" Japanese. In the case of Cuba, Puerto Rico and the Philippines it was the "evil" Spanish. Harness the Chinese resistance to do most of the fighting so that American casualties would be minimal. Once the Japanese were defeated, as the Spanish were, turn the superior American military against any Chinese resistance to American colonization. The strategy had worked in both Puerto Rico and the Philippines. It would fail miserably in China, thanks to Mao Zedong, as it would fail in Cuba because of Fidel Castro and in Vietnam because of Ho Chi Minh.

Mao called his new army the "Revolutionary army of workers and peasants," and began his guerrilla resistance in the mountains of Jiangxi. When General Chiang attacked Mao in Jiangxi, Mao eluded the general by escaping with his army to Shaanxi. This came to be known as the "Long March," from which Mao emerged as the supreme leader of the CPC. On the "Long March," Mao simultaneously defeated the local warlords while re-distributing land and recruiting the peasants to his army. Mao's strategy of harnessing the power of the masses of poor peasants increased both his popular support and that of the CPC at the expense of the KMT, General Chiang, and his American overlord.

In addition, Chiang's obsession with wiping out communism when Chinese anger was directed mostly at Japanese aggression in China, lost him further popular support. His slogan, "First internal pacification, then external resistance," did not ring true with the majority of the Chinese people.

By December 1936, Chiang's lack of popular support had reached a crisis point. He was kidnapped by his closest generals and forced to unite with the CPC against Japan, as the condition for his release. Ironically, this incident, known as the "Xi'an Incident," forced the American Empire to form a temporary alliance with *Communism* to defeat the Japanese threat to its own imperial ambition in China. In World War II, the American Empire forged alliances with both Russia and China to defeat the combined German/Japanese threat to its own hegemony. Of course, American propaganda and media were not **coerced** into referring to Russia as *Communist* Russia and China as *Communist* China, until the war had been won. Likewise, American propaganda and media were not **coerced** into calling Stalin and Mao "dictators," until the war was won.

Mao signed up with the allies in World War II both to defeat the Japanese invasion of China and to keep the American Empire from colonizing China. It was a strategy used by all colonies across the globe. Their hope was that by fighting with the allies as "equals" against the common threat from Germany and Japan, the American and European empires would be much more inclined to grant them independence after the war. China's alliance with the US during World War II meant more American troops in China. It was a necessary evil to counter the Japanese threat. After World War II the American Empire provided massive amounts of financial and military support to the KMT during China's civil war.

Mao's "army of the people," was now called the *People's Liberation Army.* It had become a well trained, disciplined fighting force able to take on the KMT and the American Empire. In January 1949, Mao captured Beijing. That was the beginning of the end for the American Empire and its KMT general. The Republic of China became the *People's Republic of China, PRC,* on October 1, 1949. Chengdu was the last KMT city to fall on December 10, 1949. Chiang was forced to flee to the island of Taiwan. The American invasion had been a dismal failure. While it was a failure of American imperialism it was seen in the West as a failure of *Capitalism*. China, like Russia before, was saved from American colonization. But the American Empire used these failures to support its propaganda that it was not seeking colonies but fighting the "evil" of *Communism*. "Red" China was demonized even more than the *Bolsheviks* had been in Russia.

The loss of China was the most significant defeat for American imperialism. Without China the American Empire had no hope of ever dominating the entire world. It had conquered the New World and made great inroads into Europe. With its conquest of Western Europe and its creation of NATO, there was always the hope of bringing Russia into its orbit. But the loss of China meant the loss of Asia and the majority of the world's population. It was for this reason that it was so determined to isolate China and support Chiang's government in Taiwan.

By continuing to support Chiang's government in Taiwan, its defeat in China would be viewed as a temporary one. It would simply wait for an opportune time to launch a third invasion of China. Unfortunately for the American Empire, subsequent military defeats in North Korea and Vietnam put an end to that dream. With current military defeats in Afghanistan and Iraq today, far from colonizing China it is on the verge of losing Taiwan, South Korea and Japan as the British Empire lost Hong Kong, Malaysia and Singapore and the Portuguese Empire lost Macau.

The Second US Invasion of Japan

The American Empire's invasions of Japan are proof positive that its invasions of Russia and China had absolutely nothing to do with the "evil" of communism. Japan had less chance of becoming a communist state than the USA. Communism has had, and continues to have, more popular, intellectual, celebrity and moral support in the US than in Japan. The American Empire's invasions of Japan, like all its invasions, had one goal. That goal is world domination by the American Empire. As in the first American invasion, the second American invasion of Japan was very much linked with its second invasion of China.

In the case of Japan, China, Hawaii, the Philippines and the islands in the Pacific, these invasions were intended to expand the American Empire westwards from its base in the New World to the Pacific, Asia and beyond. In Chapter 3 we documented the early American invasions of Japan, China and Hawaii. Like China, the 19th century invasions were intended to force Japan to trade with the American Empire on *unequal* terms. The 20th century invasions were intended to destroy Japan's competition with the American Empire for colonies in Asia. Without Asia, the American Empire could never dominate the entire world. Its domination of the New World and Europe was not enough to satisfy its insatiable appetite for more conquests and colonies. Had it succeeded in colonizing Asia it would have most certainly invaded and conquered other planets. "Legal" aliens would have entered the US to help us understand why they call "illegal" immigrants into the US, illegal "aliens."

The American Empire had awakened a "sleeping giant" when it forced Japan to open its ports to international trade. Japan's close geographical proximity to China made it see conclusively how Western imperialists such as the American Empire were willing to use the most barbaric methods, including the *opium trade,* to colonize Asia. The crucial mistake made by the American Empire in awakening this "sleeping giant" was to think that it could be easily colonized by a militarily more powerful USA. Far from permitting colonization by the American Empire, Japan copied the imperial methods of the West and soon became the American Empire's "worst nightmare" in the Pacific and Asia.

Just as the American Empire in the 21st century is wishing that it had not forced open the ports of China in the 19th century so too in the 20th century the American Empire regretted ever opening the Japanese ports in the 19th century. Japan proved to be America's most fearsome competitor in Asia throughout the 20th century just as China has become its most fearsome competitor in Asia at the dawn of the 21st century. Its numerous invasions of Japan had limited short-run successes much like its numerous invasions of China.

In the end, Japan and China will unite to bring down the once supreme American Empire. Their fortunes, their people, their history, their cultures and their geography, are more closely linked with each other and with the other powers of Asia than with the West. Had the American Empire shown any kind of virtue or leadership they may have had some reason to cooperate with it. But the American Empire was founded on false premises, lies, hypocrisy and warmongering. There is not one single virtue worth emulating, except, perhaps, McDonalds, KFC and Seven-Eleven.

Japan's Imperial Aspirations after the Meiji Restoration

While the American Empire played a supporting role to the British Empire in forcing open China to an unequal trading relationship with the West, it was the American Empire which played the leadership role in the similar forcing open of Japan to an unequal trading relationship with the West. The British had the edge in China but the Americans had the edge in Japan. It explains why the American-Japanese relationship is closer to this day compared with the Sino-American relationship.

Neither China nor Japan was willing to accept an unequal relationship with the West. However, Japan was much more successful than China in building a military force which would fight Western domination. Western domination is based on military superiority. It can only be prevented by military defence. There is absolutely no other way. In the six hundred years since the Portuguese began their exploration of the west coast of Africa the Western empires used every military weapon, including biological warfare, WMD's and ethnic cleansing, to conquer and subjugate. In every case where they were slowed or deterred it was done through military defences. Peace has never been pursued by any of the Western empires and most certainly not by the American Empire. If they are to be stopped they have to be stopped by military means or some form of military deterrent.

Japan's strategy to fight American imperialism can be best summed up as, "if you can't beat them join them." While this strategy has brought partial success to Japan it could never bring the success which Japan yearned for. Japan's strategy was to build a military force and an empire in East Asia that would equal that of the Western powers, England, France, Germany and the United States. By doing so it had hoped to become an inclusive member of that club. Even though history has proved that such hope was wishful thinking, Japan, to this day, continues to long for equal acceptance by the West. But the West is an exclusive club tied to Western Europe and those with Western European heritage such as the United States, Canada and Australia. If this exclusive club refused to accept Russia as an equal it had nothing but disdain for Japan's audacity to expect equal treatment. Japan would have been better off in the long term if it had allied with Russia and China than with the West.

Japan's colonization of Korea

In Chapter 3 we documented the "unequal treaties" imposed on Japan by the American Empire beginning in 1854 and explained how these "unequal treaties" awakened Japanese understanding of the importance of naval power in an imperial world. Japan's response of "join them if you cannot stop them," began with its competition with the West for the colonization of Korea. In the 19th century the three dominant countries in East Asia were China, Japan and Korea. The West had forced opened China and Japan. Korea was the next obvious target. The American Empire sent its first gunboat to Korea in 1853 and France invaded Korea in 1866.

Japan's strategy of invading and conquering Korea before the US, France or Britain, was one of creating a buffer colony to guard against a future American invasion of Japan while at the same time creating its own empire in a vain attempt to be treated on equal terms by Britain, France, Germany and the US. Following the example of the West in forcing open the ports of China and Japan, in 1876 Japan forced Korea to open its ports to international trade. At the time Korea had closed its borders to all foreigners except China. Japan's action in 1876 moved it closer to its goals of emulating the West while enhancing its own security but simultaneously brought it into conflict with both Korea and China. It marked the beginning of Japan's dilemma. Should it be Asian first or Western first? This is not unlike the dilemma which Britain has faced. Is Britain European first or American first?

Western first, enabled Japan to exploit Korea's resources including its reserves of iron ore and coal. To compete successfully with the West Japan must not only build a powerful navy it must also industrialize. The capitalist model of the West required colonies for raw materials and markets for its industrial products. Korea would provide both. More importantly, it would simultaneously prevent the American Empire from exploiting Korea's resources thereby giving the Japanese Empire a competitive edge over the American Empire.

The First Sino-Japanese War: 1894-95

In pursuing its strategy of "Western first," Japan was aware that it would be challenged by China. Far from Japan being concerned about China's challenge, Japan saw China's challenge as an opportunity to pursue its own desire for equal status with the Western empires by joining the Western powers in raping the resources of China in addition to those of Korea. This led to the first Sino-Japanese War of 1894-95.

Japan had prepared for this conflict by pursing a policy of rapid industrialization similar to Western Europe and the United States and by appropriately complementing its transition to Capitalism by building a navy that would be comparable to those of the Western European and American empires while simultaneously modernizing its army. In preparing its military for the war with China, Japan did not simply emulate the West but paid for military experts from Britain, France and Germany to oversee the modernization. When the first Sino-Japanese War began on August 1, 1894 Japan had a well equipped Western-style navy and army.

Japan's defeat of China by March of 1895 was no surprise. China had already suffered humiliating defeats by Britain, France and the United States. Its relevance, at the time, was a signal that the West may have to share the spoils of colonizing China, Korea and Taiwan with a non-Western power. Japan saw this sharing of the spoils as a way of achieving its goal of being treated as an equal by Britain, France, Germany and the United States.

The Western empires played along with this notion as long as it did not conflict with their own imperial and strategic goals. During the Boxer Rebellion of 1900, for example, the Western empires could count on Japan pulling its weight in helping to defeat the Chinese insurgency. For a while it appeared as if Asia had been "blessed" with its first "Western" imperial power. Japan felt vindicated in believing that it "could be one of them," when it clinched an alliance with Britain on January 30, 1902. This significant Anglo-Japanese alliance was a key factor in Japan fighting alongside the Allies during the First World War.

The Russo-Japanese War: 1904-1905

In cementing its alliance with the West through the Anglo-Japanese alliance of 1902 Japan was playing a calculated but dangerous game. Russia had been the non-Western European power trying desperately to appease the West in order to gain "equal-status recognition," for at least a century before the Japanese. It was Russia which had crushed Napoleon's army in 1812. After its conquest of China, Korea and Taiwan, Japan felt confident enough to position itself ahead of Russia in achieving "equal-status recognition," by the West.

The key benefit to Japan of the 1902 Anglo-Japanese alliance was the agreement that if Japan went to war with Russia and any Western European empire allied with Russia against Japan, the British would enter the war on the side of Japan. Russia had previously signed an alliance with France in 1892. There could be no clearer evidence that Japan was about to challenge Russia as it had challenged China in 1894. The reality was that the West never intended to give "equal-status recognition," to either Russia or Japan. They, therefore, had no qualms about playing off one against the other in order to protect and enhance their own competitive position.

While Japan's defeat of China in 1895 did not surprise any of the Great Powers its defeat of Russia in 1905 was a huge surprise to all. Russia had been on the verge of Great Power status for a much longer period than Japan. It had an army which was larger than the British or French or German army and it had begun to industrialize long before Japan had. Its navy was at least three times as large as that of Japan. But Japan had built a modern navy with technical help from Britain and France. It was the modern Japanese navy which defeated the Russians in 1904-05. Most of the major battles were fought in the Yellow Sea and in the waters around Japan and Korea. Admiral Togo annihilated the Russian fleet at the Battle of Tsushima in May 1905.

During the earlier Sino-Japanese War Japan had captured Port Arthur. The Russians had longed for an all weather port like Port Arthur. The Russian Czar, Nicholas II, was facing a peasant backed Communist revolution. Russian Marxists had founded the Social Democratic Labour Party in Russia in 1898.

Wars are popular if you win. Czar Nicholas gambled on an easy victory against Japan as a way of quelling domestic discontent as well as taking Korea, Manchuria and Port Arthur from the Japanese. That was not to be. Russia's defeat signalled the rise of Japan as next in line for membership in the exclusive Western European club of Great Powers ahead of Russia. Japan, like Russia, would never be admitted to that exclusive club. Instead, the ex-colony of Britain, the USA, would not only be admitted to that exclusive club. It would come to dominate that club and eventually, the entire world.

World War I and the Rise of the American Empire

Both Russia's French ally and Japan's British ally kept out of the Russo-Japanese War. This made it easier for Britain to sign an alliance with France in 1904 and with Russia in 1907. This meant that when World War I started Britain had signed alliances with Japan, France and Russia. Britain had a de facto unwritten alliance with the USA ever since it had been generous with the rebellious colony at the peace settlement ending the American War of Independence in 1783 and especially after it had underwritten the rather pretentious Monroe Doctrine of 1823.

The First World War devastated the economies of all of the members of the exclusive Western European club, Britain, France and Germany, thereby enabling the rise of the American, Japanese and Russian empires. Britain would maintain its unwritten alliance with the USA but would have to sacrifice its alliance with Japan to do so. America wanted exclusive imperial rights to Asia and the Pacific. There was no room in the rising American Empire for sharing the spoils of Asia with Japan. Far from admitting Japan to the exclusive Western European club America would isolate Japan and, if necessary, invade and conquer it. Britain was too weak to object.

The United States emerged from World War I as the dominant and most modern economy. By 1920 the USA produced 40 percent of the world's manufacturing output. More importantly, while Britain had led the way in the first industrial revolution it was the USA which was the leader in the second industrial revolution marked by the switch from heavy to light industries, mass production and mass consumer markets for consumer durables, cars and aircrafts.

American Isolation of Japan

America is a deeply racist society. It could never envision a time when the Japanese people could be its equal. On the other side of the coin Japan had, in some ways, distanced itself from its Asian roots to gain admittance to the Western European club. Prior to World War I American immigration laws favoured White immigrants. Japan had foolishly hoped that fighting on the side of the Allies would change America's racial view of the Japanese. That was not to be. In 1917 the USA passed a literacy test recommended by the newly founded Immigration Restriction League as a way of restricting all Asian immigration into the US. Japan was given no special treatment despite its "Great Power" status in the world. Japan was explicitly included in the *Asiatic Barred Zone.*

A much more surprising shock to Japan's pride was President Wilson's refusal to grant equal racial status to Japanese in the *League of Nations.* Woodrow Wilson, the famous American idealist, democrat and winner of the 1919 Nobel Peace Prize for his efforts to establish the League, was no less racist than his American government. There could be no clearer signal to Japan that economic and military progress would never be sufficient for an Asian Power to be respected by the West. In 1923, Japan ended its military alliance with Great Britain.

The American Empire complemented its racial isolation of Japan with economic isolation. It was less than a century before when the United States forced open Japan to international trade. Now it was imposing trade restrictions to punish and undermine Japanese competition for empire in Asia and the Pacific. High American tariffs reduced trade with Japan. The American *Smoot-Hawley tariff* of 1930 was viewed in Japan as a trade war which could lead to military conflict in Asia as Japan intensified its colonization of Asia to offset the reduction in US-Japanese trade. The American Empire was forcing a show-down with Japan for imperial hegemony in the Pacific and Asia.

The American Empire also sought to limit the size of the Japanese navy. At the *Washington Naval Conference of* 1921 Japan had agreed to limit its navy to roughly 60 percent of the size of the US navy. The *Washington Naval Treaty* was updated by the *London Naval Treaty* of 1930. The Japanese refused to participate in the second update of the *Washington Naval Treaty* of 1936 because the American Empire continued to insist that Japan must have a smaller navy than itself.

This notion that the American Empire has the legitimate right to WMD's far in excess of any other country is the single fundamental reason for the arms race. The West never chastises the American Empire because it thinks that non-Western nations and non-Western people can be easily fooled. In 1936 the Japanese were no more fooled than the Russians or Chinese today. Nor can the North Koreans or Iranians be fooled by today's Western rhetoric about nuclear non-proliferation.

In 2010, President Obama has shamefully resorted to the most outlandish propaganda by a dedicated warmonger in preaching that he wants to see a world without nuclear weapons. Here is a Western leader whose country possesses more nukes than the rest of the world combined, whose country spends more on weapons than the rest of the world combined and who has currently invaded Iraq, Afghanistan, Pakistan and Yemen, talking about a world without nuclear weapons. With the rise of the BRIC countries, Brazil, Russia, India and China, President Obama is having some difficulty fooling the world that economic sanctions against Iran is in the interests of China, Russia and the Third World.

As President Obama privately considers his option of nuking Iran to reduce American military defeats in the Middle East and protect its *uncolony* of Israel he publicly preaches nuclear non-proliferation. The non-nuclear countries, especially those in the Third World, are fed up with the Western double standard regarding nuclear weapons. Where is it written that only Western countries like the US, Britain, France and Israel, have the right to nuclear weapons? At the very least, economic sanctions against Iran to prevent Iran from acquiring nuclear weapons will require the West to agree to a nuclear-free Middle East. Of course the West would never agree to that. So President Obama is advised by his propaganda strategists to preach nuclear non-proliferation to confuse those who might otherwise see him for the dedicated warmongering imperialist he is.

As we have explained before Israel demands and gets special status among the American Empire's many *uncolonies* around the world. It's reminiscent of Britain's treatment of the 13 American colonies during the eighteenth century. The 13 American colonies demanded and received special status among the British Empire's many *colonies* around the world. For example, just as Britain paid much more to defend its 13 American colonies than its colonies in the Caribbean and Asia the American Empire pays much more to defend Israel than its other *uncolonies*. At the same time Britain could impose taxes on its Caribbean and Indian colonies but not on its American colonies just as the American Empire can make its other *uncolonies* sign the nuclear non-proliferation treaty but not Israel. Just as the British Empire could not restrain the American colonies from thefts of First Nations land the American Empire cannot restrain Israel from building settlements on Palestinian land.

The difference, of course, was that Britain had the good sense to let the American colonies seize their "independence" and fight for the American continent as an independent nation. The American Empire is either unwilling or unable to do the same with Israel. Would an "independent" Israel dominate the Middle East in the same way that an "independent" USA came to dominate the American continent? This is not an unfair question. In 1783 the USA was a tiny strip of land surrounded by the much larger English colony of Canada in the North, the Spanish, English and French colonies in the Caribbean, the older and much larger Spanish colonies in Florida, Mexico and Central America in the south and the First Nations in the vast lands to the west. Add to this the very important fact that in 1783 the USA did not possess nuclear weapons. In 2010, Israel is the only state in the Middle East which has nuclear weapons.

Israel's dastardly and unprovoked attack on the *Freedom Flotilla* of six ships taking essential humanitarian relief supplies to Palestinians in Gaza on **May 31, 2010** is a clear warning that Israel will require a concerted international effort to restrain it from using its nuclear weapons to attack and destroy Iran, Syria, Lebanon and any Arab state coming to the aid of the Palestinians. By "international" I do not mean the West since the West is either unable or unwilling to restrain Israel. In fact, Canada, for example, currently led by Israel's Prime Minister Benjamin Netanyahu's most vocal supporter of genocide against Palestinians, **Steven Harper,** can hardly wait to send its military to the Middle East to "defend" Israel. A nuclear strike by Israel will be justified by the West in the same way that the American nuking of Hiroshima and Nagasaki has been justified by the West. "International," in this context means China, Russia, Turkey, India, Brazil, Venezuela and other Third World countries. Three "asses of evil," Netanyahu, Harper and Obama, will never provide the leadership necessary to stop the genocide against the Palestinians or the nuking of Iran.

Israel combined nuclear blackmail with **piracy** in attacking the flotilla in international waters. As we have explained the Western empires have always used **piracy** as a weapon of war. As the most privileged *uncolony* of the American Empire, Israel is "above the law." Humanitarian aid is desperately needed in Gaza because of Israel's three year long blockade of Gaza. This genocide by Israel which is inflicted on the Palestinians in Gaza today is identical to the genocide inflicted on the First Nations by the American Empire, which we have documented at length. It's also reminiscent of how the West, including Canada, is of a single mind when it comes to using the most ridiculous propaganda to justify genocide against **Non-Whites.** After six centuries of genocide against the First Nations of the New World and the people of the Third World the West continues to peddle its insane ideas as to what equality, democracy and freedom means.

The Second Sino-Japanese War: 1937-1945

Japan, like the Western powers, did not end its colonizing efforts in China after the peace treaty of 1895. Like the Western powers, Japan exploited the disunity of China under the Qing dynasty and in the early years of the Chinese Republic. In fact, the period between the first Sino-Japanese war of 1894-95 and the second Sino-Japanese war of 1937-45 coincided with China's internal struggle among the War Lords, KMT and Communist Party, which we documented above. While Japan's conquests in China were opposed by the American Empire because it reduced American opportunities for further colonization the second and much more devastating Sino-Japanese War played decisively into American plans for its subjugation of Asia. Let the Japanese and Chinese inflict death and destruction on themselves for a decade, as the European empires had done for centuries, and they both become easy prey for American colonization.

The efforts of the Western empires, now led by the American Empire, to deny Japan the same respect accorded themselves was disastrous for Asia, and China, in particular. Japan could have used its rebuff by the West to become a leader in Asia. Instead it chose to use that rebuff to exploit Asia. Having conquered Korea and Taiwan during the First Sino-Japanese war it now moved to conquer parts of the Chinese mainland. It was a short-sighted policy since it would force Asia, and China, in particular, to cozy up to the same Western powers, including the American Empire, which had exploited and colonized it. Asia would no more accept Japanese colonialism than it had accepted Western colonialism. But it would co-operate with the West to fight Japanese imperialism.

Imperial rulers are incapable of seizing opportunities. The American Empire did not seize the opportunities presented to it by the fall of the Russian Empire. Likewise Japan did not seize the opportunities presented to it by the West's racial motives for respecting it only as an Asian Power not a Western Power. Its conquest of Korea and Taiwan was both a defensive move against Western dominance in Asia as well as an offensive move against China. Its offensive against China included its invasion of Chinese territory on the mainland, *Manchuria*. The peace treaty of April 17, 1895 ceded the Liaodong Peninsula in Manchuria to Japan, but diplomatic pressure from France, Germany and Russia forced Japan to relinquish their territorial conquest in Manchuria for a monetary payment of 450 million Yen.

Russia's subsequent 25 year lease of the Liaodong Peninsula in 1898 was one of the reasons for the Russo-Japanese war of 1904-05. China was caught between a rock and a hard place. While Japan saw Russia as one more Western imperialist emulating Britain, France, Germany and the United States in squeezing trade, economic and strategic concessions from a militarily weak China, instead of rallying around China and Asia, Japan chose to take for itself as much as it could prevent the Western powers from taking.

The Japanese invaded Manchuria again 1931. As in the first invasion in 1894 Japan's motives were both offensive and defensive. It was a defensive position against the Russian Empire and an offensive incursion into Chinese territory to rape and exploit its natural resources. This offensive motive was both consistent with those of the Western Powers and simultaneously aimed at countering American dominance in Asia and the Pacific. As the American Empire moved towards isolating Japan by reducing trade, immigration and respect for Japan's drive for equal imperial status with Britain, France, Germany and the US, Japan tried to compensate by raping China and Asia.

Full scale war with China broke out again in 1937. After the second invasion of Manchuria in 1931 the Japanese invader continued its push into Chinese territory on the mainland. By 1932 the Japanese controlled Shanghai and the Northern provinces. As we saw above the KMT led Chinese government had its base mostly in the south and until 1936 concentrated its military prowess on wiping out the Chinese communists rather than the Japanese invaders. Popular resentment at General

Chiang's focus on the internal strife rather than the external aggressors combined with the Japanese capture of Beijing and Tianjin in 1937 moved the KMT to engage the Japanese in open warfare. KMT forces led by General Chiang Kai-shek attacked the Japanese in Shanghai on August 13, 1937. As explained above the KMT government had the blessing of the American Empire.

The Battle of Shanghai: 1937

The KMT forces led by General Chiang Kai-shek chose to launch its full blown offensive against the Japanese invader in Shanghai on August 13, 1937. Given the huge foreign interests in Shanghai the KMT hoped that the American Empire and other Western powers would assist its offensive against Japan in Shanghai, to minimize the disruption of their commercial interests and danger to their investments in the city. Furthermore, the Japanese were now in defensive mode having conquered Northern China, thereby consolidating their huge buffer against the Russians.

Japan was well aware that a full blown war with China would only serve to undermine its hold on "Chinese territory" conquered in Northern China, Manchuria and Korea. At this time they had little desire to push further south into the Southern provinces controlled by the KMT. Further conquests of Chinese territory would spread their forces too thinly.

With this defensive stance, the Japanese were confident that they had the overwhelming firepower to quickly subdue the Chinese offensive in Shanghai. While Japan did succeed in maintaining their conquests in China, the *Battle of Shanghai* lasted much longer and was much more bloody, than the Japanese had anticipated. What the Chinese lacked in modern firepower they compensated for by having superiority in numbers. Chiang's army numbered over 1.5 million.

It was October 26, 1937 before the Japanese victories forced the Chinese to begin retreating from Shanghai. On November 5, 1937 the Japanese landed forces south of Shanghai in an effort to trap the Chinese forces retreating from Shanghai. This strategic move by the Japanese hastened the Chinese retreat out of Shanghai.

The KMT's offensive against the Japanese in Shanghai turned out to be a military disaster for Chiang. While it increased the popularity of the KMT and Chiang Kai-shek it failed to get the anticipated support from the American Empire. More importantly, it changed the Japanese stance from defensive to offensive. With Chiang's army devastated by its Shanghai offensive there was no longer any reason for the Japanese to limit its conquest to Northern China. They could now invade Southern China and still feel confident enough to hold it with sufficient forces to put down the incessant small scale Chinese rebellions.

Chiang's army never fully recovered its former strength after the Battle of Shanghai forcing Chiang to ask for assistance from the very warlords he had previously defeated in his earlier effort to unify China. Somewhat ironically, Chiang had delayed his army's retreat from Shanghai to give the American Empire time to come to his aid. This delay did not bring American help but instead destroyed his army much more than if he had retreated earlier after it was clear that victory in Shanghai, without American support, was impossible.

Chiang, like other Third World leaders who have courted American support against popular governments fail to understand the mindset of the American Empire. They never understand that they are being used by the American Empire to further the American goal of colonizing their country. It was clearly not in the interest of the American Empire to rescue Chiang's army from destruction by the Japanese. This could not be understood by a military general like Chiang. He foolishly believed that America was his friend and shared his capitalist principles. By believing in the Capitalist model of America he foolishly expected America to defend an **independent** Capitalist China.

The Japanese offensive following its defeat of the KMT's attack on Shanghai was aimed at capturing the Chinese Capital City of Nanjing. Had Chiang withdrawn his forces from Shanghai earlier, rather than prolonging the pummelling his forces suffered because of his misplaced faith in his American ally, the KMT may have been able to defend Nanjing. As it was, Nanjing fell quickly before the Japanese offensive and China's central government was forced to flee to Chongqing on December 1, 1937.

The Japanese were able to hold their expanded conquests in China until Mao's *People's Liberation Army, PLA,* launched a major offensive in the North in 1940. After 1940 the Japanese were under constant attacks from both the KMT and the PLA. In the end both Chiang and the American Empire would lose. The American decision to allow the Japanese to beat up on their "man in China" to soften up his future resistance to American colonization, backfired on the American Empire because it promoted the *PLA* to top dog in China. Unlike Chiang, Mao was no American stooge.

Short-term Gain by Japan and Russia for Long-term Pain

Russia was well aware that the Japanese invasion of China was partly motivated by its desire to create a buffer in Korea, Manchuria and Northern China against a Russian expansion into Japan. It was therefore not surprising that Russia provided some military assistance to the Chinese. Ironically, Russia's interests in Manchuria, like Japan's, were both offensive and defensive. Likewise, Russia was viewed by the West almost as much of an outsider as they viewed Japan. The long term interests of Japan, China, Russia, Korea and Taiwan would have been best served by their unified alliance against Britain, France, Germany and the United States. Instead, Japan and Russia fought each other for whatever the West deemed less strategically important to their imperial interests in Asia and the Pacific.

This short-sighted policy by both Japan and Russia served only to benefit the West. China could do nothing to assert its independence until the successful leadership of Mao Zedong. Until then it chose the lesser evil which was to seek the aid of the West against Japan. Likewise, the looming Russian-Japanese competition for strategic interests in Asia, deemed less vital to the West, forced these two outsiders to form alliances with the West, Russia with France and Japan with Britain. In the end these alliances also benefitted the Western powers, not Japan or Russia.

Japan's military defeat of Russia in 1905 only defeated what was its only *non-Western* rival in Asia. It produced some short-term gains for Japan. But by strengthening the Western alliance it brought some serious long-term pain not only to China and Asia but to Japan itself. Japan suffered the ultimate humiliation when its short-sighted policy towards China and Asia was used by the American Empire as justification for dropping atomic bombs on Hiroshima and Nagasaki. Japan had clearly fallen into the trap set for it by the American Empire. The American Empire could get world support for invading Japan by pretending that it was defending China and Asia against Japanese aggression.

It's truly amazing that even the nuking of Japan by the American Empire failed to change Japan's continued desire for respect by the West at the expense of leading Asia. As American colonization of Asia intensified following its nuking of Japan, Japan chose to ally itself with the American Empire, along with Taiwan and South Korea, against China and Asia. This continued short-sightedness by Japan would mean a much longer and difficult struggle for China and Asia against American imperialism. It would delay the inevitable decline of the American Empire.

The Japanese Attack on Pearl Harbor

By 1940 the American Empire supplied over 50 percent of Japan's oil, iron and steel. As the American Empire reduced its trade with Japan, Japan expanded its conquests across Asia moving from Korea to Taiwan to Manchuria to China to Vietnam. As the Japanese conquests across Asia expanded, the American Empire tightened its embargo on Japanese imports of gasoline, iron, steel, rubber and scrap metal. In 1941, all Japanese assets in the US were frozen and the American Empire closed the Panama Canal to Japanese shipping. Both sides moved closer and closer to military conflict but hoped that one or the other would give in to the goal of the other.

The Japanese goal was equal respect as a global power. The American goal was hegemony in Asia and the Pacific. The Japanese gambled that an attack on America's naval base in Hawaii would signal to the American Empire that it must share Asia with Japan. But the American Empire has never been interested in sharing. From its very beginning it never showed an interest in sharing a vast continent with the First Nations. Now it was unwilling to share Asia and the Pacific with Japan.

Japan interpreted American actions as one of denying it Great Power status on equal terms with the West. In reality, American actions were designed to provide an excuse for the American Empire to invade Japan and end its competition with the American Empire in Asia and the Pacific. Japan's false admiration for all things American continues to prevent Japan from making a clean break with the American Empire. It had hoped that by attacking Pearl Harbor the Americans would come to respect it. That was not to be. Instead it provided the "Day of Infamy" excuse for the second American invasion of Japan.

Japan made numerous attempts to negotiate with the American Empire. These attempts were unsuccessful because nothing short of total abandonment of colonies by Japan would appease the American Empire. By 1941, the American Empire had consolidated its hegemony in the New World. It now had its sights set on a similar hegemony on colonies in Asia and the Pacific. It was willing to share in the Pacific and Asia in the same manner as it had shared in Latin America and the Caribbean. Sharing would be with the Western empires of England and France. It would not be with an "inferior race" Asian power like Japan.

Hegemony in the Atlantic and Pacific, with some sharing of colonies with England and France, was the American Empire's unquestioned birthright . By 1941 the American Empire dreamed of ruling the world. The Second World War would make that American dream a reality. The so called "American dream" is not peace, harmony and the good life. It is conquests, colonies and military domination. Those who succumb to its propaganda are doomed to misunderstand the causes of poverty, inequality, wars, diseases, hunger, global warming, environmental degradation, dictatorships and human suffering. American propaganda continues to deceive in 2010 as much as it did in 1941.

The refusal of the American Empire to negotiate a sharing of colonies in Asia with Japan led to Japan's attack on the US naval base in Hawaii on December 7, 1941. The American Empire had expanded its Pacific base by invading and conquering the Hawaiian Islands since 1887. We documented this invasion and conquest in Chapter 3. The American Empire constructed one of its many worldwide naval bases at Pearl Harbour in Hawaii. In preparation for war with Japan the American Empire moved its Pacific Fleet from San Diego to Hawaii in 1940.

The Japanese attack on the American naval base in Hawaii, much like the more recent bombing of September 11, 2001, has received more news coverage than the creation of the universe. It has certainly received much more news coverage than the nuking of Hiroshima and Nagasaki, the fire bombing of Japan, the devastating bombing of Vietnam and Cambodia, the 12 years of bombing of Iraq, the criminal invasions of Iraq and Afghanistan and the countless crimes inflicted on the human race by the American Empire. You are somehow led to believe that there have been only **two** dastardly military attacks in the entire history of the human race and those were the rather miniscule, by comparison, air raids of December 7, 1941 and September 11, 2001. Why the world exaggerates the deaths of a few Americans and justifies the millions killed and maimed by the American Empire is a reflection of the disrespect and contempt with which the West continues to think of the people of the Third World.

The American Response to Pearl Harbor

The Japanese attack on the US naval base in Hawaii gave the American Empire the excuse it was waiting for to begin its long planned invasion and conquest of Japan. President Roosevelt's decision to invade Japan was no different from President Bush's decision to invade Iraq. These invasions were long planned by the American Empire as part of their strategy to dominate the globe. But timing of any major invasion is crucial. The American people need convincing excuses. The *December 7, 1941* attack on Pearl Harbor rallied the American people behind the invasion of Japan in the same way that the *September 11, 2001* attack on New York rallied the American people behind the invasion of Iraq.

President Roosevelt used the impending war with Japan to convince the American people to defy convention and allow him an unprecedented third term as president. As I have argued, American leaders are first *Commander-in Chief* and secondly *President*. Roosevelt, like all American presidents, preferred to govern in times of war than in times of peace. They revel in the glory of victory. Roosevelt saw an opportunity not only to be president for a third term but a "War" president. No American president would have resisted that opportunity. In the circumstances war with Japan was inevitable. Roosevelt needed the war to get a third term and to feel the "high" of commanding the greatest war machine in history.

The American dream of conquering Japan began in 1853-54 when President Millard Fillmore sent Commodore Matthew Perry to forcibly open Japanese ports to American trade and President Franklin Pierce sent Townsend Harris as US consulate to Japan. Fillmore, Perry, Pierce and Harris had led the way. Roosevelt would complete the task. Conquering Japan was the key to conquering Asia. In the period between 1853 and 2003, Japan, not China, was the dominant Asian power. Roosevelt saw the opportunity to go down in history as the *Commander-in-Chief* who secured Asia and the Pacific for the American Empire.

The American Empire declared war on Japan the day after the Japanese strike on Pearl Harbour. Let there be no doubt by anyone that Japan's attack on Hawaii was **defensive,** not offensive. As we have documented in earlier chapters the American Empire had expanded across the Pacific from its west coast to Hawaii, Midway Island, Wake Island, the Mariana Islands, Guam, Samoa and the Philippines. It was within easy striking distance of the Japanese Islands. As early as April 18, 1942 President Roosevelt was able to order an American air attack on the Japanese island of Honshu, the *Doolittle Raid.*

The closest Japanese bombers ever got to the United States, was the American *uncolony* of Hawaii. With China at war with Japan the American Empire was also free to use military bases in China to strike Japan at will. Japan had no equal strategic advantage to bomb the American mainland.

While Mao's China never had any doubt about America's true intentions in Asia, Japan remained eternally hopeful that the American Empire would be willing to share Asia. As such, it never had any ambition to invade and conquer the United States only to defend its own Asian colonies against American colonization. Between December 7, 1941 and the Battle of the Coral Sea on May 7, 1942, the Japanese won every battle against the American forces. The goal of the Japanese was to push the American Empire back across the Pacific as close to the American Mainland as possible, thereby maintaining a strategic distance between its Asian Empire and the strike force of the American Empire. The Japanese began their push back of the American Pacific Empire by capturing the Philippines, Guam and Wake Island. In addition Japan had fortified several of the Mariana Islands beginning in 1919.

Another problem for the Japanese was that the British were also heavily entrenched in Asia and the Pacific. It's no surprise that Britain declared war on Japan the same day as the American Empire. On March 11, 1942 the American General defending the American Pacific Empire, Douglas MacArthur, fled the Japanese attack on the American *uncolony* of the Philippines vowing to return. When the Japanese captured the Philippines MacArthur was able to escape to the British colony of Australia to enable him to fight the Japanese another day. While hiding out in Australia he coordinated the defence of Australia.

The Anglo-American alliance against Japan forced the Japanese to divert resources from the war with the American Empire to capture the English colonies in Asia beginning with Hong Kong and continuing with Singapore, Malaya and Burma. The French colonies of Vietnam, Laos and Cambodia and the Dutch East Indies were also captured by the Japanese, since both France and Holland were members of the Western alliance, and also to supply the Japanese war machine deprived of Western imports by the American embargo. By May 7, 1942 the Japanese had effectively driven the West out of China and Asia.

Nevertheless, Japan would suffer the same fate in Asia and the Pacific as its Western ally, Germany, in Europe. Its dream of an empire in Asia and the Pacific would be shattered and it would be reduced to another Asian *uncolony* of the American Empire. Its refusal to form an alliance with China and Russia against the West proved to be its downfall in the end. Its rise would be short-lived. Its demise would be catastrophic for itself and for Asia.

The Battle of the Coral Sea and the Battle of Midway

The ability of the American Empire to break the Japanese code was instrumental in the sudden reversal of victories by the Japanese navy. Both at the Battle of the Coral Sea, May 7, 1942 and at the Battle of Midway, June 4, 1942 the American Empire obtained advanced warnings of the Japanese invasion plans and were able to ambush the Japanese. The American ambush at the Battle of the Coral Sea stalled the Japanese expansion into New Guinea, Australia and New Zealand while the American ambush at the Battle of Midway prevented the Japanese from gaining a strategic defensive base from the Midway atoll. Midway is an ideal halfway military base in the Pacific for both Japan and the American Empire. These two defeats turned the war in favour of the American Empire and enabled the American Empire to achieve its long intended goal of invading and colonizing Japan.

After the victories of May 7 and June 4, 1942, the American Empire began to retake the Pacific islands beginning with Guadalcanal in the Solomon Islands. It was a long tough slug-match. American forces landed on Guadalcanal on August 7, 1942 and defeated the Japanese forces by February of 1943. Guam was retaken two full years later on August 10, 1944. General MacArthur did not retake the Philippines until February of 1945, almost three years after he fled from the Japanese.

During the war with the Japanese, President Roosevelt was simultaneously pursuing his complementary goal of colonizing China. Roosevelt's local henchman in China, General Chiang Kai-shek was invited to an Anglo-American conference convened in the British colony of Egypt during November 22 to 26 of 1943. One of the goals of the conference was to make it clear to Chiang that all of the spoils from an American defeat of Japan would go to the American Empire. Chiang was not sufficiently astute to understand that once Japan had been defeated and colonized by the American Empire, China would be the next immediate target for American colonization. Chiang's naivety is evidenced by his meeting with Mahatma Ghandi to support India's independence. Britain had no more interest in granting independence to India than the American Empire had in granting independence to China.

While Chiang had the lofty title of Allied Commander-in-Chief in China, the American General, Joseph Stilwell, assigned to Chiang as his Chief of Staff, was really overseeing Roosevelt's long-term plans for China. In the short-term Roosevelt saw China as essential to minimizing American casualties in his war with Japan. This was done in two ways. Use Chinese troops as much as possible instead of American troops and build airbases in China to firebomb Japan to the point where the planned invasion of Japan would involve fewer American lives.

Roosevelt's long-term plan for China was foiled by Mao Zedong. The American Empire had to settle for the island of Taiwan and South Korea while the British regained Hong Kong, Singapore, Malaya and Burma. Japan's short sighted unilateralism almost lost all of Asia and the Pacific to the Anglo-American empires. Mao's China not only prevented the American colonization of China but supported resistance to Anglo-American colonies in many other parts of Asia.

Aerial firebombing and Napalm

With the recapture of the Philippines and the Pacific islands by February of 1945 the American Empire had returned to its pre-war status and would have negotiated a peace treaty with Japan if it had no further imperial ambition in Asia as it professed. Of course, the American Empire denied imperial ambitions both when it expanded across the continent stealing the First Nations land and when it took the Caribbean and the Philippines from Spain. In like fashion it was busy selling the same propaganda of no imperial interest in Asia while militarily doing the opposite. A dedicated warmonger like the American Empire would not resist an opportunity to expand its empire. Japan and Asia would pay the price for not having the military muscle to stop the American juggernaut.

After the re-conquest of the Pacific islands and the Philippines the American Empire began its second invasion of Japan by capturing Japan's outer islands, firebombing Tokyo and using napalm. These offensive attacks on Japan by the American Empire have never been criticised by the West. The American Empire was assumed to have the moral right to punish the Japanese people for being as imperial as the West, in Asia, Japan's home turf, never mind the New World or Africa. Is it not ironic that the West would claim that the American Empire has the greater moral right to an empire in Asia than an Asian country, such as Japan?

By late 1944 the American Empire was able to dominate the skies over Japan and bomb military and civilian targets with little resistance from the Japanese Empire. Japan never came close to having any such capability to strike the American mainland. Between November 28, 1944 and the Japanese surrender on September 2, 1945 every major Japanese city was bombed continuously, killing and injuring millions of Japanese women and children. Half of Tokyo was totally wiped out and smaller cities were almost totally destroyed. Honshu Island, the target of the Doolittle Raid of 1942 was firebombed again several times beginning July 14, 1945 and causing huge civilian deaths. Another of the four main islands of Japan, Hokkaido, was bombed beginning on July 15, 1945.

Poison Gas and Nuclear Bombs

The large scale killing of Japanese civilians by the continuous firebombing of Japanese cities was followed by the nuking of Nagasaki and Hiroshima. The world's first uranium bomb was dropped on the civilian population of Hiroshima by the "Leader of the Free World" on August 6, 1945. This vile act by the world's most vicious empire is cheered by the West as a necessary evil to save freedom and democracy. Is it surprising that with that kind of cheering the "Leader of the Free World" would drop the first plutonium bomb on the civilians of Nagasaki just three days later? Only the American Empire has both the world's blessing to possess the world's largest stockpile of WMD's and the "moral authority" to use nuclear weapons. Americans kill and maim millions of innocent civilians for "a better world," according to the Western media and Western historians.

American propaganda used to convince the world that nuking Japan saved lives is still the official Western line used to defend American war crimes. Objective analysis shows that American firebombing and command of the skies over Japan had sufficiently reduced the ability of Japan to inflict much casualty on a land based invasion. The American Empire used nuclear weapons not to reduce civilian and military casualties but despite the much greater casualties caused by the nuclear weapons. The true reasons for the use of nuclear weapons include the desire to test the power and reliability of these new WMD's, the strongly held American belief that Asians are an inferior race to whites, the fear of having to share an Asian Empire with Russia as a result of Russia participating in a land based invasion and the desire to send a strong message to Russia that the American Empire would not share the world with any other imperial power because it possessed nuclear weapons and Russia did not. Most importantly, the American Empire wanted the world to know that it had no qualms about using nuclear weapons.

As a result of false American propaganda many Americans continue to accept the use of nuclear weapons by its government in invading and conquering other nations. This American willingness to use nuclear weapons puts the onus on other nations to do what they can to restrain the American Empire. Other nations, not the American Empire, must either refrain from possessing nuclear weapons or show restraint in using them should they choose to possess nuclear weapons.

The dilemma is that the best way to restrain frequent use of nuclear weapons by the American Empire as a tool of its insatiable imperial appetite is by possessing nuclear weapons and convincing the American Empire that you will use them if you are invaded to be colonized. A nuclear free world is out of the question as long as the American Empire is the dominant world power. Possession and willingness to **use** nuclear weapons is an important component of America's military superiority and its use of that military superiority to threaten the rest of the world into submission.

The land based invasion of the Japanese island was scheduled to begin on November 1, 1945. It was fortunate that Japan surrendered before then. The American land based invasion plans included the use of *poison gas,* such as mustard gas, cyanide and phosgene. Another 5 million Japanese civilians would have been killed by this lethal weapon of war. While most nations had agreed that they would not use poison gas as a weapon of war the "civilized" American Empire condoned its use against the Japanese people. The Western media is so twisted that it could loudly denounce Saddam Hussein for using the same deadly poison gas which the American Empire planned to use in their land based invasion of Japan but not condemn the American Empire for supplying Saddam with the means to produce the deadly gas.

As in any war only those who lose are guilty of war crimes. Several Japanese leaders were convicted of war crimes by an "international" war crimes tribunal. No American leaders were even tried for war crimes. No American leader was ever indicted for the American plan to invade Japan with poison gas.

American Occupation of Japan

The American Empire had finally achieved its goal of invading and colonizing Japan. As with Canada, Western Europe, Australia and New Zealand, Japan would be bullied into becoming an American satellite in fighting the Russians for American hegemony. This post-World War I strategy of giving some degree of independence to American *uncolonies* in return for their economic, military, political and propaganda support for American hegemony was more effective than conquering and policing the entire world. The British had created a "Commonwealth" to prolong their imperial hegemony. The

American Empire created capitalist "democracies" subject to guidance from Washington to prolong their imperial hegemony. Japan would be the first, but not the last, Asian country to be given this option.

At last, Japan was treated as an equal by the American Empire. It had been granted the same American *uncolony* status as Britain, France, Germany, Italy, Canada, Australia, New Zealand, Holland, Spain, Portugal, Denmark, Sweden, Finland, Ireland and Belgium, among others. It would provide one more market for American produce, one more economy for American investment and one more nation for the American Empire to indoctrinate with American lies while selling it American culture from movies to McDonalds. The Americanization of the world had gone from the New World to Europe and now to Asia. Japan was a willing patsy having secretly yearned for all things American. If it could not dominate Asia to prove to the West that it was superior to other Asians it would choose American *uncolony* status over independent status as an Asian nation.

As in the case of other conquests the American Empire constructed permanent naval bases in Japan so that its Pacific fleet would be within striking distance of Asian countries it would later invade and colonize, beginning with Taiwan and Korea.

CHAPTER 8

US Invasions of Pacific Islands, Taiwan, Korea, Vietnam, Cambodia and Laos

The Second World War had crushed the old European empires while promoting the American Empire to "Leader of the Free World." The colonies of the old European empires had fought alongside their colonial masters with the hope that they would be granted independence when the war ended. Unfortunately, they had not anticipated the rise of an American Empire intent on replacing the old colonial masters with itself as the new colonial master and working hand in glove with the old colonial masters to ensure such a transition. Where once the "West" meant the Western European empires of Britain, France, Germany, Italy, Spain and Portugal, after World War II, the "West" meant the American Empire with satellite support from Western Europe, Canada, Australia and New Zealand.

The American Empire called the shots and the satellites fell in line. A new order emerged using identical language, propaganda, mindset, tunnel vision, military muscle, "international" institutions, "morality," "democracy," consumer products, accepted culture, religion and defined common sense to control, mould and dictate to the people of the globe. Absolutely no one was permitted to think, act or speak outside this box. Political, economic, intellectual, religious and military leaders became one with this universe. Anyone daring to challenge this highly restricted view of the world was immediately marginalized, branded unpatriotic or cowardly. Worse still he or she may be accused of being a communist or traitor and harassed or imprisoned. Think inside the box and the most ignorant is portrayed as intelligent. Think outside the box and the most intelligent is portrayed as stupid.

American Invasion of the Northern Mariana Islands And the Marshall Islands

American conquests in the Pacific prior to World War II included Midway Island, Wake Island, Guam, Samoa, Baker Island, Howland Island, Jarvis Island, Johnston Atoll, Palmyra Atoll and Kingman Reef. As explained in Chapter 5 the American Empire expanded across the Pacific partly by colonizing these strategic islands as a bridge to achieving its ultimate goal of colonizing China, Japan and all of Asia. World War II provided the ideal opportunity to expand its invasion and conquest of islands in the Pacific. These islands were strategically located for both the American and Japanese empires. By declaring war on Japan the islands occupied by Japan would be targeted by the American

Empire both as a way of expanding its Pacific empire as well as providing strategic military bases for the eventual conquest of Japan.

American Invasion and Conquest of the Northern Mariana Islands

The American Empire already had an important foothold in the Mariana Islands having invaded and colonized Guam since 1898. During the Second World War the American Empire added the islands of *Saipan* and *Tinian* to its Pacific empire. These two islands in the Mariana Islands were entrusted to Japan by the League of Nations after World War I. American forces landed on Saipan on June 15, 1944 and quickly constructed B-29 air bases to enhance their firebombing of Japanese cities. Tinian Island was captured in July 1944 and turned into a giant American airbase. Some 67 Japanese cities were intensively firebombed by B-29's for over a year. A single raid on Tokyo on March 10, 1945 killed 100,000, injured thousands and destroyed a million homes.

The nuclear bombs, Little Boy and Fat Man were transported to Tinian Island on July 26, 1945. The uranium fuelled Little Boy was loaded on the American B-29, Enola Gay, and dropped on Hiroshima on August 6, 1945. It killed 140,000 civilians. The plutonium fuelled Fat Man was loaded on the American B-29, Bockscar and dropped on Nagasaki on August 9, 1945. It killed 80,000 civilians.

The American installed propaganda world body, the United Nations, UN, rewarded the American Empire for nuking Japan from the Tinian airbase by entrusting all of the 15 islands making up the *Northern Mariana Islands* to the American Empire after World War II. The largest islands are Saipan, Tinian and Rota. Most of the population are also on these three islands with Saipan being the most populous by far. The capital city is located on Saipan. The Northern Mariana Islands are strategically located north of Guam between Wake Island and China to the west, the Philippines to the south and Japan to the north. Saipan is also conveniently located for American corporations to use cheap Asian labour to boost the GDP of the American Empire.

The Northern Mariana Islands, like Hawaii, Midway Island, Wake Island, Guam and the Philippines, combined with the overwhelming superiority of the American navy after World War II puts the American Empire within easy striking distance of every country in Asia. By comparison, Russia is a land-locked behemoth incapable of launching an invasion of the United States. The evidence is clear that the American Empire has the dominant offensive capability in both the Atlantic and the Pacific. Other nations, including Russia, have to be content with purely defensive capabilities.

American Invasion and Conquest of the Marshall Islands

Prior to World War II the American Empire had already expanded south of the direct line across the Pacific stretching westwards from Hawaii to Guam, when it colonized Samoa in 1899. This southern expansion in the Pacific from Wake Island to Samoa was consolidated after World War II by colonizing the Marshall Islands. US forces landed in the Marshall Islands on January 31, 1944. The islands were heavily bombed by American B-24 aircrafts, killing Marshall Islands civilians as well as Japanese and Korean workers. US colonization of the Marshall Islands was condoned by the UN after World War II. The American Empire used many of the islands to test its growing nuclear arsenal following World War II.

The American Invasion of Taiwan

The failure to colonize China was the first of many defeats for the post World War II American Empire. Its conquest of the island of Formosa or Taiwan was part of a long term strategy to isolate and contain China while expanding its empire in Asia and the Pacific. By expanding its military and economic presence in Asia and the Pacific it hoped to increase its chances of launching a more successful future invasion of China. The key American point man commissioned by the American Empire to oversee the post World War II expansion of the empire in Asia and the Pacific was General Douglas MacArthur.

President Harry Truman appointed MacArthur as the Supreme Allied Commander to govern Japan during the Post World War II American occupation. It was from that important vantage point that MacArthur would expand the American Empire into Asia by adding Taiwan and Korea to Japan. This was a natural extension of the Japanese conquest since Japan had previously colonized both Taiwan and Korea. It is a little ironic that both Japan and the American Empire acquired Taiwan and Korea only because they failed in their ultimate goal of colonizing China. The difference, of course, was that while the American Empire's goal was the colonization of **both** Japan and China, Japan's goal was to compete with the American Empire as an equal in sharing the spoils of China, Asia and the Pacific. In addition, Japan's colonization of Taiwan and Korea was partly defensive in that they provided buffer states against an invasion of Japan by the American Empire. Despite rhetoric to the contrary the American Empire has never been threatened with invasion. Its invasions and conquests of other countries have always been purely offensive and expansionist.

When Japan surrendered to the American Empire in September 1945, the American Empire assumed that China would also become its *uncolony* under a puppet government led by General Chiang Kai-shek. Throughout the Second World War the American Empire acted and behaved as if the *Republic of China, ROC,* was the legitimate government of China and used Chiang to bolster their bargaining position against Winston Churchill and Josef Stalin. By pretending to treat China as an ally equal to Britain and Russia in the war against Japan both Roosevelt and Truman increased their leverage against the British and Russians.

The *ROC* was promoted to Great Power status by the American Empire only to serve its own selfish ends. No American president was willing to treat Japan with the respect accorded to the Western European empires even though they ranked Japan well above China. The 13 English colonies along the Atlantic seaboard had used the British to oust the French out of North America only to use the French to defeat the British in their War of Independence. In like manner the American Empire was using the *ROC* to colonize Japan so that it could use military bases in Japan as a springboard to complete its colonization of China.

Unlike the Japanese, the Chinese were never fooled into believing that the American Empire would ever treat them as equals. But Presidents Roosevelt and Truman were able to fool Chiang into believing that. Chiang never understood that Roosevelt and Truman used him and the *ROC* both to conquer Japan and to outmanoeuvre the British and Russians in sharing the spoils of the victory over Japan and its Asian empire. At the *Cairo Conference* in November 1943 Chiang was invited by Roosevelt as an equal to Churchill and Stalin, even though Stalin objected and boycotted the conference.

At the Yalta conference in February 1945 President Truman persuaded Stalin to break his five-year non-aggression pact with Japan to help him defeat the Japanese Empire. As a result, Stalin shocked the Japanese leadership when he declared war on Japan on August 8, 1945. Nevertheless, Chiang's firm support for the American Empire combined with America's willingness to use nuclear weapons ensured that all of Japan would go to the American Empire.

It was no surprise that President Truman would support the return of Taiwan to China under the *ROC* government led by Chiang Kai-shek since China under the *ROC* government would become another *uncolony* of the American Empire. The colonization of Japan was not the ultimate goal of the American Empire. It was only an essential part of its westward conquest of the First Nations lands on the American continent to Hawaii and across the Pacific to Midway Island, Guam, Samoa, the Philippines, Japan, the Mariana, Marshall, Ryukyu, Caroline, Bonin and Volcano islands and to China and beyond. Its navy and aircraft carriers would dominate the "Seven Seas" as the British navy had done before. In the post World War II period the US navy had no rival. It could act with impunity.

When the American Empire lied to the world that it had invaded Vietnam because the Vietnamese had attacked its military ships in the Gulf of Tonkin no one dared ask the obvious question. What were American warships doing in the Gulf of Tonkin and who gave the American Empire the legal right to patrol the High Seas? Piracy by countries like Somalia pales in comparison to what the American navy does in international waters. But no one is powerful enough to chastise the American Empire much less challenge it.

Mao Zedong Saves China but loses Taiwan

The American Empire fanned the flames of civil war in China as it had done in Russia. The end game was the same. Hype the propaganda that all communists were evil, encourage a civil war against the communists and invade and conquer with minimum loss of American lives. The policy failed in China as it had failed in Russia. But failures have never deterred the American Empire from future invasions and conquests. In the case of China the American Empire retreated temporarily to Taiwan to continue plotting their future colonization of China.

The Chinese civil war of 1927-1950 raged through the Japanese invasion of China, the Second World War and the immediate post war years. The American Empire was actively engaged throughout supporting their man, Chiang Kai-shek, against the *Communist Party of China, CPC.* Chiang had succeeded Dr. Sun Yat-sen the leader of the *Republic of China, ROC,* in 1925. During Sun's leadership, the ROC had friendly relations with Russia. The American Empire, having lost the civil war in Russia to the communists, was determined to make China a capitalist satellite.

Chiang was the military general willing to start a civil war in China to aid the American Empire. In 1927, Chiang began to purge the KMT, China's ruling party, of communists. Since Russia had supported the KMT under Dr. Sun Yat-sen it was slow to recognize the new reality in China. By 1927, the KMT under Chiang was funded by the American Empire to oust the communists. The CPC received relatively little financial support from Russia. They had to fight the KMT as well as the American and Japanese invaders.

The Second World War was the single greatest gift to the American Empire. Like the First World War, the American Empire benefited immensely from the sale of arms and war supplies to the Western European combatants. While its economy grew by leaps and bounds the old Western European empires were killing their economies. Unlike the First World War, Japan was not a Western ally. Between the two World Wars the American Empire had worked incessantly to make Japan its number one enemy. By instigating the *Pacific War* simultaneously with the Second World War in Europe it was setting up the Japanese Empire for defeat. Having China on its side during the conflict with Japan was the icing on the cake. It would be the equivalent of having Iraq invade Iran simultaneously with its own 2003 invasion of Iraq.

During the second Sino-Japanese War of 1937-45 China would help the American Empire achieve its life long goal of colonizing Japan. Once Japan was colonized, a weakened China would be an easier target for colonization by the American Empire especially with the help of Generalissimo Chiang Kai-shek. As in the Russian civil war the American Empire underestimated the will of the Chinese people and the strength of communist resistance to foreign domination. The American Empire would fail in China as it later did in North Korea and Vietnam. But it would colonize Japan, Taiwan and South Korea to add to the Philippines and the Pacific islands.

By 1945 the American Empire had colonized Japan but its plan for China was unravelling. Despite its willingness to use nuclear weapons to subdue its enemies Josef Stalin was far from cowering before the American juggernaut. In destroying the old European empires to achieve hegemony it had also destroyed their ability to counter the rising tide of communism in Western Europe and protect the vital oil supplies from the Middle East. War weary from the extraordinary resistance of the Japanese it now had to use some of its ill gotten gains from the Second World War to bail out Western Europe to counter the Russian invasion and aid the British in Greece, Turkey and Palestine.

With its hands full in Western Europe and its soldiers licking their wounds it could not provide the financial and military support requested by General Douglas MacArthur to achieve the mission assigned to him by President Truman. Both MacArthur and Chiang Kai-shek were frustrated by inadequate American resources. MacArthur needed resources to expand the American Empire in Asia and Chiang needed resources to defeat the communists and deliver China to the American Empire. Like the British after their massive victory over France during the Seven Years War ending in 1763, the American Empire had chewed off more than it could handle after defeating the Japanese Empire. As the British would be forced to give up the United States after the Seven Years War the American Empire would be forced to give up China after the Second World War.

President Truman determined that Western Europe and the Middle East would take priority over China and Asia in the immediate post war period. The Russians had advanced eastwards as far as East Germany and were poised to capture Turkey and Greece. The British needed reinforcements in Turkey and Greece to stop the Russian advance. Truman sent American forces into both Turkey and Greece. At the same time widespread poverty across Western Europe was enabling the rapid spread of communism even in France and Britain. American economic assistance was vital to prevent the people of many Western European countries from voting for communist party leaders in **democratic** elections. Finally, the Jews were clamouring for an American *uncolony,* Israel, on Palestinian land, thereby threatening the oil supplies from the Middle East.

With American forces in Turkey and Greece, the Marshall Plan and the creation of NATO the American Empire blocked the Soviet advance at the Berlin Wall. But stealing the oil supplies of the Middle East while creating the *uncolony* of Israel on Palestinian land proved to be much more elusive. It was the stubborn and prolonged resistance of the Middle East to American imperialism that finally hastened the decline of the most powerful empire the world had experienced and saved China, Asia and the human race from American deceit and "civilized" barbarism.

The ROC and Taiwan after the Second World War

The US army, stationed in China since the Boxer Rebellion, departed in 1948. American financial support to the ROC was estimated to be $2 billion in 1949. However, US occupation in Western Europe and the Middle East enabled Mao Ze Dong to drive Chiang Kai-shek and his American overlord off the Chinese mainland to the tiny island of Taiwan in 1949. Chiang transferred the government of the ROC from Nanjing to Taipei. The CPC created the *Peoples Republic of China, PRC,* on October 1, 1949 and established the capital in Beijing.

Both Chiang and MacArthur saw the escape to Taiwan as a temporary move much like MacArthur's escape from the Philippines to Australia in 1942. But MacArthur did not understand the new role of the American Empire. The American Empire had instigated war with Japan to dominate Asia. The collapse of the British Empire along with France and Germany forced the American Empire to postpone its imperialist expansion in Asia to divert essential resources to a leadership role in Western

Europe and the Middle East. Russian expansion into Western Europe and the Middle East was much more of an immediate threat to American hegemony than loss of China.

The ROC was directed by General MacArthur to occupy Taiwan after Japan surrendered to the American Empire in 1945. Taiwan had been a colony of Japan since 1895. The ROC's occupation of Taiwan was simply an extension of the US occupation of Japan in 1945. With the ousting of the ROC from China in 1949, Taiwan was forced by both the American Empire and the exiled ROC government of Chiang Kai-shek to begin a confrontation with China as an important part of America's cold war with the Soviet Union. The Taiwanese people had absolutely no say in the matter. This is only one more of many examples of how the West under the leadership of the American Empire spread "democracy." American "democracy" in Taiwan, as in Iraq and Afghanistan today, was imposed by brute force.

The joint American/ROC occupation of Taiwan was no less brutal than the Japanese colonization. Of course, the West had popularized the childish notion that only Western powers were capable of governing colonies. But the Taiwanese people opposed the American imposed ROC occupation even before the ROC was driven out of China. The Taiwanese people identify the beginning of the American/ROC occupation as October 1945 when Chen Yi was appointed as governor of the colony by the ROC. Chiang was forced to send reinforcements to protect Chen Yi in 1947 when violent protests erupted. The ROC government imposed martial law and executed and imprisoned thousands of Taiwanese dissidents. This is how the American Empire forced their brand of "democracy" on the Taiwanese people.

The so called "McCarthy era" in the United States came to Taiwan as early as 1947. This was no coincidence. The McCarthy witch hunts in the US were authorized by an Executive Order passed by President Truman on March 22, 1947. The long arm of the FBI reached Taiwan as the ROC imposed "democratic" government arrested and imprisoned or executed any Taiwanese opposed to American imperialism. The charge was simple. Anyone opposing American imperialism had to be a communist and all communists were **evil** and had to be punished. Even today, Canadians and Americans alike, only have to label any democratic government *communist* and no further explanation is expected.

While most Canadians are proud of their *Mixed Economy,* combining the best of *communism* and capitalism, they are equally proud of implying that they are *capitalists* when they accuse another of being *communist.* Better to be the devil incarnate than a communist. Despite the invention of other derogatory terms by the American media such as terrorist and Islamist, communist has not lost any of its stigma.

As in the US, the ROC passed laws which defined unpatriotic behaviour. In Taiwan, as in the US, it was unpatriotic to be a communist or a communist sympathiser. In the US it was unpatriotic to be anti-imperialist while in Taiwan it was unpatriotic to oppose the American/ROC occupation. The American Empire even supported a one-party state in Taiwan despite the Western propaganda that democracy cannot exist in one-party states. Chiang's KMT party found other ways of suppressing all opposition to his rule of the American *uncolony* which he called the *Republic of China.* That the American people and some other Westerners also proudly proclaimed the tiny island of Formosa the *Republic of China* is the most damning testimony to their ignorance and "Joe the plumber" IQ.

While unwilling to launch another invasion of China because of commitments in Western Europe and the Middle East the American Empire was still determined to hold the gains it had made in Japan, Taiwan and Korea as a result of the Second World War. Taiwan would therefore remain an *uncolony* of the American Empire without true independence or democracy. However, with the relative economic decline of the American Empire by 2010 and the relative economic growth of China, there is increasing economic integration of the Taiwan economy with that of China. This increased economic integration will very likely lead to political integration. Where once Taiwan held the key to a future

American conquest and colonization of China, Taiwan, together with the ex-English colony of Hong Kong and the ex-Portuguese colony of Macau, is today leading the modernization of the Chinese technology sector as China challenges the United States for economic hegemony.

Taiwan's new president, Ma Ying-jeou, is currently negotiating a free trade agreement with China. Under Ma's leadership economic, political and travel integration with China has been actively pursued. Without increased international trade with China and Asia Taiwan, once the shining example of the "Asian tiger" of the *newly industrialized countries* created by American "democracy," will stagnate and suffer the same economic fate as its colonial master, the American Empire. In the meantime Taiwan's previous pro-American puppet President, Chen Shui-bian, who ruled Taiwan between 2000 and 2008, is languishing in the Taipei Detention Center, convicted of corruption and money laundering. Chen and his wife were given life sentences for accepting bribes and embezzling funds. Chen's son and daughter-in-law were also found guilty of similar crimes.

The American Invasion and Conquest of Korea

Korea, like Japan and China, were under constant threat of colonization by the West, including the American Empire, and by Russia, and later, by Japan. The European empires began their colonization of Asia in the fifteenth century and were joined by the American Empire as early as 1784. Korea followed the example of China and Japan of closing its ports to Western ships in an effort to forestall Western colonization. We have dealt extensively with the *Unequal treaties* imposed by the American and Western European empires on China and Japan after opening their ports with military force.

The American Empire forcibly opened the Korean port of Busan in 1853, the same year that Commodore Perry arrived in Japan with orders from President Fillmore to bomb Tokyo Harbour if Japan refused to sign an *Unequal treaty*. As explained earlier the American Empire had "awakened a sleeping giant," when they forced Japan to trade with them, albeit on unequal terms. Far from making a clean sweep of colonizing China, Japan and Korea, Japan became a fearsome competitor with the American Empire until its defeat in World War II. The American Empire forced a trade treaty on Korea in 1882 but it was Japan which colonized Korea before the American Empire, only to lose it to the American Empire in 1945.

The American Empire's public propaganda for Korea, as for China, was independence. President Wilson called it "self determination." But this was a ploy to replace Japanese colonization of Korea with American colonization. The American Empire had used the same ploy in the Philippines, Cuba, Puerto Rico and the Dominican Republic against Spanish colonization. Japan was not deterred by American propaganda. It was forced to give up Korea to the American Empire only after the American Empire had firebombed its cities and nuked its women and children in Nagasaki and Hiroshima. That was President Truman's interpretation of "self determination." No Western power has ever condemned Truman.

The American colonization of Korea would be directed from Japan by General Douglas MacArthur. With the resources of the American Empire stretched by America's new role in Western Europe and the Middle East, MacArthur was forced to commandeer the military resources of the newly created American "international" institution referred to as the UN. Canada could hardly wait to provide military support for the American invasion of Korea under the guise of support for the UN "World body." The UN, like the World Bank, the IMF and the GATT, were "international" institutions in name only. They were all fronts for American domination of a world weakened by wars, capitalist exploitation, unfair trade practices, unfair global financial arrangements, racist immigration policies and fear of competition from the Soviet Union. Canada has been a zealous ally of the US when it comes to pretending that these bodies are international.

While Stalin had been duped into providing military assistance for the American conquest of Japan, Russia came away empty handed as far as Japan was concerned. Not so with Korea. Like Germany, the American Empire was forced to share Korea with its ally, Russia. But it was a short-term alliance of convenience, as are most American alliances. The American Empire wanted all of Korea and MacArthur was determined to colonize all of Korea, and if possible, make another attempt at colonizing China. Once again China would have to defend its borders as it came under attack from the American Empire. The American Empire would attack China from three sides, using the Wilsonian propaganda of self determination for Korea, Taiwan and Tibet.

Russian Interest in Korea

As we have explained before, Russian imperial interests in China and Korea long pre-dated the Second World War. Russian competition with Japan for colonies in China and Korea was a primary reason for the Russo-Japanese war of 1904-05. Russia's defeat in that war led to the rise of communism in the Soviet Union and ultimately the rise of Stalin as one of the two key players in determining the fate of Korea after World War II. Russia had lost both its foothold in China, Manchuria, and all of Korea to Japan. Thanks to Mao, China was no longer up for grabs either by Stalin or the American Empire. But Korea was, and Stalin was not going to let President Truman or General MacArthur conquer all of it.

Despite Western propaganda to the contrary, the Second World War, like all the wars before, was a **war for empire.** The Russian Empire, like the American Empire, was competing with Japan for Asia. At the same time, the Russian Empire was competing with the British and French empires for hegemony in Europe. The Anglo-French alliance needed the American Empire to defeat Germany and the American Empire needed the British to defeat Japan. Empires form temporary alliances during wars. Russia could have allied with Germany and Japan but chose to form an alliance with Britain and France in Europe and with the American Empire in Asia. Allies share the spoils of war if they are victorious. Russia fully expected to share the spoils in Europe as well as those in Asia.

Stalin was no fool. He fully expected the American Empire to take as much of the spoils of the war in both Europe and Asia as it could take by force. It was the tried and true American way. For Russia to have an equal share of the spoils it would have to secure it by force. It was able to do so in Europe and Korea but not in Japan. America's pre-emptive nuking of Japan meant that all of Japan was seized by force by the American Empire. Not so in Europe or Korea. Stalin made sure that the Russian armies were in Germany and Korea before the Americans. That way the American Empire would not have the military resources to cheat the Russians.

Russia declared war on Japan on August 6, 1945 and had troops in Korea within a few days. Russia defeated the Japanese forces in the north and secured all of Korea down to the 38th parallel. The American Empire had asked for Soviet help to defeat Japan since the Yalta Conference in February 1945. American forces arrived in Korea in September 1945, defeated the Japanese and secured the south up to the 38th parallel. There was agreement between the Russians and Americans that the 38th parallel would be the dividing line in terms of sharing Korea as part of the spoils for defeating Japan.

In 1945 the American military was not capable of conquering all of Korea. But it had no intention of letting the Russians hold on to North Korea indefinitely. As soon as it felt strong enough it would invade and capture North Korea. That was the plan. General MacArthur would have to be patient. America was temporarily war weary and also needed to divert war resources to hold back Soviet expansion into Western Europe and the Middle East since Britain and France were too weak to do that.

The Korean War Marks the Most Important Watershed in the History of the Modern World

By 1950, the American Empire had recovered from its war weariness resulting from the Second World War, had consolidated its dominant position in Western Europe and the Middle East and had grown its economy to the point that its GDP was half that of the entire world. It had acquired a nuclear arsenal far exceeding that of the Russians. Since the West had not criticized its nuking of Japan it never ruled out using nuclear weapons to achieve military victory and imperial expansion.

The American Empire had always viewed the loss of China to Mao's government and the loss of North Korea to Russia as temporary losses. By 1950 it was ready to make another attempt to invade and conquer North Korea and China. Both Generals MacArthur and Chiang Kai-shek had been waiting impatiently for the green light. Even the Dalai Lama was getting impatient with his CIA partner in crime for not providing sufficient military support to maintain serfdom in Tibet under his Buddhist monks and Lamas.

Despite military support from the UN the American Empire would fail to conquer North Korea, China, or even separate Tibet from China, as it had done with Taiwan. However, it would plant capitalism firmly in Japan, Taiwan and South Korea while continuing to promote the myth that *capitalism* and freedom was one and the same. Corrupt financial managers and presidents of multinational corporations would be *free* to earn millions for incompetence and a much larger percent of the citizens would be equally *free* to die of hunger and malnutrition. Japan, Taiwan and South Korea would seek Western adulation by following the American dream of excessive consumption and environmental degradation.

Koreans had foolishly believed American propaganda that the defeat of Japan would mean political and economic independence. When the Americans arrived in Korea in September 1945 they ignored Korean political leaders and institutions and set up an imperial administration. Adding insult to injury, American administrators were complemented by Japanese administrators. Since the American Empire had now effectively colonized Japan it was administratively efficient to keep in place as much of the Japanese colonial structure in Korea, including the police force, as was necessary to economize on the use of scarce American personnel. Upsetting the Koreans was of little concern since the Koreans did not have the military muscle to do anything about it.

In December 1945, the American Empire had agreed to a four-year joint occupation of Korea with the Soviet Union. During that four-year period the American Empire would consolidate its colonization of South Korea and destroy all guerrilla resistance to the occupation. This would prepare it for its intended invasion and conquest of North Korea from the Soviet Union. If that invasion proved to be an easy one it would advance on China. China was still the key to colonizing Asia. Japan, Taiwan and Korea were important but China was the key. With China added to Japan and Korea and its British ally still exercising significant influence in India, Pakistan, Malaysia, Ceylon, Hong Kong, Singapore and Burma, Asia would become a Western enclave of second class Americans. It would consume American products, imitate American culture, adopt American institutions and establish pretend democracies with the usual American propaganda of freedom of the press, freedom of speech, freedom of religion and freedom from the "evil" of communism. Most importantly, it would contribute vast supplies of manpower for America's incessant wars in every part of the globe.

In preparation for its colonization of all of Korea the American Empire looked for the usual indigenous dictator who would become their "s.o.b." They settled on Syngman Rhee who had been indoctrinated in the US to hate communism. He would help the US sell the notion that all Koreans opposed to American colonization were "evil' communists. The Western "free" press would have one more gift from the American Empire to peddle their wares to their gullible consumers. It would not be the American Empire making war on the hated communists in the North but freedom loving South Koreans led by President Rhee. The Americans would simply be doing their Christian duty in sacrificing their young men for the noble cause of liberating North Korea for the benefit of the Korean people.

Syngman Rhee publicly professed his dream of unifying Korea by force with the help of the American Empire. He would do for the American Empire what General Chiang Kai-shek had failed to do in China. With China surrounded by capitalist governments in Korea, Japan, Taiwan, Tibet, Hong Kong and Macau, it would simply be a matter of time before the American Empire fulfilled its dream of colonizing China. In 1950, the Soviet Union was too weak to challenge the American Empire in Asia. But once again, as with Chiang Kai-shek, it would be China which would foil the dream of Rhee and his American overlord.

North Korea, under constant threat of invasion by the American *uncolony* of South Korea, had by 1950, built a strong defensive force in the *North Korean Peoples' Army*. The American Empire, with commitments in Europe and the Middle East, was cautious. It sought the military assistance of its British, Canadian, Australian and other Western allies. Its puppet institution, the UN, was used as a front for American imperialism. Canada, for example, ever willing to follow the American lead in waging wars across the globe, used the UN to sell its warmongering to a gullible Canadian electorate. The American Empire passed a UN Security Council resolution on June 25, 1950 to the effect that Rhee's government in South Korea was the legal government of all of Korea. In 1950, neither China nor India was a member of the UN Security Council but the tiny island of Taiwan was. The Soviet Union was a member but boycotted the institution once it was clear that it was set up to serve the interest of the American Empire.

With the aid of UN forces General MacArthur invaded and captured the North Korean capital of Pyongyang by October of 1950. As the American Empire threatened to cross the Yalu River into China, Mao launched a counter offensive which successfully drove the Americans back to the dividing line of the 38th parallel agreed to by the Americans and Russians during World War II. MacArthur's dream of delivering both Korea and China to his beloved American Empire was shattered. With China encircled by the American Empire in Japan, Taiwan, Hong Kong, South Korea, Macau and Tibet, MacArthur was bent on finishing off China. He had to be stripped of his command by President Truman because he failed to understand the importance of the *nuclear deterrent*.

Up until the Second World War the American Empire could unleash its nuclear arsenal indiscriminately without fear of retaliation. No other country had nuclear weapons at the time. Stalin understood how easy it would be for the American Empire to invade and conquer Russia if Russia did not acquire a nuclear deterrent. By 1950 the Soviet Union had acquired nuclear weapons. While the Soviet Union was reluctant to fully engage the American Empire in 1950 to hold on to North Korea it drew the line when the Americans threatened to use nuclear weapons. President Truman understood that the Russians were not bluffing. MacArthur did not. He was of the old school when the American Empire seemed invincible. Of all the ironies of history the decision by the American Empire to acquire nuclear weapons to invade and conquer the world was exactly the weapon which limited its expansion. Once a country acquired a nuclear deterrent it was relatively safe from American colonization.

While America's Western allies failed to deliver North Korea to the American Empire they were instrumental in preventing the unification of Korea by the Korean people. South Korea remained an American *uncolony*. Without British forces from Hong Kong and the Far East, Canadian, Australian and other Commonwealth forces, the *North Korean Peoples' Army* would have defeated the American and South Korean forces and united Korea. General Douglas MacArthur commanded both the US forces and the forces of 15 member nations of the UN who were American allies. The Korean

War would be the first of many global wars started by the American Empire. Up until the Second World War the global wars had been started by the European empires. They fought each other for European hegemony as well as imperial expansion. The American Empire would fight for Western domination.

The Significance of the Korean War

The Korean War marks the most significant watershed in the history of the modern world. Its significance has not been analysed, much less identified, by Western historians. We will list in this section the key points of this important watershed. Firstly, it marks the division of the world into two camps. There is the *Western camp,* sometimes identified as the *First World.* This group is made up of the American Empire, the old Western European empires and English speaking ex-colonies such as Canada and Australia. The other group is the *Third World.* These are the low income non-industrialised countries scattered across the globe.

The second important feature of this watershed in history was the emergence of the American Empire as the unquestioned leader of the Western camp. In the Western press the American Empire is referred to as the US and its leadership is referred to as "leader of the free world." There is no clearly identified leader of the Third World group. However, Russia which had previously longed for inclusion as a Western nation was now firmly in the Third World camp. On the other hand, Japan, which had also longed for recognition as an equal to the Western empires was now firmly in the Western camp. Israel was fully armed by the American Empire and added to the Western camp in the strategic oil rich Middle East.

The third important feature of this watershed in history is the unquestioned use of puppet "international" institutions, set up after World War II to coerce international cooperation, by the American Empire to further its own domination of the world. The most important of these institutions is the UN because it provides military manpower. But others such as the *World Bank,* the *IMF,* and the *WTO,* are used to squeeze the Third World countries with economic and financial blackmail. When a Western leader uses the term "world community," he or she means the Western camp. Any support of the West by a Third World country is bought by the West with military threats or financial and economic blackmail.

The fourth important feature of this watershed in history is the unquestioned use of American propaganda to undermine every aspect of Third World culture, language, religion, ideas, independence, democracy, human rights, legitimacy, products, self confidence and dignity. Third World citizens are only accepted as *second class* citizens of the West if their governments promote Western values as civilized and indigenous values as backward and obstacles to economic development. Their governments must be publicly supportive of every American military invasion and economic and financial embargo.

The Western press in the US, Canada, Australia, Britain and Europe, use exactly the same language, down to the minute details, crafted in Washington. This is unabashedly promoted as "freedom of the press" and blindly accepted as such by every Western citizen, journalist and politician. As examples, China must always be referred to as *Communist* China, without exception, but never ever refer to the US either as *Capitalist* America or the *American Empire.* Muslims can be called *Islamist* extremists but Christians are never *Christianite* extremists. Israel "has a right to defend itself," no matter how many countries it invades, how much territory it occupies or how many women and children it kills. A suicide bombing is always a "cowardly" act. American bombing is always "precision" bombing no matter how many hospitals, wedding processions, funeral processions or civilians it annihilates.

The fifth important feature of this watershed in history is the recognition by both camps of how essential it is to acquire a *nuclear deterrent*. The evidence is overwhelming that the American Empire was poised to use its nuclear arsenal in the Korean War as it had used it in the Second World War. It was deterred from doing so because Russia threatened to retaliate with its nuclear weapons. The American Empire quickly provided a nuclear deterrent to Israel so that Israel could invade and bomb its neighbours without fear of retaliation. In the 21st century the American Empire chose to invade Iraq precisely because it did not have a nuclear deterrent whereas it chose not to invade North Korea precisely because the DPRK has a nuclear deterrent. Countries in the Third World camp are desperate to get nuclear deterrents against the real possibility of invasion and conquest by the American Empire. Countries in the Western camp are equally desperate to prevent Third World countries from acquiring nuclear deterrents so that they can be invaded and colonized by the West.

The final important feature of this watershed in history is a rather ironic one. In 1950, with the United States producing at least half of the world's total output of goods and services, GDP, it seemed inevitable that it would dominate the world indefinitely. It appeared as if it would only be a matter of time before it conquered China and brought all of Asia into the Western camp. The Soviet Union would be isolated and would decay and crumble. As it turned out, 1950 marked the height of the relative economic standing of the United States in terms of GDP. While the American Empire expanded globally through conquests, military ascendancy, subterfuge, threats, financial and trade embargoes and co-opting the UN, World Bank, IMF and WTO, its share of the World's GDP declined steadily to just over 16 percent by 2010. Its dominance was therefore not sustainable over the long term.

The other part to this irony is that it was not the Soviet Union which brought about the relative demise of the American Empire. If one country was most responsible it would be China. Far from conquering China as had been planned, China regained both Hong Kong and Macau while holding on to Tibet. With China's economic miracle, Japan, Taiwan and South Korea are gradually shifting their Western stance and courting China. The ex-British colonies of India, Pakistan, Singapore, Malaysia, Sri Lanka and Burma, as well as many other countries in Asia, are increasingly promoting an alternative non-Western Third World point of view. The Middle East is an American-made disaster and the American invasion of Afghanistan has pissed off every Muslim in the world. The old European empires have formed a new economic powerhouse in the European Union, EU, and are caught in the middle of a turf war between the American Empire and the Third World. Latin American nations, led by Hugo Chavez, are finally resisting American invasions in their countries. Russia's new found economic recovery based on Putin's leadership and vast oil and gas supplies is allowing Russia to flex its old Soviet-style muscle. The EU, dependent on Russian gas supplies, is also caught in the middle of a new cold war between the American Empire and Russia.

The financial and economic crises beginning in 2007 added to the woes of the American Empire. It's an empire which is increasingly forced to pay its bills by acquiring a mountain of debt. Some of that debt is held by countries in the Third World camp. With President Barack Obama taking over from President George Bush in 2009 he has to face the humiliating reality that the once powerful American Empire is held hostage by its creditors, many of whom have suffered extreme humiliation by an ignorant behemoth whose demise is absolutely essential for the progress of the human race. Adding insult to injury, just as the American economy began to show some signs of recovering from the **Great Recession** it was hit by another domestic crisis to add to its foreign policy disasters, the **Gulf of Mexico Oil Spill** on April 20, 2010. This massive deepwater oil spill was soon recognized as the worst man-made environmental disaster committed by the American Empire. The "Audacity of Hope" and "Yes We can" Barack Obama had finally inherited his "Katrina" (Hurricane Katrina,

2005) to add to his inherited foreign policy and financial crisis from the President he vilified to convince young and hopeful Americans that he stood for change.

The financial and economic cost of the Gulf of Mexico oil spill will far exceed the financial and economic cost of America's most costly hurricane, Katrina. President Obama's "Katrina" in the form of the Gulf of Mexico oil spill is a rather uncanny irony of his presidency. As Candidate Obama he convinced all of us that he would reverse the course of American foreign and domestic policies of President George W. Bush. Yet, in the foreign policy arena he expanded Bush's wars in Iraq and Afghanistan into Pakistan and Yemen. He continues to threaten Iran with invasion and possible nuclear attack. He has overseen expanded Israeli settlements on Palestinian land, a continuation of the Israeli blockade and military attacks in Gaza and the Israeli May 31, 2010 attack on the *Freedom Flotilla* taking much needed humanitarian supplies to Palestinian women and children in Gaza. Likewise in the domestic policy arena he has pursued policies favouring the financial corporations and corrupt financial executives over Americans who lost their jobs and their homes. He has responded to the Gulf of Mexico oil spill in much the same way as President Bush responded to Hurricane Katrina. Both of these disasters had their greatest effect on the people of Louisiana and the Gulf coast. Neither president gave the same kind of financial support, manpower, urgency, dedication and attention they gave to their warmongering in Iraq, Afghanistan and Palestine.

The worst irony of all is the *Christianite* perception of Obama's presidency. No president has tried harder to be a badass warmongering commander-in-chief than President Obama. No president has tried harder to portray himself and his family as *lily white* and *Christianite* Americans. But no matter how hard President Obama tries to suck up to America's *Christianite* Right he cannot shed the image of a non-White second class American born in the American *uncolony* of Hawaii to a **Black** father who had the audacity to be **Muslim** as well. Non-White comedians often joke about the comparison of racism with homophobia. Both, of course, are equally disgusting social ills in the American Empire. But there is some truth to the comedic gibe that non-whites often wish that they had a "closet" to hide in. That sums up President Obama's problem with American *Christianites*. He can think and act White but he cannot ever look White.

The Failed US Invasion of Vietnam, Cambodia and Laos

Americans did not know it at the time but their failed invasion of the countries previously colonized by France as *French Indochina* marked the beginning of the end of America's dream of governing the world by conquering Asia. After World War II, the British Empire was not the only Western European empire co-operating with the American Empire to conquer Asia. France had long competed with Britain for colonies in India, China and other parts of Asia. After World War II while the British were fighting the independence movement in India the French were fighting the independence movement in Indochina. With World War II devastating the economies of both Britain and France they looked to the United States to rebuild their economies under the *Marshall Plan* as well as provide naval and other military support to fight the independence movements in Asia.

As we explained above, the US had its hands full between 1945 and 1950, keeping the Soviet Union out of Western Europe, the Middle East, Japan, Korea and China. By 1950, the American Empire was ready to expand its military conquests in Asia by starting the Korean War, assisting the Dalai Lama in Tibet and aiding France in Indochina. The American Empire was defeated in Korea, Tibet and Indochina. The military conflict lasted from 1950 to 1973. The American Empire held on to the colonies it had acquired before and during World War II. These included the Philippines, Japan, Taiwan and South Korea. But it failed in its efforts to colonize North Korea, China, Tibet, Vietnam, Laos or Cambodia. While still dominating the high seas and the air over Asia and the

Pacific its dreams of a global empire were shattered by its disgraceful defeat in Vietnam by Asians using primitive weapons.

The relatively tiny country of Vietnam had defeated both the French and American empires in the two decades following World War II. The American Empire had conquered and colonized Western Europe but not Asia. The twenty-first century would belong to Asia not Europe or America. The World would come full circle. Asia had dominated the world for two thousand years before the industrial revolution in Western Europe and would do so again in the twenty-first century. The West had refused to extend equality to the East. It had expanded militarily to colonize and subdue the East. For its arrogance and ingrained racism it would pay the ultimate price of defeat and humiliation. America's election of its first "Black" president in 2009 will not save the West from being humbled by Asia and the Third World.

Barack Obama is not Black by either colour or outlook. One of the first acts of his presidency was to expand America's warmongering into Pakistan. Having some Black blood in you does not guarantee a Black outlook on the world, no more than a blood transfusion from a Black person to a White person changes the outlook of the White person. When history recounts the centuries, the American Empire will be a blip in time, lasting barely more than half a century.

Background to the Vietnam War

Britain and France had duked it out for European and imperial dominance for three centuries leading up to World War I. After 1870, however, they were both threatened by the rise of Germany. When their alliance proved incapable of preventing German hegemony they called on the United States, which they had both previously colonized. In both World War I and World War II they galvanized the military assistance of their worldwide colonies against Germany by promising independence. When they failed to deliver on their promises they called on the United States to come to their aid.

The American Empire willingly came to the aid of France and Britain both to defeat Germany and protect their colonies, because of its own imperial aspirations. An American alliance with France and Britain would be of immense help in achieving American hegemony. But America needed scapegoats and propaganda. Always denying its own imperial ambitions it pretended to aid Britain and France only to defend freedom and equality, first against Nazism and then against Communism. Its post-World War II attempts at colonizing Japan, Taiwan, Korea, China and Tibet were all promoted by its media and historians as defending the "free world." In 1950, it provided military support to France in Vietnam for the same professed reason.

France had colonized the countries we now know as Vietnam, Cambodia and Laos since the seventeenth century. As with European colonization in all of Asia, France began its colonization of Indochina by enforcing trade and Christianity on people who shunned the West. France consolidated its imperial dominance in Indochina when it defeated China in the Sino-French war of 1884-85 and Thailand in the Franco-Siamese war of 1893. During the Second World War, Japan colonized French Indochina. With the defeat of Japan, the American Empire effectively acquired all of the Asian countries colonized by Japan. This included Indochina.

With France and Britain joined at the hip to the American Empire during and after World War II, the American Empire returned Indochina to France. But once again, it underestimated the will of the Chinese people. As Mao Zedong had emerged in China as the leader who would defend China, and ultimately, Asia, from American imperialism, he was joined by the French educated Vietnamese, Ho Chi Minh, across the Chinese border in Indochina. Mao would come to the aid of Vietnam as he had come to the aid of Korea, to stop American imperialism from even crossing over into China, much less colonize China. The American Empire also made the mistake of camouflaging their imperialist intentions by claiming to be at war with communism. This placed the Soviet Union squarely in the Asian camp.

During the Second World War the American Empire encouraged the rise of a resistance movement in Vietnam against the Japanese colonization. This resistance movement, the *Viet Minh,* was led by Ho Chi Minh. As in China and Korea, many of the nationalists resisting Japanese imperialism were communists. The strategy of the American Empire was to coordinate the resistance movements in China, Vietnam and Korea under the overall leadership of their man in China, General Chiang Kai-shek. This would not only sideline the communists but also prevent France from reclaiming Indochina. Japan, China, Korea, Indochina and Taiwan would all become American *uncolonies.*

Japan invaded Vietnam on September 22, 1940, before the American Empire had entered into World War II. At this time the Vietnam resistance movement, the *Vietnam Liberation League,* was firmly established in Southern China, having been forced out of Vietnam. During most of World War II, Japan formed a partnership with France, in administering the colony of Vietnam. This played into the hands of the American Empire. The American Empire used the Vietnam resistance movements to oust both Japan and France by portraying France as collaborating with the enemy in Indochina.

In 1941, the China based Vietnam resistance movement established a base in Vietnam in Cao Bang province, on the border with China. This marked the birth of the *Viet Minh* under the leadership of Ho Chi Minh. Ho began to recruit and train guerrillas in Vietnam. The American Empire fully supported Ho and the *Viet Minh* guerrillas. At the time Vietnam supplied 50 percent of US imports of raw rubber. It was of strategic importance to the American Empire. With the help of the *Viet Minh* the American Empire hoped to steal Vietnam from both Japan and France.

President Roosevelt was able to persuade both Stalin and Chiang Kai-shek to oppose the return of Indochina to France. But Ho was no American puppet. He was a follower of Mao Zedong not Chiang Kai-shek. In December, 1944, Ho created the *Vietnam Liberation Army.* Ho received an unexpected gift from Japan when the Japanese chose to surrender to the *Viet Minh* instead of the American Empire. With this surrender, Ho received Japanese weapons which he would later use against the French and American empires. Ho proclaimed Vietnam an independent Republic on September 2, 1945.

The Japanese Empire was using several ports in Vietnam as transhipment points for raw materials from Southeast Asia to Japan. The American Empire began bombing these Vietnamese ports in January 1942. The American Empire continued to bomb Japanese targets in Vietnam until May, 1945. Financial aid was funnelled into Vietnam via China and the American *Office of Strategic Services.* American operations in Indochina were directed from China. Roosevelt's intension was to have Chiang Kai-shek secure both China and Indochina for the American Empire. This was not only opposed by France. Britain's Winston Churchill clearly foresaw that if the American Empire was allowed to steal the French colonies in Asia they would go after the English colonies as well. It was one of the few times when Churchill was willing to support Charles De Gaulle over his friend, FDR. Britain and France were not yet willing to hand over their empires to the American Empire. However, they would cooperate with the American Empire by allowing the American Empire to colonize those countries not previously colonized by Britain or France, especially those previously colonized by Japan or Germany.

In Vietnam, as in China and Korea, the American Empire attempted to impose its own brand of imperialism after Japan was defeated. In attempting to do so it exploited the capitalist/communist divisions in the nationalist movements. By embracing the nationalists who were anti-communists the American Empire would economize on American manpower by having pro-American locals filling many of the administrative and military positions in the American controlled colonial governments.

What the American Empire did not foresee in creating this anti-communist propaganda in Asia was inspiring a common cause against American imperialism by Chinese, Koreans and Vietnamese backed by Stalin's ever expanding Soviet Empire. True enough, American propaganda rallied capitalists and socialists across the globe to support American imperialism. But it equally rallied anti-American resentment and guerrilla operations across the Third World. It's unthinkable that the West was so naïve to believe that poor people would fight for the capitalist ideals of huge *inequalities in private property* even when offered the option of equally sharing *communal property* just because the West had the edge in media propaganda.

When Ho Chi Minh issued the proclamation of Vietnamese independence in September 1945, he had the popular support of Vietnamese throughout Vietnam, from Hanoi in the North to Saigon in the South. It was Ho's refusal to be an American puppet which led to the American support for the return of Indochina to France. If the American Empire could not colonize Indochina itself it would support French colonization over Vietnamese independence. After World War II, American policy was to co-opt the empires of France and Britain to present a unified Western domination of the globe.

The French Indochina War: 1946-54

The French Indochina War was a failed military effort by France and the American Empire to re-colonize Vietnam immediately after World War II. When Ho Chi Minh made it clear to the American Empire that he would not serve as a puppet Head of State for an American *uncolony* of Vietnam, the American Empire withdrew its military and financial support of the Viet Minh and used it to assist France during the French Indochina war. At least 80 percent of the cost of the French Indochina war was paid for by the American Empire. In Vietnam, the French and Americans were able to persuade Emperor Bao Dai to fight on their side.

Emperor Bao Dai had collaborated with both France and Japan against Vietnamese nationalists fighting for an independent Vietnam. However, once it was clear to Japan that it was facing defeat by the American Empire in 1945, Japan surrendered to the *Viet Minh* and Emperor Bao Dai abdicated on August 25, 1945. Ho Chi Minh declared Vietnam independent on September 2, 1945 with the northern city of Hanoi as its capital. On September 21, 1945 French forces occupied the southern city of Saigon. By December 1946, France had re-colonized Vietnam and Ho was forced to resort to guerrilla warfare.

Despite the best efforts of the French army in Vietnam, France was unable to defeat the *Viet Minh,* led by the very capable General Vo Nguyen Giap. With the war becoming increasingly unpopular in France, the French courted Emperor Bao Dai to head a semi-autonomous government in Vietnam. This "hand over" of Vietnam to Emperor Bao Dai was completed in 1949. The *Vietnamese National Army* was created to protect the new government from Ho and the *Viet Minh.* However, with the defeat of the American Empire in China by Mao Ze Dong in 1949, Ho could now receive military support from China. China's support of Vietnam's independence effectively neutralized the American support for French colonization. Mao was proving to be a very determined and effective warrior against American imperialism in Asia.

The American Empire made public its support for the French colonization of Vietnam by giving official recognition to the semi-autonomous government of Emperor Bao Dai. As in Korea, the official line from Washington was fighting communism. At the same time both China and the Soviet Union recognized Ho Chi Minh as the legitimate ruler of Vietnam based on his popular support by the great majority of the Vietnamese people. As the French people increasingly refused to fund another French colonial war in Asia the bulk of the cost of the French Indochina War fell on the American taxpayer.

Despite massive support from the American Empire, the French efforts to re-colonize Vietnam failed. The *Viet Minh* under General Giap, backed by both China and the Soviet Union, proved invincible. By May of 1953, the French commander, General Navarre, reported that France could not win the Indochina war. His strategy was to inflict as much punishment as possible on the insurgency to gain an edge at the inevitable peace talks. The last major battle was fought in the north at *Dien Bien Phu,* directly west of Hanoi and close to the Vietnam border with Laos. France had fortified Dien Bien Phu with state of the art defensive fortresses. This final battle began on March 13, 1954 and ended on May 8, 1954 with defeat for France and the American Empire. A tiny ex-French colony in Asia had defeated the once powerful French Empire and the newly powerful American Empire. With losses in China, Korea and Vietnam, the American Empire was failing miserably in its quest to colonize Asia.

Prelude to the American Invasion of Vietnam

The American Empire had failed in Vietnam before the Vietnam War. But it was easy to blame France for its own failure. It was the French who provided the supreme military commanders during the French Indochina War. The American Empire played the supporting role with supplies, naval and air support as well as CIA intelligence. The American Empire had three good arguments it could use to sell an American invasion of Vietnam.

The first reason was that the French failure in Vietnam was the final nail in the coffin of the French Empire. This decline of the French Empire would provide new opportunities for the American Empire. The second reason was that an American invasion would make Vietnam an American *uncolony* not restore it to France. The third reason was that the long and bloody French Indochina War had softened the Vietnamese resistance and therefore Vietnam would be an easy military target. It could be taken with minimal American casualties and financial cost.

In 1954, the Korean War was over. America was hungry for another war. Its propaganda that communism was evil was believed by capitalists and socialists in the United States and throughout the West. French defeat in Vietnam provided a timely opportunity for America's military industrial complex as well as its insatiable appetite for warmongering. While France, Vietnam, the UN, and most of the world outside the US, looked to the *Geneva Conference* to find peace, the American Empire saw Indochina as a resource rich region of Asia ripe for American colonization.

Contrary to the writings of Western historians, Vietnam was not a blunder which the American Empire foolishly stumbled into. Rather, Vietnam was the best opportunity for American imperial expansion at the time. The American Empire had failed to colonize China and North Korea, despite its best efforts. Vietnam provided one more opportunity for the conquest of Asia. At the time it seemed a much easier conquest than China or North Korea had turned out to be. It would not fail in Vietnam as it had failed in China and North Korea because the American Empire was now economically and militarily more powerful and Vietnam had been pounded for eight long years by the French. Rather than a disaster blindly sucked into, Vietnam was an opportunity the American Empire would be most foolish not to take advantage of. The American invasion of Vietnam fitted neatly and predictably into the pattern of two centuries of American expansionism.

France and Vietnam agreed to a Peace Conference in Geneva in April 1954 which concluded the French Indochina War on July 20, 1954. However, the Peace Agreement provided for a temporary division of Vietnam into North and South Vietnam. Unification would take place if the Vietnamese people voted for it in democratic elections scheduled for July 1956. The American Empire stepped in immediately to fly all pro-American supporters out of the North and into the South in anticipation of dividing Vietnam as it had divided Korea. *Operation Passage to Freedom* took place in August

1954 before the Vietnamese people even had time to celebrate their hard won freedom from French colonialism. The American Empire had signalled its intension to replace France as the imperial power in Vietnam by military force. It refused to participate in the Geneva Peace talks so that it could fully exploit the temporary division of Vietnam. In 1954, the evidence was overwhelming that the Vietnamese people would elect Ho Chi Minh as their leader of a united Vietnam over any colonial puppet, French or American.

In its effort to colonize Vietnam the American Empire found their usual local s.o.b. in Ngo Dinh *Diem,* the son of a Christian convert by Western missionaries. His Christian name was Jean-Baptiste. He initially studied to be a priest but found his true calling in engaging in anti-communist propaganda. It was that background which made him useful to the French and later endeared him to the American Empire. *Diem* collaborated with the French Empire and was rewarded with the governorship of Phan Thiet province. During the French Indochina War he opposed Ho Chi Minh. He supported the semi-autonomous government of Emperor Bao Dai, created by France in 1949 to oppose Ho.

In 1950 *Diem* travelled to the US and made contact with the officials of the American Empire. While he was well received, the Korean War was America's priority at the time and Vietnam was a French priority with only a supporting role by the American Empire. He continued to lobby American politicians while living in the US and made friends with American *Christianites* and vocal anti-communists. He made good use of the Western propaganda that America was the "leader of the free world." With the help of Wesley Fishel of the Government Research Bureau of Michigan State University, the *Vietnam Advisory Group* was established to ease the American Empire into the leadership role of colonizing Vietnam if France failed. But he would have to wait for the end of the Korean War and the defeat of the French Empire in Vietnam.

The State of Vietnam was the southern portion of the temporary 1954 division of Vietnam at the 17th parallel. Its capital was Saigon and was commonly referred to as South Vietnam. The northern portion was the Democratic Republic of Vietnam. Its capital was Hanoi and was commonly referred to as North Vietnam. Diem replaced Emperor Bao Dai as Prime Minister and Chief of State of South Vietnam on June 16, 1955.

On October 26, 1955, South Vietnam became the Republic of Vietnam and *Diem* became its first President. His mission was to invite the American Empire to colonize South Vietnam to enable him to serve as the American puppet Head of State. He needed American military intervention since he was not the people's leader but a Catholic anti-communist determined to seize power by military means. Free from the Korean War, the American Empire was in dire need of another war to keep its military-industrial complex active. It was also desperate to find another opportunity to expand its Asian Empire having failed to colonize North Korea. *Diem's* ambition to rule South Vietnam coincided with America's imperial aspirations at the time. It was a perfect fit.

In anticipation of the partnership between *Diem* and the American Empire the two future partners had cooperated in the following preparations. Firstly, neither the American Empire nor *Diem* officially participated or agreed to the Geneva Accords between France and Ho Chi Minh. Secondly, most of the one million Vietnamese who the American Empire moved from North Vietnam to South Vietnam during *Operation Passage to Freedom* were devout Catholics with extreme views similar to American *Christianites* who would blindly support *Diem* against communists since communists generally do not think much of religious fanatics. The American Empire had encouraged the flight of Catholics to South Vietnam by engaging in a high level propaganda campaign in North Vietnam that Catholics would be persecuted by a Ho Chi Minh government. When *Diem* arrived in Saigon on June 26, 1954, only pro-American Catholics welcomed him.

Thirdly, President Eisenhower was instrumental in getting Emperor Bao Dai to make Diem Prime Minister prior to Dai stepping down as Chief of State of South Vietnam. Diem's appointment was opposed by France but Dai was already looking to the American Empire to prop up his puppet government because the *Viet Minh* had defeated France. Dai had asked *Diem's* brother, Ngo Dinh *Luyen,* to negotiate with the Americans even though Dai never trusted *Diem.* Dai, like *Diem,* were political opportunists willing to sell Vietnam's freedom to any colonial power with the military muscle to take on the people's choice, Ho Chi Minh.

As soon as the French departed a referendum was called to choose between *Diem* and Emperor Dai. *Diem* rigged the elections and won with a 98 percent majority, including the infamous 133 percent majority in Saigon. *Diem* proclaimed South Vietnam a Republic and he became its first President. But he would rule only as long as the American military could back his dictatorship.

Fourthly, neither *Diem* nor the American Empire would agree to free and fair elections as specified by the Geneva Accords. American propaganda about the evils of communism and threats to nuke North Vietnam had convinced Catholics to support *Diem,* but the majority of the Vietnamese people were opposed. Both *Diem* and the American Empire knew that they would lose free democratic elections. The American Empire has a long history of publicly claiming to use military intervention to promote democracy, while secretly opposing democracy. No freely elected democracy in a Third World country would ever support American imperialism and American leaders are well aware of that fact. People in the Third World are not as gullible as people in the West. However, it is important that the American Empire publicly supports democracy to maintain its ridiculous title of "leader of the free world." Otherwise some Western countries like Canada may be a little more cautious to blindly cheer for its naked aggression in every part of the globe.

South Vietnam had developed a military force during the French Indochina War. This was the *Vietnamese National Army, VNA.* It was a modern army trained by France and it was now at *Diem's* disposal. In 1956, the VNA became the *Army of the Republic of Vietnam, ARVN.* This would be *Diem's* contribution to the American Empire's military invasion of Vietnam. American invasions have always used local puppets to minimize American casualties. American voters typically do not object to billions wasted on the most expensive military aircrafts and aircraft carriers but cringe somewhat at the loss of American lives. So called "boots on the ground" and returning "body bags" are more of a constraint on American aggression than money.

At the start of the Vietnam War the American economy had declined from its highest relative size of 50% of the world's economy in 1950, but it still accounted for over 40% of the world's GDP. With such a tiny percent of the world's population to support with over 40% of the world's GDP it could easily afford to waste a sizeable portion of its GDP on buying the most sophisticated weapons of war. It could also spend much less than one percent of its GDP on foreign aid and still be the world's largest donor to complement its naked aggression with naked propaganda.

Ngo Dinh Diem's Reign of Terror in South Vietnam

Diem's presidency did not disappoint his American benefactor. Living up to his qualification to be acceptable as an s.o.b. for the American Empire, he immediately began a reign of terror against any who opposed his illegitimate rule by branding them, communists. Taking a page from American senator Joseph McCarthy was the most obvious way of pleasing his American master. As I have explained before, the overwhelming view in the West is that all communists are evil. American democracy excludes participation by communists because the devil controls their minds. They are not free thinkers like people of the "free world." This probably explains why *Diem* received 133 percent of the votes cast by the people of Saigon in the referendum on his leadership race against Emperor Dai. American *Christianites* are very capable of producing such miracles.

Diem combined American McCarthyism with Hitler's Nazism, including use of concentration camps, in his determination to please his American master. Diem's brothers, Ngo Dinh *Nhu,* Ngo Dinh *Luyen,* Ngo Dinh *Thuc* and Ngo Dinh *Can,* formed a ruling dynasty around *Diem,* protecting his flank and implementing his despotic rule over the American *uncolony* of South Vietnam. *Luyen,* who had negotiated *Diem's* appointment as Prime Minister by President Eisenhower, was made Ambassador to England. As Archbishop of Vietnam's ancient capital of Hue, *Thuc* ensured continued support by the Catholic Church and pro-American *Christianites. Nhu* and *Can* employed secret police forces using Gestapo tactics to punish Vietnamese who dared to oppose American imperialism. The American Empire never expressed any concern over *Nhu's* public admiration for Adolf Hitler nor the Gestapo tactics of his secret police. *Can* ruled the City of Hue in the same despotic fashion as *Diem* and *Nhu.* More than 100,000 Vietnamese were killed, tortured or imprisoned.

As with all family dynasties which came to power because of the military power of the American Empire, the Ngo Dinh *Diem's* dynasty was corrupt and rotten to the core. They engaged in all of the usual tools of corruption; politics, drugs, prostitution, gambling, money laundering, smuggling, foreign bank accounts, lucrative US contracts, bribes from the wealthy, real estate and currency manipulation and religious persecution. Despite two years of overwhelming evidence to the contrary, *Diem* was greeted as a "leader of the free world" when he visited both the US and Australia in 1957. In the US he met with President Eisenhower and Eisenhower's Secretary of State, John Foster Dulles.

Opposition to *Diem's* repressive regime began from the time *Diem* made himself the President of Vietnam. However, it was not until December of 1960 that Ho Chi Minh's supporters in South Vietnam created the *National Front for the Liberation of South Vietnam, NLF.* The NLF was made up of both communists and non-communist nationalists opposed to American colonization and *Diem's* despotic rule. At the time Ho Chi Minh emphasized nationalism over communism and the NLF operated with minimal direction from Ho. The NLF gained its popular support not because of communist ideals but because *Diem* and his American master were brutally repressive. At the same time, Vietnam's religious majority, the Buddhists, were becoming more vocal about their persecution by *Diem's* Catholic minority. Vietnam's Buddhist monks would be the first to publicly humiliate the American Empire and force it to disown its s.o.b. in South Vietnam, as it would later do with Manuel Noriega in Panama and Saddam Hussein in Iraq.

The American Empire loses its local Strong Man in South Vietnam

In Chapter 5 we documented how the American Empire first promoted local strong man Manuel Noriega to "localize" their invasion and conquest of Panama but were forced by world opinion and public opinion in the US to summarily depose him from power. This long established American policy of using their control of every detail of the Western media to promote the most vile dictators as "leaders of the free world" then suddenly turn on them was the fate which awaited their man in South Vietnam, self elected president, Ngo Dinh *Diem.*

Diem was brought down by the courage and self sacrifice of several Buddhist monks who chose to follow the example of Thich Quang Duc. Duc was a Buddhist monk who found a way of focusing the world's media on America's violation of human rights in Vietnam instead on American lies about freedom, self determination and democracy. Empires fail to understand the power of the truth. Sadly, in 2010, the American Empire still steadfastly believes in the power of its propaganda to fool the world. It refuses to accept that truth will triumph in the end.

In 1963 the American Empire was forced by the actions of one Buddhist monk to retreat temporarily from its propaganda and lies, about what its man in South Vietnam was doing to the people of Vietnam. By 1963, *Diem's* persecution of Vietnam's Buddhist majority had reached such heights that one monk chose to give his life to open the eyes of the Western media to the truth about American imperialism in Vietnam. On June 11, 1963, Duc set himself on fire at the busy intersection of Phan Dinh Phung Boulevard and Le Van Duyet Street, in Saigon. He was encircled by Buddhist monks while the fire consumed his body. This picture of self sacrifice was transmitted around the world by a Western media which could no longer play the American imperialist game. Two Western reporters, Malcolm Browne and David Halberstam, even won the Pulitzer Prize for their coverage of the event. Western reporters had been forewarned of an important event but only a few, including Browne and Halberstam, had taken the warning seriously. Several other Buddhist monks put the nails in the coffin of America's *Diem,* when they also publicly burned themselves to death.

The *Diem* dynasty was so sure of America's lack of decency, integrity or self respect that they called Duc's action a "barbecue" and offered to provide free gas for further barbecues. What the *Diem* dynasty did not understand was how much the American Empire cherished its hypocrisy. While the *Diem* dynasty was correct in its knowledge that America had no desire for freedom, equality or democracy, it had failed to understand how America hungered for recognition as "leader of the free world." In the high offices of American hypocrisy *Diem* had become a liability.

The world had seen America's inhumanity and America needed a scapegoat to recharge its propaganda machine. *Diem* had to go. By using *Diem* as a scapegoat the West could also take the moral high ground that self immolation was a "barbaric" Asian practice. The West always finds a way of dumping their inherent barbarity on the Third World. US president, John F. Kennedy, was quick to distance himself from the act. The ARVN was responsible for the widespread persecution of the Vietnamese people and their Buddhist monks. President Kennedy had played an important role in this persecution since he had sent the American personnel who were responsible for training the ARVN.

The American Empire instigates another Coup in South Vietnam

The most common method used by the American Empire to remove one of their s.o.b.'s who have become a liability is to instigate a military coup. Since the local army is usually trained by the American Empire and American military advisers sway tremendous authority over local juntas it is relatively easy for the empire to replace a general/president. If the American Empire install you it can just as easily replace you. That was the situation with *Diem* and the ARVN in South Vietnam in 1963. *Diem* had to be replaced and the American Empire instigated a coup to replace him. The ARVN would take the heat for replacing the self installed president of South Vietnam and the American Empire could take credit for not supporting another vile dictator. The "free world" would cheer loudly and drown the fact that the American Empire had created and installed *Diem* and was replacing *Diem* with yet another equally vile dictator.

President Kennedy and his Ambassador to South Vietnam, Henry Cabot Lodge, Jr., worked closely with General Duong Van Minh to arrange the murder of *Diem* and his sadistic brother, Ngo Dinh *Nhu.* They were killed on November 2, 1963 and General Van Minh took over the presidency of South Vietnam. This marked the beginning of another American military government similar to those imposed in the Caribbean and Latin America. The ARVN became increasingly controlled and directed by American military personnel. A series of puppet generals were installed as presidents of South Vietnam. The *quagmire* of Vietnam had begun.

The American Empire had invaded Vietnam after the defeat of the French, expecting a quick and easy colonization of Vietnam, as a stepping stone to further conquests in Asia. They got a long and bloody war and public humiliation of their military prowess as a great Power. France had conquered and ruled all of Indochina for more than a century. The American Empire could not even conquer and hold South Vietnam even after the French had softened up the resistance and the French had trained the ARVN to fight alongside the American military.

President Kennedy launches a Full Scale Invasion of Vietnam

When Barack Obama was elected to the presidency in 2009 he was compared in a positive light to John F. Kennedy, JFK. What was unthinkable to all but a very few in 2009 was a more ominous comparison with Kennedy which we will suggest here. A Republican, Eisenhower, had started the American invasion of Vietnam just as a Republican, George W. Bush, had started the American invasion of Afghanistan. Kennedy, a Democrat, was elected to reduce American warmongering after the American Empire had participated in the Second World War, the Korean War, the Cold War, the French Indochina War and the Vietnam War. But Kennedy intensified American warmongering by launching a full scale invasion of Vietnam. He escalated a war which a Republican Administration had begun and which many Americans were questioning both because it was **evil** and unwinnable.

Likewise, Barack Obama is escalating the war in Afghanistan which was begun by a Republican Administration and which many Americans are questioning both because it is **evil** and unwinnable. Kennedy's reasons for escalating the Vietnam War mirror those of Obama for escalating the Afghanistan War. Contrary to public opinion, leaders like Kennedy and Obama are not visionaries. America never elects its visionaries to the presidency. America elects, first and foremost, those who are dedicated to warmongering. Obama, like Kennedy, is dedicated to "defending" America. Kennedy was defending America from communism. Obama is defending America from terrorism. Visionary leaders would recognize that neither communism nor terrorism is a threat to American security. They are threats imagined by American warmongers and those scared by the powerful propaganda of American warmongers. In 2009, a visionary leader would have chosen Venezuela or Cuba for the president's first foreign state visit not mundane, safe, predictable Canada led by Stephen Harper, George W. Bush's most loyal supporter after Tony Blair.

Every individual has a right to self-defence. However, most of us do not carry clubs, knives, guns, machine guns, cannons, hand grenades or other lethal weapons, as we go about our daily lives. American warmongers convince us that the American Empire must possess the most powerful weapons and aggressively use them to terrorize, kill and maim everyone *perceived* to be a threat to America's right to defend itself. In other words, it is not sufficient that you carry that cannon with you on your daily commute to work, you must unflinchingly use it to kill everyone you *think* has the *thought*, not the ability, of harming you. You never know, they may get their hands on a rock and throw it at you since your powerful cannon is not a sufficient deterrent.

This ridiculous notion of the right to self-defence was firmly held and widely publicized by Kennedy in 1960, when he became America's Commander-in-Chief, and likewise by Obama, in 2009. Yes, Kennedy and Obama have a lot in common but not what the American public, and the world at large, was thinking of in 2009.

In 1961, Kennedy became the first Catholic president to be elected by Americans. In 2009, Obama became the first "Black" president to be elected by Americans. They both rode a wave of enthusiasm by young Americans, non-white Americans, Hollywood types, left wing patriots and all Americans looking for change in America and in the world at large. Kennedy was an utter disaster as far as changing American foreign policy. Obama will prove to be equally disappointing. In 1961, Kennedy inherited an American Empire deeply mired in the firm belief that the Soviet Union threatened its hegemony. Kennedy saw his job, first and foremost, as that of conquering more territory than the Soviet Empire, beginning with Vietnam.

In 2009, Obama inherited an American Empire mired in debt and disrespected by most of the world because of its military failures in Iraq and Afghanistan. Obama saw his job, first and foremost, as that of returning the American Empire to the dominant position it held from 1950 to 2005, beginning with military victory in Afghanistan. Kennedy saw victory in Vietnam as essential for world-wide respect of American military dominance. In like fashion, Obama sees victory in Afghanistan as essential for world-wide respect of American military dominance.

When Kennedy took office in January 1961, the American Empire had been suppressing the Vietnamese for more than a decade. Vietnam had fought long and hard for freedom from French colonialism. Had the American Empire not backed France after the Second World War, Vietnam would have won that freedom much earlier. President Eisenhower admitted publicly in 1954 that Ho Chi Minh would easily get an 80 percent majority in free and fair elections. By 1961, Ho's majority would have been much larger after the terrorism inflicted by the American Empire and their s.o.b., Ngo Dinh *Diem.* Kennedy feared democracy as much as Eisenhower. He had no intention of removing American dictatorship and its military government in Vietnam. If anything, he was determined to prove that he could succeed where Eisenhower had failed.

Kennedy had made his views on the "Domino Theory" known well before his election as president. As a US Senator he had referred to the "red tide of communism" spreading across Indochina to the Philippines, Japan, India, Burma and Thailand. It was an astonishing admission that the Philippines and Japan were effectively *uncolonies* of the American Empire and that all of Indochina, as well as ex-English colonies such as India and Burma, and Thailand were immediate targets for the eventual American colonization of Asia. Kennedy's vice president, Lyndon Johnson, visited Saigon in May 1961 to assure Diem that the Kennedy Administration would not only continue the military aid provided by Eisenhower, but increase it. By 1963, Kennedy had increased Eisenhower's American manpower in South Vietnam from less than one thousand to sixteen thousand. So much for Democrats being less warmongering than Republicans!

When Kennedy was forced to kill *Diem* and his brother *Nhu* after the Buddhist focused the world's media on American atrocities in South Vietnam, the American invasion began to flounder as the world questioned America's continued denial of its imperialist ambitions in Asia. Moreover, Kennedy had grossly underestimated the power of insurgents to defeat America's supposedly invincible military machine. Vietnam was reality not a Hollywood movie where American marines are shown to be invincible against overwhelming odds. Kennedy was being sucked into a war which he foolishly thought was winnable with minimal American casualties. His propaganda to win hearts and minds had no traction with the Vietnamese people outside the Catholic *Christianites.* His unfortunate assassination in November of 1963, less than a month after he had ordered the assassination of *Diem,* at least saved him from public humiliation as America's Commander-in-Chief who was defeated by a poor Third World country in Asia.

President Lyndon Baines Johnson, LBJ, Commits American Boys to the Vietnam War and Loses the War and his Presidency

Johnson, more than Kennedy, allowed the Vietnam War to dog his presidency. The cause to which he publicly committed his presidency was "Building the Great Society." Unfortunately, America's history and ingrained psyche, pressures all of its Commander-in-Chiefs into giving the highest priority to warmongering. Imperial expansionism is a kind of obsessive compulsion throughout America's short history as a nation and empire. It was therefore not surprising that President Johnson would sacrifice his plans for the "Great Society" by trying to win the War in Vietnam. Johnson would be most remembered for the peace slogan, "Hey, hey, LBJ, How many kids did you kill today."

Johnson expanded the war by getting the US Congress to sanction military operations by the American Empire throughout Southeast Asia. His military strategy was to use America's superior air power to bomb North Vietnam into submission while simultaneously continuing the ground war in South Vietnam. This marked the origin of yet another standard tool of American Imperialism, "Bomb the enemy back to the Stone Age." This tool has since been used in Laos, Cambodia, Afghanistan, Iraq and Pakistan. In January 1965 Johnson expanded the ground war in South Vietnam into North Vietnam.

Eisenhower and Kennedy had intended to capture South Vietnam and use that as its base to invade North Vietnam, Cambodia and Laos. Once French Indochina had fallen to the American Empire other Asian countries would be colonized. Johnson decided that Vietnam would be invaded and conquered as a single country and possibly Laos and Cambodia simultaneously. His reasoning was that the area was too interconnected to disentangle and capture separately and since the long term goal was to colonize all of it anyway why not do it in a single war? With the massive airpower the American Empire possessed and the supposed invincibility of its marines it did not seem to Johnson such a formidable task and he had the backing of the US Congress and the American people.

By December of 1965, Johnson had increased the 16,000 force sent by Kennedy to South Vietnam to 200,000. This was a significant increase of American soldiers within a very short period of time. Since the average age of American forces in Vietnam was 19 years, LBJ was killing both Vietnamese and American boys. This massive increase of young American boys in Vietnam marked the beginning of US forces overshadowing the ARVN and bearing the brunt of the fighting against the forces for an independent Vietnam led by Ho Chi Minh, General Vo Nguyen Giap and the Vietnam People's Army, VPA.

The US Allies Stayed Home: Westmoreland commands SEATO Forces

General Douglas MacArthur is remembered for saving South Korea for the American Empire. As we have explained above MacArthur was after the conquest of China. He lost China and North Korea and held on to South Korea only because of UN forces. The UN had been created by the US as a puppet World Body to promote American imperialism. At the time of the Korean War it was too early for any nation to recognize this fact. Foolishly assuming that a UN resolution was an international resolution rather than a bribed and corrupted US resolution many UN member states sent their military forces to help General MacArthur defeat the Korean independence struggle. Without these UN forces the American Empire would have lost its *uncolony* of South Korea.

General William Westmoreland was America's next Douglas MacArthur who would conquer Asia and prevent the "dominoes from falling." In 1965 Westmoreland began his infamous "Search and Destroy" policy to win the Vietnam War. Fully aware that no American General would ever be prosecuted for war crimes, Westmoreland's "Search and Destroy" policy was no less than a policy of mass slaughter of every Vietnamese who opposed American colonization. Every Vietnamese civilian killed by this policy was justified by identifying the dead as "Viet Congs" or "Gooks" or "Congs." In the eyes of the West, "Vietcong" meant someone more **evil** than a communist. In the West all communists are **evil** people. But American propaganda had to portray Vietnamese communists as even more **evil** than other communists. A Vietcong or "Gook" was the devil himself. Westmoreland's

"Search and Destroy" policy combined with incessant bombing and use of toxic defoliants such as "Agent Orange" killed or maimed over 5 million Vietnamese whose only crime was to want an independent country, free from American imposed dictators.

The American public foolishly believed in Westmoreland as they had believed before in MacArthur. Westmoreland took command of the War in Vietnam in April 1964 and predicted total victory by 1967. It was somewhat ironic that under his command he was able to convince Washington to increase the number of American boys in Vietnam because he was so optimistic that he was winning the war. Each battle he won convinced Washington to honour his request for more troops. The more optimistic he became about winning the war the more American troops died in Vietnam. By 1968, American forces in Vietnam reached a staggering 550,000. His predicted 1967 victory had come and gone but he was still able to get Washington to send more boys because he was "winning." At the end of 1967 Westmoreland had told his Commander-in-Chief that the NLF had lost 90,000 men and would never be able to recruit replacements.

In reality, Westmoreland was damaging the political career of his Commander-in-Chief, Johnson, as much as MacArthur's determination to nuke China would have destroyed the political career of his Commander-in-Chief, Truman. In January 1968, the NLF launched a series of offensives with over 70,000 men. Truman had the good sense to fire MacArthur rather than expand the war into China. Likewise, Johnson chose to fire Westmoreland rather than expand the war further into North Vietnam, Laos and Cambodia. By the time Johnson fired Westmoreland in 1968, the Vietnam War had destroyed any chance of a second term for Johnson as Commander-in-Chief.

As events turned out, Westmoreland fared worse than MacArthur. MacArthur held on to South Korea. Westmoreland, like MacArthur, failed to expand America's empire in Asia but also lost South Vietnam. Westmoreland had the misfortune of not having UN forces to do his fighting as MacArthur had. He did get some help from SEATO forces. SEATO forces came from Thailand, the American *uncolonies* of the Philippines and South Korea and the English "colonies" of Australia and New Zealand. Officially, Canada followed the Mother Country, England, in not sending soldiers to Vietnam in the way in which it had sent Canadian forces to Korea. However, privately and covertly, Canada supported the Americans in the Vietnam War. Many Canadians, as many as 30,000, enlisted in the US army to fight in Vietnam. Canada was a major exporter of war supplies to the US. Canada even supplied deadly napalm and defoliants to US forces in Vietnam. Canada assisted the US in testing defoliants and allowed the US to test weapons and conduct training exercises on Canadian soil.

Barack Obama, JFK and LBJ

I have commented on the rather perverse media comparison between President Obama and JFK. I have also suggested at length that all American presidents pursue the common goal of warmongering and imperial expansion. In this section I want to comment on the eerie similarity between the response of LBJ to the Vietnam War he inherited from JFK and the response of President Obama to the Afghanistan War he inherited from George W. Bush. Both LBJ and Obama were elected on a platform emphasizing peace and hope for the creation of a better future for underprivileged Americans. Once elected both chose to end an unpopular war by expanding the war and killing more American soldiers.

We explained above that LBJ expanded US forces in Vietnam to 550,000 by 1968. Once in office President Obama succumbed to the demand from his "Douglas MacArthur," General Stanley McChrystal, for an additional 30,000 American troops as well as additional NATO troops. As with LBJ and General Westmoreland, McChrystal wanted more troops because he was winning the war in Afghanistan. President Obama, like LBJ before, responded to his general's demand to prove that he could win where his predecessor had failed. Winning a war is such a guaranteed way of boosting your popularity that no leader can resist, much less the leader of the warmongering American Empire and its military-industrial complex.

McChrystal, like MacArthur and Westmoreland, before, are depending on troops from both the US and its allies to win the war in Afghanistan. As we saw earlier, UN troops were crucial for MacArthur to colonize South Korea. But he still lost North Korea and China. Westmoreland lost all of Vietnam despite help from SEATO forces. Like Presidents Truman and Johnston before, President Obama will fire his general, McChrystal, but only after he loses in Afghanistan as MacArthur lost in North Korea and China and Westmoreland lost in Vietnam. Victory for every American Commander-in-Chief is so sweet that they ignore the parallels of their own history even when it's eerily similar.

France had supposedly made Vietnam a relatively soft target for the American Empire as a result of the pounding it inflicted on Vietnam during the French Indo-China War. But the American Empire still lost the Vietnam War. In like manner, the Russian invasion of Afghanistan in 1979 had failed the Soviet Union but supposedly made Afghanistan another soft target for the American Empire. But instead of the quick victory George W. Bush expected when he invaded Afghanistan in 2001, the American Empire is now bogged down in Afghanistan, Iraq and Pakistan. After ten years of war in this region the American Empire has nothing to show its electorate but failures. The *Bush/Wolfowitz* doctrine of unilateral pre-emptive strikes against soft targets as a key strategy of the neo-Cons to maintain American monopoly on super-power status failed miserably. Instead of the expected victories in Afghanistan, Iraq, Iran and North Korea the empire has ground to a halt in the mountains between Afghanistan and Pakistan.

President Obama, like LBJ before, ran on a ticket of hope and change. But he just cannot resist the glory of war. He believes that he can succeed where George W. Bush failed. He believes that for two reasons. The first is that Afghanistan was indeed the soft target Bush had anticipated. Bush failed not because Afghanistan was difficult to conquer but because Bush sent too few soldiers. Bush sent too few soldiers because most of the forces of the American Empire were sent to Iraq to fight an "unjust" war. Secondly, Bush was impertinent to assume that the American Empire could ever succeed with unilateralism. The American Empire needed allies in the Second World War, in Korea, in Vietnam and in the First Gulf War, Desert Storm. President Obama thinks he can succeed where Bush failed by returning to a coalition with NATO and other allies.

The Tet Offensive of 1968 Drove the American Empire out of Asia

Americans have blind faith in the prowess of their military. Even when there is overwhelming evidence that they are getting their asses royally kicked and many of their own men are complaining, deserting, depressed and suicidal, they continue to believe the lies of their politicians and generals. As it is in Iraq and Afghanistan today, so it was in Vietnam with General Westmoreland. The Tet Offensive of 1968, like the Buddhist protests of 1963, focused the World's media on Westmoreland's inability to see reality. Ho Chi Minh had warned the American Empire. If he could defeat the French Empire he would also defeat the American Empire. The Americans should have looked to their history. Without the French military support they would have had zero chance of defeating the English and securing their own independence in 1783.

Up until the Tet Offensive which began on January 31, 1968, President Johnson and General Westmoreland continued to convince the American public that America was winning the Vietnam War. American deaths averaged over 1,000 per month throughout 1967, but Americans saw that as a small price to pay to have America rather than the Soviet Union dominate the World. When the NLF and VPA launched simultaneous attacks in every city in Vietnam, including the American fortress in Saigon, Johnson and Westmoreland could no longer hide the facts from the American public.

How could an enemy who was defeated launch such massive offensives? Westmoreland's response was to request 200,000 additional American troops. As President Truman had refused MacArthur's request to nuke China, President Johnson refused Westmoreland's request for more death and destruction. The war that was begun partly because it would be so easy to win, had cost 30,000 American lives without any sign of victory. Young Americans were escaping to Canada and other countries to evade being drafted into the US army to fight an increasingly unpopular war in Vietnam. In March 1968, President Johnson announced his intention to begin Peace Talks with the Vietnamese people.

President Johnson replaced Westmoreland with General Creighton Abrams. But he had failed as Commander-in-Chief of a nation proud of its warmongering prowess. Losing a war is the most heinous crime an American president/commander-in-chief can commit. On March 31, 1968, President Johnson accepted the fact that defeat in Vietnam had ended his political career. He announced that he would not seek a second term as Commander-in-Chief. On May 10, 1968 he began Peace Talks with Vietnam. Career wise, General Westmoreland got a promotion for hiding his failures in Vietnam. He served as US Army Chief of Staff from July 3, 1968 to June 30, 1972.

Westmoreland never understood the fact that the American Empire has an almost unlimited ability to conduct aerial bombing but fails badly when it comes to "putting boots on the ground." President George W. Bush, Dick Cheney and Donald Rumsfeld made the same mistake when they so eagerly invaded Afghanistan and Iraq. That same error is being made today by President Obama as he expands the war in Afghanistan and Pakistan, and most recently, into Yemen.

President Nixon Fabricates another Deception called Vietnamization

Richard Nixon won the presidency in 1969 because Johnson had lost the war in Vietnam. His mandate was to succeed where Johnson had failed. The American public is so gullible that he was able to sell to them the most ridiculous solution. Since Johnson and Westmoreland had proved that American soldiers could never defeat Vietnamese soldiers Nixon would train Vietnamese soldiers to defeat Vietnamese soldiers. He proudly called this solution *Vietnamization* and everyone applauded. In reality, Vietnamization was another lie to continue the Vietnam War.

President Johnson had escalated American forces from 16,000 under President Kennedy to 550,000, precisely because the ARVN was incapable of defeating the NLF and VNA. Nixon's Vietnamization solution implied that combining the ARVN with 550,000 American ground troops made for a less successful fighting force than an American trained ARVN fighting on its own. So much for the fighting prowess of the American G.I?

Vietnamization was a starkly obvious military disaster but an astute political move by Nixon. The American military-industrial complex, the majority of the American people and many American politicians wanted the Vietnam War to continue. Fighting communism had become a noble cause for Americans. It was simply a case of good versus evil. A Christian nation could never stop fighting evil. That was the essence of being *Christianites*.

But Americans were tired of having their young sons die in Vietnam and new young potential recruits were exiting the country in droves. Vietnamization enabled Nixon to reduce the number of American boys sent to the killing fields of Vietnam while continuing the war on communism in Vietnam. Americans thrive on lies and deceit and Nixon had provided another big one. How wonderful to have our converted *Vietnam* Christianite brothers do the killing for us so that our own *American* boys will be safe at home?

Nixon's Vietnamization policy was another shameful war crime committed by the American Empire. It needlessly prolonged a clearly unwinnable attempt to colonize Vietnam by arming and training Vietnamese to kill and maim other Vietnamese. It also prolonged American bombing in Vietnam, Laos and Cambodia. In 1972, Nixon intensified the bombing campaigns in North Vietnam, including the city of Haiphong. In May 1972, Nixon mined Haiphong Harbour in North Vietnam.

It was natural for the American imposed Vietnamese president of South Vietnam, Nguyen Van Thieu, to continue an unwinnable war as long as President Nixon continued to pour American military aid into the economy of South Vietnam. American aid and spending by American forces was the mainstay of the South Vietnamese economy. At the same time, American bombing continued to destroy the economy of North Vietnam. But no amount of military training would ever make the ARVN an effective force against the NLF and VNA. It simply kept President Thieu in power while the US and its SEATO allies withdrew their boys from the killing fields of Vietnam.

President Nixon took three long years to withdraw all US forces from Vietnam. It was August of 1972 when the last US forces left Vietnam. This was more than four years after President Johnson had begun Peace Talks in May 1968. The people of Vietnam who had fought as America's allies during World War II, because the US had promised them their independence if they did, were forced to fight American aggression after 1950 when US forces first invaded Vietnam as "military advisers." Nixon continued to provide US aid to President Thieu up until his forced resignation in August 1974 due to Watergate. This needlessly prolonged the deaths and suffering of the Vietnamese people and the destruction of their economy.

President Ford also prolonged the war by continuing American aid to President Thieu until the US Congress finally decided to force him to end the senseless waste of American tax revenues on April 23, 1975. With American aid cut off, its puppet government in Saigon collapsed and the people of Vietnam were free to unite their country. After securing the Central cities of Hue and Da Nang, the VPA moved south and secured Nha Trang en-route to the American bastion of Saigon. Fierce fighting continued in South Vietnam until President Thieu resigned on April 21, 1975. Thieu left Vietnam for the American *uncolony* of Taiwan on April 25, 1975. With Saigon surrounded by forces of the VPA the US began a disorganized and chaotic evacuation of their personnel on April 29, 1975.

How Vietnam Represents the Failure of a Civilized and Humane West?

The so called "Western Civilization" which led the World for six centuries never tried to live up to its professed virtues of liberty, freedom, equality and democracy. The Vietnam War showed beyond any shadow of a doubt the inhumanity of Western civilization. It was the most senseless and unnecessary war which inflicted unnecessary pain and suffering on millions of innocent victims. Yet the West has never apologized for its human rights abuses in Vietnam. Far from apologizing it continued such human rights abuses in Palestine, Lebanon, Chile, Afghanistan, Iraq and other parts of the globe.

The West learnt absolutely no lessons from Vietnam. It continues to act and behave, militarily, politically and financially, in the most racist, incompetent, dictatorial, shameful and hypocritical manner in leading the world. It continues to stockpile enormous quantities of WMD's, invade countries at will, impose its will on the people of the Third World, pollute the planet with its consumption and waste, use every bully pulpit it can, stamp out free thinking and inflict the most heinous forms of human rights abuses with total impunity. Its ability to use double standards, hypocrisy, ignorance and stupidity knows no limit.

The West continues to invent threats to humanity such as communism and terrorism, scares humanity with its incessant rhetoric, and justifies its barbaric actions by claiming to defend humanity from the same evil it initially invented. This ridiculous behaviour destroys lives, property and human progress. After six disastrous centuries the West has lost all credibility of ever having the intelligence to provide any kind of leadership for the human race.

Vietnam was an opportunity to redeem itself by apologizing for its crimes. It did not apologize because it does not have the intelligence or brain capacity to understand its own mistakes. It is stuck permanently in a small box it created with its long history of lies and deception. It has no ability to think outside the box it created for itself. It is doomed to repeat those mistakes until it perishes from them. Humanity's only hope is that Asia will not copy the mistakes of the West.

My Lai, Abu Ghraib, Guantanamo, Bagram and Extraordinary Rendition

American war crimes committed in Vietnam as exemplified by the My Lai massacre were destined to be repeated as they were in Abu Ghraib, Guantanamo, Bagram in Afghanistan and American torture havens around the globe. The My Lai massacre was only one highly publicised example of the war crimes committed by President Johnson and General Westmoreland when they implemented their infamous "Search and Destroy" policy in Vietnam. US forces on "Search and Destroy" missions were given orders to kill the inhabitants of entire villages, including women and children, kill all animals and burn the villages down to the ground.

General Westmoreland was committed to the wholesale destruction of Vietnamese villages not only to kill civilians but to instil fear in the people of Vietnam. He had taken a page out of General Tecumseh Sherman's "Scorched earth" policy during the US Civil War. He wanted the people of Vietnam to fear America's penchant for brutality, human rights abuses and wanton destruction of property. He also wanted the people of Vietnam to know that Americans were "above the law." They would never be prosecuted for war crimes.

American war crimes, such as those committed at My Lai, Guantanamo, Abu Ghraib, Bagram in Afghanistan and secret prisons in the Middle East, Central Asia and Eastern Europe used for those sent by "Extraordinary Rendition," are at least as grave as those which led to convictions at the Nuremburg trials. But Americans will never be tried for war crimes because they are "above the law." The war crimes trials at Nuremberg and Tokyo sent clear messages to Germany and Japan. Those countries have not re-committed. The American Empire will re-commit over and over again precisely because it will never be tried for war crimes. The West dotes on America's desire and ability to wage wars in the most remote areas of the globe. "Those good old Yanks will defend the 'master race' in the jungles of Vietnam if they have to."

Media exposures of American war crimes such as My Lai and Abu Ghraib are rare exceptions. Every level of the American military and political leadership goes to great lengths to cover up war crimes and severely punish those who would not participate in the cover ups. Henry Kissinger, for example, as National Security Advisor to President Nixon, went to great lengths to cover up President Nixon's secret bombing of Cambodia and received the highly coveted Nobel Peace Prize for his successful cover up of American warmongering.

However, the frequency and extent of war crimes are so great and overwhelming that exposures such as My Lai and Abu Ghraib will inevitably escape through the layers of military and executive orders to cover up. The typical response to such exposures is that they are unique exceptions to overwhelmingly exemplary behaviour by American forces. The reality is that exemplary behaviour is a unique exception to brutal criminal behaviour, torture, rape, wanton killing of women and children, fear-mongering, hate, racism and inhuman conduct.

The My Lai massacre was no exception to the criminal behaviour of US forces in Vietnam. Charlie Company which gang raped and slaughtered 504 civilians in the Vietnamese villages of My Lai and Son My on March 16, 1968 was no different from other "Search and Destroy" missions ordered by General "Westy" Westmoreland during his four years as Commander in Vietnam. "Westy's Warriors," as they proudly called themselves, were only too eager to carry out these criminal missions because Vietnamese were "Congs" and "Gooks" like First Nations had been "Red Savages" during their extermination.

Americans have been trained and indoctrinated from the very beginning of the American Empire to instinctively think of all non-whites as the most primitive animals. When their orders told them to slaughter all Vietnamese and their animals they did not see a distinction between the animals they slaughtered and the Vietnamese babies, young children, mothers, old men and women. When they gang raped the Vietnamese women instead of the Vietnamese animals it was more instinct than rational choice.

Charlie Company was congratulated by General Westmoreland for wiping out every trace of life in the villages of My Lai and Son My. But a helicopter pilot, Hugh Thompson, had witnessed the massacred children, babies, women and old men, from the air. He saw unarmed women and children, crying and pleading for mercy, shot point blank. When Thompson landed his helicopter and confronted members of Charlie Company they told him in no uncertain terms that they were following orders. They continued their killing spree as Thompson departed with his helicopter. While some members of Charlie Company later testified that they were reluctant to follow orders to kill unarmed civilians many were overly zealous in executing those orders. They clearly saw their mission in Vietnam as one of wiping out the Vietnamese population in ways reminiscent of the widespread extermination of First Nations during the illegal conquest of First Nations lands. Thompson witnessed other murders on his return flight to his base and reported his observations to his commander, Major Watke. Thompson's report was corroborated by his crew and by other helicopter pilots.

President Nixon and General Westmoreland sought to cover up My Lai as much as Donald Rumsfeld and President Bush sought to cover up Abu Ghraib. But when war crimes are committed on a daily basis during decades of warfare, a "My Lai" and an "Abu Ghraib" will occasionally escape cover-up. They often escape because one exceptional and determined reporter digs and/or because one exceptional and determined soldier is overcome by his country's horrendous crimes. In the case of My Lai it was not exposed simply because of the reports of Hugh Thompson and other helicopter crews but also because of letters sent to General Creighton Abrams, President Nixon, the US Congress and State Department, by American soldiers, Tom Glen and Ron Ridenhour, and some digging by celebrated American journalist, Seymour Hersh and US Congressman, Morris Udall.

Initial investigations by Colin Powell, later US Secretary of State, Colonel Oran Henderson, who had ordered the "Search and Destroy" mission, and Henderson's commander, Major General Samuel Koster, sought only to cover up the massacre. It was more than a year after the massacre that the American public became aware of My Lai and charges were laid. As usual, Americans were convinced that My Lai was an isolated incident. They were told that barbarity was being committed on an unprecedented scale by the Viet Congs and a few American boys lost it. In the end no American leader was blamed for My Lai. One lone American soldier, Platoon leader, William Calley, took the fall and served a miserably inadequate four months prison sentence. It's essential that the World understands that Americans are "above the law," and that those who bring forward evidence of American crimes will be ostracized.

By the time Abu Ghraib occurred in 2003, My Lai had long been forgotten by a World only too eager to support American war crimes and absolve the American Empire from any and all criminal behaviour and human rights abuses. It was therefore inevitable that the American Empire would boldly and unabashedly re-commit these war crimes in Afghanistan and Iraq. And so it did. That while this **evil** empire is openly committing these atrocities and human rights abuses across the globe the Western media would focus almost exclusively on the possibility that China may be committing human rights abuses and that this same **evil** American Empire should lead a call for China to cease and desist is the most damning testimony of the ingrained bias, double standards and infantile behaviour of the Western media.

None of the social ills of the World, human rights abuses, dictatorship, racism, environmental degradation, inequality, poverty and injustice have the slightest chance of being addressed as long as the West insists on the most **evil** of all empires, the American Empire, being the "Leader of the Free World." Thank God that the empire is disintegrating from within because of its greed and incompetence. The West will not voluntarily share leadership in a fair and equitable manner. But the revolution which took the manufacturing of the World's insatiable appetite for consumer goods to Asia, in search of cheap labour, will force the West to share leadership or perish.

The American Invasions of Cambodia and Laos

The American Empire, like the French Empire before, invaded Vietnam as part of its goal of colonizing all of Indochina. This is one reason why the Vietnam War is often called the Second Indochina War. Indochina was viewed by both imperial France and Ho Chi Minh as a single struggle between imperialism and freedom. As early as 1930 Ho had become the leader of a single Indochinese Communist Party. However, as with the struggle for independence in Latin America, the independence struggle in Indochina brought to the fore divisions between North and South Vietnam as well as divisions between Vietnam, Cambodia and Laos.

In 1951, the Vietnam/Cambodia/Laos divisions in the Indochinese independence struggle were formally recognized by the Indochinese Communist Party. Three national units were recognized within the Indochinese Communist Party. Vietnam would be represented by the Vietnam Workers Party. Cambodia would be represented by the Khmer People's Revolutionary Party, KPRP. Laos would be represented by the Pathet Lao. However, Ho Chi Minh and Vietnamese nationalists played key roles in all three divisions.

In our analyses of the Vietnam War we have drawn many parallels with that American invasion and America's current invasions of Afghanistan and Iraq. Another parallel is that America's invasions of Afghanistan and Iraq were intended to be a prelude to its invasion of Iran. Likewise, colonization of Iraq, Iran and Afghanistan would be a stepping stone for conquest of the Middle East just as conquest of Indochina would be a stepping stone for conquest of Asia. Defeat in Vietnam ended America's dream of colonizing Asia and defeats in Afghanistan and Iraq will end America's dream of colonizing the oil rich Middle East.

Empires are doomed to self destruct as they endeavour to expand beyond their capabilities. They self destruct faster when their leaders are incompetent and lack vision. President Barak Obama's so called exit strategy from Iraq is one of digging a deeper and deeper hole in Afghanistan and Pakistan. His domestic economic policy is equally bankrupt as he escalates spending to cure the American disease of over-spending. Yet Obama is hailed as a visionary even though ending America's insatiable appetite for wars and for excessive consumption is nowhere on his agenda.

The public excuse used by the American Empire to invade Laos and Cambodia was the Ho Chi Minh Trail. It is the same argument used today for extending the Afghanistan invasion into Pakistan. American illegal bombing of Laos and Cambodia began as early as 1964. While this was not officially revealed to the world until 2000, it would have surprised only those who steadfastly cling to the mistaken notion that the United States is a law abiding and peaceful nation without imperial ambitions. Both countries were heavily carpet bombed by the empire's powerful B-52 bombers.

US Invasion of Cambodia led to Pol Pot and the Khmer Rouge

In 1970, the American Empire instigated a successful coup against Prince Norodom Sihanouk while Sihanouk was out of the country. Sihanouk had governed Cambodia since Cambodia ceased to be a colony of France in 1953. Sihanouk's insistence on Cambodia's neutrality made it easy for the American Empire to label him a communist. Fighting communism was America's justification for deposing a legitimate Head of Sate and replacing him with their local s.o.b. dictator, General Lon Nol. In March 1970, Lon Nol became the Head of State of the new *Khmer Republic*. The American Empire had found their man in Cambodia as they had done in South Vietnam. President Nixon had scored a temporary victory in the empire's war to colonize Indochina.

Prior to the overthrow of Sihanouk, American bombing raids into Cambodia were not only illegal, violating the 1954 Geneva Convention, but were protested by Cambodia's Head of State. Nixon escalated the bombing of Cambodia in March 1969. It was Sihanouk's constant objections to the American bombing of his people and "stone age" destruction of the Cambodian economy which led the American Empire to replace him with the American puppet, Lon Nol. The bombing destroyed the homes of over 2 million Cambodians.

In April 1970, American troops invaded Cambodia. Student protests over the illegal invasion of Cambodia led to the deaths of six American students at Kent State University and Jackson State College. The US Congress passed a special resolution to end this illegal invasion. But US bombing raids into Cambodia continued until August 1973. American bombing destabilized the puppet government led by Lon Nol. With the livelihood of millions of Cambodians destroyed by the American invasion and endless bombing, Cambodians flocked to the insurrection led by the Khmer Rouge.

The term, Khmer Rouge, had been coined by Cambodia's popular leader, Norodom Sihanouk, to refer to the Cambodian division of the Indochinese Communist Party, the KPRP. Initially led by Vietnamese nationalists, the KPRP became increasingly independent of the Indochinese Communist Party and Ho Chi minh. Its new leaders were recruited from Cambodian students educated in Marxism while studying in France. Pol Pot, who became the infamous leader of the KPRP, went to France in 1949 and returned to Cambodia in 1953. In Paris he joined the French Communist Party along with other Cambodian students who returned as leaders of the KPRP. The KPRP followed Mao Ze Dong in harnessing the power of the Cambodian peasants in the struggle against French and American imperialism.

As the US bombing disrupted peasant life in Cambodia, peasants filled the ranks of the KPRP. They launched a very effective insurgency against the American puppet, Lon Nol. In doing so they simultaneously wrested the KPRP from Vietnam's leadership. The KPRP would become anti-American as well as anti-Vietnam. There would be no unified Indochina after French and American imperialism were defeated.

While in exile in China, Sihanouk formed a tenuous alliance with his old enemies, the Khmer Rouge. The KPRP morphed into the *Communist Party of Kampuchea, CPK*. As the CPK it became the primary voice of the Cambodian insurgency against American colonization. By removing Sihanouk as Head of State the American Empire had unwittingly strengthened the indigenous communist resistance as represented by the CPK. With Sihanouk backing the CPK, Cambodians opposed to the American coup which removed Sihanouk, threw in their lot with the communists. Sihanouk's presence in Beijing also enabled him to enhance China's military support for the Cambodian insurgency. America's s.o.b. in Cambodia, Lon Nol, was doomed to fail as miserably as America's s.o.b. in South Vietnam, Ngo Dinh Diem had failed.

As the American Empire is finding out in Iraq and Afghanistan today, every Cambodian village bombed brought new recruits to the CPK. Nixon's decision to intensify the bombing was counter productive since it simply increased the number of Cambodians willing to fight American imperialism and vent their anger on Lon Nol. In January 1975 the Khmer Rouge launched their offensive against the Cambodian capital city, Phnom Penh. On April 17, 1975, the Khmer Rouge captured Phnom Penh and toppled the American imposed Lon Nol government in Cambodia.

The American Empire must be held responsible not only for the illegal bombing of the sovereign country of Cambodia but also for the deaths and destruction carried out by Pol Pot and the Khmer Rouge. American atrocities were followed by Pol Pot's reign of terror resulting from the empire's illegal bombing raids in Cambodia. American bombing killed as many as half a million Cambodian civilians and created a massive refugee problem by destroying every aspect of their economy and livelihood. Cambodia had been truly bombed back to the Stone Age as the American Empire had proudly set out to do. Another 3 million Cambodians lost their lives during the four year Khmer rule which followed the decade of illegal bombing of Cambodia by the American Empire.

US Invasion of Laos

The American Empire invaded the sovereign Kingdom of Laos during its invasions of Vietnam and Cambodia. Laos gained its independence from France in 1953 but both the French and American Empires continued to provide military support to the Laotian Monarchy. As French military support declined the American Empire increased its military support and interference in the domestic affairs of Laos. As usual, its excuse was "fighting communism." In reality, its goal was to replace French colonization of Laos with American colonization.

In pursuit of its goal to colonize Laos the American Empire began bombing Laos in 1964 and added military operations in Laos, *Operations Steel Tiger and Tiger Hound,* in 1965. Heavy bombing using B-52 bombers began in late 1965. American bombing of targets in Laos escalated threefold in 1967. During the decade after 1964 the American Empire dropped more bombs on Laos than the total bombing by all countries during the Second World War. American bombs killed half a million Laotians during that decade. In addition, children in Laos continue to die today from unexploded American bombs.

The Pathet Lao communist insurgency in Laos had fought the French and Americans in the First Indochina War. There was little reason to expect it to trade French imperialism for American imperialism. American support for the Laotian monarchy only increased the determination to overthrow both the monarchy and American imperialism. President Nixon sent South Vietnamese ground troops to invade Laos in February 1971 while simultaneously enhancing the B-52 bombing campaign. As in Cambodia, American bombing only increased the numbers joining the insurgency. With certain defeat imminent, the American Empire withdrew from Laos in 1973.

As in Vietnam, the US Congress cut off all funding for American involvement in Laos by April 1975. Without American support the Laotian monarchy was defeated. The Lao People's Democratic Republic was created in November 1975 and King Savang Vatthana abdicated on December 2, 1975. Laos had regained its independence and established a close alliance with Vietnam. It joined the ASEAN free trade area in 1997. This is an economic alliance of 10 countries in Southeast Asia including Vietnam and Cambodia. The three countries making up French Indochina had come together again as part of a larger and more viable economic, strategic and political alliance.

American defeats in China, North Korea and Indochina had stymied the American Empire's efforts to expand its Asian Empire after World War II. Massive economic growth in China, which now includes Hong Kong and Macau, and the ASEAN countries, combined with economic and military disasters by the United States, has led to America's former *uncolonies*, Japan, South Korea and Taiwan, increasing their economic and political ties with Asia. The dream of an ever expanding American Empire in Asia died with the empire's military defeat in Indochina.

CHAPTER 9

*Failed American Invasions In The Middle East Hasten
the Fall of the American Empire*

In the previous chapters we have traced the military expansion of the United Sates from its beginning in 1783 to its failed invasion of Indochina almost two centuries later. By 1983, the tiny ex-English colony on the Atlantic seaboard had become the undisputed superpower and so called "leader of the free world." This amazing achievement will be viewed by most as a testimony to American ingenuity, courage, determination and racial superiority. I see it as a dismal failure of the human race. The human race connived with and supported the rise of an imperial power which used propaganda, extreme militarism and warmongering to colonize poorer and militarily weaker nations. This imperial power imposed restrictions on freedom and democracy to stifle the natural human evolution of higher social principles, justice, international law, racial equality, income equality and simple brotherly love and respect.

The destruction of the old European empires during the Second World War made it easy for the American Empire to rise to its superpower status. But this opportunity also created the reason for its ultimate demise. With no serious challenger to its greed for imperial expansion it over expanded its reach. Ruling an entire planet even for an ambitious and unscrupulous superpower like the United Sates is impossible. By the beginning of the Second World War it had conquered the American continent and the Caribbean and begun a modest competition for Asia and the Middle East. After the Second World War it conquered Europe while simultaneously holding the Americas and expanding its Asian and Middle East acquisitions. In the previous chapter we documented its failures in Asia. In this chapter we will explain its initial successes and ultimate failures in the Middle East. Hopefully, the decline of the American Empire will deter any country from even contemplating superpower hegemony in the future.

Israel, ARAMCO, Middle East Oil and US-Saudi Alliance

American imperialism in the Middle East, like its imperialism in the Americas and Asia, began with a desire to compete with the European imperialists such as Britain and France. Britain, France, Italy and Spain had a long history of colonization in the Middle East. In fact, European colonization of the Middle East and the surrounding regions of North Africa and the Mediterranean dates back to the Roman Empire and the Christian Crusades or Holy Wars against Islam. The United States entered the imperial race for this region in 1801 when it invaded Libya.

American and Western European colonization of this region cannot be separated from the long standing religious conflict between Christianity and Islam. It is crucial that we recognize the important role which Christian religious dogma has played in Western imperialism ever since the Pope unilaterally decided that he had the supreme power to permit Spain and Portugal to colonize the entire globe. This ridiculous Christian view that the West has some kind of divine right to conquer and impose "Christian" values on all people is nowhere more significant than in the Middle East. As the centre of the Islamic world, Muslims are rightly incensed by Christian imperialism in the Middle East.

Prior to the division of the entire World between Spain and Portugal in 1493 by Pope Alexander VI, the Middle East and surrounding regions were advanced Islamic States. The Christian Crusades during the period 1095 to 1272 had failed to conquer these Muslim States. The dominant empire in this region following the Christian Crusades was the Islamic Ottoman Empire. The Ottoman Empire expanded in prestige, power and territory after the thirteenth century. North Africa, the Mediterranean, Egypt and the Middle East became relatively rich Islamic regions. But the importance of the Mediterranean as a dominant trade route declined with the discovery of the Americas and Vasco Da Gama's discovery of the oceanic route to the East around the Cape of Good Hope.

Piracy as an Important Tool of Imperialism

Western imperialism began in the fifteenth century with Spain and Portugal emerging as the dominant Western imperial powers. In competing with Spain and Portugal for colonies, Holland, France, England and the United States used piracy and privateers extensively. Without legally sanctioning privateers England would not have defeated the Spanish Empire to become the dominant seafaring nation until the Second World War. Likewise the French *Corsairs* and the Dutch *Sea Beggars* were fearsome privateers sanctioned by France and Holland, respectively, to expand their sea power as a means of imperial competition. We have examined the "legalization" of piracy by the United States in Chapter 2.

Piracy was also used as a legitimate tool of defence. England used privateers to defend England against the Spanish invasion of 1587-88 and the United States used privateers to defend against England during the American War of Independence and in the War of 1812. As in the Christian empires piracy was a legitimate tool used by Islamic States, especially those Muslim States with easy access to the Mediterranean Sea. But unlike the Christian empires, Muslim States used piracy more as a defensive weapon against the imperial expansionism by the West, including the United States, into Muslim lands. As the Christian Nations dominated the piracy based in the Caribbean Sea so did the Muslim Nations dominate the piracy based in the Mediterranean Sea.

As explained in Chapter 2, the United States sent four war ships into the Mediterranean to flex its imperial muscle outside the Americas. Piracy was the excuse used to launch an imperial invasion against the Muslim nations along the Barbary Coast, Libya, Algeria, Morocco and Tunisia. As a devoutly *Christian* nation, by invading *Muslim* countries it became impossible for the American Empire to ever convince Muslims that its future imperial aspirations were not part of a desire to wage a holy Christian war against Islam. America's current global war on "terrorism" cannot be disentangled from its war against Islam, its invasions in the Middle East and its military and economic support of Israel.

US Invasion of Libya: 1801-1805

Libya was ruled as an independent country by the Karamanli monarchy when the US invaded in 1801. It had gained its independence from the Ottoman Empire since 1711. As a relatively small independent Muslim country it seemed an easy target for the American Empire. But the American Empire has a long standing history of over estimating its military prowess. The invasion lasted four years and ended in defeat for the American Empire. The US invasion is called the *Tripolitan War* since Libya was called Tripolitania at the time. Libya's capital today is Tripoli. It is also referred to as the *First Barbary War* because Tripolitania was one of the *Barbary States.* American conquest of Libya would have enabled the American navy to patrol the Mediterranean and expand the American Empire into the Middle East.

The *Tripolitan War* lasted from 1801-1805. Despite naval reinforcements sent in 1803 and heavy bombardment of Libya in 1804, the American Empire suffered its first military defeat outside the Americas. Captain William Bainbridge was humiliated when he lost the *USS Philadelphia* in October 1803 and his entire crew of 307 American marines were imprisoned in Libya. Further humiliation followed when Lieutenant Stephen Decatur made a failed attempt to recapture the *Philadelphia* in February 1804. The worst humiliation to the American Empire came in September 1804 when Commodore Preble attempted to set fire to the Libyan navy only to sacrifice the entire crew of the *Intrepid*. The American Empire was forced to negotiate a treaty with Libya's ruling dynasty, Pasha Yusuf Karamanli, in June 1805. A ransom of $60,000 was paid for the release of American prisoners captured by Libya. Islam had registered the first of many victories against America's military superiority.

With the fall of the Karamanli monarchy, Libya once again became a colony of the Ottoman Empire in 1835. This made it much more difficult for the American Empire to conquer. In 1912, Libya became an Italian colony as a result of the Libyan War between Italy and the Ottoman Empire. Another European empire had beaten the American Empire to this valuable piece of real estate in North Africa which would have given the American Empire a strategic position in the Mediterranean. But there were other Muslim states with access to the Mediterranean. A thief always looks for the easiest target.

US Invasion of Algeria: 1815

In 1815, the American Empire invaded Algeria. As with the 1801 invasion of Libya, piracy was the excuse for waging war on another *Muslim* nation. An invasion force consisting of 10 warships was commanded by the same William Bainbridge and Stephen Decatur who had both disgraced the American Empire during the failed US invasion of Libya a decade earlier. The American Empire wrongly assumed that their experience from that earlier failed mission combined with their determination to reclaim their honour would increase the chance of a successful invasion. But once again the relatively small Muslim nation of Algeria proved to be as formidable an opponent as Libya had been. America's *Second Barbary War,* like the first, failed to add colonies to the American Empire or naval access to the Mediterranean.

The American Empire never got a second chance to conquer Algeria because it became a French colony in 1830. Likewise, in 1881 France colonized another Barbary State, Tunisia. The remaining Barbary State, Morocco had established a "Treaty of Friendship" with the United States as early as 1786. But all of the European empires, including France, Britain, Spain and Germany, competed with the US for colonial rights over Morocco. In 1912, Morocco became a protectorate of France. The American Empire had to wait for the decline of the European empires during World War II to gain naval prominence in the Mediterranean.

The First World War and the Paris Peace Conference of 1919

It is safe to say that until the First World War the British, French, Italian and German empires had succeeded in keeping the American Empire out of the Middle East and the surrounding regions of North Africa and the Mediterranean. The failed American invasions of Libya and Algeria had only served to confirm the English view that the American Empire was, at best, a "puny" empire. However, English contempt for all things American often led the English to underestimate the guile and determination of the American Empire.

British and French influence in the Middle East received a big boost as a result of the defeat of the Ottoman Empire during the First World War. As we saw above, Western European empires made numerous attempts to expand their empires into North Africa, the Mediterranean and the Middle East prior to World War I. However, the Islamic empires were largely successful in minimizing Christian conquests. At the outbreak of World War I, the dominant empire in this region was the Ottoman Empire. The Allied defeat of the Central Powers in World War I rolled back the Ottoman Empire to Turkey, thereby reducing the Islamic defence against Christianity.

The United States entered World War I belatedly in 1917. However, as a member of the Allied victory it participated in the Paris Peace Conference of 1919 which enabled the "puny" empire to begin to demand partnership with England and France in leading the Christian World against the resurgence of Islam in the Middle East, North Africa and the Mediterranean. In fact, the United States and President Woodrow Wilson were allowed to influence the peace talks in a way which far exceeded the US contribution to, and sacrifice for, the allied victory.

The peace talks were dominated by the US, Britain and France even though Russia contributed far more than the US to the allied victory. More importantly, the US was viewed by most of the parties affected by the imperialist ambitions of the West, as the more "honest broker," compared with Britain and France. President Wilson took full advantage of this view of the US to play off France and Great Britain against each other to the benefit of the US.

The European empires, including Britain and France, had never consistently lied about their imperial desires. The US, by contrast, has consistently and vehemently denied its imperial ambition. Despite its imperial expansion from the day of its birth as an independent country it has succeeded in fooling the world to this day. So it was that in 1919 it was far more trusted than Britain and France by Arab and Islamic states. Its failed invasions of Libya and Algeria had long been forgotten since those failures had prevented it from colonizing the Middle East and surrounding regions. Its conquest of the American continent and the Caribbean was ignored by the countries which would be affected by Paris Peace talks.

The Paris Peace Conference provided a new opportunity for the American Empire to envision conquests of Muslim lands. For the first time in history, Britain and France grudgingly accorded equal status to the United Sates as a Western Christian power which must be negotiated with in dividing up the spoils of Western imperialism. Prior to the Paris Peace Conference no American president had even visited Europe while in office. This new found status for the American Empire applied as much to the conquered territory of the Ottoman Empire as to other conquests during World War I.

In 1919, American interest in the conquered lands of the Ottoman Empire was viewed as marginal even by the conquered Arabs and Muslims. In fact, most of those conquered welcomed the American Empire as a useful counterbalance to the greed of Britain and France. That was a huge mistake. Fifty years later the American Empire would rule the region with an iron fist, squelching all independence struggles, controlling the vast oil supplies, promoting world-wide hatred of Arabs and Muslims and arming and condoning Israeli atrocities against Palestinians, Arabs and Lebanese. The American Empire had stolen a continent from the First Nations by guile, deceit, racism and the most savage use of military force. It would use these well honed characteristics to steal the Middle East from the Muslims and Arabs. Arab/Muslim disunity after the fall of the Ottoman Empire would make it easy for the American Empire and its Western allies, including Canada.

However, France and Britain had agreed to carve up the Ottoman Empire well before the US entry into the First World War and the subsequent Paris Peace Conference of 1919. The *Sykes-Picot Agreement* between Britain and France had been signed on May 16, 1916 but kept secret until Britain and France used the Russian revolution of 1917 as an excuse to deny Russian claims to sharing the spoils of war. President Wilson was at a clear disadvantage in somewhat belatedly pushing competing American interests against those of Britain and France. President Wilson was also relatively naïve in playing the imperial game compared with the seasoned British and French. In fact, it would be safe to say that by Britain and France trumpeting the "evils" of *Bolshevism,* Wilson and the American Empire helped France and England to increase their share of the spoils of World War I by reducing the share going to the Russians.

President Wilson had to console himself with being allowed to set up the *King-Crane Commission* to conduct an investigation of Arab views in the territories conquered from the Ottoman Empire and colonized by Britain and France. While the Commission had no power to transfer territory from Britain or France to the American Empire it marked the beginning of American involvement with the Middle East and with the *Arab-Israeli-Palestinian* conflict. The American Empire would use its efficient propaganda machine to build a lasting pro-American view by many of the Arabs and Muslims in the Middle East. To this day countries such as Saudi Arabia, Jordan and Egypt are firmly pro-American and have so integrated their economies with that of the United States that they sing the praises of American hypocrisy.

Prior to the First World War the British and French empires had ruled the world for two centuries. Russia had always been a player but somewhat of an outsider. Japan had later joined Russia as another "outsider" player. Allied victory in World War I temporarily ended the German challenge for European hegemony while strengthening the challenge from Italy. The Bolshevik revolution in Russia led to the American Empire replacing Russia as the new "outsider" threat to Britain and France. While Russia was privy to the secret *Sykes-Picot Agreement* of 1916 between Britain and France, the American Empire replaced Russia in the Paris Peace Conference of 1919. The American Empire also participated in the *Treaty of Lausanne* of July 24, 1923 which formally recognized the *Republic of Turkey.* The American Empire was represented by Admiral Mark Bristol who served as US High Commissioner to Turkey from 1919 to 1927.

ARAMCO and US Invasion of Saudi Arabia

While the American Empire first attempted to invade and conquer territories in the Middle East to expand its global empire to compete with Britain and France, it was the discovery of oil in the Middle East which made Middle East conquests a top priority for its imperial expansion. Oil was first discovered by the British in the Middle East in 1908. The British had defeated Iran in the *Anglo-Persian War* of 1856-57 and secured monopoly rights to explore for oil in Iran in 1901. With the discovery of oil in Iran in 1908 the British founded the *Anglo-Persian Oil Company* to secure the Iranian oil for Britain as well as steal most of the profits from the Iranian people.

British refusal to return Iran's oil to the Iranian people was the primary cause of the Iranian revolution of 1979 which overthrew the Western supported government of the Shah, Reza Khan. The continued sabre rattling of the West against Iran to this day is largely due to the goal of the West to steal Iran's oil. Iran's threat to acquire nuclear weapons to keep its oil supplies is the West's worst nightmare. Unfortunately for Iran, the pro-American stance of countries such as Jordan, Egypt, Saudi

Arabia and other Persian Gulf states, weaken the efforts of Iran to promote Middle East independence and sovereignty.

Iran received a new and very important ally in Turkey after the American inspired Israeli military attack on the *Freedom Flotilla* on **May 31, 2010.** After the defeat of the Ottoman Empire in World War I, Turkey became a Western ally and the only non-Western member of NATO. With the global economic shift from the West to Asia and the booming Turkish economy, Muslims in Turkey have become less fearful in criticizing the criminal invasions of the West in Palestine, Lebanon, Iraq and Afghanistan. The majority of the 663 peace activists attempting to deliver much needed humanitarian aid to the 1.5 million Palestinians in Gaza were Turkish citizens. The ship targeted by the Israeli commandos, the *MV Mavi Marmara,* flew the flag of Turkey and 400 of the passengers were Turkish citizens. The deadly and premeditated Israeli special forces military attack on peaceful civilians in international waters killed 9 passengers and injured another 60 aboard the *Mavi Marmara.* Turkey has since joined Iran in calling for an end to the American/Canadian/Israeli blockade of Gaza.

The allied defeat of the Ottoman Empire in the First World War allowed the British to colonize Iraq and exploit its oil reserves. Oil was discovered in Iraq in 1927. With the loss of Iran's oil in 1979, control of Iraq's oil supplies by the West became of paramount importance. Saddam Hussein became the US imposed s.o.b. dictator of Iraq the same year Iran took control of its oil supplies. The British and Americans have fought long and costly wars in Iraq to continue their theft of Iraq's oil.

As Britain and France have reduced their historic hold on the mind set of Muslims in the Middle East the American Empire has increased its charismatic hypnotism of the Arab intellectual to the point that they condemn their own, even more strongly than the West. To be modern, Western and "civilized" in the Middle East, after World War II, was to be more American than America. That mindset, more than anything else, is what keeps the Middle East divided and the rulers out of touch with their constituents. It was the kind of Western brainwashing that failed miserably in China but succeeded in Japan, Taiwan and South Korea. But nowhere has Western brainwashing succeeded more than among the elite of the Arab world.

The US gets a Dominant Foothold in Saudi Arabia

Britain and France may have been there first but the American Empire has secured the lion's share of Middle Eastern oil. Distrustful of Britain, Saudi Arabia, the world's largest oil producer, chose what it perceived to be the lesser evil, when it opted for American colonization over British colonialism. In 1933, *Standard Oil of California* was given the monopoly to explore for oil in Saudi Arabia. In 1933, the American Empire was still on the outside looking in, as far as the Middle East was concerned. Britain was still the dominant imperial power in the region, followed by France, Italy and Russia.

In 1933, the American Empire seemed like a good counterbalance to the long standing imperialism of Britain, France, Russia and Italy, in the Middle East. However, with the relative decline of Britain and the staggering rise of the American Empire after World War II, Saudi Arabia's choice of the US over Britain, to exploit its oil reserves, turned out to be the most detrimental decision made by a Middle Eastern state in terms of Arab and Muslim sovereignty in the region. The American Empire formed an enduring alliance with Britain and used the most barbaric forms of militarism to invade, bomb, kill, hunt, maim and humiliate Arabs and Muslims worldwide. At the same time the Western media used every form of propaganda to demonize Muslims and Arabs.

Oil was not discovered in Saudi Arabia until 1938. In that year the American Empire created the *Arabian American Oil Company, ARAMCO,* to secure the oil supplies of Saudi Arabia for the benefit of the American Empire as the British had done in Iran and Iraq for its empire. In 1946 the American Empire built a modern airbase at Dhahran to safeguard its Saudi Arabian oil. In 1951 Saudi Arabia signed a mutual defence assistance pact with the American Empire and the American Empire began to train the military force of Saudi Arabia. Saudi Arabia provided financial support for American imperialism in Afghanistan, Iraq, Ethiopia and Angola.

Saudi Arabia must be held responsible for inviting the American Empire into the region and for continuing to punish its own citizens for opposing American imperialism. While it is true that no Middle Eastern state is powerful enough to drive the Americans out of the region, the Saudi rulers are playing a dangerous game by implicitly condoning Western imperialism in the region. Furthermore, Saudi complicity provides the Western media with just the right ammunition for its propaganda campaign to discredit Iran, Syria, Hezbollah and Hamas.

Within Saudi Arabia are Islam's two most holy cities, Mecca and Medina. Mecca is the birthplace of the Prophet Muhammad and Islam's holiest city. It attracts 2 million Muslims annually for the Muslim pilgrimage of the Hajj. Muhammad was buried in Medina. Saudi Arabia uses its support for the Hajj and maintenance of these holy cities to promote itself as the leader of the Muslim World. This flies in the face of Saudi Arabia's connivance with the leader of the Christian World, the American Empire, in suppressing the freedom of Muslims in the Middle East.

The Balfour Declaration Provided a Key Opportunity for the American Empire in the Middle East

In 1917 the British Empire promised Jews that it would create a homeland for them in the Middle East. In creating the *State of Israel* in the heart of the Middle East the British provided the opportunity for the American Empire to arm and fortify an American satellite state strategically located in the oil rich Middle East. The *Balfour Declaration* of 1917 marks the beginning of the American invasions and conquests in the Middle East, barely a decade after the British had first discovered oil in Iran. In 1922 the US Congress passed a joint resolution in support of the Balfour Declaration to create a Jewish state in Palestine.

Judaism begat Christianity, with the birth of Jesus Christ, and Judaism begat Islam, with the birth of the Prophet, Muhammad. Religion has been and continues to be one of the most important forces in history. In the early years of Christianity, Jews and Christians were at constant war with each other. Today they have formed an alliance against Islam. The leader of the Christian World, the American Empire, is the most powerful empire the world has ever seen. It has chosen to arm the leader of the Jewish World, Israel, with the most sophisticated WMD's, as part of its strategy to defeat Islam while simultaneously enriching its empire with the abundance of oil which the Muslims rightly claim to be on their soil.

Columbus brought Western Europe to the Americas enabling Europe to enrich its empires with the gold and silver of the Americas. The offspring of Western Europe, the American Empire, invaded the Middle East and planted an armed Jewish nation on Muslim lands to aid their theft of "Black gold." American imperialism is the key to understanding the "Palestinian Issue," the audacity of Israel, the suffering of the Lebanese, the hostility of Muslims and Arabs, the Western wars in Iraq, Afghanistan and Pakistan, the enduring racism of Whites and the continuing poverty of the human race.

The Second World War was instrumental in creating the conditions for American conquests in the Middle East. The devastation of the Western European empires made the American Empire the leader of the Christian World. Hitler's anti-Semitic Germany provided the massive Jewish migration which the American Empire used to populate and arm the state of Israel. World opinion strongly supported a homeland for Jews because of their suffering in Europe. Since no Western country wanted that homeland in their backyard the American Empire's imperialist ambitions in the Middle East were downplayed by the world so as not to be seen as anti-Semitic or uncaring for the suffering of Jews caused by the holocaust.

It would be extremely naïve to believe that the creation and arming of a Jewish state in the heartland of Muslim territory by Western Christian powers had nothing to do with the war between Islam and Christianity. The failure of the Crusades had only temporarily halted the Christian invasions of Muslim lands. Since the voyages of Columbus and Da Gama the Christian West had prospered and the West finally re-conquered Jerusalem when the British general, Sir Edmund Allenby, defeated the Turks and entered Jerusalem on December 11, 1917.

The West had succeeded only by dividing the Muslim World. Muslim Arabs foolishly aided the West in defeating the Turkish Empire. The Muslim World continues to be divided to this day while the Christian World is not only united but has formed a solid alliance with the Jews. The American Empire is able to use its power and propaganda to continue to divide the Muslim World while protecting Israel and stealing the oil. But it is paying an increasing price as Arabs and Muslims find new ways of defending their land and their resources.

World opinion is also slowly turning away from unquestioned support for American imperialism in the Middle East and unbridled Israeli aggression against the Palestinians and Lebanese. On March 20, 2009 Canada was forced to take the unprecedented step of banning the outspoken British MP, George Galloway, from entering Canada. The 5-time elected British MP was invited by the Toronto Coalition to "Stop the War" to speak out against the plight of the Palestinians. This ban by Canada was a good example of cracks emerging in the unquestioned Western support for American and Israeli military crimes against the Palestinian people.

American-Israeli State Sponsored Terrorism

American militarism in the Middle East began by supplying arms to Jews in Israel to wage war on their Palestinian and Arab neighbours. In the Second World War the British continued to support Arab nationalism in the Middle East. This policy, begun in the First World War, was essential to the allied defeat of Germany in both wars. However, Western support for Arab nationalism during the two World Wars made it impossible for the West to create the state of Israel on Arab/Palestinian land, without military force. Most of that military force was supplied by the American Empire.

American hypocrisy has no limits. Today it claims to be at war with individual and state-sponsored terrorism. But individual and state-sponsored terrorism began with the Jews who immigrated into Israel with the blessing of the American Empire and with arms supplied or paid for by the American Empire. No other country in the world has inflicted as much pain and suffering on men, women and children, by using state-sponsored terrorism as Israel. The American Empire supplies the weapons and money for Israel to use state-sponsored terrorism. The Western media provides the propaganda to defend the use of state-sponsored terrorism by Israel. Israel's post 9-11 terrorist attacks in Lebanon and Gaza make the 9-11 attack in the US pale by comparison.

Jewish terrorists created the American-backed equivalent of Al-Qaeda, the *Haganah,* in 1920, two years before the American Congress passed the joint resolution in support of the state of Israel being created in Palestine. The most extremist terrorist branch of the Haganah was the *Irgun.* But unlike *Osama Bin Laden,* the Irgun leader, *Menachem Begin,* became the Prime Minister of Israel in 1977 with celebratory approval by the American Empire. To add insult to injury the American Empire made sure that he was awarded the now rightly maligned Nobel Peace Prize for his terrorist activities, including his bloody invasion of Lebanon in 1982 which led to the wholesale slaughter of thousands of civilians in the Palestinian refugee camps of Sabra and Shatila. For the eternally hypocritical West, there is, of course, one important difference between Osama and Menachem. Osama is a *Muslim*. Menachem was a *Jew*.

Another ironic difference between Al-Qaeda and *Irgun* is that the American Empire defended and supported the terrorist attacks on Britain by *Menachem Begin* whereas Britain has been the American Empire's number one ally in hunting down Osama Bin Laden. Begin arrived in Israel in 1942 and became the leader of Irgun the next year. Irgun had chosen to operate independently of Haganah since 1931 because it felt that the leaders of Haganah were not extreme enough in terrorizing the Palestinians and the British. At the outbreak of World War II Irgun sent a delegation to the United States to lobby for the creation of a Jewish army in Palestine. Under Begin's leadership, Irgun was very effective in significantly increasing the number of terrorist attacks.

Irgun smuggled arms into Palestine from Poland, Italy and other European countries, trained pilots to fly military aircrafts, stole arms from the British and produced some of its own arms in Palestine. Many Arab markets were mined with land mines made by Irgun. All infrastructures were sabotaged. British police officers were killed. Finance came from wealthy Jews and criminal activities. In addition to its terrorist activities Irgun arranged for thousands of "illegal aliens" to enter Palestine to recruit an increasing number of terrorists. The stated goal of Irgun was to end the British mandate over Palestine, instil fear in the Arab population and force the British to hand over Palestine to the Jews by importing millions of "illegal aliens" and committing terrorist acts. British arrests of members of Irgun had little effect on the number of terrorist acts committed. The number of terrorist acts increased steadily between 1931 and 1948 when the State of Israel was created. After 1948 the terrorist acts were conducted by the State of Israel itself and this *state terrorism* continues to this day.

The Bombing of the King David Hotel

Irgun's bombing of the King David Hotel on July 22, 1945 was simply the most widely publicised of the numerous terrorist acts committed by Irgun against the British to force Britain to hand over Palestine to the immigrant Jewish population. The King David Hotel would be the equivalent of the "Green Zone" in Iraq today. It was the Headquarters of the British Forces in Palestine as well as the offices of those administering the British Mandate over Palestine. If there was any question that the American Empire was aiding and abetting Jewish terrorists in Palestine the British Prime Minister, Clement Attlee, put that to rest after Irgun's bombing of the King David Hotel killed 91 people and injured 46 others.

Attlee called the bombing an "insane act of terrorism." Britain's famous war time Prime Minster, Sir Winston Churchill, called the members of Irgun terrorists and gangsters. One Western reporter in Jerusalem compared Irgun to the German "Gestapo." But the American Empire continued to support Jewish terrorist attacks on railroads, bridges, electrical facilities, communication facilities, police stations, prisons, immigration offices, taxation offices and other infrastructures after the bombing of the King David Hotel.

The bombing of a British Officers club in Jerusalem killed 17 British officers. British officers were kidnapped and humiliated by public beatings. On October 31, 1946, Irgun blew up the British embassy in Rome. In July, 1947, two British sergeants were kidnapped and hanged. In April 1948, 120 Palestinian civilians were killed by Jewish terrorists in the *Deir Yassin massacre.*

By the time of the outbreak of the *First* Arab-Israeli War in 1948 the American Empire, together with France and Britain, had already supplied enough arms to the Jews that the newly created State of Israel easily defeated the combined armed forces of Egypt, Iraq, Syria, Lebanon and Jordan. In 1922, Muslims outnumbered Jews, 7:1, in Palestine. Despite their numerical superiority, the Palestinians were poorly prepared for any military confrontation with the Jews. During the period between 1922, when the US Congress first passed the joint resolution in support of the creation of the State of Israel, and the formal outbreak of war in 1948, there was a steady increase of the Jewish population as Jews immigrated into Israel from all parts of the globe.

As the number of Jews increased, their acquisition of military training and weapons increased proportionately. On the other hand, many Palestinians emigrated out of Palestine to escape the conflict and the Palestinian leadership was woefully divided and disorganized relative to the Jewish leadership. The British armed the Jews to assist in dealing with the Palestinian insurgency. The French armed the Jews to have an ally in the Middle East to protect their colonies in Syria and Lebanon, and the Suez Canal in Egypt. Arms were easily purchased by the Jews from the Eastern European countries. Americans and wealthy Jews provided the money to purchase these arms.

Creation of the "Independent" State of Israel in 1947 by the American Empire

Arabs in the Middle East used the two World Wars to gain independence from the Ottoman Empire. This required an alliance with the West. We have seen before that Cuba and the Philippines allied with the American Empire to overthrow Spanish imperialism and China allied with the American Empire to overthrow Japanese imperialism. However, Arab disunity has led them to exchange Ottoman imperialism for Western imperialism. This disunity enabled the West to populate and arm Israel as an American *uncolony* in the heart of the Middle East while they fought among themselves for the lands previously colonized by the Ottoman Empire before the First World War.

By 1948, this American *uncolony,* Israel, had become strong enough to declare itself an "independent" country in the heartland of the Arab World. A tiny state had so armed itself with the best weapons the West could supply that it felt sufficiently confident to declare its "independence" even from its primary benefactor, the American Empire, by 1948. To this day no Arab state, including oil rich Saudi Arabia, has the same degree of independence as Israel. Even Iran, despite its occasional sabre rattling, must pay homage to American dictates far more than Israel.

One of the earliest uses of the UN as a puppet institution by the American Empire was the passing of *Resolution 181* on November 29, 1947. The American Empire had clearly wasted no time in using the newly created farce for a "World Body" as yet another tool in its propaganda arsenal. Canada, in particular, has been exceptionally enthusiastic in justifying all of its international atrocities by invoking UN resolutions it favoured while blatantly ignoring UN resolutions which the West opposed. It was therefore important for propaganda purposes that the US forced the Philippines, Haiti and Liberia to change their vote against UN Resolution 181 so that the resolution could pass with the required two-thirds majority.

UN resolution 181, which gave the West the "legitimate" excuse to steal Palestinian land for its *holy war* against Islam, co-opted the Jews to their cause by enabling the creation of the state of Israel. With a single UN resolution the West would:

1. Gain world-wide recognition as leading the fight against anti-Semitism
2. Protect their own overtly **racist** White population against charges of anti-Semitism
3. Reduce potential Jewish immigration into their countries
4. Encourage those Jews already in their countries to emigrate to Israel
5. Make the world believe that Muslims were anti-Semitic
6. Carve out an armed enclave in the heart of the Arab World to fortify the Christian *holy war* against Islam
7. Steal Arab oil with the aid of corrupt Arab leaders.

Resolution 181 was a clear violation of the fundamental premise for creating the UN. That fundamental premise was "self-determination" based on democratically elected governments. Resolution 181 prevented the free and fair election of a democratic government in Palestine. It imposed a government where Jews would be the ruling class and Palestinians would be second class citizens. The West would arm the Jewish ruling class to prevent the majority Palestinians from overthrowing the minority ruling class. Many Palestinians would be forced to flee Israel and become refugees in Jordan and Lebanon. Others would emigrate to the West or to neighbouring Arab states. Palestinians who remained in Israel would face permanent racial, political and economic discrimination.

An Eerie Similarity between Early American Imperialism and US-Israeli Imperialism in the Middle East

We have consistently argued that throughout the more than two centuries of American imperialism the US has used every weapon and propaganda to deny its imperialist past, present and future. It has publicly opposed imperialism while practicing it on a scale never seen before. This deception of its innate imperialist motive began immediately after its unilateral declaration of independence and during its War of Independence when it simultaneously invaded Canada. Beginning with Chapter 1, we have documented how it has expanded its empire by invading and conquering First Nations lands on the American continent. The key deception used at that time was the ridiculous notion that if you incorporate a newly conquered territory into your unified federal states then you cannot be colonizing it.

Expanding your empire by adding states to a federation may have some kind of inexplicable "Western" difference compared with the way in which Britain or France expanded their empires but was of little significance to the people whose land was conquered by force. Neither the First Nations nor the Hawaiians saw your actions as any less imperialistic. This continued attempt at deception is at the heart of why every act, every war, every invasion and every pronouncement by the American leadership is simultaneously supported 98 percent by the West and opposed 98 percent by the Third World.

And so it was that the Second World War and Hitler's campaign against the Jews provided a golden opportunity for the American Empire to use exactly the same *modus operandi* to create and expand an empire in the Middle East. It would plant a Jewish state called Israel in the heart of the Middle East and expand that state over time by conquering more and more Arab land in exactly the same way it had conquered more and more of First Nations land after 1775. It would begin this new imperialist drive for Middle East conquests in exactly the same way it had begun its conquests of First Nations land, that is, with a War of Independence. In 1775 the War of Independence was the *American War of Independence*. In 1948 it was the *Israeli War of Independence*.

The Arabs, like the First Nations before, would fight many wars to contain the expansion of the American Empire across the Middle East. Like the First Nations, the Arabs would sometimes cooperate with the American Empire and with France and Britain, and like the First Nations the Arabs would fight among themselves. The Arabs, like the First Nations before, were always on the defensive, facing the overwhelming military superiority of the West. They were forced to join with the enemy when that was the lesser evil. They were forced to fight with each other when that was the lesser evil. But like the First Nations, they could never lose sight of the fact that their land, their culture, their resources and their independence were under continuous attack by hallowed Western notions of freedom and democracy backed by the most vicious and barbaric use of sophisticated and deadly military force.

The First Nations had certainly not fought French and English imperialism to welcome American imperialism. Likewise the Arabs had not fought the Ottoman Empire in World War I and World War II to welcome French, British or American imperialism. The West would do well to remember why the Arabs fought on their side when they parade their disgusting tripe about Arab fundamentalism and terrorism. The Arabs are fighting Western imperialism which has the most modern weapons of mass destruction and mass terrorism combined with a gullible and subservient Western press only too happy to be the means by which the West projects its own dogma and fundamentalist *Christianite* beliefs.

The *First* Arab-Israeli War: 1948

The British, like the French, had firmly believed that they could colonize the Middle East once the Ottoman Empire was defeated. Unfortunately, the Second World War so destroyed their economies relative to the US that it was the American Empire, not Britain and France, which replaced the Ottoman Empire in the Middle East. The British governed Palestine after World War I under the League of Nations Mandate. Up until Hitler's persecution of the Jews in Germany the British were able to limit Jewish immigration into Palestine and keep the American Empire from inventing an excuse to colonize the Middle East.

Increased Jewish immigration into Palestine beginning in the 1930's led to the Arab uprising of 1936-39. In response to the strong Arab opposition to the high levels of Jewish immigration the British made efforts to restrict further Jewish immigration into Palestine. This provided the opportunity for the American Empire to use the propaganda of "persecuted Jews" as well as the effective **terrorist** training of Jews in Palestine, to wage a war against Britain and the Arabs in the Middle East. This American tactic had been used before in the two American invasions of Canada in 1775 and 1812 when the American Empire made war on Britain and the First Nations in Canada. In 1775 and 1812 the propaganda was that Canadians were oppressed by Britain. In the 1940's the propaganda was that the Jews needed an independent country because they were persecuted in Europe. The fact that Jews were discriminated against as much in the United States as they were in Europe during the 1940's was buried in the typical self righteousness with which the American Empire covers up its heinous crimes against humanity.

The Jewish terrorist organizations in Palestine, *Lehi* and *Irgun,* had increased their terrorist acts against the Arabs and the British while facilitating **illegal** Jewish immigration into Palestine well before the beginning of World War II. During and shortly after World War II the American Empire brought immense political pressure on Britain to end its restriction of Jewish immigration into Palestine. With the British economy devastated by World War II the British bowed to American pressure by setting up the *Anglo-American Committee of Inquiry* in early 1946 to address the question of continued Jewish immigration into Palestine. President Harry Truman publicly supported a recommendation of this Committee to allow 100,000 more Jews to immigrate into Palestine. Truman also agreed to send US troops into Palestine to stamp out the expected Arab resistance to the American sponsored immigration of such larges numbers of Jews. The American Empire had found its "politically correct" rationale for invading the Middle East.

With its economic hold on oil rich Saudi Arabia through ARAMCO the American Empire was now expanding its military presence in the Middle East by planting the "independent" Jewish state of Israel in the territory which Britain had governed under the Mandate of Palestine approved by the League of Nations on September 21, 1922. Britain was being forced out by the more powerful American Empire. As a face saving gesture Britain turned over its Mandate to the UN, the supposed successor to the League of Nations. Of course the American Empire had not been a member of the

League of Nations but the British, like all other countries, were well aware that the UN was the "politically correct" mouthpiece of the American Empire. The Americans had created this baby and controlled all its important decisions. The UN was a carefully constructed body to give the West the outer appearance of working with the emerging Third World for peace. In reality, the UN was an important instrument of post World War II Western colonization led by the American Empire. Resolution 181, creating Israel on Palestinian land, would be only the first of many UN resolutions to further American and Western imperialism.

The first of many wars waged by the American Empire in its quest to colonize the Middle East is often referred to as the *First* Arab-Israeli War. Following in the footsteps of American Imperialism the Jews proudly refer to this war as their equivalent of the American War of Independence. One of the many commonalities of these two so called "Wars of Independence," was that they were both fought for territory rightly and **legally** belonging to someone else. The *American* War of Independence was a war for First Nations land. The *Israeli* War of Independence was a war for Arab land. The other significant commonality was that both of these so called "Wars of Independence," were fought by and financed by the same American Empire. What was different was that the first was fought on the American continent while the second was fought in the Middle East.

In the first "War of Independence" the American Empire had convinced the world that its cause was just because the British had colonized them. Their "War of Independence" was never identified correctly by historians as a war for the illegal theft of First Nations land but **incorrectly** as a just war for independence from British tyranny. In the second "War of Independence" the American Empire again **incorrectly** convinced the world that this second war was also just because it was not a war for the illegal theft of Arab land, which it was, but for the independence of Jews who were escaping Western persecution, as exemplified by Hitler's Germany.

The fact that by the second "War of Independence" in1948, the American Empire had stolen so much First Nations land that it had more than enough land to create an independent Jewish state in the United States, was conveniently lost on the Western world. The West was fully aware that the American Empire chose to create an "independent" Israel in the Middle East, not simply to protect Jews from Western persecution, but mostly to expand its own empire in an area long envied by the West and now vulnerable because the West had defeated the once powerful Ottoman Empire.

Israel's Declaration of Independence and US Recognition: 1948

Israel declared its sovereignty as an independent state on May 14, 1948 and was immediately recognized as such by the American Empire. Contrary to what has been written, neither the American Empire nor Israel was fearful of a war with the Arab states. Such a war would give the American Empire and Israel an excuse to expand territory. If the once mighty British and French empires could not deter the Americans from stealing Arab land, surely a disunited and disorganized "Arab League," had zero chance of winning a war against the American Empire.

By 1948, the American Empire was the most powerful empire in existence, the European and Japanese empires having been devastated by World War II. Britain and France may have rejoiced in the fall of the Ottoman Empire but the spoils would go to the American Empire. To claim the spoils the American Empire would have to protect Israel *even* from the British.

In 1948, the Arabs had no allies. Even Stalin's Russia supported Israel and the American Empire. The Arabs also had no clearly defined goal. While Israel and the American Empire had a well defined single-minded goal of stealing as much Arab land as possible through war, the Arabs were very unsure as to which Arab state was entitled to the land given to Israel under UN resolution 181. Both Palestine and Jordan, for example, claimed the land given to Israel by UN resolution 181. That Arab disunity between states considered pro-West and states considered anti-West, continues to haunt Arab leadership to this day. As it was helpful to the West and the American Empire to encourage First Nations disunity to steal their land so it would be helpful to the West and the American Empire to encourage Arab disunity to steal Arab land and its oil.

As expected, the American Empire easily defeated the forces of the Arab League. The Arab League had been formed with the blessing of the British in 1945. The Arab League was initially made up of **seven** countries, Egypt, Saudi Arabia, Iraq, Jordan, Lebanon, Syria and Yemen. In this first of many wars against the Arabs the American Empire increased the geographical area of Israel by 50 percent over what it had first created with UN Resolution 181. Its plan to expand territory in the Middle East by continuous wars against the Arabs, as it had expanded territory in America through continuous wars against the First Nations, was firmly in place by 1949. By 1952 another 700,000 Jews had immigrated into Israel to fortify America's *uncolony* in the Middle East.

Arab-Israeli Wars: 1956-1982

American arms and military aid continued to flow into Israel turning it into the most armed state, relative to size, in the entire world. With its American installed nuclear weapons Israel can annihilate the entire Middle East. During the three decades following the *Israeli War of Independence,* the American Empire and Israel fought another **four** full blown wars against the Arabs and the Palestinian people. As with the wars against the First Nations in America, the American Empire and Israel were effectively in a constant state of war and repression against the people of Palestine. The Palestinians, like the First Nations, were defending their rights to their land against an aggressor with a far greater military superiority and propaganda machine. The American-Israeli wars in Palestine often spilled over into American wars of aggression in neighbouring Lebanon, Egypt, Jordan and Syria, reminiscent of American invasions of Mexico, Canada, Latin America and the Caribbean.

The 1956 War consolidates American Hegemony in the Middle East: End of Unilateral Actions by Britain and France in the Region.

By the outbreak of the ***Second* Arab-Israeli** in 1956 the Soviet Union had come to recognize the true nature of American imperialist expansionism in the Middle East. It therefore ceased its support for Israel and has since become part of the growing Third World denunciation of American colonialism in Palestine and the Middle East. Western countries, including Canada, continue to strongly defend America's theft of Arab oil and Israeli atrocities against Palestinian women and children. The West continues to see American aggression in the Middle East as a justified *holy war* against Islam.

They continue to dream of a day when the American Empire would be the new Roman Empire in the Middle East. The American Empire, in their view, must subjugate the Muslims like the Romans had subjugated the Jews, before Jews had converted to Christianity or Islam.

The Arabs, like the First Nations, can never hope to win a full blown war against the American Empire and Israel. They simply resist American colonization to whatever extent they can. In the five full blown wars since 1948, Israel has expanded its territory but not nearly as much as the American Empire had hoped. In the 1956 war Israel expanded its conquests by adding the *Gaza Strip* and the *Sinai Peninsula* but was forced to abandon them in 1957 because of strong protestations by the Soviet Union.

In return for the withdrawal of Israel from Egypt, the UN stationed forces in Egypt to guarantee Israel's access to the Indian Ocean via the Gulf of Aqaba. Egypt's sovereignty was once more emasculated by the West as the price it had to pay for Israel and the American Empire to retreat from

Rocky M. Mirza, Ph.D.

the Gaza and Sinai. This imperialist move by the West pushed Egypt and other Arab states into a stronger alliance with the Soviet Union.

The 1956 War was important not so much because of the territorial gains by Israel and the further weakening of the Arab League as any kind of military opposition to American expansionism in the Middle East, but for the ousting of Britain and France as key players in the region, much like the ousting of Britain and France as key players on the American continent after the American War of Independence. American propaganda had fooled the British and French for the second time in two centuries of Western imperialism. We have explained in Chapter 1 how the American Empire used the British Empire to reduce the French Empire in North America then used the French Empire to reduce the British Empire in North America. With this cunning removal of the two dominant European Empires in North America the American Empire expanded across the continent stealing every inch of First Nations land.

Like the North American continent, Britain and France had imperial ambitions in the Middle East long before the American Empire. But once again American cunning and propaganda would reduce the British and French to supporting roles in American domination of this region. Somewhat ironically it was Stalin's switch to supporting the Arab cause in 1956, as opposed to the Israeli cause in 1948, which gave the American Empire the leverage to oust the British and French.

In 1956 Britain and France could have taken on the Arab League without the American Empire. But the combined forces of Britain and France were no match for the Soviet Union. Only the American Empire could take on the Soviet Union. By refusing to take on the Soviet Union in 1956, President Eisenhower sent a clear message to Britain and France that they must play second fiddle to the American Empire in the Middle East. The American Empire will ask for British and French help when the American Empire goes to war in the region. But the American Empire would not support wars begun by Britain and France in the region.

Eisenhower's decision to refuse military support of the Anglo-French invasion of 1956 was the equivalent of a "Monroe Doctrine" for the Middle East. Like the Monroe Doctrine's declaration of American hegemony on the American continent, Eisenhower's decision to gamble on the **failure** of the Anglo-French invasion to reassert its imperial hegemony in the Middle East, was a declaration of unquestioned American hegemony in the Middle East. After 1956, the British and French, like Canada, would have to piggy-back their imperial aspirations and warmongering on the invasions initiated unilaterally by the American Empire. That they did so willingly and with such enthusiasm is another testimony to the success of American propaganda and the innate desire of the West to dominate the world and subjugate the **non-white** races.

Unlike the 1948 "War of Independence" which was instigated by the American Empire despite some opposition by Great Britain, the 1956 War was initiated by Britain and France. The Second World War had devastated the British and French economies making them dependent on American financial aid. But by 1956 the British and French economies had recovered sufficiently to prosper without further American financial aid. In that year Britain and France saw an opportunity to reassert their colonization of the Middle East. Having supported the American Empire fully in its Cold War against the Soviet Union these two Western powers foolishly assumed that the American Empire would back their imperialist actions in the Middle East, if only for the sake of the *Western-solidarity* argument, which the American Empire had always used to further its own empire. Sadly, Britain and France would learn once again, as it had with the American continent, that the United States supports only one empire, the American Empire. It uses Western nations as it uses Third World dictators to promote that single goal.

The British had a long imperial history in the Middle East and the French in North Africa. Egypt had been an important colony of Britain even before the British invasion of August 1882. French

250

imperial interests in the region led France to build and partially finance the building of the Suez Canal which opened in 1869. The Suez Canal was of strategic importance to Britain as an efficient sea route to its empire in India and Asia. Britain had forced the Ottoman Empire to allow Britain's ships free access through the canal. When the 1956 War began Britain had over 80,000 troops protecting its interest in the Canal Zone area.

Continued British colonialism in Egypt combined with the disastrous defeat by Israel in the 1948 War led to the overthrow of the Egyptian monarchy in July 1952 and the creation of a republic in June 1953. The president of the new republic, Gamal Nasser, was fully aware that his popularity depended on removing British imperialism from Egypt, including British control of the Suez Canal. In October 1954, Britain agreed to a phased withdrawal of its troops from the Canal Zone area. In anticipation of its imperial demise in Egypt Britain moved to consolidate its colonialism in Iraq and the neighbouring region by creating the *Baghdad Pact* on February 24, 1955. This was standard imperial strategy of dividing the Arab people to reduce the effectiveness of their opposition to foreign domination. President Nasser used the *Baghdad Pact* to promote Egypt to a leadership role in uniting the Arabs against British, French and American imperialism in the region.

Anglo-French control of the Suez Canal was the key symbol of continuing Western imperialism in Egypt. By 1956 the primary strategic importance of the canal was the transportation of Middle Eastern oil to Europe. President Nasser decided to challenge this Western symbol of colonialism by nationalizing the Suez Canal on July 26, 1956. Prior to this act both Egypt and Syria had increased their supplies of military equipment and military training personnel from non-Western countries in anticipation of a military attack from the West. Egypt had also formally recognized the Peoples Republic of China on May 16, 1956. This meant that both the Soviet Union and China would now oppose Western colonialism in the Middle East.

Britain and France responded to the nationalization of the Suez Canal by persuading Israel to invade the Sinai. An Anglo-French invasion would have been too overtly imperialistic. But an Israeli invasion could be more easily justified as just another attempt to acquire a defensive buffer for the Jewish state. The world was still very sympathetic to the idea of protecting Jews from world-wide persecution. Once Israel had invaded, Britain and France would send the usual Western "peace-keeping" forces and the Western media would trumpet the inherent selfless sacrifice of the West for the protection of freedom and democracy. In anticipation of the Israeli invasion France had supplied vast quantities of arms to Israel. The Western "peace-keepers" would ensure that the Suez Canal would be made into an international waterway to serve all humanity. The West would be portrayed as civilized and the east as barbaric.

The Israeli invasion began on October 29, 1956 under the command of two of Israel's future political leaders, General Moshe Dayan and Colonel Ariel Sharon. Given our assertion of important parallels between American imperial expansion in America and in the Middle East it is consistent with this assertion that military leaders in Israel would become future political leaders as in the United States. George Washington's rise to the presidency of the United States parallels David Ben-Gurion's rise to his election as the first Prime Minister of Israel. As in the United States with Washington's rise from first Commander-in-Chief to first President, Ben-Gurion's military leadership prior to the declaration of Israel's independence and subsequent rise to first Prime Minister laid the foundation for a culture of warmongering and hero worship of military leaders identical to the American Empire. See our discussion of what we have called the "Washington Syndrome" in *Rise and Fall of the American Empire*.

General Moshe Dayan was Chief of Staff of Israel's Defence Forces during the 1956 War. He had served David Ben-Gurion well during the 1948 War, rising to the position of Military Commander of Jerusalem. He was appointed to the position of Chief of Staff in 1953. He became Israel's Defence

Minister in 1967 and Foreign Minister in 1977. Major-General Ariel Sharon had also served David Ben-Gurion well. In the 1948 War he was injured but after the 1948 War he served Ben-Gurion as leader of Israel's first "special forces" unit, attacking and killing Palestinian civilians including women and children. His killing of 69 Palestinian civilians in the *Qibya massacre* in 1953 especially endeared him to Ben-Gurion. He became Israel's Minister of Defence in 1981 and was responsible for the *Sabra and Shatila massacres* of Palestinian refugees in 1982. He became Israel's Prime Minister in 2001.

The Anglo-French-Israeli war against Egypt scared the daylights out of the American Empire. Its success would restore Anglo-French imperialism in the Middle East and simultaneously restore British influence in Palestine and Israel. President Eisenhower quickly forced a cease-fire by threatening to sell the US holdings of Britain's debt incurred during World War II. Britain and France both vetoed a UN Security Council resolution to end the war only to find that their veto power had zero clout without American backing. The British economy could not survive a sell off of its US held debt. Britain abandoned France and Israel and announced a cease-fire on November 6, 1956. By March of 1957 British, French and Israeli forces had withdrawn from Egypt. Somewhat ironically the threat by the Soviet Union to intervene on behalf of Egypt played into the hands of the American Empire by scaring the Anglo-French-Israeli coalition.

President Eisenhower had sent a clear unambiguous message to Britain that its imperial aspirations in the post World War II era would be permitted only if it served the interest of the American Empire. During the nineteenth century American imperialism was permitted by Britain to the extent that it served the interest of the British Empire. Britain had now become the **junior** partner in an imperial partnership dating back to 1607, when Britain carved out and occupied the first of the 13 English colonies on First Nations land, along the Atlantic coastline of the American continent.

Israel was to be an American *uncolony* with no room for British meddling in Palestine unless Britain was requested by the American Empire to meddle for public relations or propaganda purposes. The special Anglo-American imperial partnership would continue as long as Britain did not question American motives, especially American warmongering and unilateral invasions. Britain, like Canada, would be expected to supply troops for these American invasions, if asked to do so by the American Empire. Britain and Canada must also recognize that the UN is a propaganda tool of the American Empire and must support all propaganda use of the UN to further American-British-Canadian-Western imperialism.

The PLO and the need for Guerrilla Warfare against American Imperialism in the Middle East

The American colonists had used guerrilla warfare against the superior fire power of the British to take the 13 colonies from Great Britain. With defeats in two wars against Israel the Palestinians recognized the need for guerrilla warfare. The *Palestine Liberation Organization, PLO,* was founded in 1964. It was recognized by the Arab states and the Arab League as representing the Palestinian people. Its primary goal was to "liberate" the Palestinian people from American-Israeli occupation of Palestinian land. To date it has had very little success in achieving this goal.

Israel has used its sophisticated air force to bomb PLO camps, including refugee camps and UN installations, in Jordan, Beirut, Gaza and the West Bank. Despite massive civilian casualties resulting from Israel's incessant bombing the Western press portrays Israeli atrocities as self-defence air strikes and PLO actions as **terrorism.** The killing of a single Israeli is used to justify the killing of hundreds of Palestinian women and children and the wholesale destruction of Palestinian infrastructure, homes and businesses. Israel imposes land, air and sea blockades to starve and kill the Palestinian people in the hopes that the PLO will abandon its goal of liberating the Palestinian people. Despite the unbelievable suffering inflicted by the American Empire, and the West, on the Palestinian people, the PLO continues the struggle as much as the First Nations continue to oppose the inferior status imposed on them by Canada and the US.

The Palestinian Refugee Problem

All wars create refugees. The Palestinian refugee problem is only unique because there have been so many wars and each new war adds to the number and suffering of the Palestinians. The **First** war in 1948 created as many as 800,000 Palestinian refugees. As with all wars, some Palestinians fled the war zone before the war began. Others fled during and shortly after the war. With each new war the numbers swelled. The long period of living in refugee camps, 1947-2010, led to children being born and growing up to be adults in these camps. When we include the increase from the births in the refugee camps, there are some five million Palestinian refugees today.

Palestinian refugees live in camps in Gaza and the West Bank as well as in camps in neighbouring Arab states including Jordan, Syria, Lebanon, Egypt and Saudi Arabia. With Israel and the American Empire continuing to bomb Syria, Lebanon, Gaza and Iraq, the plight of the Palestinian refugees in 2010 is worse than what it was in 1948.

Egypt Expels UN troops and is Invaded Again:
Third Arab-Israeli War: 1967

Egyptians were understandably enraged by the presence of UN forces within their borders especially when it was public knowledge that neither the American Empire nor Israel would ever permit UN forces within any territory conquered by Israel. In November 1966 Israel invaded Jordan despite Jordan's King Hussein's pro-American government. This unprovoked invasion by Israel sent a clear message to the entire Arab World that the American Empire would use Israel to expand its territory in the Middle East regardless of whether Arab governments were pro-American or pro-Soviet. King Hussein had falsely believed that an alliance with the US would guarantee Jordan's independence because of the Cold War between the US and the Soviet Union. The American Empire had forged numerous alliances with First Nations leaders only to renege on those treaties and alliances when it was sufficiently strong to conquer their lands. It would use the same strategy in the Middle East. Forge alliances with Arab leaders until it was timely to invade and conquer.

Israel's unprovoked invasion of Jordan led to heightened pressure on Egypt's President, Gamal Nasser, to expel the UN's forces stationed in Egypt. The UN had not punished Israel for its invasion of Jordan, passing yet another token resolution, Resolution 228 proposed by Nigeria and Mali, deploring the loss of life and destruction of property. On May 18, 1967, President Nasser informed the UN that its forces must leave Egypt by the end of June and that the Straits of Tiran would be closed to Israeli shipping after May 22, 1967. UN's Secretary-General, U Thant, sheepishly suggested that the UN forces be moved to Israel. It was clearly a tactless suggestion by the Secretary-General who keeps his job at the sole discretion of the American Empire. Israel not only refused UN forces on its soil but responded to Egypt's decision with a pre-emptive air strike on June 5, 1967, which totally destroyed the Egyptian air force. Israel then proceeded to re-capture Sinai and the Gaza Strip.

On the evening of June 5, 1967, the Israeli Air Force destroyed the Syrian Air Force after its successful strike in Egypt. With the Syrian Air Force destroyed Israel proceeded to conquer the Golan Heights. Jordan was convinced that one reason for Israel's unprovoked invasion in 1966 was to conquer the West Bank. With the much more powerful Egyptian air force destroyed Israel proceeded to wipe out the Jordanian air force with a single strike on June 6, 1967. Within six days, Israel had not only seized the West Bank, the Gaza Strip and Sinai but also East Jerusalem and the Golan Heights.

The American Empire was making good progress in expanding its territory in the Middle East via an expanding Israeli state.

By 1967, the American Empire had demonstrated that its modern air force could bring quick victories in a conventional war. Any country which dared to resist American aggression would have no choice but to resort to guerrilla warfare. The *Six-Day War* of June 5 to June 10, 1967, had demonstrated convincingly that the American Empire ruled the air waves much like the British Empire ruled the seas during its hegemony. The American Empire could colonize the entire Middle East by arming a tiny state like Israel with its superior firepower from the skies. Middle East and Palestinian resistance to American colonization would need to develop what may be viewed as "primitive" weapons. Methods used in countries like Vietnam to defeat American imperialism would have to be adapted to the Middle East terrain. Any "head-to-head" confrontation with an American armed Israel would be suicidal.

Using Oil as a Weapon of War: The *Fourth* Arab-Israeli War: 1973-74

By 1960, the countries in the Middle East were very much aware that they produced a commodity with high and growing demand in the West. That commodity was oil. Unfortunately, both the demand and supply was controlled by the West. The oil producers could do nothing about the demand but they could attempt to take control of the supply. One of the first steps in controlling the supply was collective action. This would be done by forming a *cartel*.

Cartels are the most common method used by countries to attempt to control the supply of a product much like the way in which a monopoly controls supply. Such cartels began in Germany since the 1870's. They are usually international because many countries, including Canada and the United States, have made domestic cartels illegal. There have been more than 200 cartels attempting to limit the supply of products such as diamonds, aluminum, steel, coffee, tin, sugar, bananas, rubber and chemicals. A cartel could never hope to exercise the same power as that of a monopoly but a cartel is the only option when there are several large suppliers.

Most cartels disintegrate within five to seven years. They suffer from two major disadvantages compared with a monopoly. Firstly, they need to agree on production quotas to limit supply. Agreement on quotas is often difficult to achieve and enforce. Members of the cartel have a profit incentive to cheat on production quotas. Secondly, countries which refuse to join the cartel will increase their supplies and new suppliers will likely enter the market. It is also important to understand that no supplier, not even a monopoly, controls demand. If demand falls more than a reduction in supply, price will still fall. There are also administrative costs to managing a cartel which can offset any price gain from a reduction of supply.

Despite the poor record of international cartels, the oil producers in the Middle East came together and formed a cartel, *OPEC,* in September 1960. While OPEC, like other cartels, was motivated by a desire to control supply by collective action to increase profits, it also understood that oil could be a weapon used to defend its territory against American colonization. OPEC had three important advantages over other cartels. The first was the strong political and military desire by its members to defend their resource and their political independence against Western imperialism. Members had both an economic and a political motivation to respect production quotas. The second advantage was that oil is a non-renewable resource. What is not produced today is saved for future profits. Countries have an incentive to conserve their non-renewable resources. The third advantage was the determination of the largest supplier of OPEC, Saudi Arabia, to cut its supplies below its quota to partially offset declines in demand.

In 1960, world demand for oil was very weak. However, government policies in the West kept oil price below the long-run free market price. This was motivated by the desire to provide consumers, especially *gas guzzling* American consumers, low gas prices. This artificially low price for oil, below $2.00 per barrel, encouraged wasteful consumption while simultaneously removing any incentive for producers to explore for new oil reserves. By 1971, 1960's excess supply had turned into *excess demand*. Price began to rise gradually from $1.80 in the 1960's to $2.24 in 1971, $2.48 in 1972 and $3.29 in 1973.

In 1973 OPEC saw an opportunity to use its oil both as a weapon of war and to boost profits. Membership in OPEC had expanded from four countries in 1960 to twelve countries in 1973. With the world market experiencing excess demand, a collective reduction in supply would boost the price of oil significantly. During the **Fourth** War against Israel in 1973-74 OPEC cut oil supplies and sent the price of a barrel of oil from $3.29 in 1973 to $11.58 in 1974. This near quadrupling of oil price made the world aware of OPEC, began a decade of high inflation in the West, sent economists scrambling to develop the AS/AD macroeconomic model to replace the outdated Keynesian model, and forced many North Americans to replace their gas guzzlers with Japanese cars which, in 1974, were poorly built and rusted quickly, but economical on gas consumption.

Egypt had paid a high price for standing up to American imperialism during the *Six-Day War* in 1967. Its leaders, first President Nasser and after his death in 1970, President Anwar Sadat, were under intense pressure from Egyptians and the Arab World to continue to oppose American and Israeli territorial expansion in the Middle East and aid the Palestinian resistance. Syria had also lost the Golan Heights in the 1967 war. Egypt and Syria formed a strong alliance to regain the territories lost in the 1967 war. Both countries looked to the Soviet Union for arms. Unfortunately, the weapons supplied to Egypt and Syria by the Soviet Union were not as technologically advanced as those provided to Israel by the American Empire. The American Empire had also aided Israel in acquiring nuclear weapons.

Despite Israel's nuclear and advanced weaponry, Egypt and Syria decided to launch a surprise pre-emptive strike against Israel on October 6, 1973. The Arab Nations had learnt how devastating a pre-emptive strike can be when Israel had used it in the 1967 war. This time the Arabs would have that advantage. In addition the Arab Nations were threatening the West with an oil embargo if they came to the defence of Israel. As we explained above OPEC was formed in 1960 partly as a weapon against Western imperialism in the Middle East. By 1973 the excess demand for oil in the world gave OPEC the economic clout it needed, compared with 1967, when oil was still in relatively plentiful supply.

Unfortunately for the Arab Nations they had three important strikes against them. Firstly, only the Western European countries took any notice of the threatened oil embargo. They ceased supplying munitions to Israel. But the key player, the American Empire, totally ignored the threat of an OPEC oil embargo. Secondly, the American Empire stood ready to supply as much war materials and economic aid as required to ensure an Israeli victory. The Soviet Union would not reciprocate either in the 1967 or 1973 war. In fact, by 1973 the Soviet leader, Leonid Brezhnev, was seeking détente with the West because of his incompetence and a crumbling Russian economy. Brezhnev was no Stalin or Khrushchev.

The Soviet Union was led by a long list of incompetents after Stalin and Khrushchev until Vladimir Putin took charge of Russia in 2000. Moreover, the Soviet Union and China began a family feud in the 1960's which worsened under Brezhnev's leadership. By 1973 both the Russian and Chinese leaders were courting friendship with the American Empire because of their deepening family feud and disastrous economic policies. Central Planning as a macroeconomic model, which could challenge the older Free Enterprise macroeconomic model of the West, was seen by Russian and Chinese leaders as responsible for the poor performance of their economies compared to those in the United States and Western Europe. They saw political co-operation with the West together with the Western Free Enterprise macroeconomic model, as their only economic salvation.

The third important strike against the Arab Nations was Israel's nuclear capability. The American Empire had used nuclear weapons against Japan and would have used them against China during the Korean War if the Soviet Union had not threatened a retaliatory strike. The pre-emptive air strikes by Egypt and Syria on October 6, 1973 had caught Israel and the American Empire by surprise. It gave the Arab Nations an advantage similar to that achieved by Israel with its pre-emptive air strike during the *Six Day War*. By October 7, Israeli losses were so great that Prime Minister Golda Meir began preparations for nuclear attacks on both Egypt and Syria the next day.

The American Empire warned Egypt of the impending nuclear strike. Egyptian President Anwar Sadat recognised the dilemma of the Arab situation. Arab victories with conventional weapons would bring nuclear retaliation by Israel. The Soviet leaders, Brezhnev and Alexei Kosygin, did not have the backbone to threaten nuclear confrontation with the American Empire as Stalin had done during the Korean War. World opinion would support Israel's use of nuclear weapons in the same way it had supported the American nuclear attacks on Japan. The Western media would pull out its massive propaganda arsenal to ensure that.

The Arab Nations would be forced to accept another military defeat by Israel. The American Empire and the West had armed Israel with nuclear weapons while denying a nuclear deterrent to the Arab Nations. This was the ultimate guarantee of continued American imperialism in the Middle East. Egyptian President, Anwar Sadat, understood this reality and chose to sacrifice the Arab/Palestinian cause for what he could achieve for Egypt.

The Soviet Union and the American Empire negotiated the terms of a cease-fire on October 22, 1973. Despite the cease-fire agreement, UN resolutions and a Geneva summit, fighting continued until May of 1974. The Egyptians decided to hold direct cease-fire talks with the Israelis on October 28, 1973. This reality check by Anwar Sadat paved the way for the *Camp David Accords* and a separate peace agreement between Egypt and Israel which was not signed until March 1979. Israel returned the Sinai Peninsula to Egypt. In return Egypt agreed to Israeli use of the Suez Canal, the Straits of Tiran and the Gulf of Aqaba. The Arab Nations felt betrayed by Sadat. With both Saudi Arabia and Egypt led by governments which favoured reconciliation with the West there seemed to be no important Arab state willing to sacrifice its economy for the Arab/Palestinian cause. Smaller states such as Libya would attempt to fill the void left by Egypt but with little success.

The 1982 War in Lebanon: The *Fifth* Arab-Israeli War

Oil and a pre-emptive air strike had not destroyed either Israel or American imperialism in the Middle East. The governments of Egypt, Jordan and Saudi Arabia had chosen to live with the reality of Israel and American imperialism despite the opposition of their people. But the war with Israel and the West was far from over. Opposition to American imperialism would spread outwards from the Middle East to a wider Muslim World and beyond. Conventional wars against the American Empire would continue but the backbone of the resistance would be guerrilla warfare. Nations would also search for ways to acquire nuclear deterrents.

The 1982 War in Lebanon is usually referred to as the **fifth** Arab-Israeli war. However, there have been **four** full blown wars and invasions of Lebanon by Israel, 1948, 1978, 1982 and 2006. Israel first invaded Lebanon during the Arab-Israeli war of 1948. Israel's victory in the 1948 war led it to occupy Southern Lebanon. During the 1948 war over 100,000 Palestinian refugees fled into

Lebanon laying the foundations of an ongoing guerrilla war against Israel that would be waged from guerrilla bases in Lebanon.

The 1982 war and invasion were waged by Israel and the American Empire to crush the guerrilla resistance by the PLO. The PLO had initially established its primary base of operations in Jordan. However, even before the creation of the PLO, Jordan and King Hussein never fully supported the land claims of the Palestinians. Jordan held fast to its own claims to territories such as the West Bank and East Jerusalem, which were claimed by the Palestinians. Despite this uneasy alliance between Jordan and the Palestinian cause, Jordan tolerated the PLO's base of operations in Jordan until "Black September" 1970.

Jordan began a military crack down against the PLO base in Jordan following the humiliating defeat of the Arab states in the Six-Day 1967 Arab-Israeli War. Jordan had always steered a middle course between support for the West and support for the Palestinian cause. But the 1967 defeat by Israel forced King Hussein to take a more militaristic stance against the PLO's guerrilla base in Jordan because of increased military attacks on Jordan by the victorious Israelis. In 1968 Israel had launched a full scale attack on the PLO base in the village of Karameh in Jordan. With the help of Jordan's military the PLO survived this Israeli invasion. But relations between the PLO and King Hussein steadily worsened.

As a guerrilla operation the PLO could not win a full frontal battle with Jordan's armed forces. With some military assistance from Israel, the United States and Britain, Jordan launched such a full frontal attack on the PLO guerrilla bases in Jordan, during September 1970. This military operation by Jordan came to be known as *Black September* and forced the gradual retreat of the PLO base in Jordan to Southern Lebanon. In Lebanon the PLO joined forces with the half a million Palestinian refugees driven from their homes by the Israeli occupation of their land and with many Lebanese opposed to American imperialism in Lebanon and in the Middle East.

In Lebanon the American Empire and Israel were generally supported by Lebanese Christians engaged in a long civil war with Lebanese Muslims. Lebanese Christians had long opposed fundamental human rights to the Palestinian refugees simply because of their religious beliefs. It was natural for the PLO, the Palestinian refugees and Lebanese Muslims to join forces against Israel, the American Empire and Lebanese Christians. As we have pointed out American imperialism is supported by many Christians everywhere who see it as a *holy war* against Islam. The Lebanese Civil War between Muslims and Christians took place between 1975 and 1990. Israel invaded Lebanon twice during its Civil War hoping to exploit the Civil War for its own desire to conquer and colonize Lebanon.

Operation Litani

Israel formally invaded Lebanon on March 14, 1978 beginning the **fifth** Arab-Israeli War which has continued to this day. Each invasion inflicts massive destruction of the Lebanese infrastructure, kills thousands of Lebanese civilians, including women and children, destroys homes and businesses, violates all UN resolutions, kills UN soldiers and destroys UN property, commits the most heinous war crimes and brings massive starvation, poverty and disease to the Lebanese people. Israel never denies these war crimes but justifies them by blaming the resistance of the people whose land it steals.

Israeli soldiers numbering over 25,000 crossed the Lebanese border during the night of March 14, 1978 with the objective of wiping out the PLO base in Lebanon. This invasion was code-named *Operation Litani* and Israel occupied Lebanese territory south of the Litani River. The invasion killed 2,000 Lebanese civilians and added to the Palestinian refugee problem. It also created a Lebanese refugee problem since many villages had been so damaged that they became uninhabitable. As usual, this addition of conquered Middle Eastern land to an ever expanding Israeli *uncolony* of the American Empire was justified as another "buffer zone" for the protection of the Jewish population. But these punitive and barbaric invasions have the single goal of expanding American imperialism in the Middle East. The people of the Middle East are not fooled by Western propaganda to the contrary. That is precisely why each war and invasion launched by Israel and the American Empire only strengthens the guerrilla resistance and adds to the number of guerrilla fighters willing to give their lives to defend their land against the overwhelming fire power, air power and media propaganda of the enemy.

Operation Peace for the Galilee

In preparation for a third war and invasion of Lebanon, Israel killed 300 civilians and wounded another 800 in a single bombing raid on July 17, 1981. This third Israeli ground invasion of Lebanon began on June 6, 1982. Its code name was *Operation Peace for the Galilee*. As in the previous invasions, Israel was supported by Lebanese Christians. The stated goal of this third invasion was to crush the PLO and expand the Lebanese territory occupied by Israel. Once again this theft and occupation of more land in the Middle East was justified on the grounds that the Jews needed to be protected. As Europeans invaded the American continent they drove the First Nations further and further west so that they could better defend the land they had stolen and occupied. In like manner Israel needed to steal and occupy more and more Muslim land to protect what they had previously stolen.

This third Israeli invasion killed another 20,000 military personnel and civilians. Another 30,000 were wounded. Israel's three wars and invasions killed over 100,000 Lebanese and wounded another 200,000. American pressure for the PLO to abandon its base in Lebanon intensified as the casualties from the Israeli invasion increased. The American military arrived in Lebanon on August 20, 1982 to force the PLO to retreat from Lebanon. This show of force by the American military led to the PLO moving its base of operations from Lebanon to Tunisia in September 1982.

The American military in Lebanon became the primary target of the guerrilla resistance against Israel and the American Empire. On April 18, 1983 the guerrillas succeeded in exploding a bomb at the US embassy in West Beirut. On October 23, 1983 a suicide bombing succeeded in killing 241 American soldiers at the US marine barracks in Beirut. Israel and the American Empire won the wars but the Arab resistance was never defeated or deterred. The 1982-83 Israeli-US invasion of Lebanon forced the PLO to retreat to Tunisia but created an even stronger guerrilla resistance movement in Lebanon, *Hezbollah*.

The Rise of *Hezbollah*

Unlike the American continent the American Empire creates more and stronger enemies in the Middle East with each new war. By 1983 the resistance coming from Egypt and Jordan had subsided but the resistance from Lebanon, Iran, Iraq and Syria was getting more determined. Israel and the American Empire had hoped to use the Lebanese Civil War to ensure an easy conquest of Lebanon. When they retreated in 1985, the Lebanese resistance led by *Hezbollah* and supported by Iran and Syria, was stronger than before their invasions of 1978 and 1982.

The fact that six Western nations, including Canada, have determined that it is vital to their propaganda campaign against Islam to declare *Hezbollah* a terrorist organization, speaks volumes to the utter failure of the American-Israeli invasions and attempted colonization of Lebanon. During the Lebanese Civil War between the Muslims and Christians, 1975-1990, Israel supplied military advisors and military equipment to the Lebanese Christians. A Christian victory would have made it easy for the American Empire to colonize Lebanon by installing a pro-American leader such as Bachir Gemayel, military leader of the Lebanese Christians. But the strategy backfired when this explicit external support of the Christian faction in a Civil War rallied the Muslim World to the plight of the Lebanese Muslims. Gemayel was assassinated on September 14, 1982 for aiding the American Empire and Israel in the invasion of his own country. Gemayel had met and colluded with both Israel's defence minister, Ariel Sharon and Israel's Prime minister, Menachem Begin. President Reagan condemned his assassination thereby implicitly condoning treason.

The formation of the Lebanese Guerrilla Resistance known as *Hezbollah* was inspired by the American-Israeli intervention in the Lebanese Civil War. The Western media's many attempts to link Iran and Syria to *Hezbollah* is laughable. Why should the Muslim World *not* support Hezbollah? The American Empire publicly supports Israel and the Lebanese Christians? The question should *not* be whether Iran or Syria supports Hezbollah? What should be questioned is the right of the West to determine who Muslims should support in the just struggle for Muslim lands in the Middle East? It's the West that is invading Muslim lands and killing Muslim women and children indiscriminately.

The world should be questioning the right of the American Empire to subjugate the peoples of the Middle East, colonize their land and steal their resources such as oil. No objective human being would question the right of Iran or Syria, or any other Muslim state, to support the resistance movement of Muslims in Lebanon against American or Israeli imperialism. Since the Second World War, every war in the Middle East, without exception, has been caused by American imperialism. The West knows that and Canada knows that. That is the reason for their incessant media propaganda against all of the Muslim resistance movements and their current paranoia at the thought of Iran enhancing its nuclear capability.

Hezbollah's primary goal is to defeat American-Israeli imperialism in Lebanon. It's no different from the earlier resistance movements in Cuba or the Philippines, born out of the need to defeat American colonization in those countries. Such resistance movements prior to the end of the cold war were branded *communists* by the Western media. Today the Western media prefer the term *terrorists*. Communism is no longer such an evil word. The propaganda aims of the Western media have not changed only the language used is revised and updated.

Israel's 2006 Invasion of Lebanon

At the time of the 1982 invasion of Lebanon by Israel, Hezbollah was a tiny unknown militia. When Israel invaded in 2006 it was not to root out the PLO guerrilla bases but the Hezbollah underground resistance movement. By 2006, Hezbollah was widely supported by all segments of the Lebanese population. It was now the most capable of the many resistance movements which had sprung up in Lebanon since the American-Israeli military invasions began in 1948. As such it was the primary target of the 2006 American-Israeli invasion.

During the 2006 war and invasion of Lebanon, Israel continued its long history of targeting the civilian population as well as destroying homes, businesses and the economic infrastructure of Lebanon. Over 1,000 Lebanese civilians, including women and children, were killed. As in the previous wars and invasions, the Lebanese people showed the world their grief and suffering, but were not defeated in their desire to defend their homeland against the most **cowardly** actions of the world's only superpower.

American and Israeli pilots rained down the most deadly and destructive bombs, safely ensconced in their fighter jets flying high above the reach of the primitive firepower of the Lebanese resistance movements. Only after they had destroyed the capability of the enemy with their aircrafts did they invade with ground forces to kill harmless civilians and frightened and disarmed guerrillas. Such **cowardice** is never reported by the Western media. Instead the Western media call the guerrilla fighters cowards. The West turns logic on its head and gets away with it.

The Gaza Massacre: 2008-2009

In December of 2008 Israel launched a full scale air and land invasion of the Gaza Strip. The Gaza Strip is a tiny 360 square kilometres of coastline on the Mediterranean Sea where close to 1.5 million Palestinians eke out a miserable living under Israeli occupation. Most of the Palestinians are refugees and descendants of refugees who fled the incessant American instigated Israeli wars. Israel occupied the Gaza Strip after invading and conquering it during the 1967 War. Israel controls all movements of people and goods in and out of Gaza by air, land and sea.

In an effort to hold the *colonized* land in Gaza, Israel began to settle Jews in Gaza. We have argued that this pattern of conquest and settlement was based on the successful conquest of First Nations land by the American Empire on the American continent. The Palestinians resisted in ways similar to all colonial peoples. One of the more successful resistance movements was *Hamas*. The easiest way to identify a **successful** resistance movement against American-Israeli imperialism is if Canada declares it a *terrorist* organization. Canada revels in being one of the most outspoken mouth pieces of the American Empire.

Hamas came to prominence in yet another of the ironies of Western double talk and conceit. Long fed up with Arafat's leadership of the Palestinian resistance, the American Empire cajoled the Palestinians into holding free and fair elections. The Palestinians, embracing any request from the West that may end their misery, decided to hold free and fair elections in January 2006. In those elections *Hamas* defeated Arafat's Fatah party, 76 seats to 43. At the time Fatah was led by Mahmoud Abbas who had succeeded Arafat after his death on November 11, 2004. In 2003, the American Empire had pressured Arafat into appointing Abbas as Prime Minister of the Palestinian National Authority.

When America's anointed Palestinian leader, Mahmoud Abbas, was trounced in the American imposed **democratic** elections, by Hamas, the American Empire determined that democracy was **evil** since it produced terrorist governments like Hamas. Canada was quick to jump on the bandwagon and denounce democracy as well.

Canada, the United States, Israel, Australia and the United Kingdom determined that the January 2006 Palestinian elections proved that *democracy* could not be trusted. Western **democracy** is only *democratic* under conditions where it produces governments subservient to the needs of American imperialism and its Western lackeys like Canada. If it produces governments which cater to the needs and interests of the electorate then those governments must be declared to be "terrorist organizations." All Western countries must stand firm on this view as it's a great excuse to widen the "war on terror."

Since the relative demise of communism as an acceptable excuse for warmongering a new **evil** must be found. That evil today is "state sponsored terrorism." **Democratically** elected governments like Hamas must be propagandized as the new threat to Western civilization. Only the West is civilized enough to know what is best for humanity. The civilized West condoned African slaves, genocide of First Nations, indiscriminate use of nuclear weapons, and abuse of children by Catholic priests in Canadian residential schools, just to mention a few of their "civilized" deeds.

The 2008 Israeli invasion of Gaza has been called a *massacre* instead of a war. It targeted Palestinian civilians, including women and children. At least 1,500 Palestinians were killed and thousands were left homeless to add to the refugee numbers. Homes, businesses, factories, government buildings, mosques, water, sewage and other infrastructure were destroyed by heavy bombing from the air. Estimated monetary cost exceeded $2 billion. The day the deadly air strikes began, December 27, 2008, has been rightly called *Massacre of Black Saturday,* because it killed 230 Palestinians and injured over 700 more, on a single day. This deadly invasion by a sophisticated air force against unarmed civilians has been condemned by the world. Yet both President **Obama** and Secretary of State **Hillary Clinton** have justified these heinous crimes against humanity by saying, "Israel has a right to defend itself." Canada continues its ridiculous assertion that Hamas, not Israel, is the terrorist organization.

When did naked aggression against civilians whose land you have colonized become self defence? As the American Empire turned the meaning of **democracy** on its head when Hamas was elected so have they turned **self-defence** on its head when they invade far off lands like Vietnam, Afghanistan, Iraq and Pakistan or Israel invades Palestinian land in the Middle East? Israel used modern heavy bombs and penetration bombs and targeted homes, killing entire families, including women and children. Civilians had no bomb shelters where they could take cover and Israel knew that. During the ground invasion which followed, Israeli soldiers later testified that there were indiscriminate civilian killings by the Israeli Defence Force, IDF.

Israel earlier denied but later admitted that its soldiers fired incendiary white phosphorous munitions at civilians. The IDF has also been accused of using civilians as human shields. Israel also made it extremely difficult for humanitarian aid to reach civilians with medical supplies, food and drinking water. Israel targeted and killed 16 health care workers employed by the World Health Organization and injured another 22. Israel also targeted and killed 5 UN personnel and injured another 11. On January 15, 2009 Israel bombed and destroyed food and fuel which the UN was storing for the one million Palestinian refugees in Gaza. Its land, air and sea blockade of Gaza has continued to this day. Gazans continue to die of starvation and children continue to die because of a lack of medical facilities. Power and fuel shortages are endemic. The Red Cross correctly points out that the blockade makes it impossible for Gazans to even begin to rebuild their war torn economy. Israel brazenly argues that its blockade is justified because the life of **one** Israeli soldier, Gilad Shalit, captured by Hamas is worth more than the lives of 1,400 Palestinians prisoners held by Israel.

President Obama is talking about negotiating a Peace Agreement between Israel and the Palestinians while sending high level American emissaries to the Middle East region. His latest public relations propaganda has been the appointment of George Mitchell as special envoy to the Middle East. Obama very cleverly ignores the decades of American-Israeli aggression against the Palestinian people and the root cause of the never ending crises in the Middle East. If there ever were an uncaring two-faced American president that would be Obama, never mind his more outspoken side-kick, Hillary Clinton. President Obama definitely speaks with a "forked tongue," and knows exactly how to fool his worldwide ardent supporters. Hillary Clinton speaks her mind defending Israel's right to self defence more than President George W. Bush ever did. If ever there was a man with so much promise and so little substance it would be President Obama. He is destined to dash the hopes and aspirations of so many. Palestinians, foolish enough to think he is any different from George W. Bush, or any previous American president, will be among the most disillusioned.

If Arab states fail to unite and drive out the American Empire from the Middle East, like China and Vietnam did from their countries, they will suffer the same fate as the First Nations of the American continent. The American Empire will never voluntarily relinquish its imperialistic and warmongering ways. Its invasions have to be defeated in battle as the Vietnamese did, as Mao Zedong did, and as the Taliban is doing now in Afghanistan. Empires will never be appeased by exemplary behaviour of their colonists. They are too greedy to share their conquests with those colonized. Empires must be forced out by long and determined resistance. Those who sacrifice their lives to bring down any empire, especially one as **evil** as the American Empire, must be praised and held in high esteem, not branded as cowards or terrorists.

There is some indication that in 2010 Arab states may rally around the Gaza blockade and Israel's attack on the *Freedom Flotilla*. It appears as if Turkey may step up to the plate and lead yet one more concerted effort by the Arab/Muslim World to roll back Western/Israeli atrocities and imperialism in the Middle East. Turkey's population of 75 million is 99 percent Muslim. Turkey's Prime Minister since 2003, Recep Tayyip Erdogan, has been the most outspoken critic of both Israel's blockade of Gaza and Israel's attack on the *Freedom Flotilla*. Erdogan is being hailed as the new "Gamal Nasser" of the Middle East. With Turkey's GDP as much as half the total GDP of the entire Middle East and its Public Debt as a percent of GDP falling to under 40% by 2010 when that of the US has risen to 100%, Turkey feels confident that it can lead a challenge to American imperialism in the region. In 2003 Turkey refused the American request to launch a ground offensive in Iraq through Turkish territory. Turkish opposition to George W. Bush's 2003 invasion of Iraq is reflected by a 2007 poll result showing only 9% of Turks having a favourable view of the US. As US-Turkey relation has deteriorated Turkey has improved its relation with Iran, Russia, Syria, Brazil, Sudan, Libya and many other states which in the past were much more anti-American than Turkey.

CHAPTER 10

Till Debt Do Us Part: How the Mighty American Empire Crumbled?

We have argued that America was a very sick society from birth. Its power and influence came, not from human values or civilized principles, but from the barrel of a gun. Its economy and military dwarfed all others. It was respected and feared because of its wealth, reckless consumerism, successful propaganda and the desperate poverty of those it ruled over with an iron fist. In the twenty-first century it faces competition from the BRIC countries, Brazil, Russia, India and China, when its own economy is sputtering and its voracious appetite for debt will bankrupt its once mighty military-industrial complex. At the height of its dominance it renewed an old war between Christians and Muslims with a confidence born out of its deep seated ignorance, unbridled arrogance and innate contempt for peace. It will lose this war along with its dominant economic status. Its sputtering economy cannot support this war and this war will bury its economy under a volume of debt the world could never have envisaged.

America has never elected visionary leaders. Their media and mindset is one of pandering to the lowest common denominator. If we look at the last three presidents, the media portrays Bill Clinton and Barak Obama as smart visionary leaders because they can read their lines correctly when they give speeches. George Bush was portrayed as less smart or even dumb because he made a few mistakes when he read his lines. In reality, Bush may very well have been smarter than Clinton or Obama. What is certain is that neither Clinton nor Obama were leaders with any kind of vision for America or the world. They had the smarts and intelligence by the criterion which the Western media and the American masses judged them. They could quickly absorb great masses of trivial information and spout it back in a reasoned and coherent way to the American people. By this criterion if you made trivial errors with data, geography, history, or political, racial, homophobic and gender sensitivities, for example, you would be deemed incompetent. No one judged you on substance because you were judged by people with even less vision than you had. If you had any vision you would have been weeded out by the political process long before you got elected as the candidate for your party. You would never have even been given the chance to run for the presidency.

Left wing supporters of Presidents Clinton and Obama are often shocked at the close friendship between Bill Clinton and both George Bush and his father, President Herbert Bush. Like President Obama, all American presidents are elected to "restore America's greatness, American principles, American superiority, American dominance, American propaganda, American religion, American know-how, American culture, American government, American media, American view of freedom,

American consumerism, American militarism, American WMD's, American foreign policy, American pride, American sovereignty, American loyalty, American prisons, American torture, American conceit and American bullying." A vision to make America or the world a better place will not get you elected to the American presidency.

Despite all the hype and rhetoric around Obama's vision for a new beginning his presidency will change nothing. He will continue the policies of George W. Bush and all those who came before him. It was not, for example, the least surprising to me that President Obama would ask the much despised former Republican President, George W. Bush, to head up his response to the devastating earthquake which struck the Caribbean island of Haiti on January 12, 2010 any more than it was surprising to me that President George W. Bush had asked former Democratic President, Bill Clinton, to head up his response to the devastating tsunami caused by the underwater Indian Ocean earthquake of December 26, 2004. Who is better qualified to use the opportunity provided by an economic disaster to strengthen American imperialism in the region receiving American economic and military aid than a former American Commander-in-Chief? These examples support my position that there is no substantive difference between Republicans and Democrats, especially when it comes to American foreign policy.

The Global Shift of Economic Power and the Great Recession of 2008-2010

America will change because the rest of the world will force America to change. America will not change because of Obama's "inspired" leadership. America will change because the rest of the world has inspired leadership. America had "piggy-backed" its empire on the European empires which came into existence after Vasco Da Gama found the sea route to Asia and Christopher Columbus re-discovered the Caribbean and the American continent. The economic base of the world was centred in Western Europe and the United States for five centuries.

In the 21st century the economic base of the world is shifting from countries with an abundance of capital to countries with an abundance of people. The West will lose its economic dominance to Asia and the Third World. At the same time the BRIC countries of Brazil, Russia, India and China, as well as other Asian and Latin American countries, are showing leadership qualities which far surpass any in the West. The lack of visionary leadership combined with relative economic decline will relegate the American Empire to a true partnership with other countries. It will no longer dictate to the world. The 21st century will see the end of American **dictatorship.** If America survives, and there is no reason to doubt that it will, it will be a smaller, kinder, gentler America minding its own business and cooperating as an equal, not as the big bully, in international trade, investment, institutions and governance, like all other large countries.

In this smaller, co-operative, role it's possible that the small minority of Americans who are the visionary leaders of the American Empire will finally get an opportunity to lead the American Empire in a new direction away from warmongering and imperial subjugation of others to peaceful coexistence with the rest of humanity. The world is full of challenging needs from eradication of diseases and hunger to natural disasters. There is absolutely no need for warmongering and military invasions to keep Americans fully employed.

Capitalism will fall in a way very different from what Karl Marx envisaged. The world is being transformed by Western capitalists taking their factories and free enterprise to the centres of cheap labour. As the masses of the densely populated Third World empower themselves with Western capital their incomes rise while real wages in the West must fall. This important change in relative wages is the key to understanding America's deep recession which no amount of massive bailouts will solve.

Unfortunately for President Obama and diehard Roosevelt Keynesians the Reaganomics Supply-siders have the better economic diagnosis and cure for what ails America in 2010. Lou Dobbs, CNN chief spokesperson on the supposed evils of outsourcing until his resignation on November 11, 2009, and other like-minded CNN reporters, may have the right propaganda, but American jobs are not being outsourced by unpatriotic American capitalists, but because of the new economic reality.

The "Lou Dobbs" solution of having the American government ban outsourcing by American corporations and reducing trade with China will grind America's economy to a halt. Outsourcing and trade with China is what props up an ailing American economy. Outsourcing keeps American corporations competitive and trade with China brings relief to relatively impoverished American consumers as their real incomes fall, as they must in the new global economy. Lower priced Chinese imports partially offset the pain of lower real wages and higher unemployment rates experienced by American workers. If America does not outsource to use cheap labour it will not be able to compete with Europe or Japan. Its exports will decline even more and the value of the once mighty greenback will fall to the level of the Mexican peso.

In the 1980's economists developed an Aggregate Supply/Aggregate Demand, AS/AD, Model to update the Keynesian Model. The Keynesian Model had worked well for FDR as a solution for the Great Depression. But the supply shock caused by the quadrupling of the price of oil in 1973-74 and growing government deficits to pay for health care, education, social welfare and other new government programs after 1973, made it clear to a growing number of economists that the Keynesian Model needed serious re-tuning. Governments cannot ignore the Supply half of their economies. The Keynesian Model is based exclusively on the Demand half of the economy.

The current American economic crisis was caused by an over stimulation of Aggregate Demand by both American consumers and the American government during the eight years of the George W. Bush administrations. It cannot be solved by the same kinds of Keynesian stimulus used by President Roosevelt during the Great Depression. It requires the Supply-side tools explained in the AS/AD model. Many die-hard Keynesians like to quote Keynes' famous line, "In the long- run we are dead," when many economists criticised Keynes for focusing exclusively on the short-run. Its time "Supply-side" economists say to President Obama and his current team of economic advisors that "Keynes is dead." Keynes' solutions for the Great Depression have no applicability to America's current economic woes. If Keynes were alive today he would be the first to recognize that.

In the AS/AD model, an important solution for any recession is a decline in real wages. There is overwhelming evidence that the shift in global production from the high wage West to the low wage Third World requires a readjustment of relative wages. American real wages must fall to enable it to compete with the Third World. Such a fall in real wages will shift the AS curve to the right and increase employment in the United States, while reducing inflation. The Obama Keynesian stimulus, on the other hand, will shift the AD curve to the right, creating only some **short-term** increase in employment at the cost of increased inflation. The employment gains will evaporate in the long-term since real wages would not have fallen as required by the new global reality. More importantly, the crowding-out effects of financing the huge deficit inherent in a Keynesian AD shift solution will also severely reduce the gain in employment as the AD curve shifts back to the left. Financing the deficit inherent in the Keynesian solution will bury the American Empire in debt.

If China, Saudi Arabia, Japan, Caribbean bankers, and other foreign lenders doubt America's ability to repay its foreign debt or meet its interest payments, they will stop lending. A foreign credit crunch will bring about both lower real wages **and** massive unemployment. While a policy induced AS shift means lower real wages, it will increase, not reduce, employment. Americans lived beyond their means during the George W. Bush years. They must reduce their real wages and their consumption to re-pay what they borrowed, with interest. In addition they must accept permanently lower real wages because of the shift of the global economy in favour of the low wage Third World workers. There is no other **long-term** solution. Americans must also reduce the drain on their standard of living caused by their desire to spend on unproductive military more than the rest of the world combined. As the war in Iraq has proved, stealing the resources of weaker countries by invading and conquering them is no longer profitable. When the cost of defending colonies exceed the economic benefits from exploiting their natural resources it's time to roll back the empire, bring the troops home and live within your defendable borders.

In this final chapter we will trace the relative economic decline of the United States since 1950. The Second World War, more than any other single incident, promoted the American Empire to top Dog, knocking off rivals such as the British Empire, the German Empire, the Japanese Empire, the French Empire and the Russian Empire. American GDP continued to grow *relative* to the world until 1950, after which, the devastated economies of Western Europe, Russia and Japan rebuilt, and the Third World economies struggled for economic independence. In this chapter we will also address the drain on America's *shrinking share* of the World's GDP as it fights the Cold War against communism, as well as hot wars in Latin America, Vietnam, Afghanistan and Iraq. This combination of the rest of the world growing faster than the American Empire and wasteful wars across the globe was bound to end America's dominance prematurely. It is true that the American Empire dominated Latin America and the Caribbean for two centuries, but in terms of being a *global* empire, like the British or Spanish or Roman, its reign will be less than a century, a mere blip in time.

Part I: America's Relative Economic Decline: 1950-2010

We begin with the economic decline because no empire can support the military and policing costs of superpower status without a large and growing economic base. For a short period, excessive costs of empire can be sustained by borrowing. But as every smart person knows you cannot sustain deficit spending for long, much less indefinitely. Historical statistics for the World economies indicate that in 1950, the GDP of the US was **27%** of the World's GDP. In addition, the 27 countries of Western Europe accounted for another 26% of the World's GDP. Adding Canada, Australia and New Zealand, the US and its closest Western allies accounted for **57%** of the World's GDP. The latest comparable data from the same source was for 2003. In 2003, the US GDP had fallen to 21% while the combined GDP of the US and its closest Western allies had fallen to **43%.** Since 1995, Asia's real GDP has grown more than twice as fast as the US and its closest Western allies. With Asia, Latin America, the Middle East and Russia growing much faster than the West during the first decade of the 21st century it is safe to say that both the GDP of the US and that of its closest Western allies have shrunk *relatively,* much more by 2010. We will provide several measures to support this claim.

We can begin to support this claim by looking at economic data on the relative **rise** of the Third World in the period 1950-2010, since the Third World is largely made up of the countries **not** recognized by the West, as among America's closest Western allies. By documenting the relative economic rise of important segments of the Third World such as Asia and BRIC, Brazil, Russia, China and India, especially in the last two decades, we provide complementary evidence of America's relative economic decline. In 1950, Asia accounted for 19% of the World's GDP. By 2003, Asia's contribution had increased to **41%.** In 1950, the contribution of the US at 27% exceeded that of Asia, at 19%. By 2003 Asia's contribution was **twice** that of the US. In 1950, the BRIC countries accounted for only 16% of the World's GDP. By 2003, the contribution of the BRIC countries had increased to **26%.** Once again, in 1950 the US contribution was larger than BRIC, 27% vs. 16%. This was reversed by 2003, 21% vs. 26%.

During the first decade of the 21st century half of the growth of the world's GDP came from Asia. Economic growth is historically linked to international trade. In 1950 the US accounted for 18% of the World's exports. By 2010 the US share of the World's exports had shrunk to 8% while that of China had grown to 10%. The other Asian giant, Japan, accounted for 5% of the World's exports in 2010. With the exception of Japan, the Asian economies have recovered much quicker from the "Great Recession" of 2008-09 than the US and its closest Western allies. Asia is projected to grow at 7% in 2011 while the US and its closest Western allies are projected to grow at only 2%.

We have argued before that the British Empire declined after World War II not only because of the relative decline in its economic base as measured by GDP, but also because of the huge debt it incurred during World War II. Likewise, the relative economic decline of the American Empire can also be gauged from its now massive dependence on foreign debt. Like the British Empire before, the American Empire moved from being the World's largest creditor nation to being the World's largest debtor nation. Wars are always waged by incurring huge debts. Wars are popular but taxes are not. The British Empire began using huge debts to finance its imperial wars beginning with the *Seven Years War*. Having defeated the French Empire it faced a new imperial rival in Germany. The huge debt incurred by the British Empire from two **imperial** wars against Germany in 1914-18 and 1939-45 marked its ultimate demise.

The American Empire rose to prominence outside the American continent precisely because the **imperial** rivalry between Britain and Germany destroyed both. Like these European empires, Portugal, Spain, Holland, France, Britain and Germany, the American Empire is obsessed with warmongering and proving its military prowess even to tiny states such as Grenada. But wars are costly. They may enrich a few but they cost the economy. People cannot eat guns and munitions. Resources used to produce guns and munitions mean there is less to produce food, clothing, houses, cars and entertainment. American consumers voted for wars but refused to pay for them with increased taxes. In the next section we will briefly review America's post World War II military adventures on the American continent and in far off places such as Korea, Vietnam, China, Iraq and Afghanistan. Here we will document its growing dependence on debt to finance these wars.

The British Empire recovered sufficiently from the debt it incurred during World War I to prevent the German Empire from toppling it from top Dog in the pre-WWII imperial race. In like manner the American Empire recovered sufficiently from the debt incurred to fight the Vietnam War to prevent the Soviet Union from toppling it from top Dog in the post-WWII imperial race. But just as the British Empire never recovered from the debt it incurred in the Second World War so too will the American Empire never recover from the debt incurred to fight the Iraq and Afghanistan wars. Britain's public debt reached 250% of GDP during World War II. The US public debt reached 100% of GDP during the Iraq/Afghan War. Germany came roaring back from its defeat in the First World War. Britain had no choice but to fight another war against Germany if it wanted to keep its imperial dominance. Not so for the American Empire. Shortly after the Vietnam War, the economy of the Soviet Union collapsed. American hegemony was assured without a war against the Soviet Union. It's therefore the American Empire's **addiction** to wars and the obsessive need to feed its military-industrial complex, as well as provide the only real economic opportunity for many of its underprivileged young men and military-based communities, which led it to the current wars in Iraq and Afghanistan.

During the Second World War the British Empire "went cap in hand" to its protégé, the American Empire, for the loans to fight the German Empire. Likewise, the American Empire first turned to its protégé, Japan, for loans to fight the Soviet Union. But more recently, it has gone "cap in hand" to China, a country which CNN reporters must still refer to as *Communist* China if they want to keep their jobs. It is the equivalent of the British going "cap in hand" to Stalin's Russia to borrow to fight the German Empire. This is one more sign of how the American Empire has such a compulsive and addictive disorder for warmongering that it would indebt its empire to those it openly declare to be its enemies to get the funds to feed this uncontrollable compulsive disorder.

The Growth of Deficits and Debt: 1980-2010

Governments incur *budget* deficits because voters demand public services but dislike paying taxes. The annual *budget* deficit is the total expenditure of the government in a given year less the tax revenues received by the government. When the cost of war is added to the growing list of peacetime public services such as health care and education, the annual deficits increase significantly. The debt is the accumulation of the annual deficits **plus** the interest cost. However, what is commonly referred to as the *National or Public Debt* in the US or Canada is only the debt incurred by the Federal government. It does not include the debt held by other levels of government. In 1980 the gross debt held by the Federal government of the US was close to 910 billion dollars or 33% of GDP.

We will restrict our analysis of the **public debt crisis** of the American Empire to the debt and *budget* deficits of its Federal government only. While this underestimates its total government debt, by excluding the debt and *budget* deficits of state and local governments, it enables us to focus on how debt, whether it is consumer debt, federal debt, or other government debt, is hastening the economic decline of the American Empire. Any government debt is bad because the tax revenues spent on paying the interest could be better spent to provide public services. Likewise consumer debt is bad because some of your hard earned income is used to pay interest instead of buying the goods and services you worked for.

Economists usually do not worry too much about the public debt if it is a *domestic* debt and if it does not increase faster than GDP. The 1980 Federal government debt of 910 billion dollars provides an *absolute* measure of the debt. The 33% of GDP provides a *relative* measure of the debt. If the absolute value of the debt grows at the rate of inflation plus economic growth the *relative* measure will remain constant. Ideally, countries should reduce the relative measure by having the debt grow less than inflation and economic growth. This will reduce the interest cost freeing up funds to increase public services without increasing taxes. Having a national debt growing faster than inflation plus economic growth is a sure sign of political manipulation of voters. It is political manipulation of voters because it promises "free" public services and wars. But public services and wars are never free. Future taxpayers will have to repay the debt incurred by the previous taxpayers **plus** the interest cost. There is no free lunch. Public services and wars must be paid for by taxes. *Budget* deficits only postpone payment and add to the cost because governments cannot borrow for free. The US Federal *budget* deficit increased from an already excessive $460 billion in 2008, to a totally irresponsible amount of $1.85 trillion in 2009.

The US Federal debt of $910 billion in 1980, increased to a staggering $12 trillion in 2009. You need to reflect on the enormity of this growth in debt. The best way to do that is to understand that this Federal debt was accumulated over more than two centuries. So let us compare its growth in the two **centuries** up to 1980 with the three **decades** after 1980. In the two **centuries** before 1980 it grew from zero in 1776 to **less** than one trillion dollars by 1980. During these two centuries there were continuous wars beginning with the War of Independence, 1776-1783. Other major wars included the countless wars in North America, Latin America and the Caribbean, the Civil War, World War I, World War II, the Korean War and the Vietnam War. Contrast that growth over two centuries with the exceedingly rapid growth in the three **decades** between 1980 and 2009. From **less** than one trillion dollars in 1980 it grew to **twelve** trillion dollars in 2009. Two **centuries** of wars and public goods and services accumulated a Federal debt under one trillion dollars. Three **decades** of wars and public goods and services accumulated a Federal debt of **eleven** trillion dollars.

The Federal debt is the accumulated annual *budget* deficits plus interest. In 2009 alone, the Federal *budget* deficit was over 13% of that year's GDP. The projected *budget* deficit for 2010 is 1.6 trillion dollars. This represents 42 percent of a total budget of 3.8 trillion dollars. In other words, almost half of the spending of the federal government in 2010 is paid for by borrowing rather than taxes. As interest rates rise the interest cost will absorb an ever increasing share of the Federal government's tax revenues. Interest rates will not remain as low as they were in 2009 and 2010. As the World's economies recover from the 2008-2010 Great Recession, interest rates will rise significantly. The US public debt and annual budget deficits are not sustainable. The interest cost alone will become exorbitant. Worse still, the Federal debt is estimated to exceed 14 trillion dollars in 2010, a **fifteen fold** increase between 1980 and 2010. The 1980 *relative* measure of the Federal debt of 33% of GDP will rise to a *relative* measure of 100% of GDP in 2010. In the next four years another five trillion dollars of deficits will be incurred. The Federal debt of the American Empire is projected to skyrocket to $19 trillion by 2014.

The American Empire's Western allies are also accumulating much more debt compared with the Third World emerging economies. In 2009 the Euro Area had a public debt of 78% of its GDP. The *Economist*, June 13-19, 2009 estimated that by 2014 the 10 Western countries in the G20 will have public debts as high as 150% of GDP while the 10 emerging Third World countries in the G20 will have public debts as low as 35% of GDP. The pattern of the "rich" American Empire borrowing from "poor" Third World countries will infect its Western allies with the same plague of living beyond their means because of obsessive warmongering combined with obsessive consumption and planetary degradation. Western consumers have become as addicted to their credit cards as their governments have become addicted to warmongering. As Western governments spend a growing portion of their tax revenues on the military and interest payments Western consumers have to pay for a growing percent of the cost of healthcare, education and other "public" services. Consumers pay by using their credit cards, racking up a growing private debt to match the growing public debt of their governments.

How is a Foreign Debt different from a Domestic Debt?

When the governments of rich nations such as the US or Canada get into debt they initially borrow from their own citizens. This is called a *domestic debt*. The major concern regarding a domestic debt is that taxes will rise in the future while public services will be reduced since the higher taxes will go to repayment of the debt and interest cost. However, the GDP of the economy is not significantly reduced since the repayments and interest will be received by Americans or Canadians, as the case may be. It's mostly a redistribution of the nation's GDP from taxpayers to those holding government securities. GDP growth is reduced somewhat because the higher interest rates caused by the public borrowing will reduce capital investment.

A *foreign debt* refers to a nation borrowing from foreigners rather than its own citizens. The way in which foreign debts are incurred is rather complex. A domestic debt is relatively easy to understand. The US Federal government, for example, sells its securities, such as treasury bills and bonds, to its citizens directly, or indirectly by selling its securities to the banks holding the savings of its citizens. Foreigners will compete with Americans for these securities if they view them as safer or yielding higher returns than equivalent securities in their home countries or other foreign countries. When foreigners buy American securities it reduces the cost to the American government. The foreign demand for American government securities is added to the American demand. This increases the total demand which increases the price of these securities. The higher price means a lower interest cost. If you do not grasp this inverse relation between the price of securities and the interest rate, just think of more lenders, not just American lenders, wanting to lend to the American government. More lenders mean that the American government is able to borrow at a better rate of interest.

There is one important factor that is *unique* to borrowing by the US Federal government which does not apply to other governments such as the Canadian government. All governments hold foreign exchange reserves to engage in international trade. Since the Second World War which led to the relative decline of Great Britain, most countries have shown a preference for the $US over the British pound, as their primary reserve currency. This is because most international transactions are conducted in $US since the Second World War. This unique feature of the $US as the World's primary reserve currency means an additional demand for the debt of the US Federal government. This is why you read in the media that major lenders to the US such as China and Japan hold large amounts of US treasury bills, which means short-term loans to the US Federal government.

With interest rates being so low today the interest cost to the US for these short-term loans, is negligible or even negative. The *real* cost is negative if the "nominal" interest rate paid by the US is less than the inflation rate. For example, a 1.5 percent interest rate on a US treasury bill means a negative *real* return of one percent for the lender, if the annual inflation rate is 2.5 percent. Foreign governments, such as the government of the Peoples Republic of China, purchase these "zero to negative real interest" US securities because of their assumed **liquidity.** A liquid asset is an asset which you can sell with zero or "minimal" capital loss. Until recently, most governments were convinced that the US "treasuries" could be exchanged for $US without capital loss. This long held confidence in a **stable value** for the US dollar is eroding fast as the ability of the American Empire to meet its foreign debt repayments **and** interest obligations, is increasingly being questioned by its foreign lenders.

Understanding a Country's Balance of Payments and How its *Foreign* Borrowing Creates its *Trade* Deficit

This section is important only because of the ever constant media rhetoric and misinformation regarding the source of the huge and growing *trade* deficit of the American Empire with the Peoples Republic of China. While a *budget* deficit is caused by the government spending more than its tax revenues in a given year, a *trade* deficit means that the value of a country's imports exceeds the value of the country's exports in the same year. It is important that you understand the difference because the media often use the term "deficit" without clarifying if it means a *budget* deficit or a *trade* deficit. Adding to the confusion is the fact that the large and growing *trade* deficits of the American Empire is caused by its foreign borrowing which, in turn, is caused by its large and growing *budget* deficits.

You will **not** get an understanding of how the *trade* deficit of the American Empire is caused by its foreign borrowing, used to pay for its wars in Iraq and Afghanistan, by listening to CNN, CBC or the BBC. Journalists have minimal or zero understanding of economic theories. What is even worse, journalists try to hide their ignorance of economic theories by pretending to understand economic theories more than economics professors and even economists who have been honoured with the Nobel Prize in economics. You will therefore need to make an effort to understand the economic theory explained in this section, so that you understand the reality of the American *trade* deficits, and why it is caused by the foreign borrowing of the American Empire to pay for its wars in Iraq and Afghanistan, **not** by currency manipulation by the Peoples Republic of China.

When a country borrows from foreigners, the annual amount borrowed shows up as a **surplus** in the capital account section of its annual balance of payments with the world. This is another complexity associated with a *foreign* debt, as opposed to a *domestic* debt, which is difficult for the public or the media to comprehend. A country's balance of payments is divided into two major parts, a current account and a capital account. Contrary to the erroneous public and media statements regarding international trade, the truth is that nations must export a value equal to the value of their imports. The only way a country can import (buy) goods from another country is to pay for the imports by exporting (sell) goods equal to the value of the imports. In this context the incessant urge by many in Canada to "buy Canadian" as if that were a good thing is totally fallacious. If we buy more imports, whether it's from the US or China, our exchange rate will adjust so that we increase the value of our exports to pay for those imports. Any jobs created by the output of goods for Canadians will be lost by an **equal** reduction of jobs in the export sector. The end result will be no net increase or loss of jobs but only a replacement of high paying jobs in the export sector with relatively low paying jobs in the domestic sector.

The value of exports does not have to equal the value of imports on an annual basis. This is because nations can borrow and lend, incur *foreign* debt, with each other. If Canada imports $10 billion in 2009 but exports $9.5 billion it can borrow $0.5 billion to pay for the short fall in 2009. The current account for 2009 will show a *deficit* of $0.5 billion and the capital account will show a *surplus* of $0.5 billion. The annual balance of payments is always zero. The key point is that nations borrow only if the value of their imports in a given year exceeds the value of their exports in that year. The more important point is that a *deficit* in the nation's current account will be matched by an equivalent *surplus* in the nation's capital account. Nations with *deficits* in their capital accounts, are called *Creditor Nations,* because they exported a value exceeding the value of their imports and are **owed** the difference. The countries they exported more to, **owe** them the difference and must repay it with interest. The only way to repay this debt is for the *Debtor Nations* to export more than they import, at some future time. This is why we say categorically that, in the long-run, each country must export a value **equal** to the value of its imports, ignoring the complication of *short-term* deficits giving rise to interest cost. The Nations with *surpluses* in their capital accounts are called *Debtor Nations.* Currently, Canada is a minor creditor nation while the US is the World's **largest** debtor nation.

As late as 1982 the US was the largest *Creditor nation* in the world. The US began lending heavily to Western Europe during and after the Second World War. Prior to the First World War, Great Britain had been the World's largest *Creditor nation.* During its economic development Canada borrowed heavily from Great Britain and the US. In the period between 1976 and 1996 Canadian governments incurred large and growing *budget* deficits which were increasingly funded by foreign debt. In the last two decades it has been the American Empire which has been funding its large and growing *budget* deficits with increased foreign debt. When *budget* deficits are funded by foreign debt it shows up as a *surplus* in the capital account of the country's balance of payments. This must be matched by an equal *deficit* in the country's current account since the overall Balance of international payments must be zero. That was the case with Canada in the two decades 1976-96 and is the case with the American Empire more recently, especially during the presidencies of George W. Bush and Barack Obama.

When Americans demand government services, including foreign wars, but do not want to pay sufficient taxes, their government must borrow. As the *budget* deficits become larger and larger each year, the demand for loans increase and the US interest rate rises. This encourages foreigners to lend to the US. This inflow of foreign lending into the US shows up as a *surplus* in the capital account of the US Balance of Payments. But foreigners can only lend to the US if they have a trade *surplus* with the US, that is, they export more to the US than they import from the US. That is the case today with many countries, including China and Japan. Furthermore, you need to understand that foreigners must first buy American dollars on the foreign exchange market in order to lend to the US Federal government. This demand for US dollars on the foreign exchange market bids up the price of US dollars relative to other currencies, including the Chinese Yuan and the Japanese Yen. This increase in the US exchange rate relative to the Chinese Yuan or Japanese Yen is part of the mechanism which enables countries like China and Japan to export more to the US than they import.

In the 1980's the US media complained incessantly about the American *trade* deficit with Japan. In the last decade China has been singled out by the media for blame. Just as the US media was wrong in the 1980's when it blamed Japan for the US *trade* deficits so it is wrong today when it blames China for the US *trade* deficits. The US *trade* deficits are caused by the American Empire living beyond its means. If the American Empire ends its warmongering in Iraq and Afghanistan it would reduce its foreign borrowing. The demand for the US dollar on the foreign exchange market would fall and the US exchange rate will fall relative to the Chinese Yuan, Japanese Yen, and other foreign currencies. This decline in the US exchange rate will increase its exports and reduce its imports. The *trade* deficit of the American Empire would disappear. On the contrary, as long as the US government continue to sell its securities to foreigners to fund its massive *budget* deficits, the American Empire must incur large *trade* deficits. If President Obama was foolish enough to impose tariffs on Chinese imports to reduce its *trade* deficit with China, the US *trade* deficit with China will fall, but the total US *trade* deficit will **not** fall. The total *trade* deficit of the American Empire must match the total foreign borrowing of the American Empire.

Why is a Foreign Debt *Much* worse than a Domestic Debt?

A domestic debt means that the US government is living beyond its means. A foreign debt means that the American Empire is living beyond its means. With a domestic debt the US government owe Americans. With a foreign debt the American Empire spends more than its GDP by using part of the GDP of China, Japan, OPEC, Brazil and other countries from whom it borrows. In the case of a domestic debt the US government can impose taxes on its own citizens or simply print money to pay the interest and repay the debt. While Americans might abhor higher taxes or the inflation caused by printing money, they will still enjoy their entire annual GDP. Not so with a foreign debt. Interest and repayments will reduce the GDP kept by Americans since an increasing part of its GDP will go to China, Japan, OPEC, Brazil and other countries which had loaned the American Empire.

Of the 14 trillion dollars of debt owed by the Federal government of the US in 2010, about 5 trillion dollars is owed to foreigners. The largest foreign lenders to the US are China, Japan, OPEC, Caribbean Bankers, Brazil, Britain, Russia, Taiwan and Switzerland. Who it borrows from is not as important as the amount it is borrowing. The once mighty American Empire is digging itself into an early grave. At the same time as its GDP is declining relative to the rest of the world it will have to take an increasing part of its shrinking GDP to send to the rest of the world to pay interest on past loans and to repay those loans. Yet, the American Empire refuses to cut back on its costly warmongering in every corner of the globe. This is yet another sign of its long historical addiction to wars and invasions.

The US economy experienced its worst recession, since the Great Depression of the 1930's, in 2009. While the official unemployment rate in July 2009 was 9.4%, at least one Federal Reserve official claimed that the real unemployment rate was 16%, when you add discouraged workers and those wanting full time jobs but finding only part time work. The official unemployment rate counts those having only part-time jobs as employed. Discouraged workers are those who have stopped looking for work because they believe that they will not find any. They are not counted as unemployed. With a falling GDP and increasing unemployment, despite an 800 billion dollars stimulus package, President Barack Obama will very likely increase rather than cut defence spending. The unusually high unemployment rate will make it easier for him to recruit the military manpower to fight his wars in Afghanistan, Pakistan and Yemen. President Obama is no less a warmonger than George W. Bush. The only difference is that Bush wanted to kill Iraqi women and children whereas Obama prefers to kill women and children in Afghanistan, Pakistan and Yemen. The foreign debt incurred by George W. Bush to fight his wars in Iraq and Afghanistan will pale in comparison to what President Obama will incur to fight his wars in Afghanistan, Iraq, Pakistan, Yemen, and possibly, Iran.

The American Empire was forced off the Bretton Woods gold-exchange standard by the cost of the Vietnam War. It was forced to float the $US dollar as its current account deficits far exceeded its gold reserves in Fort Knox. In 2010, countries are running from the $US dollar as the primary foreign exchange reserve. As more and more countries reduce their loans to the American Empire the cost of borrowing will sky rocket. The American Empire will self destruct under the weight of the enormous cost of its wars, invasions, domestic and foreign military bases, interest payments, stagnant GDP and poor leadership. The world will be **free** at last.

Part II: The American Empire's Continued Obsession With Warmongering as an Essential and Integral Part of its History and Culture: 1950-2010

The decline of the American Empire is a result of both its *relative* economic decline and the wasteful allocation of its shrinking economic resources to feed its addiction to warmongering. It is extremely important for me to make it very clear to my readers that my research of the facts and the evidence convinces me, beyond any doubt, that the vast expenditures of the American Empire on its military, military adventures globally, and countless invasions of other countries, since its birth as a nation/ empire, have absolutely nothing to do with fighting communism, terrorism, or Islamic extremism. Those are excuses for its addiction to warmongering and imperial expansion. No country in the world has either the desire or capability to invade or do harm to the United States. The American Empire's enormous and wasteful expenditures on its military is due to its inherent culture of wars and an innate need for continuous wars from the time before and after its birth as an independent nation state.

This innate need and desire for wars is due to some factors which are psychological and difficult to identify. But there are other obvious and tangible explanations. Firstly, if a large part of your economy has always been devoted to wars, cutting those expenditures will be resisted by voters and their families directly and indirectly affected by cuts in military spending. Secondly, many young Americans see the armed forces as an acceptable career. It promotes pride in their country, recognition for service to their country, education and training, a good income for their family, a decent career by American standards, participation in one of history's most powerful military machines, and the self gratification of many Americans to kill, maim and dominate those they are indoctrinated to view as inferior and primitive races.

Thirdly, the important role of the military-industrial complex in keeping the American Empire in the forefront of technology for both its military and its industry, while enriching those engaged by and employed by this large and profitable sector, is well documented elsewhere. Boeing, for example, depends on sales of both civilian and military planes. Research and tests on military planes complement research and tests on civilian aircrafts. Wars are an essential ingredient in providing opportunities for testing new and technologically sophisticated weapons. This dates back long before the decision to test its newly invented atomic weapons on Nagasaki and Hiroshima in 1945, its first *uranium* bomb on Hiroshima and its first *plutonium* bomb on Nagasaki. During the First Gulf War against Iraq in 1991 it tested its relatively new *Patriot missiles,* knocking out the *scuds* launched by Iraq. By 2009 it was testing its unmanned *drones* in Afghanistan and Pakistan.

In the post World War II period American invasions and wars increased and became more expensive. Prior to World War II American military adventures outside North America, Central and South America and the Caribbean, were small compared to those of Britain and France. With the relative decline of Britain and France, and the failure of Germany to seize imperial hegemony from Britain, the American Empire spoke for the West. As the new leader of the *uncivilized, un-free,* world, it made an implicit pact with Western Europe, Canada, Japan and Australia. It will not invade and colonize those countries if they would provide unquestioned military, political, media and propaganda support for its continued invasions in the New World as well as new invasions in Asia, Africa and Eastern Europe. The American Empire would act, speak and behave as if the Third World does not exist. It would speak for the World as if the West was the World. It would tolerate no dissent from its Western allies, including Japan, South Korea, Taiwan, Hong Kong and Singapore.

Continued Wars and Invasions in Latin America and the Caribbean

In this section we will briefly document the continued invasions and warmongering of the American Empire in the New World after World War II. One reason for this is to emphasize that when the Second World War provided the opportunity for the American Empire to expand its warmongering to the furthest corners of the universe, there was no let up of its historical warmongering in the New World. Many of these post-WWII invasions in the New World have been covered in earlier chapters. Others, including the invasions of Guyana and Grenada, have been covered in the prequel to this book, *The Rise and Fall of the American Empire.* This section will focus primarily on a few countries in the New World, which the American Empire had not invaded before World War II, but invaded after World War II. These would include the invasions of Chile, Argentina, Bolivia, Brazil, Uruguay, Paraguay and Venezuela. Of these the most widely publicized are the invasions of Chile and *Operation Condor,* which was a coordinated invasion of Argentina, Brazil, Bolivia, Uruguay and Paraguay.

US Invasion of Chile, 1973

The US invasion of Chile was typical of the hundreds of invasions executed by the American Empire worldwide. Imperialism implies subjugation of colonized peoples. This subjugation is political, economic and cultural. When a country like Chile freely elects its own democratic government that government cannot be pro-American. It cannot be pro-American because the American Empire is the foremost colonial power in all of Latin America and the Caribbean. Since the electorate is not **brain dead,** contrary to the views expressed by the Western media, given the choice to vote freely, they will always elect a government which will seek to reduce American control over their economy and their political, social and cultural institutions. Any such efforts by a democratically elected government would be denounced by Washington as *Communist.* But the people will never freely elect a government which continued to support American control of their economy and their political, cultural and social institutions.

The implication of this reasoning is that any freely elected democratic government in a Third World country will be seen by Washington as anti-American while any government in a Third World country which was pro-American would be an American imposed **dictatorship** or an elected government that was pro-American, only because it feared reprisals by the American Empire. These reprisals range from reduced American aid to financial blackmail to boycott by international institutions such as the IMF, the World Bank, the WTO, to economic sanctions, to military invasion. Without exception, countries today which are pro-American, even some in the West, but certainly all in the Third World, are not **free** to elect a democratic government. They are not free to do so because of political, economic and military blackmail by the American Empire with explicit support from Canada, the European Union, Australia, Japan and other allies of the American Empire.

Many countries have made the brave effort to elect democratic governments despite threats from the American Empire. Chile was such an example when it freely elected the government of Salvador Allende in 1970. The American Empire had begun its intervention in Chile in 1811. This was typical of American interventions throughout the New World and expressed publicly by the *Monroe Doctrine* of 1823. In the case of the later interventions in Chile, the American Empire made no attempt to hide the fact that its goal was to prevent Chile from electing a **democratic** government much like it has never hidden the fact that its public campaign against *Hamas* is intended to prevent the Palestinian people from electing a **democratic** government.

Salvador Allende began his long political career as a member of the Socialist Party of Chile. In 1938 he became Chile's Minister of Health and Social Welfare. He first ran for the presidency in 1952. After two other unsuccessful attempts in 1958 and 1964 he was elected in 1970. Throughout this period the American Empire conducted an expensive and determined campaign in Chile against Allende and Chilean **democracy.** It was this effective campaign by the American Empire which defeated Allende in 1952, 1958 and 1964. In the 1964 elections Allende was the popular favourite but lost again because of the expensive media campaign launched covertly by the CIA. As in so many other failed American interventions, the determination and longevity of the people's resistance to American imperialism prevailed, and the American Empire lost in 1970, albeit by a slim margin.

When covert political and military intervention combined with overt propaganda and fear-mongering fails, the American Empire resorts to overt military action. President Nixon ordered the CIA to depose Allende immediately after his election victory in September 1970. The CIA increased its covert media campaign against Allende with the purpose of destabilizing his government. This was combined with economic and financial blackmail. At the same time it began to put in place a plan to depose Allende by a military coup. US military aid to the Chilean army increased significantly. Good old *Henry Kissinger,* President Nixon's National Security Advisor at the time, was just the man to plan the military coup. President Nixon authorized the $10 million budget for the dirty deed. The first part of the plan was to kidnap and kill General Rene Schneider, Chile's army chief. Schneider had refused to be the American puppet. Schneider was shot on October 22, 1970 and died three days later. Kissinger had succeeded in executing the first part of his criminal action plan against Chile.

It's rather ironic that the overt American backed coup to depose the **democratically** elected Allende government of Chile succeeded on *September 11,* 1973, after a failed attempt on June 29, 1973. This sad coincidence is one more testimony to the enormous propaganda power of the so called Western "free press." Confidential American documents which clearly identified America's covert operations against the democratic government of Chile and its responsibility for the *September 11* coup were released in October 1999, a full two years before the US *September 11* of 2001. The *September 11* of 1973 was the removal of a democratically elected government by the government of the United States using both financial and military means. The *September 11* of 2001 was the actions of a few individuals and did not topple the government of the United States.

Most importantly, the 2001 *September 11* was a response to the occupation, militarization, colonization and denial of independence to the people of Saudi Arabia and the Middle East by the American Empire. The American Empire's attack on Chile on *September 11,* 1973 was never provoked by the people of Chile even though they had suffered from American imperialism since 1811. Yet the world mourns and remembers and justifies American warmongering in Iraq, Afghanistan, Pakistan, Iran, Lebanon, Yemen, and against many other Muslim states, because of the 2001 *September 11,* while conveniently ignoring the much more **evil** 1973 *September 11*. Such is the power of Western propaganda.

The 1,100 documents released by the US State Department in 1999, clearly implicated **Henry Kissinger** in both removing President Allende and installing the brutal dictator General Augusto Pinochet. Kissinger was quoted as saying, "I don't see why we need to stand by and watch a country go communist due to the irresponsibility of its own people. The issues are too important for the Chilean voters to be left to decide for themselves." For this kind of service to American imperialism and **warmongering** Kissinger was awarded the Nobel "Peace" Prize.

We have argued that there is nothing inherently evil about communism. However, there is no evidence that Chile would have become a communist state under Allende. In fact there is evidence that the Soviet Union refused to provide financial aid to Allende to counter the American economic and financial squeeze because Allende refused to convert Chile to a Soviet style Planned economy. Allende nationalized foreign corporations because they were an inherent part of American imperialism. The British Labour government nationalized many more private industries than Allende did and they were not even foreign owned. Finally, even if communism was evil and Chile would have become a communist state as Cuba had done, this does not justify American imperialism and warmongering. Communism is the excuse used by **evil** men like Kissinger to do **evil** things to the people of militarily weak states like Chile and Cuba. Kissinger's US installed s.o.b. dictator, Pinochet, killed, imprisoned and tortured thousands of Chileans during his brutal rule from 1973 to 1990.

Operation Condor: US Invasions of Argentina, Brazil, Bolivia, Uruguay and Paraguay

American military and political intervention in Chile was part of a broader program of military and political intervention in all of the *Southern cone* countries of Latin America, Chile, Argentina, Brazil, Uruguay, Paraguay and Bolivia. It is interesting that the American Empire would choose the most southern portion of the American continent to implement a coordinated attack on communism. At least that was the official line. We have argued consistently that communism was the excuse used by the American Empire to expand its empire by military aggression. Having invaded Canada twice and converted Canada to one of its primary allies in pursuing its goal of world domination, as well as added Alaska to its empire, the northernmost part of the American continent was secure. *Operation Condor* was the network of coordinated **terror** which the American Empire implemented during the *Cold War* to complete its colonization of the American continent. The American Empire set up a system of computerized links among the secret "intelligence" units of the six *Operation Condor* countries.

While *Operation Condor* was in existence before Henry Kissinger replaced Allende with Pinochet in Chile, having Pinochet as the American Empire's own s.o.b. dictator in the Southern Cone, enabled the American Empire to centralize operations in Chile. *Operation Condor* had been explicitly enunciated by American General Robert Porter since 1968. But the formal meeting to set up the network had to wait for General Pinochet's dictatorship in Chile. That meeting took place in Santiago, Chile, on November 25, 1975; two years after the American Empire had removed the **democratically** elected president of Chile. Chile had by that time instituted a **secret police**, DINA. The head of DINA, General Manuel Contreras, was a "paid CIA asset," of the American Empire. The American Empire selected General Contreras, as head of DINA, and a "paid CIA asset," to oversee *Operation Condor*. DINA and Argentina's **secret police,** SIDE, provided most of the manpower required to implement the "torture and disappearances," terror tactics of *Operation Condor*.

The decision to use "torture and disappearance" as the primary weapon of colonization of the Southern cone countries by the American Empire was copied from the French Empire which had used these methods in Algeria. Recall that the American Empire had developed a working relationship with the French Empire in Indochina. It was therefore no surprise that they would follow in the footsteps of the French Empire in South America. France had used the Catholic Church to connect with the military junta of Argentina since the 1930's. In the 1950's military officers from Argentina attended a military school in France to learn the "torture and disappearance" terror tactics used by France in Algeria. These methods were copied by a similar military school in Argentina. France also established connections with DINA in Chile. Latin American dictators, and military officers of both the American Empire and Latin American countries, were also trained in these terror tactics at the *US Army School of the Americas.* The US Army School of the Americas was first established in the American *uncolony* of Panama in 1946 and continued its training until its closure in 1984. It was subsequently re-opened in the US at Fort Benning, Georgia.

By the time the American Empire set up *Operation Condor,* DINA and SIDE officers were trained in these terror tactics. Torture and disappearances were used in all of the six *Southern cone* countries, Chile, Argentina, Brazil, Paraguay, Uruguay and Bolivia, to prevent the citizens of those countries from establishing democratic governments which would resist American imperialism. During his term as Director of the CIA, former president, George Herbert Bush, communicated to Congressman, Edward Koch, the fact that the Uruguayan branch of *Operation Condor,* had put out a contract to assassinate him, because he had sponsored a bill to cut off US military aid to Uruguay. As a result of this information, Koch asked for protection by the FBI, but protection was refused. American DINA assassin and CIA operative, Michael Townley, admitted to *Operation Condor's* role in the killing of high profile Chileans such as Orlando Letelier and General Carlos Prats, Commander-in-Chief of the Chilean army.

Orlando Letelier and his American assistant, Ronnie Moffitt, were assassinated in the US in 1976 by *Operation Condor.* Letelier had served President Allende as ambassador to the US in 1971 as well as Minister of Foreign Affairs in 1973. He was arrested by the Chilean government after the American Empire had removed President Allende and installed the dictatorship of General Pinochet. Letelier was held in several of the many concentration camps set up by the Pinochet dictatorship in Chile, and tortured. International outrage at the American Empire led to Letelier's release from prison under the condition that he will leave Chile. Letelier chose to move to the US where he became a vocal critic of the Pinochet regime as well as *Operation Condor.* In turn, *Operation Condor* took the extreme step of assassinating him on US soil. Letelier's American assistant, Ronnie Moffitt, and her husband, were in the car with Letelier, when the car was bombed by *Condor's* assassins. Letelier and Ronnie Moffitt were killed. Ronnie Moffit's husband was in the back seat and suffered a minor wound in the head.

Under pressure from the FBI, Pinochet agreed to the extradition of Michael Townley from Chile to the US in 1978, to stand trial for the murder of Letelier and Moffitt. During the trial Townley, as state's evidence, confessed to hiring five Americans, two of whom were living in Chile, to assassinate Letelier. The Three Americans living in the US were convicted in 1979. General Pinochet refused to extradite the two Americans living in Chile, and employed by Chile's secret police, DINA. During the trial it was also revealed that high profile *American terrorist,* Luis Posada Carriles, had assisted in finding the five Americans, all of whom were of Cuban origin, willing to carry out the assassination. Posada is well known to have been a CIA operative who was responsible for numerous *terrorist* acts against the Cuban people, including the 1976 bombing of a Cuban airline which killed 73 people, and an assassination attempt on Fidel Castro in 2000.

A cable from Robert White, the American Ambassador in Paraguay, to Cyrus Vance, US Secretary of State at the time, revealed that the American Empire provided the technical capability for the six military regimes supported by the American Empire during *Operation Condor* to coordinate their terror tactic of "torture and disappearances." The cable was sent in 1978 but only made public in 2001 as a result of the "Chile Declassification project," during the Clinton presidency. *Operation Condor* was allowed to use the American Empire's communications installations in Panama to coordinate the killings, torture and disappearances of their *death squads* and secret police. Henry Kissinger, US Secretary of State at the time, was fully briefed on these killings, torture methods used and disappearances. It helped him win the Nobel "Peace" prize to the extent that his actions saved the professed "Leader of the Free World," from whatever *imaginary* ghastly deeds could be inflicted on it by communists.

As a result of the declassification of US government documents, some attempts have been made to hold Henry Kissinger accountable. In May 31, 2001, for example, a French judge made the effort to serve a summons on Kissinger while he was in Paris. But Kissinger bolted out of France before the summons could be served. The intent of the summons was to question Kissinger about his role in the disappearance of five French citizens in Chile carried out by *Operation Condor.* Kissinger bolted not only because of his own guilt but the complicity of his American Empire in these disappearances. Other examples, also in 2001, were the efforts by Chilean and Argentinean judges to question Kissinger about his involvement in *Operation Condor,* and in particular, of the killing of the American journalist, Charles Horman, by *Operation Condor,* in 1973. Questions were sent from Chile and Argentina to the US through the normal diplomatic channels but never answered by Kissinger. Americans like Kissinger are "above the law."

Kissinger's involvement in *Operation Condor,* is also examined in Chapter 9, of our prequel, *Rise and Fall of the American Empire.* Somewhat ironically, Chilean human rights lawyers chose *September 11, 2001,* to file a criminal charge against Henry Kissinger for his role in the disappearance of Chileans during *Operation Condor.* Two sons of General Rene Schneider have attempted to bring a civil suite against Henry Kissinger for his role in the murder of their father, General Schneider, by the American Empire, after Schneider refused to be a party to the removal of Chile's **democratically** elected president, Salvador Allende, on *September 11, 1973.* The Supreme Court of Bolivia made a request for the extradition of Kissinger in 2007 and Brazil was forced to cancel an invitation to Kissinger to speak in Brazil in 2001 because the Brazilian government could not guarantee him immunity from prosecution in Brazil.

As of 2010, American war criminals are still "above the law." American participants in *Operation Condor* maintain their claim that it was a "legitimate" counter-terror organization and proud of its stellar assassination, torture and disappearance capabilities. They viewed their cooperation with Latin American **dictators** and secret police agencies such as DINA and SIDE, as serving the Western claims to protecting freedoms. But as the global economic power shifts from the American Empire to the rest of the world, immunity from prosecution will change. Nazi war criminals are still being brought to justice more than half a century later. The long arm of the law may still catch up with American war criminals, especially those much younger than Henry Kissinger, such as George W. Bush and Barack Obama. When Americans like Barack Obama are prosecuted for war crimes and the members of the Nobel Peace committee are held accountable for their complicity, the world would truly have changed for the better. Yes! We finally can!

US Invasion of Venezuela

The American Empire first invaded Venezuela in 1806 when President Thomas Jefferson fully supported the military invasion led by Francisco de Miranda and financed by American businessman, Samuel Ogden. As was the case with every US invasion of Spanish colonies, the American Empire pretended to invade only to free the colonists from Spanish imperialism. But in every case where the US invasion was successful, the American Empire replaced Spanish imperialism with American imperialism. The Miranda/Ogden invasion of 1806 failed for the same reason that other American invasions in Canada, Vietnam and Afghanistan, failed. Jefferson, Ogden and Miranda, overestimated the power of American propaganda to fool those whom the American Empire claim to be liberating. The hoped for "rising up of Venezuelan patriots," to welcome and fight with the American liberators, did not materialize. The Miranda invasion landed in the port of Coro and captured the city of Coro. But Venezuelans showed no preference for American imperialism over Spanish imperialism. Perhaps the American press should have been less enthusiastic with its praise of Miranda as a revolutionary fighting Spanish imperialism. Some Western writers claimed that the invasion failed only because Miranda landed in a part of Venezuela where the Venezuelans liked Spanish imperialism. To suggest that anyone likes imperialism is ridiculous. The Venezuelans were smart enough to prefer Spanish imperialism over American imperialism, just as the First Nations in Canada showed a preference for British over American imperialism.

As we have explained before, European imperialism in the New World could never have the *totality* of colonial subjugation which the "home-advantage" of American imperialism provided. In an age when transportation was primarily by ship, Europe administered its colonies from relatively remote European centres. Not so for the American *uncolonies* in the New World. The American Empire could penetrate every nook and cranny of the American continent by both sea and rail. Its imperial centre in Washington DC was never far from its colonial administrations in its New World *uncolonies.* This is the same reason why American imperialism in far off places like the Philippines, Japan, South Korea, Taiwan, Israel and the Middle East has to be less intrusive, less penetrating, less *total.* Given a choice, no colony in the New World would trade European imperialism for American imperialism. That is why Miranda failed to colonize Venezuela for the American Empire in 1806.

Venezuela is the new Cuba and Hugo Chavez is Fidel Castro's Progeny

In 2010, Venezuela is the new Cuba in America's backyard and Hugo Chavez is the rebirth of Fidel Castro. Neither Cuba before, nor Venezuela today, are military threats to the American Empire. They are important *symbolic* threats. The successful Cuban revolution and the almost *charmed* life of Fidel Castro in foiling innumerable assassination attempts by the American Empire, represented a needle constantly pricking at the heart of the American Empire's claim to be the World's leading superpower during the second half of the 20th century. Cuba and the Soviet Union formed a strong alliance which served each other immensely. Without the economic and military support of the Soviet Union it is very unlikely that Castro would have remained so popular with the Cuban people. Likewise, the Soviet Union needed a military ally in America's backyard to neutralize the effects of the nuclear missiles pointed at the Soviet Union from Turkey.

The economic collapse of the Soviet Union made the Cuban needle at the heart of the American Empire almost inconsequential. Cuba could be ignored to die a slow but painful death from the economic sanctions and American embargo which had previously proved to be so ineffective. But the long prayed for death of Cuba is the key reason for the American Empire's obsession with President Hugo Chavez of Venezuela. Having had their prayers answered with the fall of the Soviet Union making Cuba irrelevant, Venezuela snuck up on a prematurely celebrating American Empire to replace Cuba, as well as providing an equally charismatic replacement for Fidel Castro in the form of Hugo Chavez. Far from the collapse of the Soviet Union making Cuba irrelevant, Venezuela is not only replacing Cuba as the American Empire's worse thorn in its own backyard, but helping Cuba forestall its own demise. The goal of the American Empire had been to isolate Cuba from the rest of Latin America. Now Venezuela under Chavez is working very hard to isolate the American Empire from Latin America. At the same time Venezuela is helping Cuba with badly needed economic aid so that Cuba can continue to snub American overtures to renounce Castro and become the American *uncolony* it was before the Castro revolution.

Venezuela is also developing a mutually beneficial relationship with Russia similar to the symbiotic relationship between Cuba and the Soviet Union. During the Cold War the closest NATO country from which the American Empire could launch a nuclear strike on Russia was Turkey. With the fall of the Soviet Union many of Russia's allies in Eastern Europe have become *uncolonies* of the American Empire. Russia desperately needs a replacement for Cuba in America's backyard. On the other side, Venezuela needs Russian support to deter a military invasion by the American Empire. Today, Russia is arming Venezuela much as it armed Cuba during the Cold War. In 2006, President Putin reached an agreement with President Chavez to supply Venezuela with Russian military equipment. In 2008, Russia and Venezuela carried out joint naval exercises in the Caribbean. In addition to various military and nuclear agreements between Russia and Venezuela the two countries are forging a strong economic and political alliance. Russia and Venezuela speak with a single voice when it comes to opposing American colonization of the Middle East, Georgia, Kosovo or Ukraine. In economic matters Russia and Venezuela are cooperating in mining, energy, banking, transportation and space exploration.

In the Middle East, Venezuela is cooperating with Iran, Lebanon and Syria to oppose American and Israeli subjugation of Muslims, Arabs and Palestinians, in the region. President Chavez has close personal ties with President Ahmadinejad of Iran. They have great admiration for each other and a common bond inspired by their David like resistance to the American goliath. Some refer to them as "kindred spirits." They are like one in their determination to oppose a very **evil** American Empire, Israeli atrocities, Western propaganda, Western domination and Western "civilization." They are the two World leaders today who truly see the American Empire and Israel for what they really are, selfish warmongering bullies. As with Russia, Venezuela is forging strong economic, political and military cooperation with Iran. There is room for trilateral cooperation in many areas, by the three countries.

Venezuela also influences the politics of the Middle East through its membership in OPEC. Venezuela was the first country to push for an organization of oil exporting countries which would secure a higher world price for oil. Venezuela played a leading role in the creation of OPEC in 1960. Venezuela and Iran were among its **five** founding members, which also included Saudi Arabia, Iraq and Kuwait. OPEC's membership has since increased to twelve. Together, OPEC countries account for one-third of current oil output and two-thirds of oil reserves, in the world. During Venezuela's presidency of OPEC in 2000, President Chavez made a ten day tour of OPEC countries, much to the consternation of the American Empire.

Venezuela is smart enough to forge links with the World's emerging economic power house, China. Like its relationship with Russia, China and Venezuela have a mutually beneficial interest. With Russia it is a defensive one. With China it is an economic one. Today Venezuela exports 60 percent of its oil to the American Empire. As the world's **fifth** largest exporter of oil, Venezuela needs other markets to reduce its economic dependence on the American Empire. Venezuela nationalized its oil industry in 1976 and PDVSA, Venezuela's state-owned petroleum giant, controls both its oil and natural gas industries. Venezuela has an estimated 78 billion barrels of conventional oil reserves, the largest reserve of *conventional* crude in the Western hemisphere, as well as 150 trillion cubic feet of natural gas reserves. In 2007, PDVSA added electricity generation to its energy production when it purchased 82 percent of the shares of Electricidad de Caracas from its American parent, AES Corporation.

China dearly wants to help Venezuela reduce its dependence on the American market by increasing its imports of Venezuelan oil. By diverting Venezuelan oil from the United States to China, China will be diversifying its own dependence on suppliers. It's definitely a win-win situation for both countries. China can also cooperate with Venezuela in the related areas of refining, drilling, exploration and transportation of Venezuelan oil. Venezuela has the largest proven reserves of *heavy* crude oil, some 235 billion barrels, in the World. In 2005, Venezuela's state-owned oil company, PDVSA, set up an office in China, and announced plans to triple its fleet of oil tankers to ship Venezuelan oil to China. China is currently cooperating with Venezuela in building oil tankers and in refining Venezuelan *heavy* crude oil. A joint venture to drill for *extra heavy* Venezuelan crude oil was announced in September 2009. This joint venture is expected to add half a million barrels per day to Venezuela's oil production of 3.5 million barrels per day. By 2012, Venezuela is expected to export as much oil to China as it currently exports to the American Empire.

Outside the energy sector China and Venezuela are cooperating in the areas of satellite communications, railroads, culture, science and military equipment. China is increasing both its foreign trade and foreign investment with Venezuela. During the presidency of Hugo Chavez, Venezuela has become the number one recipient of Chinese foreign investment in Latin America, and foreign trade has increased an amazing *fifty-fold*. Venezuela is also forging energy cooperation with Asia's other emerging economic power house, India. In 2008 Venezuela reached an agreement with India for Indian investment in the exploration, extraction and transportation of Venezuelan oil and natural gas. This included a joint venture with PDVSA to produce Venezuelan *extra heavy* crude oil.

The 2002 Military Coup to Remove President Hugo Chavez

In 2002, the American Empire regime changed the **democratically** elected president of Venezuela, Hugo Chavez, using a military coup. But unlike Chile in 1973, the US instigated military coup in Venezuela in 2002, was a dismal failure for the American Empire. The military coup was condemned by all of the nations of Latin America. Instead of deposing Chavez permanently, the coup increased his popularity in Venezuela, in Latin America and throughout the Third World. After supporting the interim presidency of Pedro Carmona, the American Empire was forced to publicly denounce the military coup once it was clear that it had failed to permanently remove Chavez.

The US instigated military coup took place on April 11, 2002. The Venezuelan military entered the presidential palace during the evening of April 11, 2002 and demanded the resignation of President Chavez. General-in-Chief, Lucas Rincon, announced on TV in the early morning of April 12, 2002 that President Chavez had agreed to a request by the military to resign as president. President Chavez was held prisoner at Fort Tiuna and Pedro Carmona, president of the Venezuelan Chamber of Commerce, was hurriedly installed as interim president of Venezuela. Carmona issued a decree dissolving both the Venezuelan National Assembly and Supreme Court as well as suspending the most important government officials such as the Attorney General, the Comptroller General, state governors and city mayors. These actions which were intended to remove the rule of law were consistent with the actions of all US imposed **dictators,** whose actions the American Empire always claim to be the necessary methods used by the "civilized" West to bring Western democratic principles to the "uncivilized" people of the Third World. All US imposed **dictators** are "democratic" as long as they implement and support policies which the American Empire recommends.

President Chavez had won the 1988 **democratic** presidential elections on a platform of "constitutional reform." He also held a referendum on a new constitution on December 15, 1999 and 72 percent of the electorate voted in favour of it. President Chavez was re-elected in 2000 under the new constitution. This new constitution was declared null and void by interim president Pedro Carmona. The American Empire, as it often does, underestimated the will of the Venezuelan people. During the brief imprisonment of President Chavez, the public demonstrated against the coup outside the presidential palace. At the same time, the Presidential Guard, which remained loyal to President Chavez, secured the presidential palace for the president to be able to return without having to engage the military. While imprisoned at Fort Tiuna, President Chavez enlisted the help of Fidel Castro. Both on Cuban TV and the Venezuelan media, President Chavez was able to make it clear to his supporters that he had **not** resigned.

Once news got out that President Chavez had never resigned and had been imprisoned against his will, thousands of Venezuelans took to the streets outside the presidential palace to demand the return of their **democratically** elected president. By the morning of April 13, 2002, President Chavez was reinstated. The interim presidency of Pedro Carmona had lasted less than two days. We have expressed our view that the American Empire tends to exaggerate its military prowess and for that reason loses more military invasions than it wins. However, this exaggeration of military prowess was taken to new heights under President George W. Bush. The decade long economic boom in the United States, before the election of George W. Bush in 2000, the relative economic decline of Japan during that same decade, the fall of the Soviet Union, and the September 11, 2001 attack in New York, promoted the *Bush-Wolfowitz* doctrine of regime change through unilateral pre-emptive strikes by the American Empire. See chapter 9 of our prequel, *Rise and Fall of the American Empire.* As a result of this fantasy notion that the American Empire had the military capability to single-handedly invade several "rogue" states simultaneously and regime change their leaders, President George W. Bush attempted simultaneous regime change in Afghanistan, Iraq and Venezuela. He failed miserably in Venezuela.

President Hugo Chavez as the Reincarnation of Simon Bolivar

President Chavez has resurrected the earlier effort made by Latin America's most celebrated liberator, Venezuelan born, Simon Bolivar, to unite the independent nations of South America. Bolivar, like so many, was fooled into believing that the United States, which had fought for its independence from the British Empire, was a liberal, democratic, republican model, which should be followed by the Spanish colonies in South America. To this end he fought for independence from the Spanish Empire and united the Spanish colonies by creating the *Republic of Gran Colombia* in 1819. This *Republic* encompassed the present day independent countries stretching south from Venezuela to Colombia, Ecuador, Peru and Bolivia. But Bolivar lasted as President of this *Republic* only until 1830. Unlike the United States of America, which had been created out of thirteen relatively tiny English colonies, with a much shorter history of any kind of separate identities, Bolivar was attempting to unite much larger Spanish colonies with relatively longer histories of distinct identities. By 1830, Bolivar's dream of a "United States of South America," which could rival the United States of America, had self destructed.

Simon Bolivar was an iconic figure in the struggle for independence from the Spanish Empire for the Spanish colonies in South America. Unfortunately, the Spanish Empire was replaced by a much more **evil** and controlling American Empire. The *Monroe Doctrine* of 1823 was not intended to free the American colonies from imperialism. It was intended to replace European imperialism by a much more all encompassing and pervasive American imperialism. The American Empire took advantage of the disunity of Latin America after the decline of the Spanish Empire. The goal of President Hugo Chavez is to use the popularity of Simon Bolivar and his vision of a united South America to unite Latin America in its struggle against American imperialism. This unification vision has been named the **Bolivarian Revolution.** The American Empire knows that and dearly wants to cut off the head of this vision by getting rid of Chavez by any means, including military coups, assassination or military invasion. In August 2005, American *Christianite,* Pat Robertson, issued a *Christianite "fatwa"* for the assassination of President Chavez. Operation, *Plan Balboa,* is widely believed to be the code name for a planned invasion of Venezuela by the American Empire.

One of the many constitutional changes which the Venezuelan people voted for in the December 15, 1999 referendum was to change the name of Venezuela to the **Bolivarian Republic of Venezuela.** At the heart of Chavez vision for Latin America is the removal of imperialism and the creation of a true democracy, *democratic socialism.* Western democracies are elitist. They are more oligarchic than democratic. It was this elitism and concentration of wealth based on the sanctity of private property which had inspired the revolutions in the middle of the nineteenth century led by Western European intellectuals. But American leadership of the West after the Second World War instilled a fear of communism in the masses of the West which enabled the oligarchy of the West to survive. Western propaganda by this oligarchy was used at every level of society to promote the false notion that all that was required to have a democracy is two or more political parties. Furthermore, any country governed by less than two political parties could not be democratic.

This simplistic view of democracy is easy to sell to a relatively ignorant electorate. In the United States, in particular, poverty of the lower class is endemic. The so called "American dream" is as likely for these Americans as winning the lottery. Yet they believe in it and vote for it, decade after decade. Their governments spend billions on wars and weapons of mass destruction but relatively little on reducing poverty. Yet they believe the lies about threats from all nations, large and small, who envy their way of life, that is, their miserable poverty, lack of healthcare, education and protection from natural disasters such as hurricane Katrina and man-made disasters such as the Gulf of Mexico oil spill. They are led to believe that they not only have a democracy, but the greatest democracy ever created in history. They are led to falsely believe that they have the most deeply entrenched freedoms such as the freedom of the press and the freedom to be the best they can be.

President Chavez is determined to use the oil and natural gas wealth of Venezuela to make Latin America an energy self sufficient region. Venezuela will supply energy to countries in Latin America at prices less than alternative suppliers. This will wean Venezuela from its dependence on the US market. As we have explained in Chapter 6, President Chavez has fostered the growth of a Latin America free trade area which excluded membership by the American Empire. President Chavez has publicly criticized American invasions of Iraq, Afghanistan and Haiti as well as the American backed invasions of Lebanon and Gaza by Israel, during the presidency of George W. Bush. In September, 2008, Venezuela broke off diplomatic relations with the American Empire and expelled the US ambassador to Venezuela, Patrick Duddy.

President Chavez, like so many of us, had hoped that American foreign policy would change for the better under the presidency of Barack Obama. I am personally impressed at how quickly President Chavez was able to see through the false rhetoric of Obama, the candidate for presidency. While President Chavez was willing to reach out to President Obama at the Summit of the Americas in April 2009, and to re-establish diplomatic relations with the American Empire in June 2009, he is definitely not fooled by Obama. He has rightly said that Obama has "the stench of Bush," and called the peace prize awarded to Obama the "Nobel **War** prize." On a more personal note, Obama's comparison of President Chavez with Oprah Winfrey, is one more piece of evidence of the mindset of today's American leaders. In my prequel, *Rise and Fall of the American Empire,* I have used the example of Oprah Winfrey's talk show to support what I have called "the dumbing down of America." Despite the fact that Obama made the comparison because the book given to Obama by Chavez jumped to number 2 on Amazon's best selling books, much like what happens when Oprah's book club selects a book, the comparison exposes a deep ignorance by today's American leaders of substance over style.

We have commented on the fact that American voters today never select leaders with vision. They select leaders who can read lines correctly, have a superficial awareness of everything but lack depth at anything, and are popular with people who waste their lives addicted to talk shows and popular TV shows exemplified by the Oprah Winfrey talk show. That President Obama would compare a book like *Open Veins of Latin America: Five Centuries of the Pillage of a Continent,* with the relatively trivial books promoted by Oprah Winfrey, or a visionary statesman like Chavez with a talk show queen like Oprah, is a perfect example of the breadth of trivia which today's American leaders must know, combined with their astounding lack of vision or substance.

Post World War II American Invasions outside Latin America and the Caribbean

We have already documented many of the post World War II American invasions outside Latin America and the Caribbean. These include the invasions of China, Korea, Vietnam and the Middle East. Here we will document the invasions of Afghanistan, Pakistan and Yemen, which will conclude our work and bring us right up to 2010. The invasion of Afghanistan, as well as the invasions of Iraq and Iran, was also covered in our prequel, *Rise and Fall of the American Empire.* The primary focus of that coverage was Iraq. At the time it seemed as if the American Empire had successfully colonized Afghanistan but was being defeated in Iraq. As we now know, the people of Afghanistan have mounted a very determined rebellion against American colonization. While in 2006 it appeared as if Iraq would be America's latest Vietnam, it's really Afghanistan that will surpass the American defeat in Vietnam. The invasion of Afghanistan in 2001 led to the Muslim resistance to American colonization of the Middle East moving from Afghanistan to Iraq. As American forces in Iraq increased to attempt to crush the resistance, President George W. Bush's so called *troop surge,* the Muslim resistance moved back to Afghanistan and spread to Pakistan and Yemen.

The American Empire's continued military invasions and warmongering under President Obama provides support for our claim that the American Empire has been addicted to wars since its beginning as a nation state and will continue to find excuses for its inherent aggressive nature and innate cultural make-up. President Obama has expanded the American invasions in Afghanistan and Iraq into Pakistan and Yemen. He also continues the American Empire's "cold war" invasion in Iran, Lebanon, Syria and Palestine, as well. This obsession with warmongering is a costly one which is unsustainable given its relative economic decline and massive debt. With its GDP shrinking to under 20 percent of the World's GDP the American Empire continues to spend more on its military than the total expenditure of the rest of the world. In combination with the global shift in economic growth from the West to the Third World in the 21st century we are observing in 2010 the permanent demise of the most powerful but short lived empire in history.

The US Invasion of Afghanistan Brings the American Empire to its Knees

It's truly unheard of that a very poor Third World country such as Afghanistan would not only defeat both of the World's *Super Powers*, the Soviet Union and the American Empire, but deliver the death blow to their superpower status. The Western press was quick to provide that assessment for the

Soviet Union. It is suffering from a large dose of delusion when it comes to recognizing the same fate for the American Empire. Prior to the Russian and American invasions, the British Empire had also failed to conquer Afghanistan after three invasions in 1839-1842, 1878-1880 and 1919. The current American invasion can be called the *fourth* British invasion since British Prime Minister, Tony Blair, was as much a war criminal as George W. Bush, in the illegal invasion of Afghanistan in 2001.

Alexander the Great conquered Afghanistan in 327 BC. The British Empire began its efforts to conquer Afghanistan in the 1830's after it had largely colonized India and other parts of Asia. By that time most of the Afghan population had converted to Islam. Afghanistan had become a **Muslim** state since the *seventh century* after the Arabs defeated the once mighty Persian Empire. This seemingly unimportant religious conversion of the Afghan people turned out to be the single most important factor in the defeat of both the Soviet Union and the American Empire. Yet it has been largely missed by the Western press and Western writers. Western writers are so imbued with their own "superior" view of their culture, religion, and extreme bias of what is right and what is wrong, that they cannot think or write outside the box.

The West refuses to even consider the premise that the Russian and American invasions of Afghanistan re-ignited the *Holy War* between Christianity and Islam dating back to the *Crusades*. Muslims have been stifling their grudge against the growing economic, political and cultural domination of the Christian West ever since Spain defeated Granada in 1491 and sent Columbus to the West Indies. Until the Soviet invasion of Afghanistan the Muslims had laid low and had even reconciled themselves to Western domination. The Muslim world had been colonized by France, Britain, Russia and the United States. It was unthinkable for Muslims to contemplate any kind of resistance to such a formidable military and economic powerhouse as the American Empire.

The Soviet Invasion of Afghanistan in 1979 provided the unplanned opportunity for Muslims to have a re-birth of the power and prestige they had lost to the Christian West after Columbus. As the French Empire had helped the 13 American colonies to defeat the English in the New World so would the American Empire help the Muslims to defeat the Russian Empire in Afghanistan. France had unwittingly helped to create the American Empire which would wrest hegemony from both France and England. In like fashion the American Empire had helped to create a re-birth of Islamic pride which would in turn defeat the American Empire in Afghanistan. This *religious* aspect of the American invasion of Afghanistan is the key to understanding why the resistance has been so determined and has become global. Muslims everywhere, including many living in the West, now question the morality and humanity of a civilization based on lies, deceit, warmongering and the subjugation and exploitation of the **non-white** races.

Muslims are presenting an alternative to Western ideas, culture, religion and fear- mongering in both Islamic states and non-Islamic states. They have the ear of the Muslim states, the Third World and the emerging economies of China, India, Brazil, Russia, Venezuela and others as well as the non-White Asian economies of Japan, South Korea, Taiwan, Hong Kong and Singapore, previously so closely allied to the West. Western leaders, Western writers and the Western media are at a loss to comprehend this re-birth of Islam and the desire of so many to now question centuries of Western propaganda honed to perfection. The Russian invasion of Afghanistan stirred a five-century dormant religion, which has now allied itself with Russia and Cold War supporters of Russia, as well as the Third World which had been colonized, exploited and denigrated by the West because of the skin colour of their people. This alliance came about because of the American invasion of Afghanistan in 2001.

The American Empire ignites an Islamic Renaissance during the Russian Invasion of Afghanistan

As with so many of the ironies of Western imperialism it was the American support of the people of Afghanistan against the Russian invasion of 1979-89 which began the burning desire of Muslims worldwide to defeat Western domination of their lands and their culture and religion, since Columbus. The official reason for American support of the Afghan people was the Cold War against communism. The unofficial reason was the expansion of the American Empire in Asia and the Middle East. Quite apart from the insatiable appetite of the American Empire for new conquests and warmongering, the Middle East and Central Asia had massive reserves of oil and natural gas. When combined with their relatively low domestic demand for energy, this region would control about 90 percent of the world's exports of oil and natural gas.

The American Empire had been dealt a severe blow by the Iranian revolution of 1979, which overthrew the US s.o.b. **dictatorship** of the Shah, Mohammad Reza Pahlavi. Using the Russian invasion of Afghanistan as the excuse for sending US troops into Afghanistan not only gave the American Empire an opportunity to expand its empire in Asia and the Middle East, it simultaneously halted the spread of the Iranian revolution into other Muslim states, as Muslims rallied behind the American Empire in support of Muslims in Afghanistan. It was a win-win opportunity for the **evil** American Empire. But in the long term it created an enemy the American Empire would never have imagined in 1979.

American military help to defeat the Russians in Afghanistan is the single most important factor in explaining the current resurgence of the historical conflict between Christians and Muslims. Prior to the Russian invasion of Afghanistan Muslims had felt powerless to criticize, much less challenge, the five centuries of Western **Christian** domination. Today they are challenging it in their homelands and in the cities of the West where Muslims migrated to, over those five centuries. The American Empire stirred up a hornets nest that it cannot tame or control, much less dominate.

Why Did the Soviet Union Invade Afghanistan in 1979?

By the 1970's the Soviet Union was in economic decline. It had lost the Cold War with the American Empire and the West. Its influence in the Middle East had been eroded by the military victories of the American *uncolony* of Israel, the peace agreement between Israel and Egypt, and the pro-American leaders in Saudi Arabia, Jordan, Iraq and Kuwait. In 1979, Afghanistan was a *communist* state, ruled by the *PDPA,* People's Democratic Party of Afghanistan. As with all *communist* states, the American Empire was engaged in covert activities to bring about a regime change. Prior to the PDPA, Afghanistan had been a monarchy. During the long rule of King Zahir, 1933-1973, the PDPA increased its popular support. The monarchy ended in 1973 when the King's cousin and former Prime Minister, Daoud Khan, overthrew the monarchy and created a Republic. Daoud's rule was very repressive and unpopular. With the help of the Afghan army, Daoud was overthrown in 1978 and the PDPA took over the government of the newly created *Democratic Republic of Afghanistan.*

Contrary to Western propaganda, the Soviet Union was in defensive mode throughout the period of the Cold War. The West always had the economic and military advantage. The West included all of the wealthy countries of the World, the United States, Canada, Western Europe and Australia. It used its economic and military superiority to threaten, intimidate and be on the offensive. This was the situation in Afghanistan in 1979. With the loss of Iran in February 1979, the American Empire increased its covert operations in Afghanistan in an effort to maintain its influence in the Middle East by compensating for the loss of Iran with a pro-American government in Afghanistan. The

Soviet "invasion" of 1979-1989 was a typical defensive move by the Soviet Union to check the ever expanding juggernaut of the American Empire.

As in any country, the PDPA had its share of opposition. It was natural that the American Empire would aid the opposition in its covert operations to overthrow the PDPA government. Opponents of the PDPA government included the *Islamist Mujahideen Resistance.* It was this opposition party which the American Empire backed to overthrow communism in Afghanistan and chalk up one more victory in the Cold War against the Soviet Union. Of course, at the time an *Islamist* was a Western brother worthy of Western brotherly love and Western media propaganda, a freedom fighter and the moral equivalent of the founding fathers of the American Revolution, according to President Reagan. After the American invasion of 2001, the Western media turned the same freedom fighter *Islamist* into a devil worse than a communist or a terrorist.

In backing the *Mujahideen,* the American Empire inadvertently increased tensions between India and Pakistan. Historically, Pakistan had supported the Mujahideen opposition in Afghanistan while India had supported the governing PDPA. The PDPA turned to the Soviet Union for help against the American backed insurgency. As the insurgency gathered momentum as a result of increased American support following the Iranian revolution of February 1979, the PDPA requested Soviet intervention in April of 1979. Fearing reprisals by the West, the Soviet Union hesitated. But the plight of the PDPA worsened and the Soviet Union began its intervention on June 16, 1979. This Soviet intervention beginning in June 1979 has since been referred to as the Soviet invasion of Afghanistan by the Western media. In reality, it was a civil war in which the American Empire backed the opposition party while the Soviet Union backed the ruling party. Afghanistan was caught up in the Cold War. As in other communist states, including Cuba and Vietnam, it is our contention that the West was the aggressor and the Soviet Union responded to a request for help by a communist government. It has since been learnt that the strategy of the American Empire was to create conditions in Afghanistan which would force the Soviet Union to intervene.

The British Empire had long opposed Russian interest in Afghanistan. It was one of the reasons for the first British invasion of Afghanistan in 1839-1842. Afghanistan is of strategic interest to both the British and the American empires because it straddles the Middle East and Central Asia. The American Empire today, like the British Empire before, longed to control both the Middle East and Central Asia. That historical strategic interest is even greater today because of the large reserves of oil and gas in both regions. While no oil or gas has yet been found in Afghanistan, colonizing Afghanistan makes it easier to both control the oil and gas in the Middle East and Central Asia and build oil and gas pipelines through Afghanistan to transport the oil and gas to the West. It was no surprise that the British Empire quickly fell behind the American Empire, along with Pakistan and Saudi Arabia, in funding and supporting the Mujahideen opposition to the Russian backed PDPA government of Afghanistan.

Soviet intervention in Afghanistan was very costly. At a time when the Soviet economy was in decline the American intervention was funded by a growing American economy as well as by funds from the British Empire and oil rich Gulf states. By 1985, when the pro-American, Mikhail Gorbachev, became General Secretary of the Communist Party of the Soviet Union, he began to look for an exit strategy from Afghanistan. On April 14,1988, the Soviet Union signed the *Geneva Accords* with the American Empire, agreeing to withdraw Soviet troops from Afghanistan. Economic reality combined with Gorbachev's naivety with regards to the imperialist ambitions of the West to dominate the World, forced a Soviet withdrawal from Afghanistan in 1989. In 1986, Mohammad Najibullah had been elected as President of Afghanistan. With the Soviet Union indicating its intention to withdraw its support for the communist regime, Najibullah had attempted a policy of national reconciliation with the Mujahideen. But the civil war in Afghanistan continued after the Soviet withdrawal. The Najibullah government was overthrown by the Mujahideen in 1992.

Why Did the American Empire Invade Afghanistan in 2001?

By the end of the Cold War/Civil War in Afghanistan in 1992, Afghanistan was on the verge of becoming a failed state. Its economy and infrastructure had been devastated. Afghan refugees made up one-third of the total refugees in the World. Most of the Afghan refugees fled into Pakistan and Iran. Some 5 million Afghans were killed or wounded and another 5 million fled the country. Both the Soviet Union and the American Empire had continued to fund the Cold War/Civil War after signing the *Geneva Accords.* But the economic collapse of the Soviet Union forced an end to its funding of the Najibullah government. Lack of Soviet funding enabled the Mujahideen victory in 1992. With the collapse of the Soviet Union in 1991 the American Empire ended its financial support to the Mujahideen government to rebuild Afghanistan. The goal of the American intervention had been to destroy the Soviet Union and end its competition with the American Empire for World domination. That goal had been achieved.

There is an eerie similarity between the French intervention in the American War of Independence and the American intervention in the Afghan Cold War/Civil War. When the French Empire supported the rebellion of 13 tiny English colonies it never imagined in its wildest dreams that it would create a rival that would one day defeat it. Its goal had been to defeat the British Empire. In like manner the support of the Mujahideen by the American Empire was intended to defeat the Soviet Union not create a rival that would destroy it. Never in its wildest dream would the American Empire have envisaged that a rag tag group of Islamist rebels in Afghanistan would grow and become so powerful as to threaten the hegemony of the most powerful empire the World had ever seen.

Without American financial aid the Mujahideen government established in Afghanistan in 1992 came under fire from several opposition forces. Firstly, opposition came from remnants of the PDPA. Secondly, the rebels fought among themselves, dividing into various factions. Thirdly, opposition came from a *Sunni* Islamist group which we now call the *Taliban.* Its leader, Mullah Omar, has still escaped capture by the American Empire. The Taliban took advantage of the incessant fighting and disorderly behaviour among the various factions of the Mujahideen rebels to win popular support from the Afghan people for law and order. The American Empire had provided military and financial support to all Muslim groups, including the Taliban, during the Cold War/Civil War. The American ally in the Cold War/Civil War, Pakistan, continued to provide military and financial support to the Taliban after the American Empire had withdrawn its support following the fall of the Soviet Union.

The Taliban shares its *Pashtun* ethnicity with Pashtuns in Pakistan. In Afghanistan, Pashtuns have historically been the dominant and ruling ethnic group. Today Pashtuns still account for over 40 percent of the population of Afghanistan, numbering over 15 million. In neighbouring Pakistan, Pashtuns are the second largest ethnic group accounting for over 15 percent of Pakistan's population and numbering over 28 million. The Western media today speaks incessantly of the Taliban resistance to the American occupation as centred in Southern Afghanistan, *Helmand Province,* with help from Pakistanis living in North-western Pakistan bordering Afghanistan. This is no coincidence. The Taliban did not fall into Afghanistan from Mars, as the Western media would have us believe. The Pashtuns have lived in South-eastern Afghanistan and North-western Pakistan for centuries. In fact, it was the British who separated the Afghan Pashtuns from their "brothers and sisters" in North-western Pakistan when the British created the new state of Pakistan in 1947. They were there long before the West anointed the United States to lead the "unfree" World. They will be there long after the fall of the American Empire.

With Pakistan's help, the Taliban marched from its historical base in Southern Afghanistan to capture the city of Herat in September 1994. The following month the Taliban captured Kandahar City. Within a few months after the capture of Kandahar City, the Taliban had captured 12 of Afghanistan's 34 provinces from the Mujahideen. On September 27, 1996 the Taliban captured the Afghan capital of Kabul and overthrew the corrupt and dysfunctional Mujahideen government of President Burhanuddin Rabbani. Rabbani returned to Afghan politics to lead the opposition to the American installed Hamid Karzai's presidency.

The Taliban government in Afghanistan was recognized and supported by three Muslim states, Saudi Arabia, Pakistan and the United Arab Emirates. The Taliban government worked cooperatively with Pakistan to open and secure the trade route from Pakistan through Afghanistan to the newly independent Central Asian Republics of Kazakhstan, Uzbekistan, Kyrgyzstan, Turkmenistan and Tajikistan. These Central Asian states have large Muslim populations and became independent republics in 1991 as a result of the fall of the Soviet Union. This is one more example of how the American defeat of the Soviet Union in Afghanistan contributed to the current resurgence of Islam. These states are also well endowed with reserves of oil and gas which add to their common bond with the oil rich states in the Middle East.

While the reasons for the American invasion of Afghanistan in 2001 are multi-dimensional, one of those reasons was to have a government in Afghanistan that would support a pipeline through Afghanistan to transport oil and gas from the newly independent Central Asian Republics to the West. Such a pipeline would run from the Central Asian Republics through Afghanistan and Pakistan to the Indian Ocean. American oil companies had acquired the rights to produce most of the oil and gas in these republics. With the loss of Iran, a pipeline through Afghanistan rather than one through Iran became relatively more significant, as one of the reasons to invade and colonize Afghanistan.

The American oil company, *Unocal,* favoured a pipeline through Afghanistan and had talks with the Taliban government before the American invasion. These talks indicated Taliban support for such a pipeline until President Clinton decided to bomb Afghanistan in August 1998. President Clinton needed to divert public opinion from the Monica Lewinsky scandal by starting another war and invasion. The Monica Lewinsky scandal was publicized by the Washington Post on January 21, 1998. President Clinton issued his infamous denial on January 26, 1998. But the Republican Party refused to let the matter die and President Clinton was forced to admit to the affair on August 17, 1998. As we have repeated many times wars and invasions are extremely popular with the American electorate. It's the safest way of diverting public opinion from domestic mistakes. The bombing was followed with economic sanctions against Afghanistan. This made it impossible for the Taliban to support an American pipeline through Afghanistan. It became very clear to the post-1998 American administrations that *regime change* in Afghanistan was a pre-requisite for an American pipeline through Afghan territory.

The United Islamic Front, UIF: Northern Alliance

With *regime change* as the post-1998 goal of the American Empire, the American Empire looked for an Afghan **Islamic** alternative to the Taliban. It turned to the *United Islamist Front or UIF.* However, with its so called "War on terror," recognized by most as an anti-Islamic war, the American Empire could not risk confusing its ignorant supporters by publicly allying itself with another *Islamist* group. Such a public alliance with one *Islamist* group to fight another *Islamist* group would compromise its propaganda efforts to associate terrorists with Islamists. It therefore chose the name of the *Northern Alliance* to publicly refer to its alliance with the *United Islamic Front.*

As we said before the Taliban's base is in Southern Afghanistan. After taking control of the Afghan government in 1996, the Taliban never subdued anti-Taliban resistance in Northern Afghanistan. The *UIF* was largely made up of remnants of the Afghan government overthrown by the Taliban in 1996 with a strong base in Northern Afghanistan. To call the *United Islamist Front* the Northern Alliance is the equivalent of calling the Taliban the *Southern Alliance.* At the beginning of the American invasion of Afghanistan in 2001, the *United Islamist Front* exercised military and political control over about 30 percent of Afghans comprised largely of three ethnic groups, Tajiks, Uzbeks and Hazara, living in the northern provinces of Afghanistan.

One rather interesting outcome of this new American alliance with *Islamists* in Afghanistan is that the *Mujahideen,* which the American Empire allied with to overthrow the Soviet Union is now divided. The *Mujahideens* who follow the leadership of Osama bin Laden and Ayman al-Zawahiri are clearly opposed to the American colonization of Afghanistan. On the other hand, the *United Islamist Front* has the support of many of the *Mujahideens* who had formed the government of Afghanistan under President Burhanuddin Rabbani. The "regime change" by the American Empire in 2001 was to a large extent a return to the *Islamist* government overthrown by the Taliban in 1996.

The important difference between the pre-Taliban *Mujahideen* government in Afghanistan and the post-Taliban *Mujahideen* government in Afghanistan is that the post-Taliban *Mujahideen* government is a puppet government of the American *uncolony* of Afghanistan. The American Empire had withdrawn from Afghanistan after the defeat of the Soviet Union. Its mission in Afghanistan was to defeat the Soviet Union and that mission had been accomplished. Its current mission in Afghanistan is the colonization and subjugation of Afghanistan. This will not only give it the power to build pipelines in Afghanistan to transport Central Asian oil and gas but an important strategic location to oppose Iran and support its long standing interest in colonizing the Middle East.

The role of *9/11* in the American Invasion of Afghanistan

Just as the American Empire did not enter World War II because of the Japanese attack on Pearl Harbour, the American Empire did not invade Afghanistan because of the *9/11* attacks on the Twin Towers in New York. In both cases they were important catalysts in initiating long held plans of imperial expansion. As we explained the American Empire entered World War II to prevent an alliance between Germany and Mexico to recapture Mexican territory colonized by the American Empire and to compete with Japan for Asia and the Pacific. Likewise the American Empire invaded Afghanistan and Iraq to expand its empire in the Middle East and Central Asia.

The Second World War was a war of aggression by the Western empires. How else can anyone explain the unexploded bombs in Africa today resulting from the massive tank warfare between Germany and Britain on African soil? How can anyone justify foreigners using a militarily weak country as their backyard to devastate and pummel each other? If that is how you preserve freedom and democracy I can live without that kind of freedom and democracy. No. The Brits and Germans fought in Africa and elsewhere during the Second World War to colonize Africa, Egypt, the Suez Canal, the Middle East and the World. Likewise the Americans fought the Second World War to colonize Asia, the Pacific, Latin America, the Caribbean and the World.

Just as the American Empire used the Japanese attack on Pearl Harbour to justify its warmongering and imperialism during World War II the American Empire used *9/11* to justify its warmongering and imperialism in the first decade of the 21st century. This decade of American invasions and warmongering marks an unbreakable continuous history of wars and invasions by the American

Empire since, and even before, its birth. It's an empire founded on lands stolen from the First Nations by fighting, killing, enslaving, dehumanising and imprisoning First Nations in reserves. It's an empire founded on African slavery and the transatlantic slave trade. It's an empire founded on the sanction of piracy. It's an empire founded on lies, deceit, propaganda, suppression of freedoms, weapons of mass destruction, racism, hypocrisy, addiction to warmongering, addiction to frivolous consumption, waste and planetary degradation.

There is very little that the West, and its anointed leader, the American Empire, can offer humanity. In the six centuries it has dominated the World it has promoted the most primitive and inhumane idiocy that nations must be at constant war to live in peace. Every new war it starts and engages with great vigour is yet another war to make us live in peace. That is the dumbest and most stupid idea that a brain dead Western civilization has bequeathed to the human race during its six centuries of leadership. Even those who criticize these endless wars as counter productive quickly defend the military and the soldiers absolving them from any blame or responsibility for fear that the establishment would say that they are unpatriotic or, heaven forbid, cast aspersions on "our brave boys in uniform" who are making the ultimate sacrifice for our protection and freedom. The fact that these "brave boys" are the primary cause of the deaths of millions of innocent women and children seems to conveniently escape even these critics of war. In Afghanistan alone these "brave boys" have killed as many as **seven million.** A Western soldier fully armed with the most sophisticated killing machine is promoted to the status of hero worship while a primitively armed resistance fighter is branded a coward, a terrorist, an Islamist and a non-combatant who is not entitled to the protection of the Geneva Convention against torture. The Western World is truly an "upside Down" World.

Operation Moshtarak: Are Canadians Warmongers, Stupid, Misinformed, or Simply the Worst Hypocrites?

In 1980 Canada boycotted the Olympics in Russia. The reason for the Canadian boycott was the Russian Invasion of Afghanistan. The beginning of the *Vancouver* Olympic Games in Canada on *February 13, 2010,* coincided with the launch of *Operation Moshtarak,* a massive military offensive by the American Empire in Southern Afghanistan. Canada proudly used the Vancouver Olympics to encourage its military to invade, conquer and subjugate the people of Afghanistan, participating in the killing of a hundred thousand defenceless men, women and children, between 2001 and 2010. Canadian forces and their families participated in the torch relay across Canada in a deliberate attempt by Canada to get support for its **illegal** invasion of Afghanistan. Even the Paralympics torch was carried by one Canadian veteran wounded in Afghanistan.

The February 2010 Western offensive in *Helmand* province, the largest military offensive in Afghanistan following the overthrow of the Taliban government, was widely publicized as one of using overwhelming firepower against civilians and primitively armed Taliban freedom fighters. Canada used its Chinook helicopters to drop heavily armed Western soldiers into *Helmand* province, Southern Afghanistan. It represented the largest use of Canadian helicopters in a single operation in Afghanistan. With 4,000 British troops involved it was also the largest single British support for the American invasion. In general the Brits and Canadians have been the most willing of the American allies to send their soldiers to kill innocent and defenceless Afghan men, women and children, and be killed, in turn. Is there something about the Anglo race that makes them more diehard warmongers than other Western imperialists? One brain-dead British General remarked that it was important to convince the Afghans in *Marjah* that they "come in peace." I guess that would explain why they came with the most massive firepower of the entire invasion. His remark was as asinine as the typical US marine's attempt to win "hearts and minds" by pointing a gun and commanding the insurgent to "love me or I will shoot." President Obama added 30,000 of these armed idiots to those sent by President George W. Bush to win "hearts and minds" by killing their women and children.

On February 13, 2010, as the Olympic races in Whistler, Cypress and Richmond, began in Western Canada, Canadian soldiers participated in the "search and destroy," mission in *Marjah* and *Nad Ali,* in Southern Afghanistan. Canadian commanders, Colonel Christian Drouin and Lieutenant Colonel Jeff Smyth, boasted about the lack of resistance from the Taliban. But the invaders still killed at least 30 Afghans. The following day, *February 14, 2010,* while the second day of Olympic competition continued in Western Canada, Canada was a proud participant of a "Valentine Day massacre," when the American Empire's "precision" rockets killed 12 Afghan civilians hiding in their home in *Nad Ali.* Canada dismisses these acts of savagery against unarmed Third World *non-Whites* as "collateral damage." Canadians mourn the deaths of their soldiers, who they have sent thousands of miles with the mission to kill and maim the defenceless people of the Third World, but never mourn the many who are killed by their soldiers. It's as if the lives of the people of the Third World have little significance compared to the lives of Canadians.

It was no coincidence that *Operation Moshtarak* began the same day as the Winter Olympics in Canada. *Operation Moshtarak* is a desperate attempt by the increasingly unpopular Obama administration to salvage some kind of "victory" from the Afghanistan disaster. As the most willing participant in the massacre of innocent women and children by the American Empire, Canada's Prime Minister, Steven Harper, was only too happy to use the Winter Olympics in Canada to take the eyes of the World's media off the massacre of innocent Afghans in *Marjah* and *Nad Ali* by having them focused for two weeks on Vancouver and Whistler in British Columbia, Canada. Every intelligent Western critic of the War in Afghanistan has correctly concluded that there is absolutely nothing to be gained by *Operation Moshtarak* except senseless killing on both sides. The evidence that the Taliban cannot be defeated is now overwhelming. The American Empire knows that and Canada knows that. It was therefore important for this senseless bloodbath to take place while the Western media had the Winter Olympics in Canada to keep it occupied.

The lesson we must take away from Canada's double standard is that imperialism, invasions and subjugation of the people of the Third World, such as the people of Afghanistan, is only bad if the imperial power is **communist.** In such a case the Olympics must be used to punish the imperialist. If the imperial power is **capitalist,** like Canada, then imperialism, invasion and subjugation is good. The Olympics must be used to reward the imperialist. When Canada boycotted the 1980 Olympics in Russia, Canada's athletes were bitterly disappointed. Years of training were sacrificed. But Canada's government, and the Canadian people, convinced the athletes that their sacrifice was for a just cause. In 2010, The Canadian government and the Canadian people used the Olympics, and the Canadian athletes, to promote warmongering. The irony is that in both 1980 and 2010, the same country, Afghanistan, was being illegally invaded and colonized. In 2010, one of the invaders was Canada. How can Canadians not see the hypocrisy?

Before the Winter Olympics ended on February 28, 2010, the American Empire had captured *Marjah* and "democratically elected" an Afghan imprisoned for four years in Germany for assaulting his step son, *Abdul Zahir,* as the new mayor. When criticized for imposing an ex-criminal as mayor, British Major General, Nic Carter, the allied commander in Southern Afghanistan, defended the imposition by saying, "there was no reason to suppose that *Zahir* was any worse than other Afghan politicians," imposed by the invaders. Canadians can be proud to have done their part to preserve freedom and democracy in this small town of 75,000 souls in Southern Afghanistan. How much more "civilized" than preventing the Church of Latter-day Saints from exercising their **illegal** rights to polygamy and exploiting women and young girls in *Bountiful, British Columbia,* the same

Canadian province hosting the Winter Olympics? The church leader, Winston Blackmore has a mere 19 wives.

Mayor Abdul Zahir has been given the task of convincing the inhabitants of *Marjah* that the killing and maiming of their family and relatives as well as the wanton destruction of their homes and livelihood by the Western invaders was done to bring Western democracy and freedom into their lives. General Stanley McChrystal, President Obama's "Douglas MacArthur," in Afghanistan, personally attended a council meeting called in *Marjah* to allow Afghans to complain or vent their anger, or praise, this very "civilized" Western invention. After this very "civilized" Western democratic process McChrystal proudly announced to reporters that the key was to get the locals to shape the process because "they will know best." Canadians can take heart that they helped the American Empire to "regime change" the government of Afghanistan by using overwhelming military force because Afghans know what is best for them. Am I the only one confused by this kind of logic?

Like every country which the American Empire colonized in Latin America, Afghanistan today is a dirt poor country with no security, no government representing the people, destroyed homes, infrastructure, dreams and opportunities. Some 60 percent of Afghanistan's very low post-American invasion GDP comes from illegal drugs such as opium and heroin. Western imposed politicians are mostly drug lords and war lords or ex-criminals like Mayor Zahir in Marjah. There is massive unemployment. Women's rights and opportunities have deteriorated since the American invasion. Most importantly is the massive bombing and killing of innocent civilians and a legacy of unexploded bombs which will continue to kill children for many decades as unexploded American bombs continue to kill the children of Cambodia today. The West, including Canada, has a lot of innocent blood on its hands and must change its **evil** behaviour before it can preach to others.

American invasions, such as its current invasion of Afghanistan, represent far worse examples of naked aggression against military weak states than Hitler's invasion of Poland in 1939. As we said before, even the Soviet invasion of 1979, inexcusable as it was, could be forgiven as a defensive move against the American Empire during the Cold War. There are no such defensive arguments for the American invasions in Afghanistan or Iraq. They are the purest form of **naked and wanton aggression** by a superior military power. Absolutely no one can provide even the tiniest piece of justification for such **naked aggression.** The American Empire, and countries contributing men and arms for such examples of **naked aggression,** has lost the moral right to scold or chastise any country for human rights abuses or acquiring nuclear weapons or aggression against neighbouring states. The West needs to look inwards at six centuries of warmongering, amassing of weapons of mass destruction, imperialism, human rights abuses and **crimes against humanity.** It must first change its own **evil** deeds before criticizing or scolding any other nation.

The *New* Cold War and the Dangerous American Rolling of the Pakistani Dice

President Obama's expansion of military activity into nuclear armed and politically volatile Pakistan, begun under President George W. Bush, is the most dangerous misadventure of the American Empire since the Korean War. The so called "War on Terror," is nothing other than a **new** *Cold War* to replace the old Cold War which ended in 1991, with the collapse of the Soviet Union. During the old Cold War from 1945 to 1991 there were many "hot wars" fought in Korea, Vietnam, Latin America and elsewhere. In like manner, the American invasions of Iraq and Afghanistan are the identical equivalent "hot wars," of what I now call a **new** Cold War. This **new** Cold War has nothing to do with a revitalised Russia under Vladimir Putin. It is simply the necessary replacement for an American Empire **addicted** to warmongering.

While the American invasions of Vietnam, Iraq and Afghanistan have been military disasters for the American Empire it was the American invasion of Korea which most resembles its current spill-over invasion from Afghanistan into Pakistan. I say this because the Korean invasion spilled over into China bringing the American Empire to the brink of nuclear war with Russia. At the time China had no nuclear weapons but the decision of General MacArthur to invade China from Korea brought nuclear armed Russia to China's defence. MacArthur was fired and nuclear holocaust averted. See my prequel, *Rise and Fall of the American Empire.*

The American Empire threatened to invade China after it was losing its invasion of Korea. A bully threatens those who aid its victims. In like manner, the American Empire today is invading and threatening to expand its invasion of Pakistan because it is losing its invasion of Afghanistan. Its earlier threat to invade China backfired by increasing Chinese support for Koreans against its invasion of Korea. China had long historical ties with the people of Korea. In like manner its current threat to Pakistan will very likely backfire. The people of Pakistan share a common religion, Islam, with the people of Afghanistan. They have long historical ties with each other. Many in both countries recognize the American Empire for what it is, the World's most powerful bully. The people of Pakistan also know that it is possible to defeat the American Empire with guerrilla warfare. As a last resort Pakistan's nuclear arsenal is the safest defence it has against all out American aggression or bullying.

The January 21, 2010 *Report to the US Senate Committee on Foreign Relations,* concluded that Al Qaeda was pushed into Pakistan's *Federally Administered Tribal Authority* region which borders Afghanistan. This region has an area of over 27,000 square kilometres and is guaranteed autonomous governance by the various tribes inhabiting this inhospitable mountainous area, by the constitution of Pakistan. One of the tribes inhabiting this region is the *Pashtun* tribe. The American Empire fully understands that its war on the *Pashtuns* in Afghanistan will spill over into Pakistan's *Federally Administered Tribal Autonomous Region* because of the *Pashtun* inhabitants in that region. As usual it uses its time honoured propaganda machine to convince the gullible American electorate that it is losing the war in Afghanistan because Pakistan is supporting the "terrorists" in Afghanistan.

In the Vietnam War the American Empire convinced the American electorate that it needed to invade Cambodia and Laos to win the Vietnam War because the "Congs" were using Cambodia and Laos to transport weapons into South Vietnam. In reality it was the excuse to expand its warmongering in Indochina. In like manner it is using Pakistan today as its scapegoat to get the support of the American people to expand its warmongering in the Middle East and Central Asia. "Congs" have been replaced by "Islamists." The American people are so naïve that they refuse to accept the fact that a Pakistani born American, *Faisal Shahzad,* attempted to explode a bomb in New York's Time Square on Saturday, May1, 2010, for one reason and one reason only. He wants the American Empire out of Pakistan. The American people continue to believe the lies of their government propaganda that this Pakistani born American is jealous of the "freedoms" which Americans enjoy or that he is some kind of misguided religious fanatic like their own *Christianites* such as Rush Limbaugh.

What is laughable about this attempted bombing is the media's spin on the ineptitude of the "would be" bomber. How many of us have the knowledge to successfully and efficiently make a bomb and detonate it? The lesson should be that the people invaded by the American Empire are so fed up with American invasions which kill and maim so many innocent men, women and children that they are willing to strike back with the most primitive weapons and know how? Furthermore, failure of a bomb to detonate and kill or maim, does not negate its effect in making a bold and courageous statement against Western imperialism nor negate the perceived failure of the American Empire to protect Americans, despite its vast expenditures on its military and supposedly military invincibility.

It's no surprise to me that it was later discovered that *Faisal Shahzad* had visited the *Pashtun* city of Peshawar, Pakistan where his father and relatives now live, in July 2009, while he was on a six months holiday in Pakistan. It's the same reason that President Obama and other Western politicians visit Afghanistan and Iraq. They want an up close and personal assessment of what is happening. As a cousin of Faisal's father, Kifyat Ali, surmised correctly, President Obama will use Faisal's attempt at defending his native country of Pakistan, as an excuse to kill more *Pashtuns.* We have also explained the ethnic link between the Taliban and the Pashtuns. The American invasions of Iraq, Afghanistan and Pakistan represent simultaneously a war against Islam, a war against the Taliban, a war against Al Qaeda and a war against the Pashtuns. The Western media belatedly came around to the fact that it was the American invasion of Iraq which begat *Al Qaeda in Iraq.* Yet this same Western media seems incapable of forming the obvious conclusion that it is the current American invasion of Pakistan that created *Al Qaeda in Pakistan* and the *Pakistani Taliban.* Just as *Al Qaeda in Iraq* had absolutely nothing to do with religious fanaticism but everything to do with resisting American imperialism so too does *Al Qaeda in Pakistan* and the *Pakistani Taliban* have nothing to do with religious fanaticism and everything to do with resisting American imperialism.

Contrary to comments by prominent Americans, including popular comedian, *Bill Maher,* it is not "Muslim fanatics" that are killing Westerners, it is the West that is killing Muslims. The West has both the military firepower and the addiction to warmongering to kill millions of Muslims. Even if Muslims were religious fanatics and the Koran preached Jihad, as *Bill Maher* claimed on CNN's *Larry King Live* only a few days after *Shahzad's* attempted bombing in Times Square, they lack the military firepower to kill Christians in the kind of numbers even close to the thousands of Muslims being killed each month by Christians in Iraq, Afghanistan, Palestine, Lebanon, Pakistan and Yemen. Americans like *Bill Maher* are so full of their innate conceit based on their Western "superiority," that they miss even the most rudimentary facts.

Pakistani resistance to the American invasion of Pakistan is strongest in Pakistan's North-West Frontier Province, the smallest of Pakistan's four provinces. *Pashtuns* are the dominant ethnic group of this province and Peshawar is the capital city with 3 million inhabitants. It's also the city that the American Empire used as its head quarters to train and arm the *Mujahideen* to fight the Russians in Afghanistan. American created "terrorist" *Osama bin Laden* arrived in Peshawar in 1980 to co-ordinate the resources of Saudi Arabia with those of the American Empire in a joint *Western-Islamist* assault on the Soviet Union. Both Al-Qaeda and the Taliban were born in this region of Pakistan precisely because the American Empire took advantage of its relative lack of control by the Pakistani government and Pakistani military as well as its *Pashtun* ethnicity.

Thousands of Afghan refugees from the two-decade American-Soviet inspired Civil War in Afghanistan later fled to this province of Pakistan increasing the *Af-Pak* connection. Now the American Empire is bullying the same Pakistani government and military to clean up the *jihadist* movement it created there in the 1980's. Another irony is that current American aid to Pakistan goes to the Pakistani government in Islamabad to bribe the Pakistani government and Pakistani military to kill *Pashtuns* in its *North-West Frontier Province.* But aid is most needed in Pakistan's *North-West Frontier Province* because of the massive influx of Afghan refugees and orphaned children which fled the American created Civil War in Afghanistan in the 1980's and 1990's. In the 1980's the American Empire conspired with the *Pashtuns* to increase their independence from Pakistan's central government in Islamabad. In 2010, the Obama administration is funding a Civil War in Pakistan against *Pashtun* independence.

Pashtuns in Pakistan's *North-West Frontier Province* are as opposed to the American invasion of Pakistan as Pashtuns in Pakistan's *Federally Administered Tribal Autonomous Region* which we have referred to above as the focus of the January 21, 2010 Report to the US Senate Committee on

Foreign Relations. In fact, the American invasion of Afghanistan has led to Pashtuns in Afghanistan uniting with Pashtuns in both Pakistan's *North-West Frontier Province* and *Federally Administered Tribal Areas* to contemplate the creation of a new independent state of *Pashtunistan.* Such a state would simultaneously oppose American imperialism while promoting Pashtun nationalism. Having lost East Pakistan to the independent state of *Bangladesh* after the 1971 Civil War the Muslim state of Pakistan carved out of India by Britain in 1947 must feel rightly confused and frustrated by the simultaneous American financial aid and threat to "bomb it back to the stone-age" if it does not do the bidding of the American Empire.

American Invasion of Yemen

Yemen is the most recent target of America's so called "War on Terror." The *Report to the US Senate Committee on Foreign Relations* in January of 2010, referred to above, concluded that the pummelling of Iraq, Afghanistan and Pakistan by the military forces of the American Empire and NATO countries has pushed Al Qaeda into bases in Yemen, Somalia, North Africa and Southeast Asia. That is great for the military-industrial complex of the West but disastrous for those who love peace and had naively hoped that the election of a "Black" president in the White House would have wined down America's fabricated "War on Terror."

As the US invasion of Afghanistan in 2001 widened to Iraq and then back to Afghanistan and into Pakistan it is now certain to escalate across the entire region into Yemen, Somalia, North Africa and beyond. At least one online public opinion poll claimed that 71 percent of Americans favour a US invasion of Yemen. Senator Joe Lieberman called for a pre-emptive strike on Yemen reminiscent of President George W. Bush's pre-emptive strike on Iraq. There is no evidence that in 2010 the majority of Americans, or Westerners in general, see that this two-decade old Western "War on Terror" is counter-productive. Nor do they recognize the dismal failure of the *Bush-Wolfowitz doctrine* of unilateral pre-emptive strikes by the American Empire. I can understand why the military-industrial complex wants this war to escalate. It's more difficult to comprehend why the majority of the people in the West wants this war to escalate? As this senseless war escalates the killing and maiming of the innocent and the defenceless will far exceed the staggering numbers who have already been victims.

President Reagan recruited Yeminis as "freedom fighters" in his *holy jihad* against the Soviet Union in Afghanistan during the 1980's. With a population of almost 30 million and one of the poorest countries in the oil rich Middle East, Yemen supplied significant numbers of "freedom fighters" for President Reagan's Cold War efforts in Afghanistan. Osama bin Laden's Yemini roots stemming from his Yemini father and close historical ties between Yemen and Saudi Arabia was an advantage to President Reagan in recruiting Yemenis to his Christian "jihad" against the Soviet Union in Afghanistan. But Reagan's Yemeni "freedom fighters" supported Osama bin Laden, not Saudi Arabia, when the first President Bush, Herbert Bush, launched the Gulf War against Saddam Hussein in 1990. It was especially galling to both the American Empire and Saudi Arabia when Yemen, as a non-permanent member of the UN Security Council, voted against the American UN resolution to authorize the American invasion of Iraq and Kuwait to roll back the Iraqi occupation of Kuwait. We have addressed at some length the fact that Osama bin Laden did a 180 degree reversal of support for both the American Empire and his native Saudi Arabia when Saudi Arabia chose the American Empire over him to drive Iraq out of Kuwait in our prequel, *Rise and Fall of the American Empire.*

As a result of Yemen's refusal to support the 1990 American invasion of Iraq the American Empire declared war on Yemen. It withdrew all financial aid and backed military attacks on Yemen by Saudi Arabia and other neighbouring states which had voted for the 1990 American invasion of Iraq. Yemen responded as every state has responded for the last six centuries when attacked by a militarily superior empire, guerrilla warfare. As we have explained the West now uses the term *terrorism* when it means guerrilla resistance against imperial invasion for propaganda purposes only. This Yemeni resistance to American aggression in Yemen is referred to by the American Empire as *Al Qaeda in Yemen*. As in Iraq, Afghanistan and Pakistan the American Empire exploits historical divisions among the Yemeni population. Among these historical divisions is the dispute between North and South Yemen, reminiscent of disputes between North and South Korea and between North and South Vietnam previously exploited by the American Empire to expand its empire in Asia.

North Yemen became an independent state after the Ottoman Empire was defeated by the West in World War I. **Shiite** Muslims are the dominant religious group in **North** Yemen. **South** Yemen became a British colony and did not secure its independence from Britain until 1967. **Sunni** Muslims are the dominant religious group in **South** Yemen. Like North Korea and North Vietnam, **South** Yemen was continuously harassed by the American Empire throughout the old Cold War period because of its supposedly pro-communist stance. At the same time the American Empire supplied arms and military aid to **North** Yemen as it had done to South Korea and South Vietnam. With the collapse of the Soviet Union the continued economic and military harassment of **South** Yemen by the West caused the disintegration of the **South** Yemini economy and government and the merger of South Yemen with North Yemen in 1990. But Yemen's UN vote against the American invasion of Iraq in 1990 led the American Empire to wage war against all of Yemen.

Yemini resistance to America's undeclared war with Yemen got the attention of the Western media when Yemen was blamed for the October 2000 attack on the *USS Cole* while anchored in the Yemini port of Aden, killing 17 American sailors. With the American Empire suffering humiliating defeats in Somalia, Lebanon, Iraq, Afghanistan and Pakistan, Yemen received zero respect from the Western media until December 25, 2009. As with the attempted Time Square bombing of May 1, 2010 which brought home to Americans their empire's warmongering in Pakistan so did the attempted Christmas Day bombing bring home to Americans their empire's warmongering in Yemen. The would be "panty-bomber" of the Northwest Airlines flight on December 25, 2009, *Umar Farouk Abdulmutallab,* appears to be linked to *Al Qaeda in Yemen.*

Yemini resistance has formed links with Somalia's long resistance to American invasions. In addition to proven reserves of oil and gas Somalia's strategic location on the coast of the Arabian Sea makes it an important target of American imperialism in the Arabian Sea. Somalia's resistance to American imperialism became *infamous* when the Somali resistance shot down two American Black Hawk helicopters and damaged three others in October 1993. The American Empire had trained "freedom fighters" in Afghanistan how to use rocket-propelled grenade launchers to shoot down Russian helicopters. Somewhat ironically it was Pakistani forces stationed in Somalia by the American puppet international body, the UN, using Pakistani tanks, which rescued the trapped Americans from certain death by the Somali resistance during this *Battle of Mogadishu.* Today Somalia is using its strategic coastline and another Western warmongering tool, *piracy,* to harass the West and the American Empire. Just as the spill-over of the American invasion of Afghanistan into Pakistan is now referred to as Obama's *Af-Pak* invasion, President Obama's 2010 intensification of the American invasions of Somalia and Yemen has now become Obama's *Yem-Som* War. As the Taliban can easily move back and forth across the *Af-Pak* border *Yem-Som* "freedom-fighters" can easily cross the straight which separates Yemen from Somalia.

As we have mentioned the January 21, 2010 *Report to the US Senate Committee on Foreign Relations* singled out not only Pakistan and Yemen as countries resisting the American invasions in the Middle East and Asia but North Africa, Southeast Asia and Somalia, as well. It also makes reference to *Al Qaeda in the Arabian Peninsula*. Nigeria has also surfaced in the Western media as a possible country opposed to the American invasions of Muslim countries because *Umar Abdulmutallab* is a 23 year old Nigerian and Nigeria has both oil and a very large Muslim population. Nigerians were included in a list of 14 Nationals targeted for special scrutiny at American airports following the attempted December 25, 2009 bombing of the Northwest Airline flight. This latest list is another example of an ever increasing number of countries, Pakistan, Yemen, Somalia, Sudan, Algeria, Libya, Syria, Lebanon, Saudi Arabia, Iran, Cuba, Afghanistan and Iraq, which the Obama administration plans to target militarily, economically and politically in its bid to expand its artificial "War on Terror" to appease the military-industrial complex and feed America's **insatiable** appetite for warmongering.

President Obama's response to the recent media focus on Yemeni resistance to American invasions of Muslim countries has so far been primarily, though not exclusively, one of training and paying Yemenis to kill their own. As I have explained before the American Empire has massive firepower but limited manpower to put "boots on the ground." Yemen has a larger geographical area than Iraq with terrain almost as challenging as Afghanistan. As in other invasions the American Empire promotes and supports a local pro-American s.o.b. dictator to do its dirty work. In the case of Yemen President Obama has found his American s.o.b. dictator in Field Marshall *Ali Abdullah Saleh*. President Obama can exploit Yemen's historical North-South and ethnic divisions and semi-Civil War caused by the merger of the two independent states in 1990. President Obama's so called military and development aid to *Saleh* for 2010 is $70 million. An added bonus for President Obama is that America's ally, Saudi Arabia, supports the Yemini government led by President *Saleh* while Iran supports the resistance led by the Northern Shiites.

President Obama's next book should be entitled *The Audacity of Global War*. America's propaganda "War on Terror" was begun by the *Neo-Cons* led by President George W. Bush, falsely imbued by the supposedly unlimited and invincible military and economic resources of the World's only super power. But it will be the supposedly pro-peace Democratic and Nobel Peace Prize President Obama who will bring the once mighty American Empire to its knees by expanding the *Neo-Cons* false "War on Terror" to an unwinnable global war against Islam. Prior to the George W. Bush's invasion of Afghanistan none of us had heard of *Al Qaeda* or the *Taliban*. By invading Iraq in 2003 the Bush presidency created *Al Qaeda in Iraq*. In like manner it is President Obama's invasion of Pakistan that created *Al Qaeda in Pakistan* and the *Pakistani Taliban*. It is President Obama's invasion of Yemen that has created *Al Qaeda in Yemen*. The key to understanding why the American Empire will self-destruct under President Obama is to simply reverse the Western propaganda as to the reason for the Islamic victories. Muslims are absolutely **not** opposing American and Western imperialism because of religious fanaticism. They are resisting American imperialism because of American atrocities against Palestinians, Lebanese, Iraqis, Iranians, Afghans, Pakistanis, Libyans, Syrians, Yemenis, Somalis and against Muslims even in those Muslim states whose governments may be pro-American, such as Saudi Arabia, Jordan and Egypt.

The increasing shift of economic power from the West to Asia and the Third World combined with the Western debt crisis, as exemplified by Greece, Spain, Ireland and other countries in the Euro zone as well as the United Kingdom and the United States, means that the West can no longer ignore the Third World countries and dominate "international" institutions such as the WTO, the World Bank, the UN and the IMF. The G-20, founded in December 1999, has already replaced the G-8 as the World's dominant economic forum. This new international body includes "Third World" countries such as China, India, Brazil, Argentina, Mexico, Turkey, Indonesia and Saudi Arabia. Many of these emerging economies will likely support Muslim states for strategic, economic, cultural or political reasons. As we have explained before Western "democracies" are incapable of producing visionary leaders. Far from improving the quality of their leadership they celebrate the "dumbing down" of the leadership produced by their false democracies. The West is stuck in a mindset which originated six centuries ago when Portugal succeeded in exploring the coast of West Africa to begin the enslaving of Africans and Spain succeeded in reaching the New World to begin the enslaving of First Nations.

CONCLUSION

In 2010 the world has a small window of opportunity for real change. This window of opportunity has been provided by the military defeats of the American Empire in Iraq and Afghanistan and the severe economic recession in the homeland. Those of us who had hoped that change would come from an inspired President Barak Obama are very sadly disappointed. President Obama has made it crystal clear in the first year of his administration that he intends to be as **White** as every previous American president and equally **warmongering.** There is absolutely no sign that President Obama wants to change the course set by President George W. Bush and his predecessors for American foreign policy. President Obama has expanded the war in Afghanistan and across the Afghan border into Pakistan. He continues the colonization of Iraq and continues to threaten Iran and North Korea. He has made no effort to restrain Israel or provide any support for the Palestinian people. He has even begun a new war and occupation in Yemen which will likely expand into Somalia.

President Obama, out of necessity, not choice, has continued the disastrous foreign policy of George W. Bush by switching from American unilateralism to American multilateralism. Bush was able to use the unilateral approach because a decade ago the American Empire was much stronger economically and militarily. Obama uses a multilateral approach only because the American Empire today is both economically and militarily weak. Obama does not have a choice. Obama's multilateral approach has not so far changed the agenda of American foreign policy. It's a continuation of the foreign policy set by the West six centuries ago. When George W. Bush invaded Iraq he was unable to cajole two Western leaders, President Jacques Chirac of France and Chancellor Gerhard Schroder of Germany, into supporting his **illegal** invasion. But the other Western leaders were on board. Far from the Western alliance falling apart or Britain being isolated from Europe because Tony Blair supported the American invasion, France and Germany are now one with Britain and the American Empire. The Western alliance today is more solid than it has ever been. President Obama is clever enough to make full use of that solidarity to pursue exactly the same course set for US foreign policy by George W. Bush.

What I called the "three asses of evil," Bush, Blair and Harper, in my *Rise and Fall of the American Empire,* was replaced by three new "asses of evil," Obama, Brown and Sarkozy. President Nicolas Sarkozy of France joined with Chancellor Angela Merkel of Germany to repair what they saw as a small crack in the historic alliance between the American Empire and Western Europe. Gordon Brown replaced Tony Blair as "poodle" to the American president. Canada's Steven Harper became a marginal player. Britain is once again united with Europe in ensuring that the American Empire will not have to stand alone in its pursuit of Western supremacy.

One conclusion I am sure of. The removal of the American Empire as the leader of the World is a **necessary** condition for change. It many not be sufficient for change. But it is necessary and essential. I reached that conclusion once I was convinced that President Obama is following the same course as all American presidents beginning with George Washington. The American Empire will never elect an American leader who will change course. That is clearly the will of the electorate. The American Empire effectively has a one-party "democracy," despite its rhetoric to the contrary. Whether the people elect Democrats or Republicans the fundamentals of its policies, both domestic and foreign, remain those of a warmongering behemoth with the same three centuries of tunnel vision. It will never be an empire which will bring peace to the world, inspire the human race to develop, maximize resources devoted to reducing poverty, reduce excessive consumption and planetary degradation or work towards racial equality and equality of opportunities. It will never inspire the world to create just societies, true democracies, and true freedom of the press.

China holds the Key for Real Change

The opportunity for change in my lifetime rests solely with China. The West desperately wants to co-opt China to its cause as it did with Japan after the Second World War. The West has been courting China's subservience ever since President Richard Nixon visited China in 1972. This began as a strategy to isolate the Soviet Union and win the Cold War. With the collapse of the Soviet Union the American Empire became invincible and no longer needed allies. That was why George W. Bush made American foreign policy unilateral.

In 2010, President Barak Obama desperately needs China on side to continue the Western colonization of the Middle East and prevent countries like Iran and North Korea developing nuclear **defence** capability. This need to co-opt China as a means of maintaining Western hegemony is far greater in 2010 than it was in 2000. In addition to the relative economic and military decline of the American Empire in the last decade Russia has regained some of its Cold War power and prestige after Vladimir Putin replaced Boris Yeltsin as president in 2000.

What does Co-opting China mean?

To a large extent the West has already co-opted China to its cause. That cause is the preservation of a Western culture which began with the Spanish victory over the Muslims in Grenada in 1491. This Western culture spread from Western Europe to the New World following the discoveries of Christopher Columbus and to Asia and Africa following the discovery of the sea route to India and the beginning of the transatlantic **slave** trade. The foundations of this Western culture, which has dominated the World for six centuries now, can be summarized as follows:

1. Begin with, and maintain at all cost, the unquestioned view that the **White** race is superior to all other races.
2. Enslave or subjugate all **Non-Whites** you conquer and permanently deny full and equal citizenship rights to Non-Whites.
3. Begin with, and maintain at all cost, the unquestioned view that **Christianity** is the only civilized religion.
4. Begin with, and maintain at all cost, military superiority over those who may challenge Western hegemony.
5. Engage in constant wars, domestic and foreign, to make the military and warmongering deeply entrenched institutions in every facet of society so that no one would ever contemplate a world without wars. Fight with Western states as well as non-Western states. Make your citizens depend on wars for their livelihoods, careers, promotion, recognition, political and economic advancement.
6. Develop a media which promotes this culture and defends it with biased and selective reporting.
7. Instil in citizens the pride of defending the military, the constitution, the warmongering, the foreign invasions, the expansion of empire, the denigration of non-Western culture, values and religious beliefs.
8. Use every form of propaganda and hypocrisy to defend and promote false interpretations of Western culture, Western domination, Western aggression, Western warmongering, Western invasions, Western values and Western beliefs.
9. Confuse the citizenry as to what governments do, lie, deceive and threaten, punish dissent, promote and reward subservience, use colourful and loaded language, educate with biased and indoctrinated professors and historians.

10. Institute a **legal** as opposed to a **justice** system to maintain and enhance the status quo, easily punish those who dare to threaten it, defend those who commit crimes against humanity.

11. Maintain the sanctity of private property, promote the illusion of equal economic and political opportunities but maintain inequality of wealth, power, prestige and influence.

12. Promote the unchallenged view that non-Western values are primitive, uncivilized, barbaric, homophobic, intolerant of religious freedom, demeaning to women, communist, dictatorial, unjust and undemocratic.

13. Keep the people of the West, including intellectuals, viewing the World from a narrow, tunnel vision, fish bowl, constrained perspective. This prevents any true development or progress of humanity which could lead to a challenge of six centuries of stagnation and fear.

14. Minimize resources spent on the eradication of poverty, diseases, natural disasters, environmental conservation, equality of opportunity, promotion of peace and security, promotion of justice as opposed to enforcement of laws, promotion of leisure over frivolous consumption, promotion of social values over individual competition, promotion of communist and cooperative values and behaviours over private and selfish behaviours and the development of the human spirit, brotherly love, respect, non-violence and an end to **all** wars.

Co-opting China means getting China onboard to implicitly or explicitly buy into and support the fourteen pillars of Western culture listed above, in the same way that countries like Japan, Taiwan, Hong Kong, South Korea, the Philippines and Singapore, were previously seduced into with Western investment in their economic development. China is still a relatively poor country with two-thirds of its people yearning for the standard of living of Japan, Taiwan, Hong Kong, Singapore and South Korea. China could be swayed by this quicker road to economic prosperity by giving up its ability to change the course of history from the path dictated by the West for six centuries.

What if China refuses to be Co-opted by the West?

When Japan decided to be co-opted by the West in exchange for rapid economic development it lost an opportunity to lead Asia and the Third World. That may have been a sensible choice in the immediate post World War II years. In 2010, the centre of economic success has shifted somewhat from North America and Western Europe to Asia and the Third World. This time it is China, not Japan, which has the opportunity to lead Asia and the Third World along a path quite different from that charted for six centuries by the West.

There are several important reasons why China can succeed today while Japan may very well have failed earlier. The world yearns for relief from American hegemony and Western dogma. People in Asia, in the Third World, and in the West want the opportunity to try an alternative to warmongering, demonising Muslims and communists and increased expenditures on security at airports. Rather than responding to imagined threats by terrorists by killing their families people long for the alternative of withdrawing from global conflicts and imperial dictates. China could provide the leadership for this alternative. Western Europe has so far refused to.

China is well aware that Asia dominated the world for at least 18 of the last 20 centuries and can do so again. With this opportunity to lead not only Asia but the Third World, including an Africa fed up with six centuries of Western colonialism, it may very well choose the alternative to cooperating with the West as a second class player. When the people of Africa are so afraid of a return of British colonialism that they would choose the "dictatorship" of a **Robert Mugabe** over the slightest chance of a return of British colonialism, the evidence is overwhelming that the people of the Third World want relief from Western domination.

As we said before the Western semi-colonies of Macau, Hong Kong, Singapore, Malaysia, Indonesia, Philippines, Taiwan, South Korea and Japan which once saw their future as integration with the West have reversed course and increased trade and integration with China in the last three decades. The other emerging Asian giant, India, is also increasingly cooperating with China.

Resource rich Third World countries want to know that by switching from Western markets to China they are getting a genuine alternative to centuries of economic colonialism by the West. Ever since the West created the United Nations as a "World" body to "govern" the world in a truly democratic way the Third World has yearned for some country to stand up to the American bully in that institution. They hope that China will be that country where once they had hoped it would have been the Soviet Union.

Non-whites re-taking New World/Old World from Whites

Another new development complementing the global shift of economic power from the West to the East has been increased immigration of **non-Whites** into the West. This is happening in the US, in Canada, in Australia and in Western Europe. The West had severely restricted **non-White** immigrants into their countries for five centuries. But during the last half a century barriers to **non-White** immigrants have been gradually eased. In addition, **non-Whites** have found new ways of immigrating into Western countries "illegally."

It's unclear how this increased percent of **non-Whites** in the West will change the historical behaviour of the West. **Non-Whites** are indoctrinated into thinking and behaving as **Whites** even before they immigrate into the West. This indoctrination continues during their lifetime in the West and is passed on to their children. When **White** Canadians, for example, say that **non-White** immigrants should become "Canadians" they certainly do not mean First Nations. They mean **White/Anglo** Canadians. French-Canadians rightly complain bitterly about being treated as second class Canadians by Anglo-Canadians, even though they were here "first." But French-Canadians see no contradiction in considering themselves superior to First Nations.

It would be interesting to see the dynamics between **Whites, non-Whites** and First Nations in Canada and the US as the percent of **non-White** second and third generation immigrants increase in these two Western countries. Blacks, Hispanics and Asians will compete with each other as well as with **Whites** and First Nations. Add to these facts the increasing numbers of inter-racial marriages in all of the Western countries. Will the West continue with the ridiculous notion that someone with 10 percent Black blood and 90 percent White blood is **Black?** Will another person with the same racial mixture as President Obama be still considered a "Black" president?

One fact is undeniable. The world is changing in two fundamental and complementary ways. Since the Korean War the world was explicitly divided into East and West. The West used every kind of "dirty trick," including the ridiculous notion of racial superiority of **Whites,** to colonize and subjugate the majority of the world's people who happen to live in the East. Since the economic resurgence of Asia there has been a re-balancing of the wealth of the globe in favour of the East. At the same time the percent of **non-Whites** in the West has increased significantly as barriers to **non-White** legal and illegal immigration have been broken down and mixed-race marriages have increased.

Those who mistakenly think that race has not been important in Western domination will dismiss the relevance of increased numbers of **non-Whites** living in the West. But my thesis is that **race** has been the most significant factor in explaining the hypocrisy of the West since Portugal began to make

slaves of Africans and Spain defeated the Moors in Granada during the fifteenth century. Race is a very visible and easily identifiable way of demonizing and discriminating against people. It has been used very effectively by the West. This fact leads me to the inevitable conclusion that the increasing percent of **non-Whites** in the West will change the view of the West. This will, of course, take time. **Non-Whites** in the West will not have much power and influence in the institutions of the West for this generation or the next. Those institutions will continue to be controlled by **Whites** for the foreseeable future.

I am very happy to conclude this book on a very optimistic note. The relative decline of the American Empire will remove this "Rome-like imperial" suffocation of the human race. People will be allowed to breathe freedom and make choices. Some will make poor choices. Some will make mistakes. But in the end we develop as human beings only when we have the freedom to choose. Countries like Canada and many in Western Europe will find this freedom from American paranoia both stimulating and fulfilling. Young people will dream of a better world and strive to make it so. The **non-White** people of the Third World will finally have an opportunity to contribute much more equally in the development of institutions, culture, products and **leadership.** Most importantly, the insane amount of money spent by the West on its military which is used to kill and main innocent and defenceless men, women and children in the Third World can now be spent on alleviating hunger, malnutrition, diseases, global warming and natural disasters. The world will be both safer and more prosperous.

Bibliography and References

Most of the references below are from the internet. I have listed the main articles which has links to several other articles that I have used but not referenced. In particular I wish to express special thanks to Wikipedia as my primary source for many of the facts used in this book. I have, of course, checked the accuracy of those facts from other sources. As in all cases I have used the facts only. The interpretation of those facts are entirely my own.

1. afghanistan.blogs.cnn.com/category/operation-moshtarak/
2. AL QAEDA IN YEMEN AND SOMALIA: A TICKING TIME BOMB: A REPORT to the Committee on Foreign Relations: US Senate: www.gpoaccess.gov/congress/index.html
3. Argueta, Al: Guatemala: Moon Books, 2nd. Edition, Avalon Travel Publishing, USA, 1977
4. Axelrod, Alan: The Complete Idiot's Guide to American History, Third Edition, Alpha Books, Indianapolis, 2003
5. Bakewell, Peter: A History of Latin America, second edition, Blackwell Publishing, USA, 2004
6. Boorstin, Daniel J and Kelley, Brooks Mather: A History of the United States: Prentice Hall, Englewood Cliffs, 1989
7. Brinkley, Douglas: History of the United States, Viking Penguin, New York, 1998
8. Brown, Brian A.: Your Neighbor as Yourself: Race, Religion and Region: North America into the Twenty First Century, Cross Cultural Publications, Indiana, 1997
9. Buckman, Robert T.: Latin America 2001, Stryker-Post Publications, USA, 2001
10. caribbean-guide.info/past.and.present/history/seven.years.war/: Caribbean History: Seven Years War
11. Chandler, Gary and Prado, Liza: Honduras and the Bay Islands, Lonely Planet Publications, Singapore, 2007
12. countrystudies.us/panama/11.htm: Panama: United States Intervention
13. en.wikipedia.org/wiki/Vermont
14. en.wikipedia.org/wiki/George Washington
15. en.wikipedia.org/wiki/Battle of Valcour Island
16. en.wikipedia.org/wiki/Lewis and Clark Expedition
17. en.wikipedia.org/wiki/Ohio
18. en.wikipedia.org/wiki/Thomas Jefferson
19. en.wikipedia.org/wiki/Napoleonic Wars
20. en.wikipedia.org/wiki/Royal Proclamation of 1763
21. en.wikipedia.org/wiki/Battle of Queenston Heights
22. en.wikipedia.org/wiki/Maine
23. en.wikipedia.org/wiki/Florida
24. en.wikipedia.org/wiki/Michigan
25. en.wikipedia.org/wiki/Mexico
26. en.wikipedia.org/wiki/Northwest Indian War
27. en.wikipedia.org/wiki/Texas
28. en.wikipedia.org/wiki/Iowa
29. en.wikipedia.org/wiki/Wisconsin
30. en.wikipedia.org/wiki/Oregon
31. en.wikipedia.org/wiki/Minnesota
32. en.wikipedia.org/wiki/Fort Leavenworth
33. en.wikipedia.org/wiki/Ostend Manifesto

34. en.wikipedia.org/wiki/James Gadsden

35. en.wikipedia.org/wiki/Antonio López de Santa Anna

36. en.wikipedia.org/wiki/Declaration of Paris

37. en.wikipedia.org/wiki/Teller Amendment

38. en.wikipedia.org/wiki/Theodore Roosevelt

39. en.wikipedia.org/wiki/Abraham Lincoln

40. en.wikipedia.org/wiki/Townsend Harris

41. en.wikipedia.org/wiki/First Sino-Japanese War

42. en.wikipedia.org/wiki/Three-fifths compromise

43. en.wikipedia.org/wiki/Bleeding Kansas

44. en.wikipedia.org/wiki/History of the United States Republican Party

45. en.wikipedia.org/wiki/James Dole

46. en.wikipedia.org/wiki/Pearl Harbor

47. en.wikipedia.org/wiki/Wake Island

48. en.wikipedia.org/wiki/Benjamin Harrison

49. en.wikipedia.org/wiki/Russo-Japanese War

50. en.wikipedia.org/wiki/Abolitionism

51. en.wikipedia.org/wiki/Confederate States of America

52. en.wikipedia.org/wiki/Nevada

53. en.wikipedia.org/wiki/West Virginia

54. en.wikipedia.org/wiki/Montana

55. en.wikipedia.org/wiki/Washington

56. en.wikipedia.org/wiki/Idaho

57. en.wikipedia.org/wiki/Wyoming

58. en.wikipedia.org/wiki/Utah

59. en.wikipedia.org/wiki/Ute Tribe

60. en.wikipedia.org/wiki/Fallujah

61. en.wikipedia.org/wiki/Guam

62. en.wikipedia.org/wiki/Cochise

63. en.wikipedia.org/wiki/Martyrs' Day (Panama)

64. en.wikipedia.org/wiki/Iran hostage crisis

65. en.wikipedia.org/wiki/April 1983 U.S. Embassy bombing

66. en.wikipedia.org/wiki/George P. Shultz

67. en.wikipedia.org/wiki/Ferdinand Marcos

68. en.wikipedia.org/wiki/United Fruit Company

69. en.wikipedia.org/wiki/Luis Posada Carriles

70. en.wikipedia.org/wiki/Shogun

71. en.wikipedia.org/wiki/Philippines

72. en.wikipedia.org/wiki/Katipunan

73. en.wikipedia.org/wiki/William McKinley

74. en.wikipedia.org/wiki/American Samoa

75. en.wikipedia.org/wiki/Puerto Rico

76. en.wikipedia.org/wiki/New Mexico

77. en.wikipedia.org/wiki/Trans-Alaska Pipeline System

78. en.wikipedia.org/wiki/Costa Rica

79. en.wikipedia.org/wiki/Hurricane Mitch

80. en.wikipedia.org/wiki/Central America

81. en.wikipedia.org/wiki/Daniel Ortega

82. en.wikipedia.org/wiki/Haiti

83. en.wikipedia.org/wiki/Dominican Republic

84. en.wikipedia.org/wiki/Navassa Island

85. en.wikipedia.org/wiki/Russian Civil War

86. en.wikipedia.org/wiki/Soong Ching-ling

87. en.wikipedia.org/wiki/Soong May-ling

88. en.wikipedia.org/wiki/History of Japan

89. en.wikipedia.org/wiki/History of Korea

90. en.wikipedia.org/wiki/Russo-Japanese War

91. en.wikipedia.org/wiki/Second Sino-Japanese War

92. en.wikipedia.org/wiki/Korean War

93. en.wikipedia.org/wiki/Battle of Dien Bien Phu
94. en.wikipedia.org/wiki/Army of the Republic of Vietnam
95. en.wikipedia.org/wiki/Vietnam War
96. en.wikipedia.org/wiki/William Westmoreland
97. en.wikipedia.org/wiki/Canada and the Vietnam War
98. en.wikipedia.org/wiki/Tet Offensive
99. en.wikipedia.org/wiki/My Lai massacre
100. en.wikipedia.org/wiki/Khmer Republic
101. en.wikipedia.org/wiki/Laotian Civil War
102. en.wikipedia.org/wiki/Cambodian Civil War
103. en.wikipedia.org/wiki/Ho Chi Minh
104. en.wikipedia.org/wiki/Pathet Lao
105. en.wikipedia.org/wiki/ASEAN
106. en.wikipedia.org/wiki/Paris Peace Conference, 1919
107. en.wikipedia.org/wiki/King-Crane Commission
108. en.wikipedia.org/wiki/Sykes-Picot Agreement
109. en.wikipedia.org/wiki/San_Remo conference
110. en.wikipedia.org/wiki/Menachem Begin
111. en.wikipedia.org/wiki/Six-Day War
112. en.wikipedia.org/wiki/History of Afghanistan
113. en.wikipedia.org/wiki/Soviet war in Afghanistan
114. en.wikipedia.org/wiki/Cartel
115. en.wikipedia.org/wiki/Yom Kippur War
116. en.wikipedia.org/wiki/Palestine Liberation Organization
117. en.wikipedia.org/wiki/Suez Crisis
118. en.wikipedia.org/wiki/History of Egypt
119. en.wikipedia.org/wiki/Multinational Force in Lebanon
120. en.wikipedia.org/wiki/Litani River
121. en.wikipedia.org/wiki/Gaza War
122. en.wikipedia.org/wiki/Gaza Strip
123. en.wikipedia.org/wiki/Pacific War
124. en.wikipedia.org/wiki/Operation Condor
125. en.wikipedia.org/wiki/Salvador Allende
126. en.wikipedia.org/wiki/Letelier case
127. en.wikipedia.org/wiki/United States–Venezuela relations
128. en.wikipedia.org/wiki/Cold War
129. en.wikipedia.org/wiki/Ma Ying-jeou
130. en.wikipedia.org/wiki/Deepwater Horizon oil spill
131. Ferguson, Will: Canadian History for Dummies, John Wiley & Sons, Ontario, 2005
132. Francis, R. Douglas, Jones, Richard and Smith, Donald, B.: Origins: Canadian History to Confederation, Third Edition, Harcourt Brace, Toronto, 1996
133. Glassman, Paul: Central America Guide, Open Road Publishing, New York, 1995
134. Grenier, John: The First Way of War: American War Making on the Frontier, 1607-1814, Cambridge University Press, New York, 2005
135. McDougall, Walter A.: Freedom Just Around the Corner: A New American History: 1585-1828, Harper Collins Publishers, New York, 2004
136. Miller, James and Thompson, John: Almanac of American History, National Geographic, Washington, D.C.
137. Mirza, Rocky M.: Rise and Fall of the American Empire: A Re-Interpretation of History, Economics and Philosophy: 1492-2006, Trafford Publishing, Victoria, BC, Canada 2007
138. Morton, Desmond: A Military History of Canada, Hurtig Publishers, Edmonton, 1985

139. Pearcy, Thomas L.: The History of Central America, Palgrave Macmillan, New York, 2006

140. Riendeau, Roger: A Brief History of Canada, Fitzhenry & Whiteside, Ontario, 2000

141. Scowen, Peter: Rogue Nation: The America the Rest of the world Knows, McClelland & Stewart, Quebec, 2003

142. Sinclair, Andrew: A Concise History of the United States, Sutton Publishing, Gloucestershire, 1999

143. Stewart, Ian: A Rough Guide to Guatemala, third edition, Rough Guides, New York, 2006

144. The *Economist,* June 13-19, 2009 and February 27, 2010

145. www.globalexchange.org/campaigns/cafta/

146. www.suite101.com/article.cfm/pirates/96570: American Privateers: An Introduction

147. www.city-journal.org/html/17_2_urbanities-thomas_jefferson: Jefferson Versus the Muslim Pirates

148. www.s4c.co.uk/americagaeth/e_caethfasnach-amp.php: The Slave Trade: The Second "Middle Passage."

149. www.army.mil/cmh-pg/books/amh/AMH-06.htm: Chapter 6: The War of 1812

150. www.wsu.edu/~dee/MODCHINA/SUN.HTM: Modern China: Sun Yat-sen

151. www.worldfreeinternet.net/archive/arc10.htm: The Story of the Usurpation of the Kingdom of Hawaii

152. www.assumption.edu/ahc/Kansas/default.html: Bleeding Kansas: A narrative Guide to the Sources

153. www.ggdc.net/maddison/Historical.../horizontal-file_03-2007.xls: *Historical Statistics for the World Economy*

154. www.econlib.org/library/Enc/OPEC.html

155. www.alternet.org/.../has_the_u.s._invasion_of_pakistan_begun/